Engineering Analysis with SolidWorks Simulation 2010

***Paul M. Kurowski**, Ph.D., P.Eng.*

Schroff Development Corporation

Design Generator, Inc.

Schroff Development Corporation
P.O. Box 1334
Mission KS 66222
(913) 262-2664
www.SDCpublications.com

Publisher: Stephen Schroff

Trademarks and Disclaimer

SolidWorks® is a registered trademark of Dassault Systémes SolidWorks Corp.

Microsoft Windows® and its family products are registered trademarks of the Microsoft Corporation.

Every effort has been made to provide an accurate text. The author and the manufacturers shall not be held liable for any parts or products developed with this book or held responsible for any inaccuracies or errors that appear in the book.

Examination Copies:

Books received as examination copies are for review purposes only and may not be made available for student use. Resale of examination copies is prohibited.

Electronic Files:

Any electronic files associated with this book are licensed to the original user only. These files may not be transferred to any other party.

About the cover

The image on the cover presents the deformations plot of SPRING experiencing large displacements. This model is presented in Chapter 15.

About the Author

Dr. Paul Kurowski obtained his M.Sc. and Ph.D. in Applied Mechanics from Warsaw Technical University. He completed postdoctoral work at Kyoto University. Dr. Kurowski is an Assistant Professor in the Department of Mechanical and Materials Engineering, at the University of Western Ontario. His teaching includes Finite Element Analysis, Product Design, Kinematics and Dynamics of Machines and Mechanical Vibrations.

Dr. Kurowski is also the President of Design Generator Inc., a consulting firm with expertise in Product Development, Design Analysis, and training in Computer Aided Engineering. His interests focus on Computer Aided Engineering methods used as tools of product design.

Dr. Kurowski has published many technical papers and taught professional development seminars for the Society of Automotive Engineers (SAE), the American Society of Mechanical Engineers (ASME), the Association of Professional Engineers of Ontario (PEO), the Parametric Technology Corporation (PTC), Rand Worldwide, SolidWorks Corporation and others.

Dr. Kurowski is a member of the Association of Professional Engineers of Ontario and the Society of Automotive Engineers. He can be contacted at www.designgenerator.com

Acknowledgements

This book is already in its eighth release counting from the first one "Engineering Analysis with COSMOSWorks 2003". In the 2009 release, the book title has been changed to "Engineering Analysis with SolidWorks Simulation 2009" to address the product re-naming implemented by the SolidWorks Corporation. The book takes a unique approach by bridging lightly treated theory with examples showing the theory's practical implementations.

The book evolves together with SolidWorks Simulation software and I hope that every year it offers better value to students who use it in the introductory course in the Finite Element Analysis with SolidWorks Simulation.

Writing and updating this book every year to the new software release has been a very substantial effort that would not have been possible without the help and support of my professional colleagues. I would like to thank the students attending my various courses for their valuable comments and questions. I would like to thank Tomasz Kurowski for editing and proof reading the text and the exercises. I thank my wife Elzbieta for her support and encouragement that made it possible to write this book.

Paul Kurowski

Table of contents

Before You Start

Notes on hands-on exercises

This book goes beyond a standard software manual because its unique approach concurrently introduces you to SolidWorks **Simulation** software and the fundamentals of Finite Element Analysis (FEA) through hands-on exercises. We recommend that you study the exercises in the order presented in the book. As you go through the exercises, you will notice that explanations and steps described in detail in earlier exercises are not repeated in later chapters. Each subsequent exercise assumes familiarity with software functions discussed in previous exercises and builds on the skills, experience, and understanding gained from previously presented problems. Exceptions to the above are chapters 21, 22 and 23 which do not include hands-on exercises.

The functionality of SolidWorks **Simulation** depends on which software **Simulation** product is used. The functionality of different products is explained in the following table:

MECHANICAL DESIGN PRODUCTS | DATA MANAGEMENT PRODUCTS | ANALYSIS PRODUCTS

	SolidWorks Premium	SolidWorks Simulation Professional	SolidWorks Simulation Premium	SolidWorks Flow Simulation
Design Validation				
Tolerance Stack-up Validation	✓			
Assembly Simulation	✓	✓	✓	
Mechanism Simulation	✓	✓	✓	
Simulate Welded Structures	✓	✓	✓	
Product Failure Prediction		✓	✓	
Compare and Optimize Design Alternatives		✓	✓	
Simulate Natural Frequencies		✓	✓	
Predict Buckling or Collapses		✓	✓	
Simulate Heating or Cooling		✓	✓	
Simulate Drop Test or Prod Failure		✓	✓	
Simulate Repeat Loading		✓	✓	
Simulate Forced Vibrations			✓	
Non-Linear Dynamics			✓	
Simulate Plastic Parts			✓	
Fluid Flow Simulation				✓

This **Simulation** product matrix is available at:
http://www.solidworks.com/sw/mechanical-design-software-matrix.htm

Most exercises in this book will require SolidWorks **Simulation** Professional. Exercises limited to static analysis can be completed in SolidWorks Premium. Some exercises in chapter 15 and all exercises in chapters 18 and 19, require SolidWorks **Simulation** Premium. All exercises use SolidWorks models, which can be downloaded from http://www.schroff.com/resources. These exercises do not contain any **Simulation** studies; you are expected to create all studies and results plots and graphs yourselves. The only exceptions are exercises in chapter 20 which come with some **Simulation** studies fully or partially defined.

This book is not intended to replace regular software manuals. While you are guided through the specific exercises, not all of the software functions are explained. We encourage you to explore each exercise beyond its description by investigating other options, other menu choices, and other ways to present results. You will soon discover that the same simple logic applies to all functions in SolidWorks **Simulation**.

Prerequisites

We assume that you have the following prerequisites:

- An understanding of Mechanics of Materials
- Experience with parametric, feature based solid modeling using SolidWorks
- Familiarity with the Windows Operating System

Selected terminology

The mouse pointer plays a very important role in executing various commands and providing user feedback. The mouse pointer is used to execute commands, select geometry, and invoke pop-up menus. We use Windows terminology when referring to mouse-pointer actions.

Item	Description
Click	Self explanatory
Double-click	Self explanatory
Click-inside	Click the left mouse button. Wait a second, and then click the left mouse button inside the pop-up menu or text box. Use this technique to modify the names of folders and icons in SolidWorks **Simulation** Manager.
Drag and drop	Use the mouse to point to an object. Press and hold the left mouse button down. Move the mouse pointer to a new location. Release the left mouse button.
Right-click	Click the right mouse button. A pop-up menu is displayed. Use the left mouse button to select a desired menu command.

All SolidWorks file names appear in CAPITAL letters, even though the actual file names may use a combination of capital and small letters. Selected menu items and SolidWorks **Simulation** commands appear in **bold**, SolidWorks configurations, SolidWorks **Simulation** folders, icon names and study names appear in *italics* except in captions and comments to illustrations.

Notes:

1: Introduction

What is Finite Element Analysis?

Finite Element Analysis, commonly called FEA, is a method of numerical analysis. FEA is used for solving problems in many engineering disciplines such as machine design, acoustics, electromagnetism, soil mechanics, fluid dynamics, and many others. In mathematical terms, FEA is a numerical technique used for solving field problems described by a set of partial differential equations.

In mechanical engineering, FEA is widely used for solving structural, vibration, and thermal problems. However, FEA is not the only available tool of numerical analysis. Other numerical methods include the Finite Difference Method, the Boundary Element Method, and the Finite Volumes Method to mention just a few. However, due to its versatility and numerical efficiency, FEA has come to dominate the engineering analysis software market, while other methods have been relegated to niche applications. When implemented into modern commercial software, both FEA theory and numerical problem formulation become completely transparent to users.

Finite Element Analysis used by Design Engineers

FEA is a powerful engineering analysis tool useful in solving many problems ranging from very simple to very complex. Design engineers use FEA during the product development process to analyze the design-in-progress. Time constraints and limited availability of product data call for many simplifications of analysis models. On the other hand, specialized analysts implement FEA to solve very complex problems, such as vehicle crash dynamics, hydro forming, and air bag deployment.

This book focuses on how design engineers use FEA implemented in SolidWorks **Simulation** as a design tool. Therefore, we highlight the most essential characteristics of FEA as performed by design engineers as opposed to those typical for FEA preformed by analysts.

FEA for Design Engineers: another design tool

For design engineers, FEA is one of many design tools that are used in the design process and include CAD, prototypes, spreadsheets, catalogs, hand calculations, text books, etc.

FEA for Design Engineers: based on CAD models

Modern design is conducted using CAD, so a CAD model is the starting point for analysis. Since CAD models are used for describing geometric information for FEA, it is essential to understand how to prepare CAD geometry in order to produce correct FEA results, and how a CAD model is different from an FEA model. This will be discussed in later chapters.

FEA for Design Engineers: concurrent with the design process

Since FEA is a design tool, it should be used concurrently with the design process. It should drive the design process rather than follow it.

Limitations of FEA for Design Engineers

An obvious question arises: would it be better to have a dedicated specialist perform FEA and let design engineers do what they do best – design new products? The answer depends on the size of the business, type of products, company organization and culture, and many other tangible and intangible factors. A general consensus is that design engineers should handle relatively simple types of analysis, but do it quickly and of course reliably. Analyses that are very complex and time consuming cannot be executed concurrently with the design process, and are usually better handled either by a dedicated analyst or contracted out to specialized consultants.

Objectives of FEA for Design Engineers

The ultimate objective of using FEA as a design tool is to change the design process from repetitive cycles of "design, prototype, test" into a streamlined process where prototypes are not used as design tools and are only needed for final design verification. With the use of FEA, design iterations are moved from the physical space of prototyping and testing into the virtual space of computer simulations (Figure 1-1).

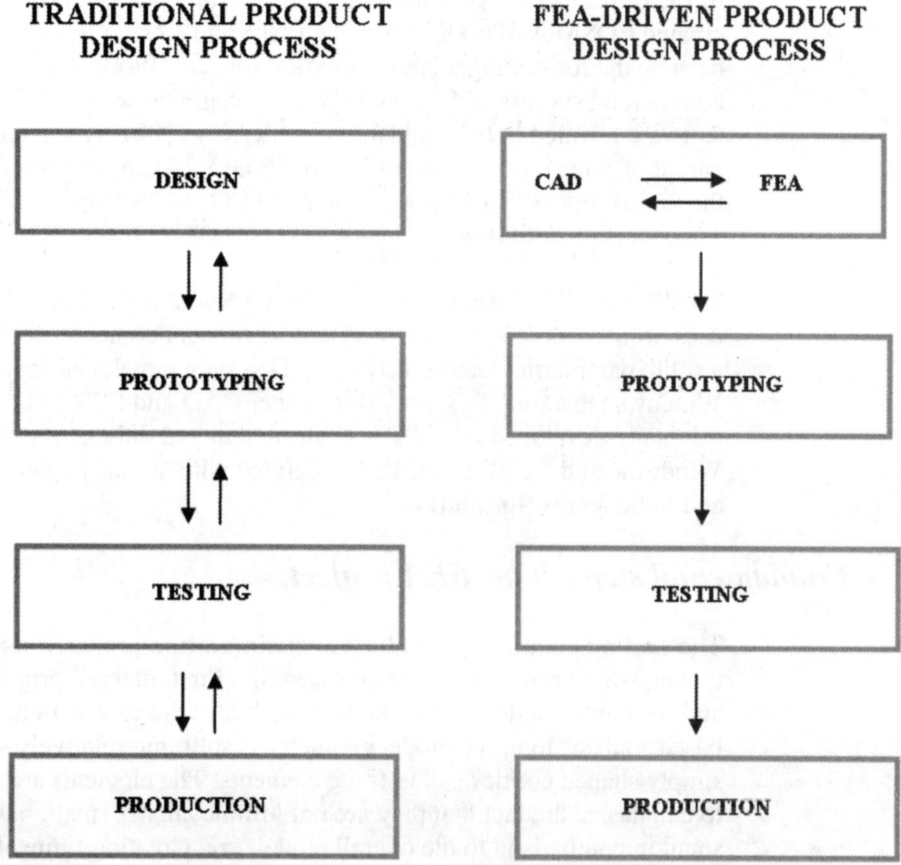

Figure 1-1: Traditional and. FEA-driven product development

Traditional product development needs prototypes to support a design in progress. The process in FEA-driven product development uses numerical models, rather than physical prototypes to drive development. In an FEA-driven product, the prototype is no longer a part of the iterative design loop.

What is SolidWorks Simulation?

SolidWorks **Simulation** is a commercial implementation of FEA capable of solving problems commonly found in design engineering, such as the analysis of displacements, stresses, natural frequencies, vibration, buckling, heat flow, etc. It belongs to the family of engineering analysis software products originally developed by the Structural Research & Analysis Corporation (SRAC). SRAC was established in 1982 and since its inception has contributed to innovations that have had a significant impact on the evolution of FEA. In 1995 SRAC partnered with the SolidWorks Corporation and created COSMOSWorks, one of the first SolidWorks Gold Products, which became the top-selling analysis solution for SolidWorks Corporation. The commercial success of COSMOSWorks integrated with SolidWorks CAD software resulted in the acquisition of SRAC in 2001 by Dassault Systèmes, parent of SolidWorks Corporation. In 2003, SRAC operations merged with the SolidWorks Corporation. In the 2009 COSMOSWorks has been re-named SolidWorks **Simulation**.

SolidWorks **Simulation** is integrated with SolidWorks CAD software and uses SolidWorks for creating and editing model geometry. SolidWorks is a solid, parametric, feature-driven CAD system developed specifically for the Windows Operating System. Many other CAD and FEA programs were originally developed in a UNIX environment and only later ported to Windows, and therefore are less integrated with Windows than SolidWorks and SolidWorks **Simulation**.

Fundamental steps in an FEA project

The starting point for any SolidWorks **Simulation** project is a SolidWorks model, which can be a part or an assembly. First material properties, loads, and restraints are defined. Next, as it is always the case with using any FEA-based analysis tool, the model geometry is split into relatively small and simply shaped entities called finite elements. The elements are called "finite" to emphasize the fact that they are not infinitesimally small, but relatively small in comparison to the overall model size. Creating finite elements is commonly called meshing. When working with finite elements, the SolidWorks **Simulation** solver approximates the sought solution (for example stress) by assembling the solutions for individual elements.

From the perspective of FEA software, each application of FEA requires three steps:

- Preprocessing of the FEA model, which involves defining the model and then splitting it into finite elements
- Solving for desired results
- Post-processing for results analysis

We will follow the above three steps in every exercise.

From the perspective of FEA methodology, we can list the following FEA steps:

- Building the mathematical model
- Building the finite element model by discretizing the mathematical model
- Solving the finite element model
- Analyzing the results

The following subsections discuss these four steps.

Building the mathematical model

The starting point to analysis with SolidWorks **Simulation** is a SolidWorks model. Geometry of the model needs to be meshable into a correct finite element mesh. This requirement of meshability has very important implications. We need to ensure that the CAD geometry will indeed mesh and that the produced mesh will provide the data of interest (e.g. stresses or temperature distribution) with acceptable accuracy.

The necessity to mesh often requires modifications to the CAD geometry, which can take the form of defeaturing, idealization, and/or clean-up:

Term	Description
Defeaturing	The process of removing geometry features deemed insignificant for analysis, such as external fillets, chamfers, logos, etc.
Idealization	A more aggressive exercise that may depart from solid CAD geometry by, for example, representing thin walls with surfaces and beams with lines.
Clean-up	Sometimes needed because geometry must satisfy high quality requirements to be meshable. To cleanup, we can use CAD quality-control tools to check for problems like sliver faces, multiple entities, etc. that could be tolerated in the CAD model, but would make subsequent meshing difficult or impossible.

It is important to mention that we do not always simplify the CAD model with the sole objective of making it meshable. Often we must simplify a model even though it would mesh correctly "as is", but the resulting mesh would be too large (in terms of the number of elements) and consequently, the meshing and the analysis would take too long. Geometry modifications allow for a simpler mesh and shorter meshing and computing times.

Sometimes, geometry preparation may not be required at all. Successful meshing depends as much on the quality of geometry submitted for meshing as it does on the capabilities of the meshing tools implemented in the FEA software.

Having prepared a meshable, but not yet meshed geometry, we now define material properties (these can also be imported from a CAD model), loads and restraints, and provide information on the type of analysis that we wish to perform. This procedure completes the creation of the mathematical model (Figure 1-2). Notice that the process of creating the mathematical model is not FEA specific. FEA has not yet entered the picture.

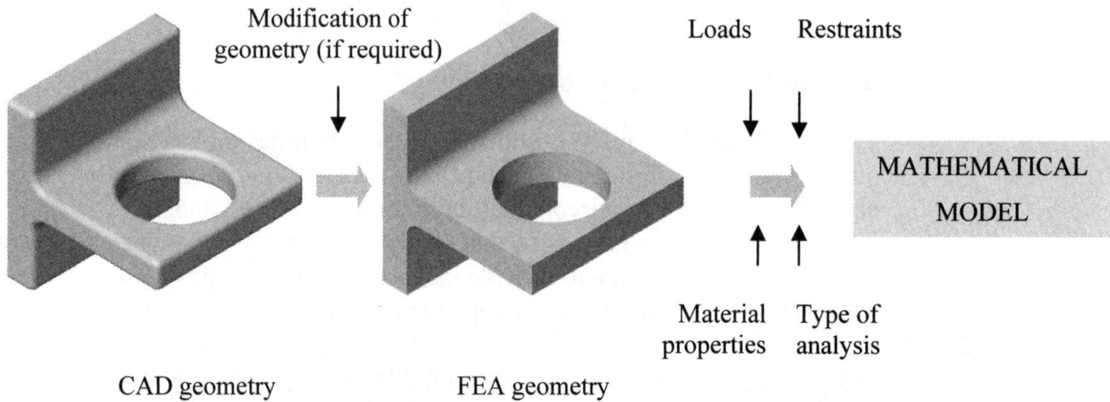

Figure 1-2: Building the mathematical model

The process of creating a mathematical model consists of the modification of CAD geometry (here removing external fillets), definition of loads, restraints, material properties, and definition of the type of analysis (for example static) that we want to perform.

Building the finite element model

The mathematical model now needs to be split into finite elements in the process of discretization, more commonly known as meshing (Figure 1-3). Geometry, loads, and restraints are all discretized. The discretized loads and restraints are applied to the nodes of the finite element mesh.

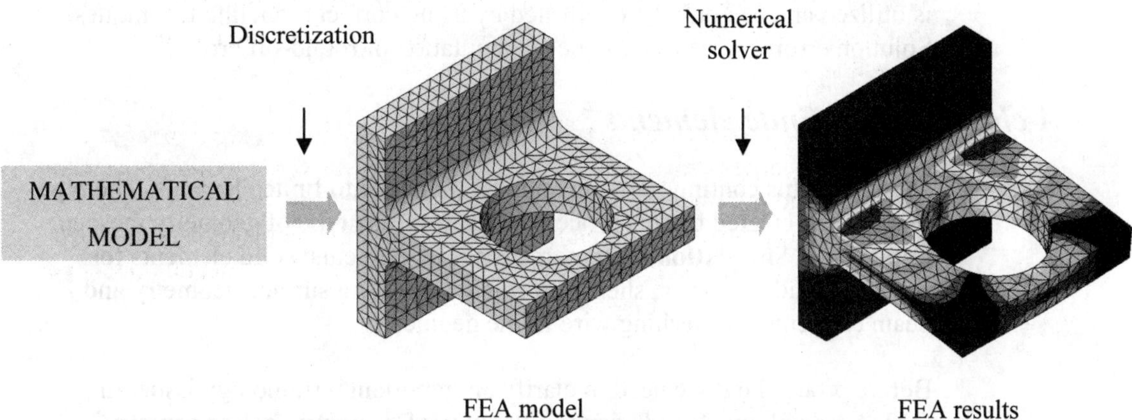

Figure 1-3: Building the finite element model

The mathematical model is discretized into a finite element model. This completes the pre-processing phase. The FEA model is then solved with one of the numerical solvers available in SolidWorks Simulation.

Solving the finite element model

Having created the finite element model, we now use a solver provided in SolidWorks **Simulation** to produce the desired data of interest (Figure 1-3).

Analyzing the results

Often the most difficult step of FEA is analyzing the results. Proper interpretation of results requires that we understand all simplifications (and errors they introduce) in the first three steps: defining the mathematical model, meshing, and solving.

Errors in FEA

The process illustrated in Figure 1-2 and Figure 1-3 introduces unavoidable errors. Formulation of a mathematical model introduces modeling errors (also called idealization errors), discretization of the mathematical model introduces discretization errors, and solving introduces solution errors. Of these three types of errors, only discretization errors are specific to FEA. Modeling errors affecting the mathematical model are introduced before FEA is utilized and can only be controlled by using correct modeling techniques. Solution errors are caused by the accumulation of round-off errors.

A closer look at finite elements

Meshing splits continuous mathematical models into finite elements. The type of elements created by this process depends on the type of geometry meshed. SolidWorks **Simulation** offers three types of elements: solid elements for meshing solid geometry, shell elements for meshing surface geometry and beam elements for meshing wire frame geometry.

Before proceeding, we need to clarify an important terminology issue. In CAD terminology, "solid" denotes the type of geometry: solid geometry (as opposed to surface or wire frame geometry). In FEA terminology, "solid" denotes the type of element used to mesh the solid CAD geometry.

Solid elements

The type of geometry that is most often used for analysis with SolidWorks **Simulation** is solid CAD geometry. Meshing of this geometry is accomplished with tetrahedral solid elements, commonly called "tets" in FEA jargon. The tetrahedral solid elements in SolidWorks **Simulation** can either be first order elements (draft quality), or second order elements (high quality). The user decides whether to use draft quality or high quality elements for meshing. However, as we will soon prove, only high quality elements should be used for an analysis of any importance. The difference between first and second order tetrahedral elements is illustrated in Figure 1-4.

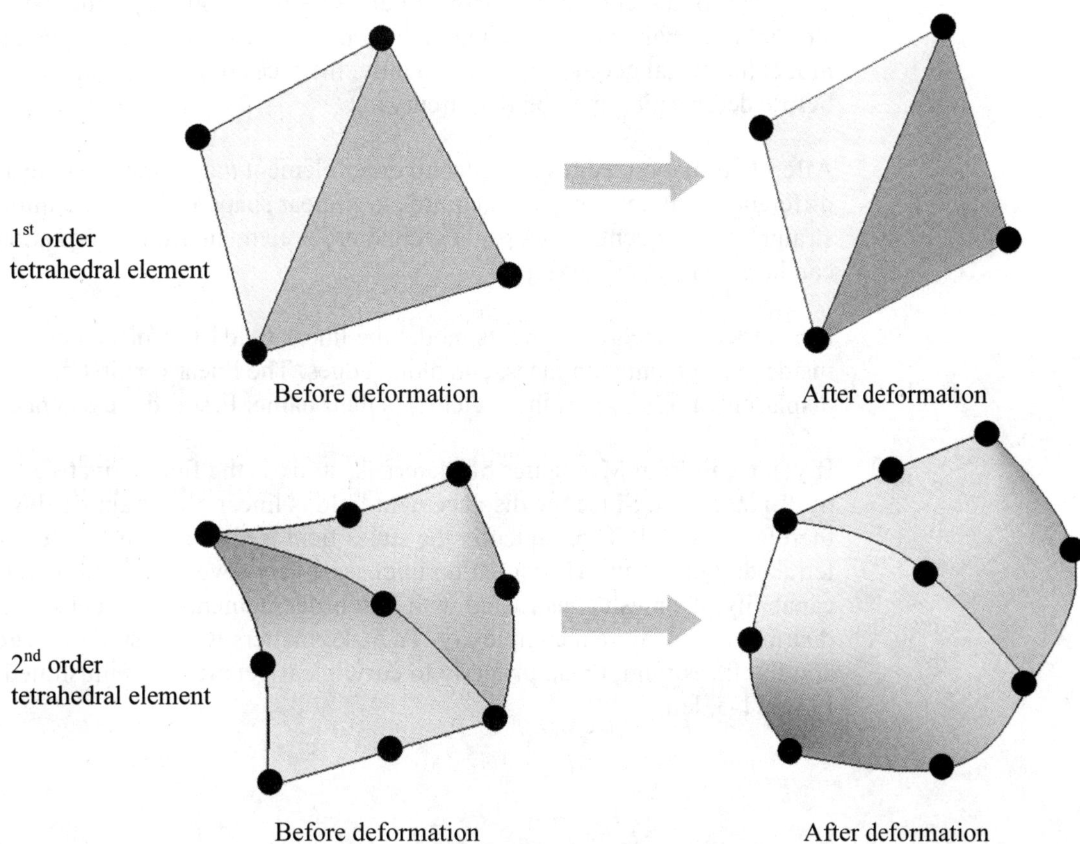

Figure 1-4: Differences between first and second order tetrahedral elements

First and second order tetrahedral elements are shown before and after deformation. Note that the first order element only has corner nodes, while the second order element has both corner and mid-side nodes (one mid-side node is not visible for the second order element in this illustration). Single elements seldom experience deformations of this magnitude, which are exaggerated in this illustration.

In a first order element, edges are straight and faces are flat. After deformation the edges and faces must retain these properties.

The edges of a second order element before deformation may either be straight or curvilinear, depending on how the element has been mapped to model the actual geometry. Consequently, the faces of a second order element before deformation may be flat or curved.

After deformation, edges of a second order element may either assume a different curvilinear shape or acquire curvilinear shape if they were initially straight. Consequently, faces of a second order element after deformation can be either flat or curved.

First order tetrahedral elements model the linear field of displacement inside their volume, on faces, and along edges. The linear (or first order) displacement field gives these elements their name: first order elements.

If you recall from Mechanics of Materials, strain is the first derivative of displacement. Since the displacement field is linear, the strain field is therefore constant. Consequently the stress field is also constant in first order tetrahedral elements. This situation imposes a very severe limitation on the capability of a mesh constructed with first order elements to model stress distribution of any real complexity. To make matters worse, straight edges and flat faces cannot map properly to curvilinear geometry, as illustrated in Figure 1-5, left.

Second order tetrahedral elements have ten nodes (Figure 1-4) and model the second order (parabolic) displacement field and first order (linear) stress field in their volume, on faces and along edges. The edges and faces of second order tetrahedral elements can be curvilinear before and after deformation, therefore these elements can map precisely to curved surfaces, as illustrated in Figure 1-5 right. Even though these elements are more computationally demanding than first order elements, second order tetrahedral elements are used for the majority of analyses with SolidWorks **Simulation** because of their much better stress modeling capabilities.

A tetrahedral solid element is the only type of solid element available in SolidWorks **Simulation**.

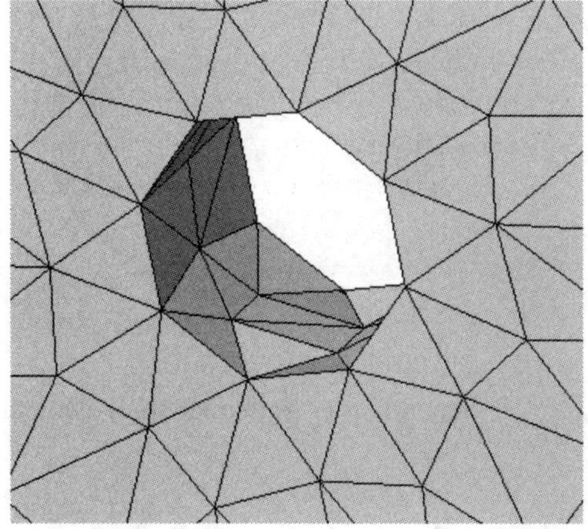

First order solid tetrahedral elements

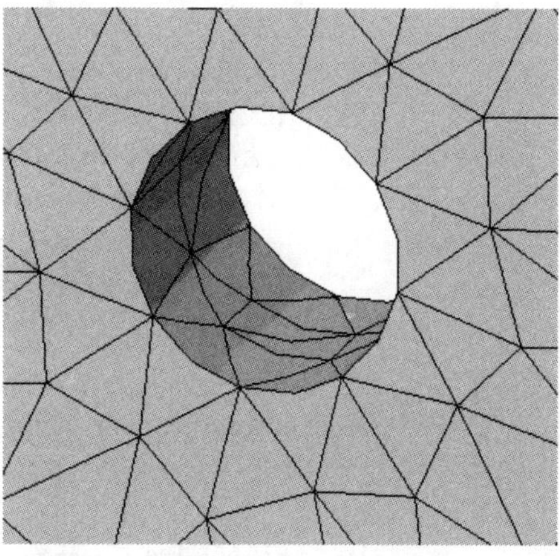

Second order solid tetrahedral elements

Figure 1-5: Failure of straight edges and flat faces to map to curvilinear geometry when using first order elements (left), and precise mapping to curvilinear geometry using second order elements (right)

Notice the imprecise first order element mapping of the hole; flat faces approximate the face of the curvilinear geometry. Second order elements map well to curvilinear geometry.

Shell elements

Shell elements are created by meshing surfaces or faces of solid geometry. Shell elements are primarily used for analyzing thin-walled structures. Since surface geometry does not carry information about thickness, the user must provide this information. Similar to solid elements, shell elements also come in draft and high quality with analogous consequences with respect to their ability to map to curvilinear geometry, as shown in Figure 1-6.

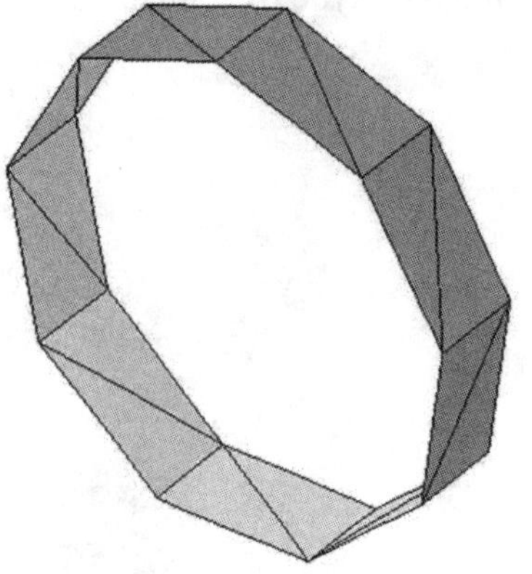

First order triangular shell elements

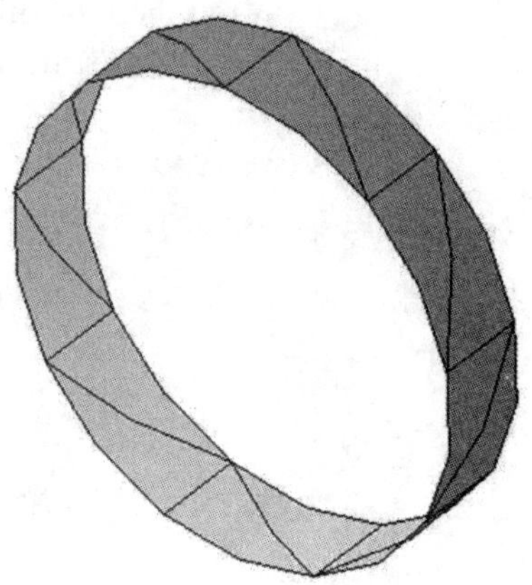

Second order triangular shell elements

Figure 1-6: First order shell elements (left) and second order shell elements (right)

The shell element mesh on the left was created with first order elements. Notice the imprecise mapping of the mesh to curvilinear geometry. The shell element mesh on the right was created with second order elements, which map correctly to curvilinear geometry.

We need to make two important comments about Figure 1-6. First, a mesh should never be that coarse. We use a coarse mesh only to show the differences between first and second order elements clearly. Second, notice "kinks" on the side of second order elements; they indicate locations of mid side nodes. The second order element does map precisely to second order geometry.

As in the case of solid elements, first order shell elements model the linear displacements and constant strain and stress. Second order shell elements model the second order (parabolic) displacement and linear strain and stress.

The assumptions of modeling first or second order displacements in shell elements apply only to in-plane directions. The distribution of in-plane stresses across the thickness is assumed to be linear in both first and second order shell elements.

Triangular elements are the only type of shell elements available in SolidWorks **Simulation**.

Certain classes of shapes can be modeled using either solid or shell elements, such as the plate shown in Figure 1-7. Often the nature of the geometry dictates what type of element should be used for meshing. For example, a part produced by casting would be meshed with solid elements, while a sheet metal structure would be best meshed with shell elements.

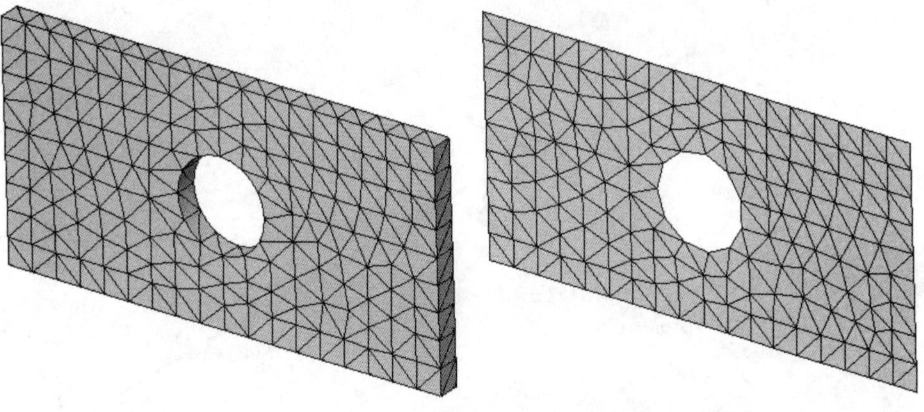

Figure 1-7: Plate modeled with solid elements (left) and shell elements (right)

The actual choice between solids and shells depends on the particular requirements of analysis and sometimes on personal preferences.

Beam elements

Beam elements are created by meshing curves (wire frame geometry). They are a natural choice for meshing weldments. Assumptions about stress distribution in two directions of the beam cross section are made.

A beam element does not have any physical dimensions in the directions normal to its length. It is possible to think of a beam element as a line with assigned beam cross section properties (Figure 1-8).

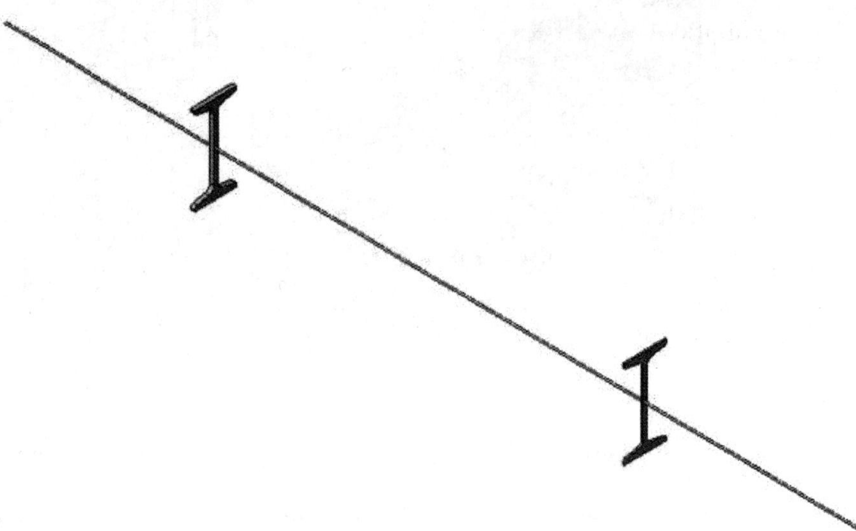

Figure 1-8: Conceptual representation of a beam element

A beam element is a line with assigned properties of a beam cross section as required by beam theory. This illustration conceptualizes how a curve (here a straight line) line defines an I-beam and does not represent actual stored geometry.

Figure 1-9 presents the basic library of elements in SolidWorks **Simulation**. Solid elements are tetrahedral, shell elements are triangles and beam elements are straight lines. Elements such as hexahedral solids, quadrilateral shell or curvilinear beams are not available in SolidWorks **Simulation**.

	Shell elements	**Solid elements**	**Beam elements**
First order element Linear displacement field Constant stress field			
Second order element Parabolic (second order) displacement field Linear stress field			

Figure 1-9: Basic element library of SolidWorks Simulation

The vast majority of analyses use the second order tetrahedral element.

The degrees of freedom (DOF) of a node in a finite element mesh define the ability of the node to perform translation and rotation. The number of degrees of freedom that a node possesses depends on element type. In SolidWorks **Simulation**, nodes of solid elements have three degrees of freedom, while nodes of shell elements have six degrees of freedom.

In order to describe transformation of a solid element from the original to the deformed shape, we only need to know three translational components of nodal displacement. In the case of shell elements, we need to know the translational components of nodal displacements and the rotational displacement components.

What is calculated in FEA?

Each degree of freedom of a node in a finite element mesh constitutes an unknown. In structural analysis, nodal degrees of freedom represent displacement components, while in thermal analysis they represent temperatures. Nodal displacements and nodal temperatures are the primary unknowns for structural analysis and thermal analysis, respectively.

Structural analysis finds displacements, strains and stresses. If solid elements are used, then three displacement components (three translations) per node must be calculated. With shell elements, six displacement components (six translations) must be calculated. Strains and stresses, are calculated based on the nodal displacement results.

Thermal analysis finds temperatures, temperature gradients, and heat flow. Since temperature is a scalar value (unlike displacements, which are vectors), then regardless of what type of element is used, there is only one unknown (temperature) to be found for each node. All other thermal results such as temperature gradient and heat flux are calculated based on temperature results. The fact that there is only one unknown to be found for each node, rather than three or six, makes thermal analysis less computationally intensive than structural analysis.

How to interpret FEA results

Results of structural FEA are provided in the form of displacements and stresses. But how do we decide if a design “passes” or “fails”? What constitutes a failure?

To answer these questions, we need to establish some criteria to interpret FEA results, which may include maximum acceptable displacements, maximum stress, or the lowest acceptable natural frequency.

While displacement and frequency criteria are quite obvious and easy to establish, stress criteria are not. Let us assume that we need to conduct a stress analysis in order to ensure that stresses are within an acceptable range. To judge stress results, we need to understand the mechanism of potential failure. If a part breaks, what stress measure best describes that failure? SolidWorks **Simulation** can present stress results in any desired form, but it is up to us to decide which stress measures should be used to analyze results.

Discussion of various failure criteria would be out of the scope of this book. Any textbook on the Mechanics of Materials provides information on this topic. Here we will limit our discussion to three commonly used failure criteria: Von Mises Stress failure criterion, Maximum Shear Stress failure criterion and Maximum Normal Stress failure criterion.

Von Mises Stress failure criterion

Von Mises stress, also known as Huber stress, is a stress measure that accounts for all six stress components of a general 3-D state of stress (Figure 1-10).

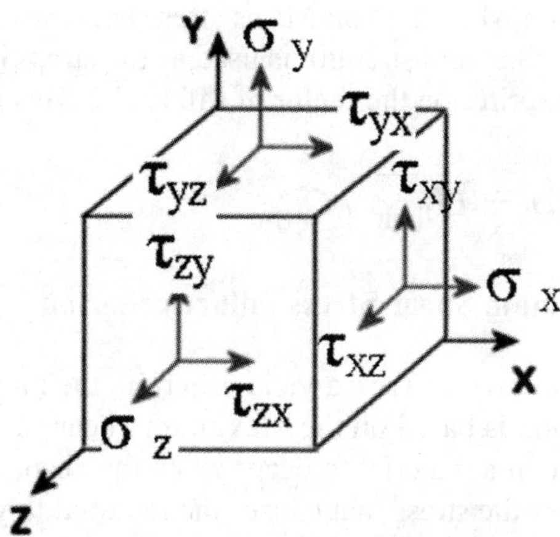

Figure 1-10: General state of stress represented by three normal stresses: σ_x, σ_y, σ_z and six shear stresses

Two components of shear stress and one component of normal stress act on each side of this elementary cube. Due to symmetry of shear stresses, the general 3-D state of stress is characterized by six stress components: σ_x, σ_y, σ_z *and* $\tau_{xy} = \tau_{yx}$, $\tau_{yz} = \tau_{zy}$, $\tau_{xz} = \tau_{zx}$

Von Mises stress σ_{vm}, can be expressed either by six stress components as:

$$\sigma_{vm} = \sqrt{0.5*[(\sigma_x - \sigma_y)^2 + (\sigma_y - \sigma_z)^2 + (\sigma_z - \sigma_x)^2] + 3*(\tau_{xy}^2 + \tau_{yz}^2 + \tau_{zx}^2)}$$

or by three principal stresses (Figure 1-11) as:

$$\sigma_{vm} = \sqrt{0.5*[(\sigma_1 - \sigma_2)^2 + (\sigma_2 - \sigma_3)^2 + (\sigma_3 - \sigma_1)^2]}$$

Note that von Mises stress is a non-negative, scalar stress measure. Von Mises stress is commonly used to present results because the structural safety for many engineering materials showing elasto-plastic properties (for example, steel) can be evaluated using von Mises stress.

The maximum von Mises stress criterion is based on the von Mises-Hencky theory, also known as the shear-energy theory or the maximum distortion energy theory. The theory states that a ductile material starts to yield at a location when the von Mises stress becomes equal to the stress limit. In most cases, the yield strength is used as the stress limit. According to von Mises failure criterion the factor of safety (FOS) is expressed as:

$$FOS = \sigma_{limit} / \sigma_{vm}$$

Maximum Shear Stress failure criterion

Also known as Tresca yield criterion, the maximum shear stress failure criterion is based on the Maximum Shear stress theory. This theory predicts failure of a material to occur when the absolute maximum shear stress (τ_{max}) reaches the stress that causes the material to yield in a simple tension test. The Maximum shear stress criterion is used for ductile materials. According to the Maximum Shear stress failure criterion, the factor of safety is expressed as:

$$FOS = \sigma_{limit} / (2\tau_{max})$$

Maximum Normal Stress failure criterion

By properly adjusting the angular orientation of the stress cube in Figure 1-10, shear stresses disappear and the state of stress is represented only by three principal stresses: σ_1, σ_2, σ_3, as shown in Figure 1-11. In SolidWorks **Simulation**, principal stresses are denoted as P1, P2, and P3.

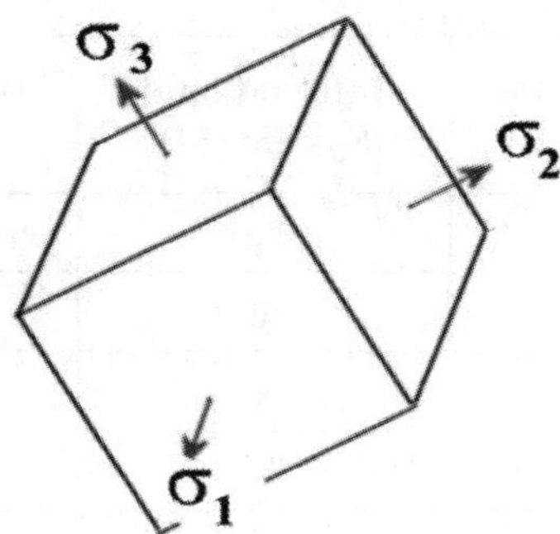

Figure 1-11: General state of stress represented by principal stresses: σ_1, σ_2, σ_3

This criterion is used for brittle materials. It assumes that the ultimate strength of the material in tension and compression is the same. This assumption is not valid in all cases. For example, cracks considerably decrease the strength of the material in tension while their effect is not significant in compression because the cracks tend to close. Brittle materials do not have a specific yield point and hence it is not recommended to use the yield strength to define the limit stress for this criterion.

This criterion predicts failure will occur when σ_1 exceeds stress limit, usually the Ultimate strength. According to maximum principle stress failure criterion the factor of safety FOS is expressed as:

$$FOS = \sigma_{limit} / \sigma_1$$

Units of measure

Internally, SolidWorks **Simulation** uses the International System of Units (SI). However, for the user's convenience, the unit manager allows data entry in any of three systems of units: SI, Metric, and English. Results can be displayed using any of the three systems. Figure 1-12 summarizes the available systems of units.

	International System (SI)	**Metric (MKS)**	**English (IPS)**
Mass	kg	kg	lb
Length	m	cm	in
Time	s	s	s
Force	N	Kgf	lbf
Gravitational acceleration	m/s^2	G	in/s^2
Mass density	kg/m^3	kg/cm^3	lbf/in^3
Temperature	K	°C	°F

Figure 1-12: Unit systems available in SolidWorks Simulation

SI, Metric, and English systems of units can be interchanged when entering data and analyzing results in SolidWorks Simulation.

As SolidWorks **Simulation** users, we are spared much confusion and trouble with systems of units. However, we may be asked to prepare data or interpret the results of other FEA software where we do not have the convenience of the unit manager. Therefore, we will make some general comments about the use of different systems of units in the preparation of input data for FEA models. We can use any consistent system of units for FEA models, but in practice, the choice of the system of units is dictated by what units are used in the CAD model. The system of units in CAD models is not always consistent; length can be expressed in [*mm*], while mass density can be expressed in [kg/m^3]. Contrary to CAD models, in FEA all units *must* be consistent. Inconsistencies are easy to overlook, especially when defining mass and mass density and can lead to serious errors.

In the SI system, which is based on meters [*m*] for length, kilograms [*kg*] for mass, and seconds [*s*] for time, all other units are easily derived from these basic units. In mechanical engineering, length is commonly expressed in millimeters [*mm*], force in Newtons [*N*], and time in seconds [*s*]. All other units must then be derived from these basic units: [*mm*], [*N*], and [*s*]. Consequently, the unit of mass is defined as a mass which, when subjected to a unit force equal to 1N, will accelerate with a unit acceleration of 1 mm/s^2. Therefore, the unit of mass in a system using [*mm*] for length and [*N*] for force, is equivalent to 1000 kg or one metric ton. Therefore, mass density is expressed in metric tonnes [$tonne/mm^3$]. This is critically important to remember when defining material properties in FEA software without a unit manager. Notice in Figure 1-13 that an erroneous definition of mass density in [kg/m^3] rather than in [$tonne/mm^3$] results in mass density being one trillion (10^{12}) times higher.

System SI	**[m], [N], [s]**
Unit of mass	kg
Unit of mass density	kg/m^3
Density of aluminum	2794 kg/m^3

System of units derived from SI	**[mm], [N], [s]**
Unit of mass	tonne
Unit of mass density	$tonne/mm^3$
Density of aluminum	2.794×10^{-9} $tonne/mm^3$

English system (IPS)	**[in], [lb], [s]**
Unit of mass	slug/12
Unit of mass density	$slug/12/in^3$
Density of aluminum	2.614×10^{-4} $slug/12/in^3$

Figure 1-13: Mass density of aluminum in the three systems of units

Comparison of numerical values of mass densities of 1060 aluminum alloy defined in the SI system of units with the system of units derived from SI, and with the English (IPS) system of units.

Using on-line help

SolidWorks **Simulation** features very extensive on-line Help and Tutorial functions, which can be accessed from the Help menu in the main SolidWorks tool bar (Figure 1-14 top). The Study advisor can be accessed from the Study drop down menu (Figure 1-14 bottom).

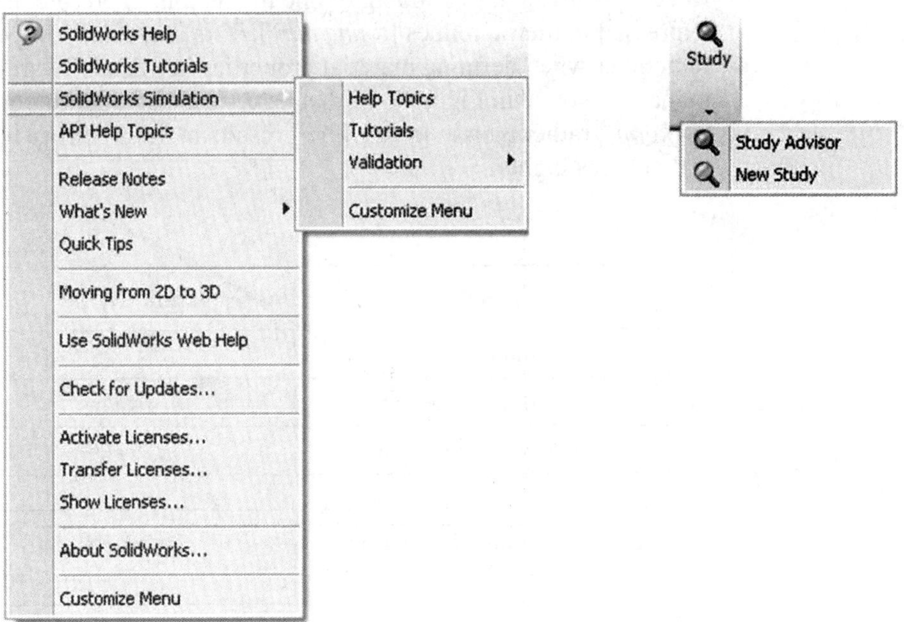

Help Topics, Tutorials, Validation

Study Advisor

Figure 1-14: Accessing the on-line Help, and Study Advisor

On-line Help, Tutorial and Validation can be accessed from the main SolidWorks toolbar (left). The Study Advisor can be accessed from the Study drop down menu (right).

Limitations of SolidWorks Simulation Professional

We need to appreciate some important limitations of SolidWorks **Simulation** Professional: material is assumed as linear, and loads are static.

Linear material

Whatever material we assign to the analyzed parts or assemblies, the material is assumed as linear, meaning that stress is proportional to strain (Figure 1-15).

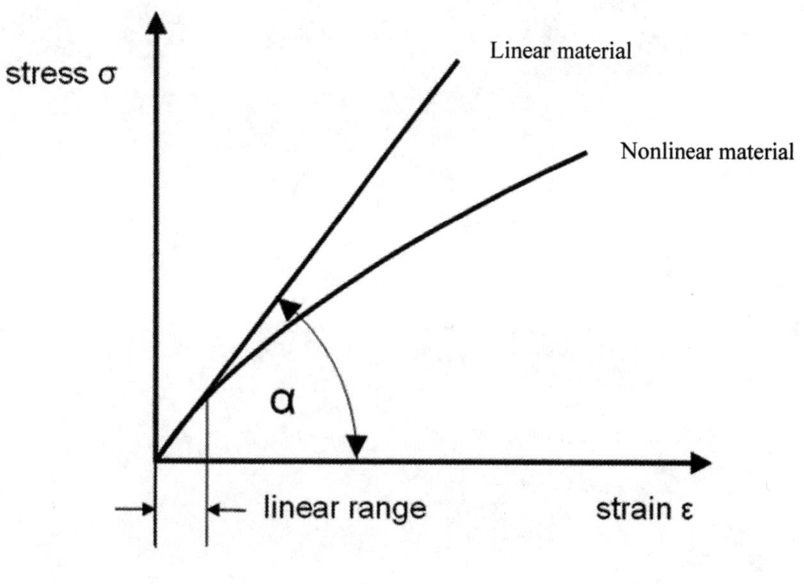

$$E = \frac{\sigma}{\varepsilon} = \tan\alpha$$

Figure 1-15: Linear material model assumed in SolidWorks Simulation

In linear material, stress is linearly proportional to strain. The linear range is where linear and nonlinear material models are not significantly different.

Using a linear material model, the maximum stress magnitude is not limited to yield or to ultimate stress as it is in reality. Material yielding is not modeled, and whether or not yield may in fact be taking place can only be established based on the stress magnitudes reported in results. Most analyzed structures experience stresses below the yield stress, and the factor of safety is most often related to the yield stress. Therefore, the limitations imposed by linear material seldom impede SolidWorks **Simulation** Professional users.

Static loads

All structural loads and restraints are assumed not to change with time. Dynamic loading conditions cannot be analyzed with SolidWorks **Simulation** Professional (the only exception is **Drop Test** analysis). This limitation implies that loads are applied slowly enough to ignore inertial effects.

Nonlinear material analysis and dynamic analysis can be performed with SolidWorks **Simulation** Premium.

2: Static analysis of a plate

Topics covered

- Using SolidWorks **Simulation** interface
- Linear static analysis with solid elements
- Finding reaction forces
- Controlling discretization errors by the convergence process
- Finding reaction forces
- Presenting FEA results in desired format

Project description

A steel plate is supported and loaded, as shown in Figure 2-1. We assume that the support is rigid (this is also called built-in support or fixed support) and that a 100000N tensile load is uniformly distributed along the end face, opposite to the supported face.

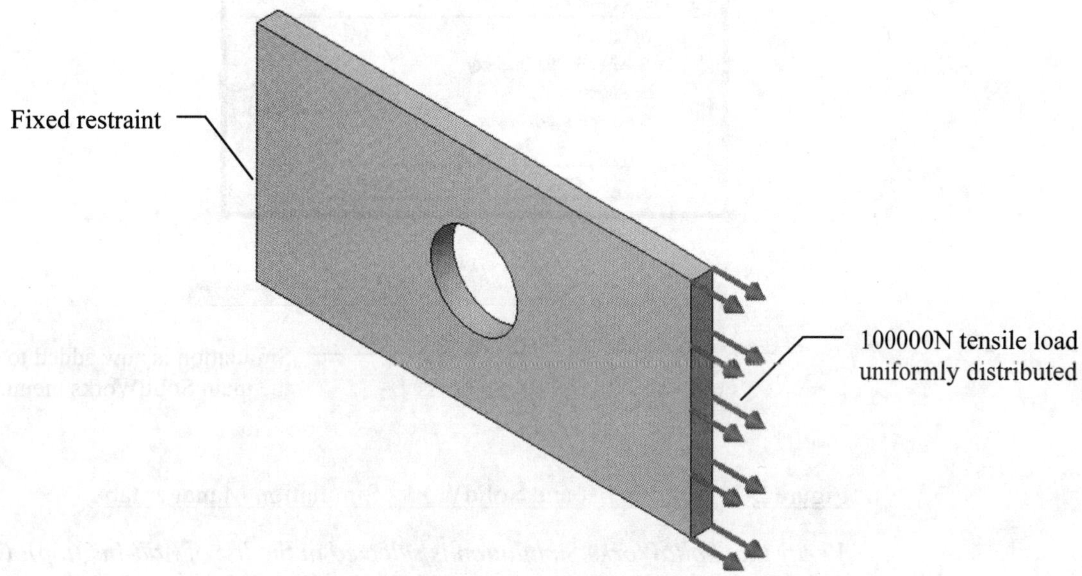

Figure 2-1: SolidWorks model of a rectangular plate with a hole

We will perform displacement and stress analysis using meshes with different element sizes. Note that repetitive analysis with different meshes does *not* represent standard practice in FEA. The process does however produce results which are useful in gaining more insight into how FEA works.

Procedure

In SolidWorks, open the model file called HOLLOW PLATE. Verify that SolidWorks **Simulation** is selected in the **Add-Ins** list (Figure 2-2).

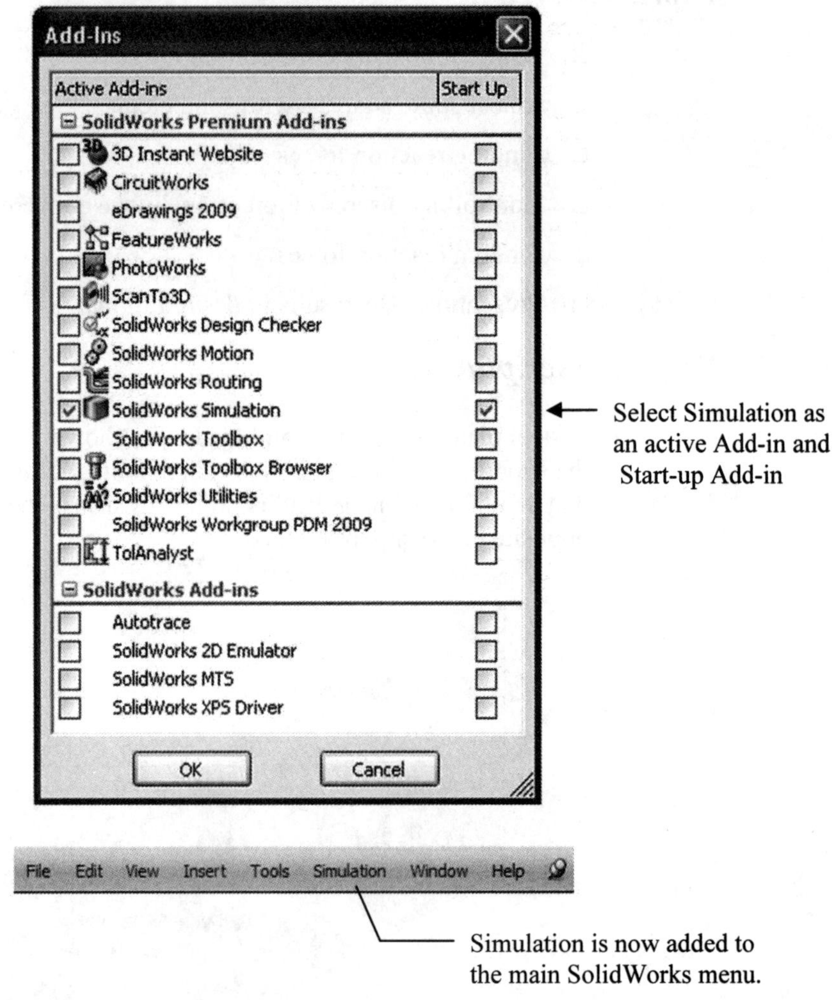

Figure 2-2: Add-Ins list and SolidWorks Simulation Manager tab

Verify that SolidWorks Simulation is selected in the list of Add-Ins (top). Once Solid Works Simulation has been added, Simulation shows in the main SolidWorks tool menu (bottom).

It is necessary to add the **Simulation** tab to the **Command Manager** if it is not visible. If the **Simulation** tab has been added but is still not showing, follow steps explained in Figure 2-3.

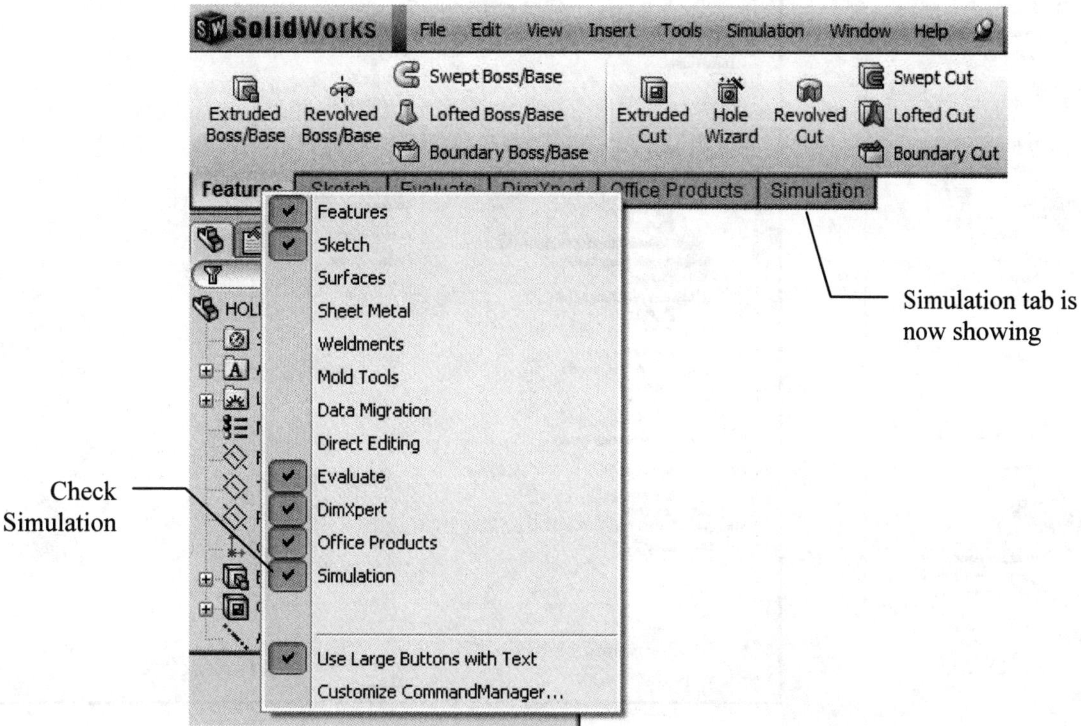

<u>Figure 2-3: How to display Simulation tab in SolidWorks Command Manager</u>

Right-click any tab in Command Manager and check "Simulation" from the pop-up menu to make the Simulation visible.

Before we create the FEA model, let's review the **Simulation** main menu along with its **Options** window (Figure 2-4).

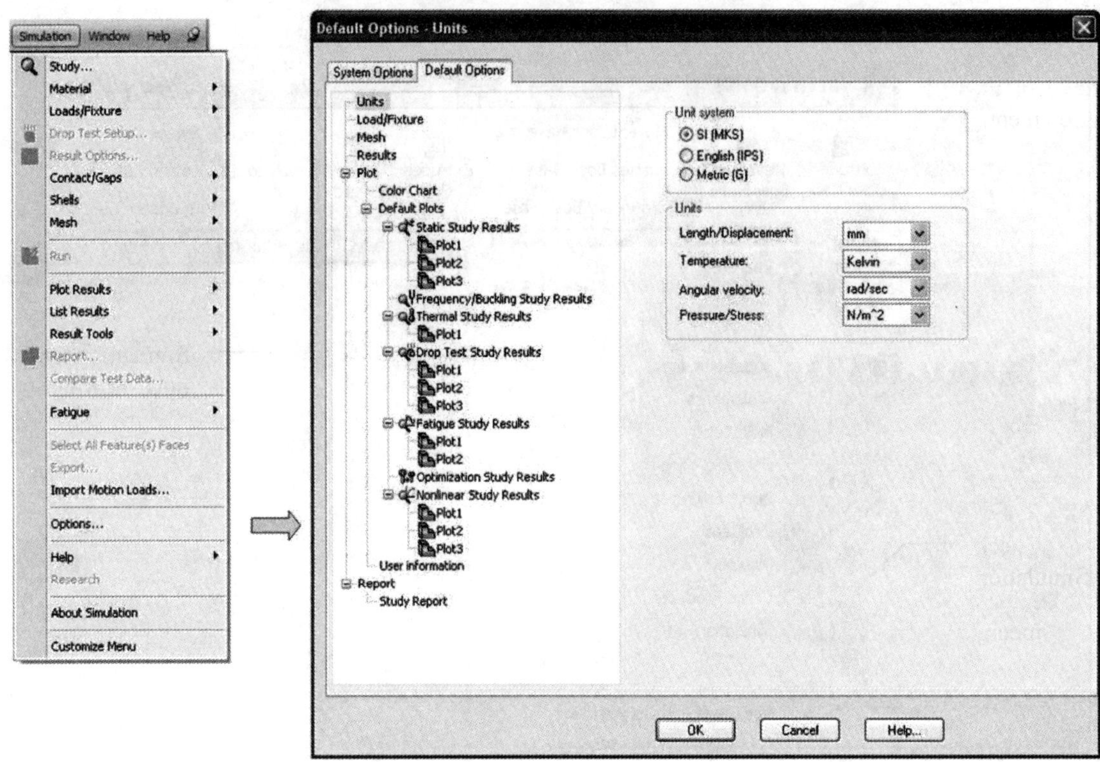

Figure 2-4: Simulation main menu (left) and Options window; shown is Default Options tab

The Default Options window has two tabs. Review both tabs before proceeding with the exercise. Note that Default Plots can be added, deleted or grouped into sub-folders which are created by right-clicking on the Static Study Results folder, Thermal Study Results folder etc. As shown above, we use the SI system as specified in Default Options tab.

Creation of an FEA model starts with the definition of a study. To define a new study, select **New Study** either from the **Simulation** menu (Figure 2-5 left) or the **Simulation** Command Manager (Figure 2-5 right). Name the study *tensile load 01*.

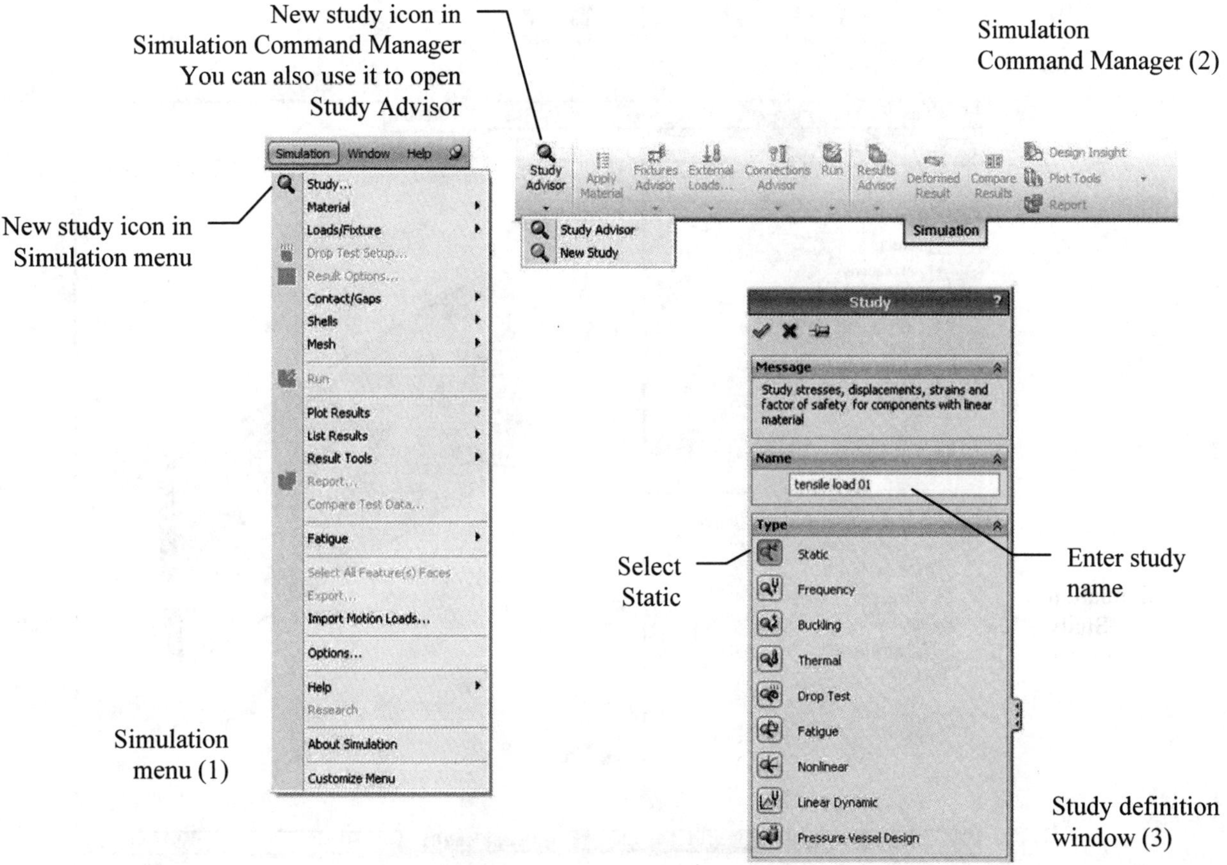

Figure 2-5: Creating a New Study

A study can be created either using Simulation menu (1) or Simulation Command Manager (2) Also shown is Study definition window (3)

Once a new study has been created, all Simulation Commands can be invoked in three ways:

- ❑ From the Simulation main menu
- ❑ From the Simulation tab in Command Manager
- ❑ By right-clicking appropriate items in the study window

In this book, we will most often use the third method.

When a study is defined, SolidWorks **Simulation** creates a study window located below the SolidWorks **Feature Manager** window and places several folders in it. It also adds a study tab that provides access to the window (Figure 2-6).

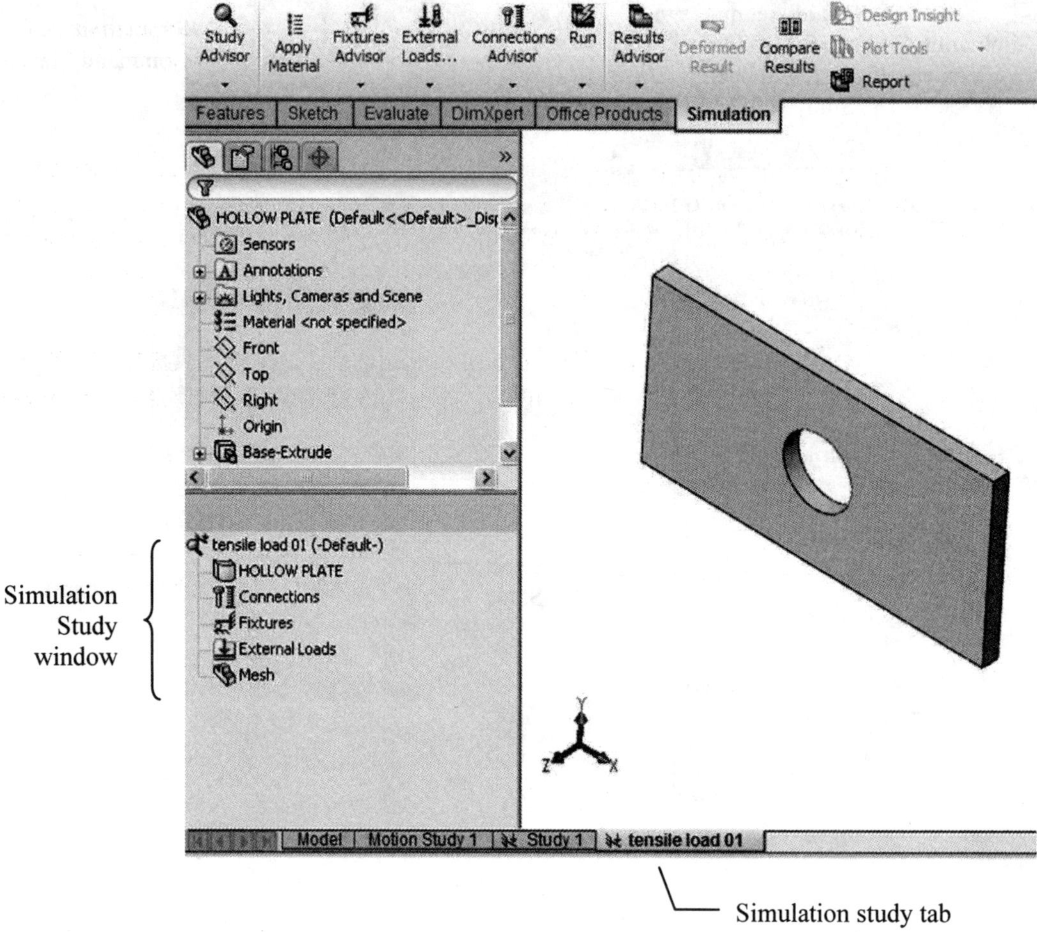

Figure 2-6: Simulation window and Simulation tab

You can switch between SolidWorks Model, Motion Studies and Simulation Studies by selecting the appropriate the tab.

We are now ready to define the analysis model. This process generally consists of the following steps:

- CAD geometry idealization and/or simplification in preparation for analysis. This is usually done by creating analysis specific configuration and making your changes there
- Material properties assignment
- Restraints application
- Load application

In this case, the geometry does not need any preparation because it is already very simple, therefore we can start by assigning material properties.

Notice that if a material is defined for a **SolidWorks** part model, material definition is automatically transferred to the **Simulation** model. Assigning a material to the SolidWorks model is actually a preferred modeling technique, especially when working with an assembly consisting of parts with many different materials. We will do this in later exercises.

To apply material to the **Simulation** model, right-click the HOLLOW PLATE folder in the *tensile load 01* simulation study and select **Apply/Edit Material** from the pop-up menu (Figure 2-7).

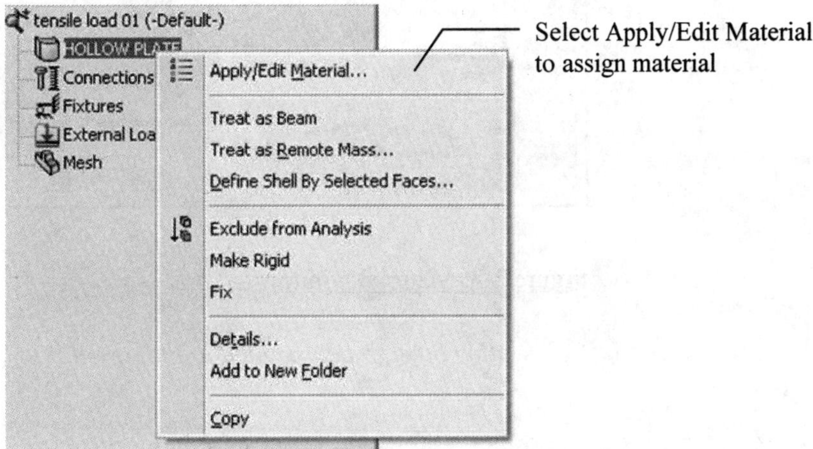

Figure 2-7: Assigning material properties

The action in Figure 2-7 opens the **Material** window shown in Figure 2-8.

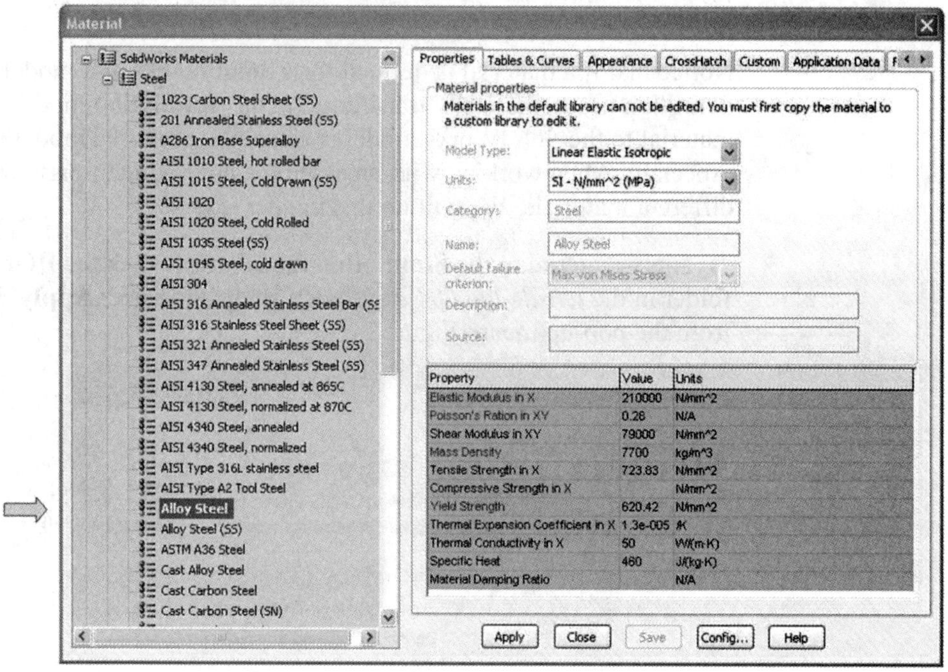

Figure 2-8: Material window

Select Alloy Steel to be assigned to the model.

In the **Material** window, the properties are highlighted to indicate the mandatory and optional properties. A red description (Elastic modulus, Poisson's ratio) indicates a property that is mandatory based on the active study type and the material model. A blue description (Mass density, Tensile strength, Compressive strength, Yield strength, Thermal expansion coefficient) indicates optional properties. A black description (Thermal conductivity, Specific heat, Material damping ratio) indicates properties not applicable to the current study.

In the **Material** window select **From library files** in the **Select material source** area, and then select **Alloy Steel.** Select **SI** units under the **Properties** tab (other units could be used as well). Notice that the *HOLLOW PLATE* folder in *tensile load 01* study now shows a check mark and the name of the selected material to indicate that a material has been assigned. If needed, you can define your own material by selecting **Custom Defined** material.

Material definition consists of two steps:

- Material selection (or material definition if a custom material is used)
- Material assignment (either to all solids in the model, selected bodies of a multi-body part, or to selected components of an assembly)

Having assigned the material, we now move to defining the loads and restraints. To display the pop-up menu that lists the options available for defining restraints, right-click the *Fixtures* folder in the *tensile load 01* study (Figure 2-9).

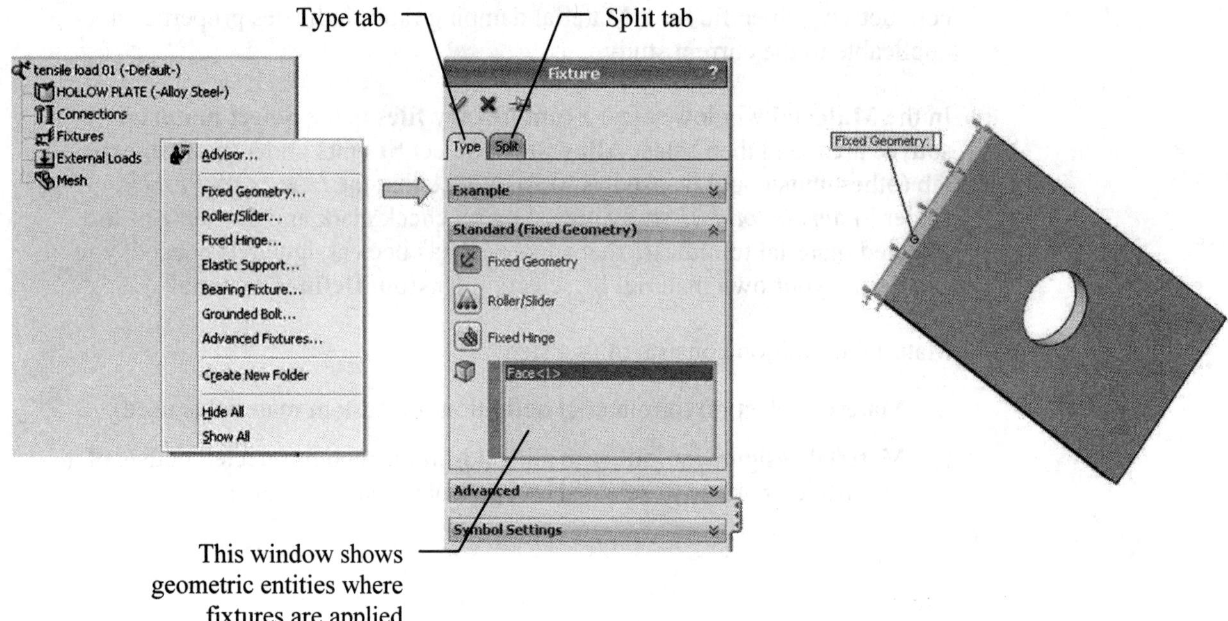

Figure 2-9: Pop-up menu for the Fixtures folder and Fixture definition window

All restraints definitions are done in the Type tab. The Split tab is used to define a split face where a restraint is to be defined. The same can be done in SolidWorks by defining a Split Line.

Once the **Fixtures** definition window is open, select the **Fixed Geometry** restraint type. Select the end-face entity where the restraint is applied.

Note that in SolidWorks **Simulation,** the term “Fixture” implies that the model is firmly “fixed” to ground. However, aside from **Fixed Geometry**, which we have just used, all other types of fixtures restrain the model in certain directions while allowing movements in other directions. Therefore, the term “restraint” may better describe what happens when choices in the **Fixture** window are made. In this book we will switch between terms “fixture” and “restraint” freely.

Before proceeding, explore other types of restraints accessible through the **Fixture** window. All types of restraints are divided in two groups: **Standard** and **Advanced**. Review animated examples available in the **Fixture** window and study the following chart.

Standard Fixtures	
Fixed	Also called built-in or rigid support, all translational and all rotational degrees of freedom are restrained.
Immovable **(No translations)**	Only translational degrees of freedom are constrained, while rotational degrees of freedom remain unconstrained. If solid elements are used (like in this exercise), **Fixed** and **Immovable** restraints would have the same effect because solid elements do not have rotational degrees of freedom. Therefore, **Immovable** restraint is not available if solid elements are used.
Hinge	Applies only to cylindrical face and specifies that the cylindrical face can only rotate about its own axis. This condition is identical to selecting the **On cylindrical face** restraint type and setting the radial and axial components to zero.
Advanced Fixtures	
Symmetry	Applies symmetry boundary conditions to a flat face. Translation in the direction normal to the face is restrained and rotations about the axes aligned with the face are restrained.
Roller/Sliding	Specifies that a planar face can move freely on its plane but not in the direction normal to its plane. The face can shrink or expand under loading.
Use reference geometry	Restrains a face, edge, or vertex only in certain directions, while leaving the other directions free to move. You can specify the desired directions of restraint in relation to the selected reference plane or reference axis.
On flat face	Provides restraints in selected directions, which are defined by the three directions of the flat face where restraints are being applied.
On cylindrical face	This option is similar to **On flat face**, except that the three directions of a cylindrical face define the directions of restraints.
On spherical face	Similar to **On flat face** and **On cylindrical face**. The three directions of a spherical face define the directions of applied restraints.
Cyclic symmetry	Allows analysis of a model with circular patterns around an axis by modeling a representative segment. The segment can be a part or an assembly. The geometry, restraints, and loading conditions must be identical for all other segments making up the model. Turbine, fans, flywheels, and motor rotors can usually be analyzed using cyclic symmetry.

When a model is fully supported (as it is in our case), we say that the model does not have any rigid body motions (the term "rigid body modes" is also used), meaning it cannot move without experiencing deformation.

Note that the presence of restraints in the model is manifested by both the restraint symbols (showing on the restrained face) and by the automatically created icon, **Fixture-1**, in the *Fixtures* folder. The display of the restraint symbols can be turned on and off by either:

- Right-clicking the *Fixture*s folder and selecting **Hide All** or **Show All** in the pop-up menu shown in Figure 2-9 , or
- Right-clicking the fixture icon and selecting **Hide** or **Show** from the pop-up menu.

Now define the load by right-clicking the *External Loads* folder and selecting **Force** from the pop-up menu. This action opens the **Force** window as shown in Figure 2-10.

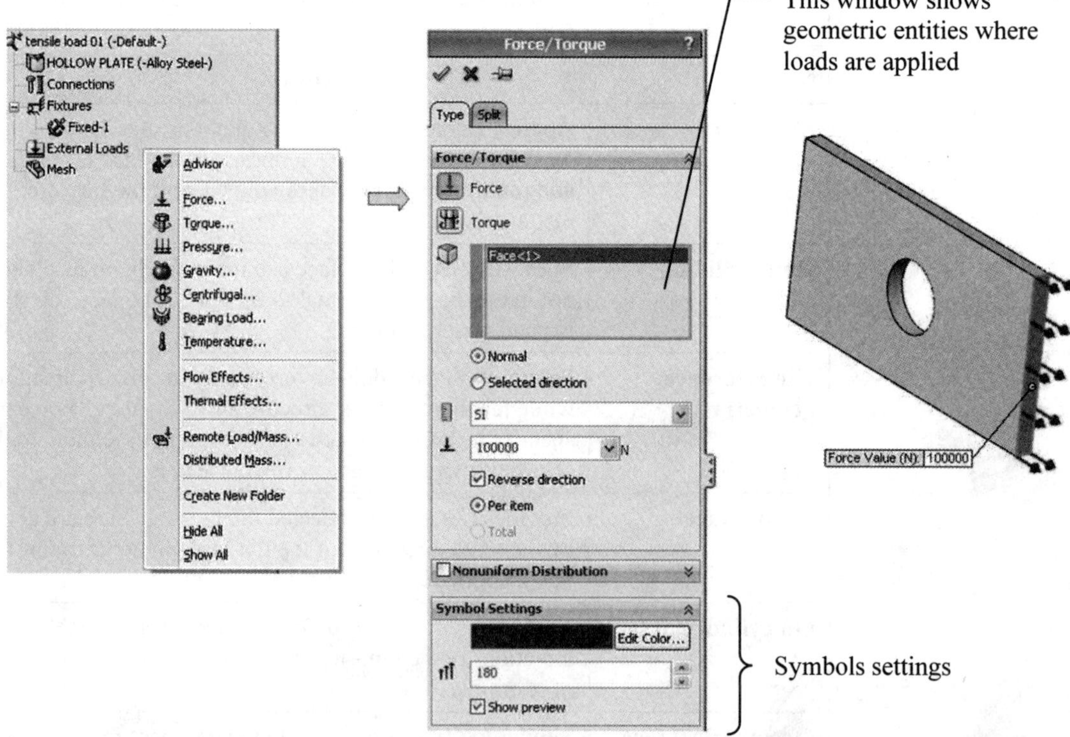

Figure 2-10: Force window

The Force window displays the selected face where the tensile force is applied. If only one entity is selected, there is no distinction between Per Item and Total. This illustration also shows the model with symbols of applied restraint and load. Load symbols have been enlarged by adjusting the Symbols Settings.

In the **Type** tab, select **Normal** in order to load the model with a 100000N tensile force uniformly distributed over the end face, as shown in Figure 2-10. Check the **Reverse direction** option to apply a tensile load.

Generally, forces can be applied to faces, edges, and vertices using different methods, which are reviewed below:

Force normal	Available for flat faces only, this option applies load in the direction normal to the selected face.
Force selected direction	This option applies a force or a moment to a face, edge, or vertex in the direction defined by the selected reference geometry. Moments can be applied only if shell elements are used. Shell elements have six degrees of freedom per node: three translations and three rotations, and can take a moment load. Solid elements only have three degrees of freedom (translations) per node and, therefore, cannot take a moment load directly. If you need to apply moments to solid elements, they must be represented with appropriately applied forces.
Torque	This option applies torque (expressed by traction forces) about a reference axis using the right-hand rule.

Try using the click-inside technique to rename the **Fixture-1** and **Force/Torque-1** icons. Note that renaming using the click-inside technique works on all icons in SolidWorks **Simulation**.

The model is now ready for meshing. Before creating a mesh, let's make a few observations about defining the geometry, material properties, loads and restraints.

Geometry preparation is a well-defined step with few uncertainties. Geometry that is simplified for analysis can be compared with the original CAD model.

Material properties are most often selected from the material library and do not account for local defects, surface conditions, etc. Therefore, definition of material properties usually has more uncertainties than geometry preparation.

The definition of loads is done in a few quick menu selections, but involves many assumptions. Factors such as load magnitude and distribution are often only approximately known and must be assumed. Therefore, significant idealization errors can be made when defining loads.

Defining restraints is where severe errors are most often made. For example, it is easy enough to apply a fixed restraint without giving too much thought to the fact that a fixed restraint means a rigid support – a mathematical abstraction. A common error is over-constraining the model, which results in an overly stiff structure that underestimates displacements and stresses. The relative level of uncertainties in defining geometry, material, loads, and restraints is qualitatively shown in Figure 2-11.

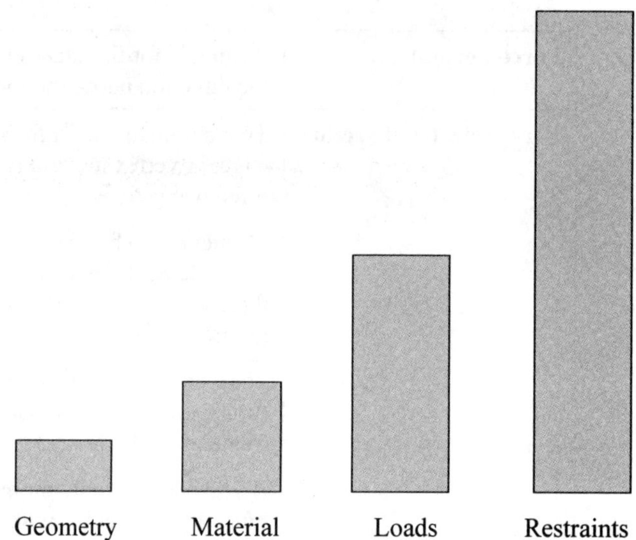

Figure 2-11: Qualitative comparison of uncertainty in defining geometry, material properties, loads, and restraints

The level of uncertainty (or the risk of error) has no relation to time required for each step, so the message in Figure 2-11 may be counterintuitive. In fact, preparing CAD geometry for FEA may take hours, while applying restraints and loads takes only a few clicks.

In all of the examples presented in this book, we assume that definitions of material properties, loads, and restraints represent an acceptable idealization of real conditions. However, we need to point out that it is the responsibility of the FEA user to determine if all those idealized assumptions made during the creation of the mathematical model are indeed acceptable.

Before meshing the model, we need to verify under the **Default Options**' **Mesh** tab that **High** mesh quality is selected. The **Options** window can be opened from SolidWorks **Simulation** menu as shown in Figure 2-12.

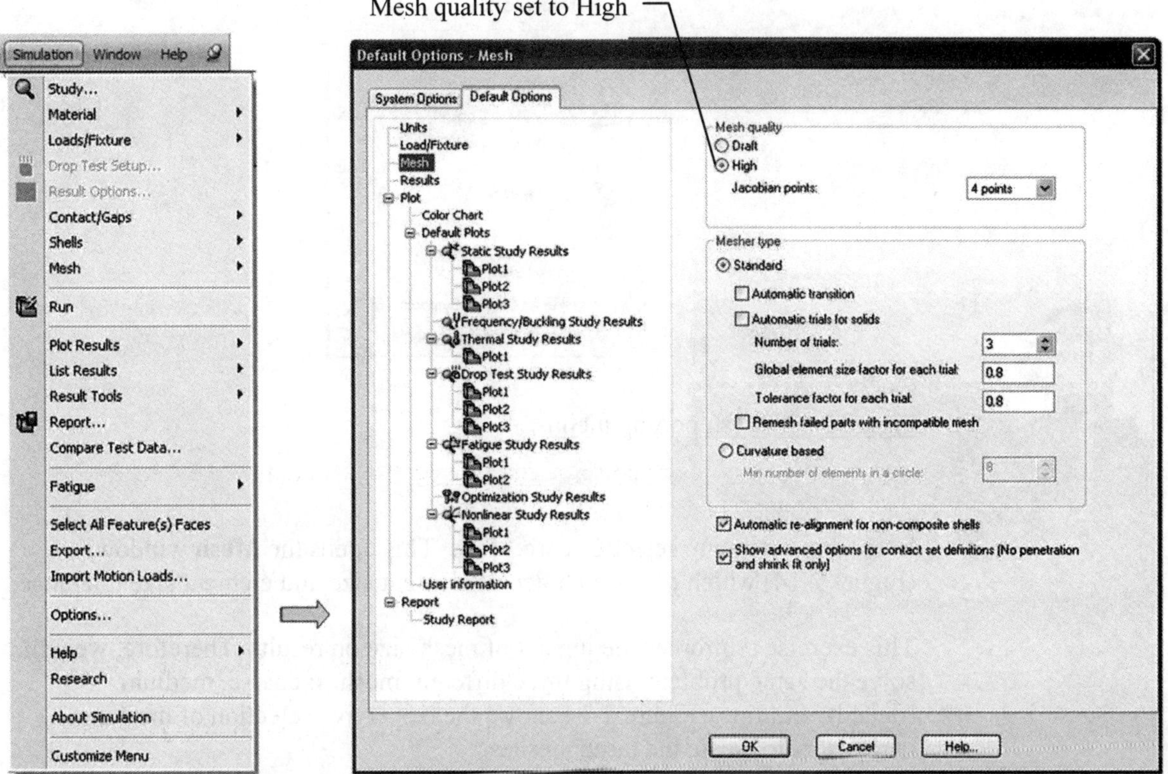

Figure 2-12: Mesh settings in the Options window

Use this window to verify that mesh quality is set to High.

The difference between **High** and **Draft** mesh quality is that:

- Draft quality mesh uses first order elements
- High quality mesh uses second order elements

Differences between first and second order elements were discussed in chapter 1.

Now, right-click the *Mesh* folder to display the pop-up menu (Figure 2-13).

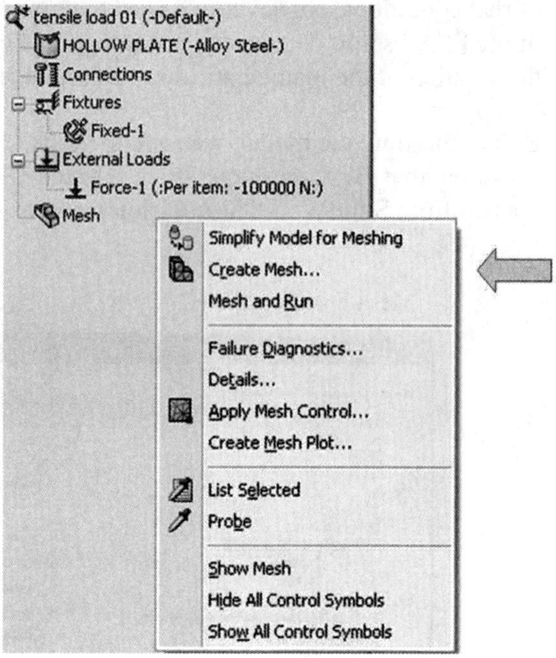

Figure 2-13: Mesh pop-up menu

In the pop-up menu, select **Create Mesh**. This opens the **Mesh** window (Figure 2-14) which offers a choice of element size and element size tolerance.

This exercise reinforces the impact of mesh size on results. Therefore, we will solve the same problem using three different meshes: coarse, medium (default) and fine. Figure 2-14 shows the respective selection of meshing parameters to create the three meshes.

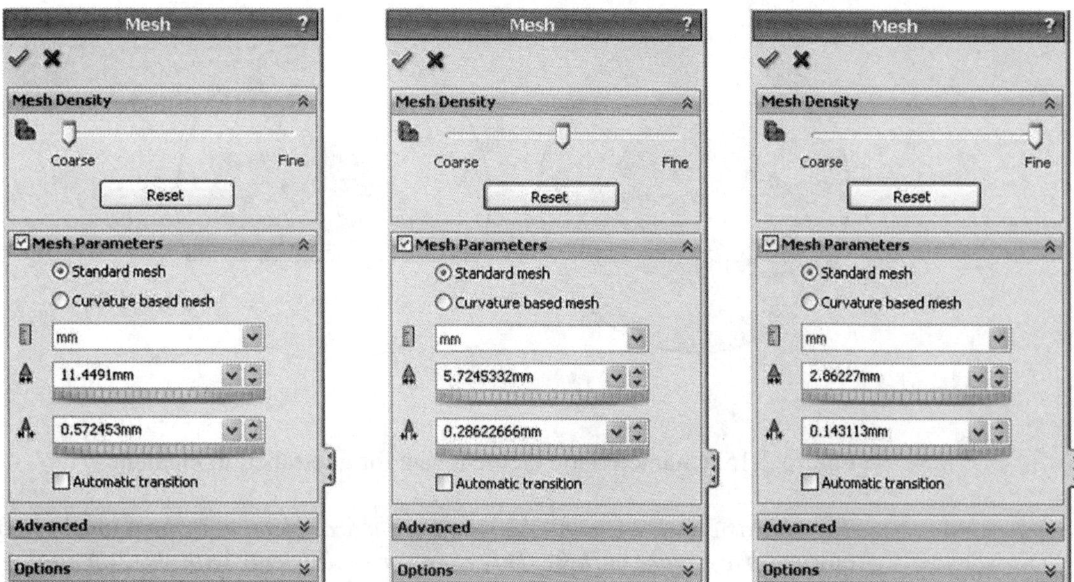

Figure 2-14: Three choices for mesh density from left to right: coarse, medium (default), and fine

Select mesh Parameters to see the element size. In all three cases use Standard mesh. Note different slider positions in the three windows.

The medium mesh density, shown in the middle window in Figure 2-14, is the default that SolidWorks **Simulation** proposes for meshing our model. The element size of 5.72 mm and the element size tolerance of 0.286mm are established automatically based on the geometric features of the SolidWorks model. The 5.72-mm size is the characteristic element size in the mesh, as explained in Figure 2-15. The default tolerance is 5% of the global element size. If the distance between two nodes is smaller than this value, the nodes are merged unless otherwise specified by contact conditions (contact conditions are not present in this model).

Mesh density has a direct impact on the accuracy of results. The smaller the elements, the lower are the discretization errors, but the meshing and solving time both take longer. In the majority of analyses with SolidWorks **Simulation**, the default mesh settings produce meshes that provide acceptable discretization errors, while keeping solution times reasonably short.

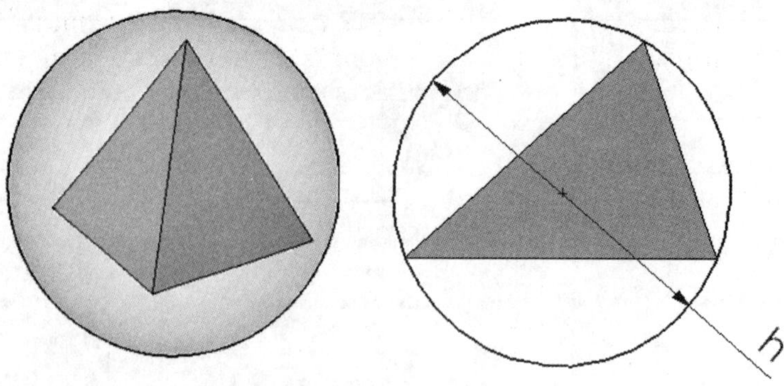

Figure 2-15: Characteristic element size for a tetrahedral element

The characteristic element size of a tetrahedral element is the diameter h of a circumscribed sphere (left). This is easier to illustrate with the 2-D analogy of a circle circumscribed on a triangle (right).

Right-click the *Mesh* folder again and select **Create…** to open the **Mesh** window.

With the **Mesh** window open, set the slider all the way to the left (as illustrated in Figure 2-14, left) to create a coarse mesh, and click the green checkmark button. The mesh will be displayed as shown in Figure 2-16.

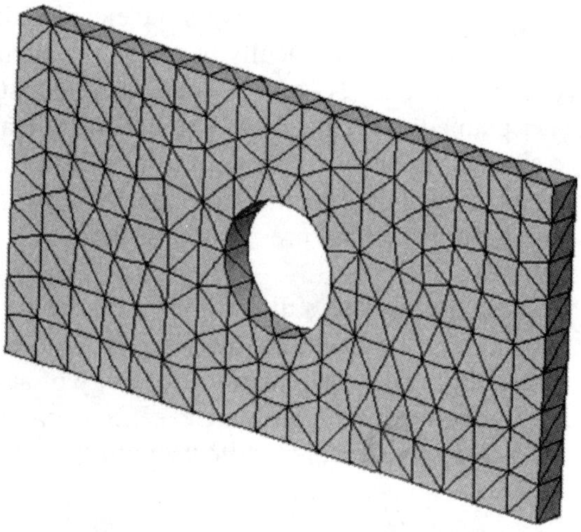

Figure 2-16: Coarse mesh created with second order, solid tetrahedral elements

You can control the mesh visibility by selecting Hide Mesh or Show Mesh from the pop-up menu shown in Figure 2-13.

To start the solution, right-click the *tensile load 01* study folder which displays a pop-up menu (Figure 2-17). Select **Run** to start the solution.

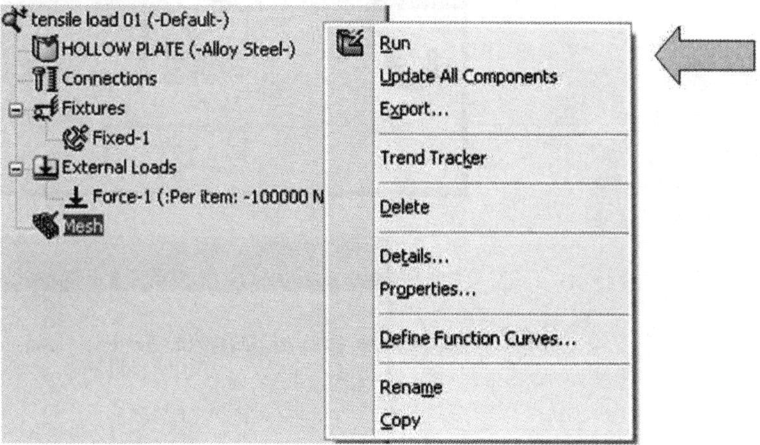

Figure 2-17: Pop-up menu for the *Study* folder

Start the solution by right-clicking the tensile load 01 folder to display a pop-up menu. Select Run to start the solution.

The solution can be executed with different properties, which we will investigate in later chapters. You can monitor the solution progress while the solution is running (Figure 2-18).

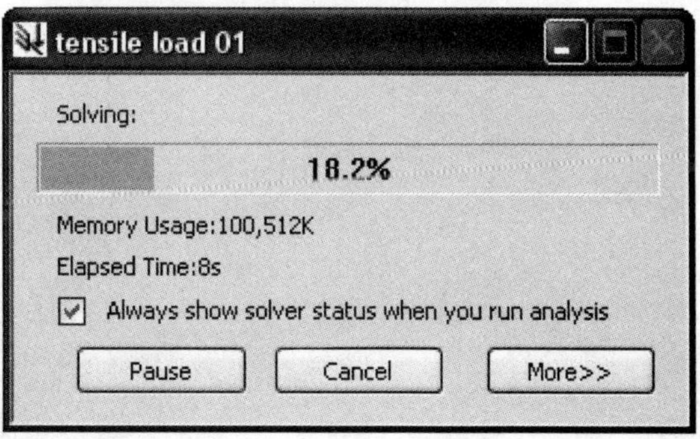

Figure 2-18: Solution Progress window

The Solver reports solution progress while the solution is running.

If the solution fails, the failure is reported as shown in Figure 2-19.

Linear Static
No restraints are defined.
You may use Soft Spring or Inertia Relief options.
OK

Simulation
HOLLOW PLATE-tensile load
01 : Failed
OK

Figure 2-19: Failed solution warning window

Here solution of model with no restraints was attempted. Once the error message has been acknowledged (top), solver displays the final outcome of solution (bottom).

When the solution completes successfully, **Simulation** creates a *Results* folder with result plots which are defined in **Simulation Default Options** as shown in Figure 2-20.

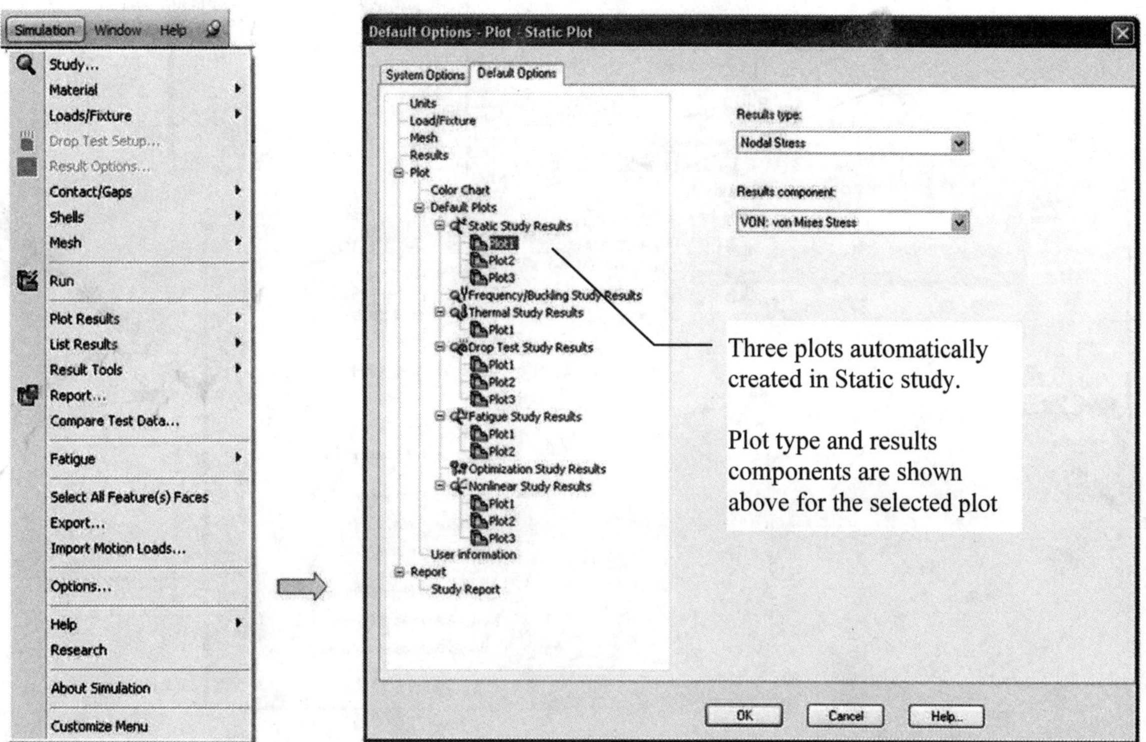

Figure 2-20: Plots that are automatically placed in *Results* folder are defined in Simulation Default Options

Review the definition of all plots in a Static study.

In a typical configuration three plots are created automatically in the Static study:

- *Stress1* showing von Mises stresses
- *Displacement1* showing resultant displacements
- *Strain1* showing equivalent strain

Make sure that the above plots are defined in your configuration, if not, define them.

Once the solution completes, you can add more plots to the *Results* folder. You can also create subfolders in the *Results* folder to group plots (Figure 2-21).

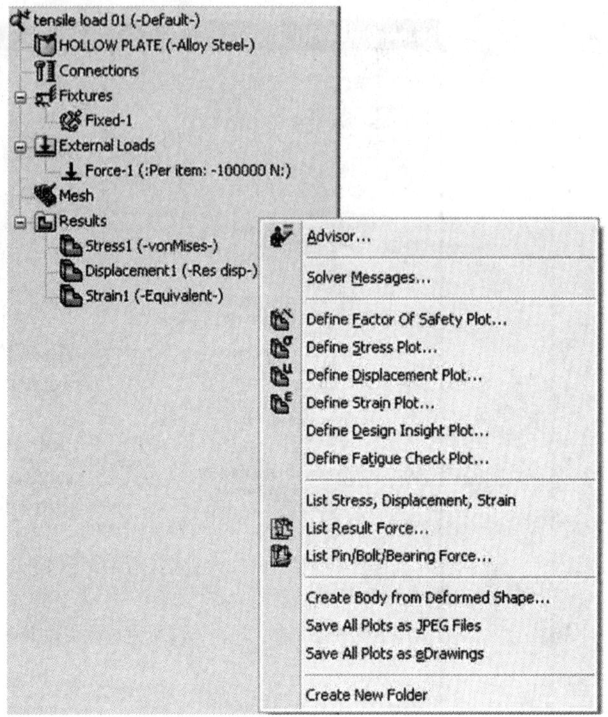

Figure 2-21: More plots and folders can be added to *Results* folder

Right-clicking on Results activates this pop-up menu from which plots may be added to the Results folder.

To display stress results, double-click on the **Stress1** icon in the *Results* folder or right-click it and select **Show** from the pop-up menu. The default stress plot is shown in Figure 2-22.

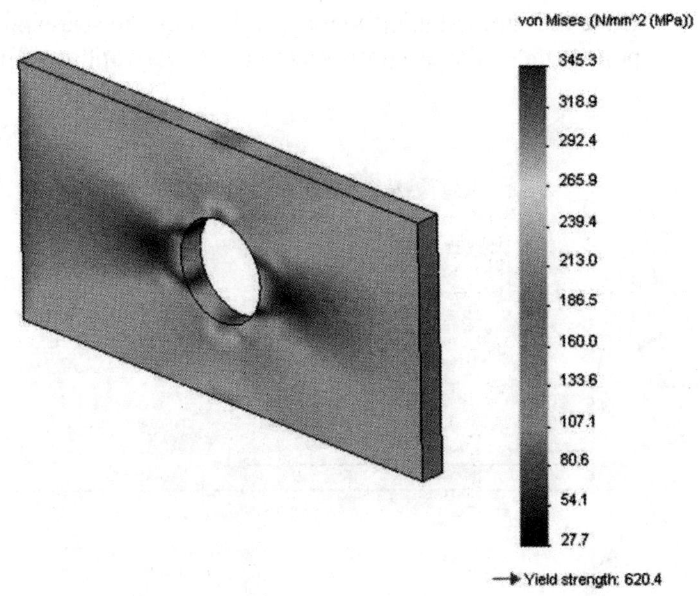

Figure 2-22: Stress plot displayed using default stress plot settings

Von Mises stress results are shown by default in the stress plot window. Notice that results are shown in [MPa] and the highest stress 345 MPa is below the material yield strength 620 MPa. The actual numerical results may differ slightly depending on solver, software version and service pack used.

Once the stress plot is showing, right-click the stress plot icon to display the pop-up menu featuring different plot display options (Figure 2-23).

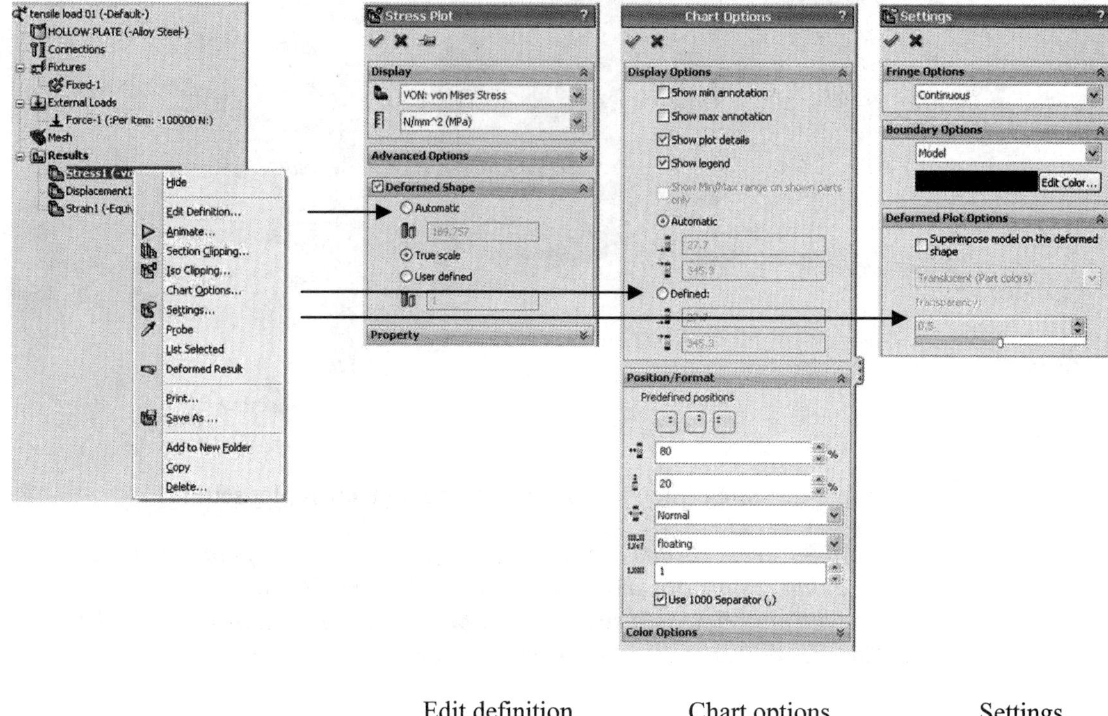

Edit definition Chart options Settings

Figure 2-23: Pop-up menu with plot display options

Any plot can be modified using selections from the pop-up menu (left). Arrows relate selections in the pop-up menu to the invoked windows. Explore all selections offered by these three windows. In particular explore color Options accessible from Chart Options, not shown in the above illustration.

We now examine how to modify the stress plot using the **Settings** window shown in Figure 2-23. In **Settings,** select **Discrete** in **Fringe options** and **Mesh** in **Boundary options** to produce the stress plot shown in Figure 2-24.

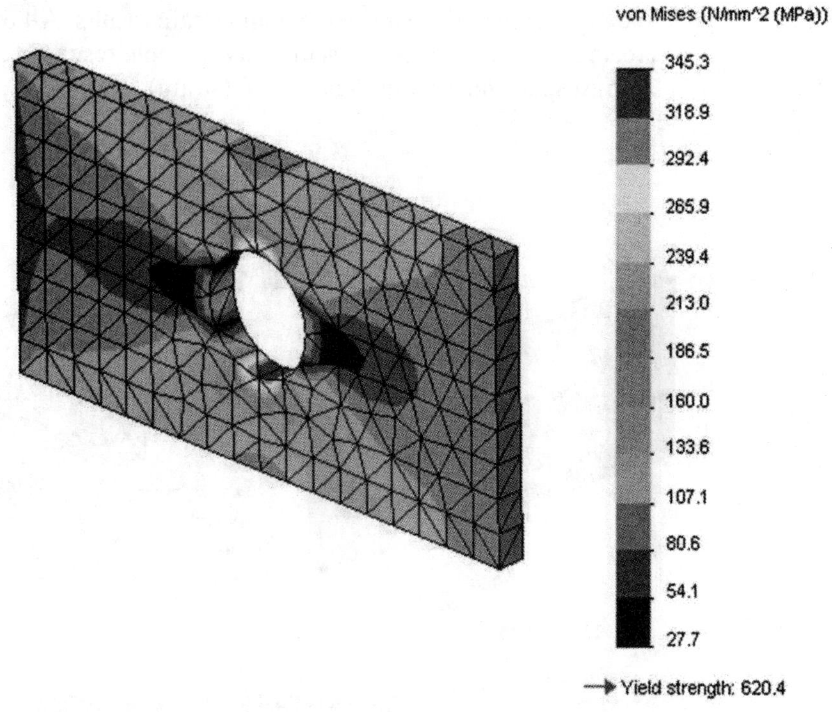

Figure 2-24: The modified stress plot is shown with discrete fringes and the mesh superimposed on the stress plot

The Stress plot in Figure 2-24 shows node values, also called averaged stresses. Element values (or non-averaged stresses) can be displayed by proper selection in the **Stress Plot** window in **Advanced Options**. Node values are most often used to present stress results. See chapter 3 and the glossary of terms in chapter 23 for more information on node values and element values of stress results.

Before you proceed, investigate this stress plot with other selections available in the windows shown in Figure 2-23.

We now review the displacement and strain results. All of these plots are created and modified in the same way. Sample results are shown in Figure 2-25 (displacement) and Figure 2-26 (strain).

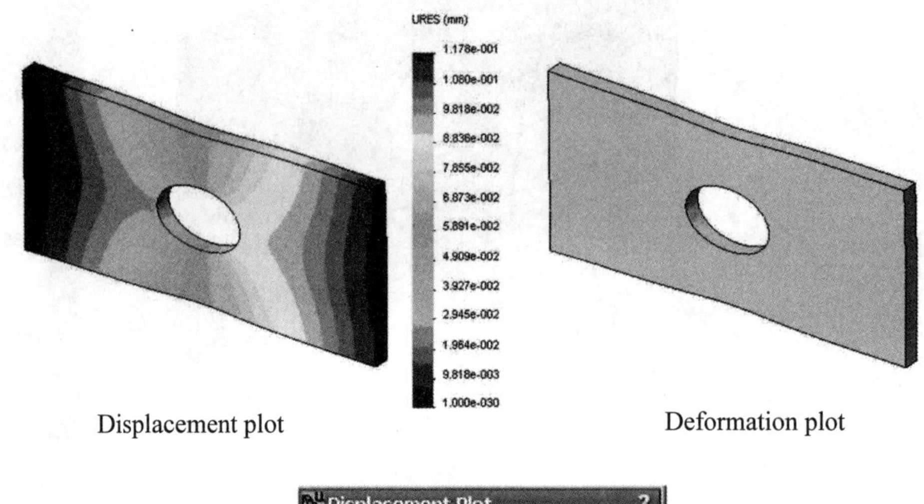

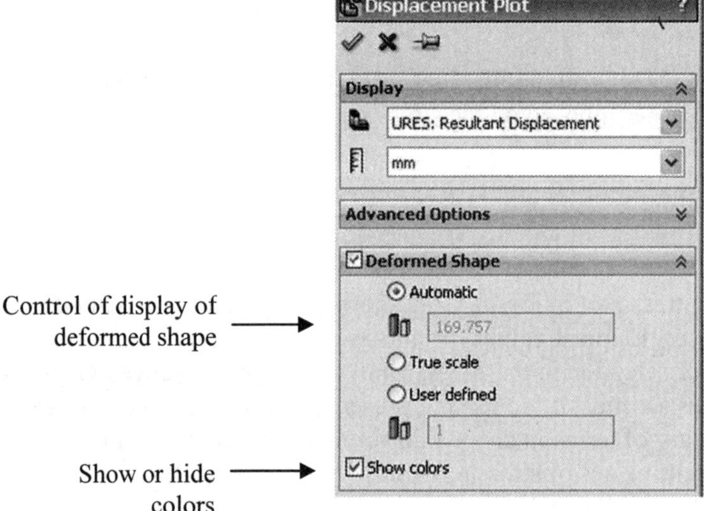

Figure 2-25: Displacement plot (left) and Deformation plot (right)

A Displacement plot can be turned into a Deformation plot by deselecting Show Colors in Displacement Plot in Edit Definition window. The same window has the option of showing the model with an exaggerated scale of deformation as shown above.

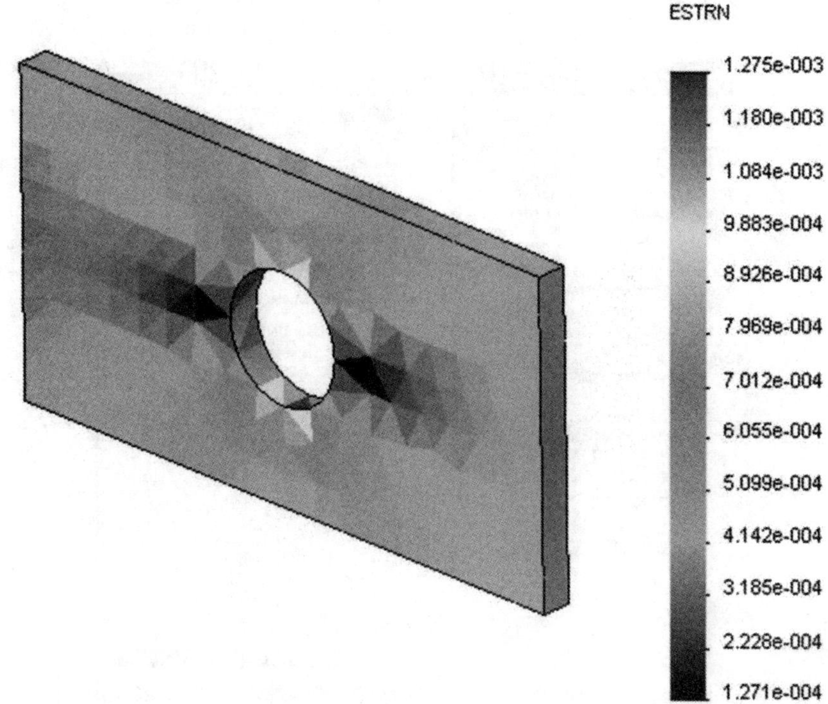

Figure 2-26: Strain results

Strain results are shown here using Element values.

The plots in Figure 2-25 show the deformed shape in an exaggerated scale. You can change the display from deformed to undeformed or modify the scale of deformation in the **Displacement Plot**, **Stress Plot**, and **Strain Plot** windows, activated by right-clicking the plot icon, then selecting **Edit Definition**.

Now, construct a **Factor of Safety** plot using the menu shown in Figure 2-21. The definition of the **Factor of Safety** plot requires three steps. Follow steps 1-3 using the selection shown in Figure 2-27. Review Help to learn about failure criteria and their applicability to different materials.

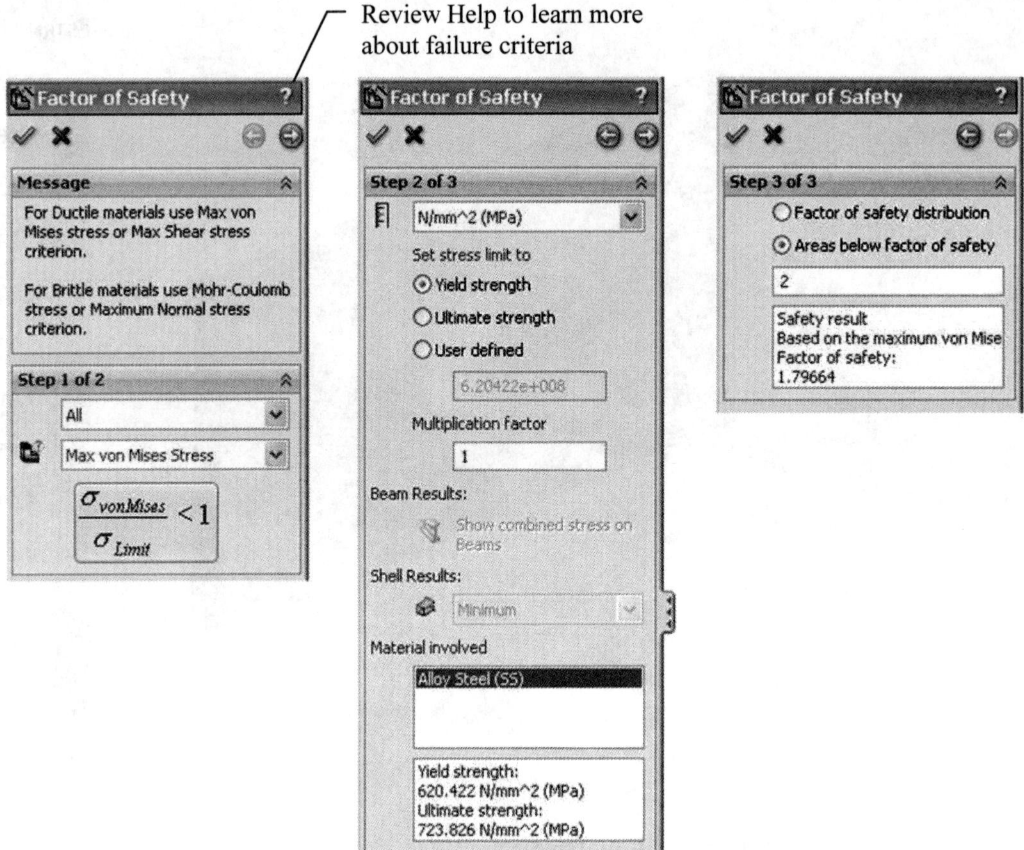

Figure 2-27: Three windows show the three steps in the Factor of Safety plot definition. Select Max von Mises Stress criterion in the first window.

To move through steps, click on the right and left arrows located at the top of the Factor of Safety dialog.

Step 1 selects the failure criterion, step 2 selects display units and sets the stress limit, step 3 selects what will be displayed in the plot. Here we select areas below the factor of safety 2.

The factor of safety plot in Figure 2-28 shows the area where the factor of safety is below the specified.

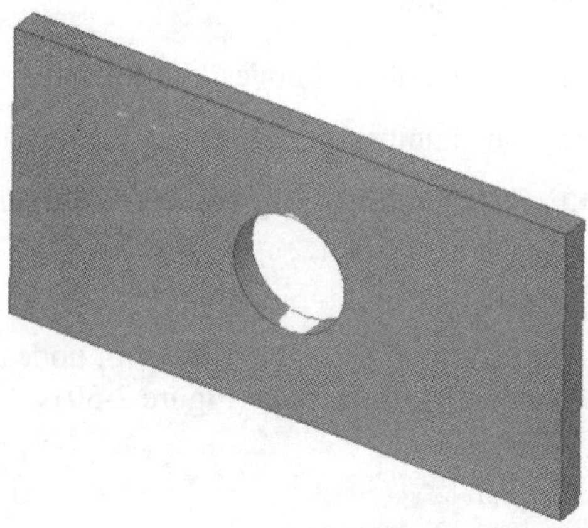

Figure 2-28: Red color (shown as white in this grayscale illustration) displays the areas where the factor of safety falls below 2

We have completed the analysis with a coarse mesh and now wish to see how a change in mesh density will affect the results. Therefore, we will repeat the analysis two more times using medium and fine density meshes respectively. We will use the settings shown in Figure 2-14. All three meshes used in this exercise (coarse, medium, and fine) are shown in Figure 2-29.

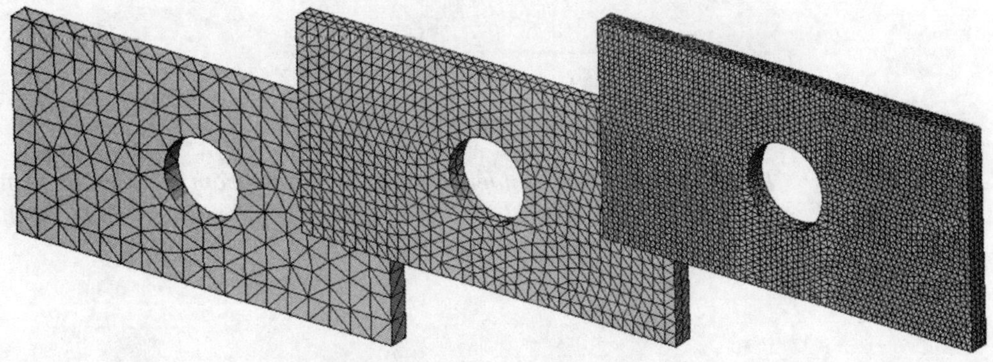

Figure 2-29: Coarse, medium, and fine meshes

Three meshes used to study the effects of mesh density on results.

To compare the results produced by different meshes, we need more information than is available in the plots. Along with the maximum displacement and the maximum von Mises stress, for each study we need to know:

- The number of nodes in the mesh.
- The number of elements in the mesh.
- The number of degrees of freedom in the model.

The information on the number of nodes and number of elements can be found in **Mesh Details** (Figure 2-30).

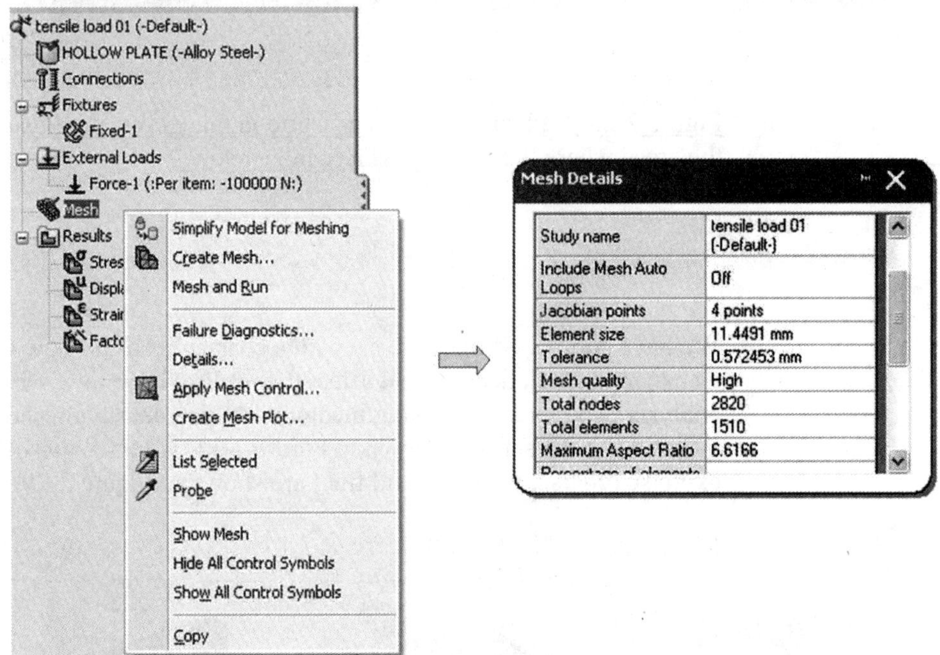

Figure 2-30: Meshing details window

Right-click the Mesh folder and select Details from the pop-up menu to display the Mesh Details window. Note that information on the number of degrees of freedom is not available here.

The most convenient way to find the number of nodes, elements and degrees of freedom is to use the pop-up menu activated by right-clicking on the *Results* folder (Figure 2-31).

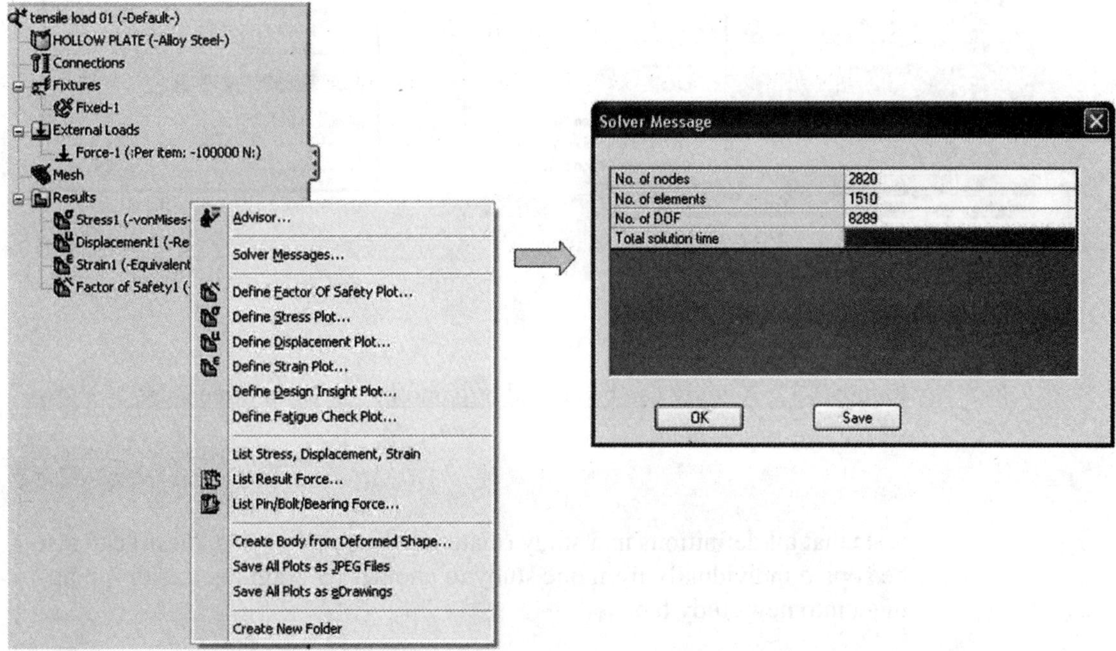

Figure 2-31: The Solver Message window lists information pertaining to the solved study

Right-click on the Results folder and select Solver Messages from the pop-up menu to display the number of nodes, elements and degrees of freedom.

Now create and run two more studies: *tensile load 02* with default element size and *tensile load 03* with fine element size, as shown in Figure 2-14. To create a new study we could just repeat the same steps as before but an easier way is to copy a study. To copy a study, follow the steps in Figure 2-32.

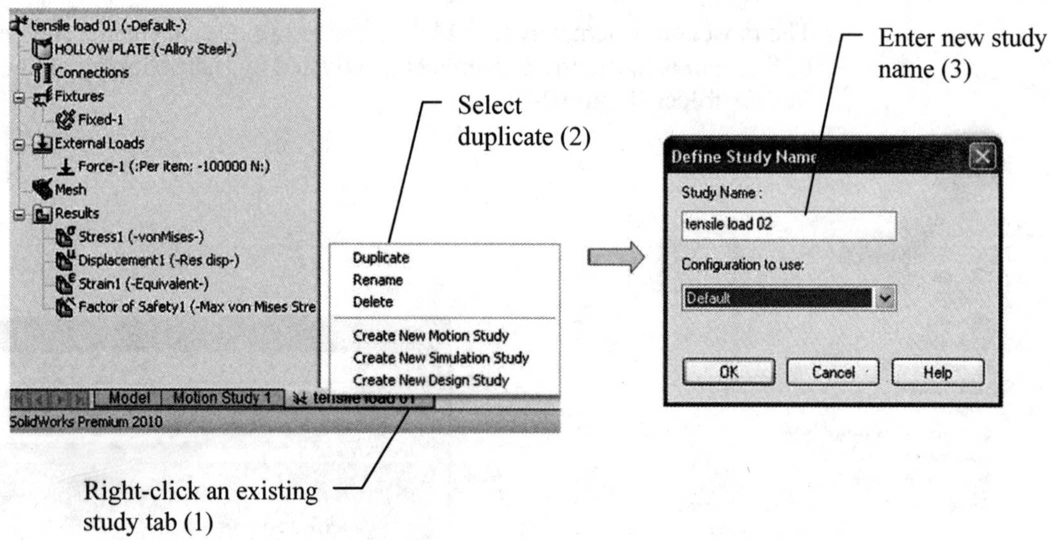

Figure 2-32: A study can be copied into another study in three steps as shown

Note that all definitions in a study (material, restraints, loads, mesh) can also be copied individually from one study to another by dragging and dropping them into new study tab.

A study is copied complete with results and plot definitions. Before remeshing, study *tensile load 02* with the default element size mesh, you must acknowledge the warning message shown in Figure 2-33.

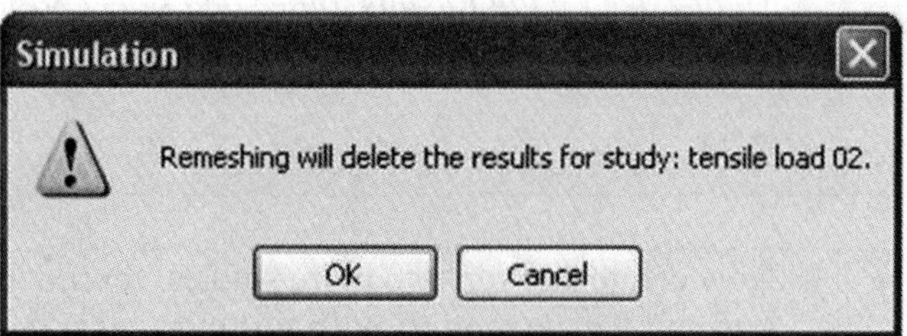

Figure 2-33: Remeshing deletes any existing results in the study

The summary of results produced by the three studies is shown in Figure 2-34.

Study	Element size [mm]	Max. resultant displacement [mm]	Max. von Mises stress [MPa]	Number of elements	Number of nodes	Number of DOF
tensile load 01	11.45	0.1178	345	2820	1510	8289
tensile load 02	5.72	0.1180	372	12204	7024	36057
tensile load 03	2.86	0.1181	378	84427	55222	251796

Figure 2-34: Summary of results produced by the three meshes

Note that these results are based on the same problem. Differences in the results arise from the different mesh densities used in studies tensile load 01, tensile load 02, and tensile load 03.

The actual numbers in this table may vary slightly depending on type of solver and release of software used for solution.

Figure 2-35 shows the maximum resultant displacement and the maximum von Mises stress as function of the number of degrees of freedom. The number of degrees of freedom is in turn a function of mesh density.

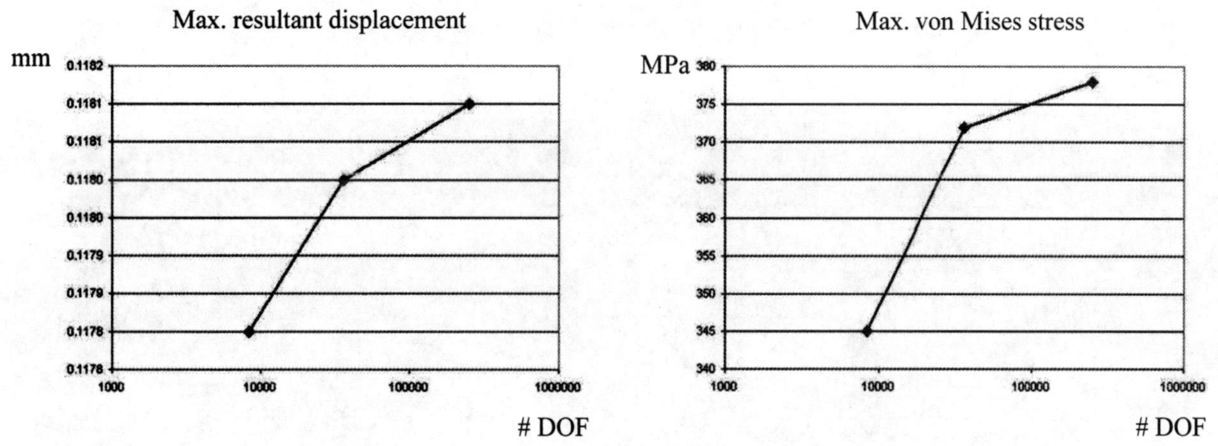

Figure 2-35: Maximum resultant displacement (left) and maximum von Mises stress (right)

Both are plotted as a function of the number of degrees of freedom in the model. The three points on the curves correspond to the three models solved. Straight lines connect the three points only to visually enhance the graphs.

Having noticed that the maximum displacement increases with mesh refinement, we can conclude that the model becomes "softer" when smaller elements are used. With mesh refinement, a larger number of elements allows for better approximation of the real displacement and stress field. Therefore, we can say that the artificial constraints imposed by element definition become less imposing with mesh refinement.

Displacements are the primary unknowns in structural FEA, and stresses are calculated based on displacement results. Therefore, stresses also increase with mesh refinement. If we continued with mesh refinement, we would see that both the displacement and stress results converge to a finite value which is the solution of the mathematical model. Differences between the solution of the FEA model and the mathematical model are due to discretization errors, which diminish with mesh refinement.

We will now repeat our analysis of the HOLLOW PLATE by using prescribed displacements in place of a load. Rather than loading it with a 100000N force that has caused a 0.118 mm displacement of the loaded face, we will apply a prescribed displacement of 0.118 mm to this face to see what stresses this causes. For this exercise, we will use only one mesh with default (medium) mesh density.

Define the fourth study, called *prescribed displ*. The easiest way to do this is to copy study *tensile load 02*. The definition of material properties, the fixed restraint to the left-side end-face and mesh are all identical to the previous design study. We need to delete the load (right-click the load icon and select **Delete**) and apply in its place the prescribed displacement.

To apply the prescribed displacement to the right-side end-face, create a new **Fixed Geometry** by right-clicking the **Fixtures** folder and select **Advanced Fixtures** from the pop-up menu. This opens the **Fixture** definition window. Select **On Flat Face** from the Advanced menu and define displacement as shown in Figure 2-36. Check **Reverse direction** to obtain displacement in the tensile direction. Note that the direction of a prescribed displacement is indicated by a restraint symbol.

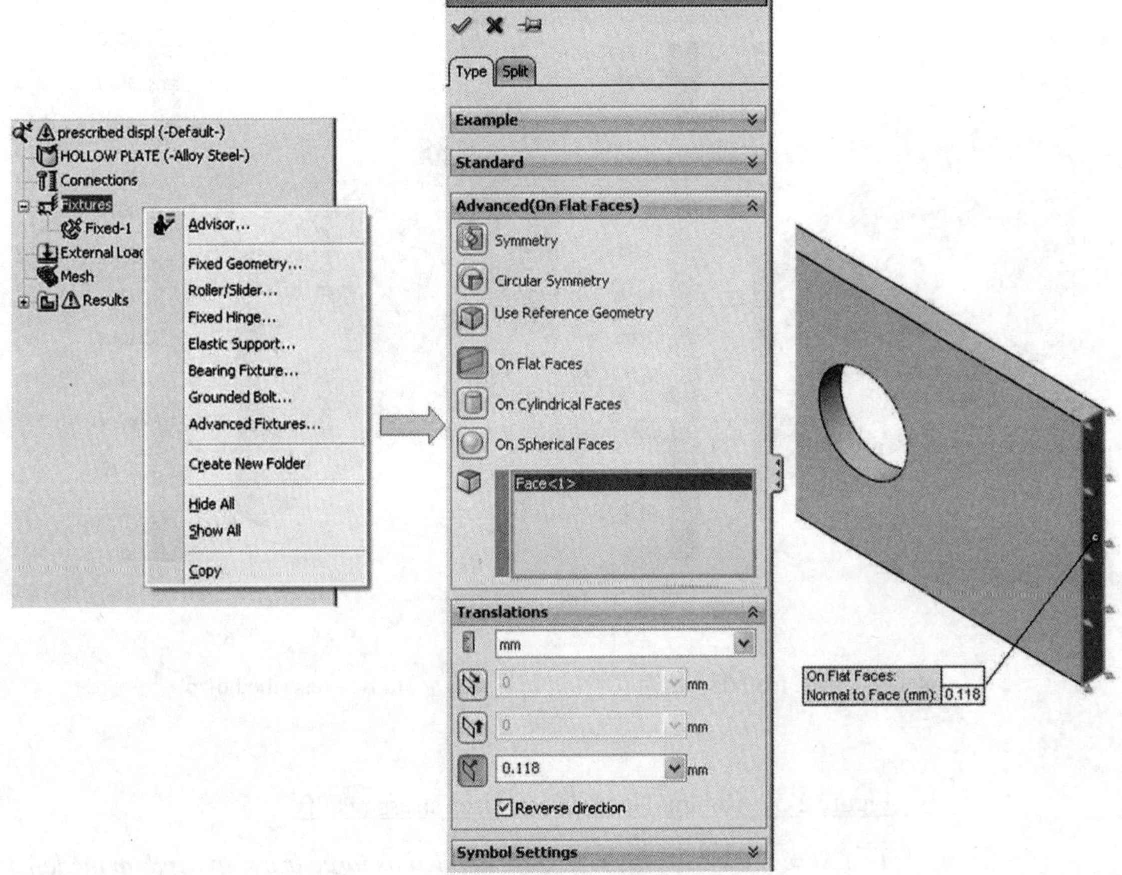

Figure 2-36: Restraint definition window

The prescribed displacement of 0.118 mm is applied to the same face where the tensile load of 100000N had been applied. The size and color of this symbol can be changed using Symbol Settings. The color and size of all load and restraint symbols is controlled the same way.

The visibility of all load and restraints symbols is controlled by right-clicking the symbol and making the desired choice (**Hide/Show**). All load symbols and all restraint (fixture) symbols may also be turned on/off all at once by right-clicking **Fixtures** or **External loads** folders and selecting **Hide all/ Show all** from the pop-up menu.

Once prescribed displacement is defined to the end face, it overrides any previously applied loads to the same end face. While it is better to delete the load in order to keep the model clean, the load has no effect if a prescribed displacement is applied to the same entity and in the same direction.

Figures 2-37 compares stress results for the model loaded with force to the model loaded with prescribed displacement.

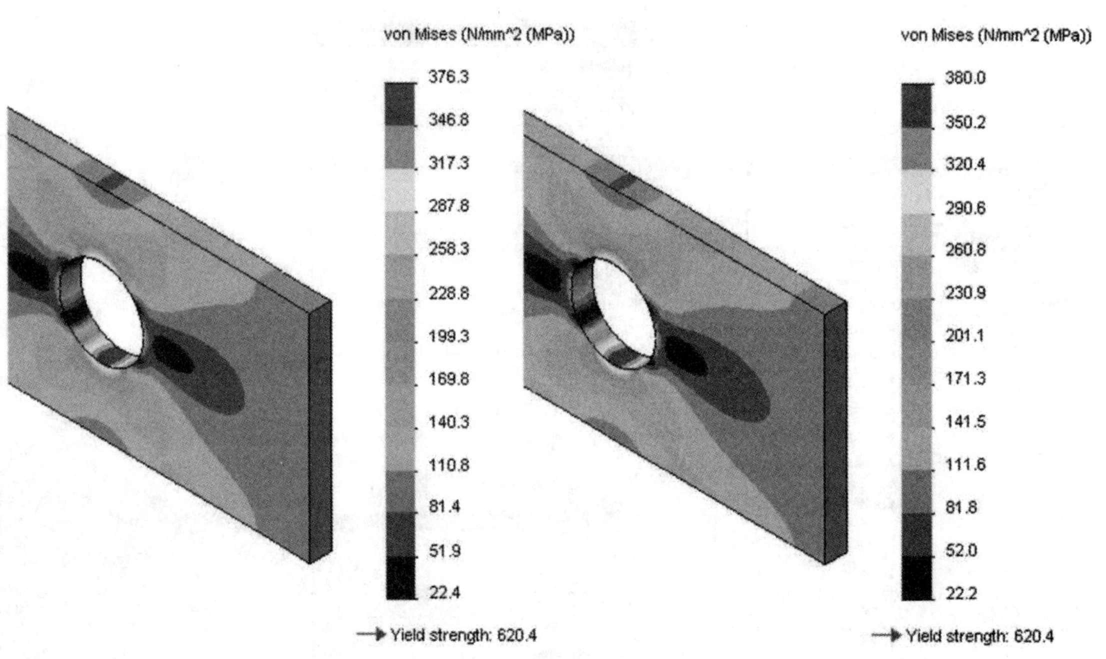

Study: tensile load 02

Study: prescribed displ

Figure 2-37: Comparison of von Mises stress results

Von Mises stress results with load applied as force are displayed on the left and Von Mises stress results with load applied as prescribed displacement are displayed on the right.

Results produced by applying a force load and by applying a prescribed displacement load are very similar, but not identical. The reason for this discrepancy is that in the model loaded by force, the loaded face is allowed to deform. In the prescribed displacement model, this face remains flat, even though it experiences displacement as a whole. Also, while the prescribed displacement of 0.118 mm applies to the entire face in the prescribed displacement model, it is only seen as a maximum displacement in one point in the force load model. You may plot displacement along the edge of the end face by following the steps in Figure 2-38.

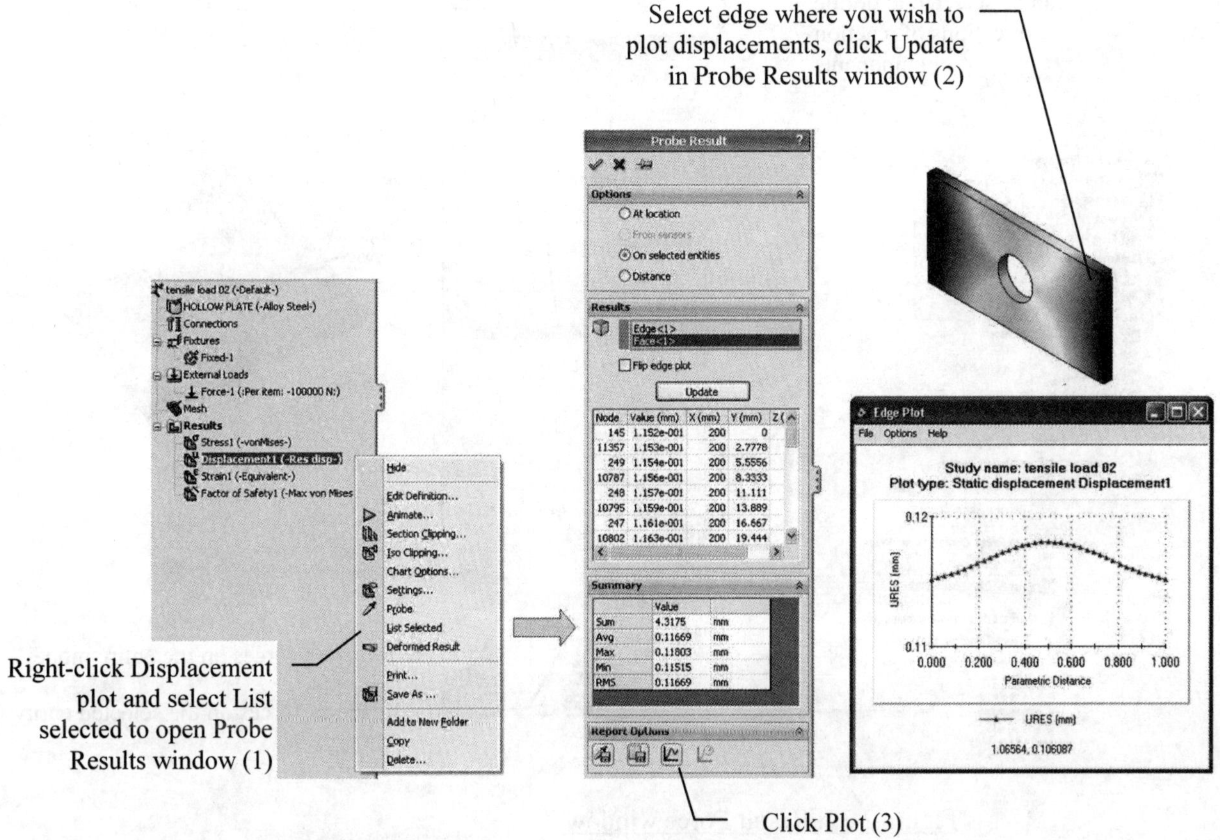

Figure 2-38: Plotting displacement along the edge of force loaded face in study *tensile load 02*

Follow steps 1, 2, and 3 to produce a graph of displacements along the loaded edge. Repeat this exercise for a model loaded with prescribed displacement to verify that displacement is constant along the edge.

We conclude the analysis of the HOLLOW PLATE by examining the reaction forces using the results of study *tensile load 02*. In the study *tensile load 02*, right-click *Results*. From the pop-up menu, select **List Result Force** to open the **Result Force** window. Select the face where the fixed restraint is applied and click the **Update** button. Information on reaction forces will be displayed as shown in Figure 2-39.

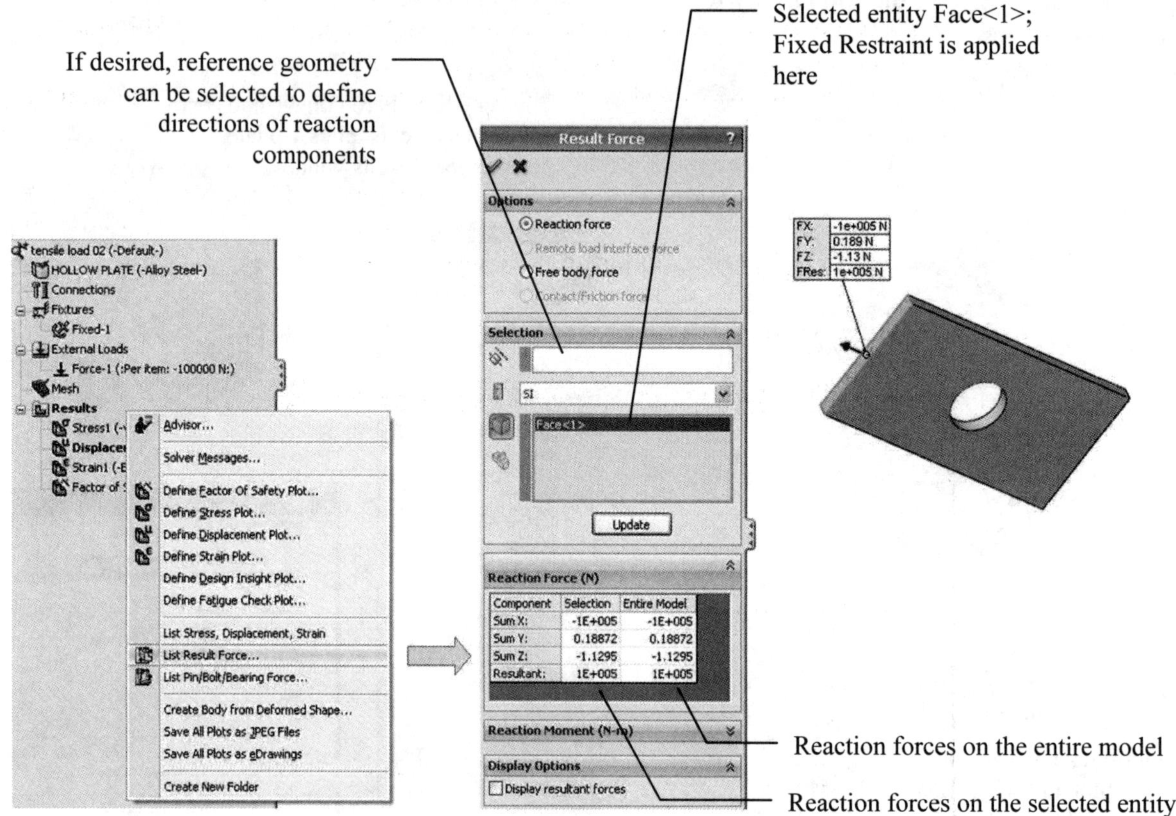

Figure 2-39: Result Force window

Reaction forces can also be displayed in components other than those defined by the global reference system. To do this, reference geometry such as plane or axis must be selected.

A note on where **Simulation** results are stored: All studies are saved with the SolidWorks part or assembly model. Mesh data and results of each study are stored separately in *.CWR files. For example, the mesh and results of study *tensile load 02* have been stored in the file:

HOLLOW PLATE-tensile load 02.CWR.

When the study is opened, the CWR file is unzipped into a number of different files depending on the type of study. Upon exiting SolidWorks **Simulation** (which is done by means of deselecting SolidWorks **Simulation** from the list of add-ins, or by closing the SolidWorks model), all files are compressed back allowing for convenient backup of SolidWorks **Simulation** results.

The location of CWR files is specified in the **Default Options** window which is called from Simulation main menu first shown in Figure 2-4. For easy reference, the **Default Options** window is shown again in Figure 2-40).

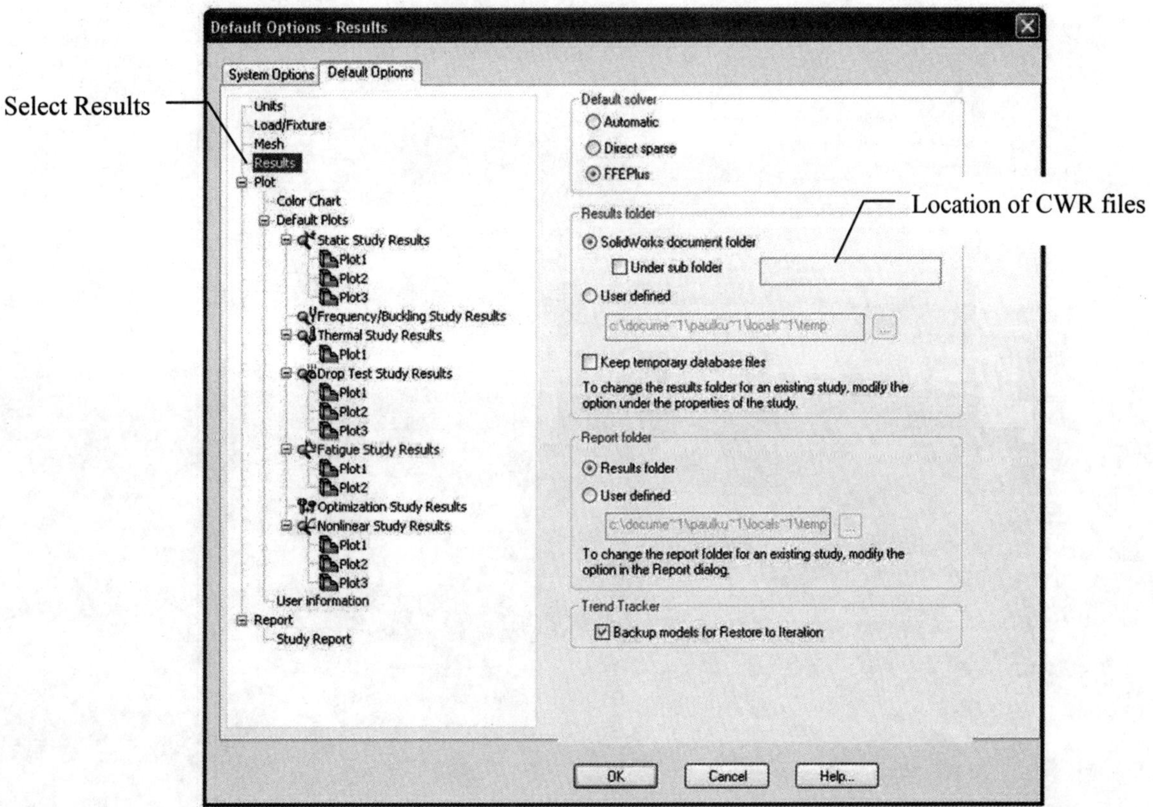

Figure 2-40: Location of solution database files

Using these settings, CWR files are located in SolidWorks document folder.

Notes:

3: Static analysis of an L-bracket

Topics covered

- Stress singularities
- Differences between modeling errors and discretization errors
- Using mesh controls
- Analysis in different SolidWorks configurations
- Nodal stresses, element stresses

Project description

An L-shaped bracket (in the file called *L BRACKET* in SolidWorks) is supported and loaded as shown in Figure 3-1. We would like to find the displacements and stresses caused by a 1000N bending load. In particular, we are interested in stresses in the corner where the 2mm fillet is located. Since the radius of the fillet is small compared to the overall size of the model, we decide to suppress it. As we will soon prove, suppressing the fillet is a bad mistake!

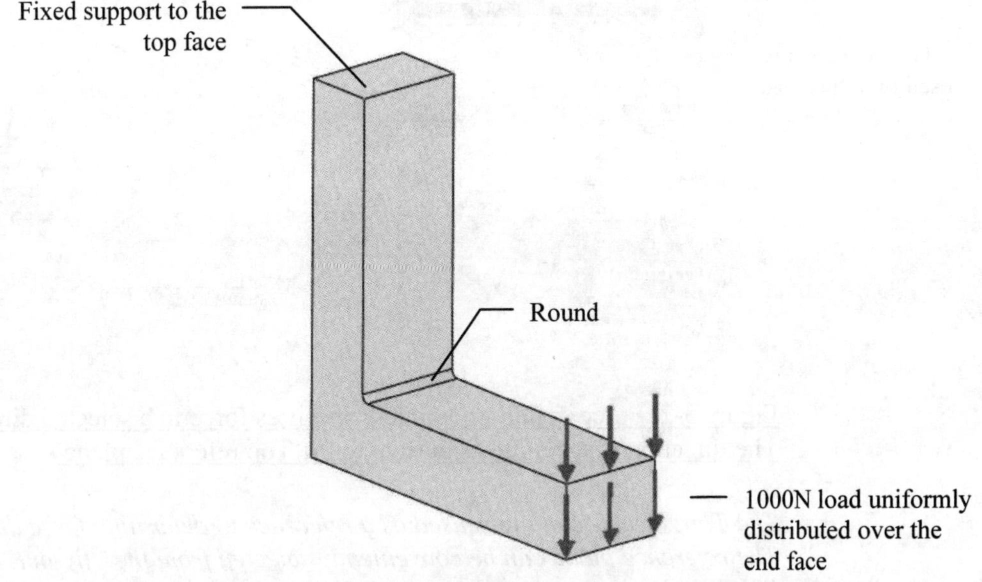

Figure 3-1: Loads and supports applied to the L BRACKET model

The geometry of the L BRACKET includes a fillet, which will be mistakenly suppressed, leaving in its place a sharp re-entrant corner.

The *L BRACKET* model has two configurations: *01 sharp edge* and *02 round edge*. Change to the *01 sharp edge* configuration. The material (Alloy steel) is applied to the SolidWorks model and is automatically transferred to SolidWorks **Simulation**

Procedure

Make sure the model is in configuration *01 sharp edge*. Following the same steps as those described in chapter 2, define a study called *mesh 1* and define a **Fixed** restraint to the top face shown in Figure 3-1. Define the load using the **Force/Torque** window choices shown in Figure 3-2.

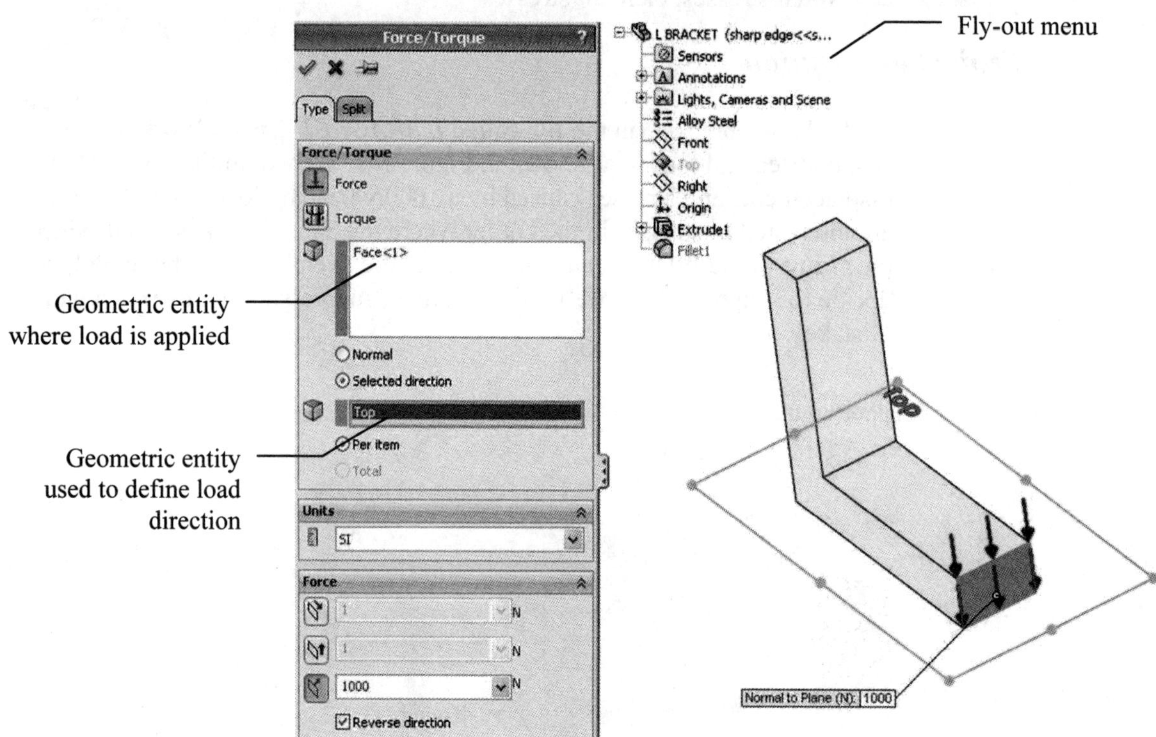

Figure 3-2: Force definition window specifies force in a selected direction. The direction is specified as normal to the Top reference plane.

The Top reference plane is used as a reference to determine force direction. The reference plane can be conveniently selected from the "fly-out" SolidWorks menu.

Next, mesh the model with second order tetrahedral elements, accepting the default element size. The finite element mesh is shown in Figure 3-3.

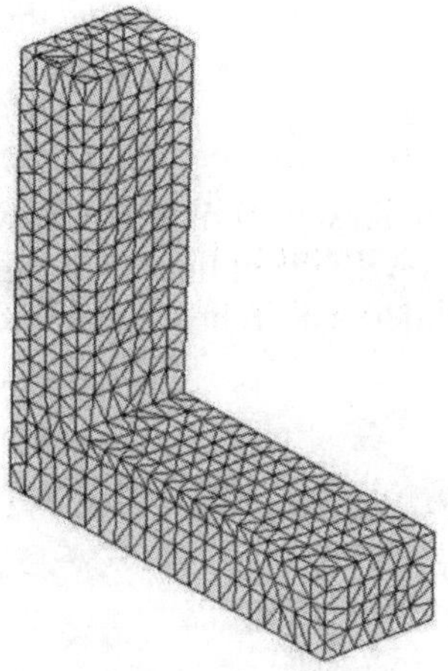

Figure 3-3: Finite element mesh created with the default settings of the mesher

In this mesh, the global element size is 4.76 mm.

The displacement and stress results obtained in the *mesh 1* study are shown in Figure 3-4.

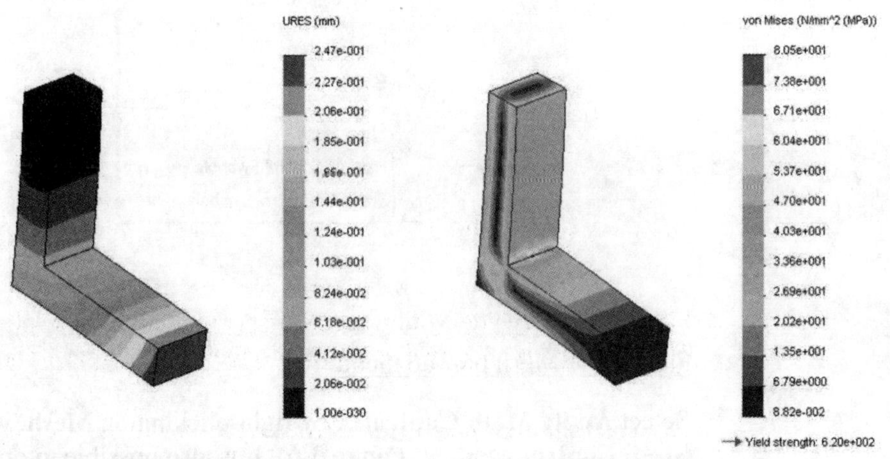

Figure 3-4: Displacements and von Mises stresses results produced using study *mesh 1*

The maximum displacement is 0.247 mm and the maximum von Mises stress is 81 MPa. As explained later, these stress results are meaningless.

Now we will investigate how using smaller elements affects the results. In chapter 2, we did this by refining the mesh uniformly so that the entire model was meshed with elements of a smaller size. Here we will use a different technique. Having noticed that the stress concentration is near the sharp re-entrant corner, we will refine the mesh locally in that area by applying mesh controls. The element size everywhere else will remain the same as it was before: 4.76mm.

Copy the *mesh1* study into a new study "*mesh2*". Select the edge where mesh controls will be applied, then right-click the *Mesh* folder in the *mesh2* study (this folder is currently empty) to display the pop-up menu shown in Figure 3-5.

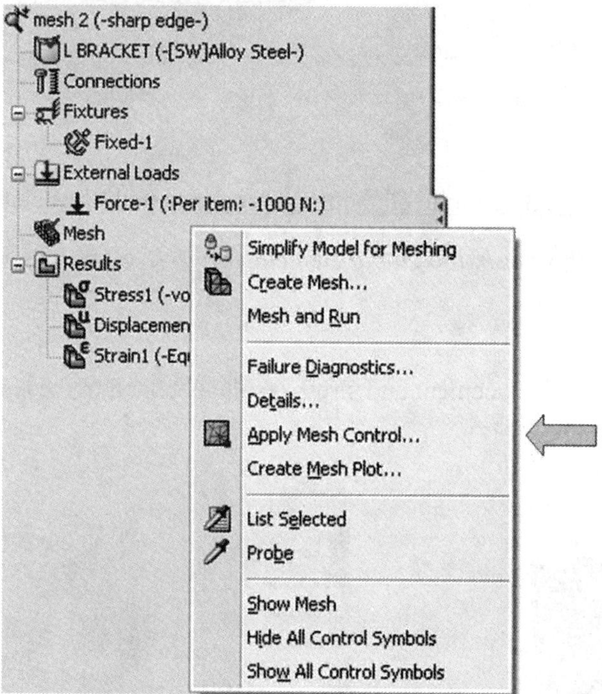

Figure 3-5: Mesh pop-up menu

Select **Apply Mesh Control...** by right-clicking on **Mesh**, which opens the **Mesh Control** window (Figure 3-6). It is also possible to open the **Mesh Control** window first and then select the desired entity or entities (here the re-entrant edge) where mesh controls are being applied.

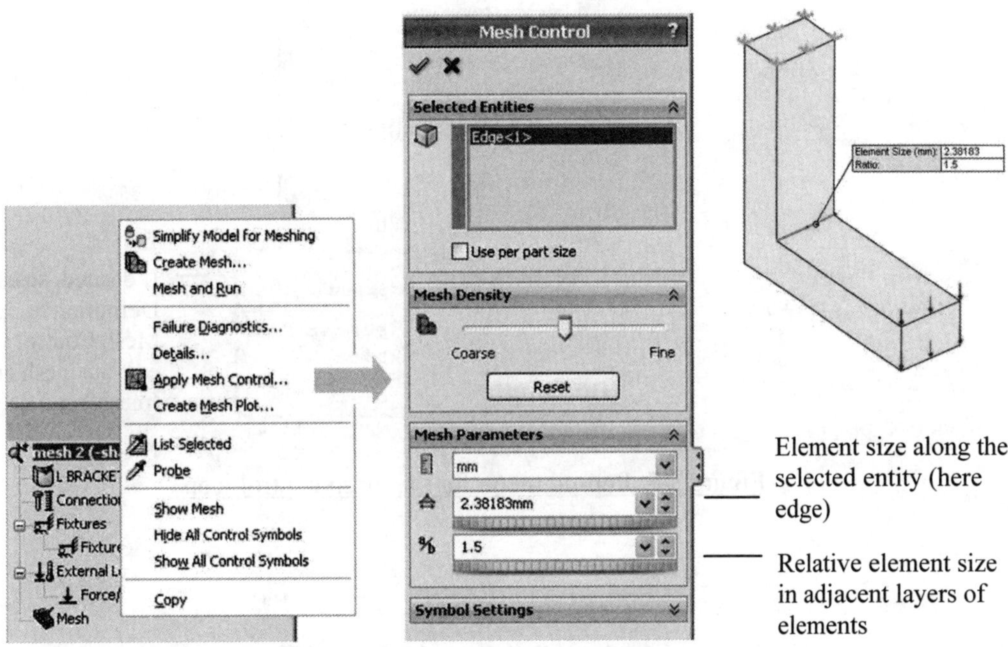

Figure 3-6: Mesh Control window

Mesh controls allow for the definition of a local element size on selected entities. Accept the default values of the Mesh Control window.

The element size along the selected edge is now controlled independently of the global element size. Mesh control can also be applied to vertices, faces and to entire components of assemblies. Having defined the mesh control, create a mesh with the same global element size as before (4.76 mm), while making elements along the specified edge to be 2.38 mm. The added mesh controls display as thc **Control-1** icon in the *Mesh* folder and can be edited using a pop-up menu displayed by right-clicking the mesh control icon (Figure 3-7).

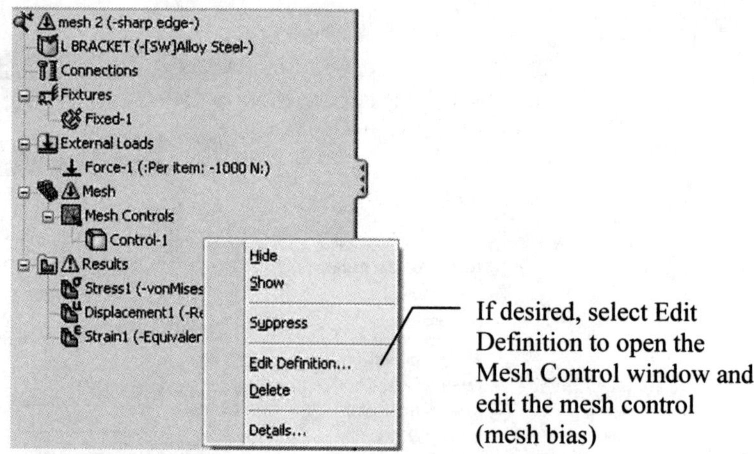

Figure 3-7: Pop-up menu for the mesh control icon

The mesh with applied control (also called mesh bias) is shown in Figure 3-8.

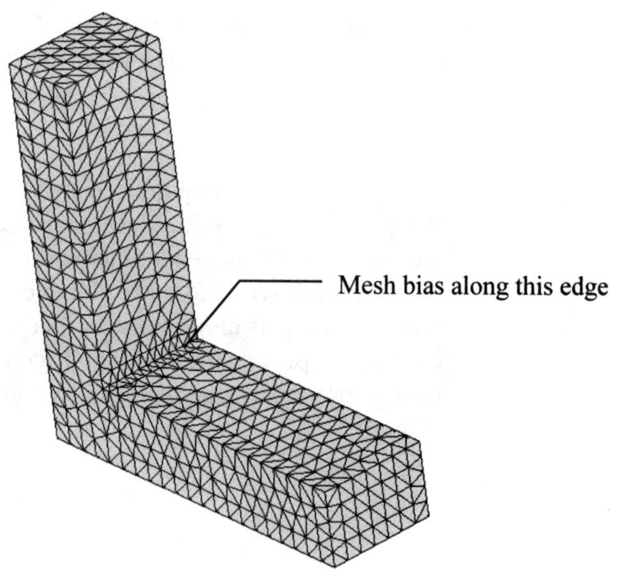

Figure 3-8: Mesh with applied controls (mesh bias)

Mesh in study mesh2 is refined along the selected edge.

The maximum displacements and stress results obtained in study *mesh2* are 2.47697 mm and 74.1 MPa respectively. The number of digits shown in a result plot is controlled using **Chart Options** (right-click plot and select **Chart Options)**.

Now repeat the same exercise three more times using progressively smaller elements along the sharp re-entrant edge. Create three studies with element size along the sharp-re entrant edge as shown in Figure 3-9.

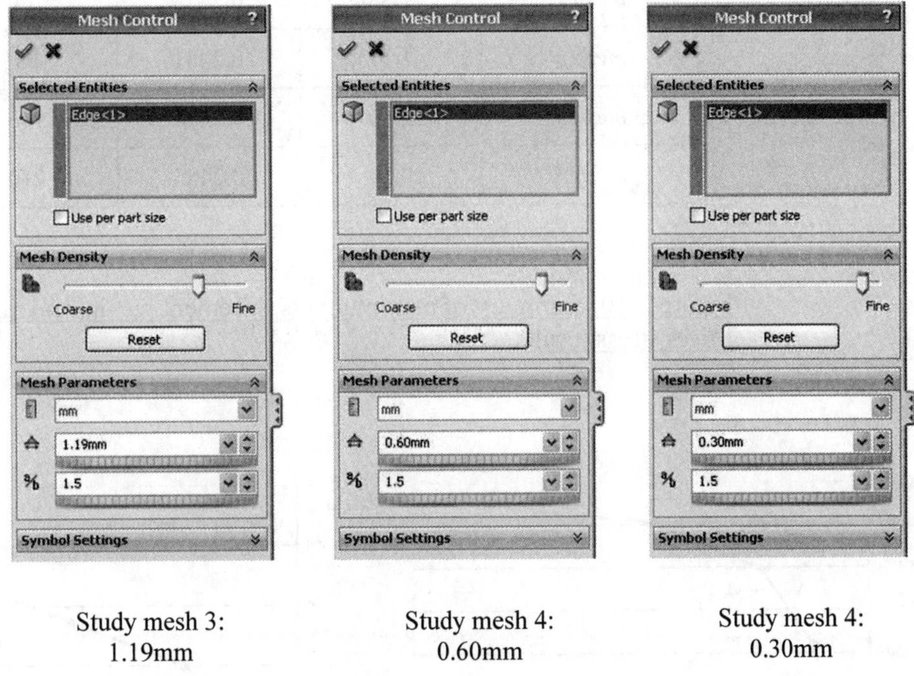

Figure 3-9: Mesh Control windows in studies *mesh3*, *mesh4*, and *mesh5* defining the element size along the sharp re-entrant edge.

The summary of results of all five studies is shown in Figures 3-10 and 3-11.

Study	Element size h [mm]	Max. resultant displacement [mm]	Max. von Mises stress [MPa]
mesh 1	4.76	0.2473	81
mesh 2	2.38	0.2478	74
mesh 3	1.19	0.2481	99
mesh 4	0.60	0.2484	136
mesh 5	0.30	0.2485	210

Figure 3-10: Summary of maximum displacement results and maximum von Mises stress results

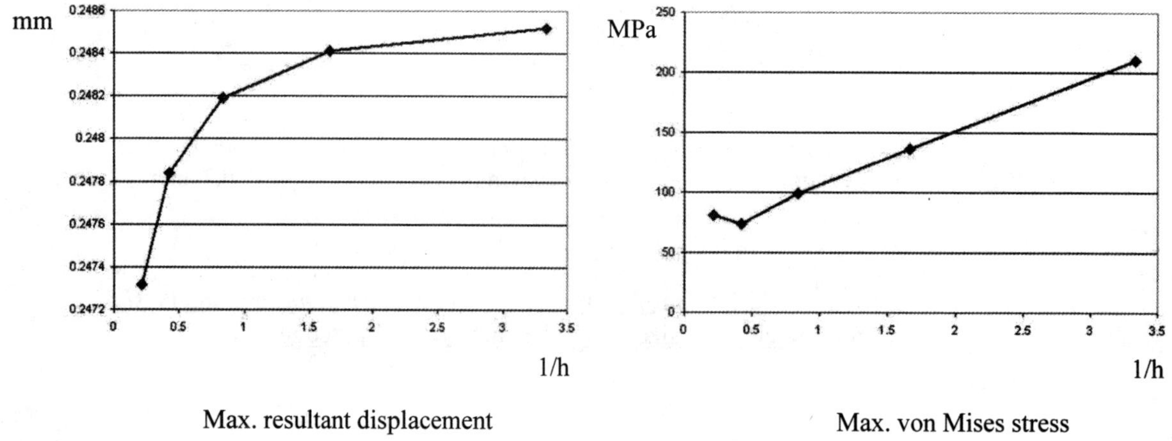

Figure 3-11: Max. resultant displacement (left) and max. von Mises stress (right) as function of 1/h (h is the element size (Figure 2-15) along the sharp re-entrant edge

The local drop in stress magnitude for study mesh 2 is caused by shifting the maximum stress location between studies mesh1 and mesh2.

Upon examining Figures 3-10 and 3-11 we notice that while each mesh refinement brings about an increase in the maximum displacement, the difference between consecutive results decreases. The absolute increases in displacement results are so minute that results need four decimal places to show the difference. The first study, without any mesh refinement provides accurate displacement results.

The stress behaves very differently. Each mesh refinement brings about an increase in the maximum stress. The difference between consecutive results increases, proving that the maximum stress result is divergent.

We could continue with this exercise of progressive mesh refinement either:

- Locally, near the sharp re-entrant, as we have done here by means of mesh controls, or
- Globally, by reducing the global element size, as we did in chapter 2.

Given enough time and patience, we can produce results showing any stress magnitude we want. All that is necessary is to make the element size small enough! We should avoid a temptation to make any conclusions based on stress graph in Figure 3-11 because all these results are meaningless!

The reason for divergent stress results is not that the finite element model is incorrect, but that the finite element model is based on the wrong mathematical model.

According to the theory of elasticity, stress in a sharp re-entrant corner is infinite. A mathematician would say that stress in a sharp re-entrant corner is singular. Stress results in a sharp re-entrant corner are completely dependent on mesh size: the smaller the element, the higher the stress. Therefore, we must repeat this exercise after un-suppressing the fillet, which is done by changing from configuration *01 sharp edge* to *02 round edge* in the SolidWorks Configuration Manager.

Notice that after we return from the Configuration Manager window to the SolidWorks **Simulation** window, all studies pertaining to the model in configuration *01 sharp corner* are not accessible. They can be accessed only if the model configuration is changed back to *01 sharp corner* (Figure 3-12).

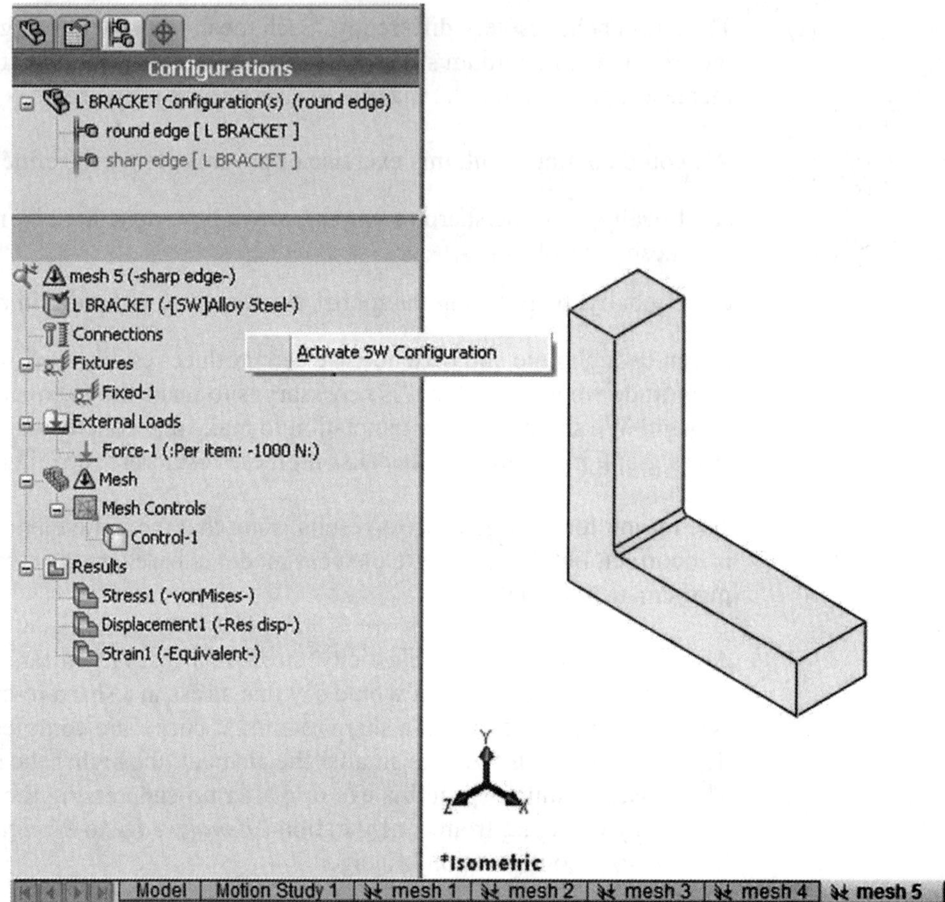

Figure 3-12: Studies become inaccessible when the model configuration is changed to a configuration other than that corresponding to now grayed-out studies.

The SolidWorks model can be changed to a configuration corresponding to a given study by right-clicking the study icon and selecting Activate SW configuration.

To analyze the bracket with fillet, define a study named *round edge*. Copy the *Fixtures* and *External Loads* folders from any inactive studies to the *round edge* study (Figure 3-13).

.

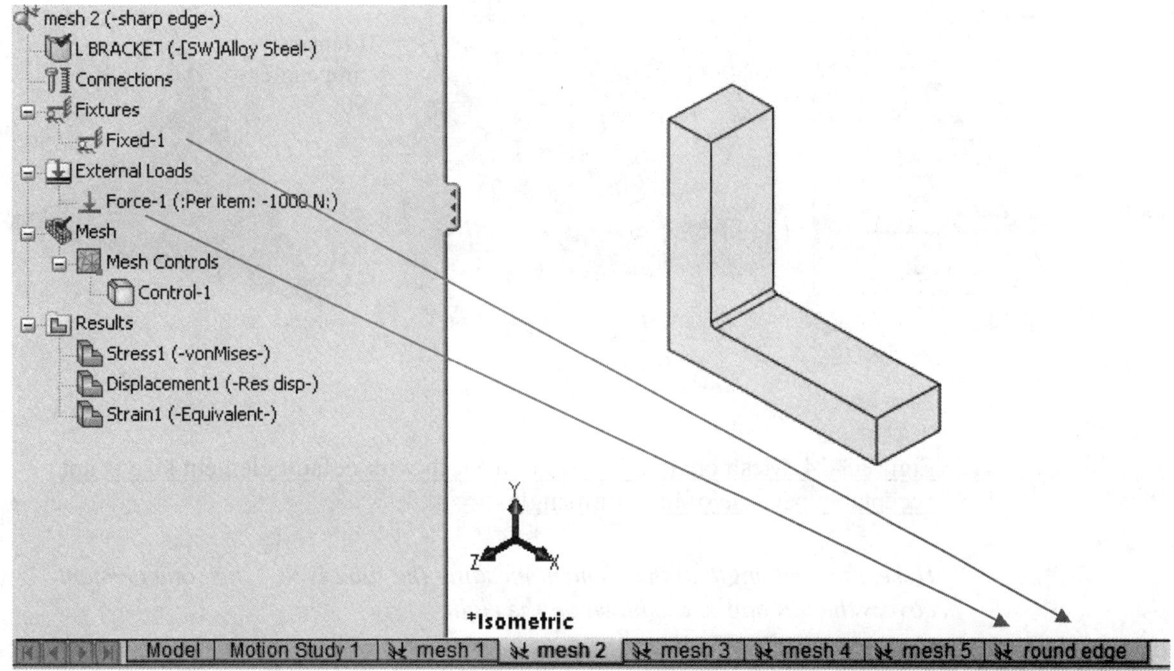

Figure 3-13: Copying *Fixtures* and *External Loads* from study *mesh2* to *study round edge*

Entities can be copied between studies by dragging them and dropping into study tab as shown.

Meshing with the default element size and Standard Mesh selected produces elements with an excessive turn angle in the area where it is particularly important to have correct mesh (Figure 3-14).

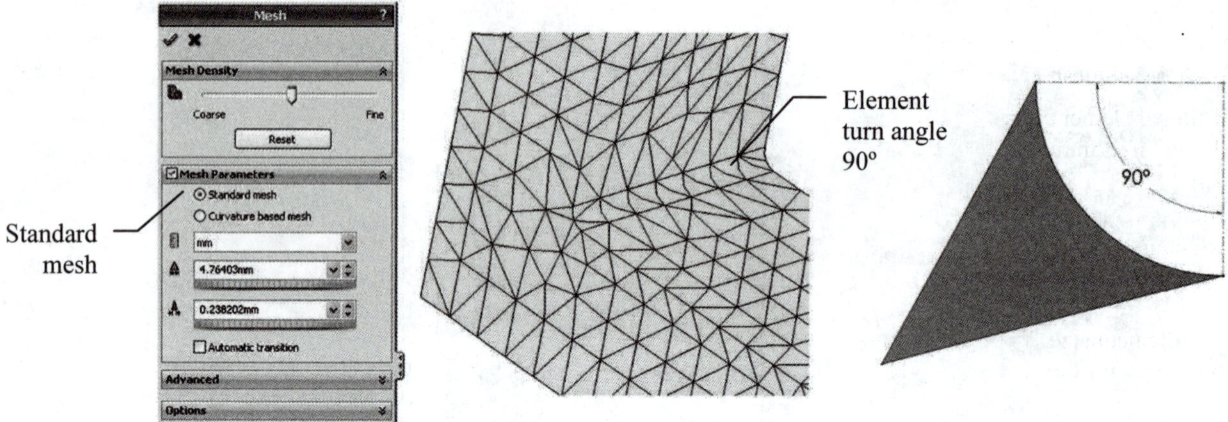

Figure 3-14: Mesh created as Standard Mesh with default element size is not acceptable because of high turn angle

Here, the turn angle of the element meshing the fillet is 90°. Just one element covers the 90° angle, as shown on the right.

To eliminate excessive turn angles from areas where stresses are of particular interest we use the **Curvature based mesh** option (Figure 3-15).

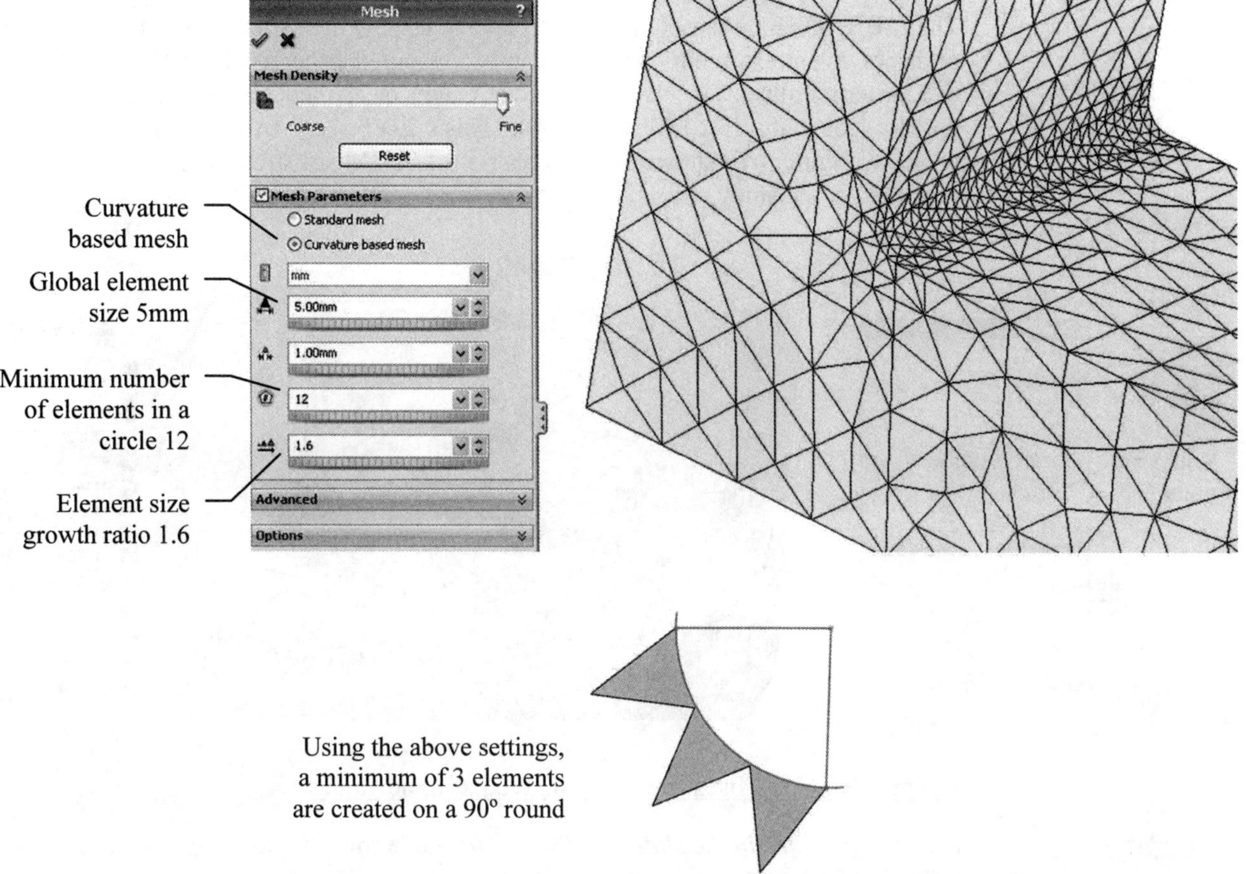

Figure 3-15: Curvature based mesh assures correct meshing of curved faces

Minimum number of elements in a circle (360°) set to 12 means that element turn angle is 360°/12=30°.

Element size growth ratio control transition between refined mesh on curved faces and coarser mesh on flat faces.

It is generally recommended that the turn angle does not exceed 30° in "sensitive" locations where stresses must be correctly modeled.

The L-BRACKET example is a good place to review the different ways of displaying stress results. Stresses can be presented either as **Node Values** or **Element Values**. To select either node values or element values, right-click the plot icon and select **Edit Definition**. This will open the **Stress Plot** window. Figure 3-16 shows the node values of von Mises stress results produced in the study *round edge*.

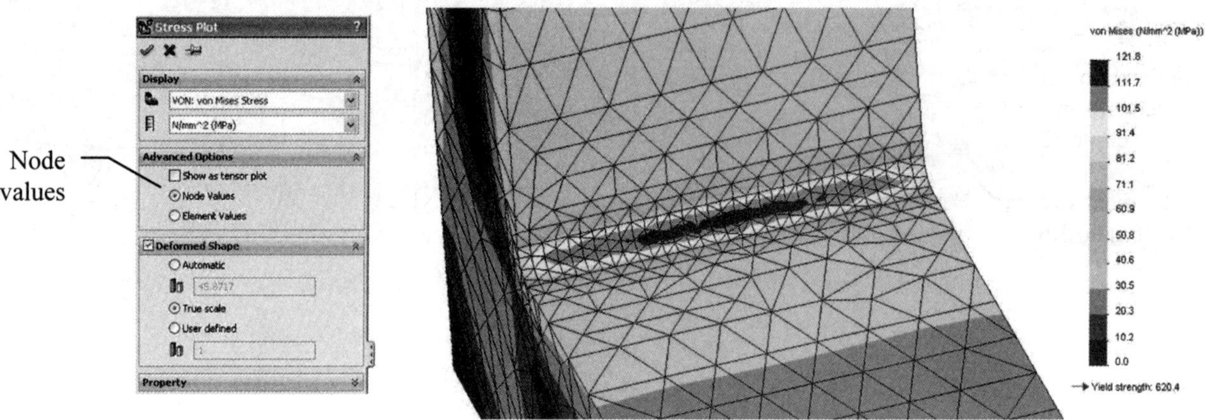

Figure 3-16: Von Mises stresses displayed as node values

The irregularities in the shape of discrete fringes showing nodal stress results (left) may be used to decide if more mesh refinement is needed in the area of stress concentration. Here, regular shapes indicate sufficient mesh refinement.

The maximum stress (121MPa) is now bounded. In the convergence process it will converge to a finite value, close to the one shown in Figure 3-16. Again, we must resist temptation to compare this result to maximum stress results produced by studies with sharp re-entrant edge because all these results are meaningless.

Figure 3-17 shows the element values of von Mises stress results produced in the study *round edge*.

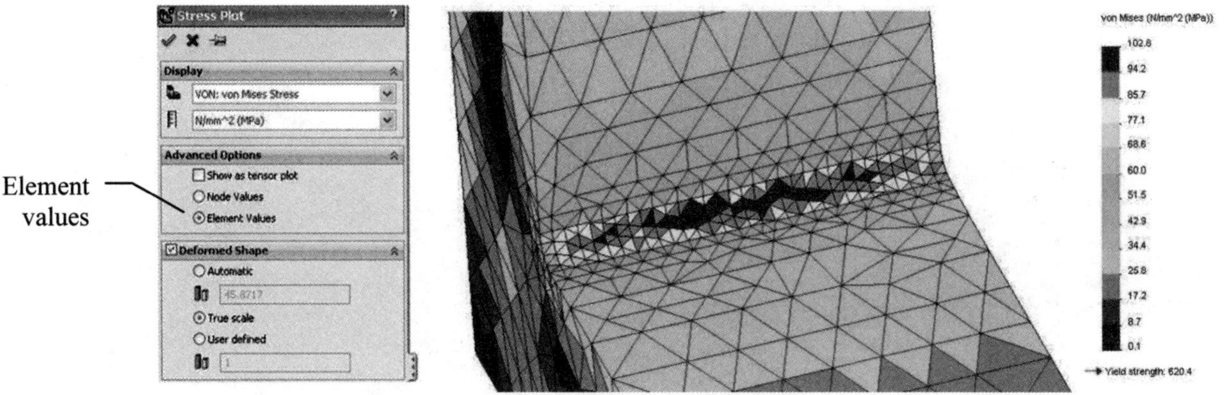

Figure 3-17 Von Mises stresses displayed as element values

Element values are not averaged across different elements. A single stress value is assigned to each element.

As we explained in chapter 1, nodal displacements are computed first, from which strains and then stresses are calculated. Stresses are first calculated inside the element at certain locations, called Gauss points. Next, stress results are extrapolated to all of the elements' nodes. If one node belongs to more than one element (which is always the case unless it is a vertex node), then the stress results from all the elements sharing a given node are averaged and one stress value, called a node value, is reported for each node.

An alternate procedure to present stress results is by obtaining stresses in Gauss points, then averaging them in-between themselves. This means that one stress value is calculated for the element. This stress value is called an element value.

Node values are used more often because they offer smoothed out, continuous stress results. However, examination of element values provides important feedback on the quality of the results. If element values in two adjacent elements differ too much it indicates that the element size at this location is too large to properly model the stress gradient. By examining the element values, we can locate mesh deficiencies without running a convergence analysis.

To decide how much is "too much" of a difference requires some experience. As a general guideline, we can say that if the element values of stress in adjacent elements are apart by several colors on the default color chart, then a more refined mesh should be used.

Notes:

4: Stress and frequency analyses of a pipe support

Topics covered

- Use of shell elements
- Frequency analysis

Project description

We will analyze a support bracket (shown in Figure 4-1) with the objective of finding stresses and the first few modes of vibration. This will require running both static and frequency analyses. Open part model PIPE SUPPORT with assigned material properties of Galvanized Steel, and begin a **Static** analysis.

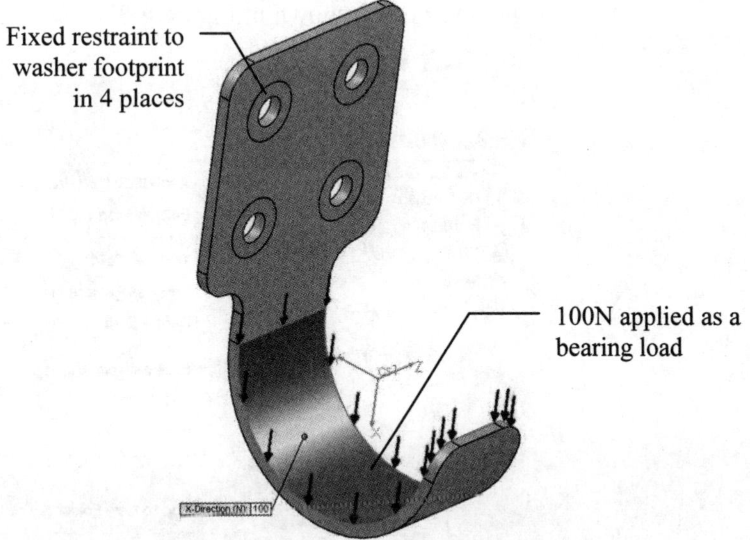

Figure 4-1: PIPE SUPPORT model

Note that model has been designed in SolidWorks as sheet metal.

Procedure

Before defining the study, consider that thin wall geometry would be difficult to mesh with solid elements. Generally it is recommended that two layers of second order tetrahedral elements be used across the thickness of a wall undergoing bending. Therefore, a large number of solid elements would be required to mesh this thin model.

A sheet metal model has inherently thin walls. Therefore, when a sheet metal model is presented to SolidWorks **Simulation**, it is by default designated for meshing with shell elements. Create a **Simulation** study *analysis1* and note that the familiar **Solid** folder is replaced with **Shell** folder (Figure 4-2).

Solid folder from chapter 2 **Shell** folder in this exercise

Figure 4-2: Solid folder in study from chapter 2 and shell folder in present study

The presence of the Shell folder indicates that model will be meshed with shell elements.

If solid elements are preferred after all, the default designation **Shell** can be changed to **Solid** as shown in Figure 4-3.

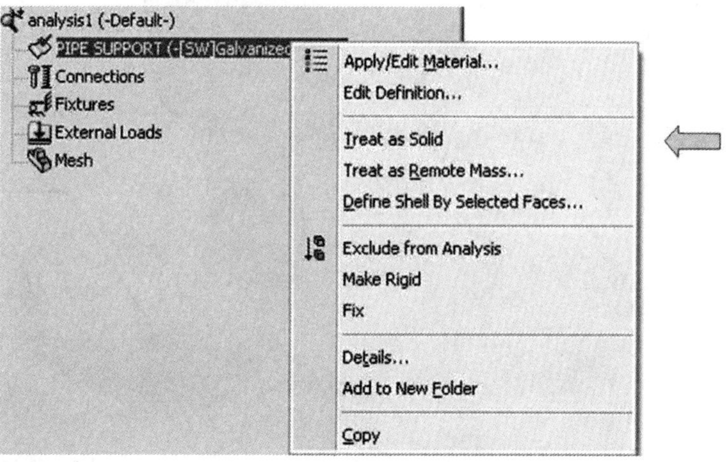

Figure 4-3: Changing from Shell to Solid element

If you want to mesh the sheet metal model with solid elements, right click Shell folder and select Treat as Solid. This exercise uses shell elements. This illustration is for information only.

*Apply a fixed restraint to the four washer footprints, as shown in Figure 4-1 and repeated in Figure 4-4. Review split lines in the SolidWorks model that define split faces where restraints are applied. Split faces are commonly used in preparation of CAD models for analysis with SolidWorks **Simulation**.*

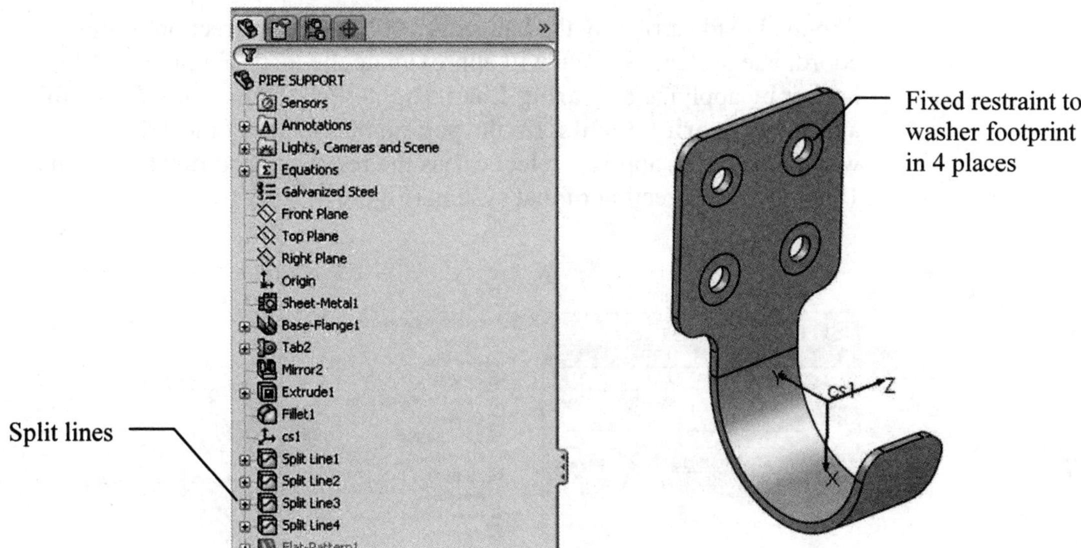

Figure 4-4: Split lines in SolidWorks model

Adding split lines is a technique frequently used in preparation of a CAD model for analysis with FEA. In this model, the split line defines the face where the bearing load and restraints will be applied.

The total load carried by the hanger is 100N in the x direction of the coordinate system **cs1**. We will approximate the load of a pipe onto the hanger by applying a **Bearing Load**. Right-click the *External Loads* folder and select **Bearing Load** form the pop-up menu. Select the cylindrical face where the load is applied, select **cs1** as the reference coordinate system and 100N in the x direction of that system (Figure 4-5).

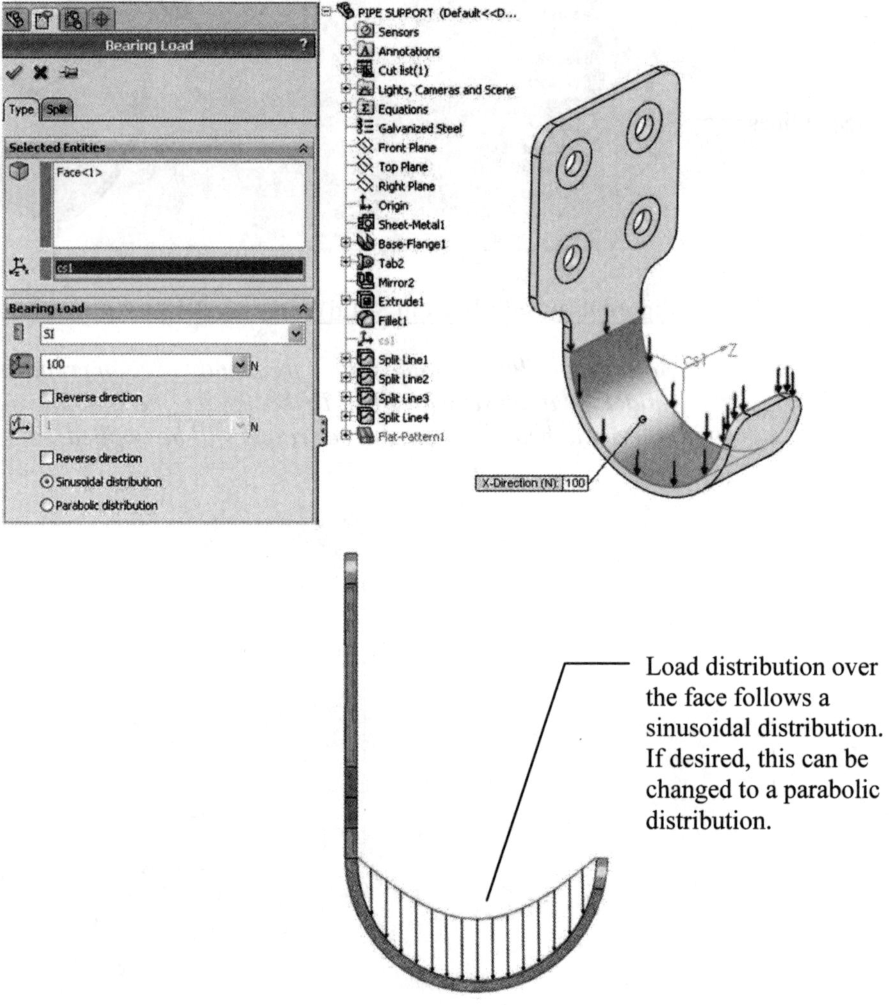

Figure 4-5: Bearing Load definition

Bearing load can only be applied to a cylindrical face. It is not uniformly distributed over the face but follows a sinusoidal or parabolic distribution. A typical application of a Bearing Load is modeling interactions between shafts and housings.

The model is now ready for meshing (right-click the *Mesh* folder, **Create Mesh**). Use default element size. The shell element mesh is shown in Figure 4-6.

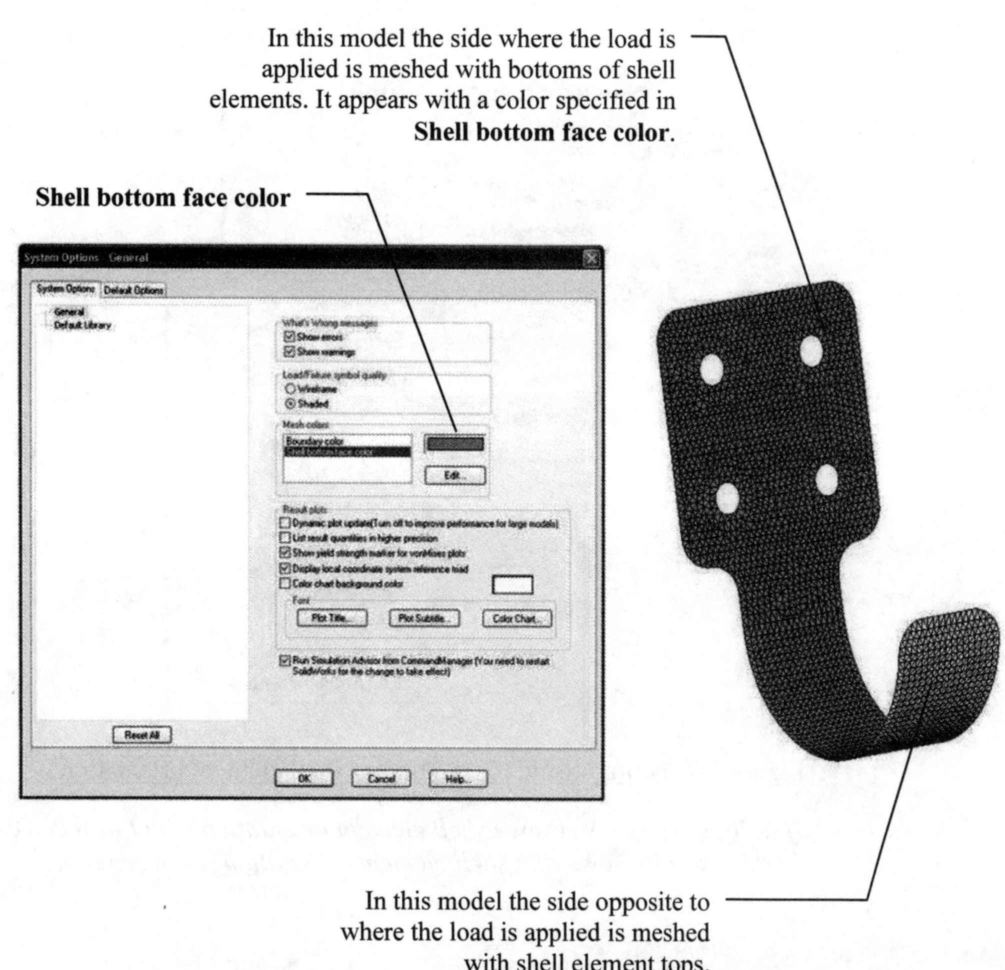
In this model the side where the load is applied is meshed with bottoms of shell elements. It appears with a color specified in **Shell bottom face color**.
Shell bottom face color
In this model the side opposite to where the load is applied is meshed with shell element tops.

Figure 4-6: Shell element mesh. Mesh elements have been placed in mid surface between the faces which define the thin wall.

Different colors distinguish between the top and bottom of the shell elements. The bottom face color is specified in the System Options window (see Figure 2-40), System Options tab under Mesh Options. The top face color is the same as the color of the SolidWorks model.

Review the mesh colors to ensure that the shell elements are aligned. Try reversing the shell element orientation: select the face where you want to reverse the orientation, right-click the *Mesh* folder to display a pop-up menu and select **Flip shell elements** (Figure 4-7).

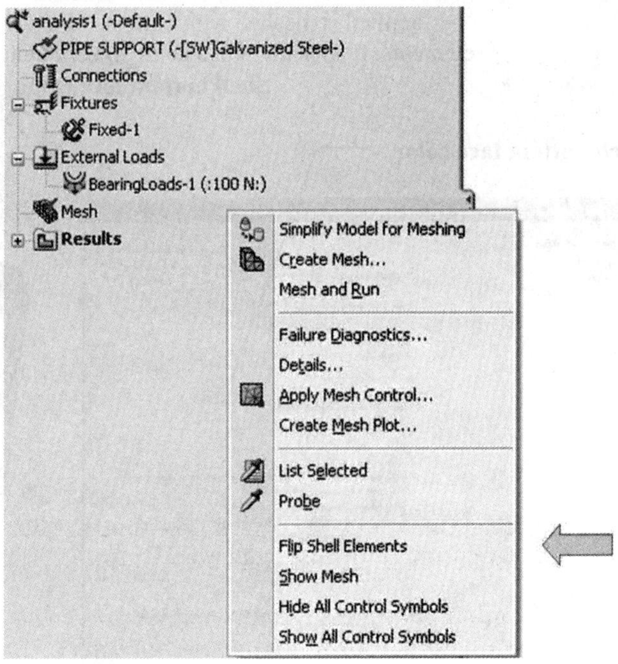

Figure 4-7: Pop-up menu for modifying shell element orientation

If desired, you may reverse shell element orientation with this menu choice. In this exercise reversing shell element orientation is not required.

Misaligned shell elements lead to the creation of erroneous plots like the one shown in Figure 4-8, which shows a rectangular plate undergoing bending.

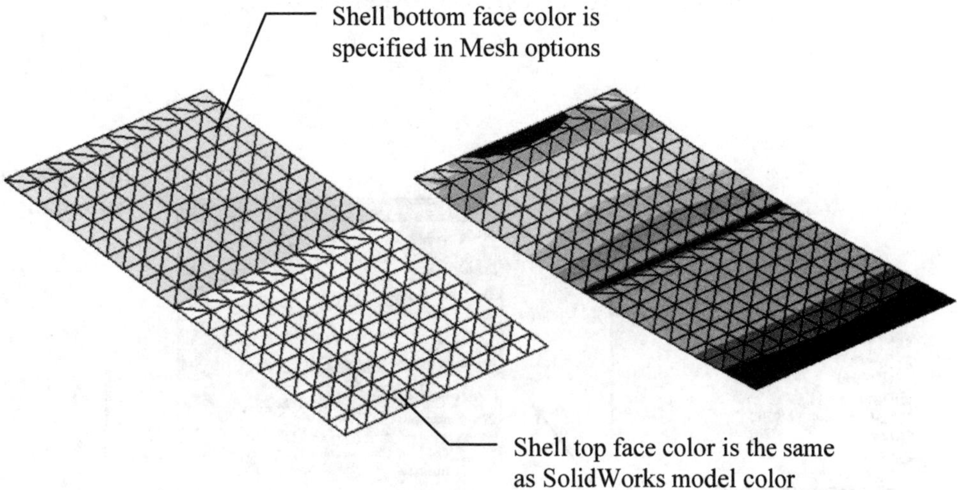
Shell bottom face color is specified in Mesh options
Shell top face color is the same as SolidWorks model color

Figure 4-8: Misaligned shell elements and erroneous von Mises Stress plot resulting from this misalignment

The misaligned shell element mesh (left) and erroneous von Mises Stress plot are the result of shell element misalignment. This model is unrelated to our exercise.

Obtain the solution and display displacement results. Select the **Superimpose model on the deformed shape** option. This option is available in plot settings (Figure 4-9).

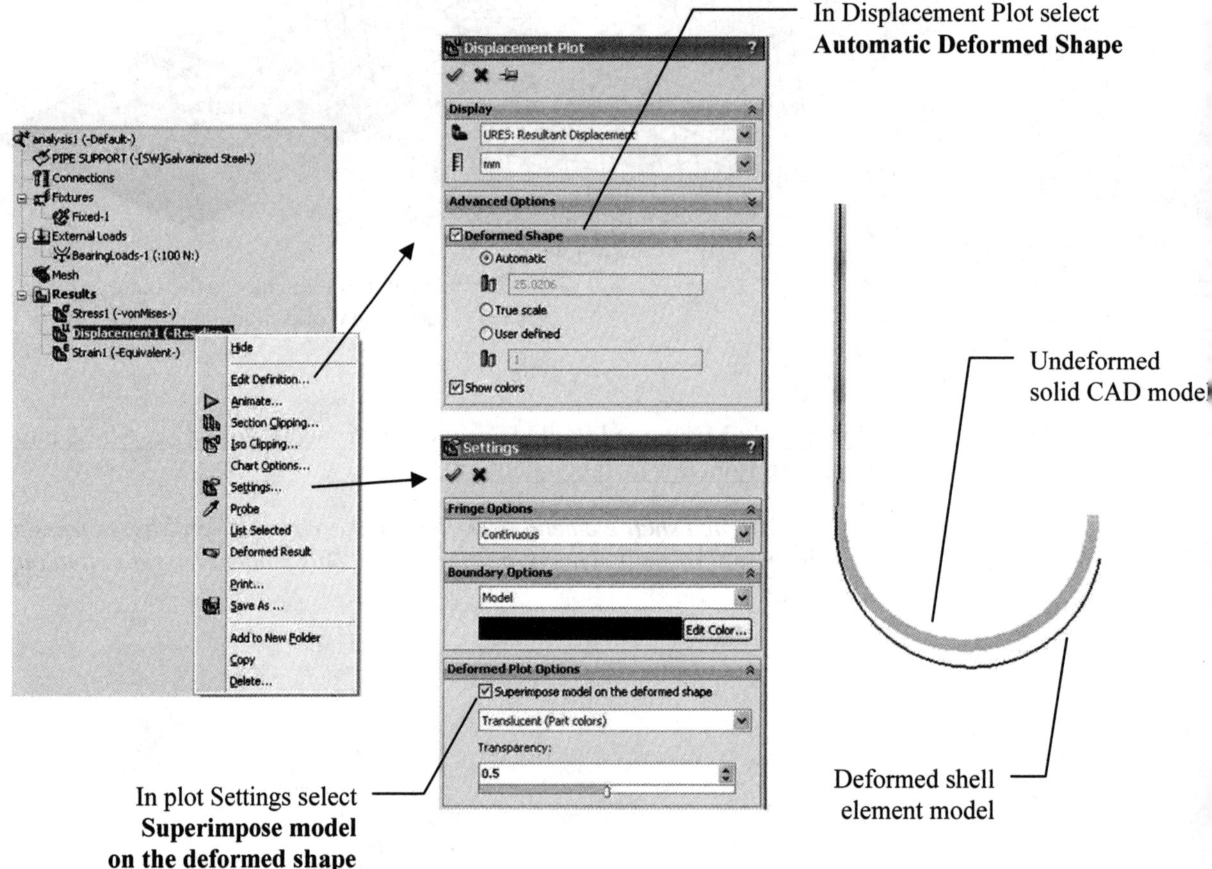

Figure 4-9 The undeformed model is superimposed on the deformed shape

This plot clearly shows that the shell element mesh has been placed in the mid-plane of solid the CAD model. The plot shows the deformed model. The Show color option has been deselected, therefore the color legend is not showing.

Shell elements differentiate between stress results on the top and bottom of the element. In the case of bending, one side will show tensile stress, the other compressive stress. For correct interpretation of results we must know on which side of the element results are presented. To illustrate this, we prepare two stress plots

- P1 stress (maximum principal stress) on the tensile side of the model. The tensile side corresponds to the bottom of shell elements (Figure 4-10)

- P3 stress (minimum principal stress) on the compressive side of the model. The compressive side corresponds to the top of shell elements. Note that P3 is the maximum compressive stress (Figure 4-11).

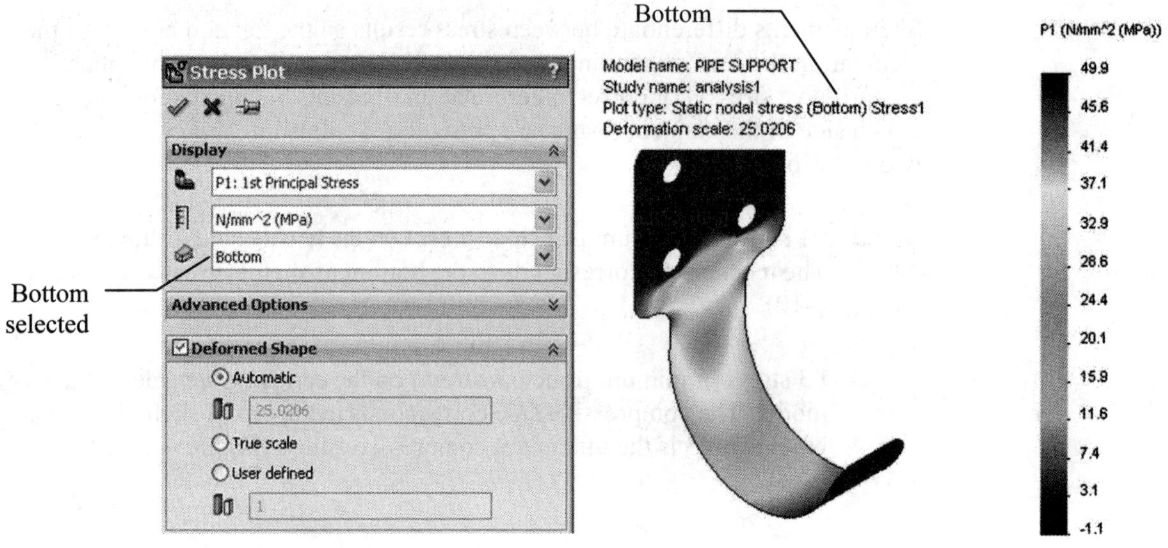

Figure 4-10: Maximum principle stress (P1) results for the bottom faces of the shell elements - on the tensile side of the model

Information on the element side is shown in Plot details. This can be turned off in Chart Options.

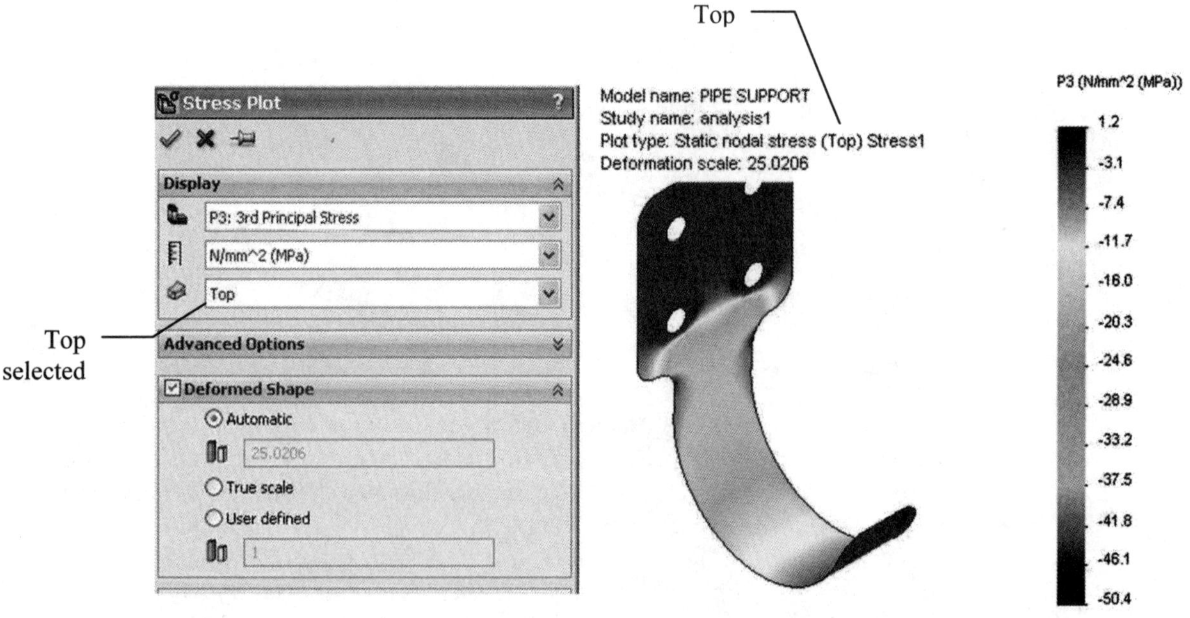

Figure 4-11: Minimum principle stress (P3) results for the top faces of the shell elements - on the compressive side of the model

In Figure 4-10 we are looking at bottom faces of shell elements. Still, stress results are displayed for the top side (which is "underneath" the model) of the elements, as if the shells were transparent. What stress is visible (top or bottom) does not depend on view direction (which side is visible) but only on the selection made in the **Stress Plot** window.

The structural analysis of the support bracket has been completed. We now proceed to calculate natural frequencies for the same bracket.

This requires a frequency analysis also known as modal analysis. Create a new study and name it *analysis2* (Figure 4-12).

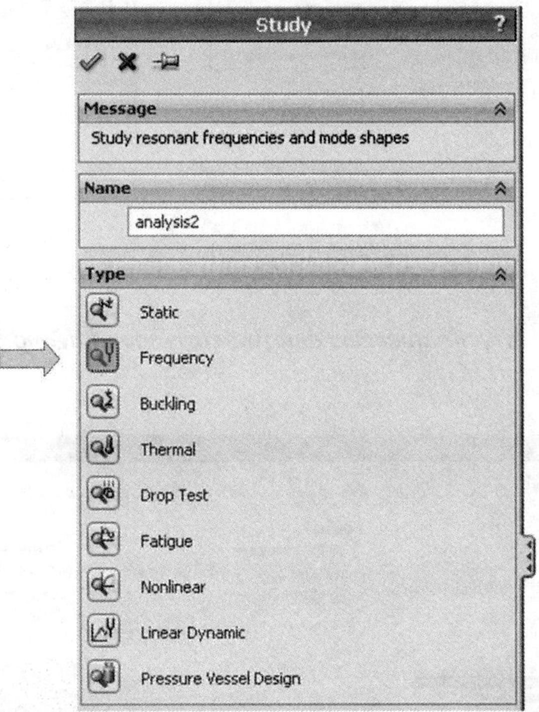

Figure 4-12: Frequency study definition

You can copy restraints and mesh definitions from the static study to the frequency study by dropping them into the frequency study tab. No loads are defined in this frequency study. We assume that loads, if any are present, will not significantly affect the natural frequencies.

In the properties of the **Frequency** study, verify that five modes will be calculated (Figure 4-13). In **Simulation Default Options**, verify that displacement plots are automatically created in the *Results* folder for all calculated modes (Figure 4-14).

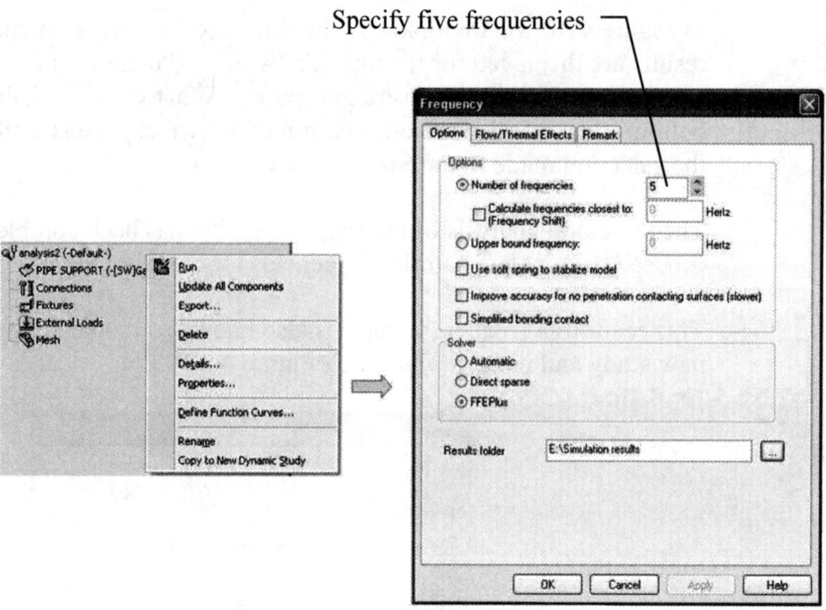

Figure 4-13: Properties of frequency study

Five frequencies and five corresponding modes of vibration will be calculated.

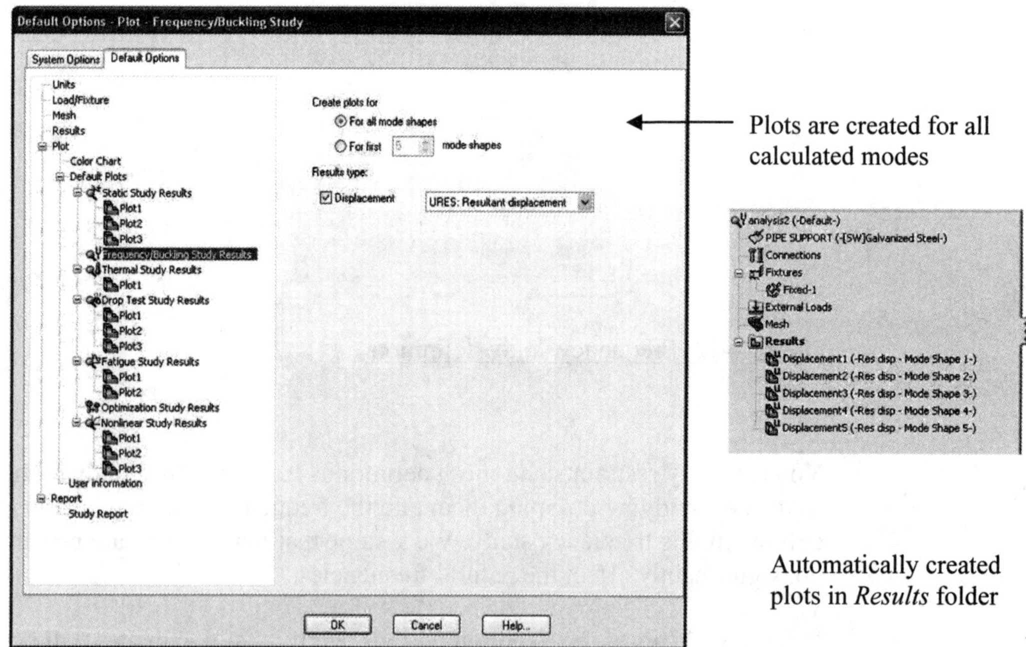

Figure 4-14: Using the above settings, displacement plots are automatically created for all the modes of vibration specified in the Options of the Frequency study window (fig. 4-13)

Run the solution and verify that five displacement plots are in the *Results* folder. Right-click any displacement plot icon and select **Edit Definition** to open the **Mode Shape/Displacement Plot** panel. Try displaying the mode shape plot with and without colors by making the appropriate selection shown in Figure 4-15.

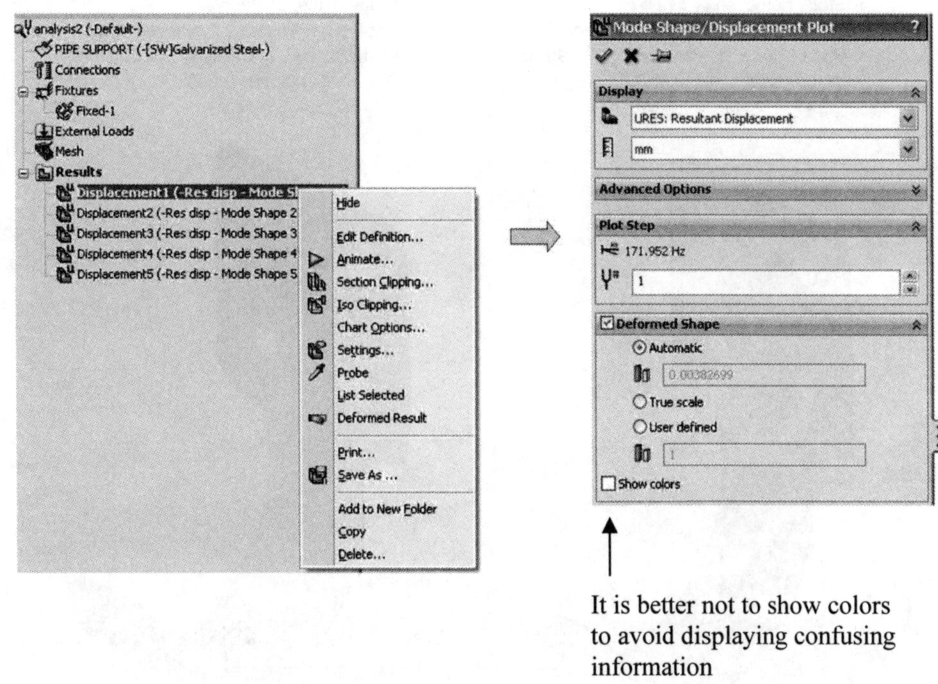

Figure 4-15: Mode Shape/Displacement Plot definition window

You can switch between Mode Shape and Displacement plot showing or hiding colors. However, you must remember that absolute displacements values are meaningless. Only ratios between displacements are valid.

Figure 4-16 shows the first mode of vibration presented as a mode shape and as a displacement plot.

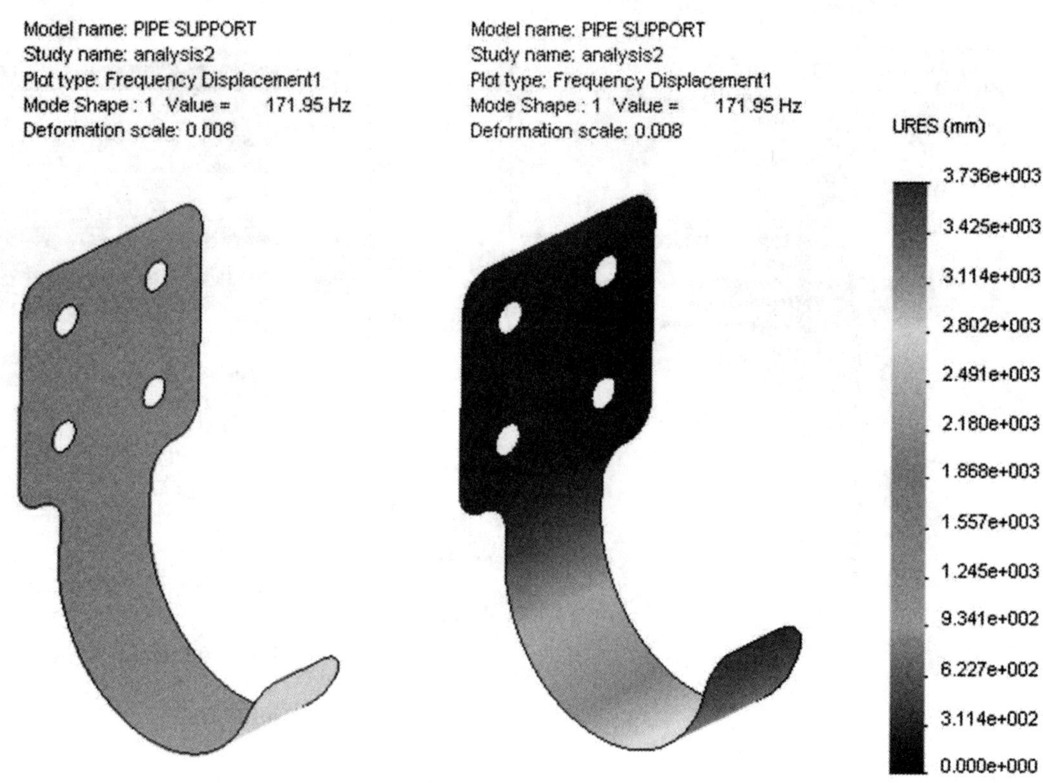

Figure 4-16 Mode shape plot (left) and Displacement plot (right)

Both plots show the vibration frequency associated with this mode, here 172Hz. Even though the displacement plot does show displacement magnitude, the absolute displacement results are meaningless

Once again note that the magnitudes of displacements shown in Figure 4-16 are meaningless. Displacement results are purely qualitative and can be used only for qualitative comparison of displacements within the same mode of vibration. Relative comparison of displacements between different modes is invalid.

The magnitude of the deformed shape is selected for the best visualization of the mode of vibration. One of the worst errors an FEA user can make is to take displacement results from modal analysis for their face value!

Examine deformation plots of higher modes (Figure 4-17) to notice that higher modes are associated with more deformation. The best way to analyze the results of a frequency analysis is by examining the animated deformation plots.

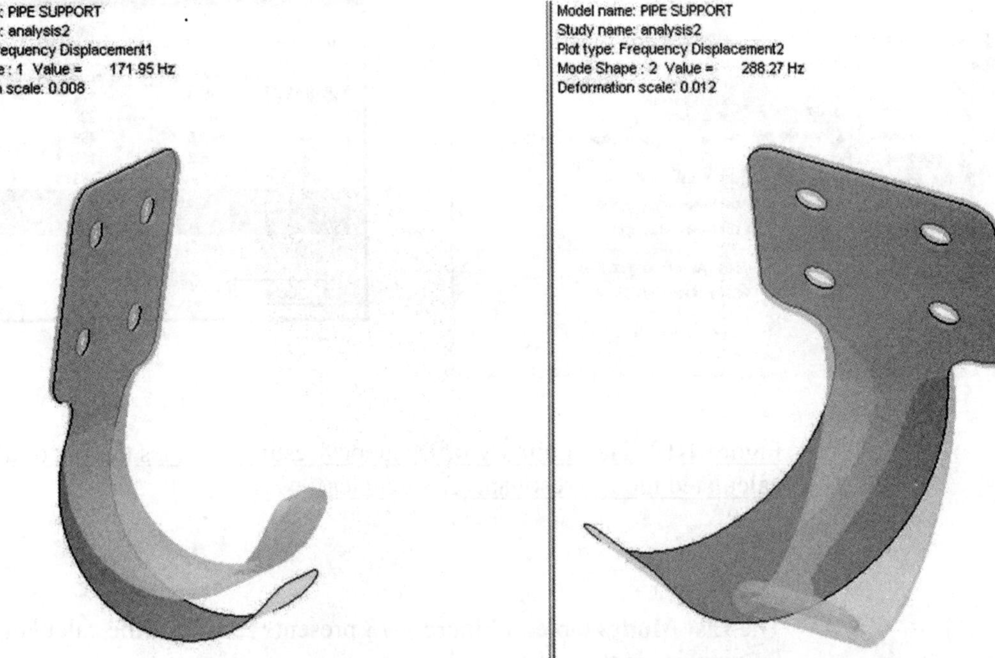

Figure 4-17: Deformation plots showing the shape of deformation (mode shape) of the first two modes

SolidWorks Simulation results plots can be viewed more than one at a time using the SolidWorks split window technique. The deformation scale in these plots has been changed to better show the deformed shape superimposed on the undeformed shape.

To animate any plot, right-click an active plot icon to display an associated pop-up menu, and then select **Animate**.

To **List Resonance Frequencies** right-click *Results* folder and make the selection as shown in Figure 4-18.

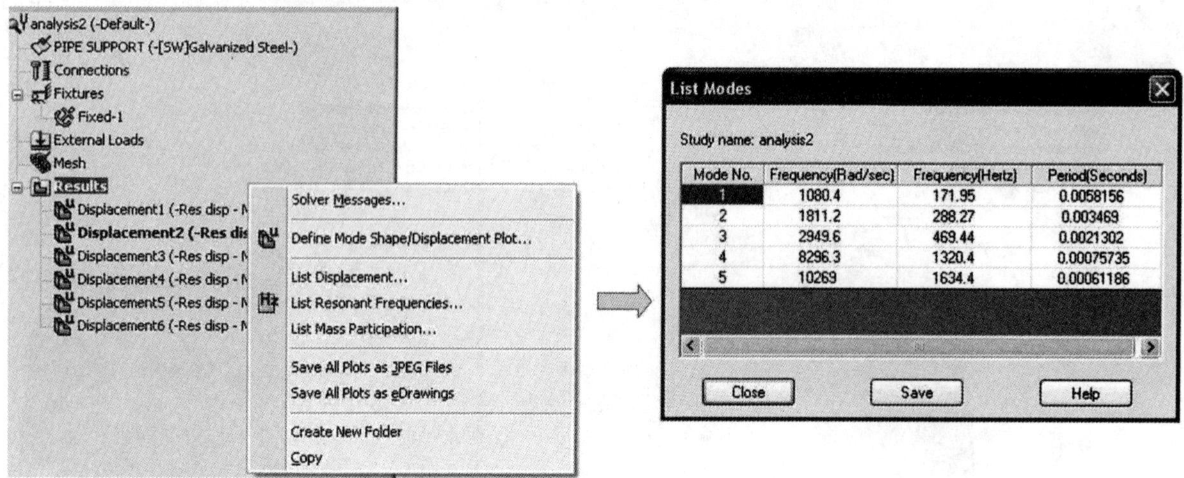

Mode No.	Frequency(Rad/sec)	Frequency(Hertz)	Period(Seconds)
1	1080.4	171.95	0.0058156
2	1811.2	288.27	0.003469
3	2949.6	469.44	0.0021302
4	8296.3	1320.4	0.00075735
5	10269	1634.4	0.00061186

Figure 4-18: The summary of frequency results includes the list of all calculated modal (resonant) frequencies

The **List Modes** table in Figure 4-18 presents results of the calculated frequencies in three different ways:

- ❑ circular frequency ω [rad/s]
- ❑ frequency f [Hz]
- ❑ vibration period T [s]

The above quantities are related as follows:

$$\omega = 2\pi f$$

$$f = \frac{1}{T}$$

5: Static analysis of a link

Topics covered

- Symmetry boundary conditions
- Preventing rigid body motions
- Limitations of small displacements theory

Project description

We need to calculate displacements and stresses of the link shown in Figure 5-1. The link is supported by tight-fitting pins in the two end holes and is loaded by a loose fitting pin at the central hole with a force of 100000N. The other two holes are not loaded. Open part file LINK. It has assigned material properties of Chrome Stainless Steel.

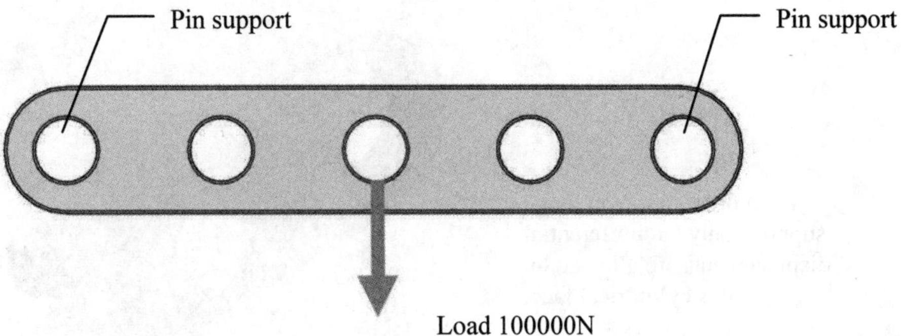

Figure 5-1: CAD model of the link

Note that the supporting pins and the loaded pin are not present in the model. All filleted edges have no structural significance and will be suppressed to simplify meshing.

Procedure

One way to conduct this analysis would be to model both the link and all three pins, and then conduct an analysis of the assembly. However, we are not interested in the contact stresses that will develop between pins and the link. Our focus is on deflections and stresses that will develop in the link. Therefore the analysis can be simplified; instead of modeling the pins, we can simulate their effects by properly defining the restraints and the load. Notice that the link geometry, restraints, and load are all symmetrical. We can take advantage of this symmetry and analyze only half of the model, replacing the other half with symmetry boundary conditions.

To work with half of the model, switch to the *02 half model* configuration. This also suppresses all the small fillets in the model. The fillets have negligible structural effect and would unnecessarily complicate the mesh. Removing geometry details deemed unnecessary for analysis is called defeaturing.

Finally, note a split face in the middle hole that defines the area where the load will be applied. Geometry in FEA-ready form is shown in Figure 5-2. Figure 5-2 also explains how restraints should be applied.

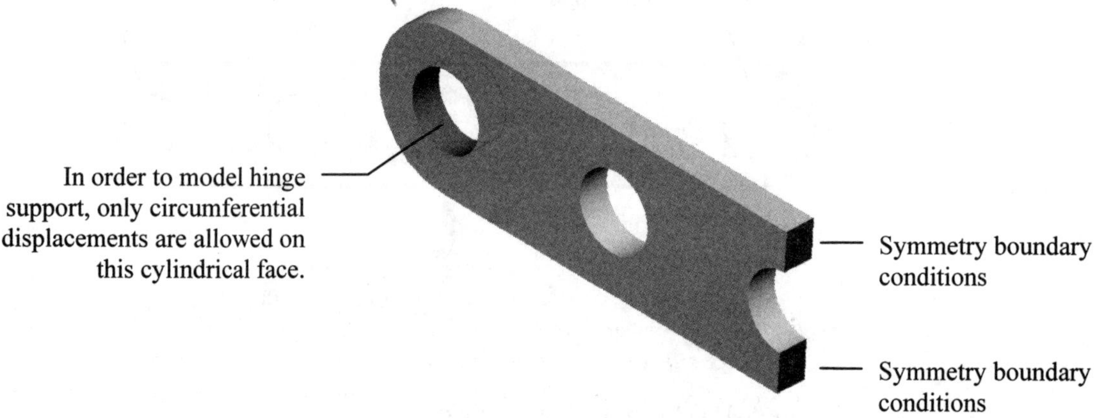
In order to model hinge support, only circumferential displacements are allowed on this cylindrical face.
Symmetry boundary conditions
Symmetry boundary conditions

Figure 5-2: Half of the link with restraints explained

The applied restraints: a hole where the pin support is simulated and two faces in the plane of symmetry where symmetry boundary conditions are required.

The model is ready for the definition of supports – the highlight of this exercise. Move to SolidWorks **Simulation** and define a static analysis study.

Right-click the *Fixtures* folder and select **Fixed Hinge** from the pop-up menu. This opens the Fixture window with the **Fixed Hinge** button already selected (Figure 5-3). This restraint simulates hinge support.

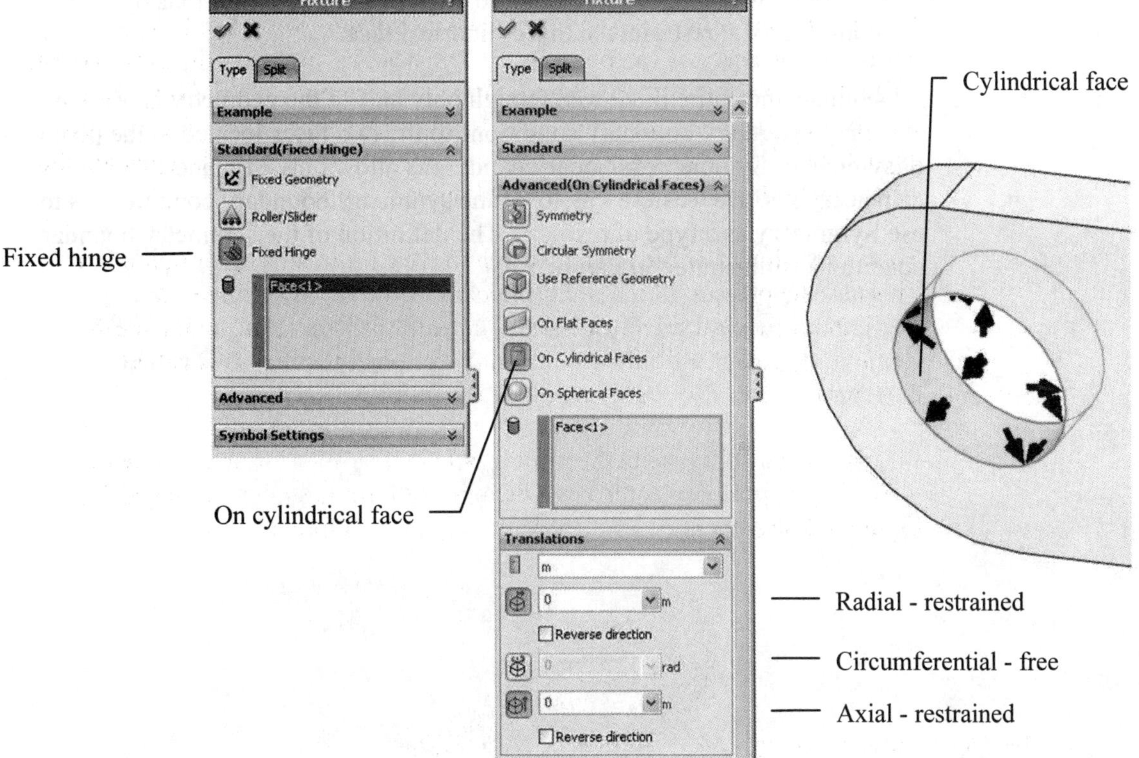

Figure 5-3: Fixture window defining hinge support

An identical restraint can be obtained using either Hinge or On Cylindrical Face (with suppressed radial and axial directions). Once the Fixture definition window has been opened, you can move between different types of restraints. You are not committed by the selection made in the pop-up menu choice.

When the **Fixture** definition window specifies the restraint type as **Hinge** or **On cylindrical face**, the restraint directions are associated with the directions of the cylindrical face (radial, circumferential, and axial), rather than with global directions x, y, z.

To simulate a pin support that allows the link to rotate about the pin axis, radial displacement needs to be restrained and circumferential displacement allowed. Furthermore, displacement in the axial direction needs to be restrained in order to avoid rigid body motions of the entire link along this direction.

Using **Hinge** support is easier but has less learning benefit, so the **On cylindrical face** restraint method is used here instead.

Notice that while we must restrict the rigid body motion of the link in the direction defined by the pin axis, we can do this by restraining any point of the model. It is simply convenient to remove rigid body motions by applying the axial restraints to this cylindrical face.

To simulate the entire link, even though only half of the geometry is present, we apply symmetry boundary conditions to the two faces located in the plane of symmetry. Symmetry boundary conditions allow only in-plane displacements. The easiest way to define symmetry boundary conditions is to use **Symmetry** as a type of restraint. The definition of the symmetry boundary conditions is illustrated in Figure 5-4.

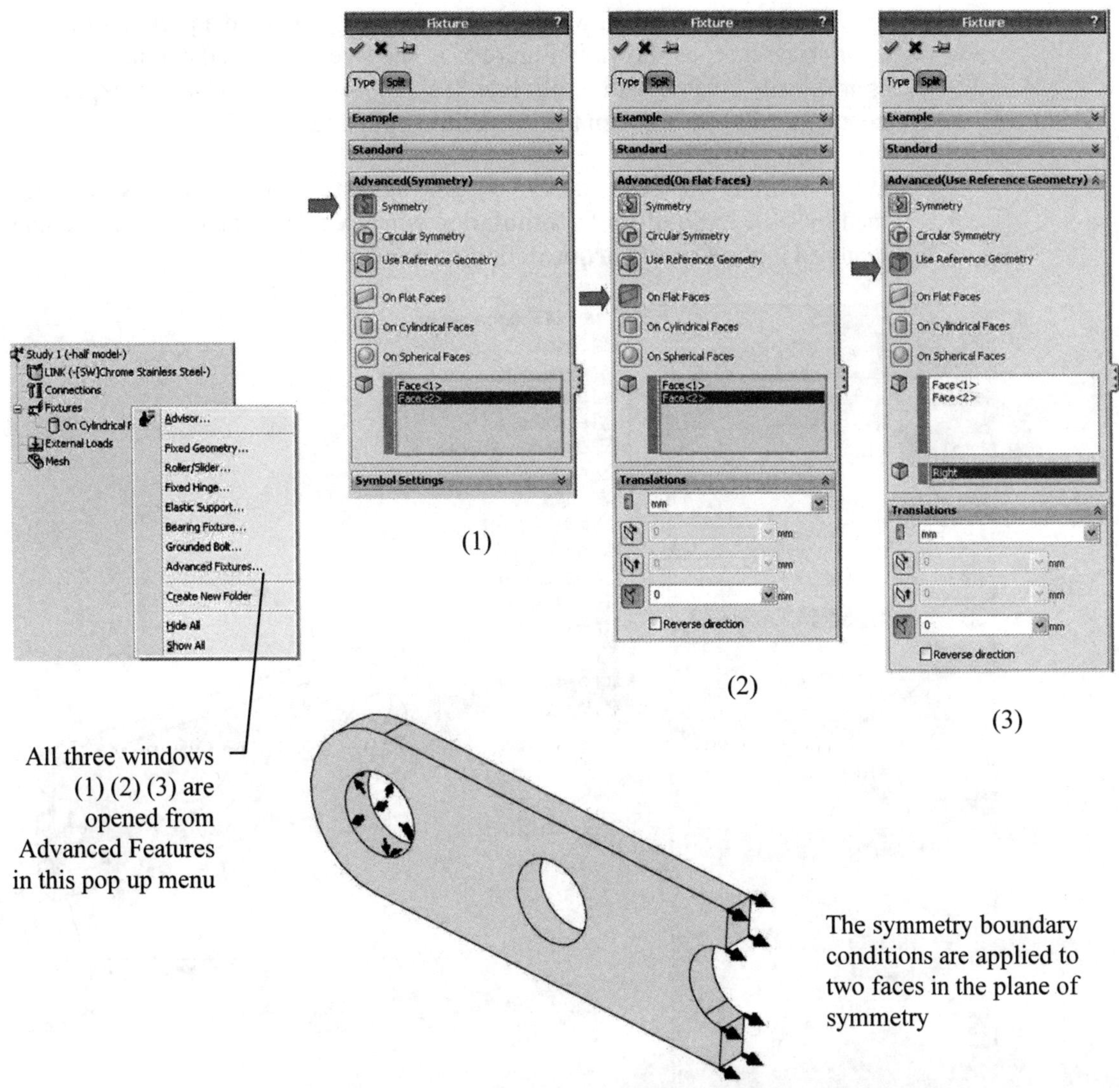

Figure 5-4: Definition of symmetry boundary conditions

The same could be defined using:

(1) Symmetry restraint

(2) On Flat Face restraint where both in-plane displacements are allowed, but displacement in the direction normal to the face is set to zero

(3) Use Reference Geometry where free and restrained directions are defined with reference to selected reference geometry here, the Right reference. The reference plane can be selected from a fly-out menu not shown here.

Recall from Figure 5-1 that the link is loaded with 100000N. Since we are modeling half of the link, we must apply a 50000N load to a portion of the cylindrical face, as shown in Figure 5-5. The size of the load application area is arbitrarily created with a split line. It should be close to what we expect the contact area to be between the loose fitting pin and the link.

When defining the load (Figure 5-5), take advantage of SolidWorks' fly-out menu visible in SolidWorks **Simulation** window to select the reference plane required in the **Force/Torque** definition window.

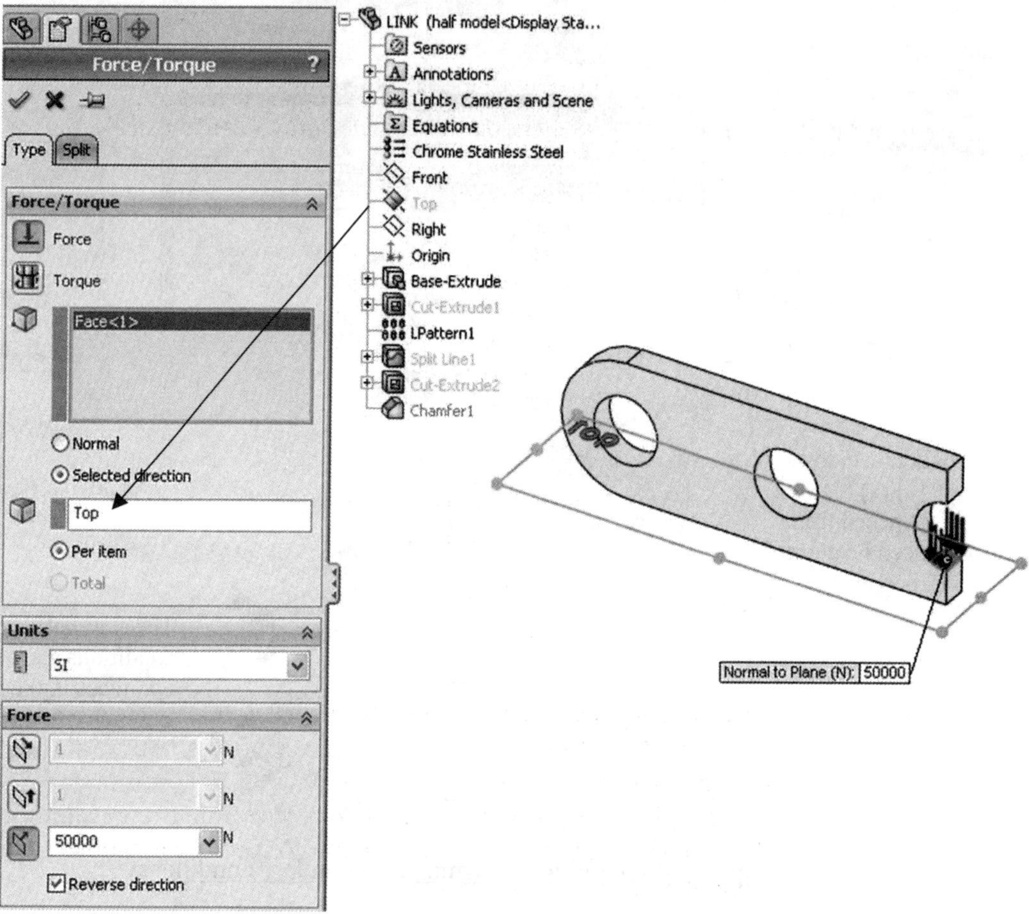

Figure 5-5: 50000N force applied to the central hole

Force is applied in the Selected direction. The Top reference plane is used to determine the load direction. Notice that the load is distributed uniformly. We are not trying to simulate a contact stress problem.

The last task of model preparation is meshing. Right-click the *Mesh* folder to display the related pop-up menu, and then select **Create…**. Verify that the mesh preferences are set on high quality (meaning that second order elements will be created) and mesh the geometry using the default element size. For more information on the created mesh, you may wish to review **Mesh Details** (Figure 5-6).

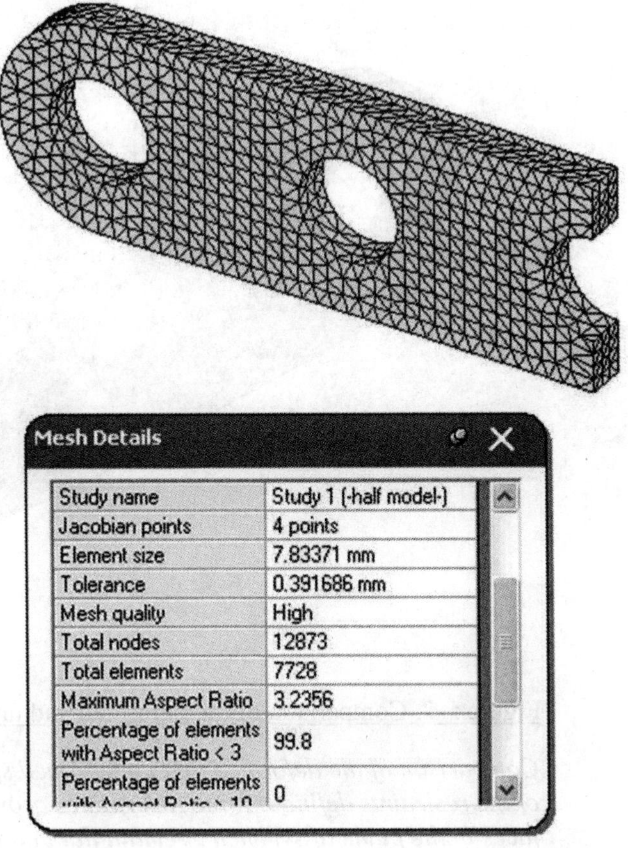

Mesh Details
Study name
Study 1 (-half model-)
Jacobian points
4 points
Element size
7.83371 mm
Tolerance
0.391686 mm
Mesh quality
High
Total nodes
12873
Total elements
7728
Maximum Aspect Ratio
3.2356
Percentage of elements with Aspect Ratio < 3
99.8
Percentage of elements
0

Figure 5-6: Mesh Details window shown over the meshed model

After solving the model, we first need to check if the pin support and symmetry boundary conditions have been applied properly. This includes checking whether the link can rotate around the pin and whether it behaves as a half of the whole link. This is best done by examining the animated displacements, preferably with both undeformed and deformed shapes visible (Figure 5-7).

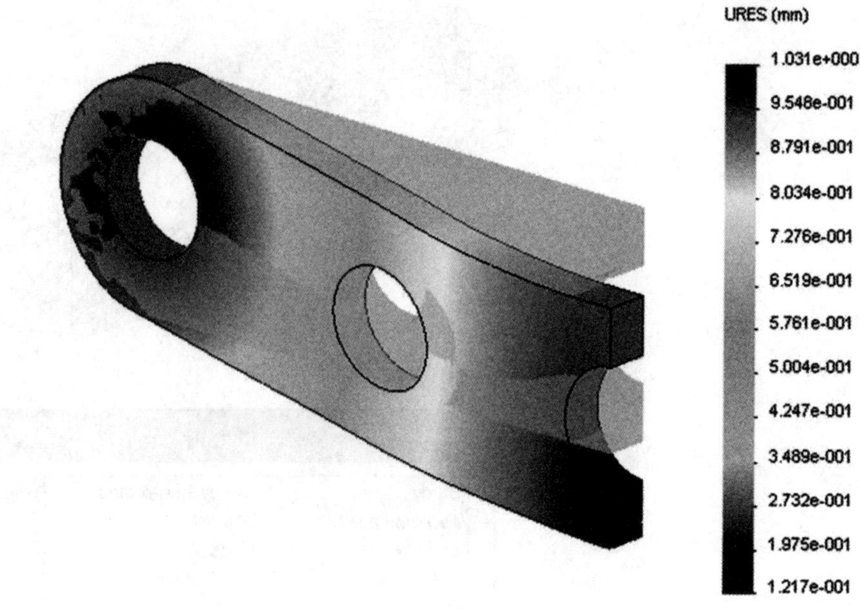

Figure 5-7: Comparison of the deformed and undeformed shapes

Comparison of the deformed and undeformed shapes verifies the correctness of the restraints definition: the link rotates around the imaginary pin while faces in the plane of symmetry remain flat and perform only in-plane translations.

To conclude this exercise, review the stress results. Examine the different stress components, including the maximum principal stresses, minimum principal stresses, etc.

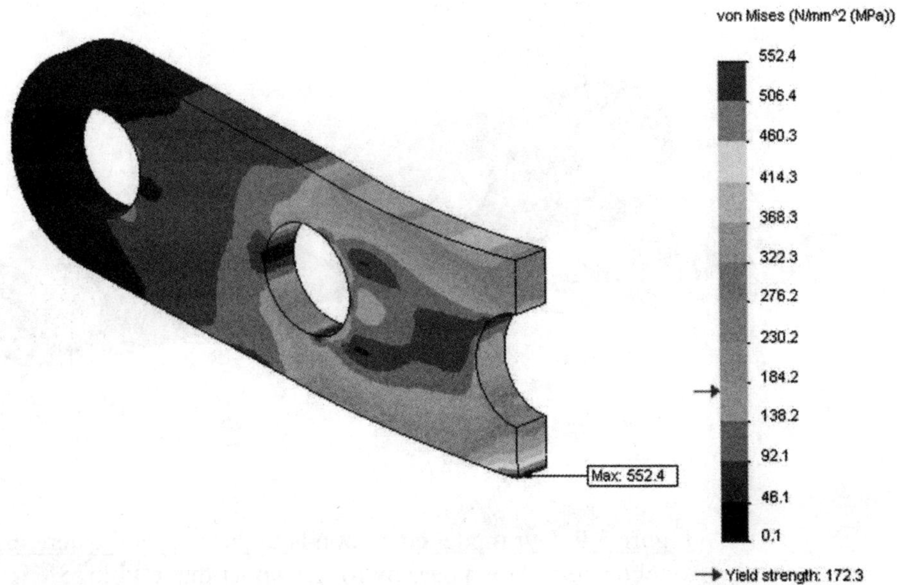

Figure 5-8: Sample of stress results: von Mises stress

In this plot, the location of the maximum stress is shown, as requested in the Chart Options window.

Note that model is severely overloaded. The maximum von Mises stress read 562MPa as compared to the yield strength 172MPa. Material yielding is of course not modeled here because we ran a linear analysis.

Repeat this exercise using the full model to perform an analysis of the complete model without using symmetry boundary conditions.

Before finishing the analysis of LINK, we should notice that the link supported by two pins as modeled in this exercise corresponds to the configuration shown in Figure 5-9, where one of the hinges is free to move horizontally.

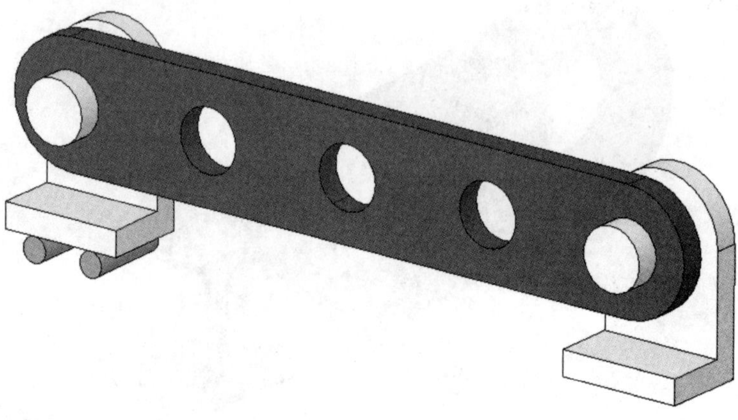

Figure 5-9: Our model corresponds to the situation where one hinge is floating, symbolically shown here by rollers under the left hinge

Since linear analysis does not account for changes in model stiffness during the deformation process (nor does it account for material yielding), linear analysis is unable to model stresses that would have developed if both pins were in a fixed position. If both pins were fixed, a nonlinear geometry analysis would be required to analyze the model. Refer to chapter 15 for more information on non-linear analysis.

6: Frequency analysis of a tuning fork and a plastic plate

Topics covered

- Frequency analysis with and without supports
- Rigid body modes
- The role of supports in frequency analysis
- Symmetric and anti-symmetric modes

Project description

Structures have preferred frequencies of vibration, called resonant frequencies. A mode of vibration is the shape in which a structure will vibrate at a given natural frequency. The only factor controlling the amplitude of vibration in resonance is damping. While any structure has an infinite number of resonant frequencies and associated modes of vibration, only a few of the lowest modes are important to describe their response to dynamic loading. A frequency analysis calculates these resonant frequencies and their associated modes of vibration.

Open the part file called TUNING FORK. It has material properties already assigned (Chrome Stainless Steel). The model is shown in Figure 6-1.

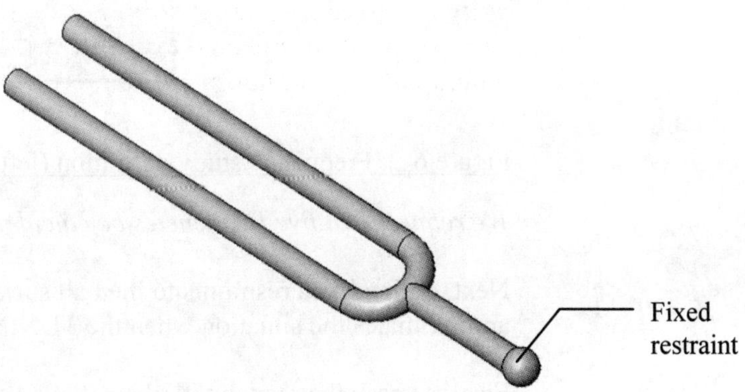

Figure 6-1: Model of TUNING FORK

A fixed restraint is applied to the surface of the ball. Do not apply On spherical face restraint.

A quick inspection of the CAD geometry reveals a sharp re-entrant edge. This condition renders the geometry unsuitable for stress analysis, but is acceptable for frequency analysis unless the omitted round significantly changes the model stiffness.

Procedure

Define a **Frequency** study *TUNING FORK*. Once the study has been created right-click it to open pop-up menu and select Properties (Figure 6-2).

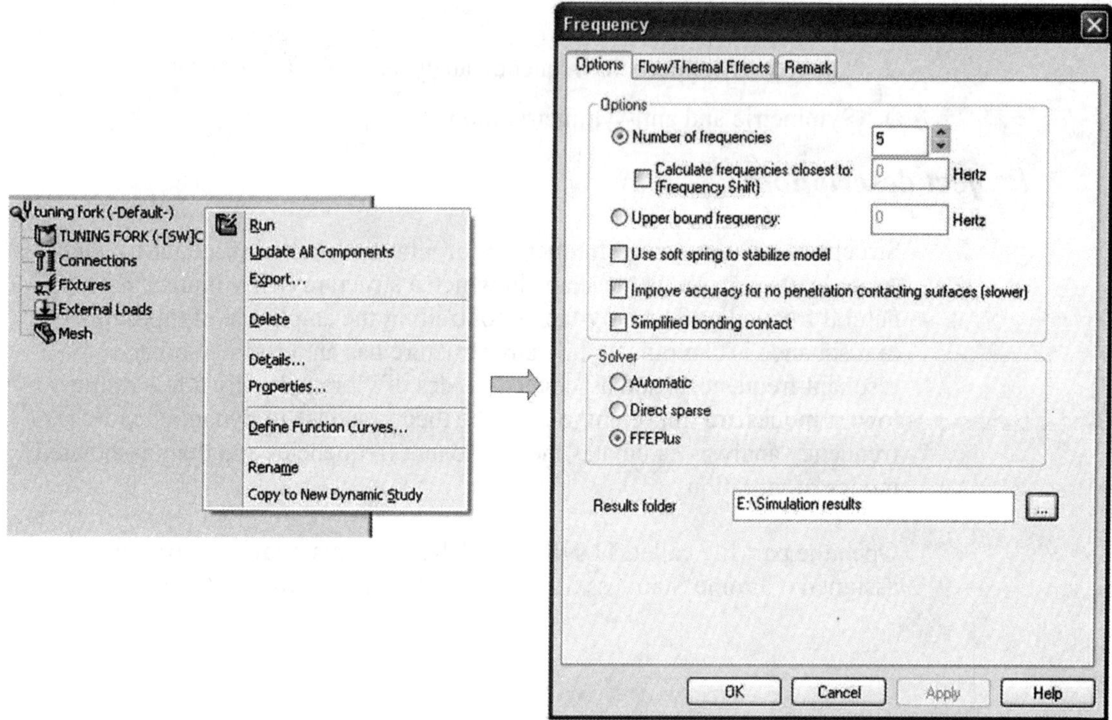

Figure 6-2: Frequency study definition (left) and study properties (right)

We request that five frequencies be calculated using the FFEPlus solver.

Next, define fixed restraints to the ball surface, as shown in Figure 6-1. This approximates the situation when the TUNING FORK is held with two fingers.

Finally, mesh the model with the default element size. The meshed model is shown in Figure 6-3. The mesher selects the element size to satisfy the requirements of a stress analysis. A frequency analysis is less demanding on the mesh, so generally, a less refined mesh is acceptable. Nevertheless, since this is a very simple model, we accept the mesh without making an attempt to simplify it.

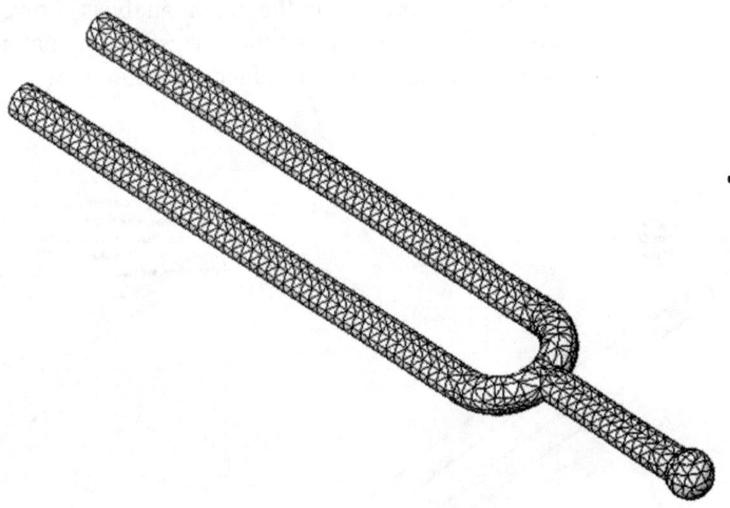

Figure 6-3: Meshed model of the TUNING FORK

After the solution is complete, SolidWorks **Simulation** automatically creates displacement plots (Figure 6-4). For reasons already explained in chapter 4, we ignore displacement results. Using the **Mode Shape/ Displacement** window we deselect colors, turning the displacement plot into a deformation plot. We call the **Displacement** plot without colors a **Mode Shape** plot.

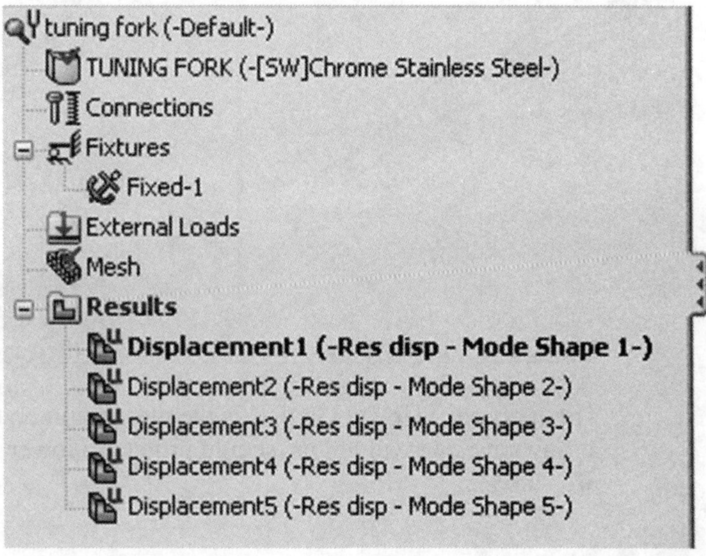

Figure 6-4: Five Displacement plots are created automatically

Plot Displacement1 shows Mode Shape 1 etc.

The **Mode Shape** plot in the modal analysis shows the associated modal shape of vibration and lists the corresponding natural frequency. The first four modes of vibration are presented in Figure 6-5.

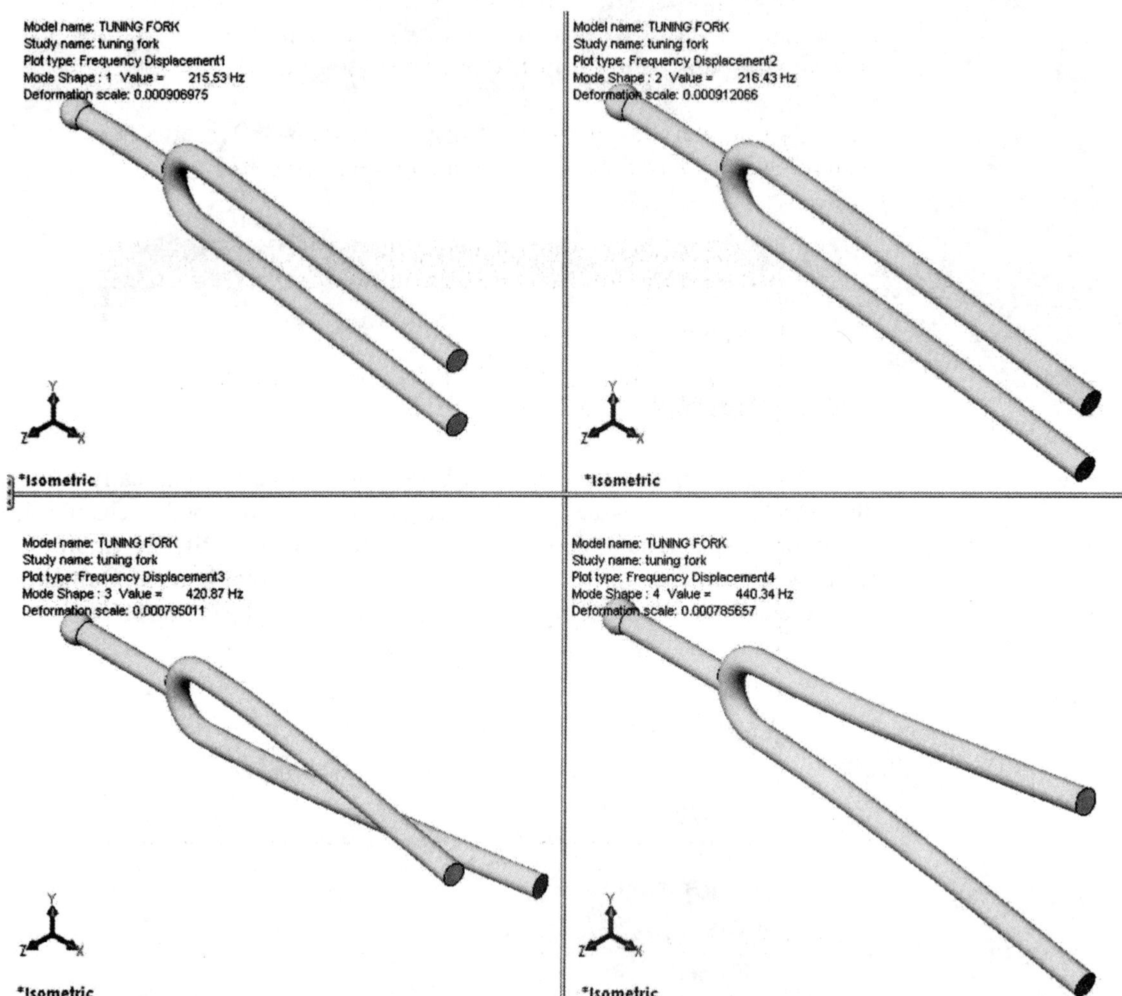

Figure 6-5: First four modes of vibration and their associated frequencies

The analyzed TUNING FORK is the most common type of tuning fork and, as any musician will tell us, should produce a lower A sound, with frequency of 440 Hz.

However, the lower A frequency of 440 Hz, which we were expecting to be the first mode, is actually the fourth mode. Before explaining the reasons for this, let's run the frequency analysis again, this time without any restraints. We need to define a new frequency study, which we will call *tuning fork no supports*.

The easiest way is to do this is to copy the existing *TUNING FORK* study and either delete or suppress the restraint (right-click the restraint icon and make proper selection).

In the **Options** tab of the Frequency window in the *tuning fork no supports* study, we again specify that five modes be calculated (no change compared to previous study). After the solution is has been completed, right-click the *Deformation* folder and select **List Resonant Frequencies**.

Here, we find that the highest calculated mode is mode 7 (Figure 6-6) even though we asked that only five modes be calculated.

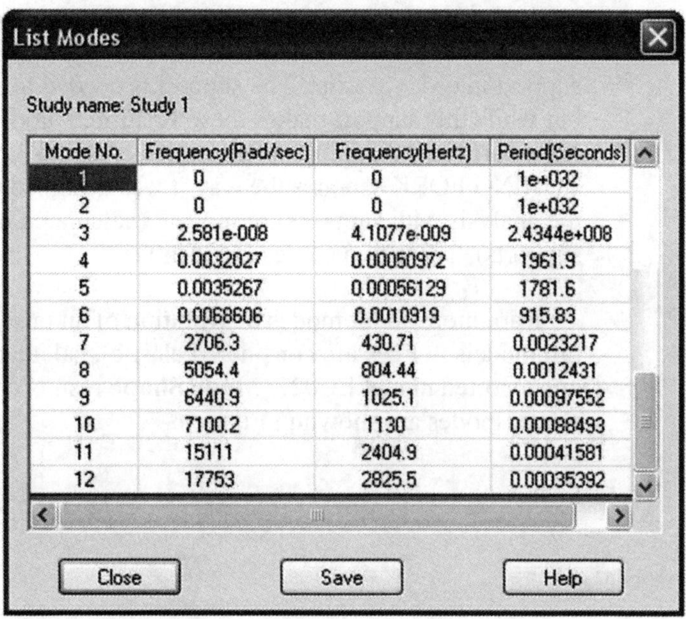

List Modes

Study name: Study 1

Mode No.	Frequency(Rad/sec)	Frequency(Hertz)	Period(Seconds)
1	0	0	1e+032
2	0	0	1e+032
3	2.581e-008	4.1077e-009	2.4344e+008
4	0.0032027	0.00050972	1961.9
5	0.0035267	0.00056129	1781.6
6	0.0068606	0.0010919	915.83
7	2706.3	430.71	0.0023217
8	5054.4	804.44	0.0012431
9	6440.9	1025.1	0.00097552
10	7100.2	1130	0.00088493
11	15111	2404.9	0.00041581
12	17753	2825.5	0.00035392

Close Save Help

Figure 6-6: **List Modes** window

Modes 1-6 are rigid body modes. Mode 7 is the first elastic mode of vibration. This illustration has been modified to show all calculated modes without scrolling.

We also notice that the first six modes have the associated frequency 0 Hz or very close to 0Hz (with-in solution error). Why? The first six modes of vibration correspond to rigid body modes. Because the TUNING FORK is not supported, it has six degrees of freedom as a rigid body: three translations and three rotations.

SolidWorks **Simulation** detects those rigid body modes and assigns them zero frequency (0 Hz). The reason why modes 4, 5, 6 do not have a frequency of exactly zero is solution error. Having detected rigid body modes, the solver expanded the number of modes to be calculated to include the first two elastic modes; therefore the total number of modes is eight.

The first elastic mode of vibration, meaning the first mode requiring the fork to deform is mode 7, which has a frequency of 440.2 Hz. This is close to what we were expecting to find as the fundamental mode of vibration for the TUNING FORK.

Why did the frequency analysis with the restraint not produce the first mode with a frequency near to 440 Hz? If we closely examine the first three modes of vibration of the supported TUNING FORK, we notice that they all need the support in order to exist. The support is needed to sustain these modes, but while this support makes these first three modes possible, in reality it also provides damping. After modes 1, 2, and 3 have been damped out, the TUNING FORK vibrates the way it was designed to: in mode 4 (calculated in the analysis with supports) or mode 7 (calculated in the analysis without supports). These two modes are identical.

To learn more about modes of vibration of an unsupported elastic model (all models in FEA are considered elastic), calculate six elastic modes of the unsupported model EC027. **Mode Shape** results corresponding to the first six elastic modes are shown in Figure 6-7.

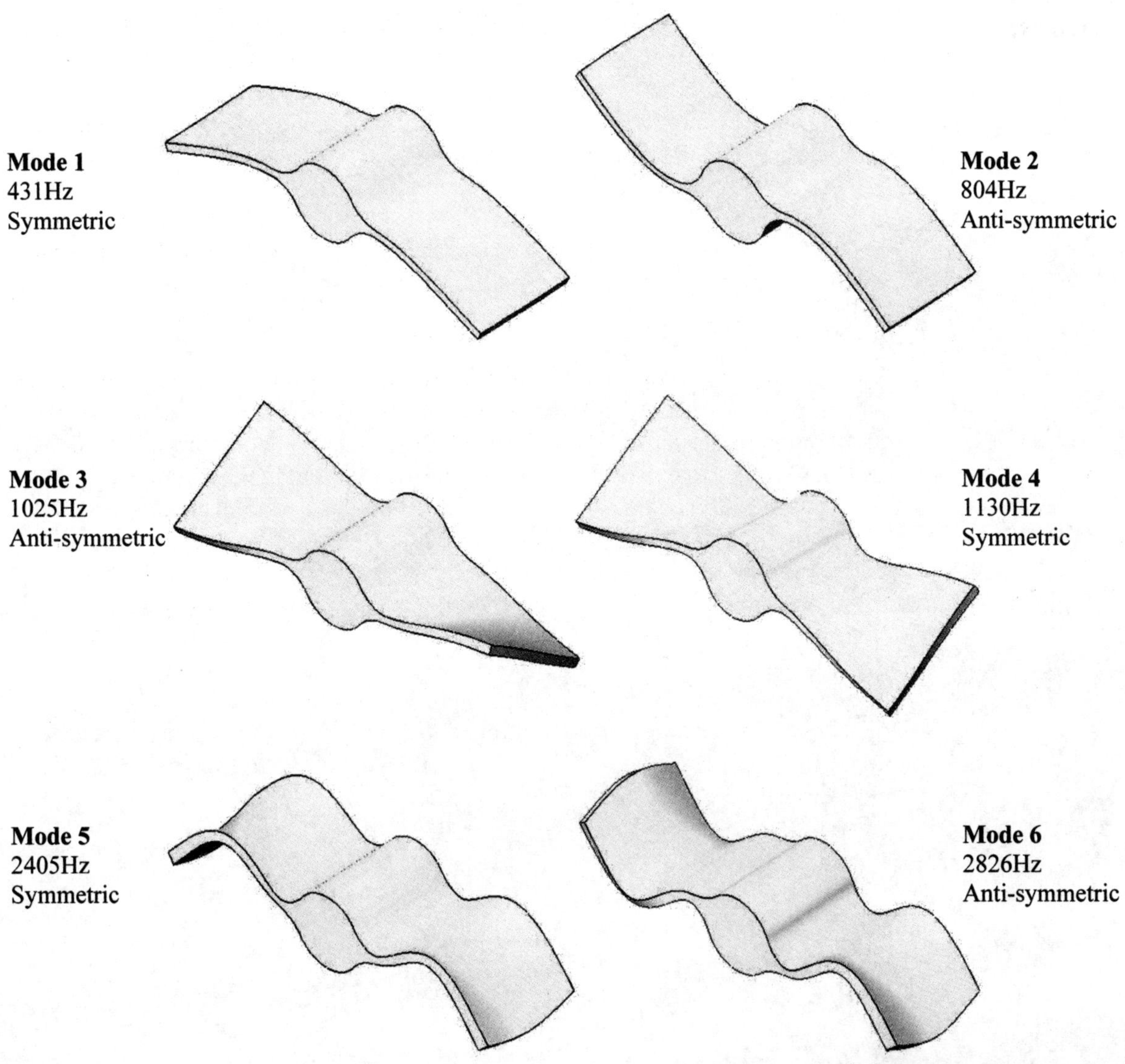

Figure 6-7: The first six elastic modes of vibration of the unsupported model EC027

Based on deformation results of PIPE SUPPORT, TUNING FORK and EC027 we can make an interesting observation about the nature of modes of vibration. If a model is symmetric and has symmetric restraints (or no restraint at all), then its modal shapes are either symmetric or anti-symmetric.

Notes:

7: Thermal analysis of a pipeline component and a heater

Topics covered

- Analogies between structural and thermal analysis
- Steady state thermal analysis
- Analysis of temperature distribution and heat flux

Project description

So far, we have performed static analyses and frequency analyses, which both belong to the class of structural analyses. Static analysis provides results in the form of displacements, strains, and stresses, while frequency analysis provides results in the form of natural frequencies and associated modes of vibration. We will now examine a thermal analysis. Numerous analogies exist between thermal and structural analyses. The most direct analogies are summarized in Figure 7-1.

Structural Analysis	Thermal Analysis
Displacement [m]	Temperature [K]
Strain [1] (dimensionless)	Temperature gradient [K/m]
Stress [N/m^2]	Heat flux [W/m^2]
Load [N] [N/m] [N/m^2] [N/m^3]	Heat source [W] [W/m] [W/m^2] [W/m^3]
Prescribed displacement [m]	Prescribed temperature [K]

Figure 7-1: Selected analogies between structural and thermal analysis with corresponding units in SI system.

A negative heat source is a heat sink.

Procedure

Open part model CROSSING PIPES. Our objective is to find the steady state temperature of the part when prescribed temperatures are applied to end faces as shown is Figure 7-2. As indicated in Figure 7-1, prescribed temperatures are analogous to prescribed displacements in structural analyses.

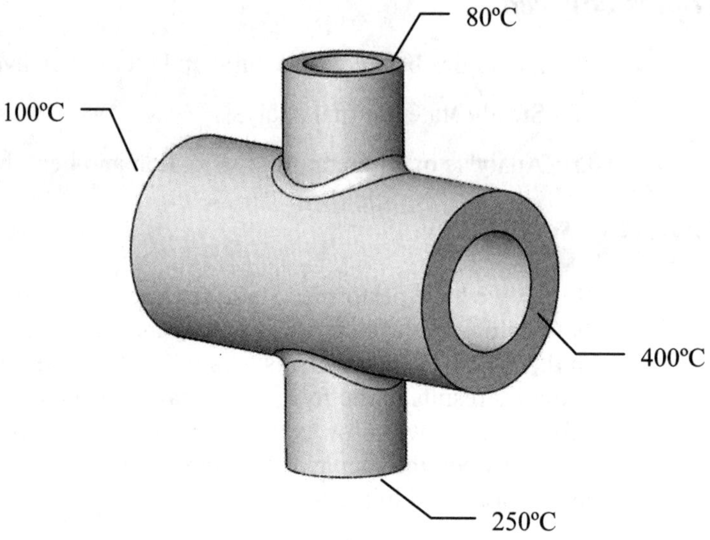

Figure 7-2: CAD model of two crossing pipes

Also shown are the prescribed temperatures, applied to the end faces as temperature boundary conditions. Note that the units are in degrees Celsius. Fahrenheit or Kelvin degrees can be used as well.

Since no convection coefficients are defined on any faces, heat can enter and leave the model only through the end faces with prescribed temperatures assigned. Even though the problem has little relevance to real heat transfer problems, it helps us understand the basics of thermal analysis.

The first step is study definition. Call this study *crossing pipes* and define it as shown in Figure 7-3.

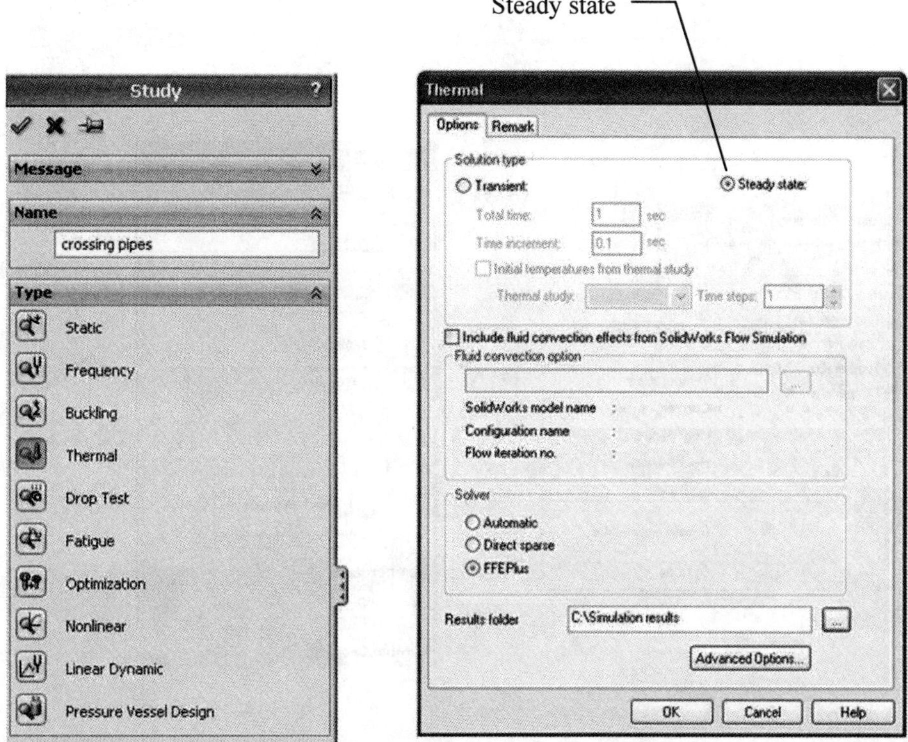

Figure 7-3: Definition of *crossing pipes* thermal study

The Study is defined as Steady state.

In **Steady state** thermal analysis, it is assumed that enough time has passed since thermal conditions have been applied and therefore, all parameters characterizing heat flow no longer change with time.

To define the prescribed temperature, right-click the *Thermal Loads* folder and select **Temperature** to open the **Temperature** definition window. Define prescribed temperatures to the four faces in four separate steps as in Figure 7-2.

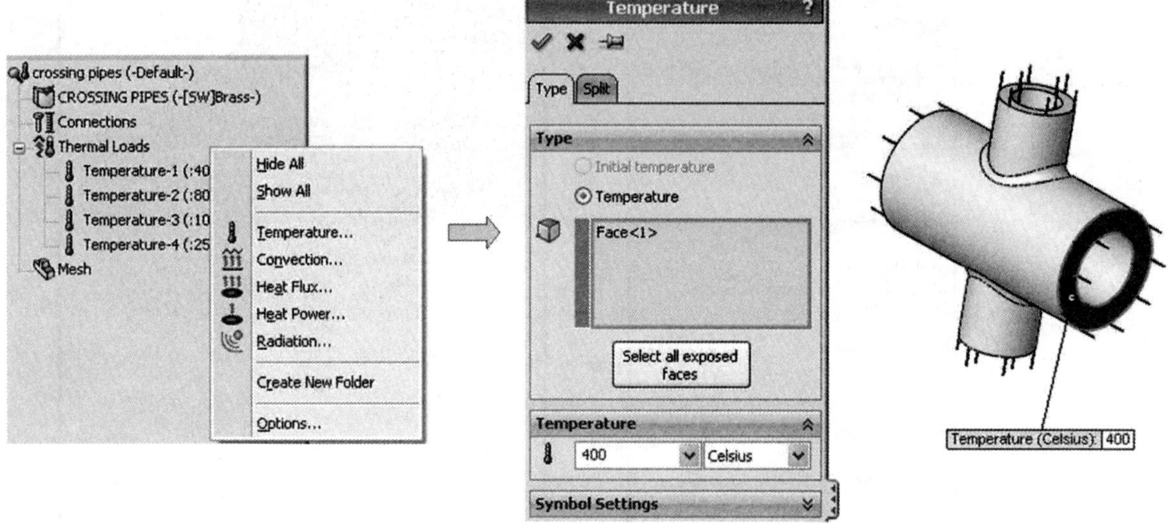

Figure 7-4: Defining prescribed temperature on the end face

Right-click the Thermal Loads folder and select Temperature from the pop-up menu. Define prescribed temperatures in the Temperature definition window.

Mesh the model using the settings shown in Figure 7-5.

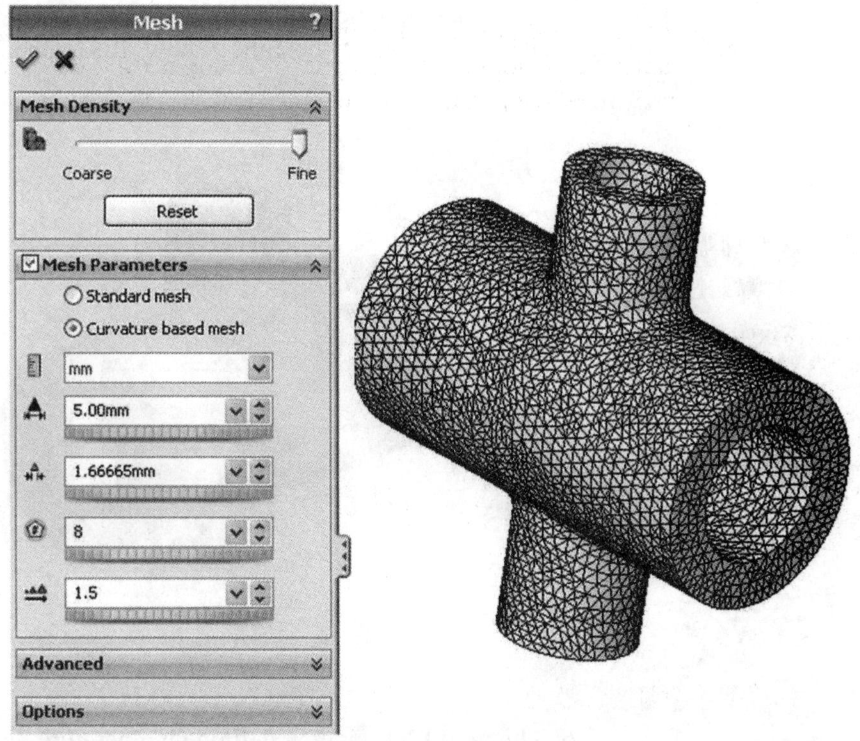

Figure 7-5: Curvature based mesh is used to assure correct meshing of fillets

A 5mm element size gives at least two elements across the wall. Eight elements in a circle are specified to assure low element turn angle.

After solving the model, notice that only one result folder called *Thermal* is present and has one plot. By default, it shows the temperature distribution (Figure 7-6).

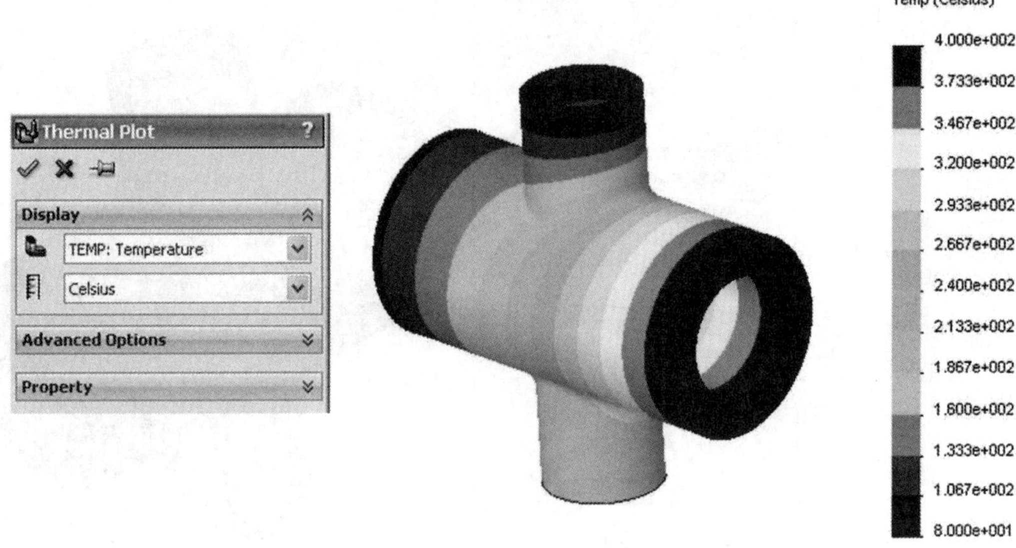

Figure 7-6: **Thermal Plot** window defining temperature distribution and corresponding plot

Create a plot showing resultant heat flux (Figure 7-7).

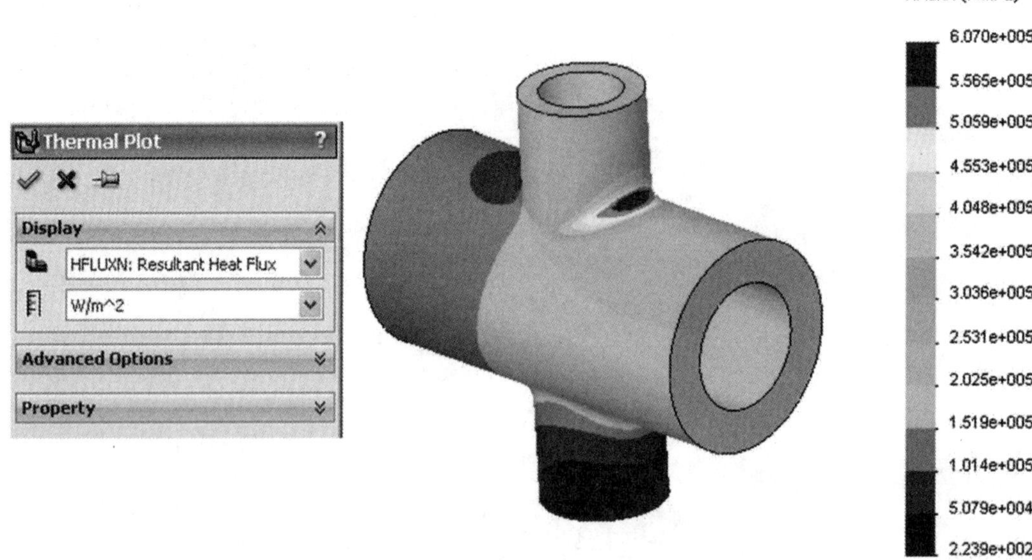

Figure 7-7: **Thermal Plot** window defining heat flux plot and the corresponding plot

Since heat flux is a vector quantity, it lends itself well to be presented as a vector plot. Follow the steps in Figure 7-8 to define and edit a vector plot of heat flux.

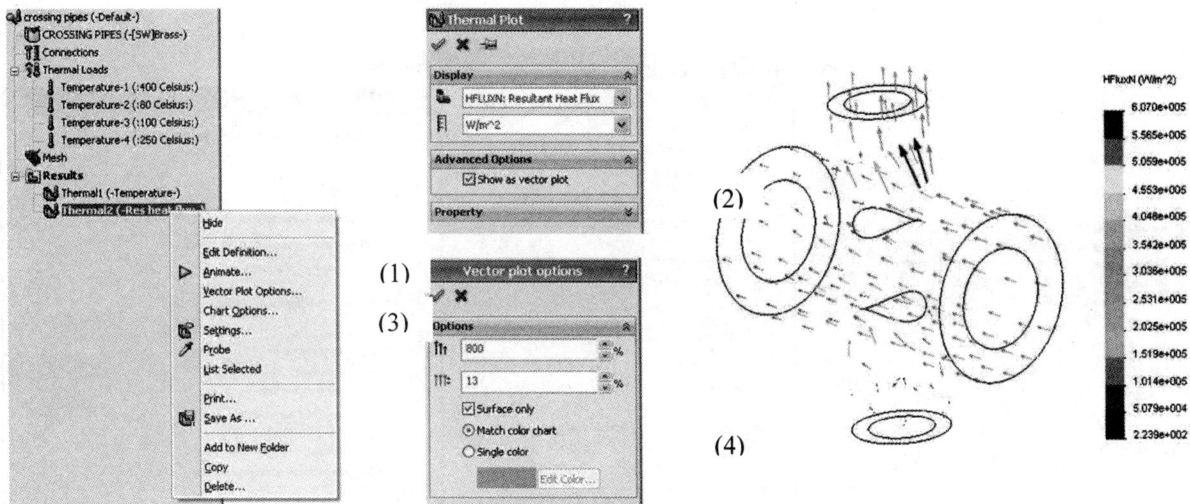

Figure 7-8: Heat flux result presented as a vector plot

Proceed as explained below to produce a heat flux vector plot.

To display a vector plot, right-click the existing heat flux plot to open the pop-up menu (1), select **Edit definition** to open the **Thermal Plot** window. In **Advanced Options**, select **Show as vector plot** (2). Once the vector plot is showing, right-click its icon again and select **Vector Plot Options** from the pop-up menu (3) to open the **Vector plot options window** (4). Adjust the settings to have a clear plot. In particular select **Surface only** in **Vector plot options**.

The non uniform temperature that establishes itself in the model (Figure 7-6) produces thermal stress due to non uniform thermal expansion of different portions of the model. We will now analyze those thermal stresses. Define a static study, *thermal stresses*, with the properties shown in Figure 7-9.

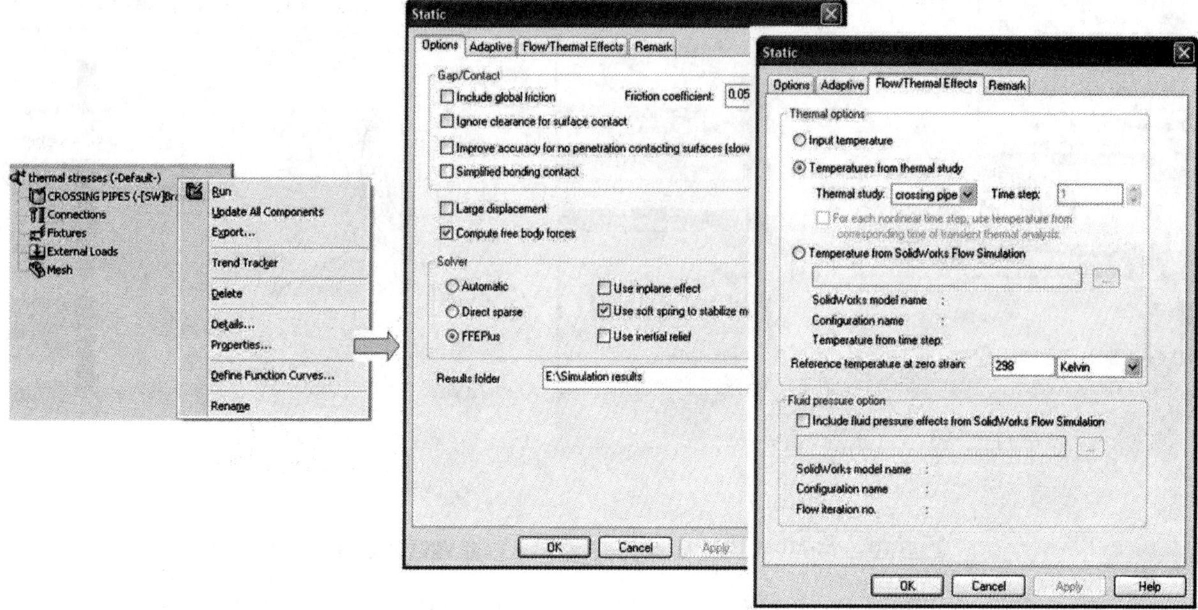

Options tab Flow/Thermal Effects tab

Figure 7-9: Properties of study intended for analysis of thermal stresses are defined under two tabs

Proceed as explained below to define Options and Flow/Thermal Effects tabs.

In the **Options** tab select **Use soft springs to stabilize model**. This is because in static analysis, the model will not be subjected to any structural loads or restraints. This way the pure effect of temperature is shown. The model is under internally balanced loads, but due to numerical errors, would experience rigid body movement. Soft springs eliminate those rigid body movements by attaching springs of very low stiffness to all nodes.

In the **Flow/Thermal Effects** tab specify **Temperature from thermal study** *crossing pipes*. This will import temperature results from the completed *crossing pipes* study.

A static study with temperatures imported from a thermal study must use a mesh that is identical to the one used in the thermal study. To make sure the mesh is identical, copy the mesh from the thermal study *crossing pipes* to the static study *thermal stresses*. To copy the mesh, drag it into the *thermal stresses* study tab.

Run the thermal stresses study and display a von Mises stress plot (Figure 7-10).

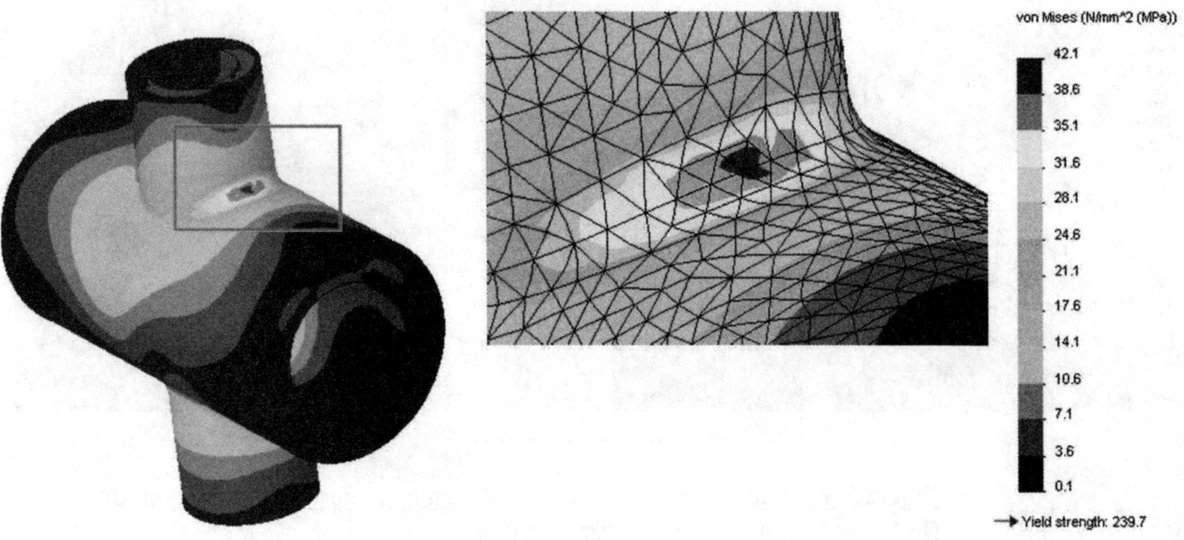

Figure 7-10: Thermal stresses due to non uniform temperature distribution

Note the irregular shape of fringes.

Analysis of the results in Figure 7-10 reveals irregularly shaped fringes. This is due to a coarse mesh. As it turns out, the mesh was adequate for the analysis of temperature and heat flux, but not sufficiently refined for an analysis of thermal stresses. Repeat the analyses (both thermal and static) with a more refined mesh to see the effect of element size and "regularity" of fringe plots (Figure 7-11).

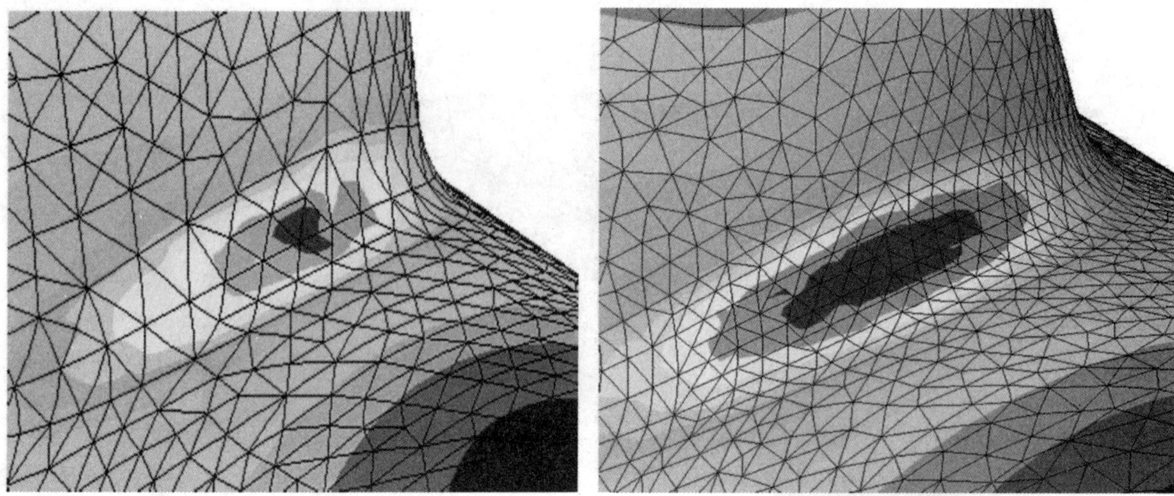

Figure 7-11: Thermal stress results produced by a mesh used in this study (left) and by a more refined mesh (right)

The left plot is a repetition of Figure 7-10. You can use the "regularity" of fringe plots to decide if a mesh needs to be refined.

We will now conduct a thermal analysis of a pipe with cooling fins. The objective of this analysis is to find how much heat is dissipated by a 50mm long section (Figure 7-12). Open part model HEATER, and begin a **Thermal** study.

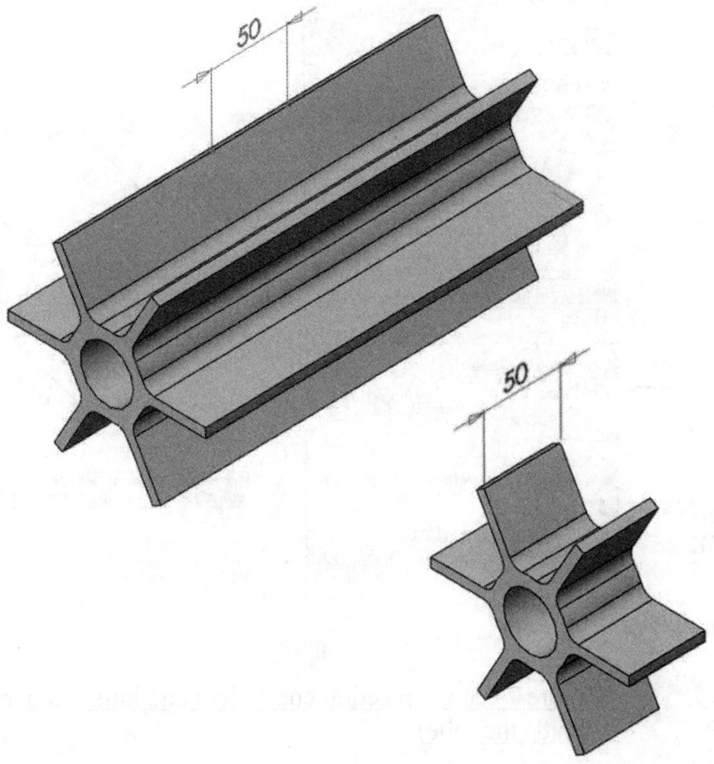

Figure 7-12: Analysis of a pipe with cooling fins (left) is conducted on the model of a section 50mm long (right)

Hot water at 100°C flows inside the heater. The coefficient of thermal convection between water and the heater face is 1000 W/(m^2/K), meaning that each 1m^2 of the surface exchanges (gains or looses) 1000W heat if the temperature difference between the face and water is 1K. The coefficient of thermal convection between outside faces and air is 20 W/(m^2/K). The ambient air temperature is 27 °C or 300K.

Note that we are using somewhat arbitrary values of convection coefficients. Finding convection coefficients that correctly describe the problem is often the most difficult part of thermal analysis.

Define convection coefficients and bulk temperatures as shown in Figures 7-13 and 7-14.

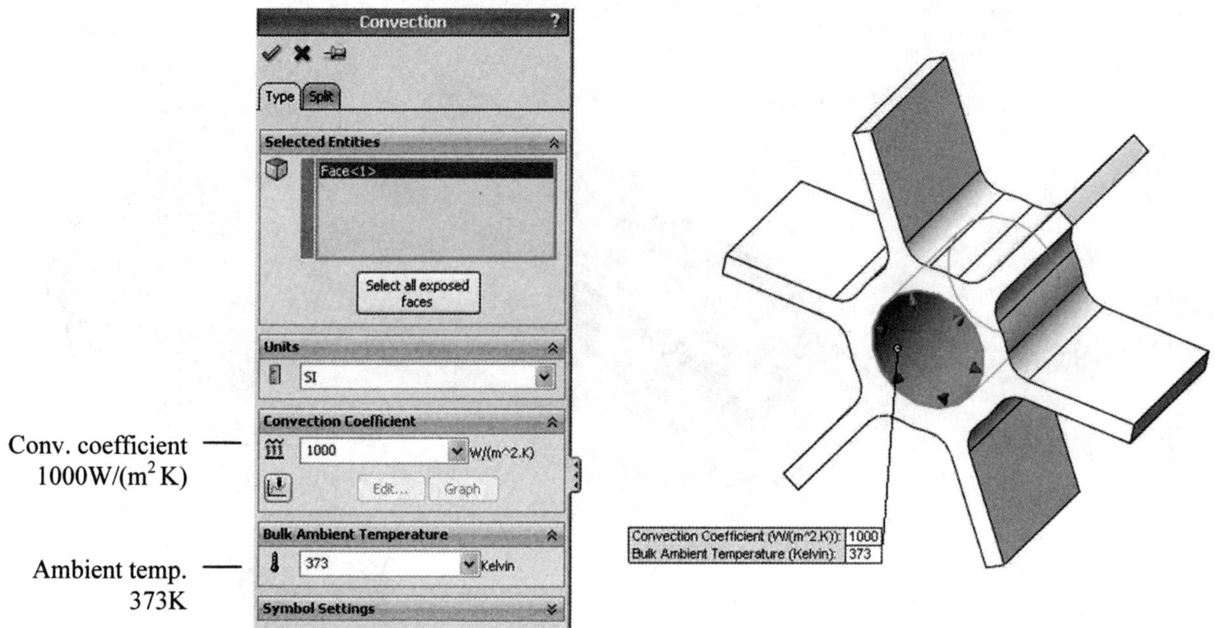

Figure 7-13: Convection coefficient and bulk temperature on the water side (inside the tube)

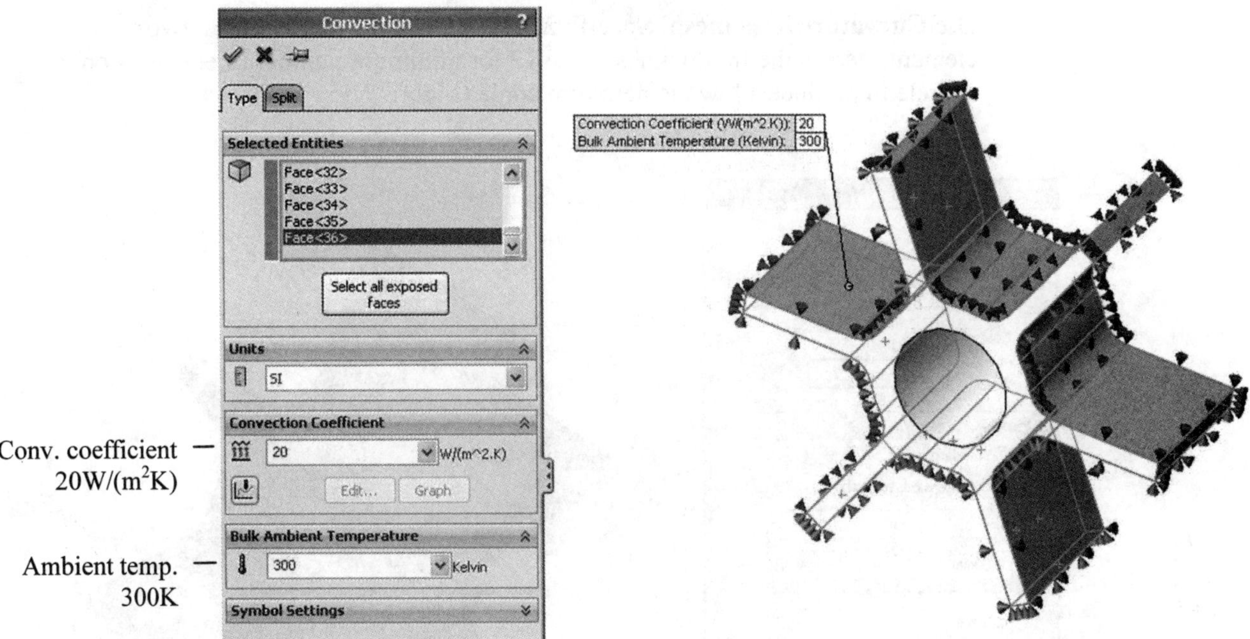

Figure 7-14: Convection coefficient and bulk temperature on the air side (outside)

Since the model represents a section of a longer pipe, we assume that there is no heat exchange through the end faces. Therefore we do not define any convection coefficients on the end faces, treating them as insulated.

Use **Curvature base mesh**. Specify 2.5mm global element to create two elements across the fin thickness. Use 12 for minimum number of elements on a circle to produce a low element turn angle (Figure 7-15)

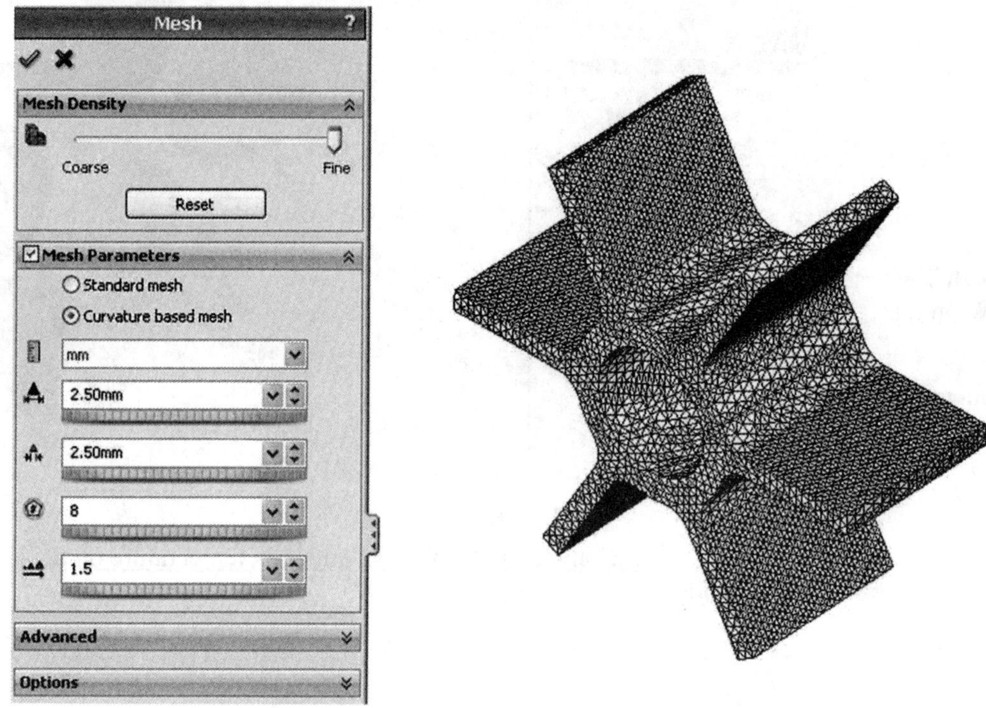

Figure 7-15: Curvature based mesh type is used to control element turn angle in fillets

Solve the study and display the resultant heat flux plot. Right-click the plot icon and select **List selected** (1) from the pop-up menu to open the **Probe Result** window. In the model window select the inside face (water side), then click the **Update** button (3) in the **Probe Result** window. The total heat entering the model through the selected face is shown in the lower portion of the **Probe Result** window (4) as shown in Figure 7-16.

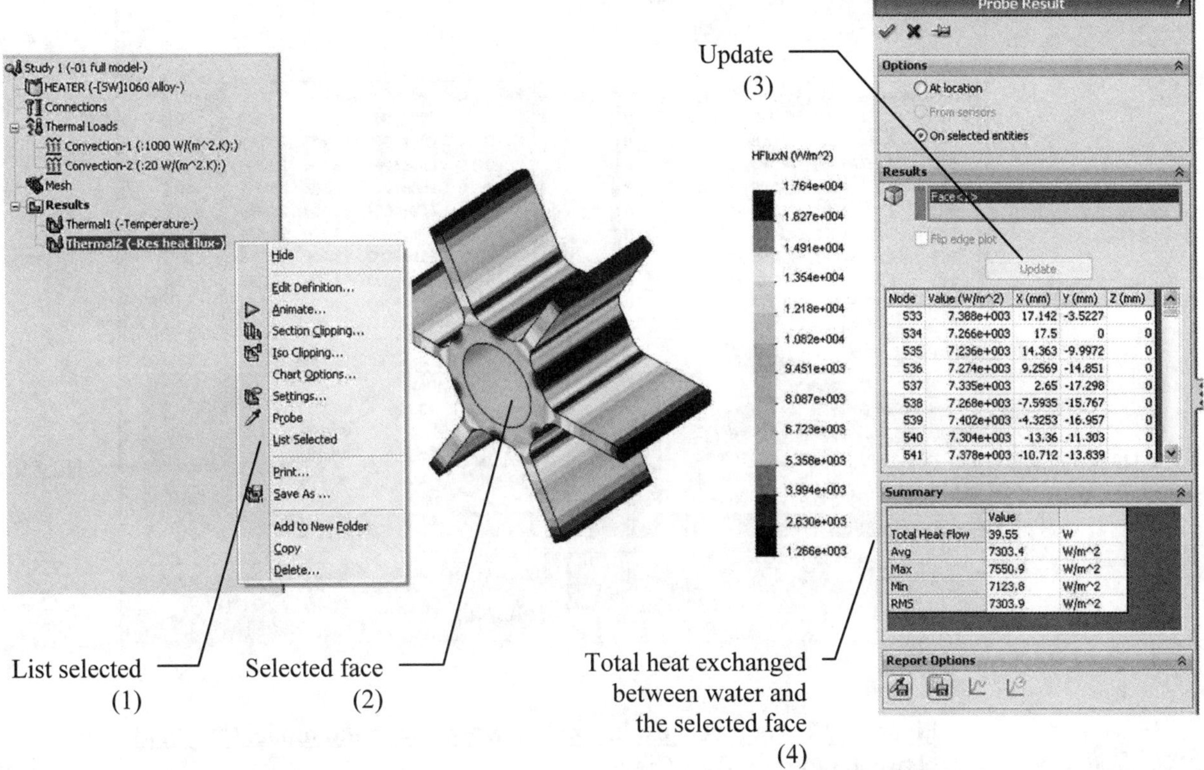

Figure 7-16: Total heat exchanged between the water and the model is 39.5W

The positive sign indicates that the model gains heat from the water. This can be visualized by constructing a vector plot of resultant heat flux.

Alternatively we can obtain the same results by selecting all faces on the air side (Figure 7-17). Selection of multiple entities requires pressing and holding ctrl key and is somewhat difficult because of poor visual feedback on the plot.

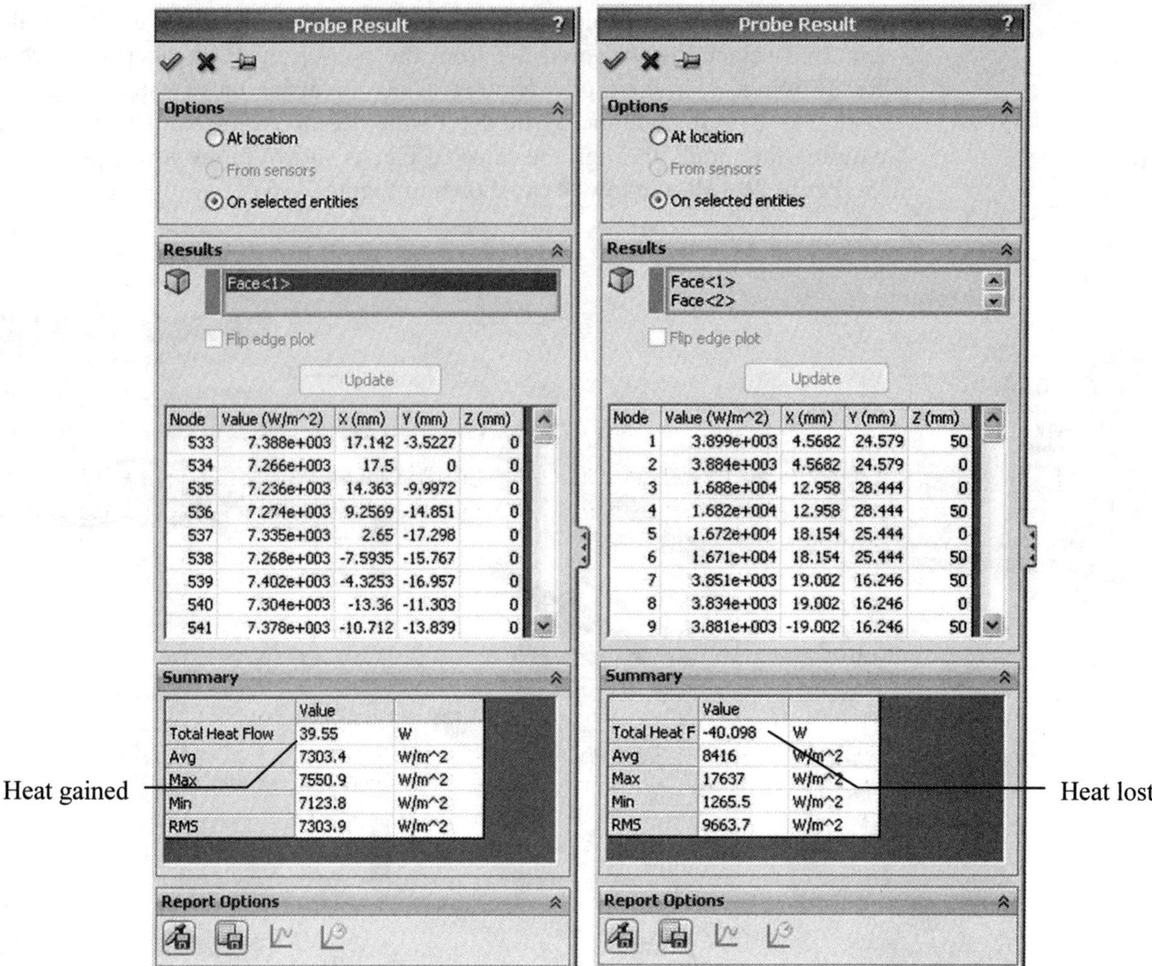

Figure 7-17: Total heat exchanged between water and model (left) and between model and air (right)

The heat gained from the water is +39.55W. The heat lost by the model to air is -40.10W. The difference is due to the numerical error.

Since this is a steady state thermal analysis, the amount of heat entering the model and the amount of heat dissipated by the model must be equal. Any small discrepancies are due to numerical error.

The analysis can be significantly simplified by noticing that heat flow through the model has the property of axial symmetry. Therefore, instead of analyzing the entire model, we can analyze just one radial section (Figure 7-18).

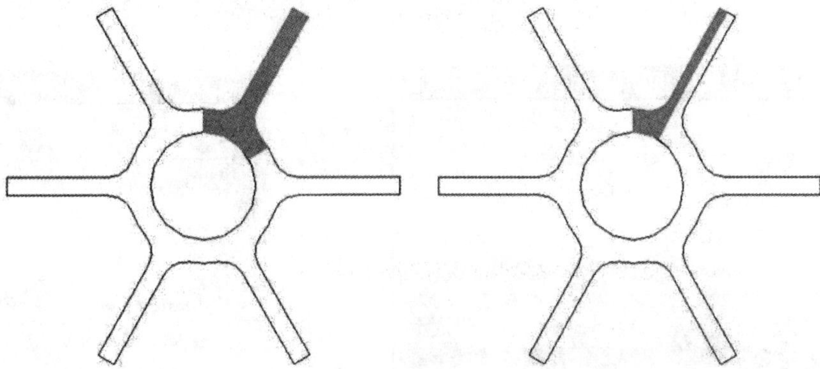

Figure 7-18: The model can be simplified to a radial section. While 60° section (left) appears the most obvious at he first sight, the smallest repeatable section is 30° (right).

You are encouraged to repeat the analysis in model configuration *30 degrees section or 60 degrees section*. Do not apply any convection conditions on faces created by radial cuts and remember to multiply the total heat either by 6 or by 12 depending on which configuration you use for analysis (Figure 7-19).

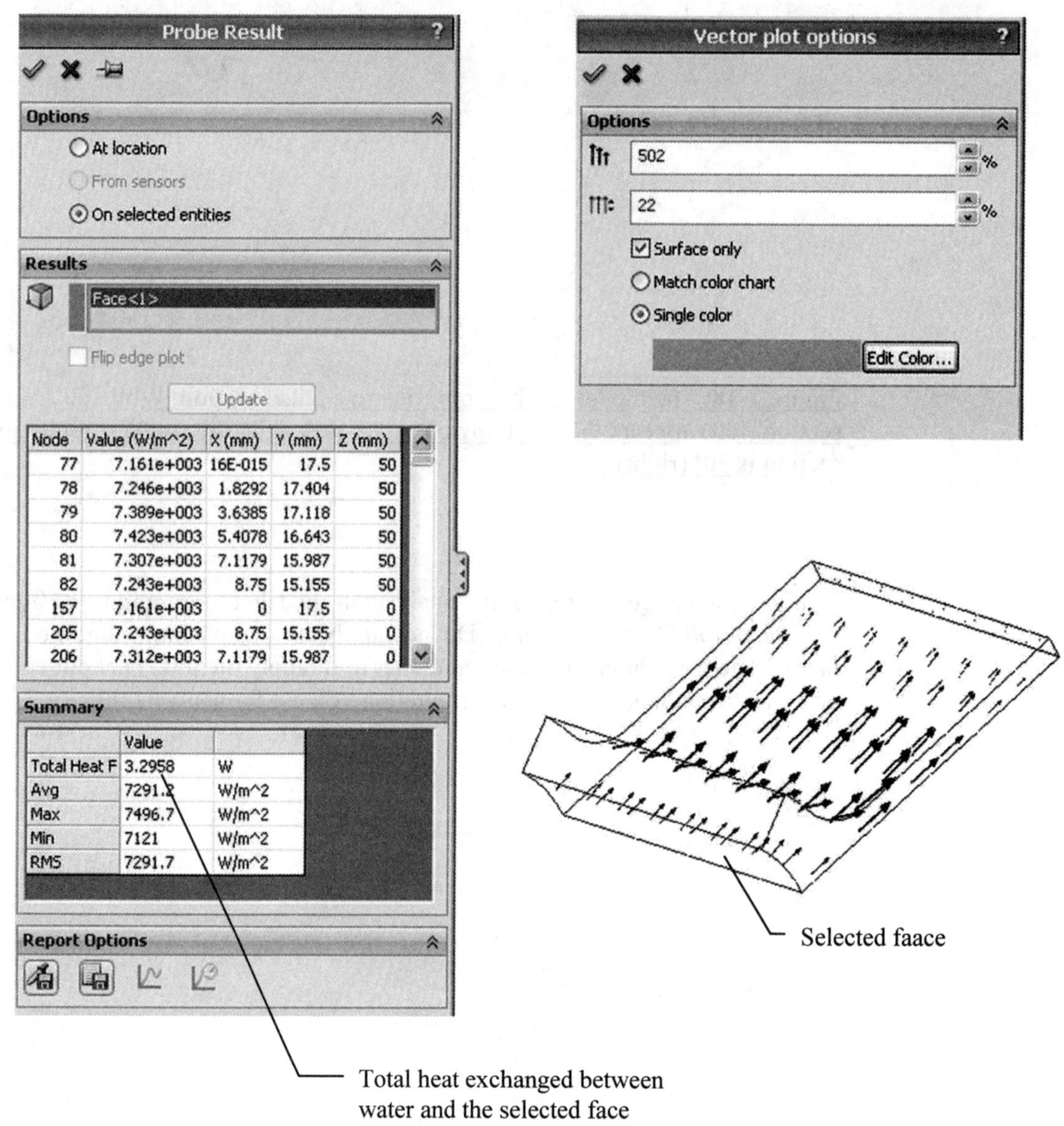

Figure 7-19: Total exchanged between water and the selected face of 30° section

Total heat gained from the water by the model is 3.3 x 12 = 39.6W.
Heat flow is presented using a vector plot with the above shown settings

8: Thermal analysis of a heat sink

Topics covered

- Analysis of an assembly
- Global and local Contact/Gaps conditions
- Steady state thermal analysis
- Transient thermal analysis
- Thermal resistance layer
- Use of section views in result plots

Project description

In this exercise, we continue with thermal analysis. However, this time we will analyze an assembly rather than a single part. Open the assembly HEAT SINK (Figure 8-1).

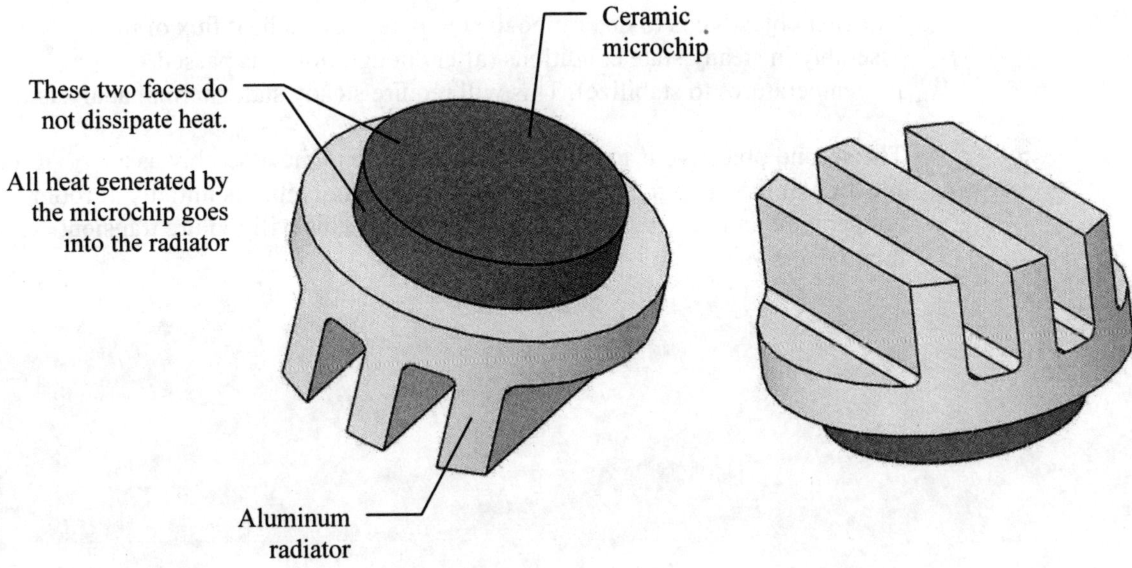
Ceramic microchip
These two faces do not dissipate heat.
All heat generated by the microchip goes into the radiator
Aluminum radiator

Figure 8-1: Assembly model of a heat sink using a radiator

Two views of the HEAT SINK assembly. The model consists of two components: a ceramic microchip and an aluminum radiator.

Analysis of an assembly allows assignment of different material properties to each assembly component. Notice that the *Solids* folder contains two icons corresponding to the two assembly components with material properties already assigned. This is because material has been assigned to parts which are assembly components: Ceramic Porcelain material to the microchip and 1060 Alloy to the radiator.

The ceramic insert generates a heat power of 25W and the aluminum radiator dissipates this heat. The ambient temperature is 27ºC (300K). Heat is dissipated to the environment by convection through all exposed faces of the radiator. We assume that the microchip is insulated, meaning it can not dissipate heat directly to ambient air, but only through the face touching the radiator. The convection coefficient (also called the film coefficient) is assumed to be $25W/m^2/K$ in this model. This means that if the difference of temperature between the face of the radiator and the surrounding air is 1K, then each square meter of the radiator surface dissipates 25W of heat. This value of the convection coefficient corresponds to natural convection without a cooling fan.

Heat flowing from the microchip to the radiator encounters thermal resistance on the boundary between the microchip and radiator. Therefore, a thermal resistance layer must be defined on the interface between these two components.

Our first objective is to determine the temperature and heat flux of the assembly in steady state conditions (after enough time has passed for temperatures to stabilize). This will require steady state thermal analysis.

The second objective is to study the temperature in the assembly as a function of time in a transient process when the assembly is initially at room temperature and power is turned on at time t=0. This will require transient thermal analysis.

Procedure

Create a thermal study called *heat sink steady state*. Before proceeding, we need to investigate the folder called *Connectors* which is found in the *heat sink steady state* study. By default, Global Contact is Bonded. As the name implies, all parts in assembly behave as one. We need to change it by defining a Contact Set. Right-click the *Connectors* folder to open the pop-up menu, and apply the settings shown in Figure 8-2.

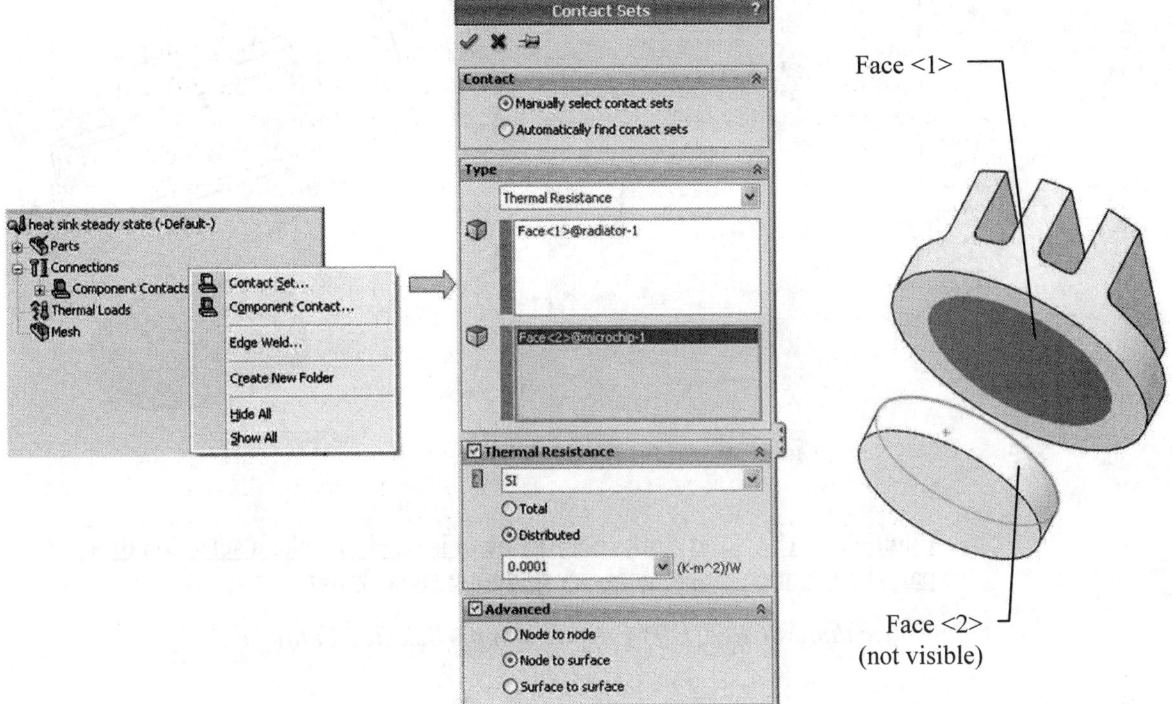

Figure 8-2: Definition of Thermal Resistance Contact Set

We need to define a local Contact Set for contacting faces in order to introduce a thermal resistance layer between the contacting faces. This can only be done as a local Contact Set using the Node to surface option in Advanced settings. Use the exploded model view to define the Contact Set.

Right-click the *Connectors* folder and select **Contact Set** to open the **Contact Set** window shown in Figure 8-2. Select **Thermal Resistance** with **Node to surface** as the contact type. This contact condition overrides the global Bonded contact condition. Select the contacting faces and enter **Distributed Thermal Resistance** as 0.0001Km^2/W (this value is usually obtained by testing). Note that the units of thermal resistance are the reciprocal of units of thermal convection.

Next, specify the heat power generated in the microchip. To do this, right-click the *Thermal loads* folder to open the pop-up menu. Select **Heat Power…** to open the **Heat Power** window (Figure 8-3), then from the SolidWorks fly-out menu select the *MICROCHIP* assembly component and define a 25W heat power. This applies heat power to the entire volume of the selected component.

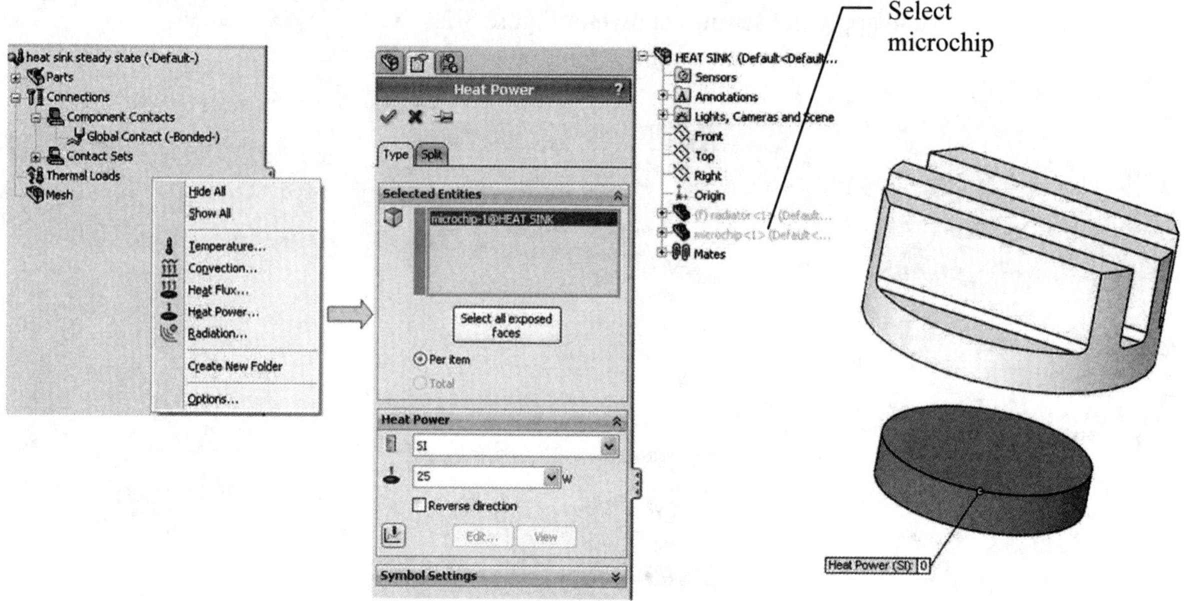

Figure 8-3: The SolidWorks pop-up menu is used to make a selection of the part (here a microchip) necessary to define Heat Power

Notice that MICROCHIP-1 appears in the Selected Entity field.

So far we have assigned material properties to each component, and also defined the heat source and the thermal resistance layer. In order for heat to flow, we must also establish a mechanism for the heat to escape the model. This is accomplished by defining convection coefficients.

Right-click the *Thermal Loads* folder to open a pop-up menu and select **Convection…** to open the **Convection** window (Figure 8-4). Select all faces of the RADIATOR except the one touching the microchip. Don not select any face of the MICROCHIP. Enter 25 W/(m^2K) as the value of the convection coefficient for all selected faces and enter the ambient temperature (bulk temperature) as 300K.

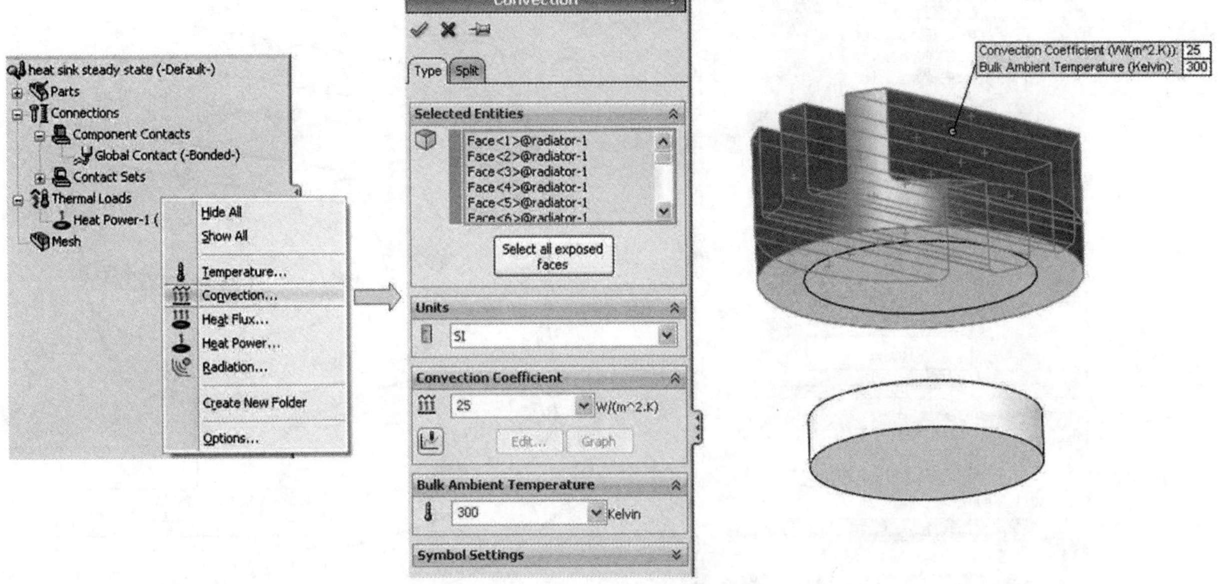

Figure 8-4: Convection window

Use this window to specify both the Convection Coefficient and the Bulk Temperature.

The last step before solving is creating the mesh. For accurate heat flux results apply mesh controls to all six fillets as shown in Figure 8-5. A similar effect can be obtained using **Curvature based mesh**.

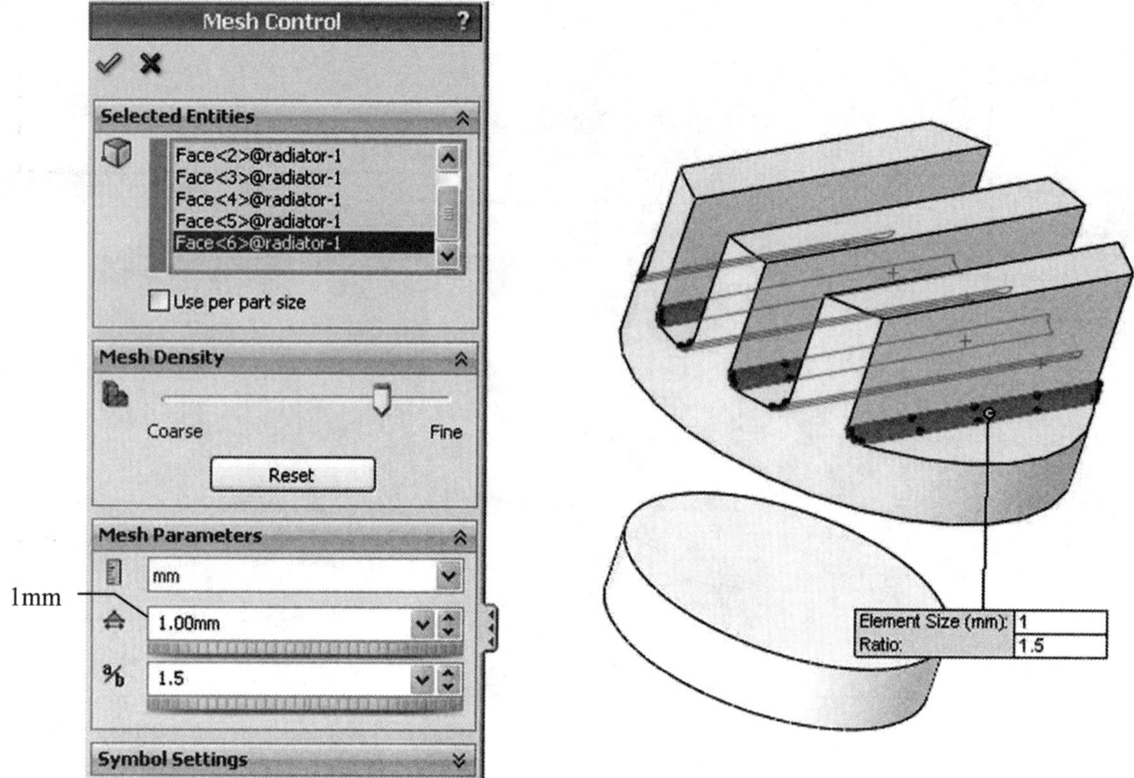

Figure 8-5: Mesh control applied to all fillets in the RADIATOR component

Now mesh the assembly with the default global element size to produce a mesh, as shown in Figure 8-6.

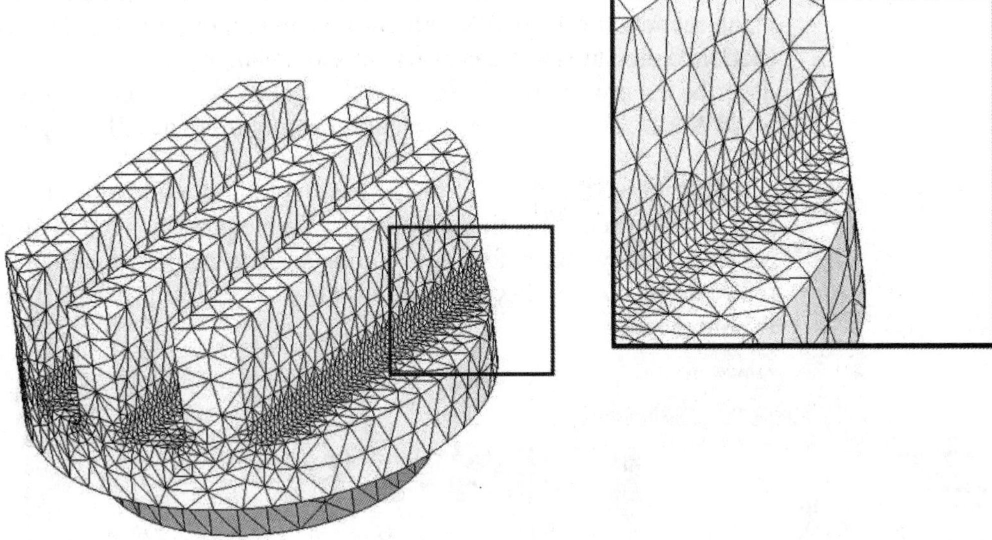

Figure 8-6: View of the meshed assembly

Note that two elements are placed across the thickness of each cooling fin, and that the mesh control assures a low element turn angle at the base of each fin.

Once the solution is ready, examine two plots: temperature and resultant heat flux. The temperature plot is created automatically in the *Results* folder. The required choices for both plots are shown in Figure 8-7.

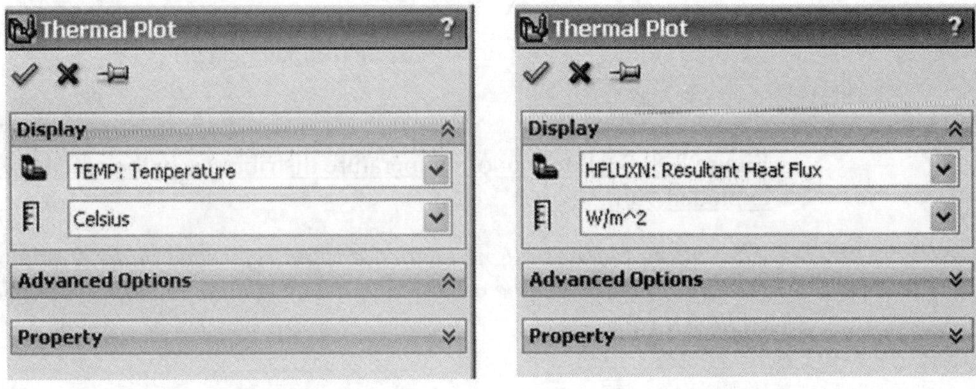

Temperature distribution

Heat flux

Figure 8-7: Thermal Plot definition window for temperature distribution plot (left) and heat flux plot (right)

Both temperature and heat flux result plots are more informative if presented using section views. SolidWorks **Simulation** offers a multitude of options for sectioned plots which are easier to practice than to read about. Here we describe the procedure of creating a flat section result plot using one of SolidWorks' default reference planes, but any reference plane can be used.

To show the section view of the temperature distribution plot, right-click the plot icon and select **Section Clipping** from the pop-up menu to open the **Section** window. By default, the cutting surface is aligned with the **Front** reference plane. To select another cutting plane select it from the SolidWorks fly-out menu.

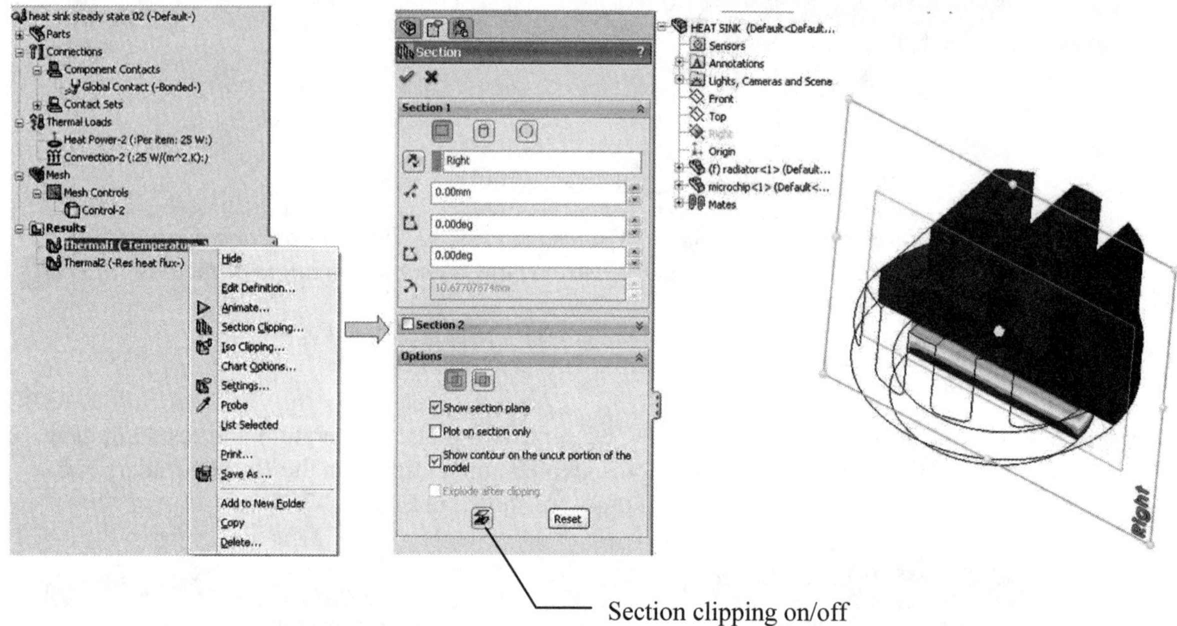

Figure 8-8: Section plot of temperature distribution in the assembly using exploded view

The cutting plane is aligned with the Right reference plane. The position of the cutting plane can be modified in a way similar to modifying a SolidWorks exploded view.

Experiment with different options in the **Section** window, and then construct a section plot of heat flux. Since heat flux is a vector quantity, heat flux results lend themselves well to representation with vector type plots. Follow the steps described in chapter 7 to create a heat flux vector plot. In addition to using a vector plot, use the exploded view to produce a heat flux plot similar to the one shown in Figure 8-9.

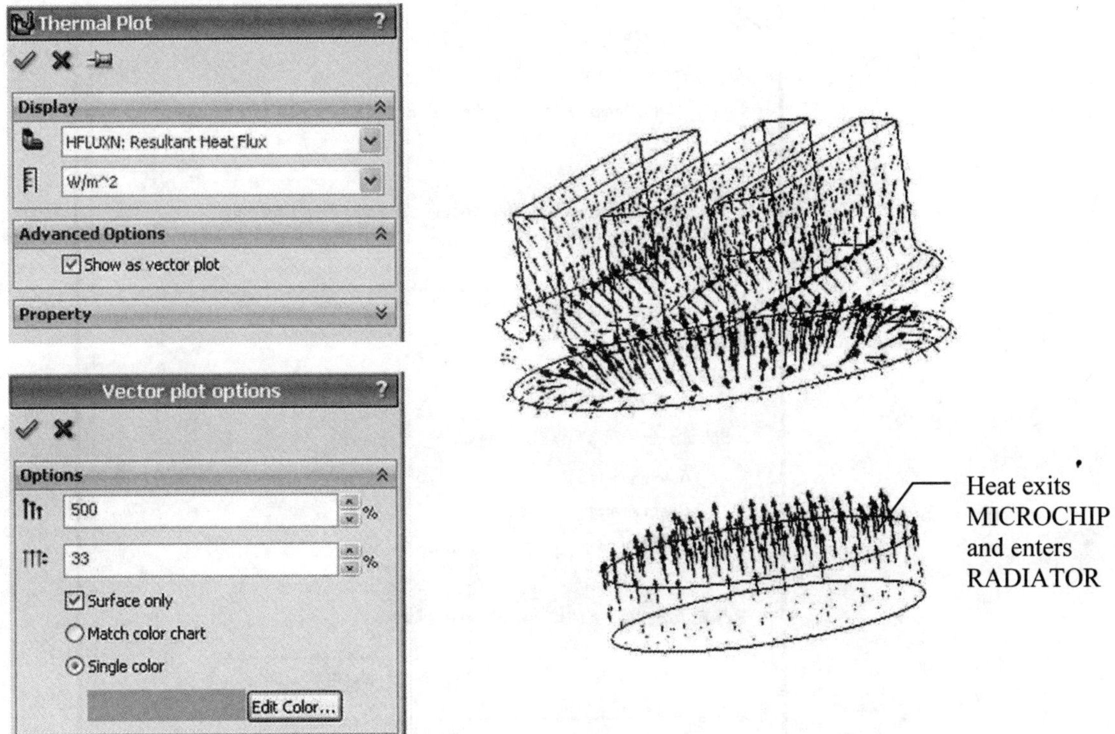

Figure 8-9: Vector plot of heat flux in the assembly using exploded view

Note that arrows "coming out" of the microchip visually represent where heat leaves the microchip. Vectors are tangent to faces where no convection coefficients have been defined.

Examine the vector plot in Figure 8-9 to see the heat flux exiting the MICROCHIP and entering the RADIATOR.

This completes the steady state thermal analysis of the HEAT SINK assembly. We now proceed with transient thermal analysis. Copy the study *heat sink steady state* into a new study named *heat sink transient*. Right-click the study *heat sink transient* folder and select **Properties** to open the window shown in Figure 8-10.

Select **Transient** analysis (**Steady state** is the default option). Our objective is to monitor temperature changes every 360 seconds during the first 3600 seconds with particular attention to the vertex location shown in Figure 8-1. Enter 3600 as **Total time** and 360 as **Time increment**.

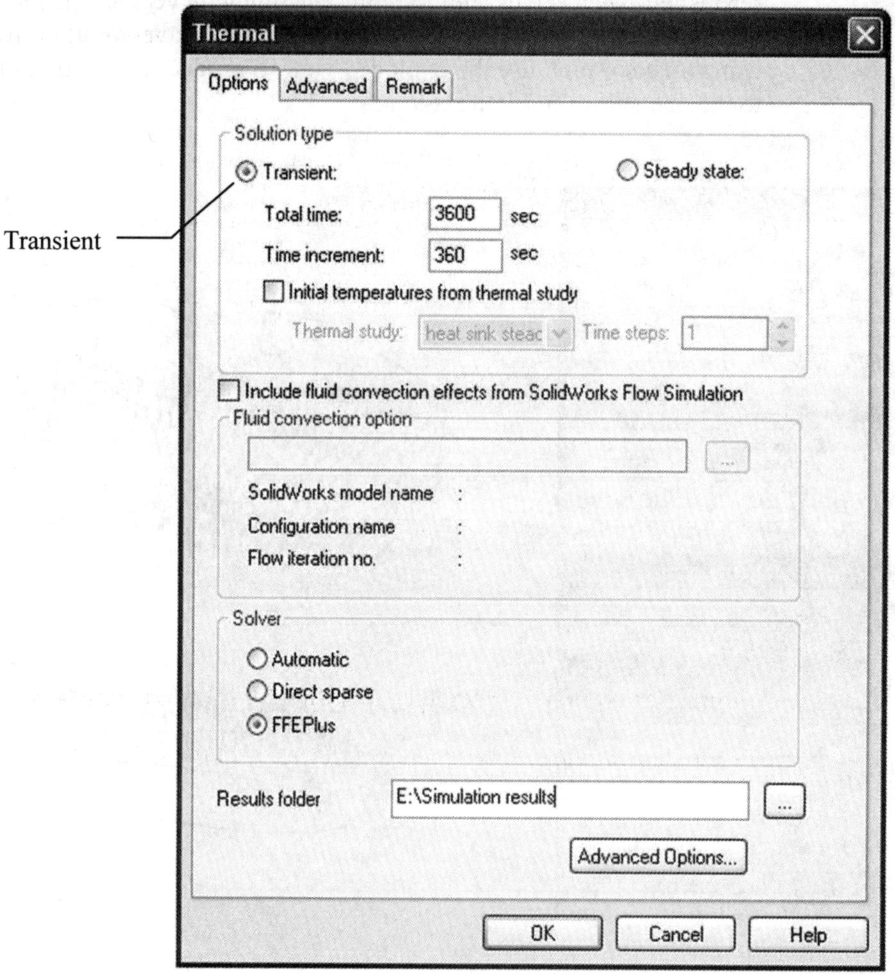

Figure 8-10: **Transient** thermal analysis is specified in thermal study **Options**

Analysis will be carried on for 3600 seconds with results reported every 360 seconds.

Transient thermal analysis requires that the initial temperature of the model be defined in addition to the already defined **Heat Power** and **Convection** coefficients which can be copied from the steady state study. Contact conditions and the mesh can also be copied from the steady state study.

We assume that both components have the same initial temperature of 300K. Right-click the *Thermal Loads* folder in the *heat sink transient* study and select **Temperature** to open the window shown in Figure 8-11. Select **Initial Temperature** and enter 300K. From the fly-out menu select both assembly components.

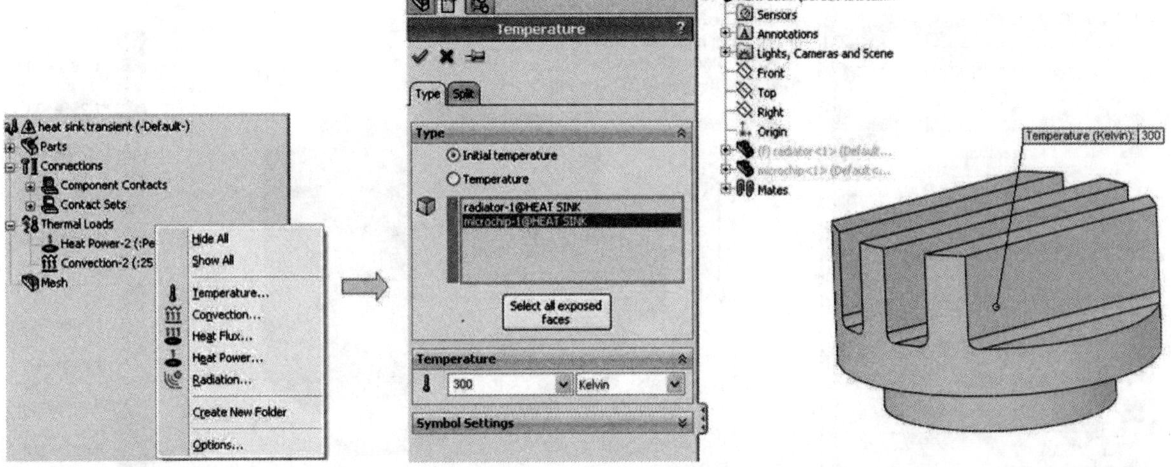

Figure 8-11: Initial Temperature specified for both assembly components

Assembly components can be selected from the SolidWorks fly-out menu.

Now run the analysis and display the temperature plot. Display the temperature plot for the last step (step number 10) by right-clicking the plot icon, selecting **Edit Definition** and setting **Plot Step** to 10 (Figure 8-12).

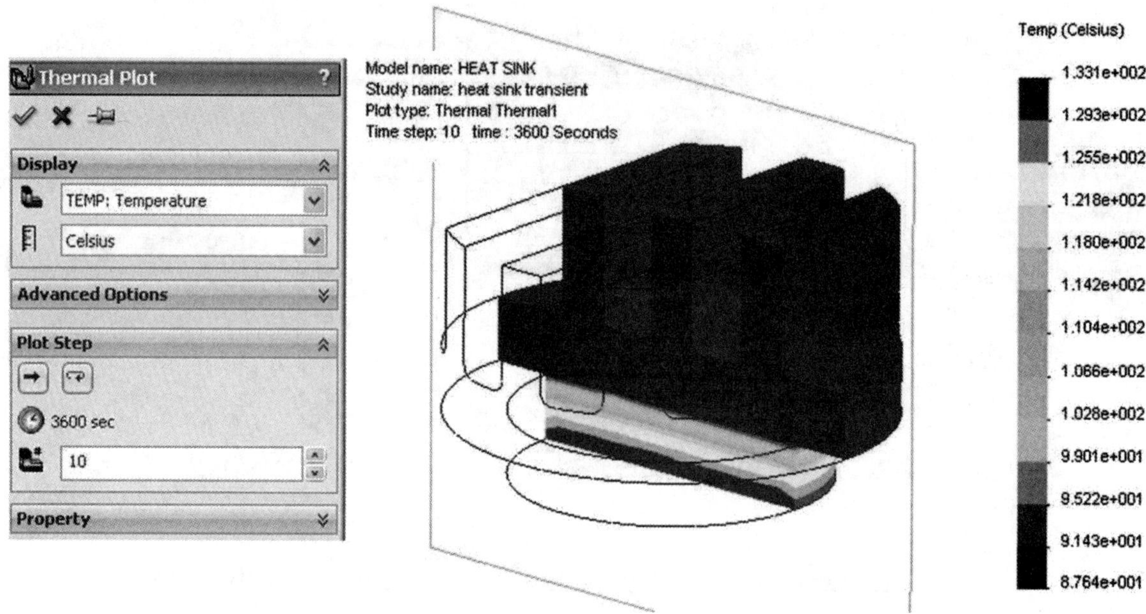

Figure 8-12: Temperature distribution after 3600 seconds (step 10) since heat has been turned on. Temperature results shown in degrees Celsius

Since we have not specified heat power as function of time, it is assumed that the full power is turned on at time t=0, when the assembly is at an initial temperature of 300K. Figure 8-12 shows the temperature distribution after 3600 seconds. Notice that this result is very close to the result of steady state thermal analysis, meaning that after 3600 seconds, the temperature of assembly has almost stabilized.

To see the temperature history at selected locations of the model, proceed as follows: make sure the temperature plot is showing, right-click its icon, and select **Probe** to probe temperature in the location shown in Figure 8-13. This probing opens the window shown in Figure 8-14.

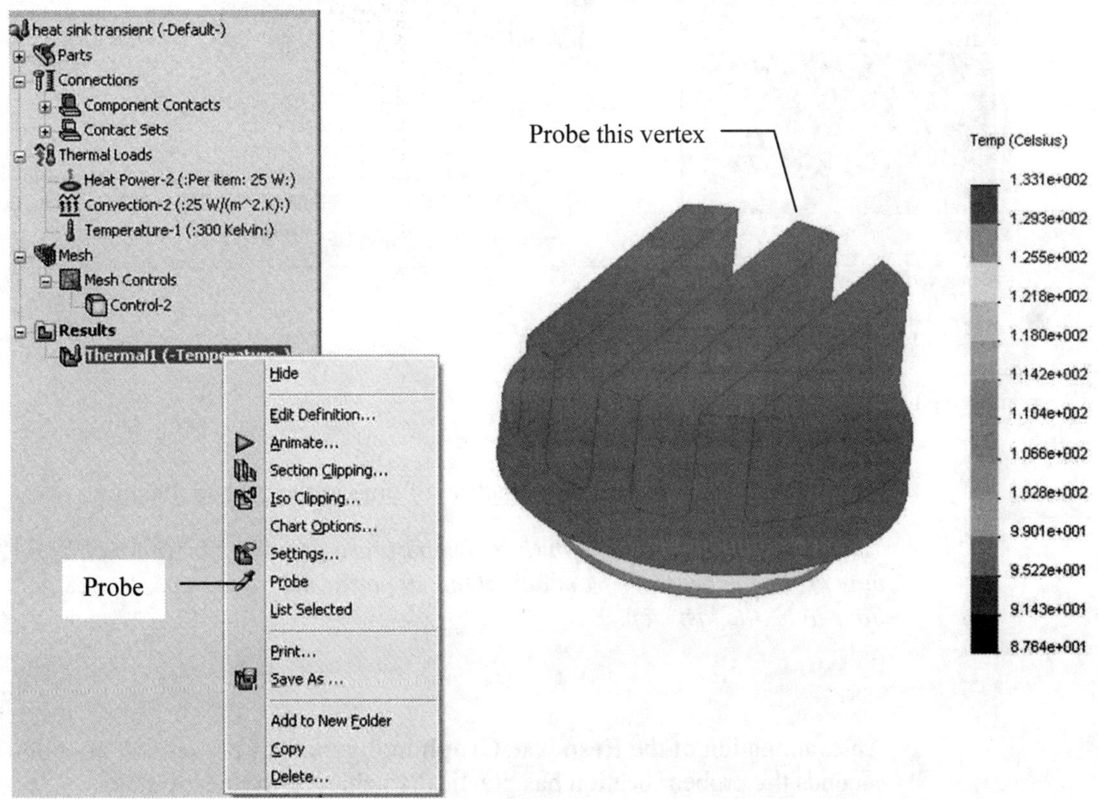

Figure 8-13: Temperature is probed in the indicated location.

Select **Response** in the **Probe Results** window (Figure 8-14) to display a graph showing the temperature at the probed location as a function of time (Figure 8-14).

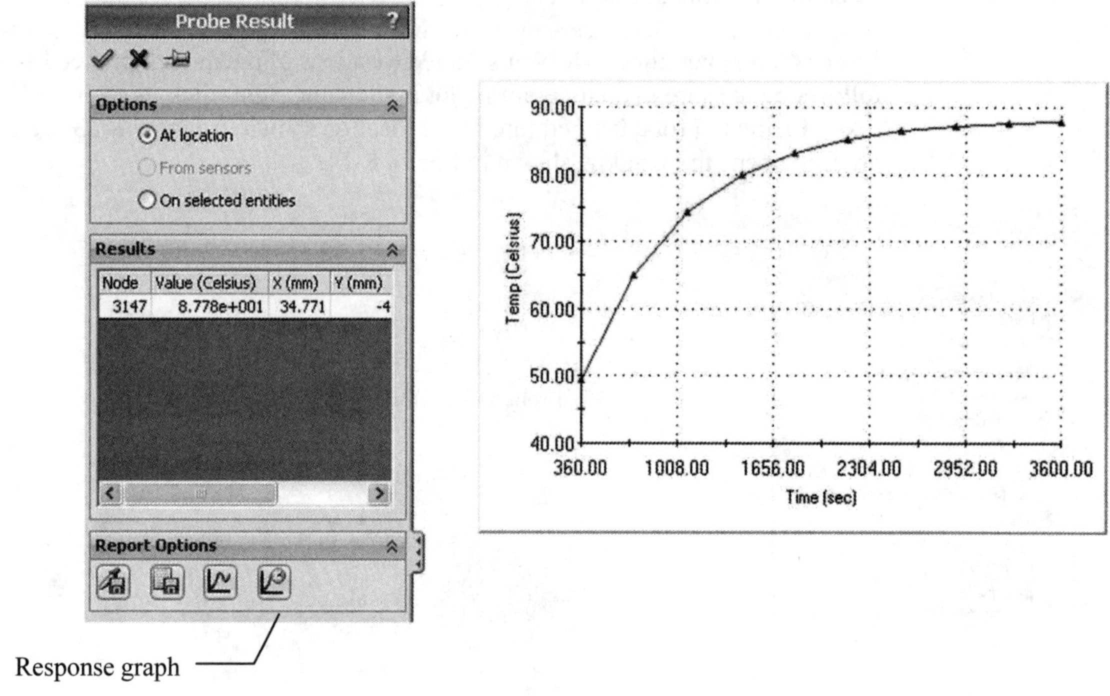

Figure 8-14: Temperature as a function of time in the probed location

To produce a response graph (here temperature as a function of time), you may probe temperature from any of the 10 performed time steps. It does not have to be the last step.

An examination of the **Response Graph** in Figure 8-14 proves that after 3600 seconds the probed location has practically achieved the steady state temperature.

To conclude the thermal analysis of the MICROCHIP assembly, we'll study the effect of the thermal resistance layer. Change to exploded view and show any **Temperature** plot, here we use the plot from the last step of transient thermal analysis. Probe temperatures in corresponding locations on two contacting faces separated by the layer of thermal resistance and notice that a temperature gradient exists due to the presence of the thermal resistance layer (Figure 8-15). The temperature gradient is required to "push" heat through the layer of thermal resistance. Temperature time history in two locations can be seen on a graph created as shown in Figure 8-14.

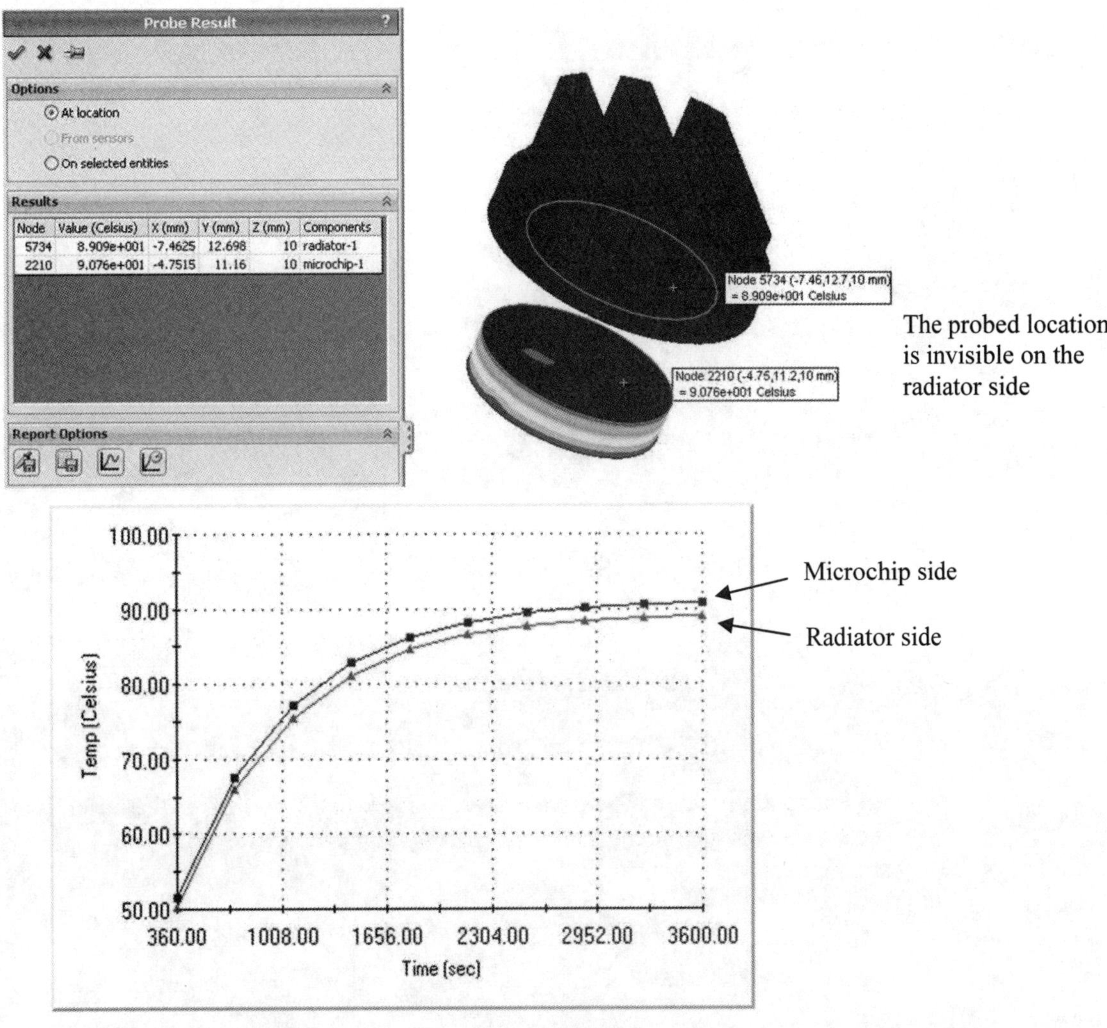

Figure 8-15: Temperature difference on two contacting faces separated by the layer of thermal resistance.

The presence of the thermal resistance layer creates a temperature gradient shown in the probed results and in the temperature time history graph.

Notes:

9: Static analysis of a hanger

Topics covered

- Static analysis of an assembly
- Global and local Contact conditions
- Hierarchy of Contact/Gaps condition

Project description

In this exercise we introduce structural analysis of assemblies. To begin, we review different options available for defining the interactions between assembly components (we began exploring this topic in the previous exercise).

Open the HANGER assembly and create a Static study. Right-click **Global Contact** in the **Components Contact** folder to open the **Component Contact** window (Figure 9-1).

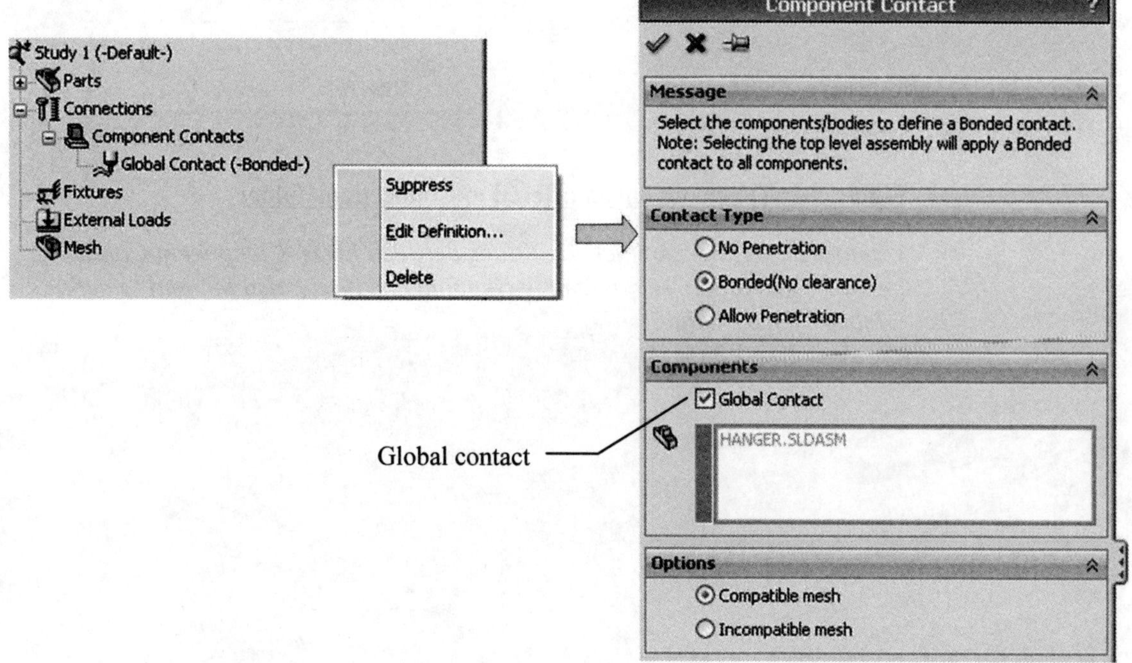

Figure 9-1: *Component Contact* menu

Component Contact distinguishes between Global Contact and Component Contact. Global Contact set as Bonded is default.

Right-click the **Component Contacts** folder to invoke a pop-up menu that offers two more types of contact: Component Contact and Contact Set (Figure 9-2).

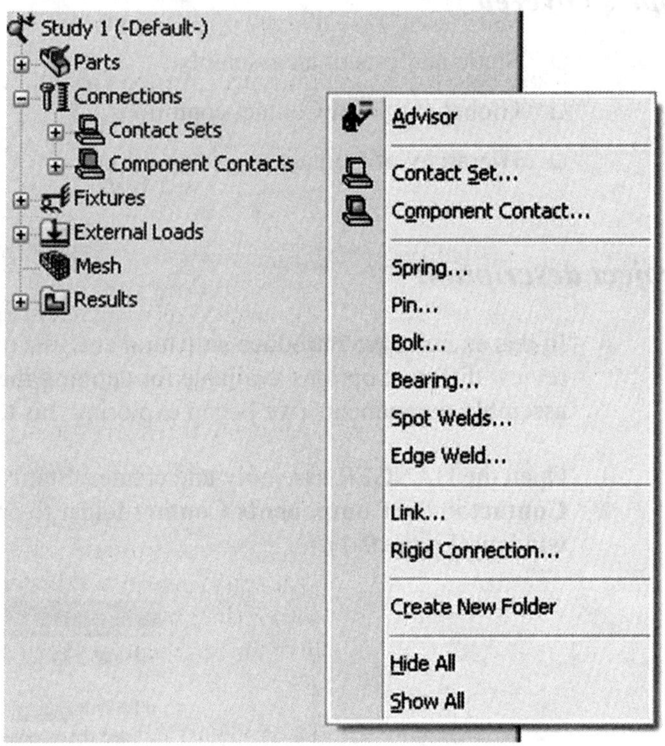

Figure 9-2: Types of contact offered in Connections folder

Contact Set defines contact conditions between faces. Component Contact defines contact between assembly components. It can also be used to define Global Contact conditions.

The differences between the available Contact Type conditions are as follows:

- Global Contact - affects all faces in an assembly
- Component Contact - affects one component
- Contact set - affects only two specified faces (which must belong to different components of an assembly)

More detailed descriptions are given in the following tables:

GLOBAL	
Option	**Description**
Touching Faces: **Bonded**	Touching areas of different components are bonded. This option is available for structural (static, frequency, and buckling) and thermal studies. If touching faces are left as **Bonded** and Global conditions are not overridden by Component or Local conditions, then an assembly behaves as a part. This contact condition comes with two options: **Compatible mesh** and **Incompatible mesh**. Using the **Compatible mesh,** nodes located on touching faces are shared by elements on both sides of these touching faces. If a **Compatible mesh** causes meshing difficulties, then an **Incompatible mesh** option can be used. Meshes on each face are then created independently but are automatically constrained to each other.
Touching Faces: **Allow Penetration (Free)**	The mesher treats parts as disjointed bodies. This option is available for structural (static, frequency, and buckling) and thermal studies. For static studies, the loads can cause interference between parts. Using this option can save solution time if the applied loads do not cause interference. For thermal studies, there is no heat flow due to conduction through touching faces.
Touching Faces: **No penetration**	The mesher creates compatible meshes on overlapping parts of touching faces. The program creates gap elements connecting the coincident nodes. This option is available for static, nonlinear, and thermal studies. For static studies, a gap element between two nodes prevents part interference, but allows the two nodes to move away from each other.

COMPONENT	
Option	**Description**
Touching Faces: **Bonded**	The mesher will bond common areas of the selected components at their interface with all other components. This option is available for structural (static, nonlinear, frequency, and buckling) and thermal studies. This contact condition comes with two options: **Compatible mesh** and **Incompatible mesh**. Using the **Compatible mesh** option, the two components are just meshed across the touching faces. Nodes located on touching faces are shared by elements on both sides. If a **Compatible mesh** causes meshing difficulties then an **Incompatible mesh** option can be used. Meshes on each face are then created independently but are automatically constrained to each other.
Touching Faces: **Free**	The mesher will treat the selected components as disjointed from the rest of the assembly. This option is available for structural (static, frequency, and buckling) and thermal studies. For static studies, the loads can cause interference between parts. Using this option can save solution time if the applied loads do not cause interference.
Touching Faces: **No penetration**	The mesher will create compatible meshes on overlapping areas of touching faces. The nodes associated with the two parts on the common areas are coincident but different. The program creates a gap element connecting each two coincident nodes. This option is available for static, nonlinear, and thermal studies. For static studies, a gap element between two nodes prevents part interference but allows the two nodes to move away from each other.

LOCAL	
Option	**Description**
No penetration	Available for static, drop test, and nonlinear studies only. This contact type prevents interference between source and target entities but allows gaps to form.
Bonded	The source and target entities are bonded. The entities may be touching or within a small distance from each other. The program gives a warning if the distance between bonded entities is larger than the average element size of the associated elements. Only source and target entities are required to define this contact type.
Shrink fit	Valid for faces from two components which show interference. This interference is eliminated after solution.
Free	The selected faces are disjoined and can freely go through each other with no interaction.
Virtual wall	This contact type defines contact between the source entities and a virtual wall defined by a target plane. The target plane may be rigid or flexible. You can define friction between the source and the target plane.
Insulated	Available for thermal studies only. This option is similar to the Free option for structural studies. The program treats the source and target faces as disjointed and therefore prevents heat flow due to conduction through the source and target entities.
Thermal resistance	Specifies thermal resistance between source and target faces.

Local conditions can be defined either with the **Node to Node** option available for touching source and target faces only, or with one of two surface options: **Node to Surface** or **Surface to Surface,** which do not require compatible source and target meshes. We will now discuss the important differences between **Node to Node** and **Surface** conditions.

A **Node to Node** condition can be applied to faces that overlap. The faces do not have to be the same size, but do need to share some common area. **Node to Node** conditions can be specified between two:

- ❑ Flat faces
- ❑ Cylindrical faces of the same radius
- ❑ Spherical faces of the same radius

With these options, the mesh on both faces in the area where they overlap is created in such a manner that there is node to node correspondence (nodes are coincident) on both touching surfaces - hence the name **Node to Node**.

Surface contact may be specified between two faces of different shapes and can only be specified as a local condition. Initially, faces can either touch or not touch, but are expected to come in contact once the load has been applied to the model. The **Surface to Surface** condition is more general, but less numerically efficient than **Node to Surface** condition. Any contact could be defined as a **Surface** condition, but this would unnecessarily complicate the model.

The difference between **Node to Node** and **Surface** conditions is illustrated in Figure 9-3.

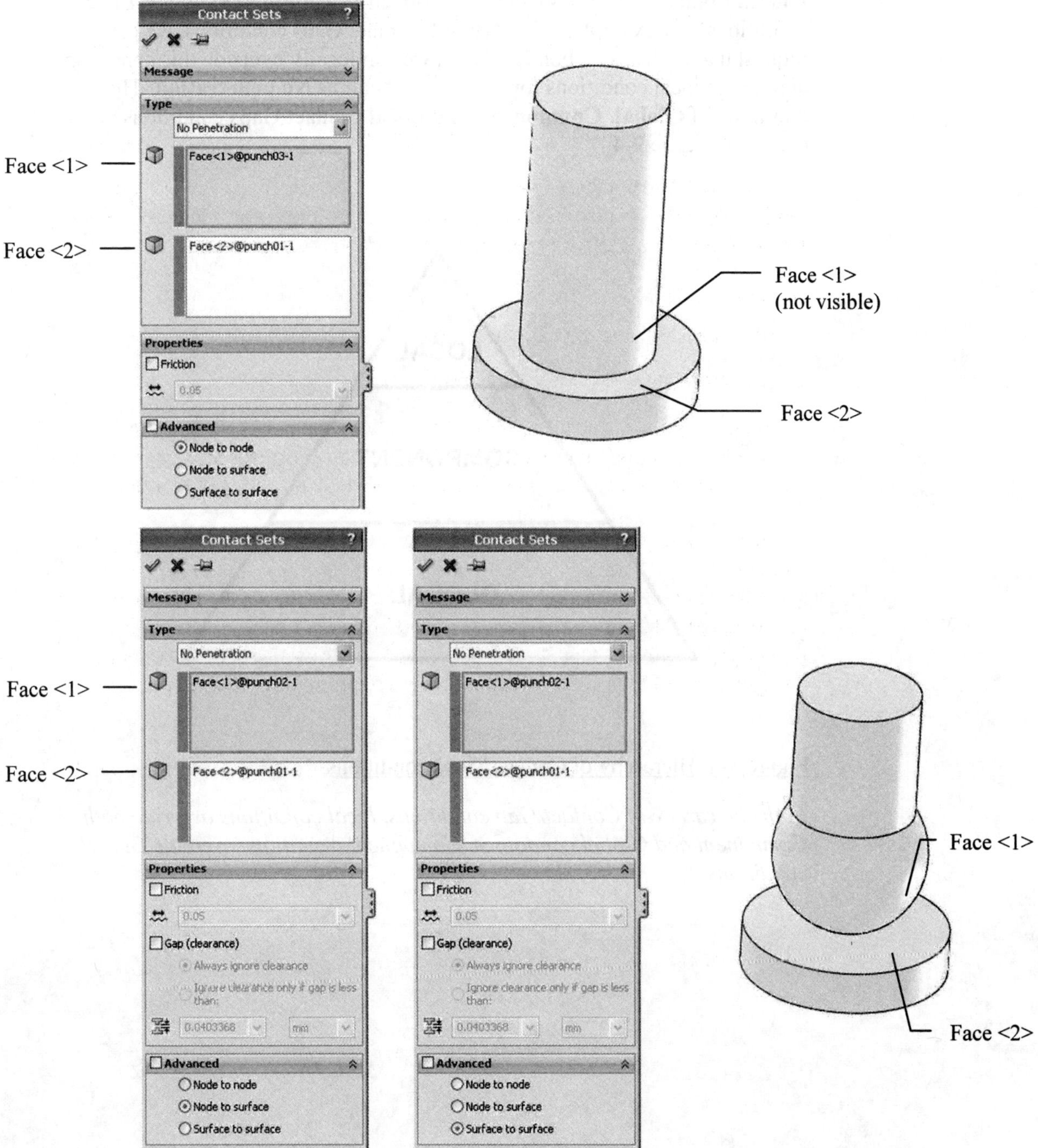

Figure 9-3: The contact between a flat end punch and a plate (top) is defined as a Node to Node contact. The contact between a spherical punch and a plate (bottom) can be defined either as Node to surface or Surface to surface contact.

Faces in Surface to Surface contact conditions don't have to touch initially, but they are expected to come in contact under the load.

Global Contact conditions can be overridden by **Component** and/or **Local** conditions. For example, using **Global** Contact/Gaps conditions, we can request that all faces be bonded. Next, we can locally override this condition and define local conditions for one or more pair as **No penetration**. The hierarchy of **Global**, **Component**, and **Local** Contact/Gaps conditions is shown in Figure 9-4.

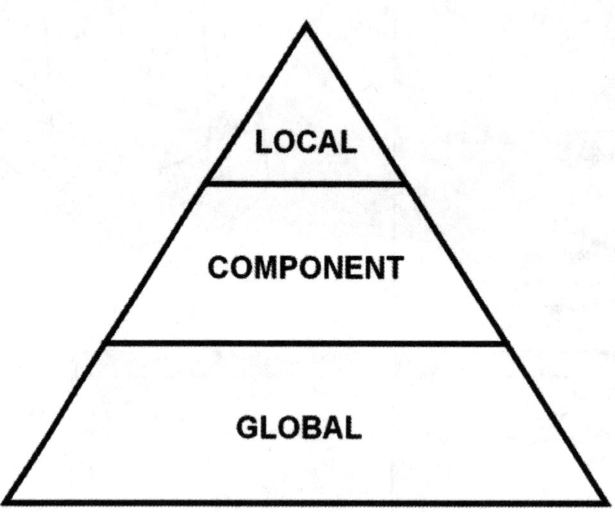

Figure 9-4: Hierarchy of Contact/Gaps conditions

In the hierarchy of Contact/Gap conditions, local conditions override both Component and Global conditions. Component conditions override Global conditions.

Procedure

The assembly HANGER (Figure 9-5) consists of three components, material (AISI 304) is assigned to all assembly components.

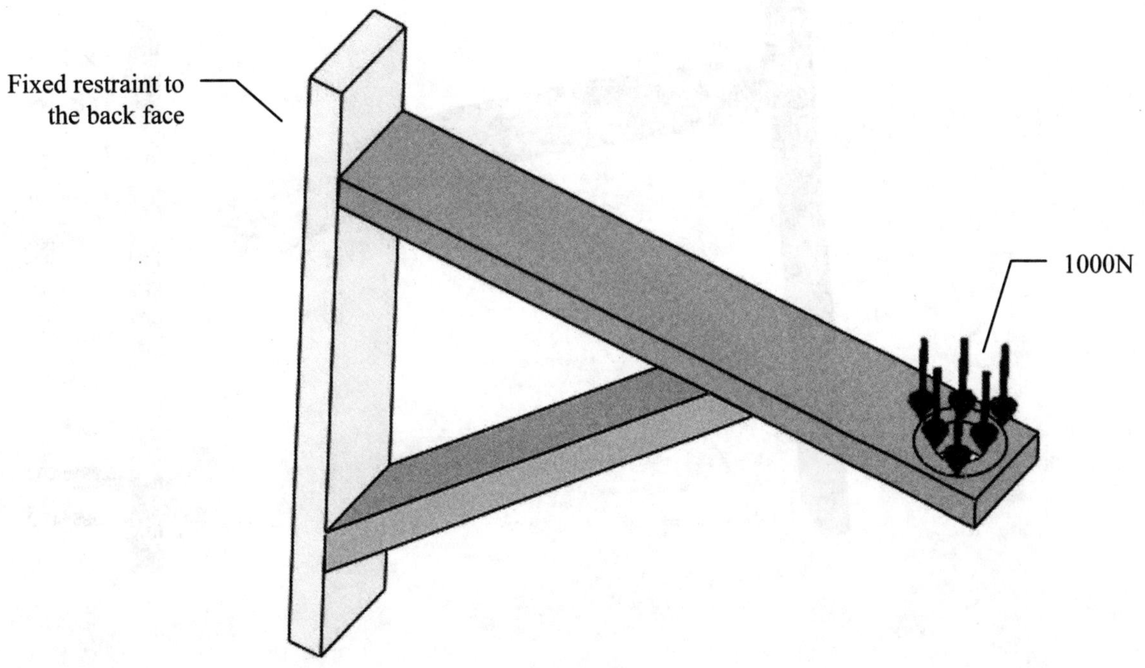

Figure 9-5: HANGER assembly

The HANGER assembly consists of three parts (compare with Figure 9-7). A 1000N load is applied to the split face (washer footprint), and support is applied to the back of vertical component.

If you do not modify the Contact/Gaps conditions, then by default all touching faces are bonded, and the assembly will behave as one part. A sample result is shown in Figure 9-6.

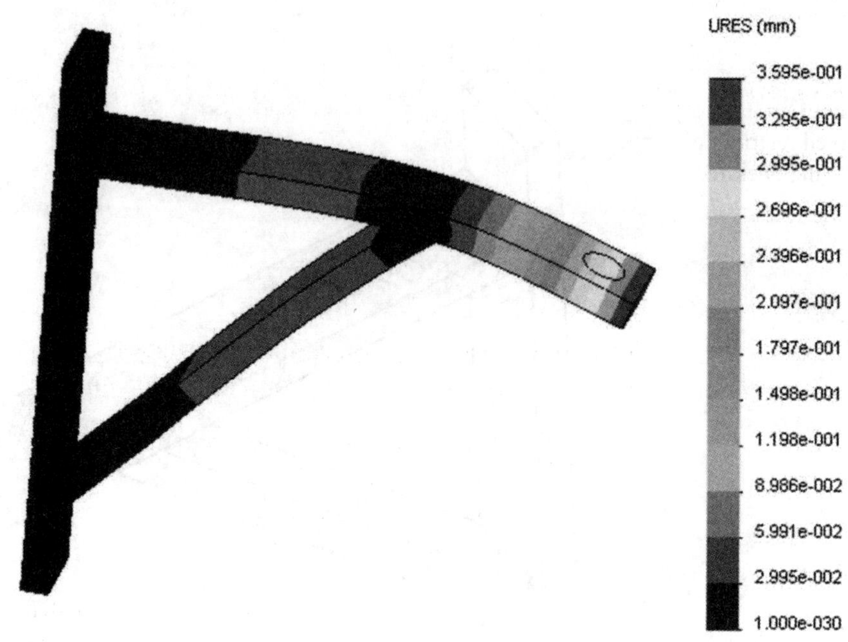

Figure 9-6: Displacement results for a model with all touching faces bonded. The assembly behaves as one part.

Notice that the HANGER assembly model is adequate for analysis of displacements. However, due to stress singularities in the sharp re-entrant corners, it is not suitable for analysis of stresses in these corners.

Now, we modify the Contact conditions on selected touching faces. We leave the global conditions as **Touching Faces: bonded**, but locally we override them by defining a local **Contact** condition. One of the three pairs of touching faces (Figure 9-7) will be defined using the local condition **Free**, meaning that there is no interaction between the faces. These faces will be able to either come apart or "penetrate" each other with no consequences.

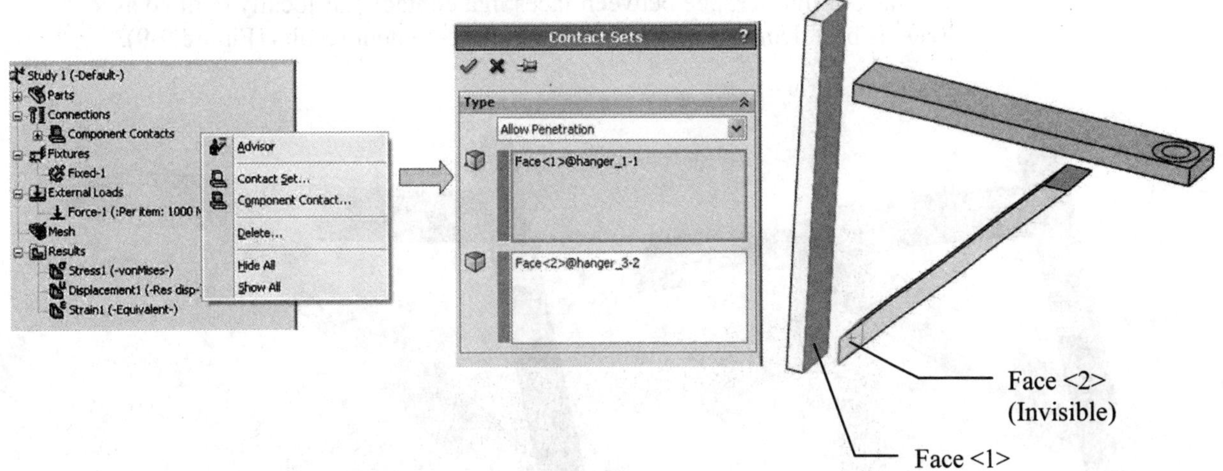

Figure 9-7: Touching Faces: Allow Penetration. When faces 1 and 2 are locally defined as **Allow Penetration**, there is no interaction between them.

An exploded view of the HANGER makes it easier to define a local Contact Set.

Once a Contact Set has been defined, an icon is placed in the *Connectors* folder, as shown in Figure 9-8. Every time Contact/Gaps conditions are changed, a new mesh needs to be created (Figure 9-8).

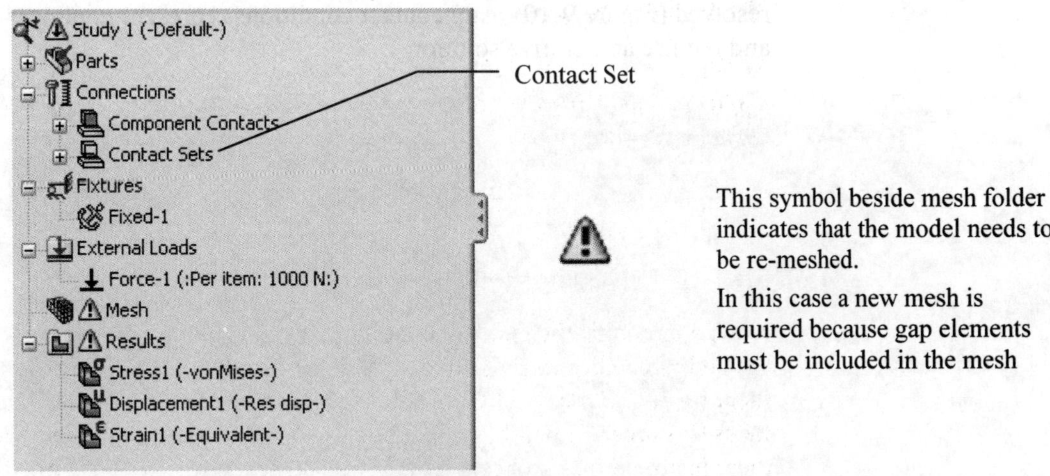

Figure 9-8: Any change in Connections invalidates the mesh and requires remeshing

Remeshing deletes the previous results. If we wish to keep the earlier results, we need to define local Contact conditions in a new study.

The lack of interference between faces in a contact pair locally defined as **Free**, is best demonstrated by showing displacement results (Figure 9-9).

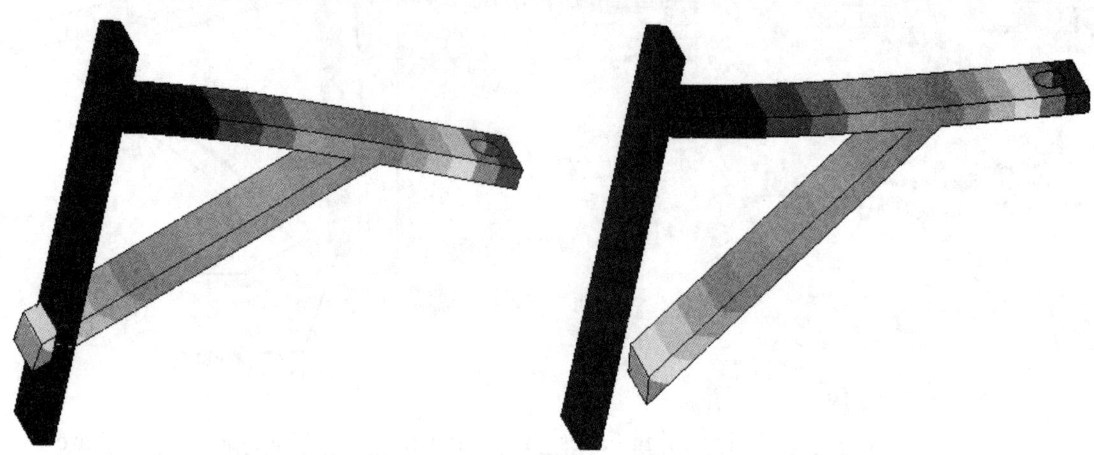

Figure 9-9: Displacement results in a pair defined as **Free**

The plot on the left shows results for a load directed downwards and the plot on the right has the load direction reversed.

Let's now change the local contact conditions between the faces shown in Figure 9-7 from **Free** to **No penetration** using the **Node to node** option. Remesh the model, and run the solution again. Notice that the solution now requires much more time to run because the contact constraints must be resolved (Figure 9-10). Any contact conditions represent nonlinear problems and require an iterative solution.

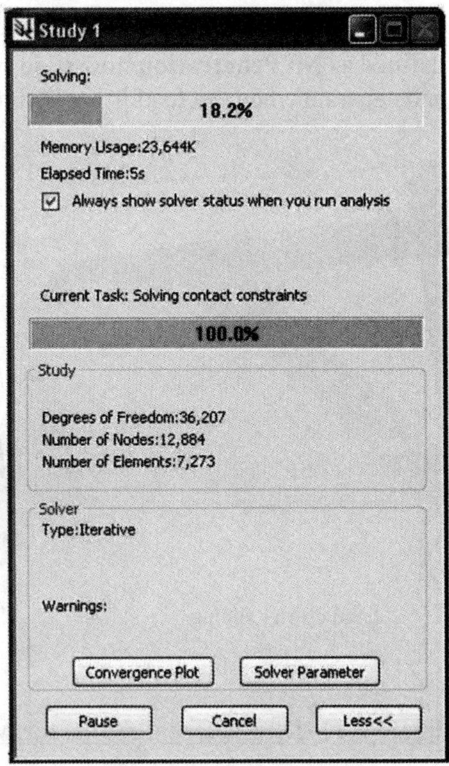

Figure 9-10: Iterative solution for the HANGER assembly using a No Penetration condition

A No Penetration condition requires an iterative solution to solve contact constraints and takes significantly longer to complete than a linear solution.

The displacement results, displayed in Figure 9-11, show that the two faces defined as **No Penetration** now slide when a downward load is applied (left) and separate when the load is applied upward (right).

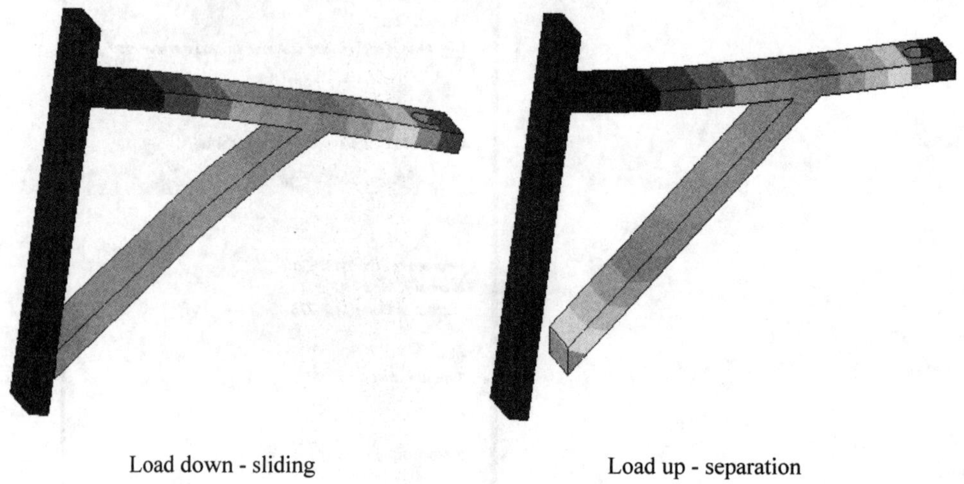

Load down - sliding

Load up - separation

Figure 9-11: Displacement results for two locally defined Node to Node faces

The two faces in the pair defined locally as Node to Node sliding (left) or separation (right) depending on the load direction.

Closer examination of the displacement results for the sliding faces (Figure 9-12) shows that the sliding faces partially separate.

Figure 9-12: Partial separation of the sliding faces

Only a portion of face 1 contacts face 2. The mesh in the contact area is too coarse to allow for the analysis of contact stresses.

While the mesh is adequate for the analysis of displacements, the mesh is not sufficiently refined for the analysis of the contact stresses that develop between the two sliding faces.

Notes:

10: Analysis of contact stresses between two plates

Topics covered

- Assembly analysis with surface contact conditions
- Contact stress analysis
- Avoiding rigid body motions

Project description

We will perform an analysis of contact between two plates in the assembly model named TWO PLATES. The model consists of two identical plates that touch each other on their curved outside surface (Figure 10-1). The material for both parts is Nylon 6/10 and has already been assigned to the parts. Our objective is to find the distribution of von Mises stress and the maximum contact stresses under a 1000N of compressive load.

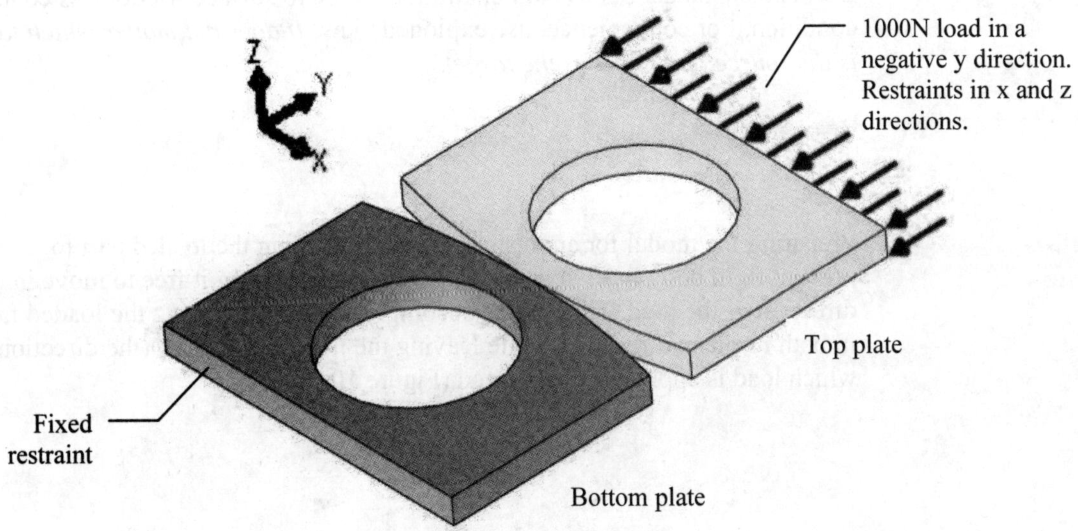

Figure 10-1: Load and restraints on the model of TWO PLATES with their cylindrical surfaces in contact

Define a Contact Set between the two cylindrical faces as shown in Figure 10-2.

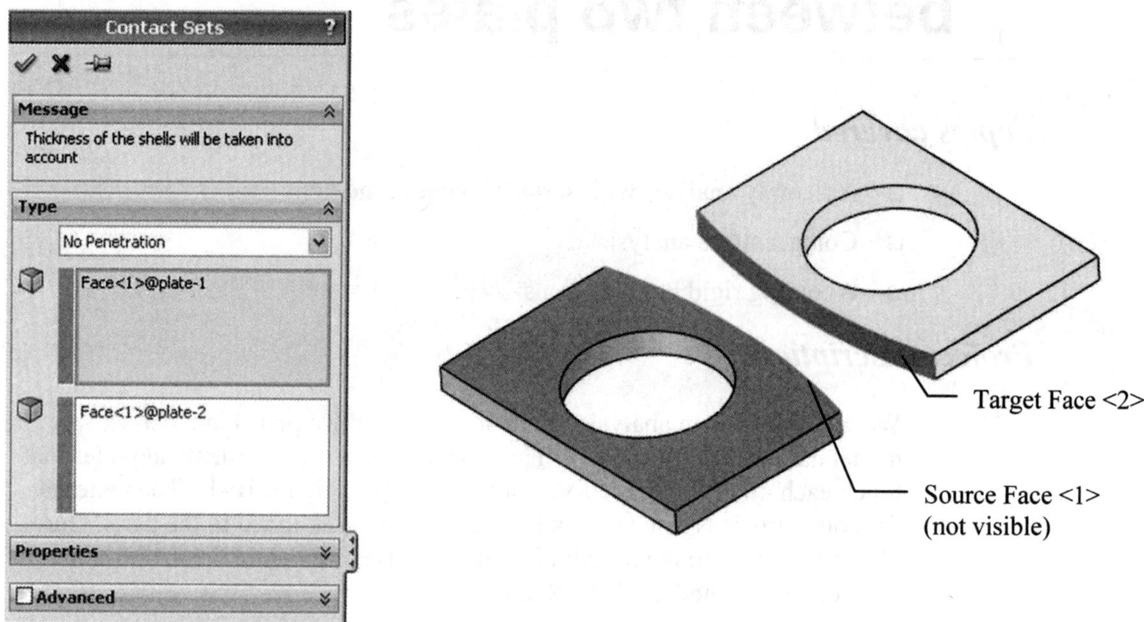

Figure 10-2: Contact Sets window

Define the Contact Set as No Penetration, Node to surface frictionless contact condition. For convenience, use exploded view. *It does not matter which face is the source and which is the target.*

Preparing the model for analysis requires restraining the loaded part to prevent rigid body motion and at the same time, making it free to move in the direction of the load. This can be accomplished by restraining the loaded face in both in-plane directions while leaving the normal direction (the direction in which load is applied) unrestrained (Figure 10-3).

The restraints shown in Figure 10-3 are required to prevent rigid body motions: rolling motion and sliding top plate off the bottom plate. The analyzed contact problem is frictionless.

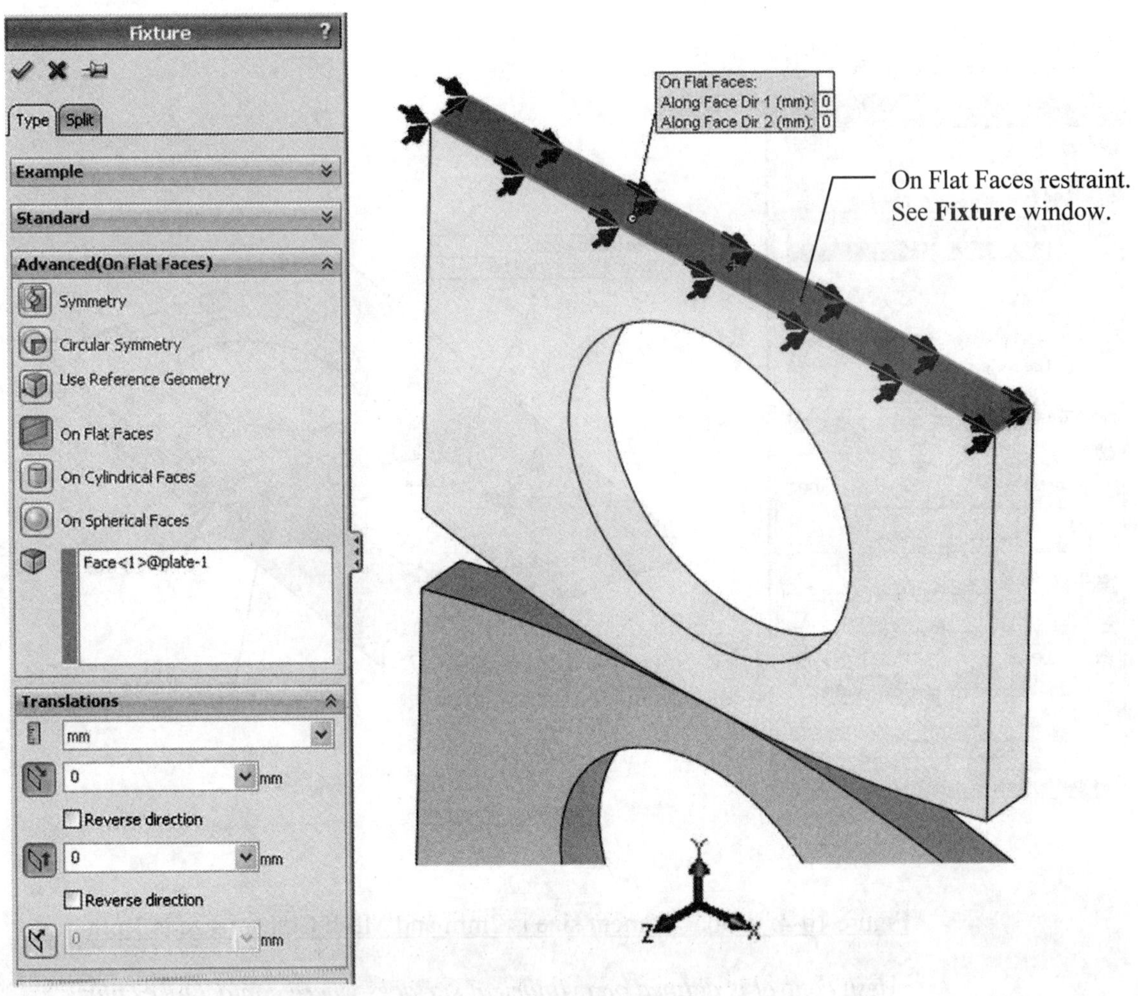

Figure 10-3: Restraints and loads definition

Note that no restraint is applied to the top face in the direction of load. Otherwise the load would have no effect.

Apply load to the top plate and a fixed restraint to the bottom plate as shown in Figure 10-1.

We are now ready to mesh the assembly model. Adequate mesh density in the contact area is of paramount importance in any contact stress analysis. It is the responsibility of the user to make sure that there are enough elements in the contact area to properly model the distribution of contact stresses. In this exercise we use a default global element size and apply mesh controls to contacting faces as shown in Figure 10-4.

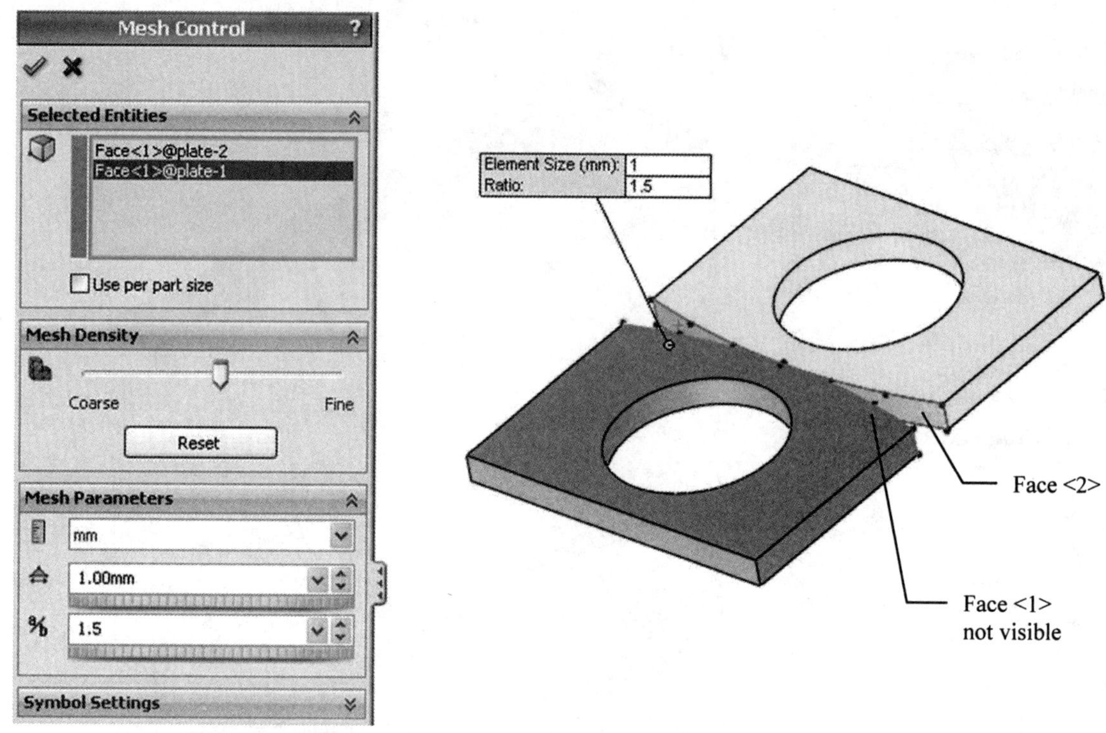

Figure 10-4. Global element size is 2mm and Mesh Control size is 1mm

Mesh control is defined on cylindrical surfaces where contact takes place.

Shown in Figure 10-5 is a contact pressure plot and associated windows used to define it.

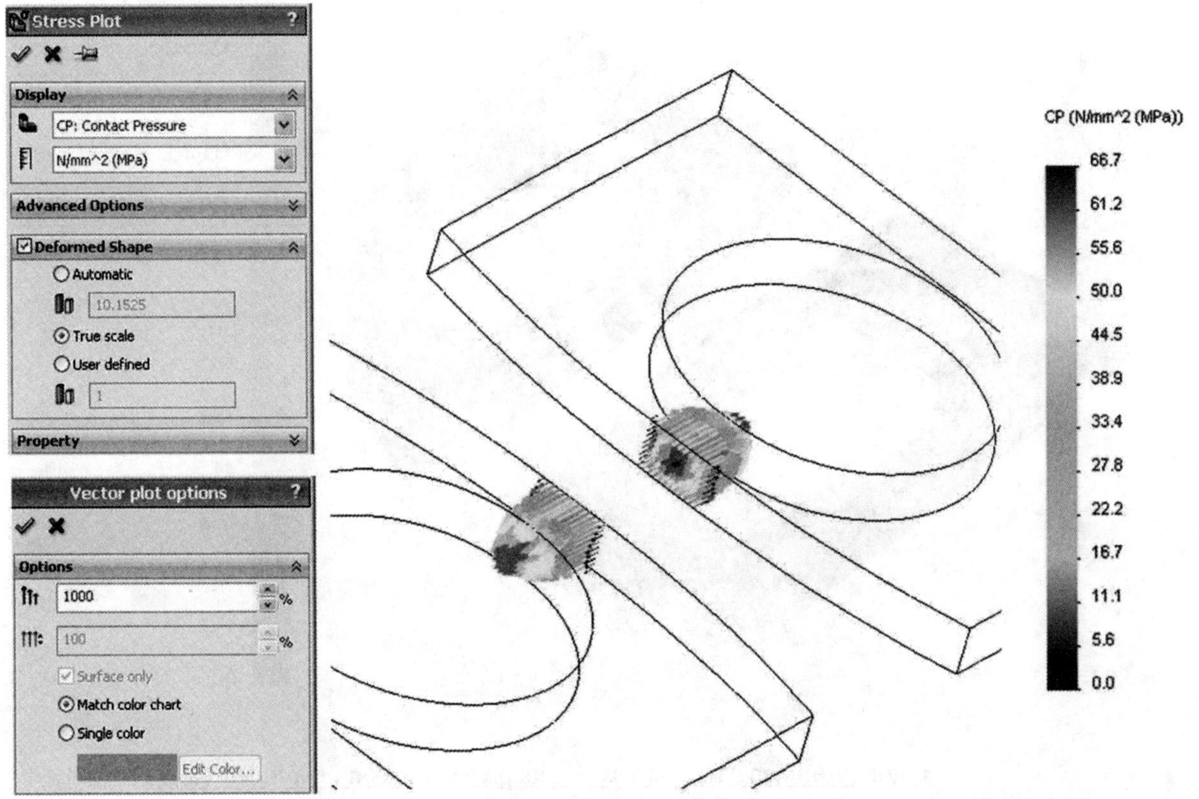

Figure 10-5: Contact stress results for the coarse mesh presented using an exploded view. The maximum contact stress is 67 MPa.

The plot presents Contact pressure defined in the Stress Plot window (left top). A contact pressure plot uses a Vector type of display which can be modified using the Vector plot options window (bottom left).

Von Mises stresses are shown in Figure 10-6.

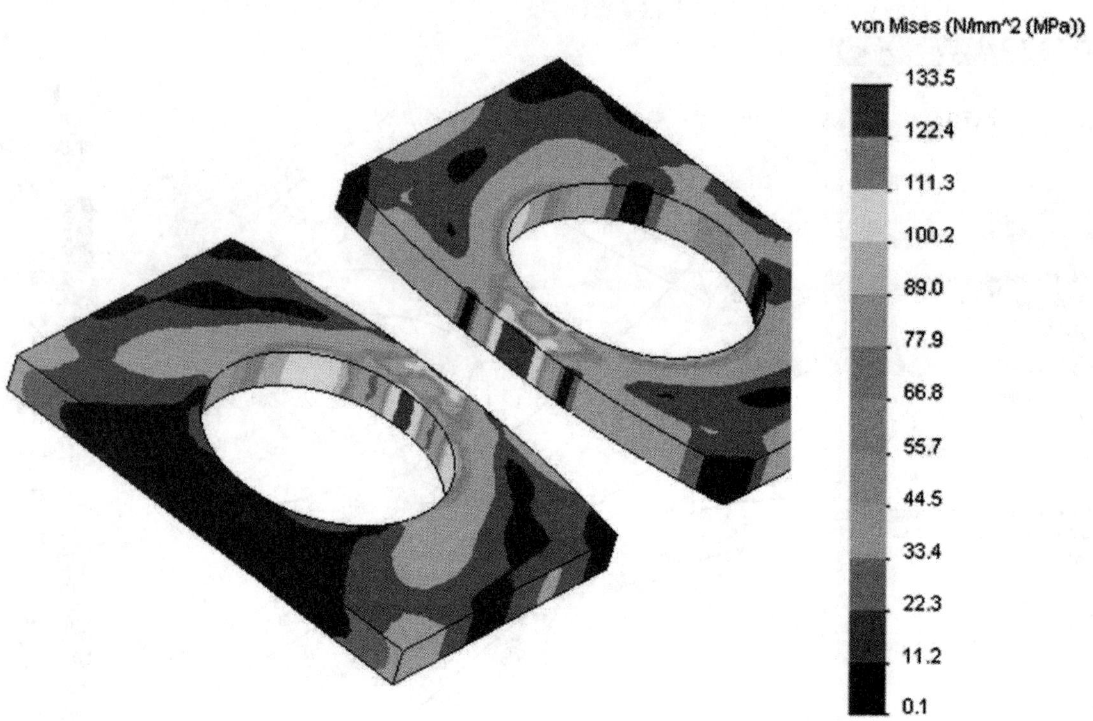

Figure 10-6: Von Mises stress results presented using exploded view

We leave it to the reader to decide if this stress level (the maximum von Mises stress in the contact area is 134MPa) is acceptable for Nylon 6/10 material which has yield stress of 139 MPa..

Before concluding this exercise, further investigate the effects of mesh refinement and type of material (such as steel or aluminum) on contact stresses. Note that our mesh is adequate for modeling contact stresses between two Nylon parts because the low modulus of elasticity of Nylon makes the contact area quite large. The same mesh will prove too coarse when analyzing more rigid materials.

11: Thermal stress analysis of a bi-metal beam

Topics covered

- Thermal stress analysis
- Shear stress analysis

Project description

The temperature of the entire bi-metal beam, shown in Figure 11-1, increases uniformly from an initial 298K to 400K. We need to find displacements and thermal stresses induced by this increase in temperature.

Procedure

Open the assembly BIMETAL PLATE and examine material properties assigned to each part.

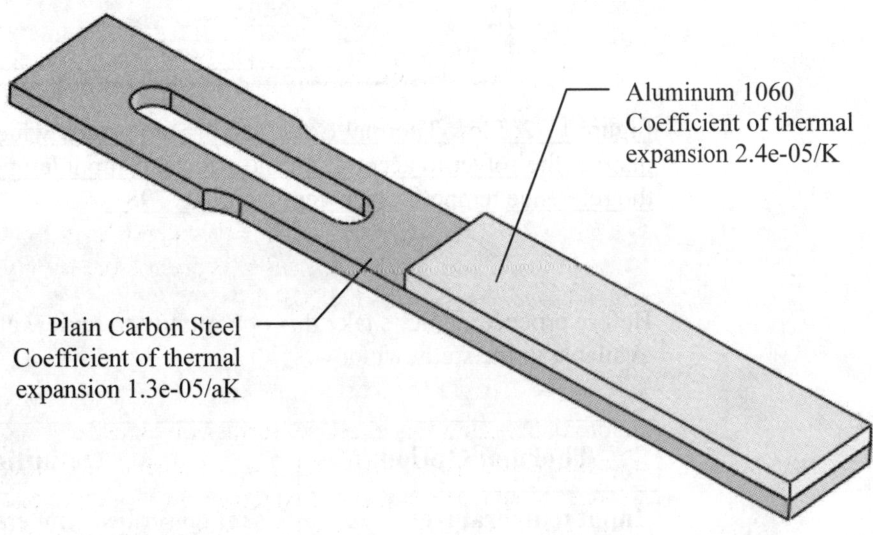

Figure 11-1: Bi-metal beam consisting of bonded steel and aluminum strips

The bi-metal beam will deform when heated because of the different thermal expansion coefficients of steel and aluminum.

To account for thermal effects we define the study as **Static,** and in the **Properties** of this study, under **Flow/Thermal Effects** select the option **Input temperature** (Figure 11-2).

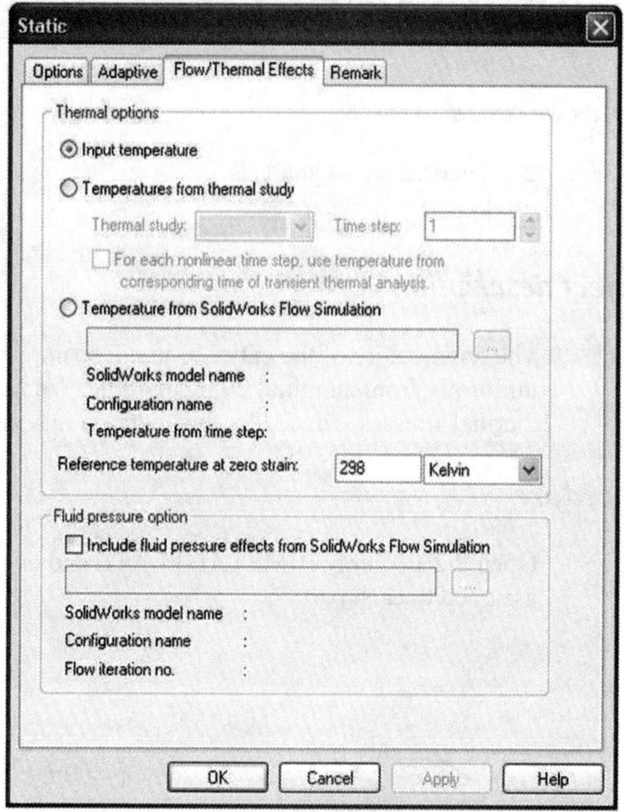

Figure 11-2: Flow/Thermal Effect tab in Static study window, where we instruct the solver to account for the effects of Input temperature and define the reference temperature at zero strain, as 298K

Before proceeding, let's take this opportunity to review all thermal options available in the study window.

Thermal Option	Definition
Input temperature	Use if prescribed temperatures will be defined in the *Load/Restraint* folder of the study to calculate thermal stresses. This is our case.
Temperature from thermal study	Use if temperature results are available from a previously conducted thermal study.
Temperature from SolidWorks Flow Simulation	Use if temperature results are available from a previously conducted SolidWorks Flow study.

An important part of this exercise is applying restraints. Restraints should eliminate Rigid Body Motions but should allow the restrained entity to expand due to temperature increase. This can be accomplished in three steps as explained in Figure 11-3.

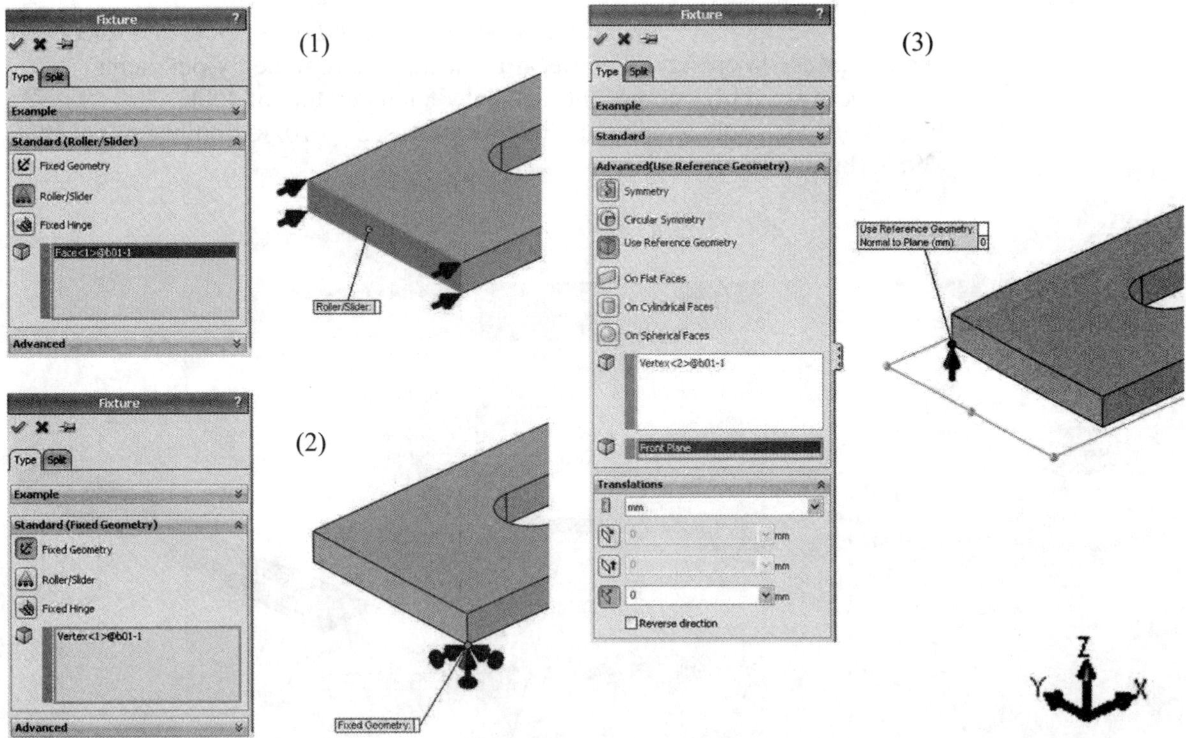

Figure 11-3: Definition of restraint to the end face

(1) ***Roller/Slider*** *restraint is applied to the end face to eliminate translations in the direction normal to the face. The same could have been accomplished by defining symmetry restraint or On Flat Faces with suppressed normal direction*

(2) One corner is restrained in all tree translation directions. Note that even though ***Fixed Geometry*** *restraint is used, this will not prevent the model from rotating about this point. Solid elements do not have rotational degrees of freedom so rotational restraint can not be applied.*

(3) With restraint (1) and (2) in place, the model still has one rigid body motion left. To eliminate this remaining rigid body motion we eliminate translation of the opposite corner in the direction normal to the Front reference plane with ***Use Reference Geometry*** *restraint.*

Note that for clarity of illustrations in Figure 11-3 only the symbol of restraint applied in the given step is shown. Symbols of restraints applied in previous steps are not repeated in illustrations pertaining to other steps.

To apply a temperature load, right-click the *External Loads* folder and select **Temperature** to open the **Temperature** window. From the fly-out menu, select both assembly components and enter a temperature of 400K. This means that assembly temperature will be increased by 102K from the initial 298K (Figure 11-4).

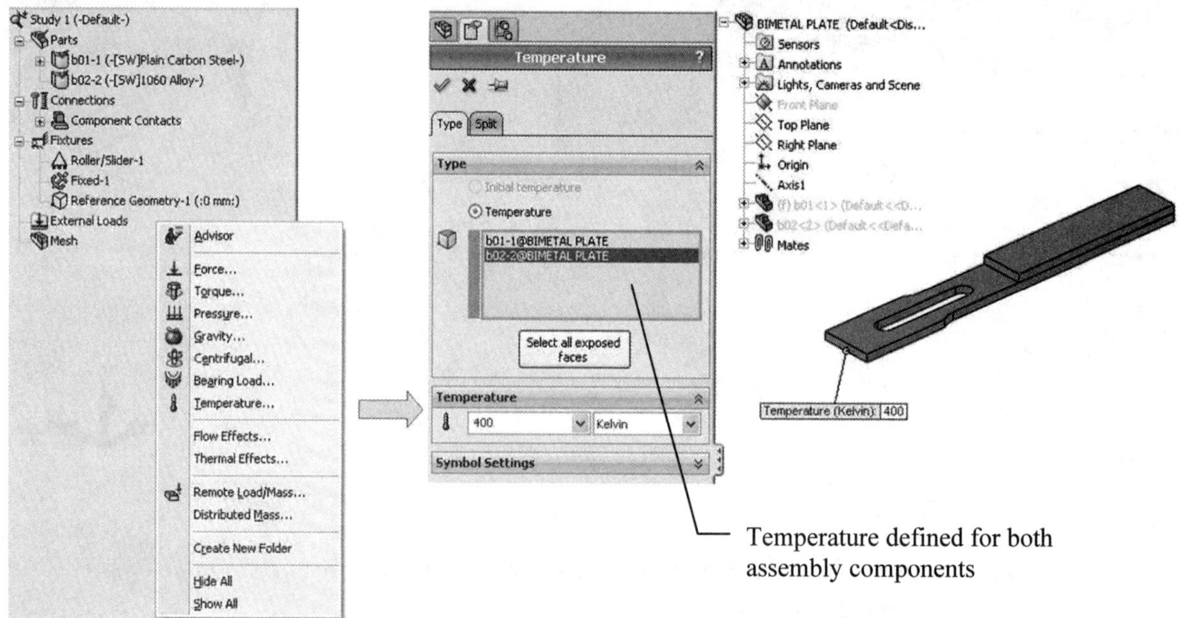

Figure 11-4: A temperature of 400K is applied to both assembly components, which are most conveniently selected from the SolidWorks fly-out menu

Select both components from the fly-out menu

Mesh the model with a 1mm element size to create a total of four layers of elements across the entire thickness (two layers across each component).

Displacement results are shown in Figure 11-5, von Mises stress results are shown in Figure 11-6.

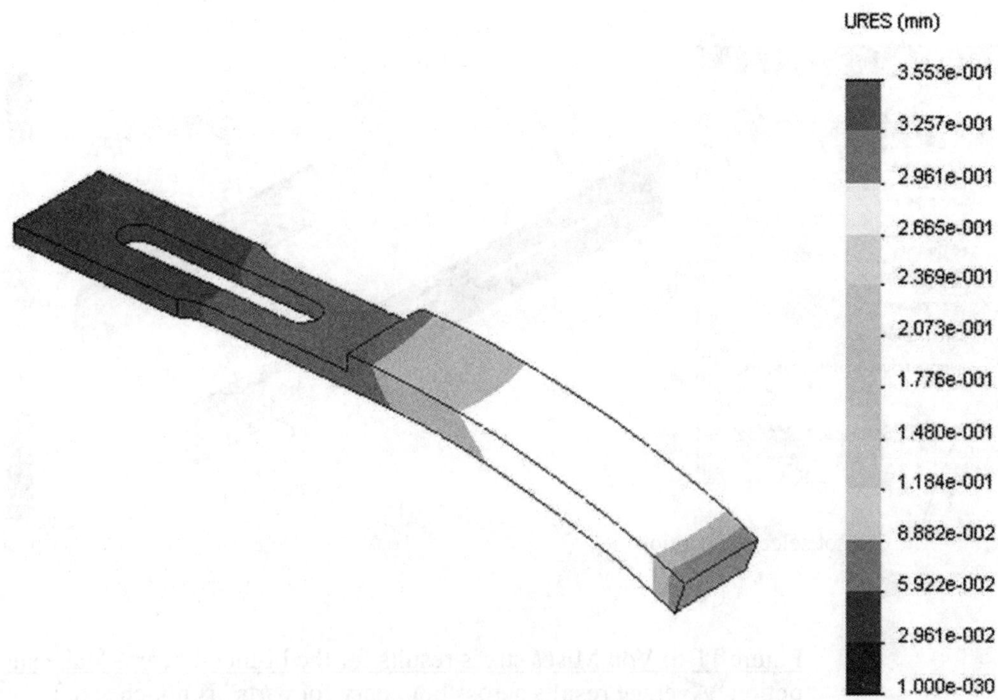

Figure 11-5: Displacement results for the bi-metal beam

Due to the different thermal expansion ratios of steel and aluminum, thermal strains develop and bend the bimetal beam.

Von Mises stresses in both components are shown in Figure 11-6. Because of different materials, stresses should not be averaged across the boundary separating these two components.

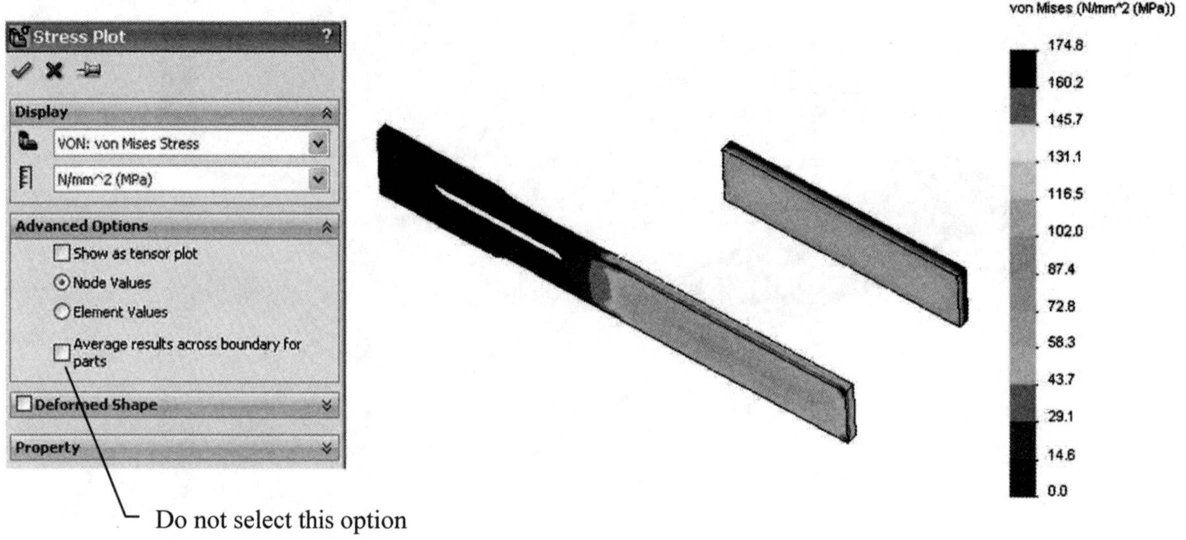

Figure 11-6: Von Mises stress results for the bi-metal beam. Make sure that the option "Average results across boundary for parts" is not checked.

Note the unavoidable stress singularities along the edges and in the corners of the contacting faces. Stress singularities are present because of the rapid change in the material properties across the touching faces.

Because of stress singularities along the edges of touching faces, the maximum stress strongly depends on the mesh size. You are encouraged to repeat analysis with different mesh densities to see this effect. Also try probing stress results at a location away from the edges to see that stresses there are not singular and converge to a finite value while mesh is refined.

To review stresses in the longitudinal direction and stresses in the transverse direction, follow instructions shown in Figures 11-7 and 11-8.

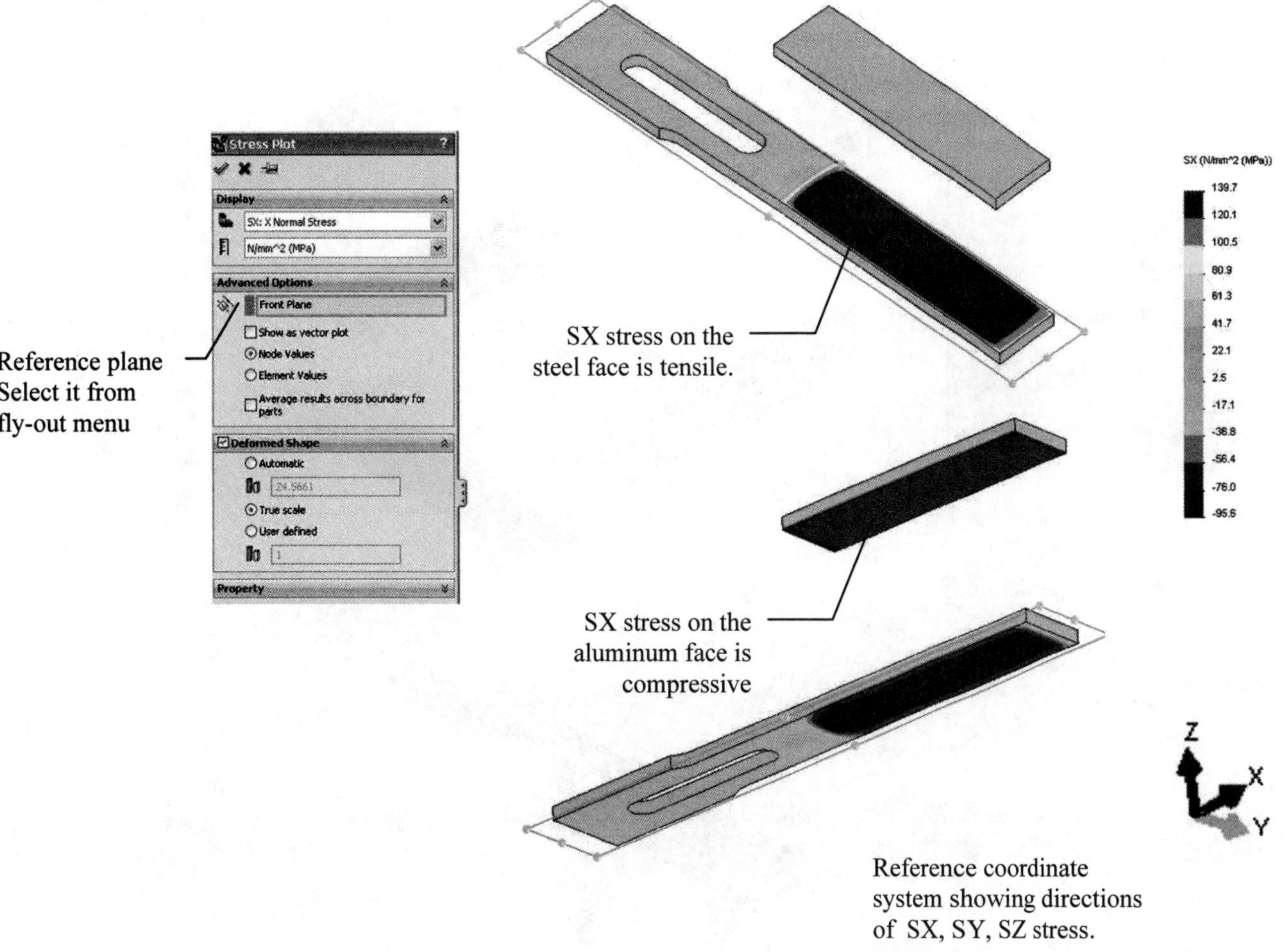

Figure 11-7: Analysis of SX stresses SX (in the longitudinal direction of bimetal beam) on the contacting faces.

If we select Front Plane as reference geometry, we need to specify the SX stress component in order to see stresses in the longitudinal direction. Vector display is useful to visualize stresses, harder to see here due to black and white illustration. A stress vector directed in the positive reference direction denotes positive (tensile) stress. Exploded view is used.

The orientation of this coordinate system may be the same or different from the orientation of the global coordinate system. In this case it is the same so we could have defined SX in the global coordinate system as well.

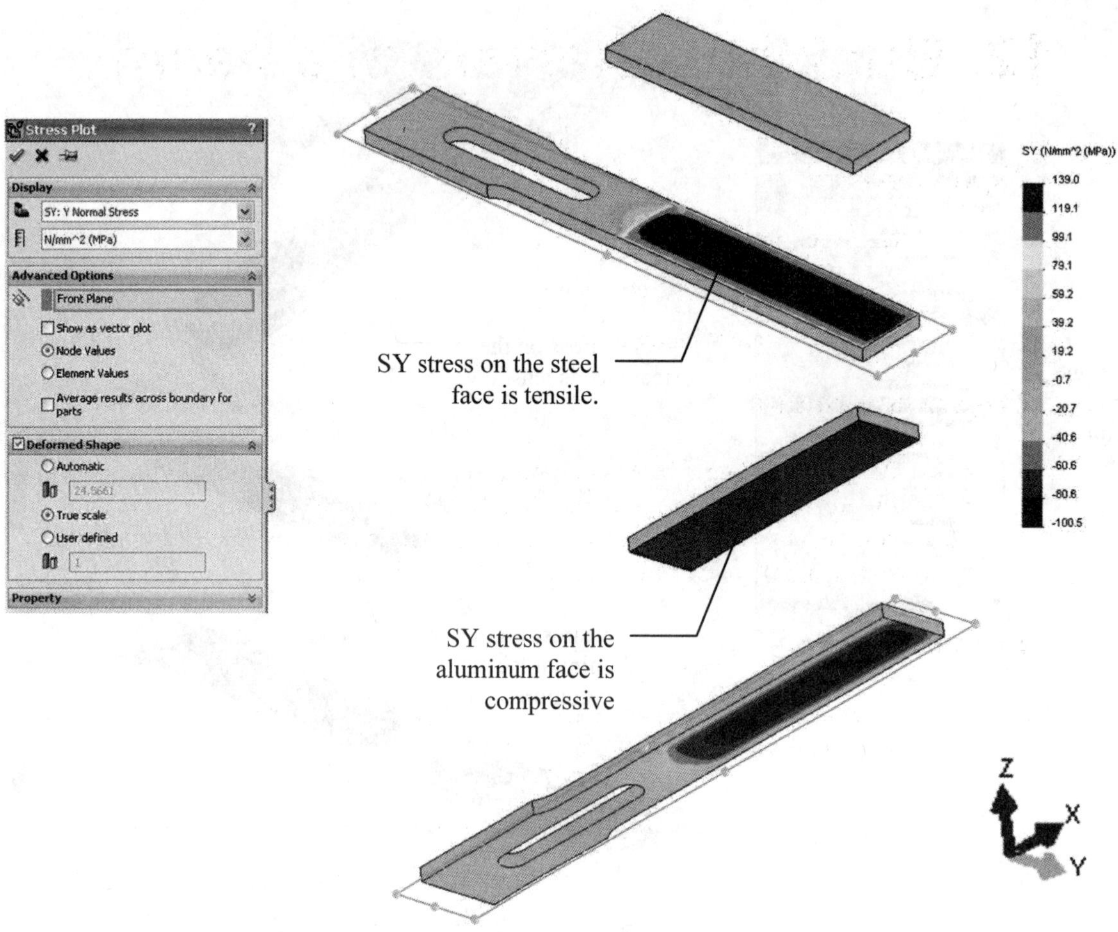

<u>Figure 11-8: Stresses SY (in the transverse direction of bimetal beam)</u>

Repeat analysis of SX and SY stress components on the touching faces using vector display.

Review of results of stresses on the contacting faces (Figures 11-7 and 11-8) demonstrates that due to higher coefficient of thermal expansion of aluminum tensile stresses develop on the steel face and compressive stresses develop on the aluminum face.

12: Buckling analysis of a beam

Topics covered

- Buckling analysis
- Buckling load safety factor
- Stress safety factor

Project description

A perforated angle beam is compressed with a 30000N load, as shown in Figure 12-1. The material has already been assigned to the assembly components. Our goal is to calculate the factor of safety related to the yield stress and the factor of safety related to buckling.

Procedure

Open the assembly file L BEAM. The beam and endplates material is alloy steel with a yield strength of 620 MPa.

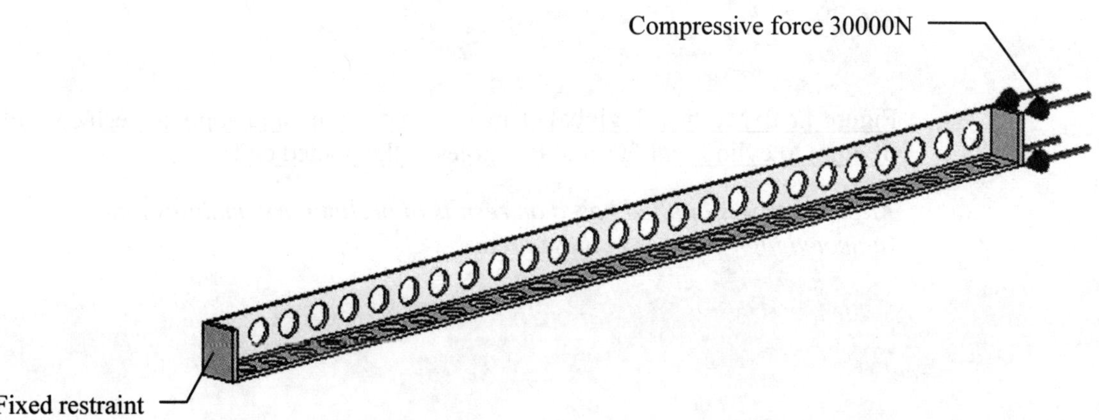

Figure 12-1: L-beam assembly model

A perforated angle is compressed by a 30000N force uniformly distributed over the ENDPLATE.

Before we run a buckling analysis, let's first obtain the results of a static analysis based on the load and restraint shown in Figure 12-1. Name this study *stress analysis*. Prepare mesh as shown in Figure 12-2.

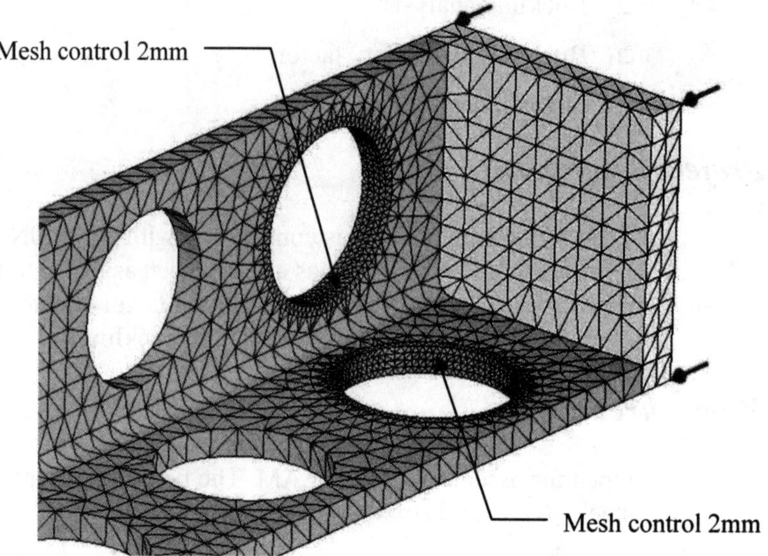

Figure 12-2: Mesh with global element size of 8mm, and apply a mesh control of 2mm to cylindrical faces of two holes at the loaded end

Mesh control is applied based on results of preliminary analyses that indicated high stresses in these areas.

The results of the static analysis show the maximum von Mises stress 447Mpa which is below the yield strength 620 MPa. Figure 12-3 identifies the location of the highest stress.

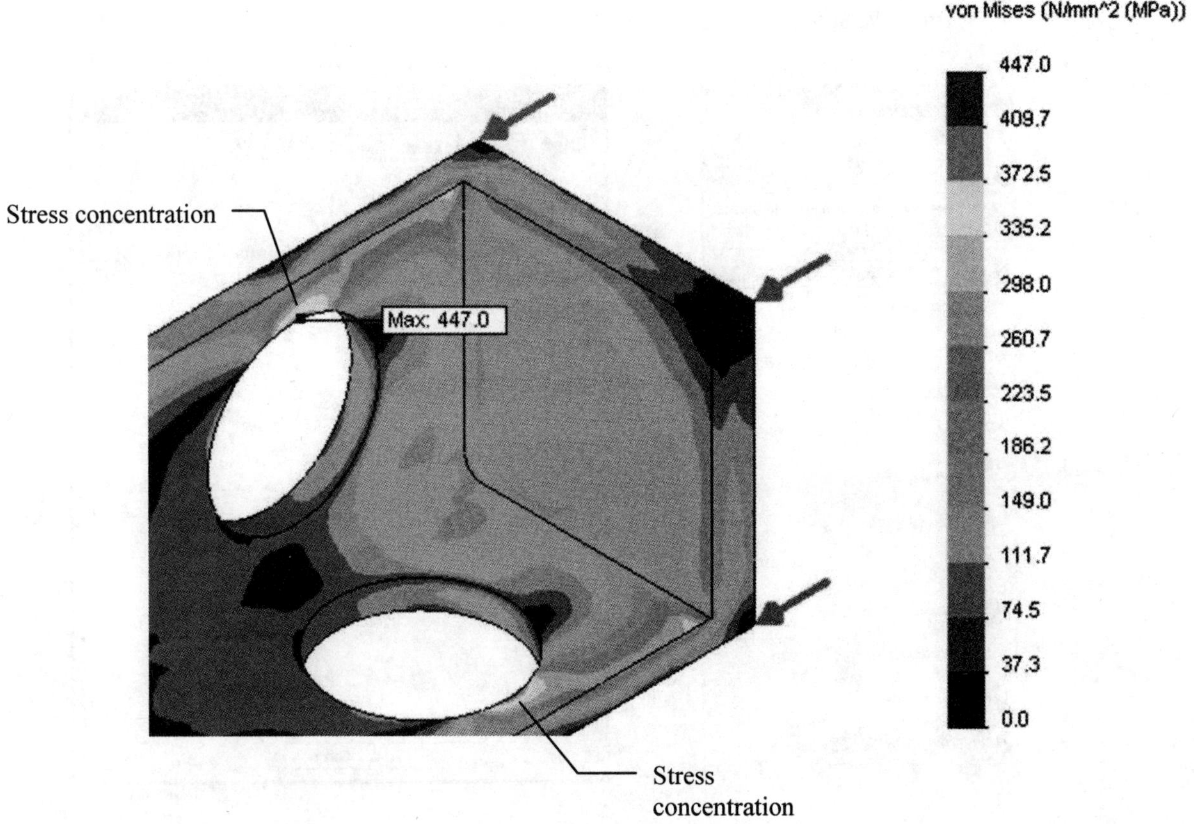

<u>Figure 12-3: Location of the maximum von Mises stress is close to the loaded ENDPLATE</u>

The plot displays the location of the maximum stress and uses floating format to display numerical values. Both are selected in Chart Options.

Base on the results shown in Figure 12-3, the factor of safety to yield is:

$$FOS_{yield} = \frac{\text{yield strength}}{\text{max von Mises stress}} = \frac{620\text{MPa}}{447\text{MPa}} = 1.39,$$

meaning that the beam's material is below yield.

As is always the case with slender members under a compressive load, the factor of safety related to material yield stress may not be sufficient to describe the structure's safety. This is because of the possible occurrence of buckling. We need to calculate the buckling safety factor which requires running a buckling study created as shown in Figure 12-4.

Copy loads and restraints from the *stress analysis* study to the *buckling analysis* study.

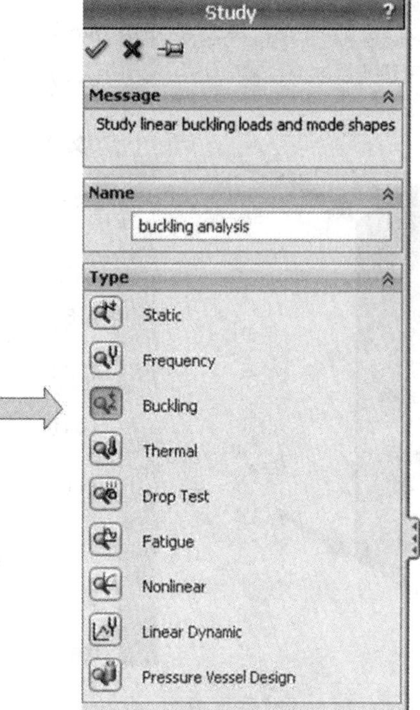

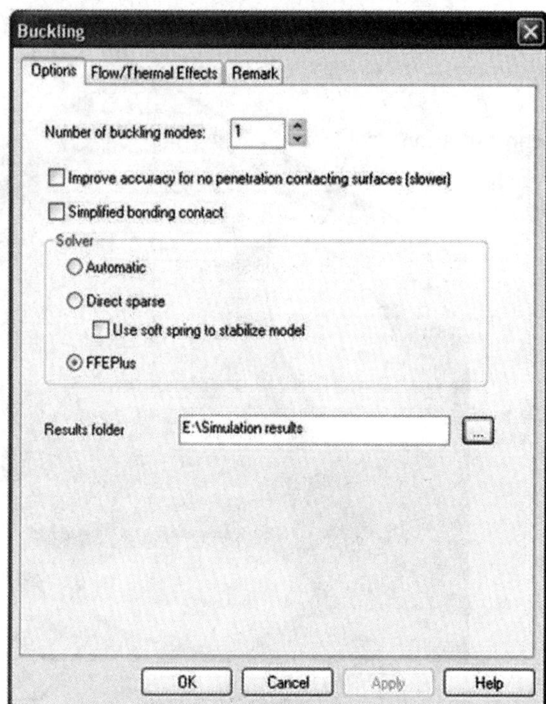

Figure 12-4: Definition of a buckling study (left) and the Buckling study window, where properties are defined for a buckling study

Defining a buckling study requires specifying the number of desired buckling modes. Here we ask for the first buckling mode.

When defining a buckling study, we need to decide how many buckling modes should be calculated. This is a close analogy to the number of modes in a frequency analysis. In most practical cases, the first buckling mode determines the safety of the analyzed structure. Therefore, we limit this analysis to calculating the first buckling mode. Once the buckling analysis has been completed, SolidWorks **Simulation** creates a result folder: *Displacement*.

Even though displacement results can be shown in color, they do not provide any useful information just like in modal (frequency) analysis. In a buckling analysis, the magnitude of displacement is meaningless, just like in frequency analysis. The **Mode Shape** plot shown in Figure 12-5 does not include confusing information on the magnitude of displacement; it lists the buckling load factor related to the displayed buckling mode.

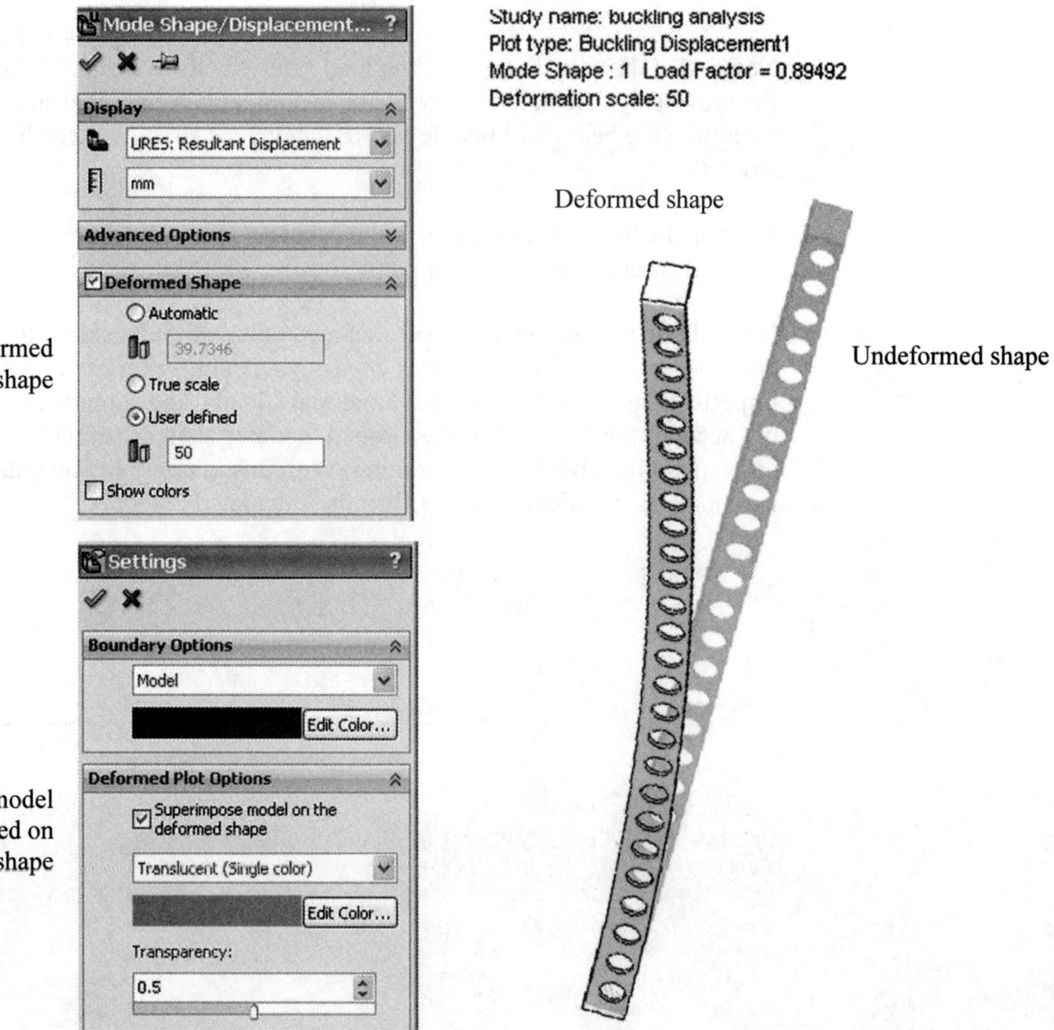

Figure 12-5: The deformation plot provides visual feedback on the shape of the buckled structure. It also lists the buckling load factor, here equal to 0.89.

This plot shows the buckled shape along with the undeformed model.

The buckling load factor provides information on how many times the load magnitude would need to be increased in order for buckling to actually take place. In our case, the magnitude of load causing buckling is 0.89*30000N = 26,700N. Therefore, buckling will take place because the actual load is 30000N. The buckling load factor can also be called the buckling load safety factor.

$$FOS_{buckling} = 0.89$$

Notice that the calculated buckling load safety factor is actually lower than the previously calculated safety factor related to material yield strength. Therefore the beam will buckle before it develops stresses exceeding the yield strength.

Our conclusion is that buckling is the deciding mode of failure. Also notice that high stress affects the beam only locally, while buckling is global.

It should be pointed out that the calculated value of the buckling load is non-conservative, meaning that it does not account for the always-present imperfections in model geometry, materials, loads, and supports. Also, it does not account for the fact that the meshed model is stiffer than the corresponding model before meshing. With this in mind, the real buckling load may be significantly lower than the calculated 26,700N.

13: Static analysis of a bracket using adaptive solution methods

Topics covered

- H-adaptive solution method
- P-adaptive solution method
- Comparison between h-elements and p-elements

Project description

A bracket shown in Figure 13-1 is supported along the backside. A 10000N load is uniformly distributed over a face surrounding the hole as shown in Figure 13-1. We need to find the location and magnitude of the maximum von Mises stress. Open the part BRACKET with material AISI 304 assigned.

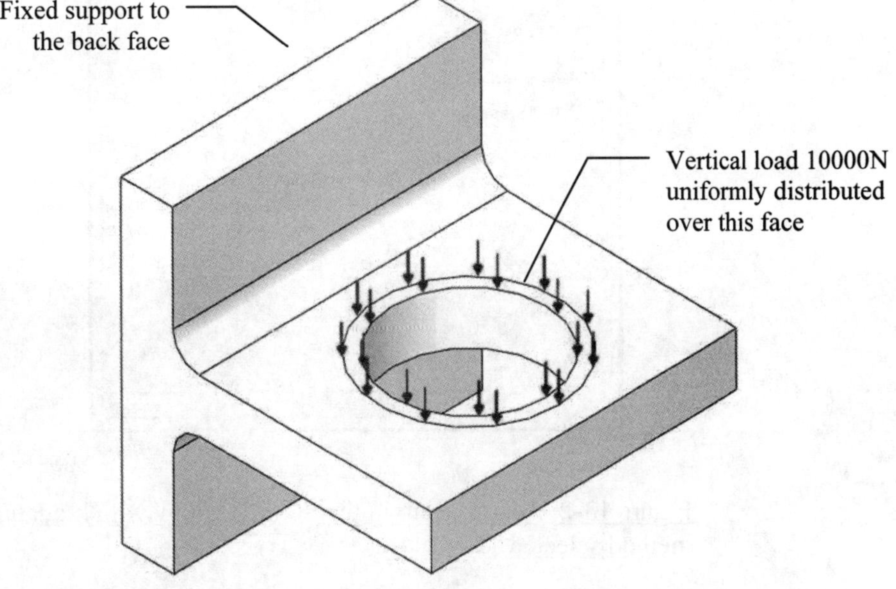

Figure 13-1: Hollow cantilever bracket under a bending load

Due to the symmetry of the BRACKET geometry, loads and supports, we could simplify the geometry by cutting it in half along the plane of symmetry, but decide against it because the work involved would not save much time overall.

We use this simple problem to introduce two new solution methods: the h-adaptive and the p-adaptive solution methods. Both are available only for **Static** studies using solid elements.

We start with a description of the **h-adaptive** solution method. In several previous occasions, we performed mesh refinements to investigate the effect of mesh density on results. We also added mesh controls to analyze stresses more accurately in "difficult" locations. In this chapter we demonstrate that the h-adaptive solution method automates the mesh refinement process and, to some extent, relieves users from having to make meshing decisions such as selecting element size and applying mesh controls.

Figure 13-2 shows properties of an h-adaptive study. **Target accuracy, Accuracy bias** and **Maximum number of loops** control the iterative process of mesh refinement.

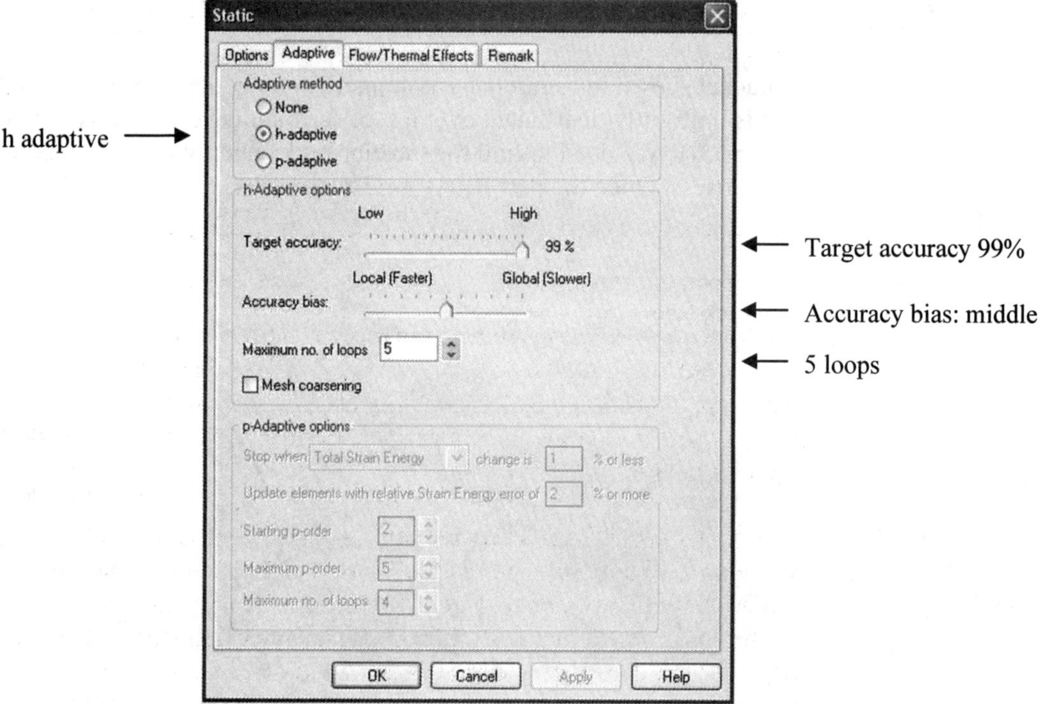

Figure 13-2: Adaptive tab in the Static window with h-adaptive solution method selected

The selection "h-adaptive" made in the Adaptive tab in the Static study window (selectable by right clicking the Static study and selecting Properties...) activates the use of the h-adaptive solution method. For the h-adaptive solution presented in this chapter, we use the settings as shown in this illustration.

H-adaptive solution options are explained in the table below.

Setting	Definition
Target accuracy	Sets the accuracy level for the strain energy norm. This is NOT the stress accuracy level. However, a high level of accuracy in the convergence of the strain energy norm indicates more accurate stress results.
Accuracy bias	You can also move the slider towards Local to instruct the program to concentrate on getting accurate peak stress results using a fewer number of elements. You can also move the slider towards Global to instruct the program to concentrate on getting overall accurate results.
Maximum no. of loops	Sets the maximum number of loops allowed when you run the study. The maximum possible number of loops is five.
Mesh coarsening	Check this option to allow the program to coarsen the mesh in regions with low error during the adaptive loops. The number of elements in consecutive loops may increase or decrease depending on the model and the initial mesh. If this option is not checked, the program does not change the mesh in regions with low errors.

The h-adaptive solution method is called "adaptive" because mesh refinement is "adapted" to the stress pattern and the mesh is refined only where it is necessary to produce results satisfying accuracy requirements specified in **Study** Properties. H-elements retain their order; they cannot be upgraded to a higher order.

Now let's look at the **p-adaptive** solution method. If you recall, in chapter 1 we mentioned that SolidWorks **Simulation** can use either first order elements (called draft quality), or second order elements (called high quality). Furthermore, recall that first order elements model a linear (or first order) displacement distribution and constant stress distribution, while second order elements model a parabolic (second order) displacement distribution and linear stress distribution. We now have to amend the above statements.

Aside from first and second order elements, SolidWorks **Simulation** can also work with elements of "floating" order which can change order during the iterative solution process. The highest available order is five. These elements of "floating" order are called p-elements and are available when the **p-adaptive** option is selected as the solution method in the **Study** window under the **Adaptive** tab (Figure 13-3). This option is available only for static studies using solid elements.

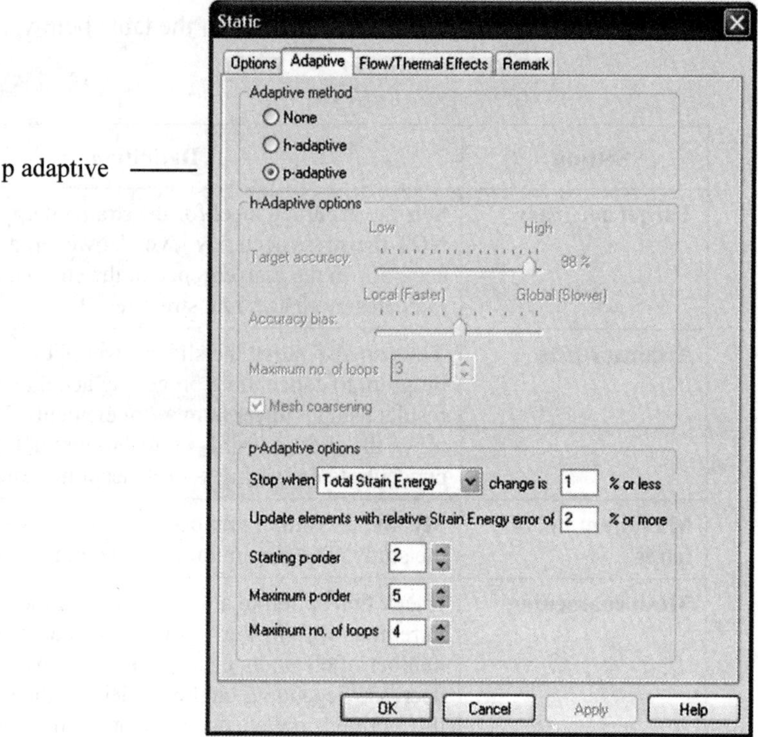

<u>Figure 13-3: Adaptive tab in the Static window with p-adaptive solution method selected</u>

The selection "p-adaptive" made in the Adaptive tab in the Static study window activates the use of the p-adaptive solution method. For the p-adaptive solution presented in this chapter, we use the settings as shown in this illustration.

P-adaptive solution options are shown in Figure 13-3 and explained in the table below:

Setting	Definition
Stop when	Iterations (looping) increase element order until the change in Total Strain Energy (or other measures like RMS resultant displacement or RMS von Mises stress) between the two consecutive iterations is less than the specified value (default is 1%) shown in the p-adaptive options area. If this requirement is not satisfied, then looping will stop when the elements reach the fifth order; this will be the fourth loop.
Update elements with relative Strain Energy error of …	This setting controls which elements are upgraded during the iterative solution. By default, elements with relative Strain Energy error of 2% or more are updated.
Starting p-order	Initial order of elements. Usually the starting p-order is set to 2, which means that all elements are defined at start as second order elements.
Maximum p - order	The actual highest order to be used in p-adaptive solution. The highest order available in SolidWorks **Simulation** is the fifth order.
Maximum no. of loops	Sets the maximum number of iterations (loops) allowed when the p-adaptive study is run. The maximum possible number of loops is four.

Let's pause for a moment and explain some terminology. Refer to Figure 2-15 which explains that *h* denotes the characteristic element size. While the mesh is refined during convergence process, the characteristic element size *h* becomes smaller. Therefore the mesh refinement process that we conducted in chapters 2 and 3 is called the h-convergence process, and the elements used in this process arc called h-elements. An h-adaptive solution is an iterative solution where the h-element mesh is automatically refined in several iterations.

When p-elements are used, the iterative process does not involve mesh refinement. While the mesh remains unchanged, the element order changes from the second all the way to the fifth. The iterations may also stop sooner if the convergence criterion (here the change in **Total Strain Energy**) is satisfied before the fifth order is reached.

The order of any element is defined by the order of polynomial functions that describe the displacements in the element. Because the polynomial order experiences changes in the p-adaptive solution, the process of consecutive element order upgrade is called a p-convergence process, and the upgradeable elements used in this process are called p-elements.

Not all p-elements are upgraded during the solution process. Which elements are updated depends on the selection made in the field **Update elements with relative Strain Energy error of ___ % or more**. Here we set it to 2%, meaning that only those elements that do not satisfy the above criterion will be upgraded (investigate other criteria as well). Therefore we say that the element upgrading is "adaptive", or driven by the results of consecutive iterations.

The p-adaptive solution process is analogous to the process of mesh refinement, which also continues until the change in the selected result is no longer significant.

Procedure

We will solve the same problem in five different ways:

1. Using one mesh of h elements
2. Using one mesh of h elements with mesh controls added
3. Using h-adaptive solution method
4. Using p-adaptive solution method with default **p-adaptive** solution settings
5. Using p-adaptive solution method with modified **p-adaptive** solution settings

First, solve the model using second order solid tetrahedral h-elements using default element size. Name the study *standard*. Von Mises stress results with superimposed mesh are shown in Figure 13-4.

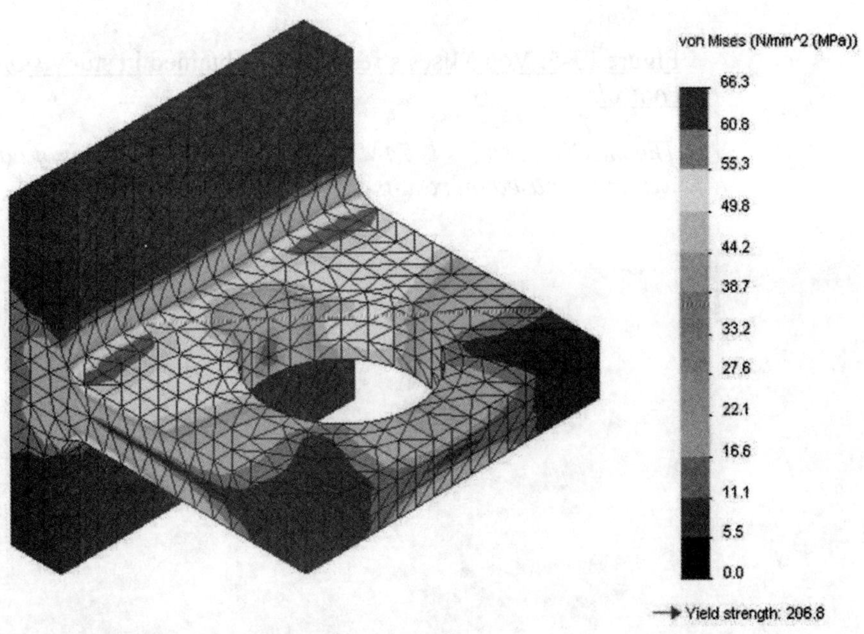

Figure 13-4: Von Mises stress results obtained in standard study

The maximum stress is 66MPa.

We now repeat analysis using a mesh with default mesh controls applied to both fillets (top and bottom). Name the study *standard with mesh controls.* Von Mises stress results produced by this study are shown in Figure 13-5.

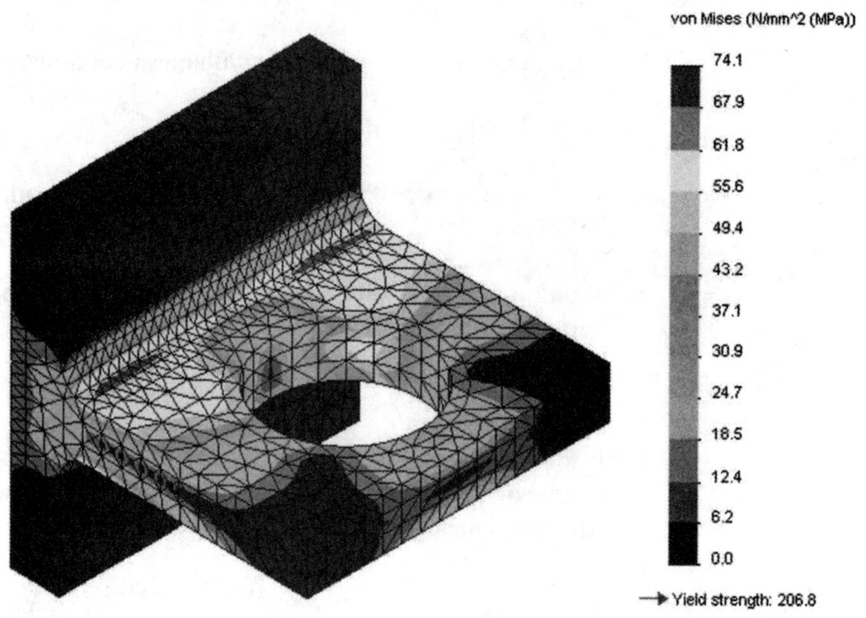

Figure 13-5: Von Mises stress results obtained in study *standard with mesh controls*

The maximum stress is 74MPa. Note that the decision of adding mesh controls was made based on results from the previous study.

Now, create a new study *h adaptive* identical to *standard* study (the one without mesh control) except in the study window under the **Adaptive** tab, select **h-adaptive**. Use settings shown in Figure 13-2: **Target accuracy 99%**, no **Accuracy bias** (slider in the middle), **Maximum no. of loops 5.**

As we have previously mentioned, the finite element mesh is refined during the h-adaptive solution. The results are reported for the mesh from the last performed iteration (the most refined one). Run the solution of the *h-adaptive* study and display the results as shown in Figure 13-6.

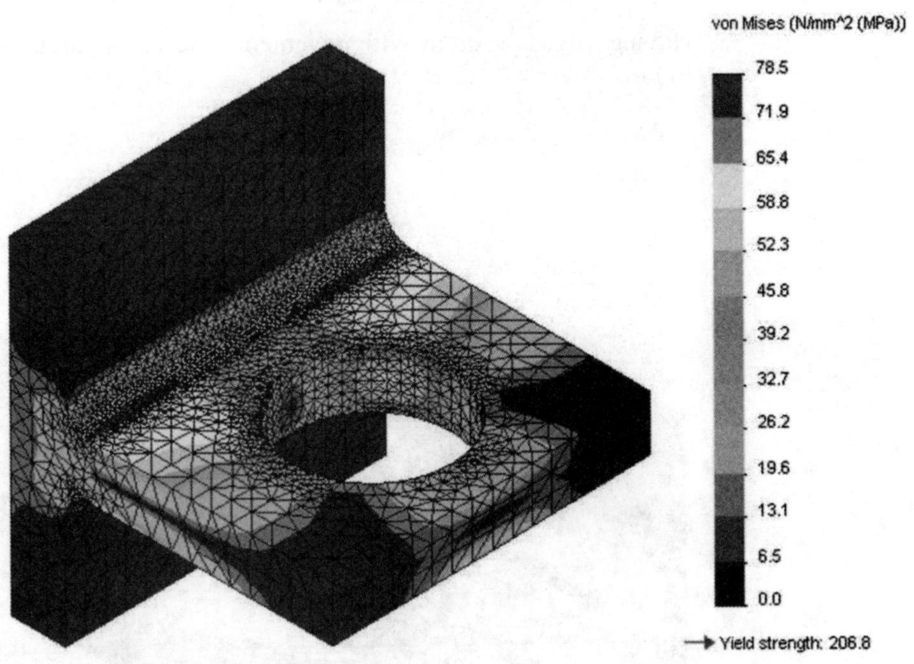

Figure 13-6: Von Mises stress results obtained with an h-adaptive solution

Notice that the mesh has been automatically refined as compared to the initial mesh visible in Figure 13-4. The maximum von Mises stress is 79MPa.

Now, create a study called *p-adaptive 01*. In the study window under the **Adaptive** tab, select **p-adaptive**: Use all defaults for a p-adaptive study definition as shown in Figure 13-3. **Restraints** and **Loads** can be copied from any of the two previous studies.

Considering that the p-adaptive solution will be used, we can manage with a mesh without bias (no controls need to be applied). Therefore, copy the mesh from the *Standard* study. Using higher order elements, which is equivalent to refinement of an h-element mesh, our mesh without bias will still deliver results with acceptable accuracy.

Having solved the study with p-elements, the stress plot produced is shown in Figure 13-7.

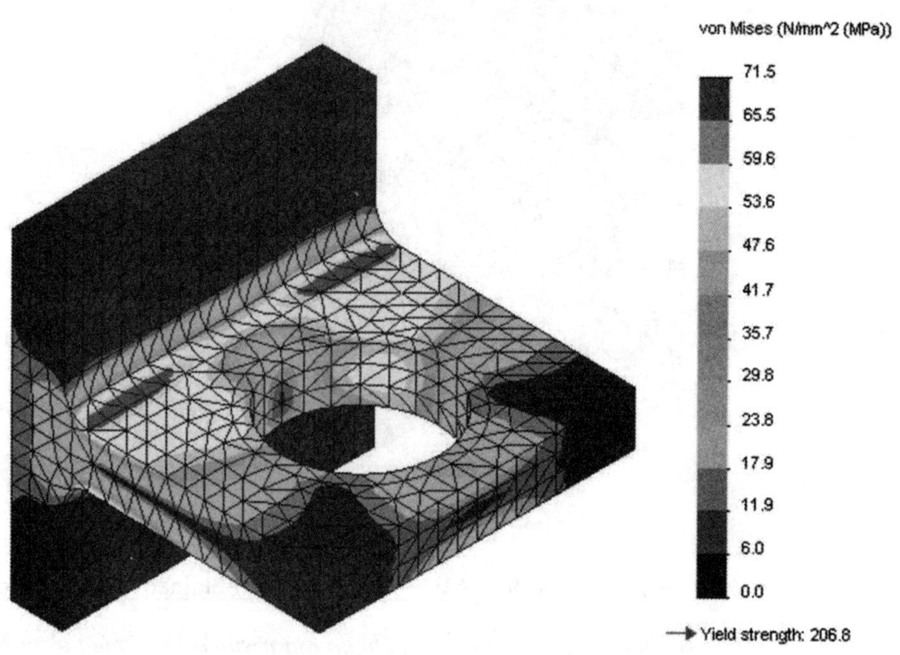

Figure 13-7: Von Mises stress results obtained using p-adaptive

Mesh is identical to the mesh visible in Figure 13-4. The maximum von Mises stress is 72 MPa.

To illustrate the iterative nature of h-adaptive and p-adaptive solutions, create convergence graphs which are available for both types of adaptive solutions.

To create a convergence graph, right-click *Results* folder and select **Define Adaptive Convergence Graph**. For both studies select **Maximum von Mises Stress** in the **Convergence Graph** window (Figure 13-8). Later try experimenting with other **Convergence Graph** options.

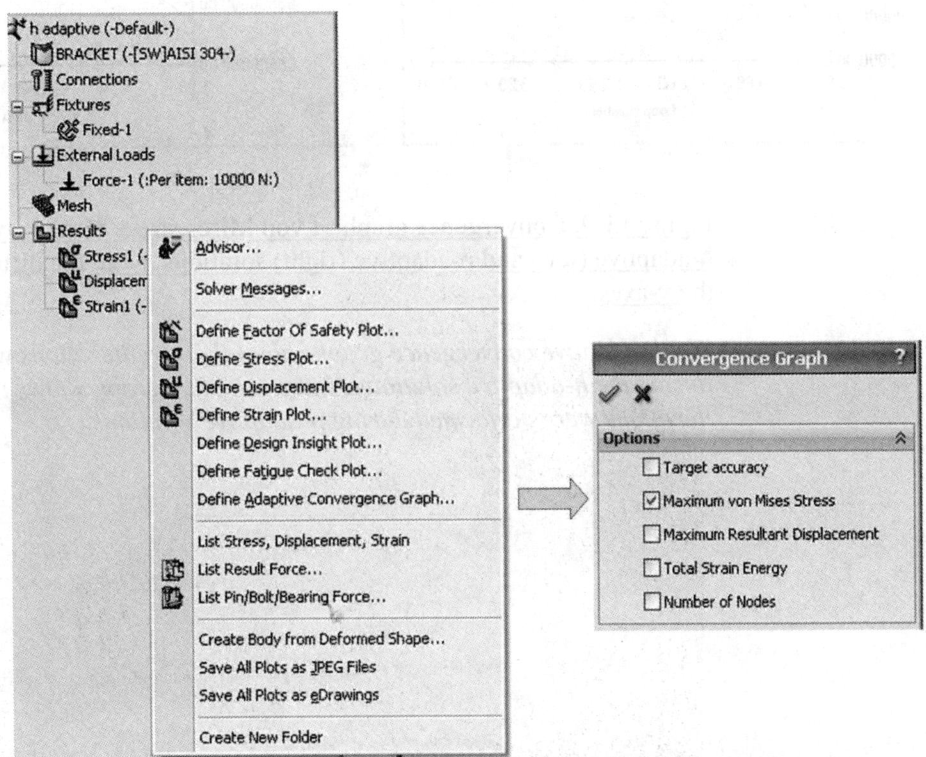

Figure 13-8: Defining a convergence graph for h-adaptive or p-adaptive solution

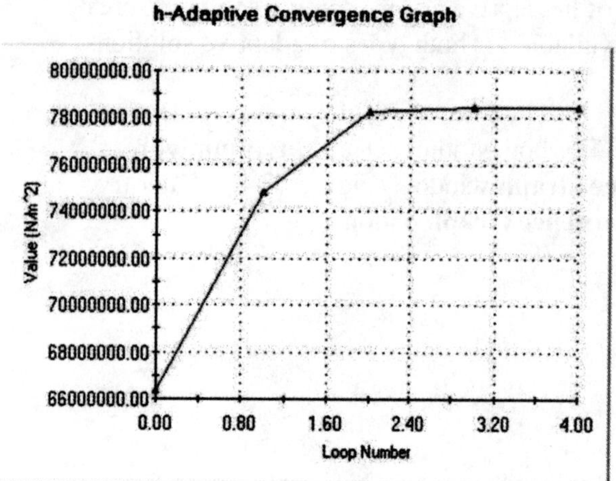

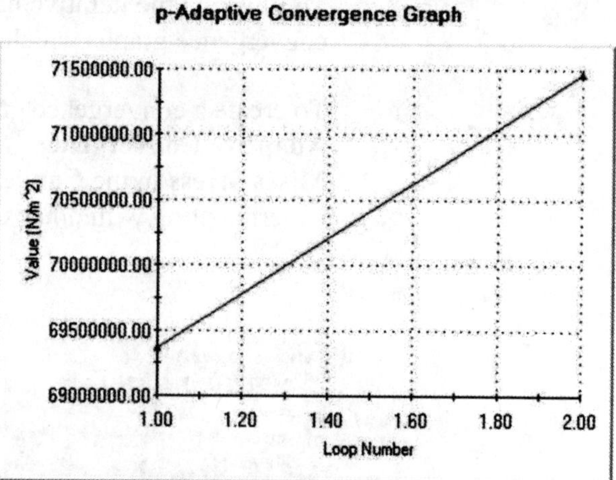

Figure 13-9: Convergence graph of von Mises stress results obtained in h-adaptive (left) and p-adaptive (right) solutions. Note the different scales on the y-axes.

The h-adaptive convergence graph shows that five iterations were performed during the h-adaptive solutions. The p-adaptive graph shows that only two iterations were performed during p-adaptive solutions.

The maximum number of iterations in the h-adaptive process is five and as Figure 13-9 indicates, all five iterations were performed because we used a very demanding 99% for **Target accuracy** specified in settings of h-adaptive study. **Target accuracy** indirectly controls the number of iterations performed during the h-adaptive solution. Try experimenting with a less demanding setting of **Target accuracy** to see that the solution will stop without using up all available iterations.

The maximum number of iterations in a p-adaptive study is four. Figure 13-9 shows that only two were performed, so the iterative solution must have stopped due to convergence requirements being satisfied before all available iterations were "used up".

Create the last study and call it *p adaptive 02* (you may copy study *p adaptive 01*). Define much more demanding convergence requirements (Figure 13-10) to force the solver into using all available element orders.

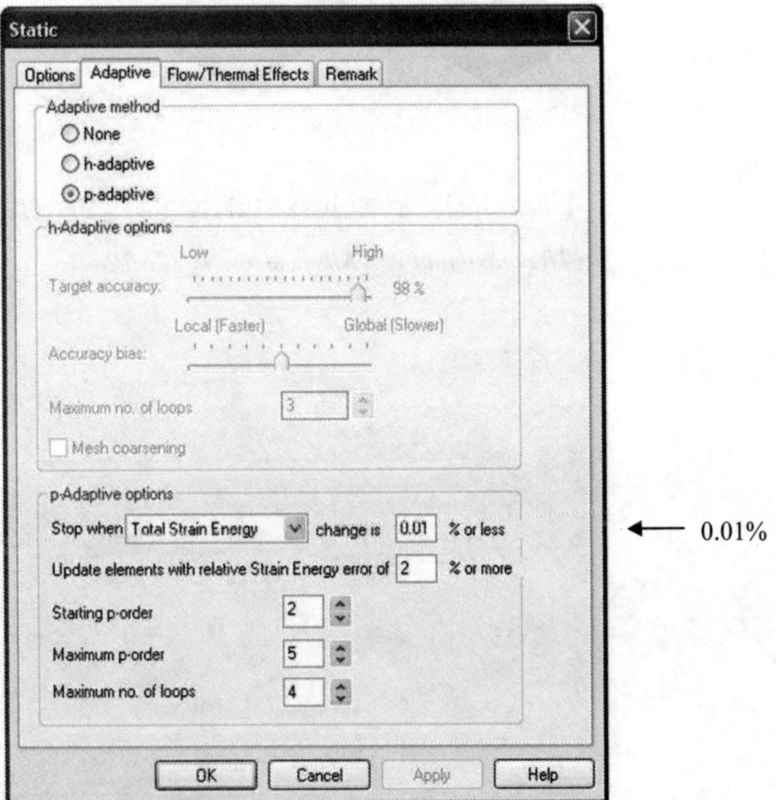

Figure 13-10: p-adaptive solution settings for study *p adaptive 02*

A very demanding convergence requirement forces the solver to go up to the highest available p order (5) and hence to perform the maximum possible number of iterations (4).

Von Mises stress results of study *p adaptive 02* are shown in Figure 13-11.

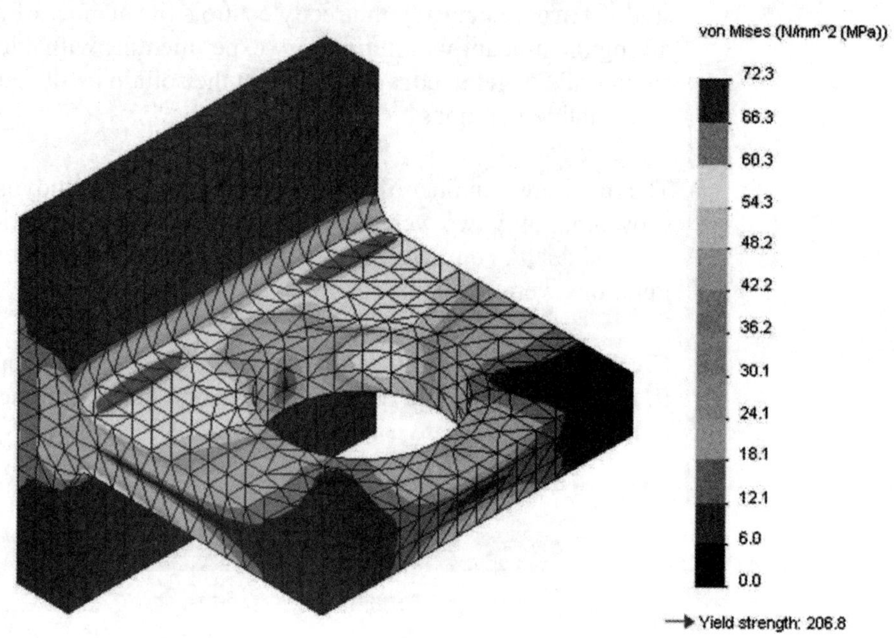

Figure 13-11: Von Mises stress results of study *p adaptive 02*

The maximum von Mises stress is 72MPa.

Convergence of von Mises stress results obtained in the *p adaptive 02* study is shown in Figure 13-12.

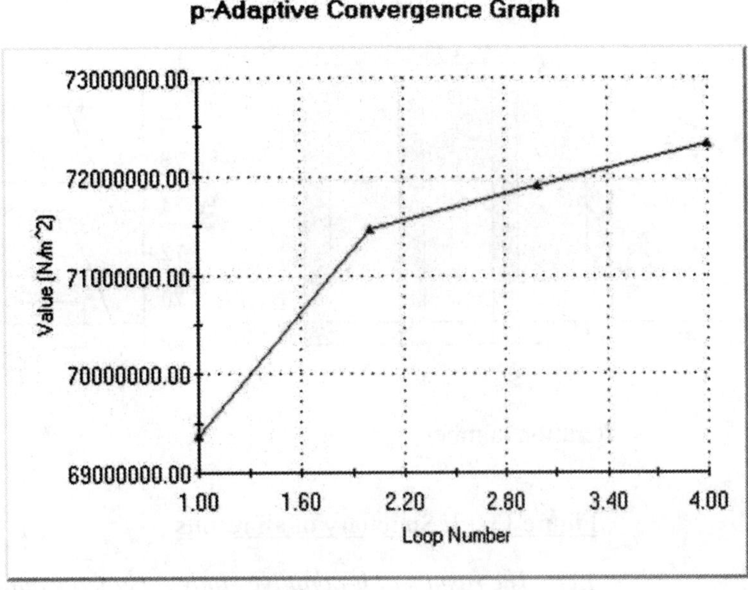

Figure 13-12: Convergence of von Mises stress results obtained in *p adaptive 02* study

The p adaptive convergence graph shows that four iterations were performed.

When the maximum number of iterations is performed as shown in Figure 13-12, we get no feedback as to whether the solution stopped because the specified accuracy in study properties was achieved, or because the maximum allowed number of iterations was reached. In the h-adaptive solution the maximum number of iterations is 5, in p-adaptive solution the maximum number of iterations is 4 and coincides with the highest available element order 5.

A summary of results obtained in all studies is shown in Figure 13-13. These graphs were prepared outside of SolidWorks **Simulation** based on data exported from SolidWorks **Simulation** graphs.

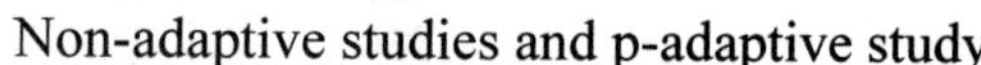

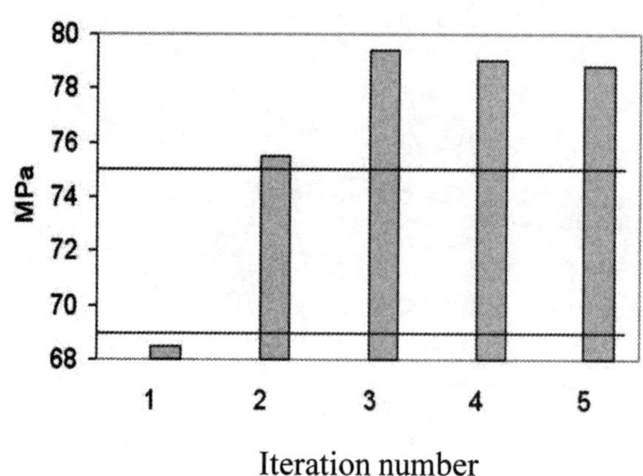

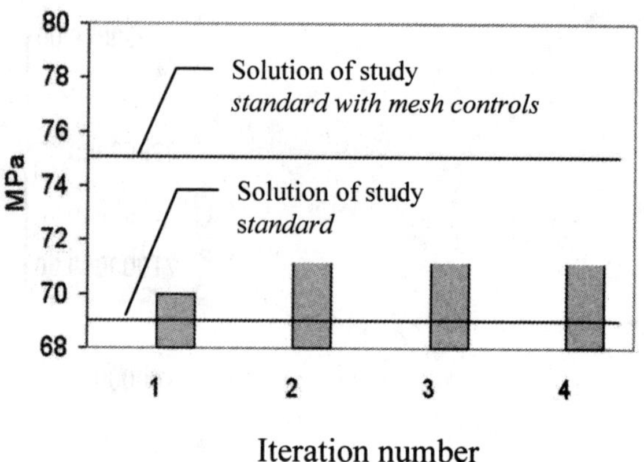

Figure 13-13: Summary of all results

***Left**: The results of h-adaptive study repeated from Figure 13-9*

***Right**: The results of two non adaptive studies shown with the horizontal lines and the results of p adaptive studies shown with bars.*

Examine the right graph in Figure 13-13 and notice that the first two iterations are the results of study *p adaptive 01*. All four iterations 1,2,3,4 are the results of study *p adaptive 02*. The difference between studies *p adaptive 01* and *p adaptive 02* is that in study *p adaptive 02,* two more iterations were performed because of more demanding study settings.

You are encouraged to repeat both h and p convergence studies using an initially more refined mesh and different convergence criteria.

Which one of the three solution methods is preferred? The "regular" method using h-elements (here studies *standard* and *standard with mesh controls*), the h-adaptive solution (*h adaptive* study), or the p-adaptive solution (*p adaptive 01* and *p adaptive 02* studies)?

Experience indicates that second order h-elements offer the best combination of accuracy and computational simplicity. For this reason, the SolidWorks **Simulation** mesher is tuned to create h-element meshes. This makes h-elements preferable over p-elements. Also, a p-adaptive solution is much more computationally intensive than a standard or adaptive h-element solution. For these reasons, the p-adaptive solution should be reserved for special cases where solution accuracy must be known according to the settings available in the p-adaptive study.

This leaves us with the choice between standard and h-adaptive solution methods. The h-adaptive solution is more computationally demanding and more time-consuming than the standard solution. At the same time, it offers a very important advantage: it relieves users from the need to exercise judgment over meshing choices. In a standard solution users must decide if a default mesh is acceptable and how it should be modified by specifying mesh controls and/or global refinement. The h-adaptive solution automatically takes care of refining the mesh (both globally and locally).

With increasing computational power and decreasing cost of computer hardware, the h-adaptive solution is becoming the preferred solution method in SolidWorks **Simulation**.

Both h-adaptive and p-adaptive methods are great learning tools, leading to better understanding of element order, the convergence process, and discretization error. For this reason, readers are encouraged to repeat some, if not all of the previous exercises using both adaptive solution methods presented in this chapter.

Notes:

14: Drop test of a porcelain ring

Topics covered

- Drop test analysis
- Stress wave propagation
- Direct time integration solution

Project description

A ceramic porcelain ring is dropped from the height of 500mm and lands flat on a flat and horizontal rigid floor (Figure 14-1). We will simulate the impact using a **Drop Test** analysis.

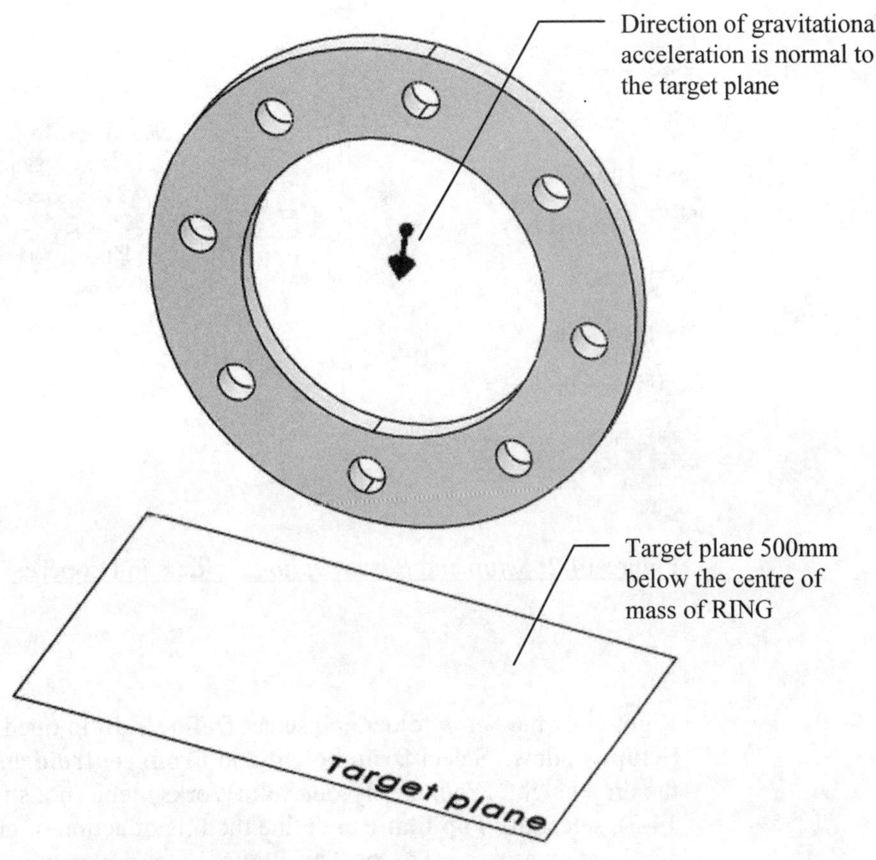

Figure 14-1: RING landing square on a rigid floor

Procedure

Open the part file called RING. It has ceramic porcelain material properties already assigned. Note the split lines added to the RING geometry.

Create a study *drop* specifying **Drop Test.** SolidWorks **Simulation** creates two folders in the **Drop Test** study: *Setup* and *Result Options* (Figure 14-2).

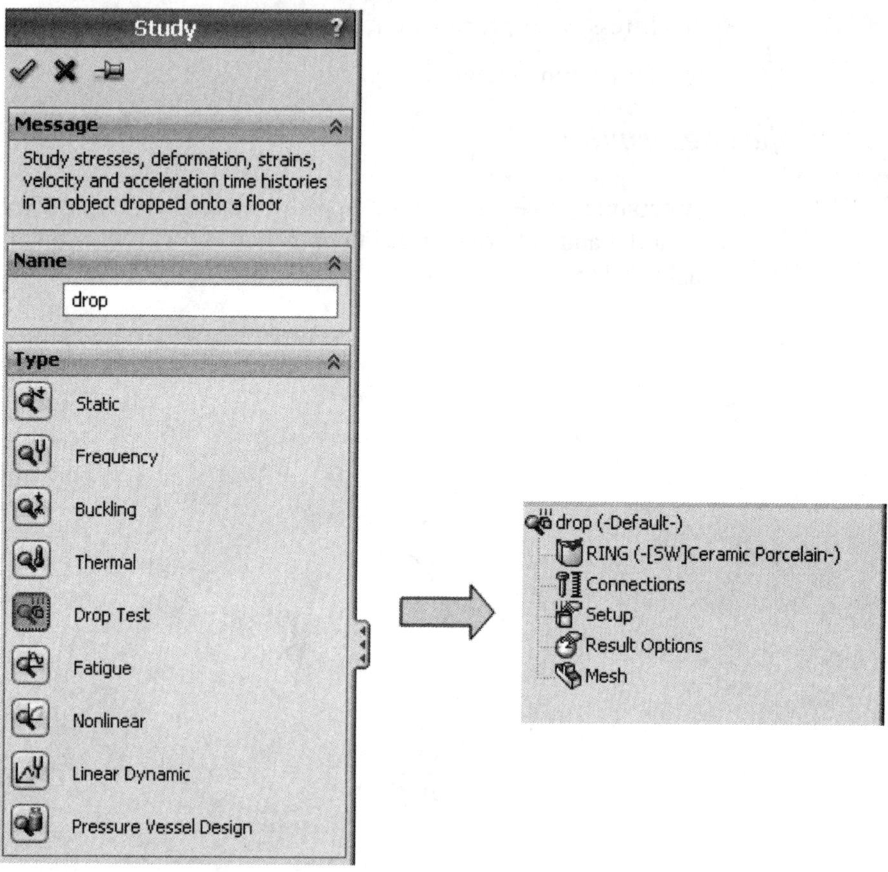

Figure 14-2: *Setup* and *Result Options* folders in Drop Test study

Right-click the *Setup* folder and select **Define/Edit** to open the **Drop Test Setup** window. Select **Drop height** and **From centroid** and enter 500mm as the drop height. From the fly-out SolidWorks menu (not shown in Figure 14-3), select the **Top Plane** to define the line of action of gravitational acceleration as normal to the **Top Plane**. Enter the magnitude of gravitational acceleration as $9.81 m/s^2$. Finally, select **Normal to gravity** as **Target Orientation**. After completing the exercise, try experimenting with a different **Target Orientation** using the **Parallel to Ref. Plane** option in the **Drop Test Setup** window (Figure 14-3).

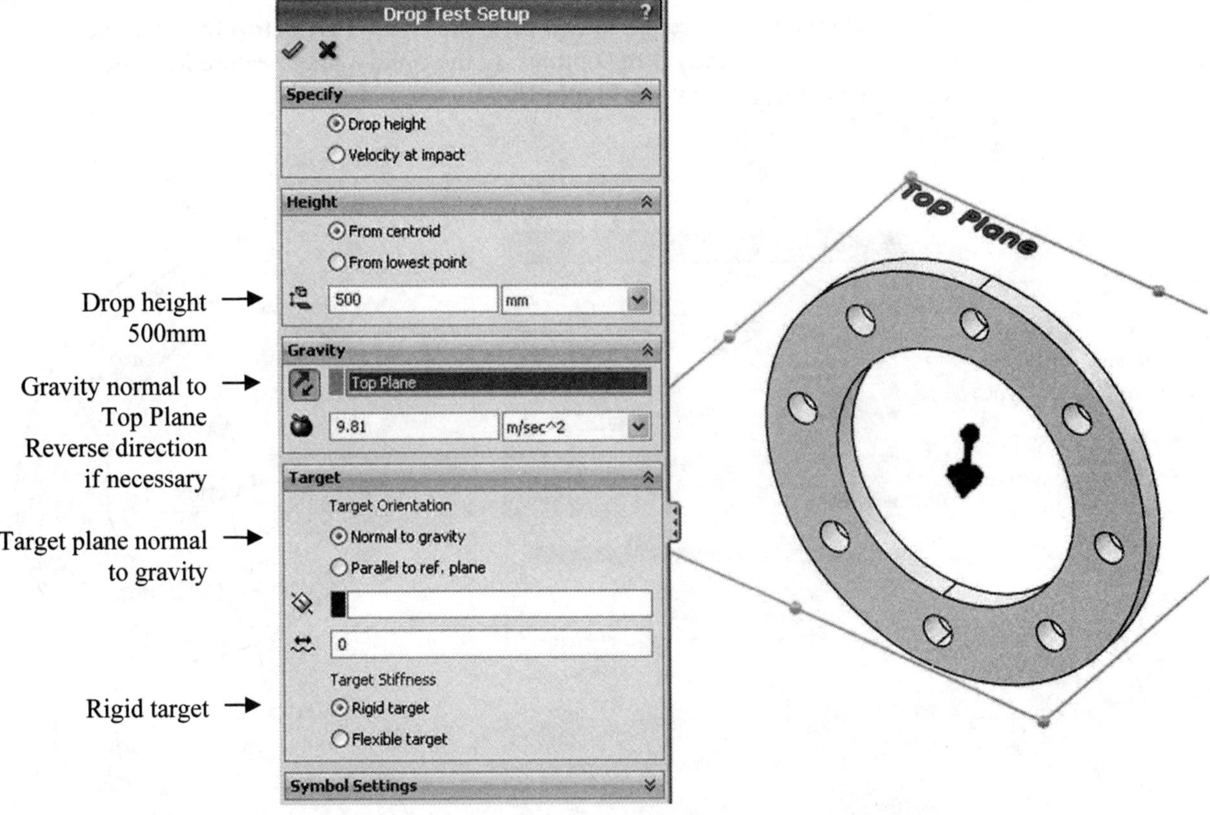

Figure 14-3: **Drop Test Setup** window

RING landing perfectly square on a rigid floor may not be a realistic scenario but allows for an illustrative review of Drop Test.

Make sure the gravity is pointing down. Reverse the direction if necessary.

Having defined all the required entries in the **Drop Test Setup** window, we now need to define the results options. In the SolidWorks Feature Manager, define a **Sensor** as shown in Figure 14-4.

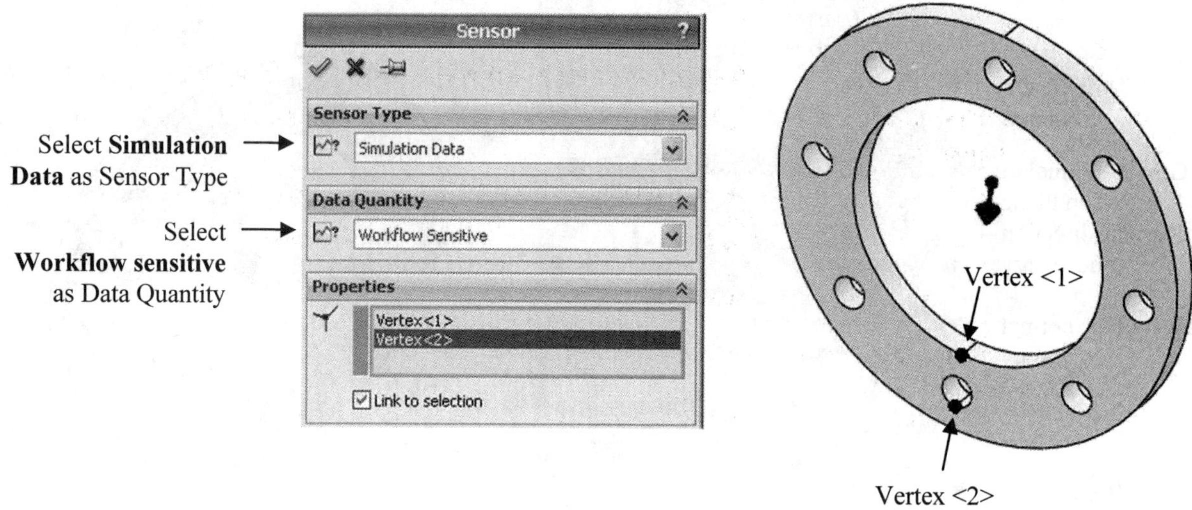

Figure 14-4: Sensor defined in two locations

Locations of vertices used in Results Options. Vertices are created by split lines in the SolidWorks model.

Referring to Figure 14-4, note that sensors are defined where we expect the highest P1 stress. Note that the maximum principal stress relates to the failure of porcelain, which is a brittle material.

Right-click the *Result Options* folder to open the **Result Options** window.

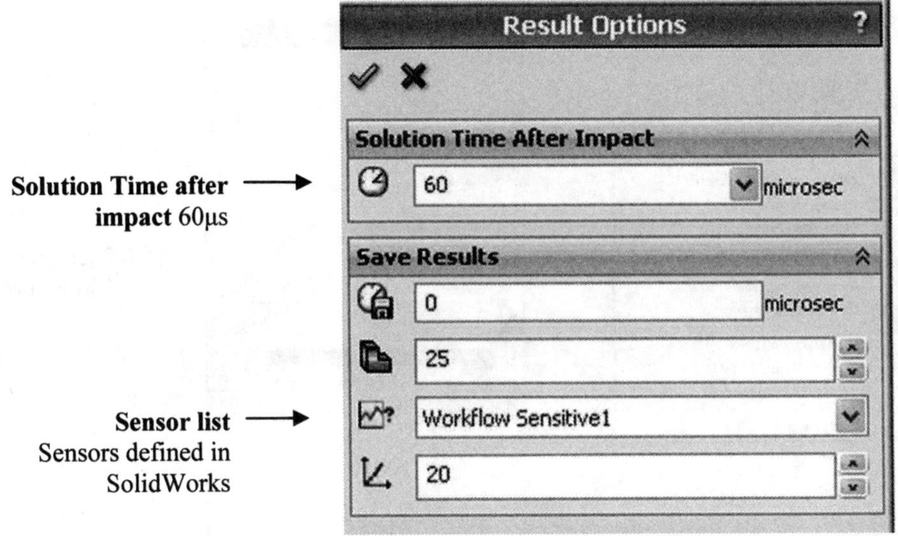

Figure 14-5: Result Options window

To monitor what happens to the ring during the first 60 microseconds after the first impact, enter 60 as **Solution time after impact**. See SolidWorks **Simulation** help for more information.

In the **Save Results** area of the **Result Options** window, accept the default 0 (microseconds) meaning that results will be saved immediately after the first impact. Also, accept the default 25 for the **No. of plots**. This means that the solution time is divided into twenty five intervals and full results (available as plots) are saved only for these intervals.

Note that full results are saved for the 25 plots spaced out evenly over a 60 microseconds time period.

Since the impact time is very short, it is measured in microseconds. The maximum displacements or stress may occur during the first impact, or later when the model is rebounding. A sufficiently long solution time needs to be specified to capture maximum displacement and stress.

Mesh with default element size and run the solution. Upon completion of the solution, SolidWorks **Simulation** creates the following result folders: *Stress, Displacement and Strain*. To view a time history graph, right-click the *Results* folder and select **Define Time History Plot** (Figure 14-6).

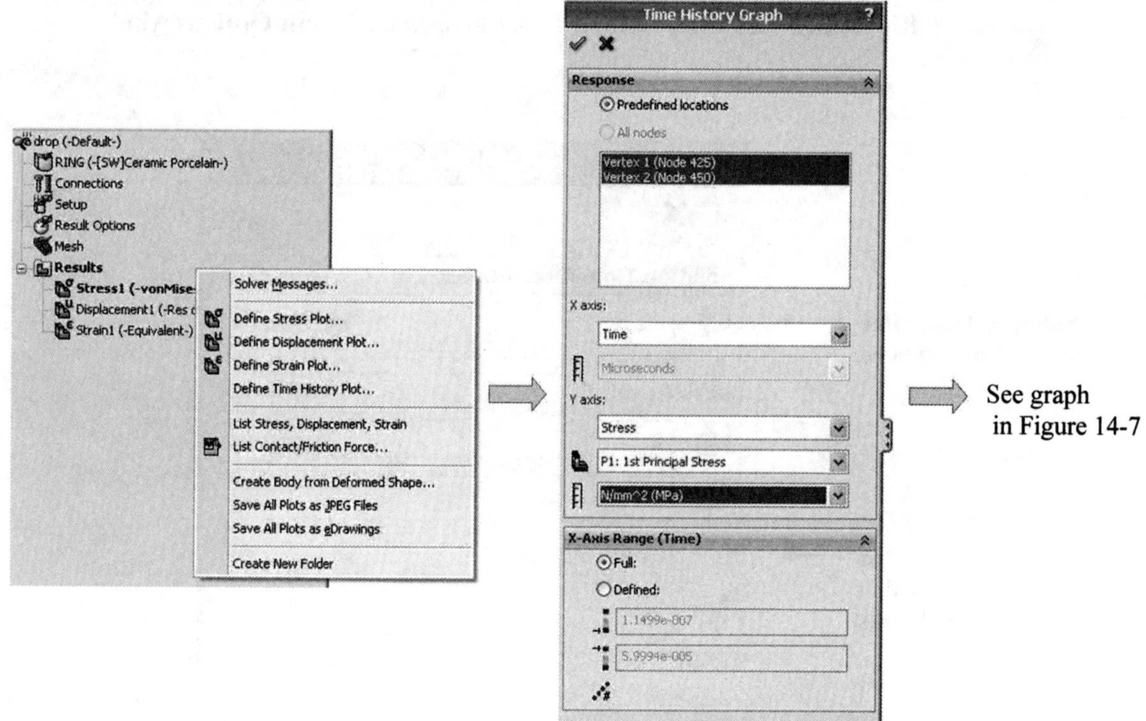

Figure 14-6: Define Time History Graph creates graphs of stress, displacement, velocity and acceleration as functions of time

Graphs are created for locations defined by sensors.

Based on the review of the **Time History Graph** we find that the highest P1 stress occurs at a time of 24 microseconds (move the cursor over the plot to find this time value). Therefore, we can create a P1 stress plot that approximately corresponds to this time point (Figure 14-7).

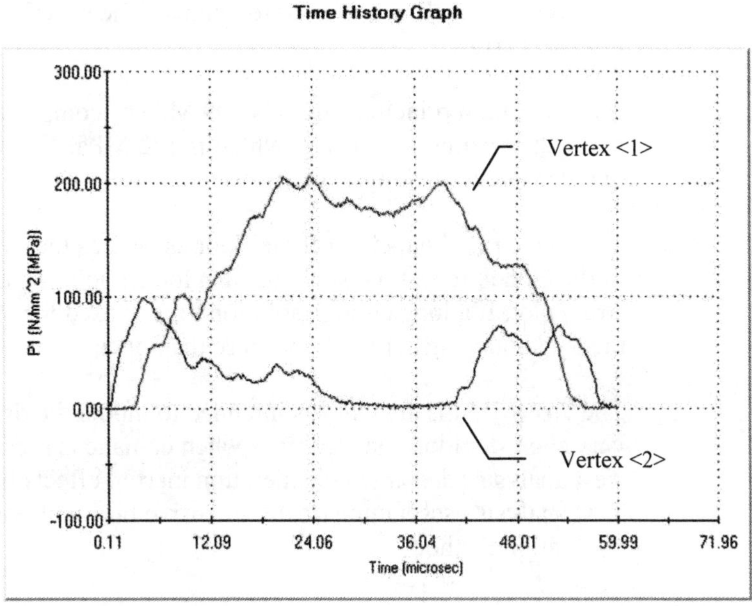

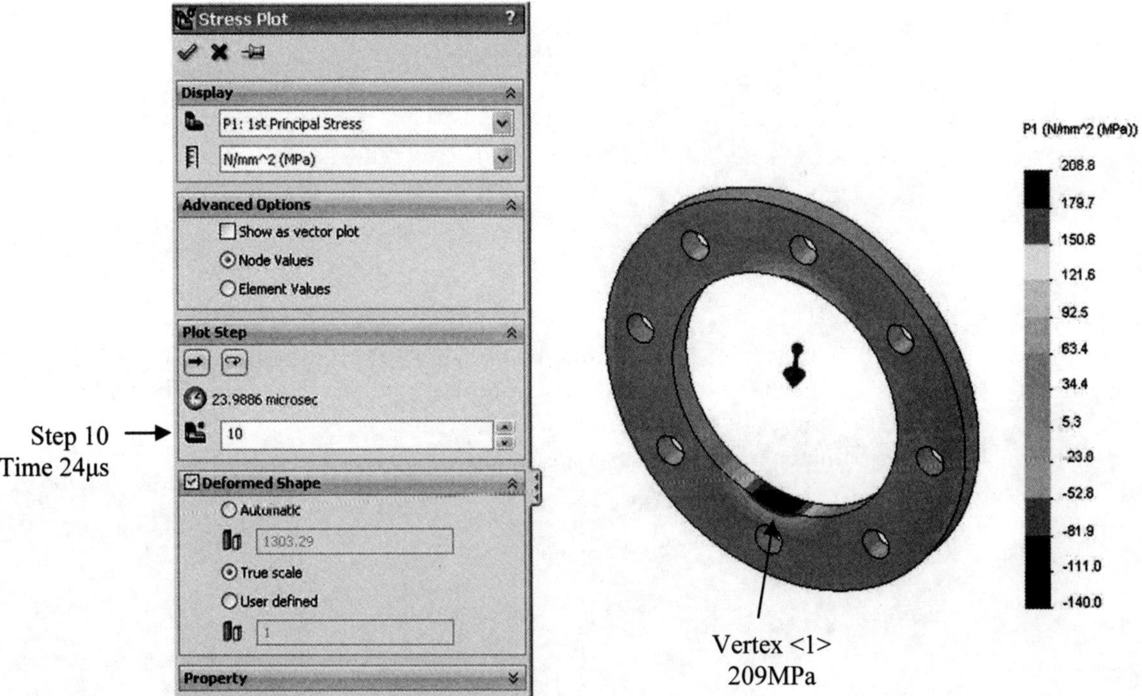

Figure 14-7: The highest P1 stress plot during the analyzed 60μs of impact

Animate this plot to see dynamic impact.

Will the ring break? The **Drop Test** analysis does not directly provide pass/fail results. It is best used to compare the severity of impact for different drop scenarios.

The maximum principal stress is 209 MPa as compared to the ultimate strength of ceramic porcelain which is 172 MPa. This comparison indicates that damage to the ring is likely.

To see the ring bouncing off the floor as well as the stress wave propagating in the model, repeat the study using a longer solution time and animate the stress plot. If a long enough solution time is used for the analysis you will see the ring bouncing off the floor more than once.

The **Drop Test** is an analysis intended to model the dynamic impact force of very short durations, since this is when damage is most likely to occur. **Drop Test** analysis takes into consideration inertial effects but no damping. **Drop Test** analysis uses a numerically intensive but stable direct (explicit) time integration method.

15: Selected nonlinear problems

Topics covered

- Large displacement analysis
- Membrane effects
- Following and non following load
- Non-linear material analysis
- Residual stress

In all previous exercises we assumed that the model stiffness did not change significantly when the model deformed due to the applied load. Consequently, the stiffness only needed to be calculated once, before any load had been applied. Since this stiffness adequately described model behavior during the entire loading process, the model stiffness did not have to be updated and the load could be applied in one single step. The only time we departed from these assumptions was in the analysis of the contact problem.

We will now discuss a few problems where the stiffness changes globally due to the model displacing under a load (not local, as in the contact problem). These problems require **Large displacement** formulation which is an option in a **Static** study (Figure 15-1).

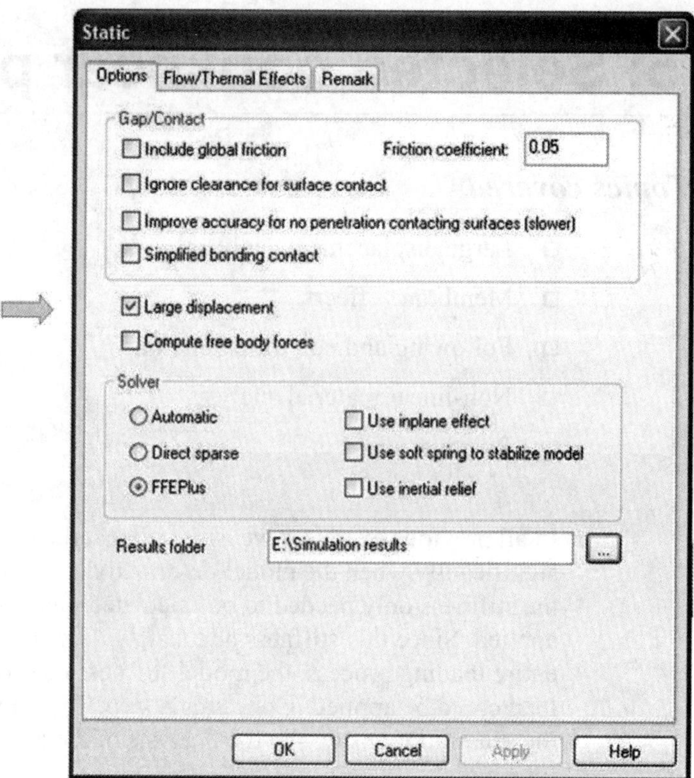

Figure 15-1: Large displacement option in Static study

You may always select the Large displacement option, whether necessary or not. However, this significantly increases solution time.

Open model NL002 and review SolidWorks Feature Manager. Note that an offset surface has been inserted in the middle of beam thickness and solid bodies have been deleted. Therefore, the model contains only surface geometry. **Simulation** will recognize it and will mesh the model with shell elements.

Create two static studies: *linear* and *nonlinear.* Check the **Large displacement** option in the properties of the *nonlinear* study. This is the only difference between these two studies.

When a study is created using a model with surfaces only, we need to define shell thickness. Note that this was not required in chapter 4 where a sheet metal model was analyzed. This was because shell thickness was taken from solid model geometry. Right-click the shell folder and select **Edit Definition** from the pop-up menu. In the **Shell Definition** window, select **Thin** as the shell element type and enter 2mm for shell thickness (Figure 15-2). Material properties are transferred automatically from the SolidWorks model.

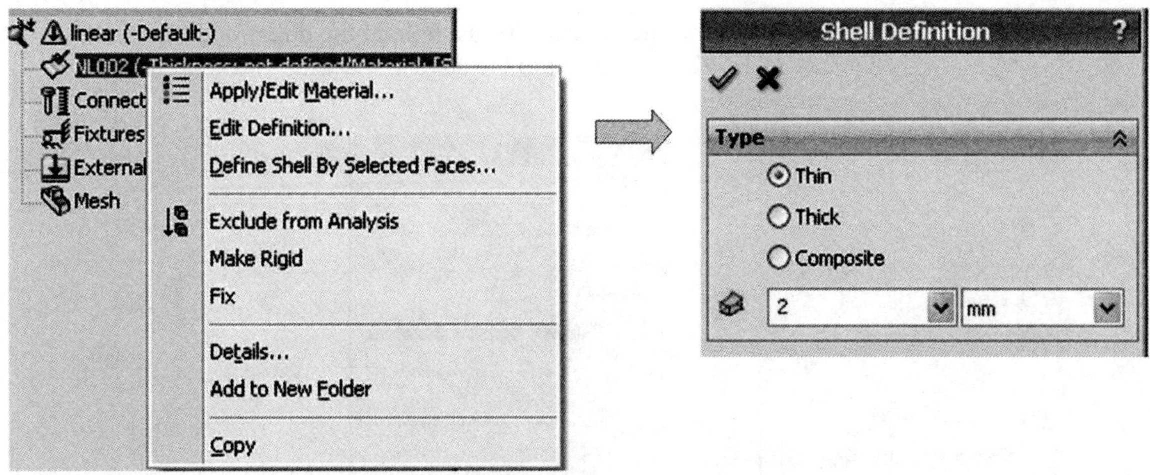

Figure 15-2: Shell Definition window

Thin shell and thick shell models respectively, have a constant and parabolic transverse shear stress distribution across their thickness. Refer to Simulation help for information on Composite shells.

Apply a 10N force to the edge of the last hole in the direction normal to the Top plane, and a **Fixed** restraint to the edge at the wide end (Figure 15-3).

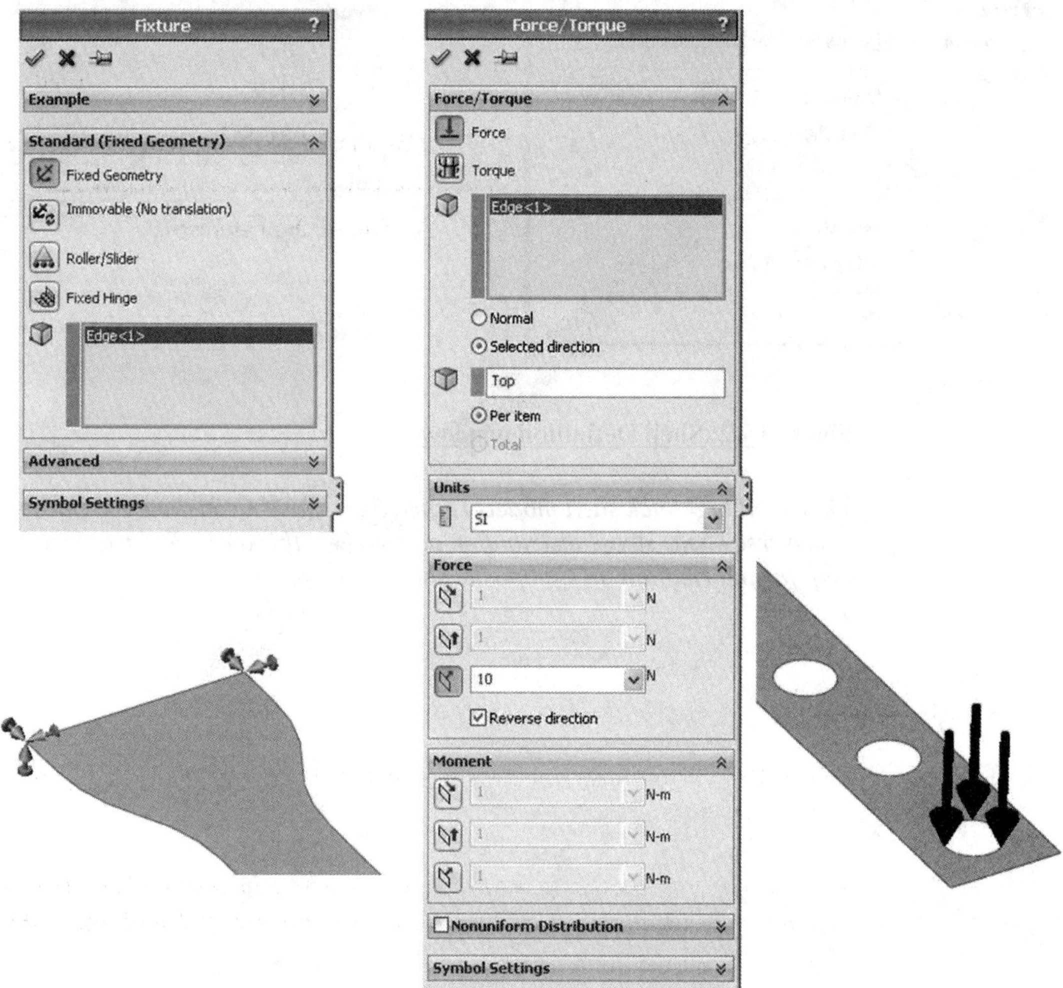

Figure 15-3: Loads and restraints

Note that the Fixture window offers the choice Immovable. This is because shell elements are analyzed. In our case, defining restraint as Immovable would result in a hinge.

Now mesh the model with shells (Figure 15-4).

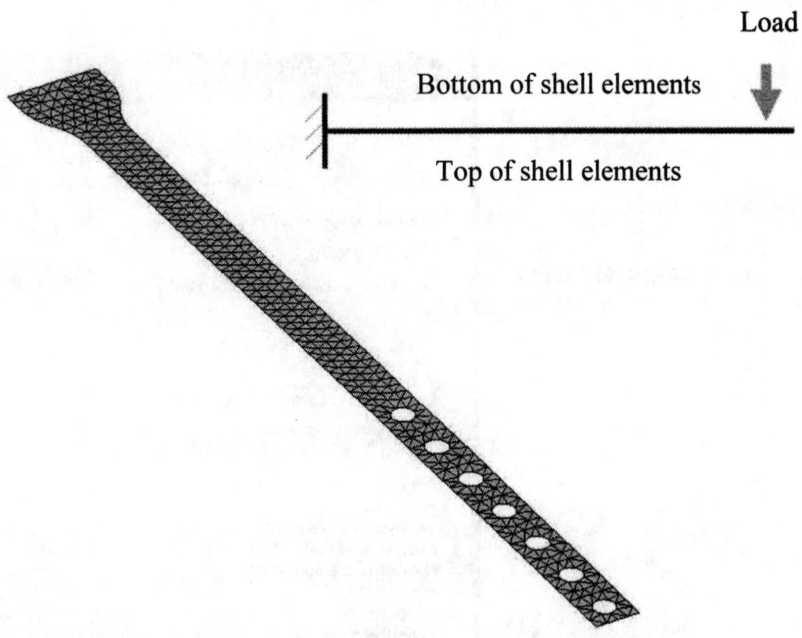

Figure 15-4: Shell mesh orientation is such that bottoms of shell elements are on the load side

This mesh shows orange in color on the side where load is applied. As you remember for chapter 4, bottoms of shell elements are by default marked with orange color.

Solve the study *nonlinear* with the **Large displacement** option checked. Solving with the **Large displacement** option is a nonlinear solution, which progresses in iterations. The load is increased in automatically determined steps while the model stiffness is updated according to progressing displacement (Figure 15-5).

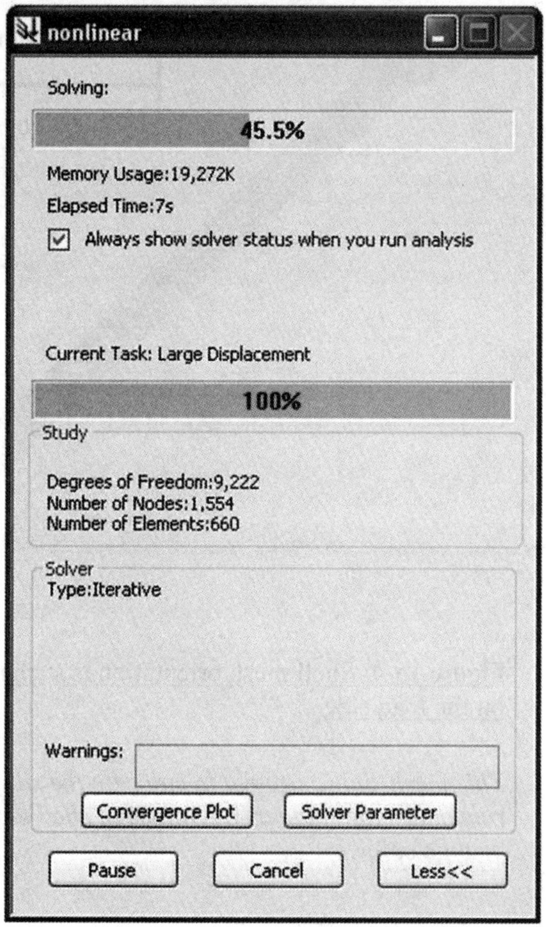

Figure 15-5: Nonlinear solution (with Large displacement option) progresses in iterations while the load gradually increases and the stiffness is updated

Due to the iterative nature of the Large displacement solution, the solution time is much longer in comparison to the corresponding linear solution.

The solution without the **Large displacement** option displays a warning message (Figure 15-6) that must be acknowledged to complete the solution process.

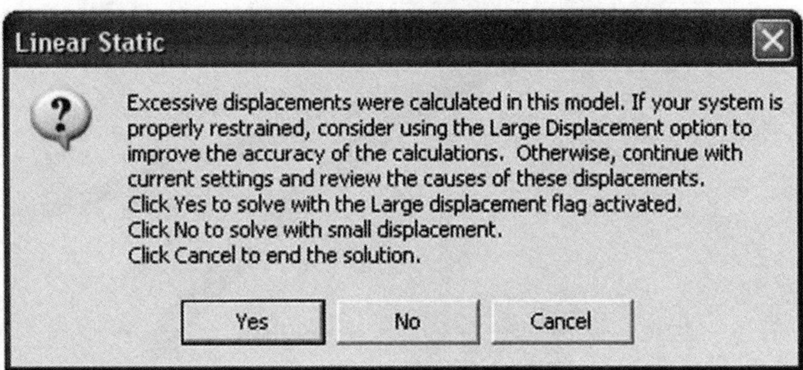

Linear Static
Excessive displacements were calculated in this model. If your system is properly restrained, consider using the Large Displacement option to improve the accuracy of the calculations. Otherwise, continue with current settings and review the causes of these displacements.
Click Yes to solve with the Large displacement flag activated.
Click No to solve with small displacement.
Click Cancel to end the solution.
Yes
No
Cancel

Figure 15-6: A warning message displayed by the solver if large displacements are detected and Large displacement option is NOT checked

To obtain a linear solution select No.

The above message is displayed if the maximum resultant displacement is larger than the default element size. Depending on the problem, it may be okay to ignore it.

Create displacement plots obtained from the nonlinear and linear solutions (Figure 15-7). Use a 1:1 scale of deformation for both plots.

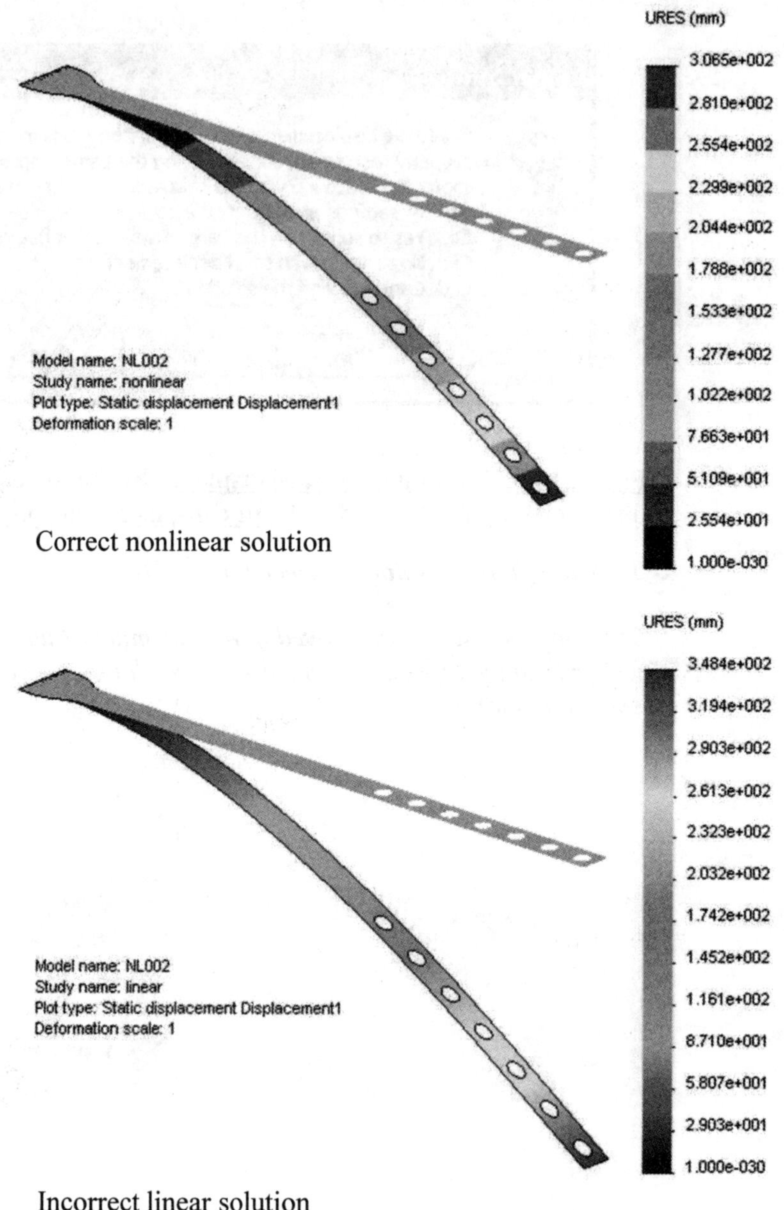

Figure 15-7: Nonlinear solution (top), obtained with the Large displacement option shows the deformed model. Compare this with the incorrect linear solution (bottom)

The undeformed model is superimposed on both plots. Note that the linear solution produces an incorrect pattern of deformation where the tip of the beam travels along a straight line and the beam appears to be stretching out.

Now create two stress plots based on the nonlinear solution using a 1:1 scale of deformation. Create a von Mises stress plot for the bottoms of shell elements and for the tops of shell elements

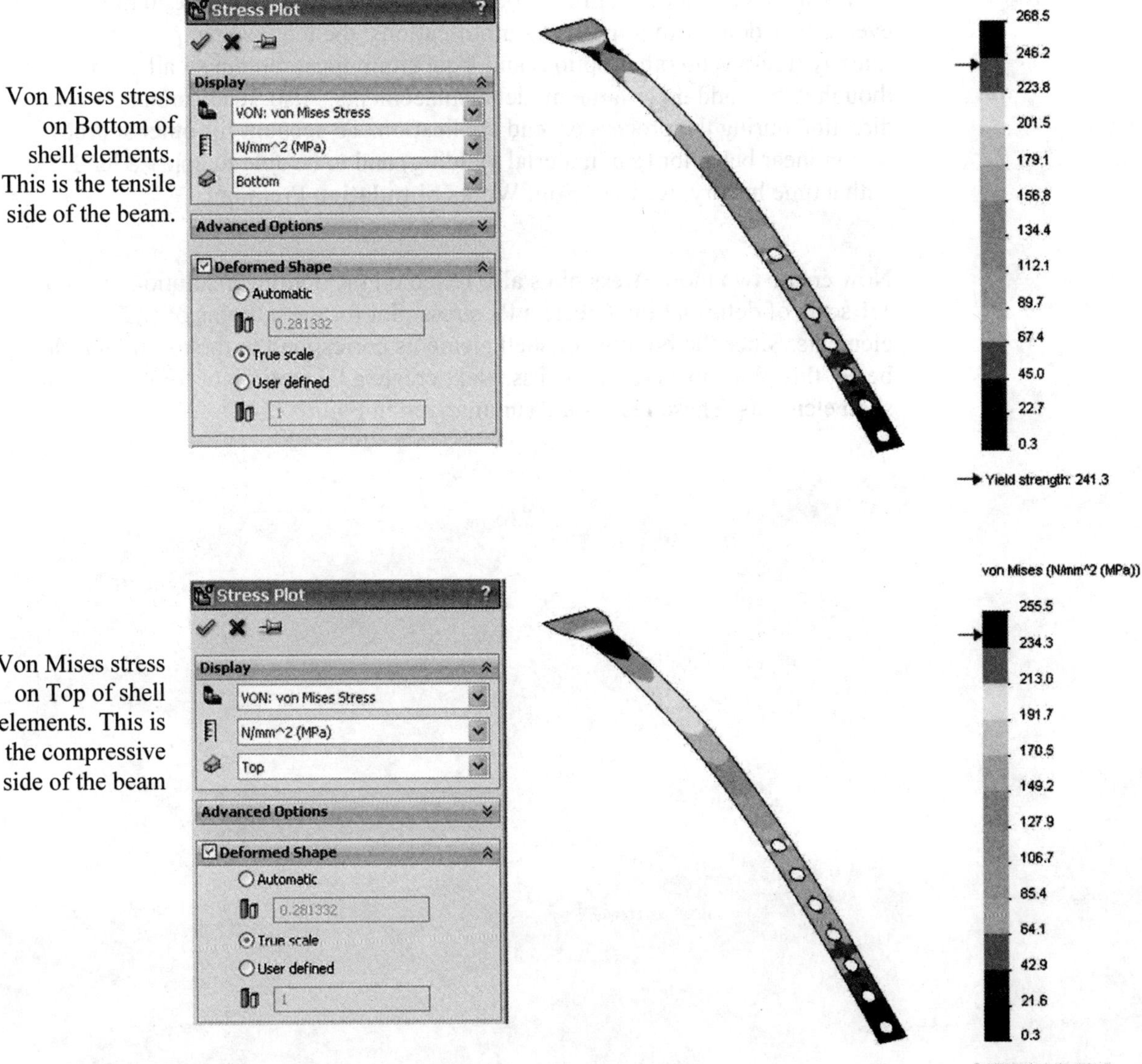

Figure 15-8: Von Mises stress results for element Bottom (top illustration) and element Top (bottom illustration)

Both plots show similar stress magnitudes because von Mises stress is not sensitive to stress sign. Tensile and compressive stresses equally contribute to von Mises stress.

Examine the plots in Figure 15-8 to notice that von Mises stress on the bottom side (tensile side) is 269MPa, and that von Mises stress on the top side (compressive) side is 256MPa. Both values are above yield. Even though we run a nonlinear analysis, the only source of nonlinear behavior is the large displacement. Material yield is not modeled. SolidWorks **Simulation** Professional can model nonlinear behavior due to **Large displacement** and even that is done with important simplifications; the load is "ramped up" linearly (there is no other option) and local strain must remain small even though it may add up to large model displacements. Also, load cannot change direction during the process of load application. To account for other sources of nonlinear behavior (e.g. material yielding) and to be able to apply a load with a time history, we need SolidWorks **Simulation** Premium.

Now create two more stress plots also based on the nonlinear solution using a 1:1 scale of deformation. Create a P1 stress plot for the bottoms of shell elements. Since the bottoms of shell elements correspond to the top side of the beam, this plot shows tensile stress. Next create a P3 stress plot for the tops of shell elements. These results are summarized in Figure 15-9.

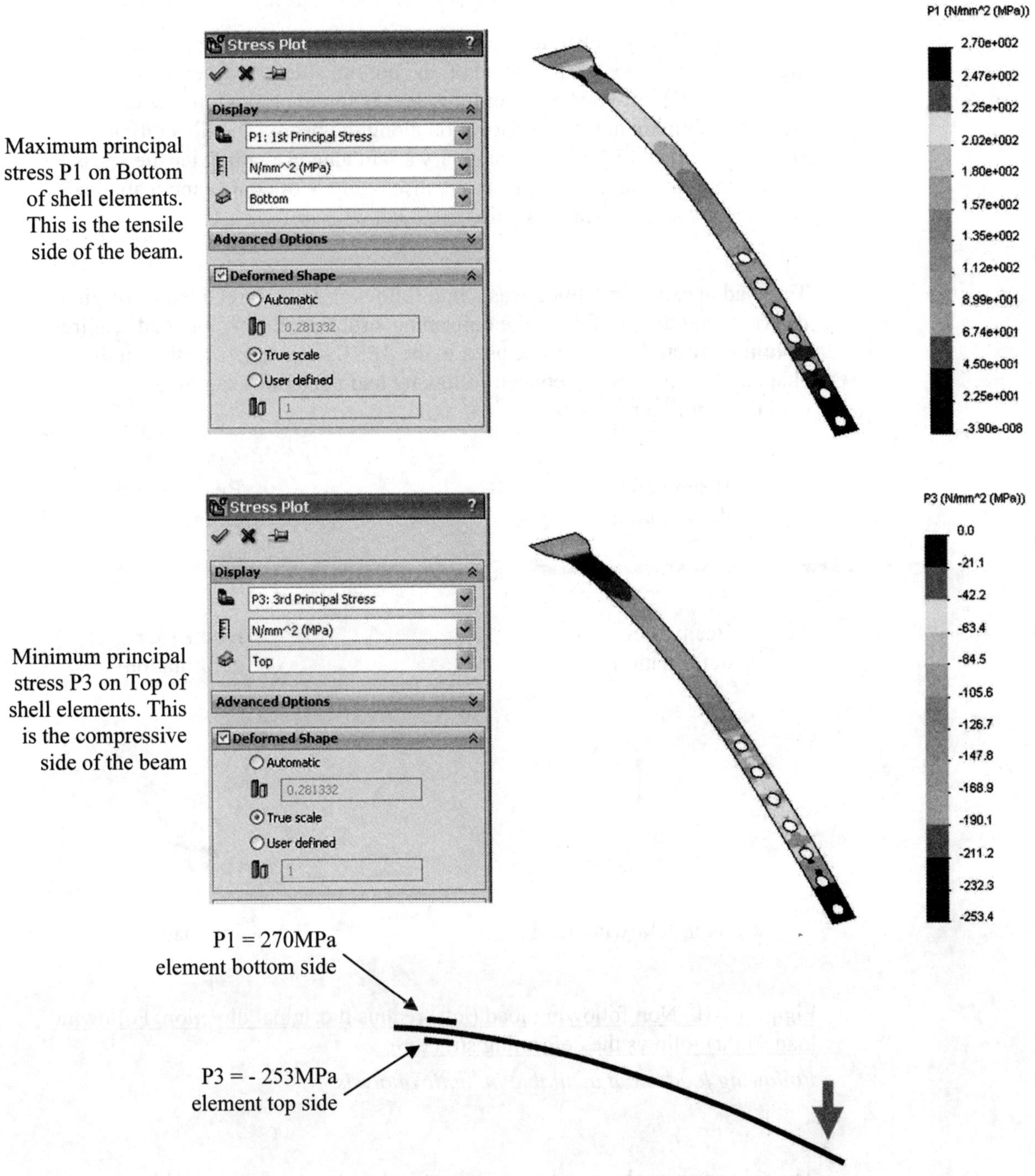

Figure 15-9: P1 stress results for element Bottoms (top illustration) and P3 stress results element Tops (bottom illustration)

Figure 15-9 clearly illustrates shell element capability to model bending. The highest P1 stress (tensile) is found on the bottom side of elements and the numerically lowest P3 stress (compressive) is found on the top side of elements, both are in the same location along the beam. The illustration in the bottom of Figure 15-9 shows imaginary strain gauges reading tensile stress P1 and compressive stress P3. The above discussion is of course applicable to both linear and nonlinear analysis

The load in example NL002 was a non following load; it retained its original direction and did not follow the deforming structure. Following load requires a **Nonlinear** study and will be used in the SPRING example further in this chapter. The difference between following and non-following load is explained in Figure 15-10.

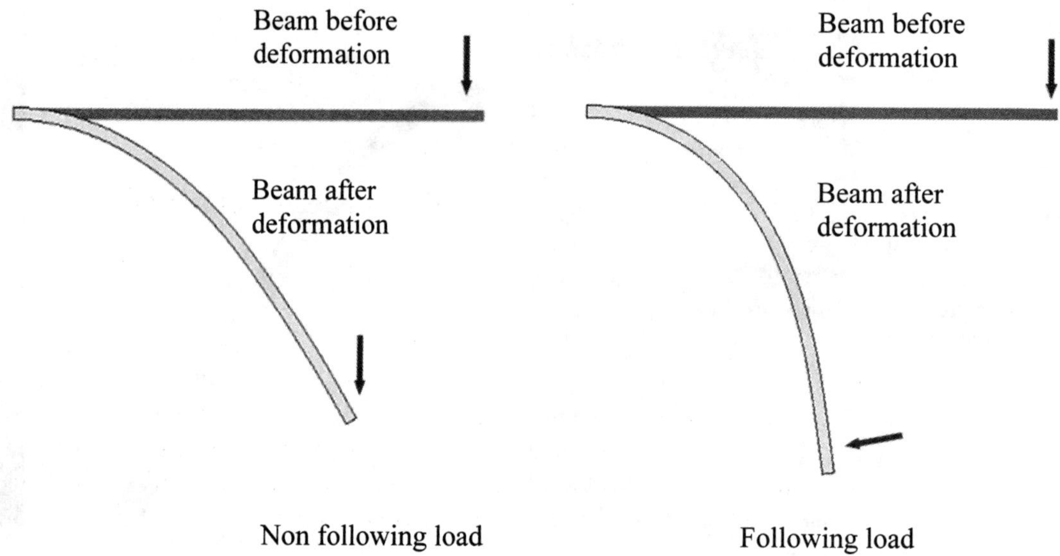

Figure 15-10: Non following load (left) retains it original direction. Following load (right) follows the deforming structure

Following load is not available in Static analysis

The second example introduces a large displacement combined with a contact problem. To illustrate this nonlinear contact problem, we analyze a plastic part CLIP (Figure 15-11).

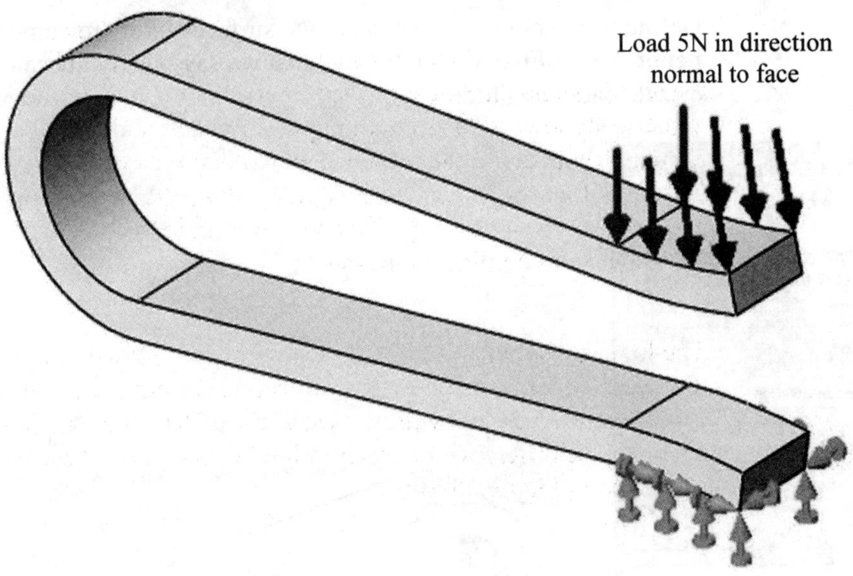

Figure 15-11: The CLIP model complete with load and restraint

Two surfaces, defined in a contact pair, will experience large displacement (even though not quite as large as in NL002 example) before contacting each other. Therefore, the **Large displacement** option must be selected in the properties of the **Static** study. There are two sources of nonlinear behavior we have to account for: large displacement and contact.

Define local contact set between two surfaces likely to come in contact as: **No penetration** (Figure 15-12). Note that we say "likely" because this depends on the load magnitude.

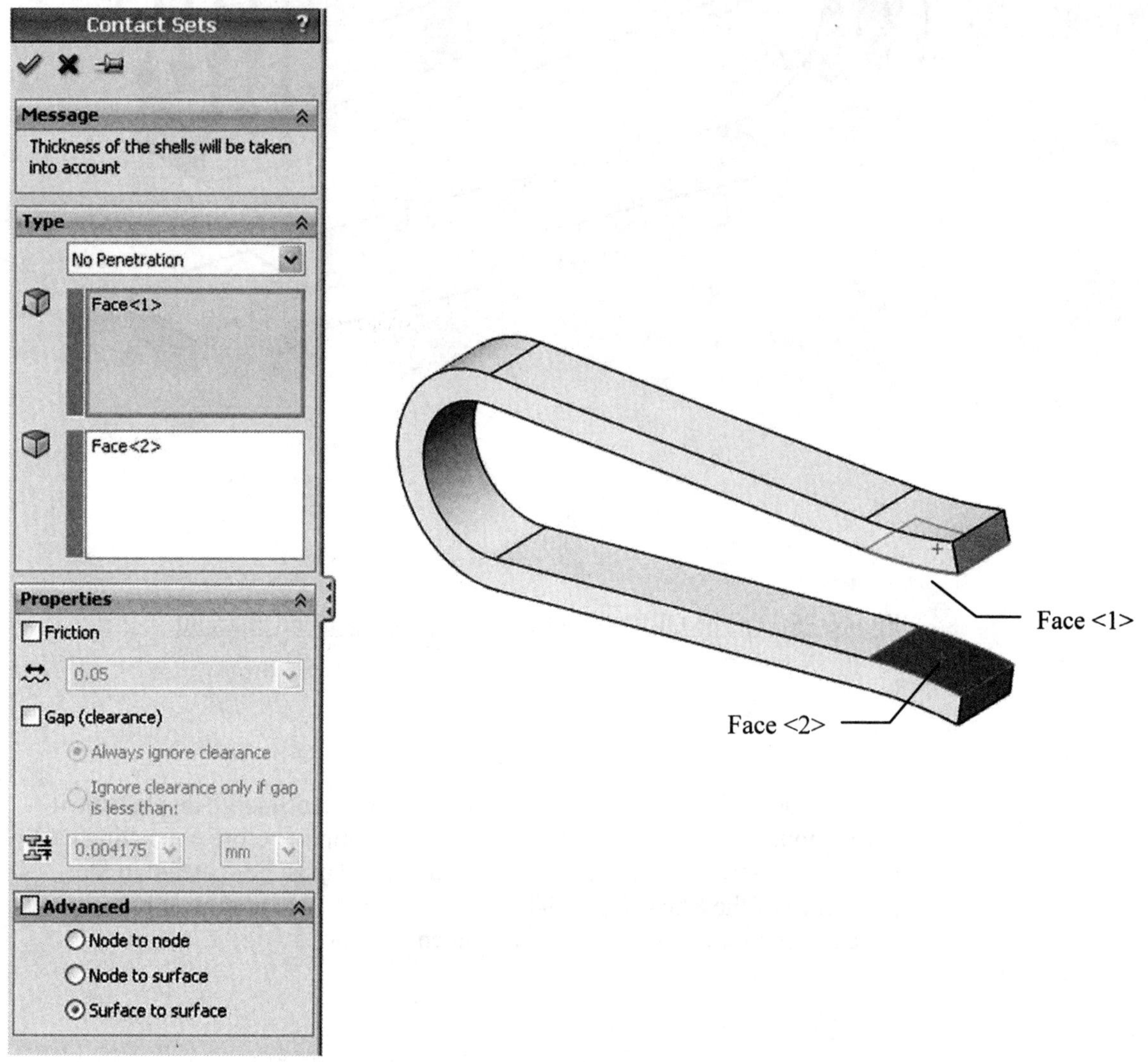

Figure 15-12: Definition of Contact Set. Surface to surface contact is required when faces are not initially touching but may come in contact under the applied load.

Split lines in the SolidWorks model define small faces that may come in contact. The smaller size of the contacting faces shortens the solution time.

Mesh the assembly with the default element size, and then obtain two solutions: one with the **Large displacement** option selected, and the other without. Compare the displacement results obtained from these two studies (Figure 15-13).

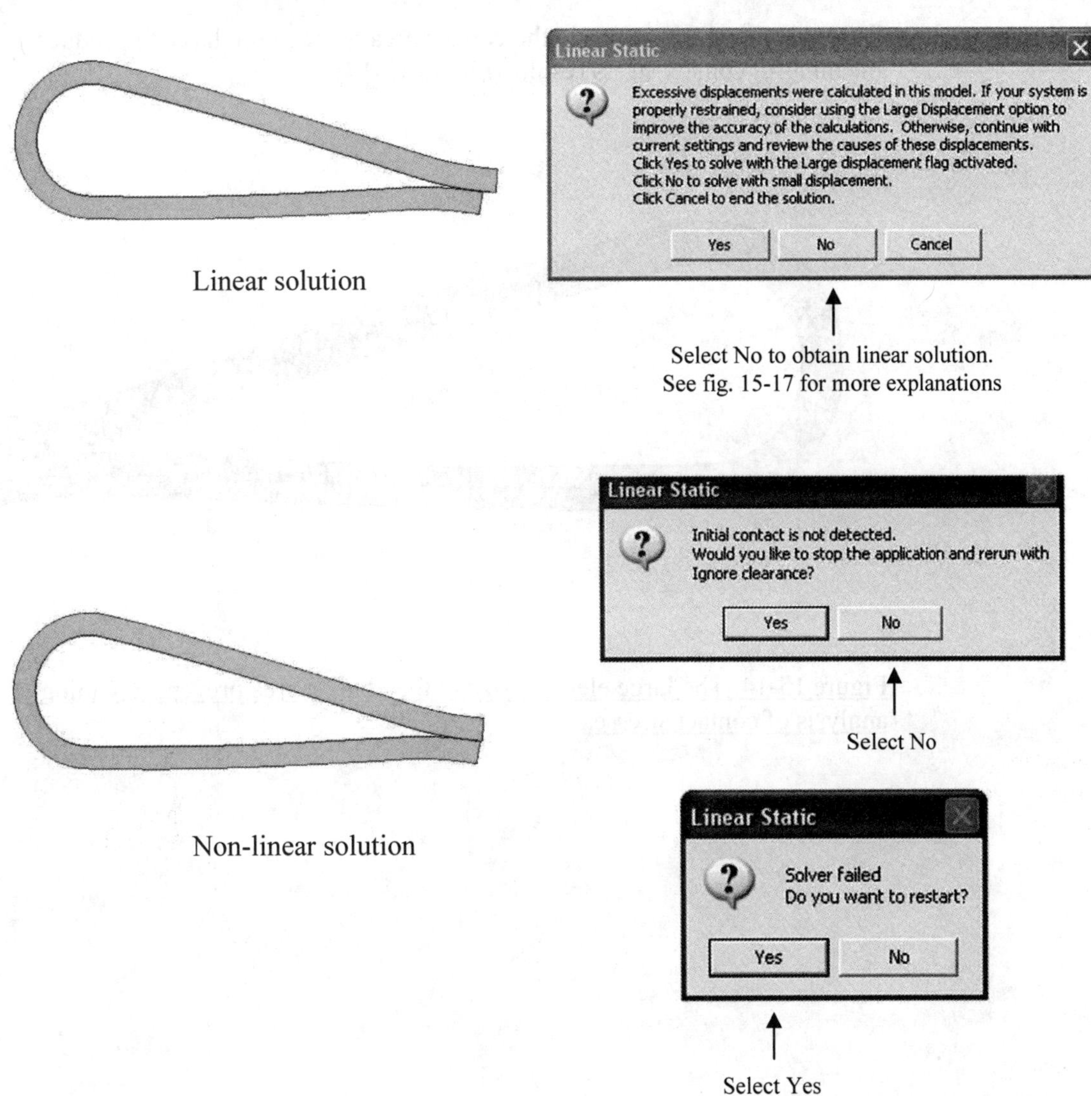
Linear Static
Excessive displacements were calculated in this model. If your system is properly restrained, consider using the Large Displacement option to improve the accuracy of the calculations. Otherwise, continue with current settings and review the causes of these displacements.
Click Yes to solve with the Large displacement flag activated.
Click No to solve with small displacement.
Click Cancel to end the solution.
Yes
No
Cancel
Linear solution
Select No to obtain linear solution.
See fig. 15-17 for more explanations
Linear Static
Initial contact is not detected.
Would you like to stop the application and rerun with Ignore clearance?
Yes
No
Select No
Non-linear solution
Linear Static
Solver failed
Do you want to restart?
Yes
No
Select Yes

Figure 15-13: Incorrect displacement results produced without **Large displacement** option (top) and correct displacement results produced with the **Large displacement** option selected (bottom). The Gap did not close properly in the solution executed without the Large displacement option.

Also shown are solver messages that need to be acknowledged in each solution. The solver messages depend on the type of solver used. The incorrect linear solution was obtained with Direct Sparse solver. Try obtaining the same with the iterative solver FFEPlus to see that solution becomes numerically unstable and produces completely meaningless results.

The iterative solver FFEPlus was used to obtain the correct, non linear solution. The Direct Sparse solver produced the same results within the range of numerical error. The solver is selected in Study properties.

If the solution fails, choose to restart the analysis.

Note that the element size in the contact area is much too large to produce meaningful contact stress results (Figure 15-14).

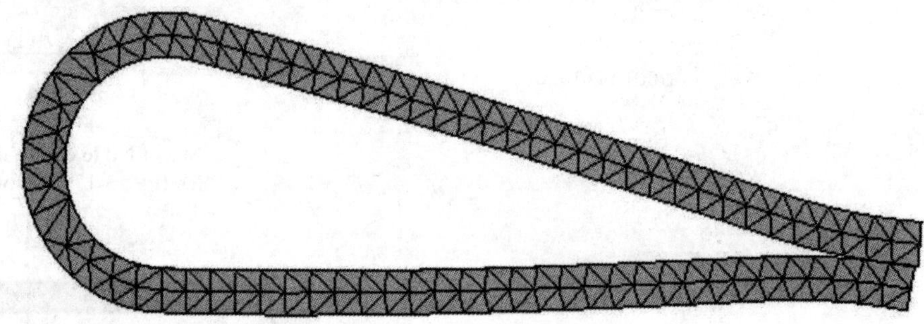

Figure 15-14: The large element size in the contact area prevents meaningful analysis of contact stresses

The deformed shape can be saved as another configuration in the same model or as another part. To save the deformed shape as SolidWorks geometry, follow the steps in Figure 15-15.

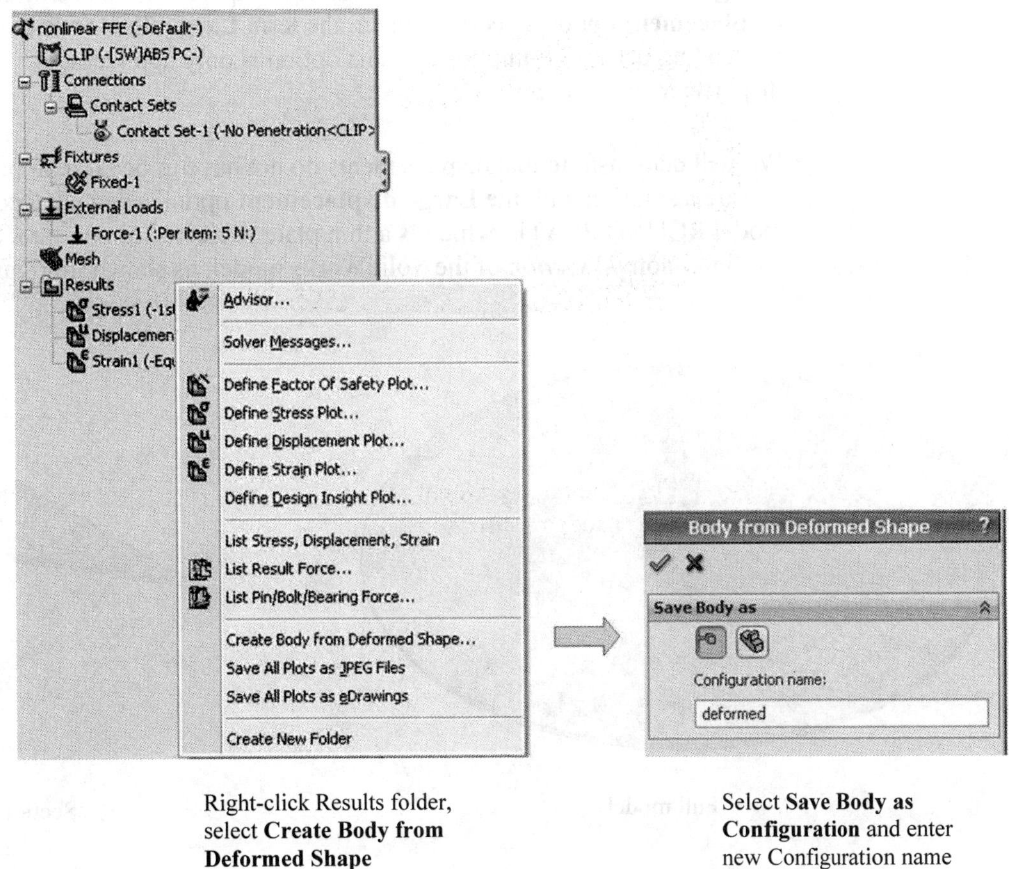

Right-click Results folder, select **Create Body from Deformed Shape**

Select **Save Body as Configuration** and enter new Configuration name

Figure 15-15: Model can be saved in deformed configuration

Examine SolidWorks Feature Manager to see that the new configuration in shown as imported geometry

To complete the exercise, review the stress results and notice that a more refined mesh would be required for detailed stress analysis.

The two pervious exercises (NL002 and CLIP) required the **Large displacement** option because displacements were indeed large. However, there are problems where displacements are small, yet they significantly change model stiffness. These problems still require solutions with the **Large displacement** option selected. In fact, the term **Large displacement** may be misleading because it implies that this option is only applicable if displacements are large.

We will demonstrate that displacements do not have to be large in order to require a solution with the **Large displacement** option selected. Open the model ROUND PLATE, which is a thin plate subjected to pressure. Switch to configuration *02 section* of the SolidWorks model, as shown in Figure 15-16.

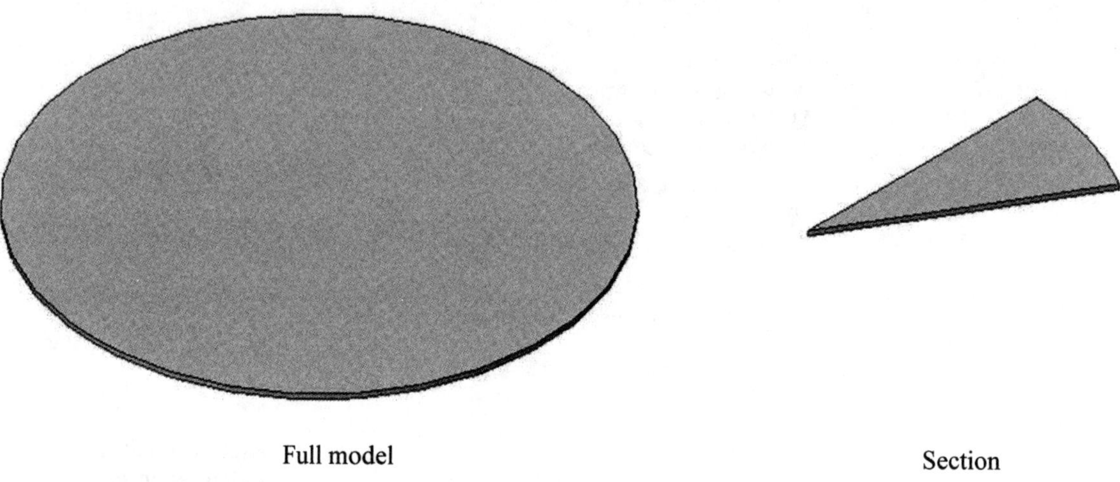

Full model Section

Figure 15-16: The full ROUND PLATE model (left) and a section obtained by switching to configuration *section*

Since there is axial symmetry in the geometry, loads, and restraints, an arbitrary slice with applied symmetry boundary conditions correctly represents the plate's response to pressure. Symmetry boundary conditions are required to enforce flatness of radial faces in the Section model.

Create a static study with a **Solid mesh** and apply **Symmetry** restraints to both radial faces created by the cut. Next, apply a **Fixed Geometry** restraint to the cylindrical face on the plate circumference and a pressure of 0.3MPa to the top face (Figure 15-17).

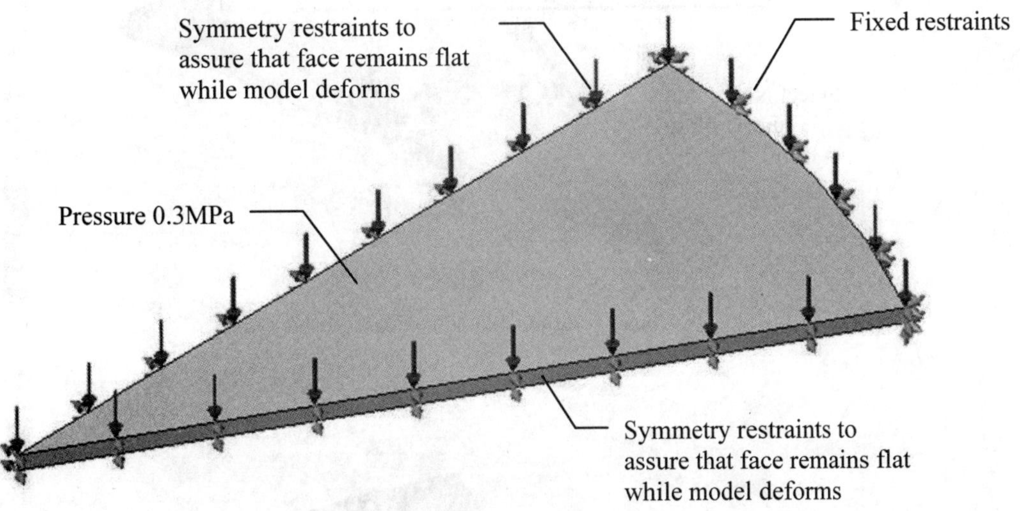

Figure 15-17: Load and restraints applied to the ROUND PLATE model

Even though the pressure symbols are shown only along the edges, the pressure is applied to the entire top face. The name "Symmetry" may be confusing here, it is used just to enforce flatness of the radial faces.

Obtain two solutions: with and without the **Large displacement** option and compare the displacement results (Figure 15-18).

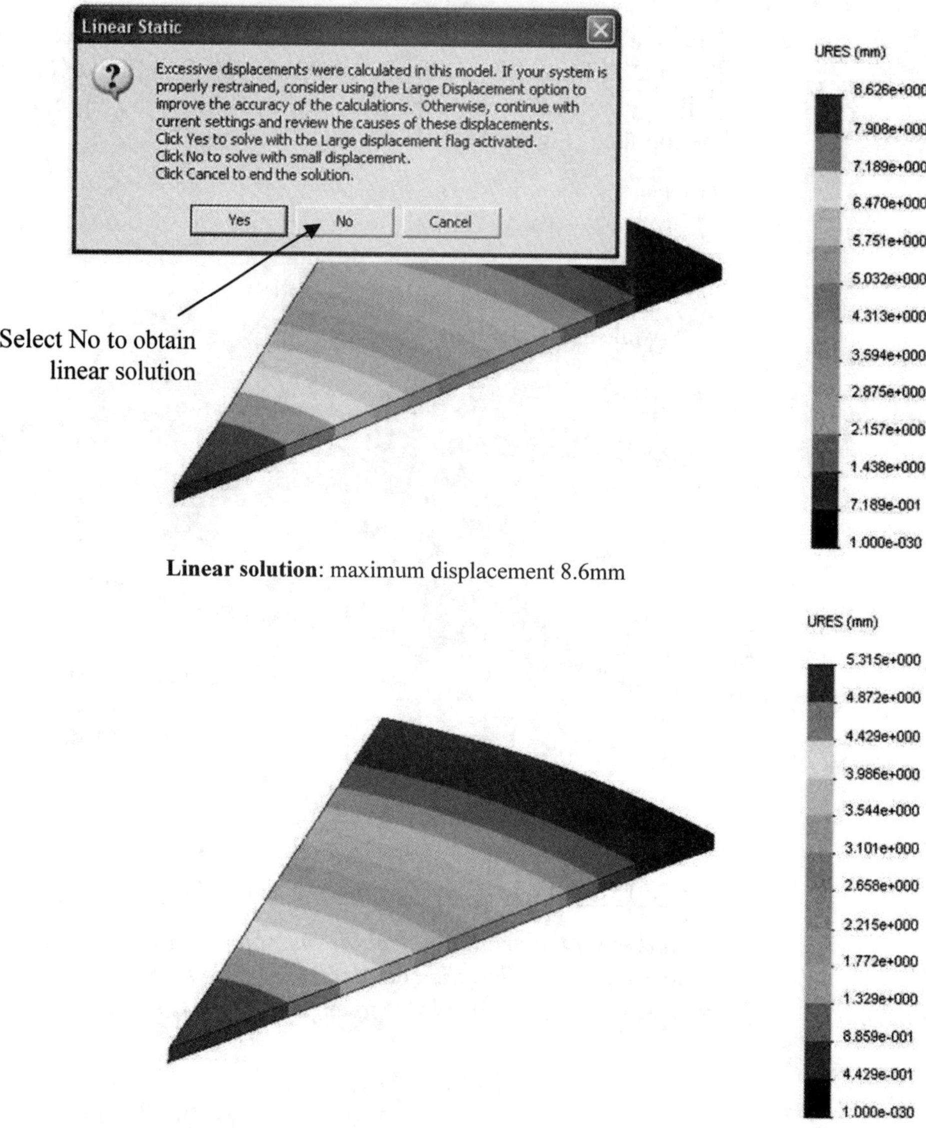
Linear Static
Excessive displacements were calculated in this model. If your system is properly restrained, consider using the Large Displacement option to improve the accuracy of the calculations. Otherwise, continue with current settings and review the causes of these displacements.
Click Yes to solve with the Large displacement flag activated.
Click No to solve with small displacement.
Click Cancel to end the solution.
Yes
No
Cancel
Select No to obtain linear solution
URES (mm)
8.626e+000
7.908e+000
7.189e+000
6.470e+000
5.751e+000
5.032e+000
4.313e+000
3.594e+000
2.875e+000
2.157e+000
1.438e+000
7.189e-001
1.000e-030
URES (mm)
5.315e+000
4.872e+000
4.429e+000
3.986e+000
3.544e+000
3.101e+000
2.658e+000
2.215e+000
1.772e+000
1.329e+000
8.859e-001
4.429e-001
1.000e-030

Linear solution: maximum displacement 8.6mm

Nonlinear solution: maximum displacement 5.3mm

Figure 15-18: Displacement results obtained without the Large displacement option (linear solution) (top) and displacement results obtained with the Large displacement option (nonlinear solution) (bottom).The nonlinear model deforms less than the linear model meaning that the nonlinear model is stiffer.

The message "Excessive displacements were calculated..." is displayed by the linear solver when the maximum resultant displacement exceeds the default element size. The decision whether to change to Large displacement formulation is left up to the user.

A flat plate under pressure is a classic case where the assumption of small displacements leads to erroneous results. The analysis requires a **Large displacement** option even though displacements are small in comparison to the size of the model.

The need to use the **Large displacement** option is due to the change of shape (from flat to curved) altering the mechanism of resisting the load; a deformed plate is able to resist pressure with membrane (tensile) stress additionally to the original bending stress (Figure 15-19).

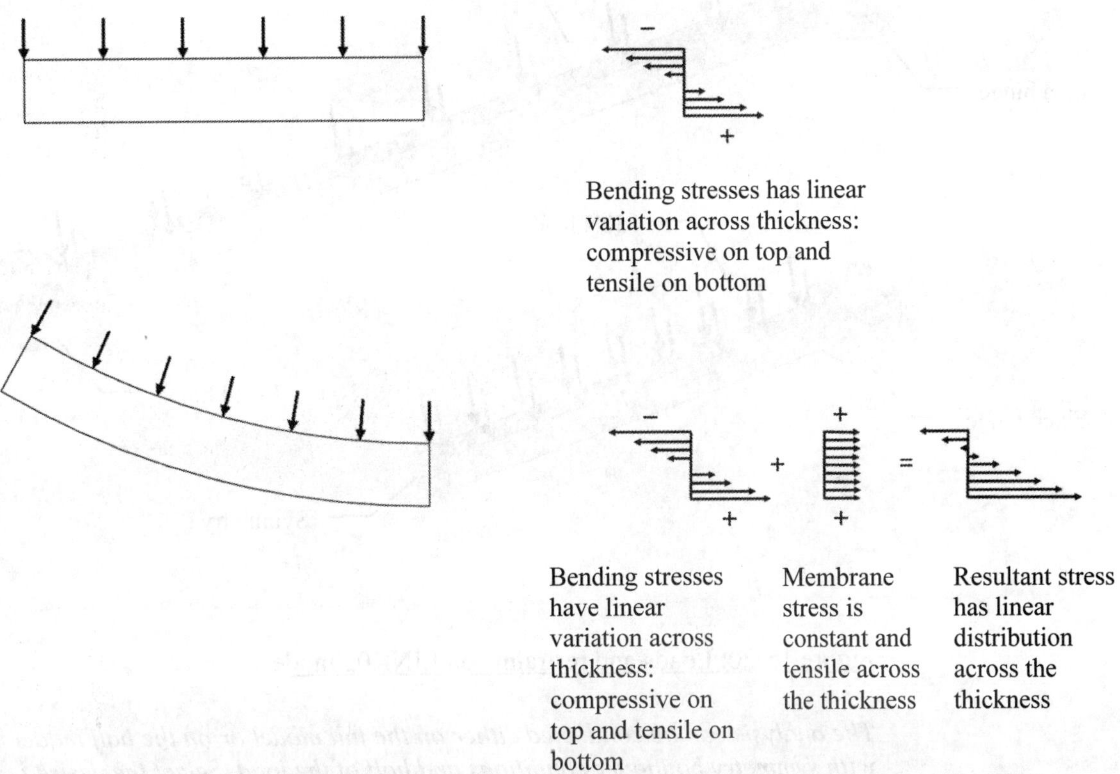

–
+
Bending stresses has linear variation across thickness: compressive on top and tensile on bottom
–
+
+
+
+
=
Bending stresses have linear variation across thickness: compressive on top and tensile on bottom
Membrane stress is constant and tensile across the thickness
Resultant stress has linear distribution across the thickness

Figure 15-19: Pressure resisting mechanism in an undeformed plate (top) and in a deformed plate (bottom)

To account for the change of plate stiffness that takes place due to deformation (even though the deformation is small), the stiffness must be updated during the deformation process. This is only possible if a nonlinear analysis is executed. The linear analysis only takes into account the initial bending stiffness, which is the reason why the linear model is softer that the corresponding nonlinear model.

We will illustrate the same problem with one more example, similar to LINK described in chapter 5. Open the model LINK02 and note that the material properties of ABS have been assigned to this model. Due to this material's low stiffness, the model will experience large deformation which will make it easy to show the difference between the correct nonlinear (**Large displacement**) solution and incorrect linear solution. Apply a 300N load to the top face and hinge restraints to the "eyes" (Figure 15-20).

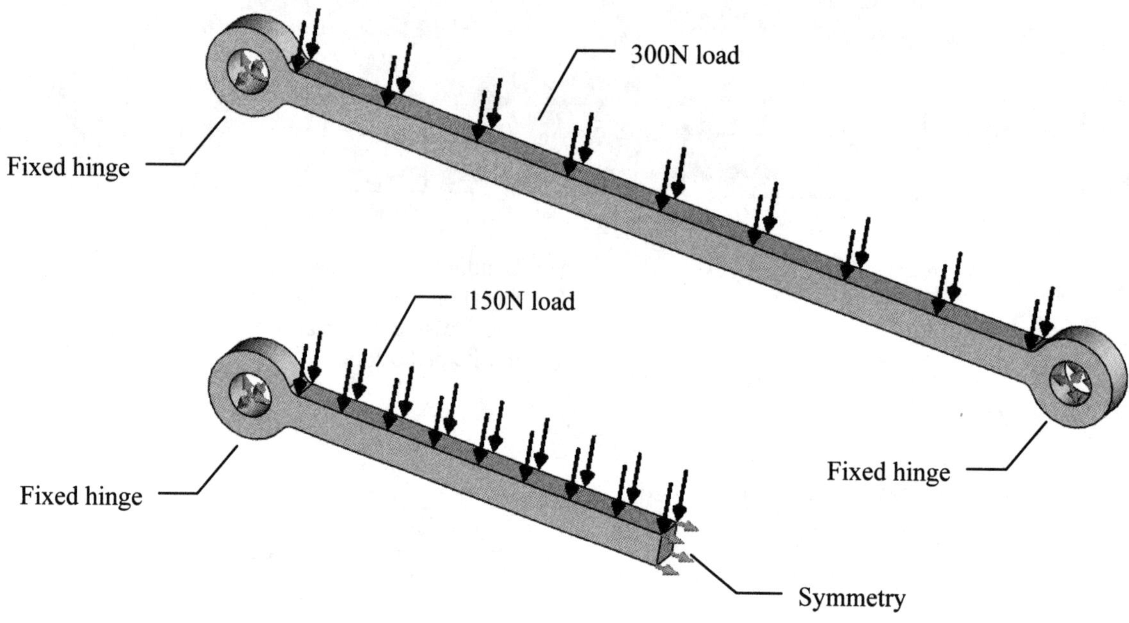

Figure 15-20: Loads and restraints on LINK02 model

The analysis can be conducted either on the full model or on the half model with symmetry boundary conditions and half of the load. Select the desired model configuration.

Obtain nonlinear and linear solutions and compare von Mises stress results from both solutions (as shown in Figure 15-21).

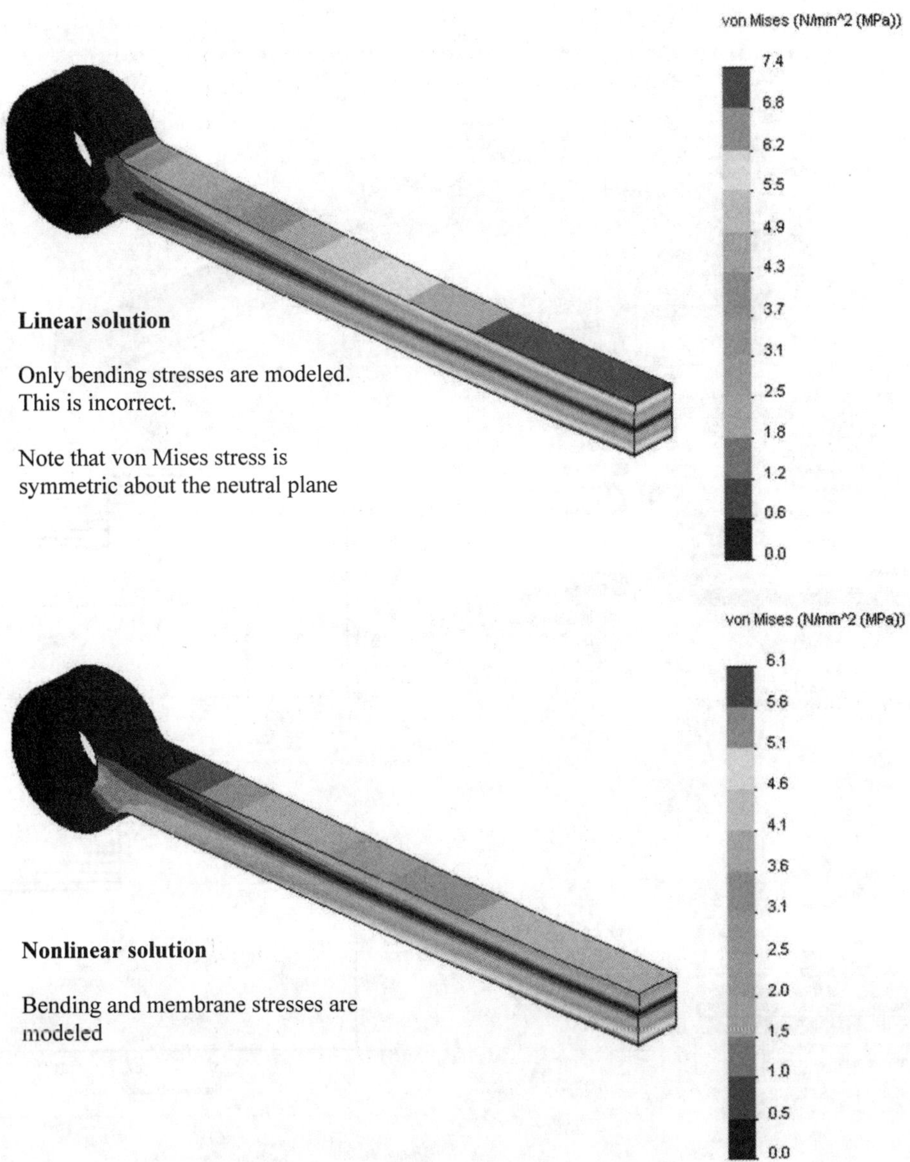

Figure 15-21: Linear and nonlinear Von Mises stress results for the same problem

The absence of membrane (tensile) stresses in the linear solution is illustrated by the symmetric distribution of von Mises stresses in the section stress plot (top).

The von Mises section plot obtained in the nonlinear (large displacement) solution shows non symmetric distribution stresses proving the presence of membrane (tensile) stresses (bottom).

Another way to demonstrate the presence of membrane stress is to examine a graph of SX stress distribution across the height of the link. To create a plot of SX stresses, follow the steps in Figure 15-22.

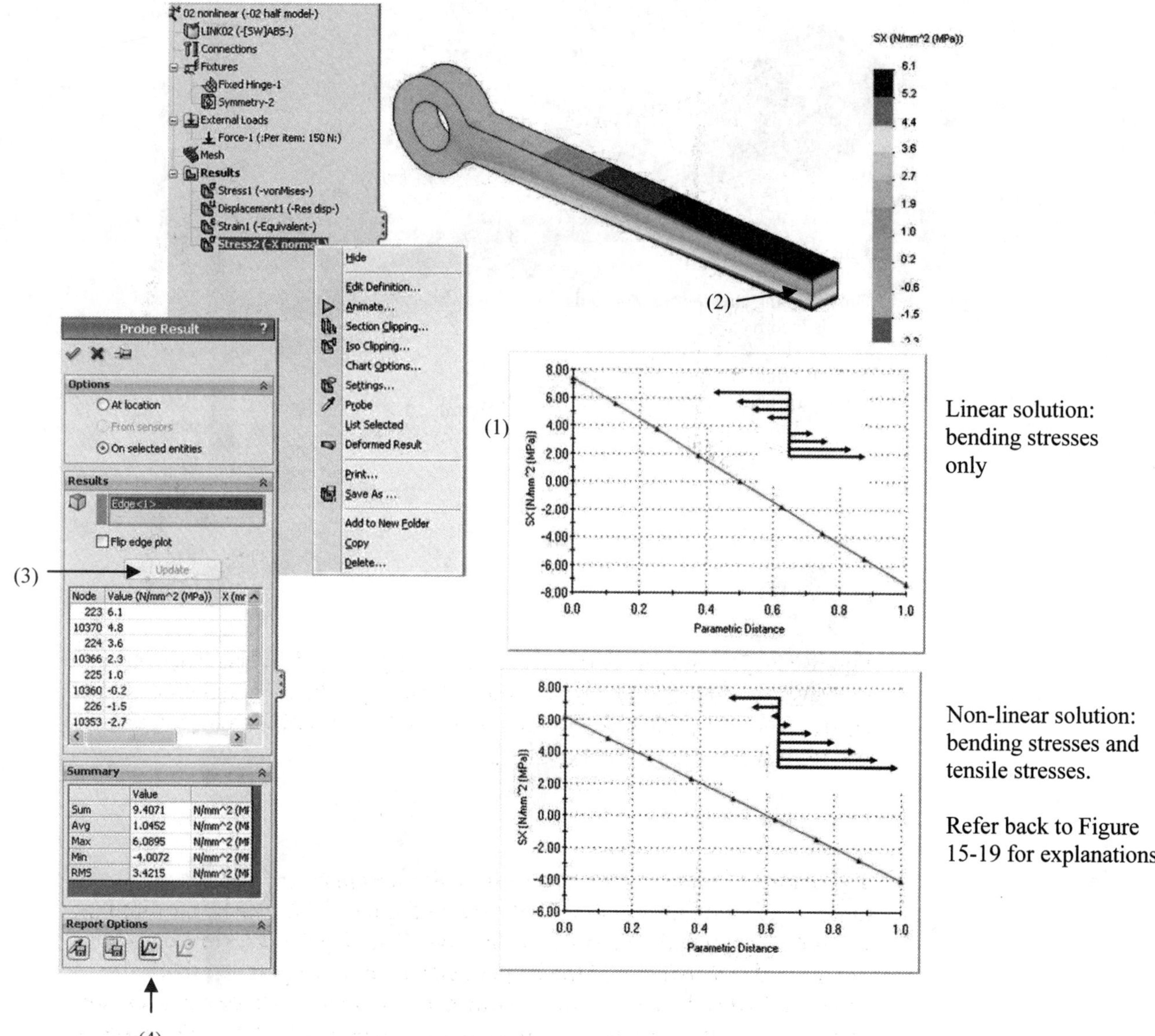

Figure 15-22: Distribution of SX stress component across the thickness can be graphed by following steps explained in this Figure.

(1) Right-click SX stress plot and select List Selected
(2) Select the vertical edge (or split line if you are using the full model), this opens the Probe Result window.
(3), (4) In the Probe Results window click Update and Graph to produce a graph of the SX stress distribution along the entity selected in (2)

The difference between a linear and nonlinear solution is schematically shown in Figure 15-23.

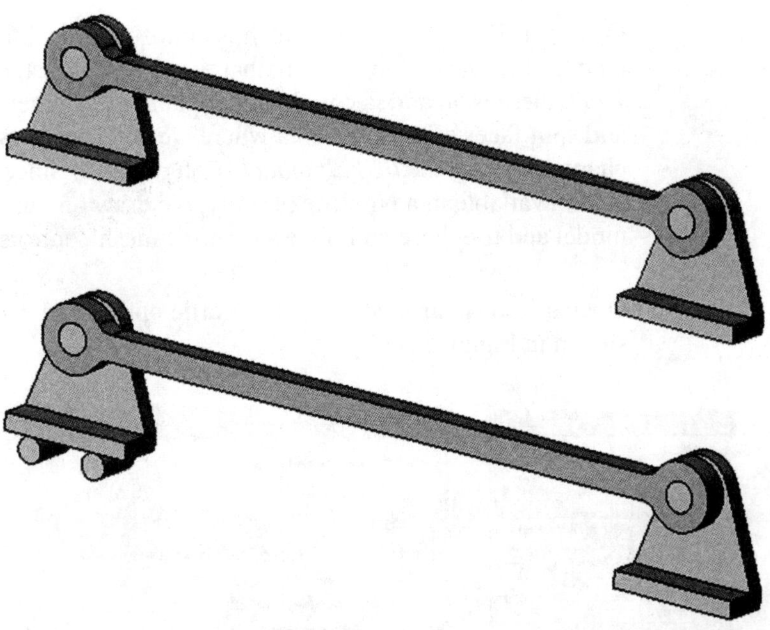

Figure 15-23: The nonlinear solution correctly models displacements and stresses in a hinge supported link where the distance between hinges can not change (top). The linear solution can only model the configurations where one of the hinges is floating (bottom).

The nonlinear solution correctly models displacements and stresses in a hinge supported link as shown at the top of Figure 15-22. The linear solution can not model membrane stresses that develop during the deformation, so this link is modeled as if one of the hinges had a floating support (symbolically shown in Figure 15-22 as rollers). Note that horizontal displacements are not modeled in a linear solution, even if floating support is modeled. Therefore, a linear model can not distinguish between the two configurations shown in Figure 15-22.

All nonlinear problems presented in this chapter owe their nonlinearity to changes in geometry taking place during the loading process. They can be solved using a **Static** study with the **Large displacement**. Now we present a problem where nonlinear behavior is caused by nonlinear material. This example requires SolidWorks **Simulation** Advanced Professional.

Open part BRACKET NL, which is almost identical to the model analyzed in chapter 14. The differences are that the assigned material is aluminum alloy 1060, there is an added cut along the plane of symmetry to simplify the model, and split faces exist in the area where we detected stress concentrations in chapter 13. Use the *02 half model* configuration. Since an h-adaptive solution is not available in a **Nonlinear** study, we draw on our past experience with the model and use these split faces to define mesh controls.

. Open a **Nonlinear** study with the **Static** option and define its properties as shown in Figure 15-24.

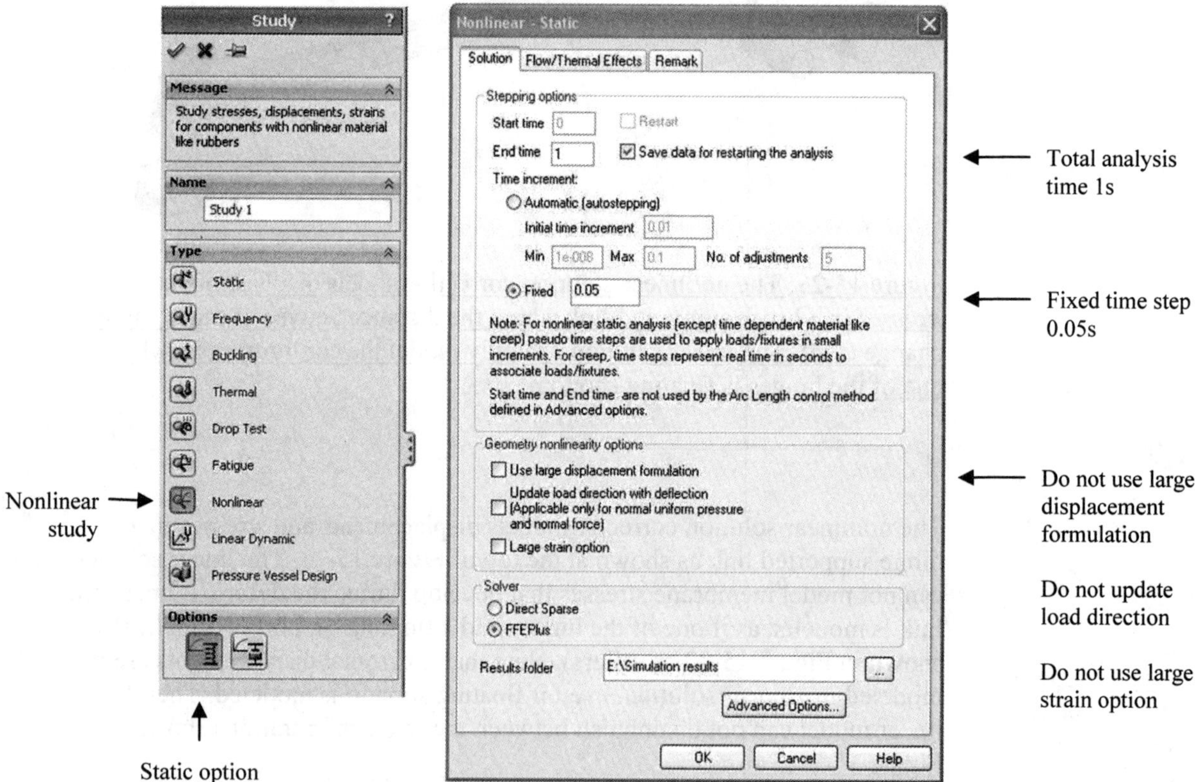

Figure 15-24: Non linear study definition and study properties

Make selections as shown above. We do not expect large displacements so load direction does not need to be updated during the load application process and fixed time stepping can be used. We also do not expect large strain magnitudes, therefore the Large strain option should not be selected.

Following the selections shown in Figure 15-24, the load application will take 1s. Considering the fixed time step of 0.05s, the load will be applied in 20 steps. It is important to remember that in our case of static analysis, time is only used to define the shape of the load history curve. The same results are obtained if the analysis time is 1s and the time steps are 0.05s or if the analysis takes 1000s and a time step of 50s. To differentiate it from "real" time used in a dynamic analysis, the time used to defined the load history curve is called "pseudo time".

The ability to control the load time history is an important difference between a **Static** study executed with the **Large displacement** option and a **Nonlinear** study. In a **Static** study executed with the **Large displacement**, a load can only be increased linearly in automatically determined steps. Without the **Large displacement** option, a load in a **Static** study is applied just in one step.

Now we define a nonlinear material. We use the simplest type of nonlinear material called elastic-perfectly plastic model. Its stress-strain curve is shown in Figure 15-25.

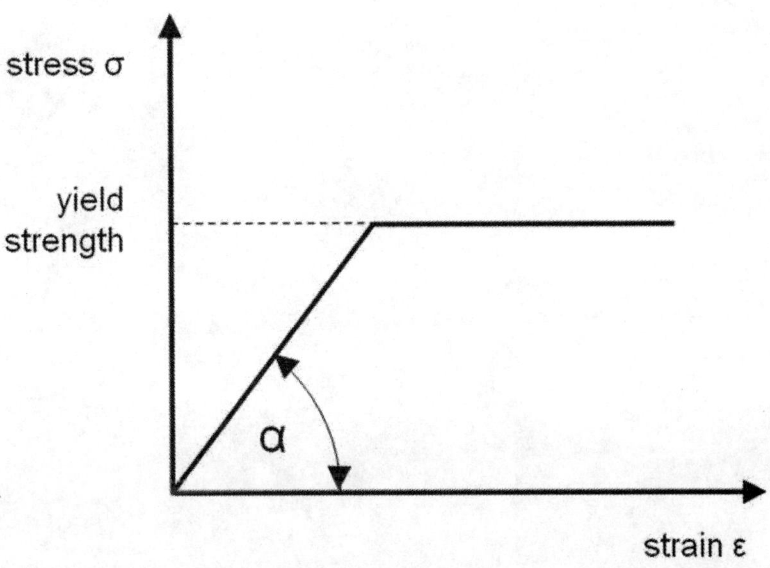

Figure 15-25: Stress-strain curve of elastic-perfectly plastic material

According to an elastic-perfectly plastic material model, stress is proportional to strain until the stress magnitude reaches yield stress. After that, stress becomes constant, regardless of the magnitude of strain.

The modulus of elasticity of a material in the linear elastic range is $E = \tan \alpha$. The modulus of elasticity of material in the plastic range is zero.

To define an elastic-perfectly plastic material model we need to know the material modulus of elasticity describing its behavior in the elastic range and the magnitude of the yield stress. We also need to decide how to determine if yield stress is reached. In this example we compare von Mises stress to yield stress. Once von Mises stress reaches yield stress, the material modulus of elasticity becomes zero. In SolidWorks **Simulation** this material is called **Plasticity – von Mises**.

Edit the material properties of 1060 Alloy assigned in the SolidWorks model to change it into **Plasticity – von Mises** (Figure 15-26).

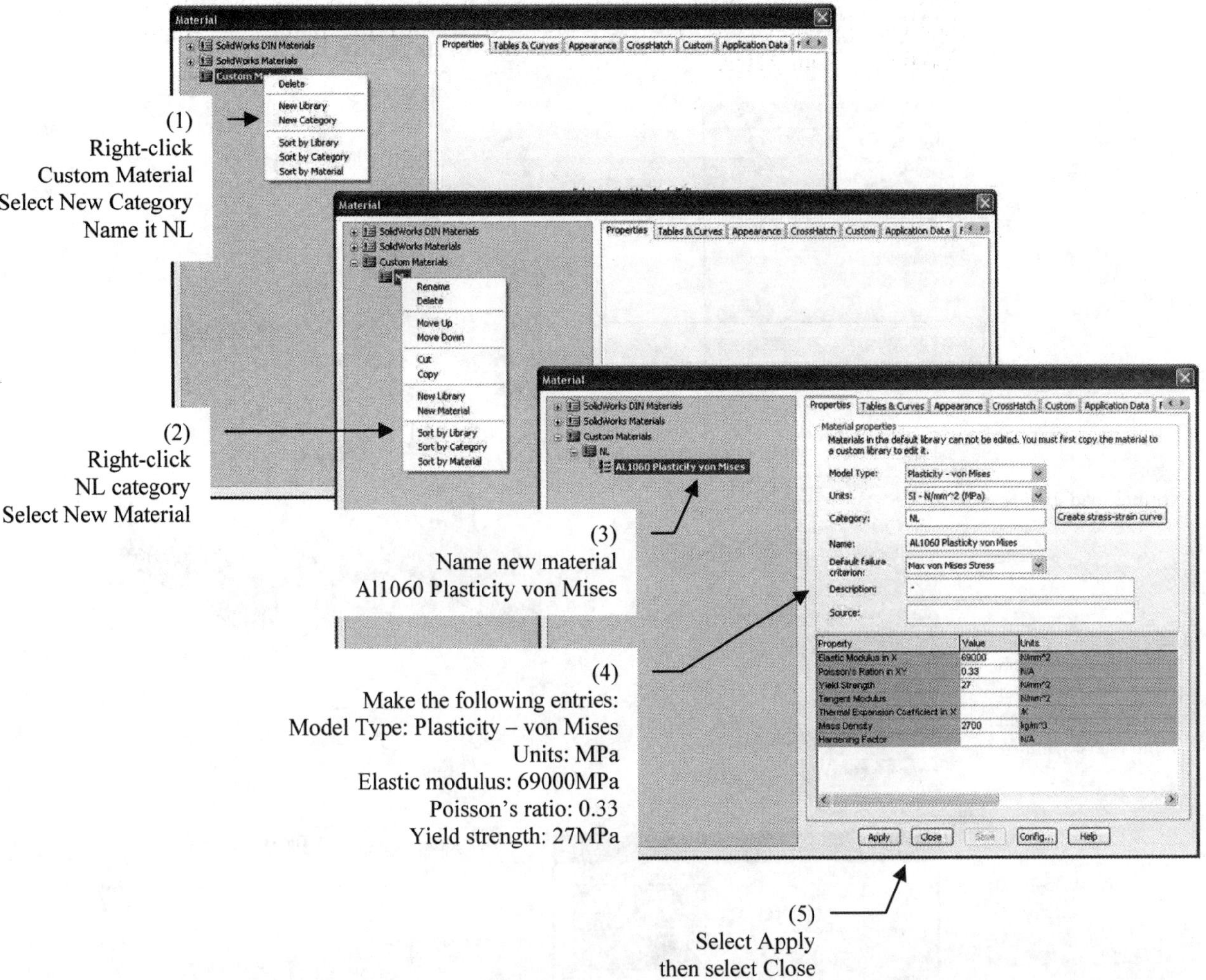

Figure 15-26: Plasticity – von Mises material definition. Follow the above steps to define custom material

A yield stress of 27MPa is the highest von Mises stress magnitude that model will see.

Define a **Fixed** restraint on the back side and **Symmetry** restraint to the faces created by the symmetry cut.

The total load on the model is 5000N. Apply it the same way as in chapter 13. Here, remember to apply only 2500N because we are working with one half of the model geometry. The load application requires definition of the load time history. We want to "ramp-up" the load to the maximum value to see the maximum stresses, then we will drop it back down to zero to examine the residual stresses. The load definition is shown in Figure 15-27.

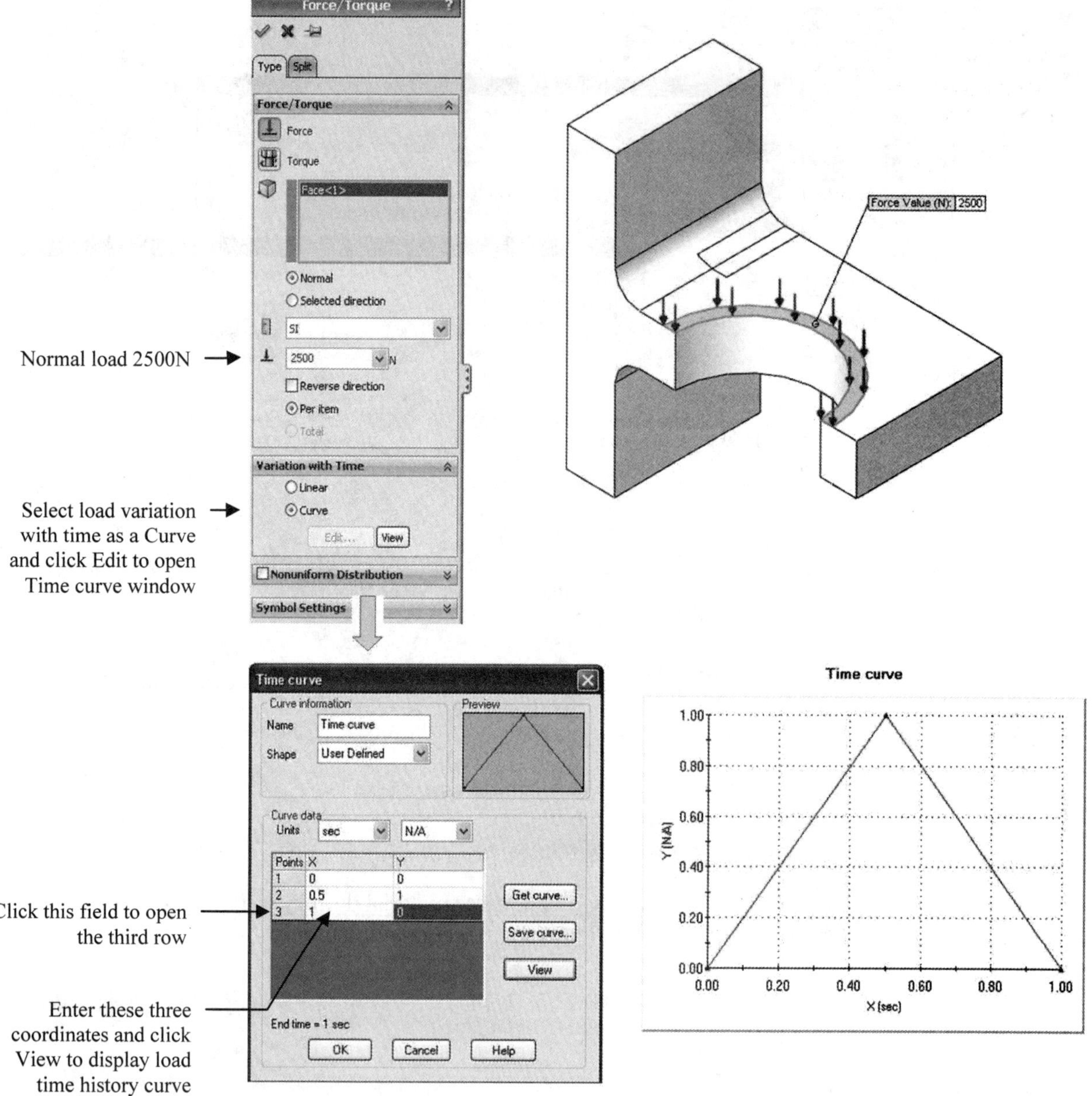

Figure 15-27: Load definition

Y values of load time history are load multipliers. The maximum load takes place at time t=0.5s. At t=1s, the load is back to zero.

In SolidWorks Feature Manager, define a **Sensor** in the location indicated in Figure 15-27. Return to **Simulation** study, right click *Result Options* folder to open **Results Option** window. Specify solution steps 1-20 with increment 1, specify **Response Plots** as **Workflow Sensitive**. This links **Result Option** to the Sensor (Figure 15-28).

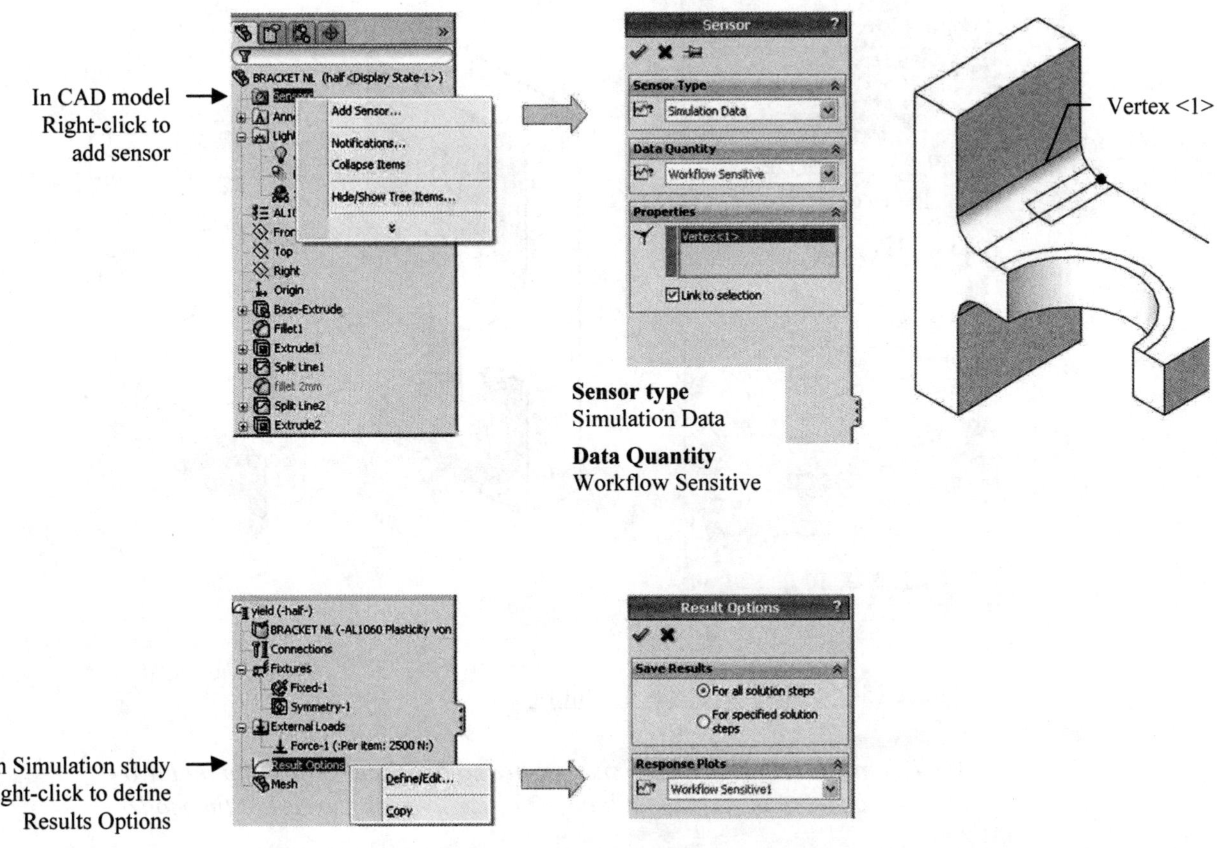

Figure 15-28: Sensor definition (top) and Results Options definition (bottom)

Select the vertex where high stresses are expected.

Apply mesh controls as shown in Figure 15-29. Defining these mesh controls requires knowledge of where stress concentrations will be located. We investigated this in chapter 13.

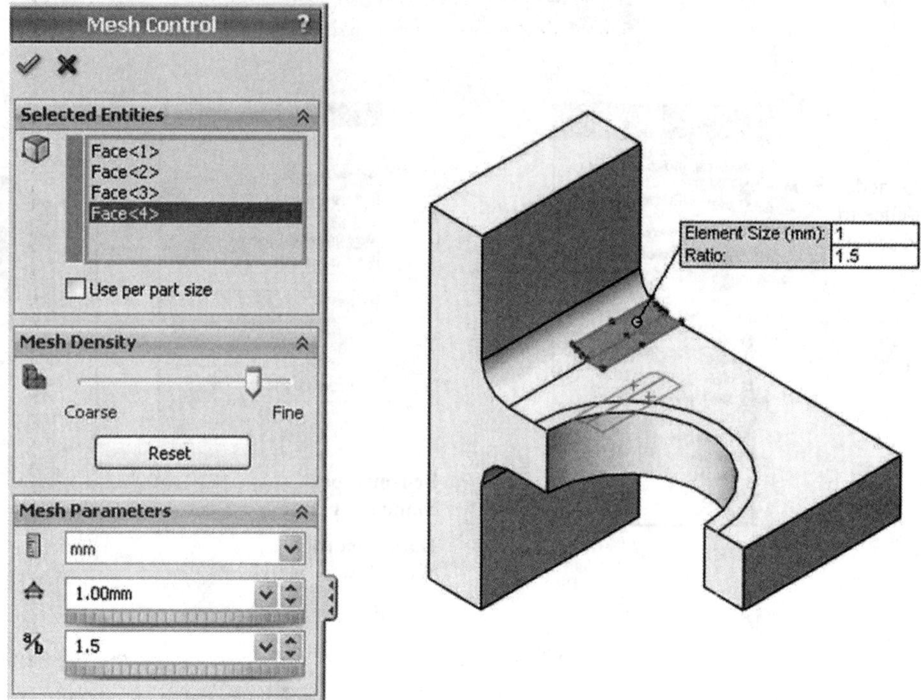

Figure 15-29: Mesh controls definition

Mesh controls (element size 1mm) applied to two faces on the top and two faces on the bottom. Use default element size to mesh the rest of the model.

Execute the solution of the nonlinear study and observe solution progress in the Solver window. Be prepared for a solution time much longer than a typical linear analysis. The nonlinear solver window is shown in Figure 15-30.

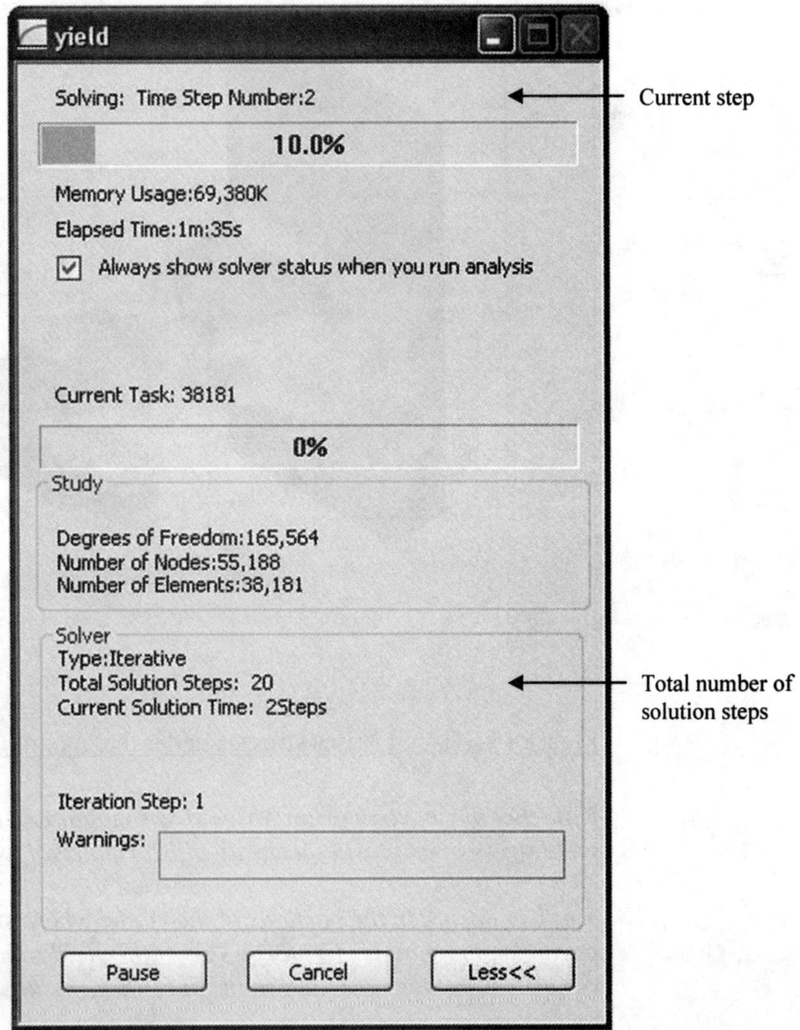

Figure 15-30: Nonlinear solver window

The nonlinear solver window shows the solution progress: here, step 1 of 20.

Von Mises stress results for the maximum load (time step 10) are shown in Figure 15-31.

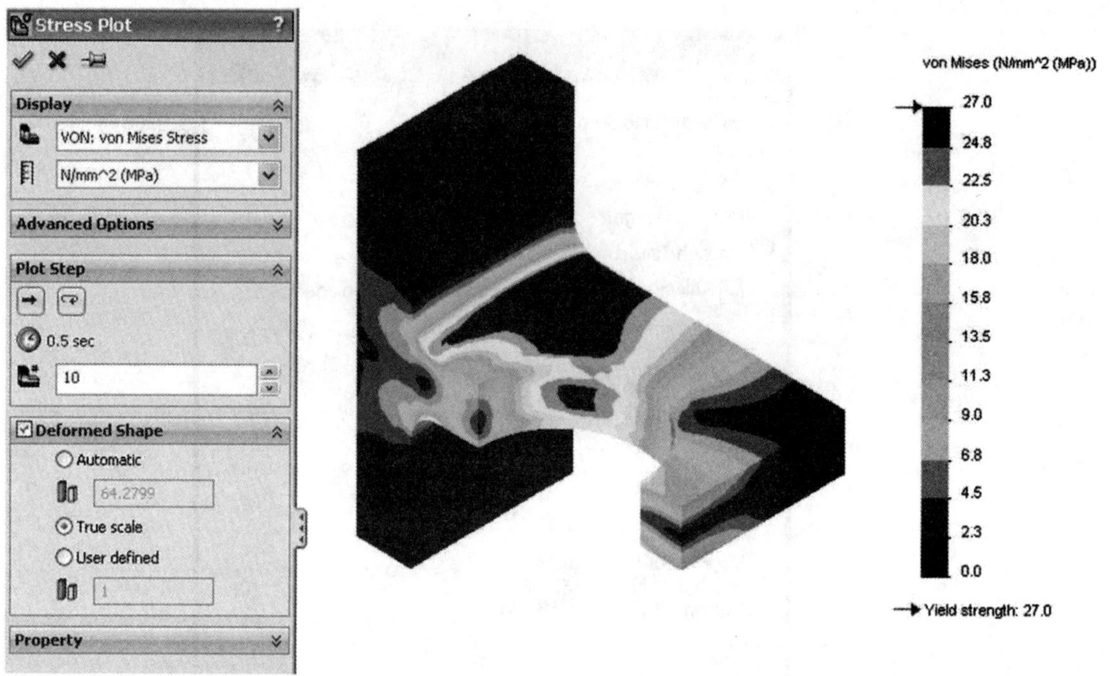

Figure 15-31: Von Mises stresses under the maximum load, time step 10

Note that the maximum von Mises stress magnitude is 27MPa, which is the yield stress of an elastic-perfectly plastic material we used in the analysis.

Yielding occurs in the portions of the model where stress reaches the maximum magnitude. The large size of the yield zone indicates that the mesh controls were not necessary to produce these results.

Von Mises stress results for the zero load (time step 20) are shown in Figure 15-32. These are residual stresses “left over” after completing the load cycle.

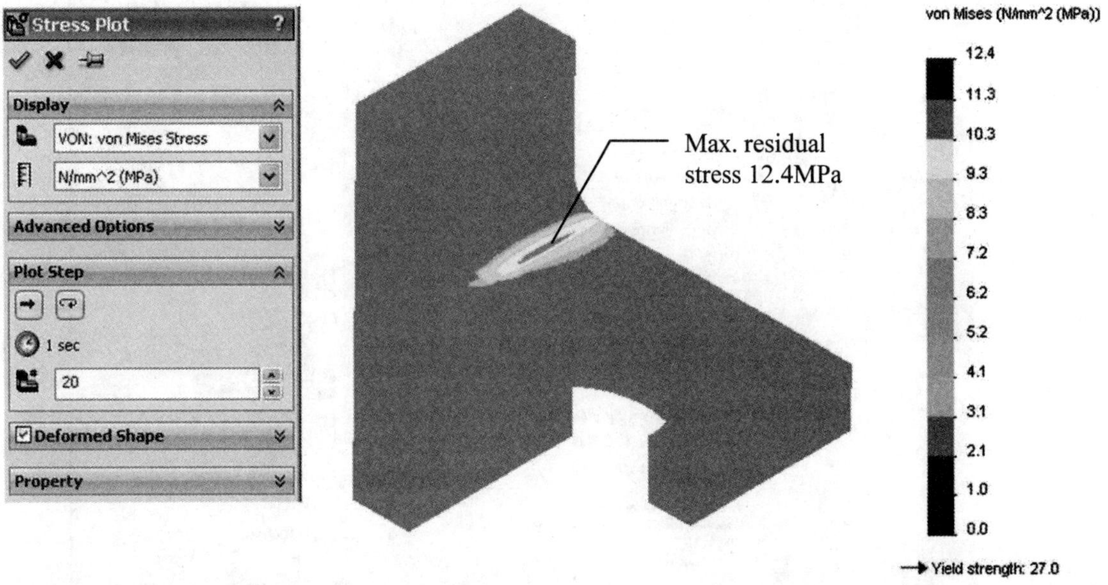

Figure 15-32: Residual von Mises stresses left after load has been removed; time step 20

Residual stresses reach 12.4MPa in the area that experienced plastic deformation (yield). The small size of the high stress zone indicates that the mesh controls were necessary to produce these results.

Follow the steps in Figure 15-33 to display the maximum von Mises stress as a function of time step number.

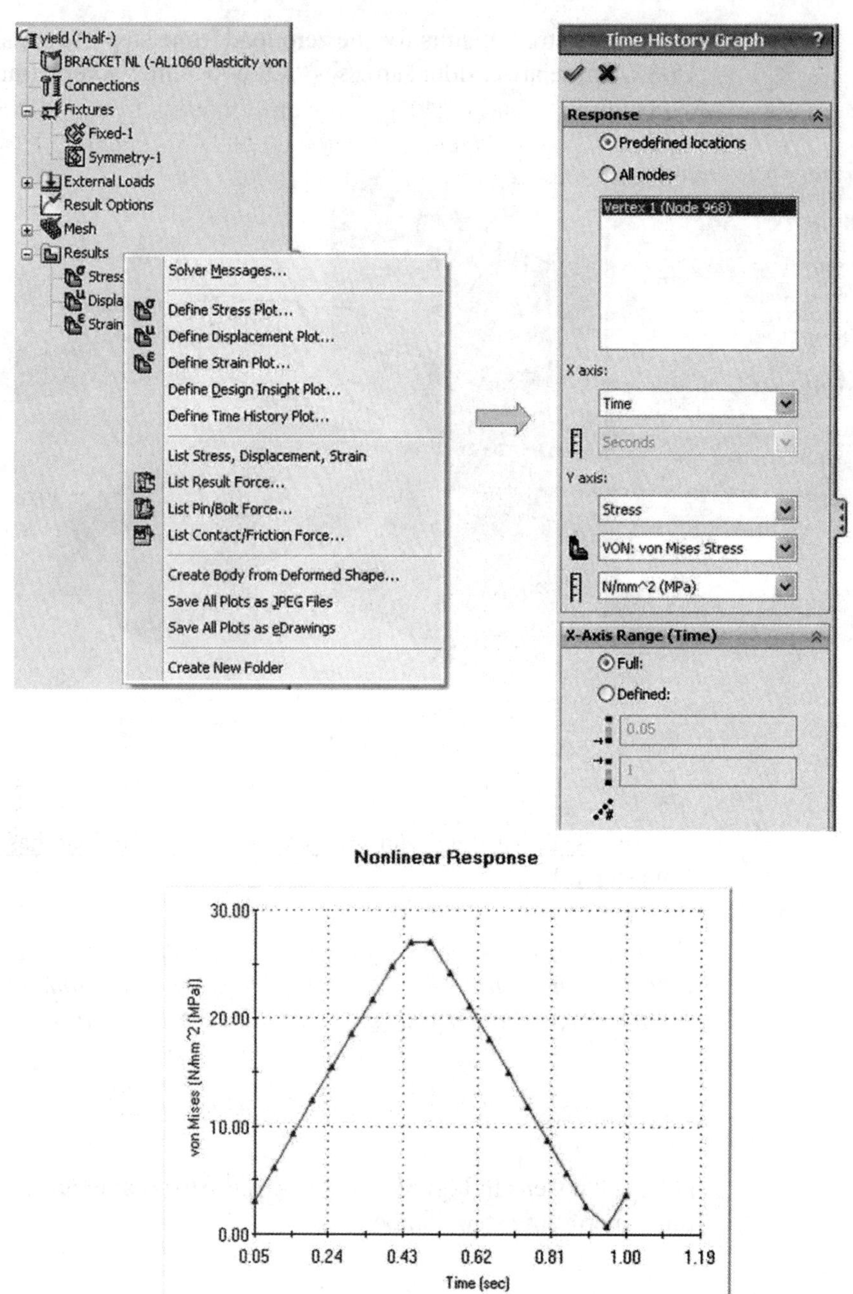

Figure 15-33: Maximum von Mises stress as function of time step

*Right-click the Results folder and select Define Time History Plot to open the Time History Graph window. Select von Mises stress for the only location available to display the graph. The maximum stress is 27MPa, which is the yield stress. If desired, the graph can be saved as a *.csv file for editing in Excel.*

To continue with the theme of elastic perfectly plastic material, open model SPRING, create a nonlinear study and define elastic-perfectly plastic material with the following properties: modulus of elasticity E = 200000MPa, Poisson's ratio 0.29 and yield strength 689.48MPa (100000psi). Apply loads and restraints as shown in Figure 15-34.

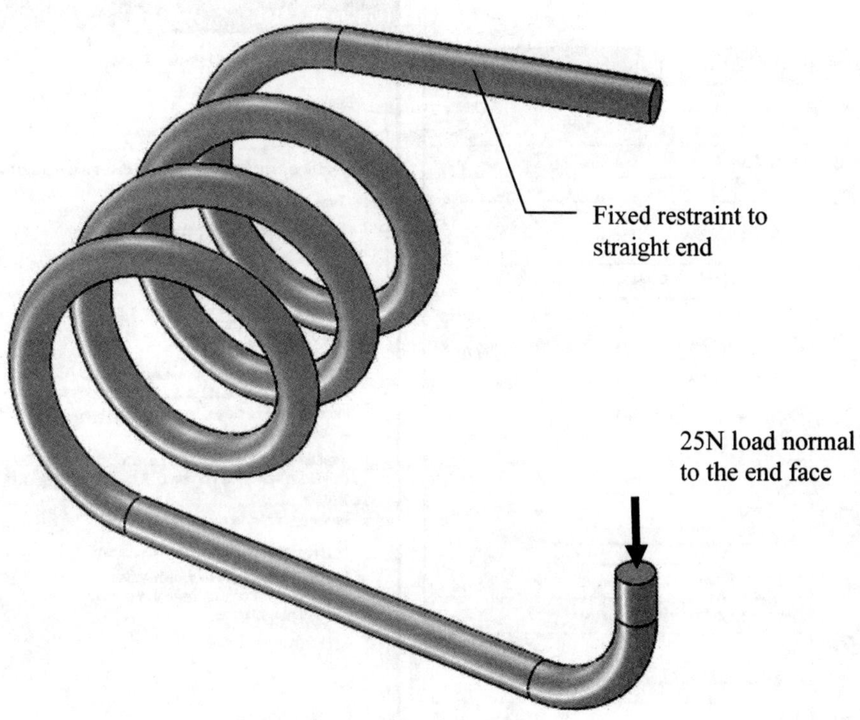

Figure 15-34: Restraint and load of SPRING model

Load remains normal to the face while SPRING deforms

Mesh the model with Curvature Base mesh and select options **Use large displacement formulation** and **Upload load direction with deflection** in study property (Figure 15-35). This option defines a following load, one that changes direction to follow the deforming model during the loading process. Even though the model will experience large displacement, strain won't be large, so the **Large strain** option does not have to be selected.

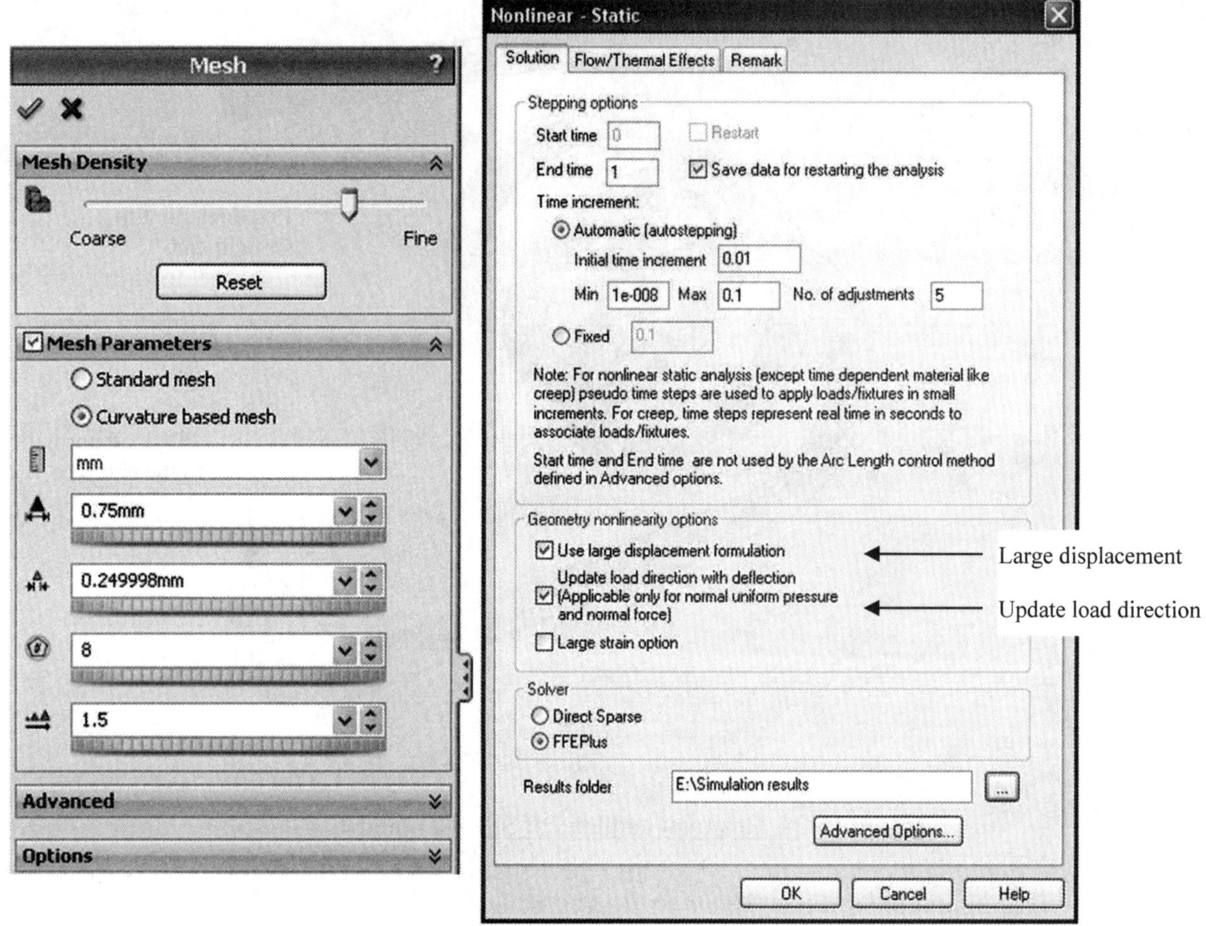

Figure 15-35: Mesh parameters and study Properties

Large displacement formulation and Update load direction with deflection are selected

Be prepared for a long solution time when you run the study. Review displacement results and note the large displacement that the model has experienced under the load (Figure 15-36). Next, review Von Mises Stress and examine the portions of the model that reached yield stress (Figure 15-37).

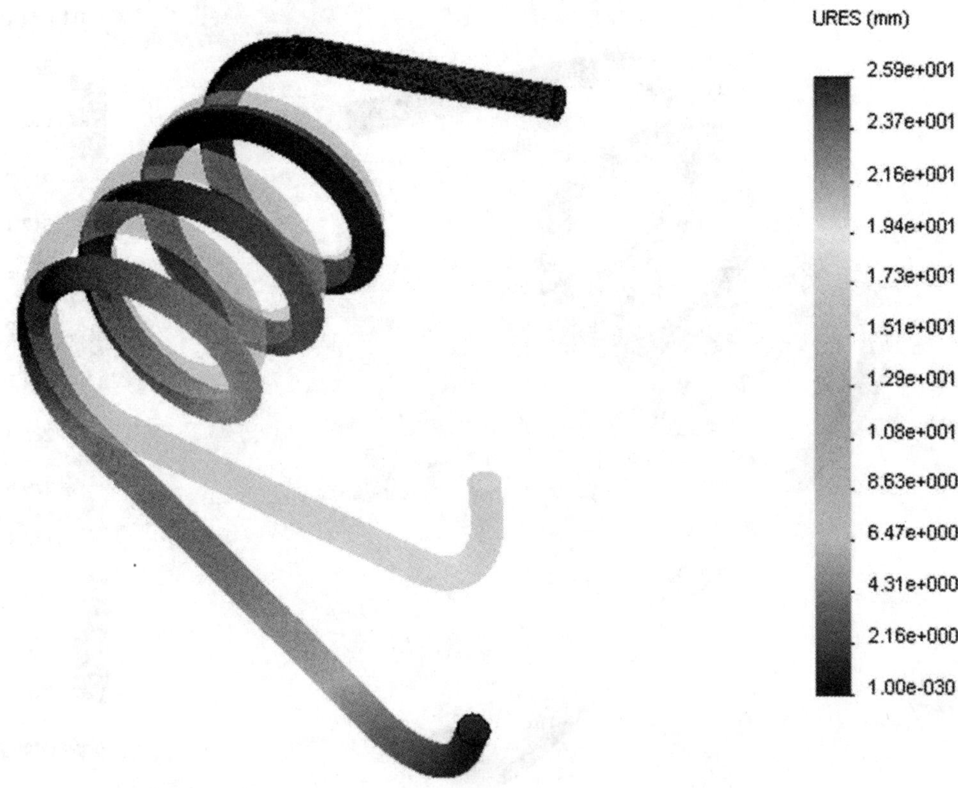

Figure 15-36: Displacement results plot shows that the model has experienced large displacement under the applied load.

The undeformed model is superimposed on the deformed plot.

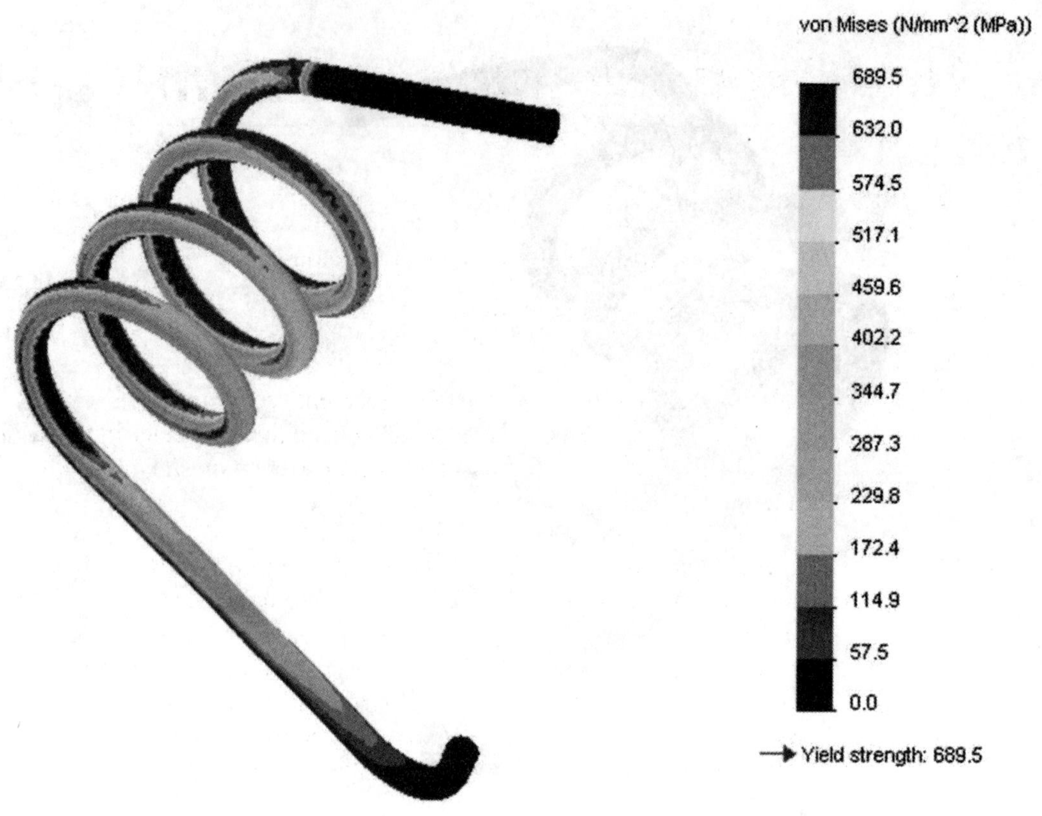

Figure 15-37: Von Mises stress plot shows that large portions of the model have yielded

The model shows large areas at yield stress 689.5MPa.

You may want to experiment with the model by increasing the load until the solution crashes, meaning that the entire spring cross section has yielded and it is no longer capable of resisting the applied load.

16: Mixed meshing problem

Topics covered

- Using solid and shell elements in the same mesh
- Mixed mesh compatibility

While in previous exercises we used different types of meshes such as solid and shell meshes, we have never used them together in the same model. This exercise introduces the use of different mesh types within the same model.

Open the part model WHEEL. Note that the "bulky" hub and rim are connected by thin spokes. Since the spokes are thin, using a solid element mesh to model them would require a large number of small solid elements. Therefore, to reduce the problem size, the hub and rim will be meshed with solid elements and spokes with shell elements. To accomplish this, model geometry must be prepared in SolidWorks. Start the exercise by examining the SolidWorks Feature Manager and Figure 16-1.

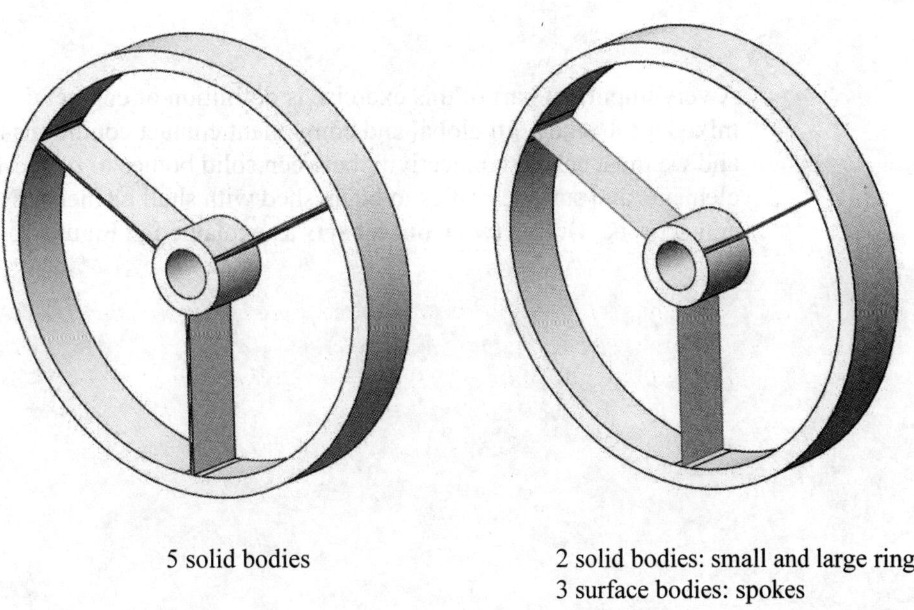

5 solid bodies

2 solid bodies: small and large ring
3 surface bodies: spokes

Figure 16-1: Spokes are represented by surfaces

Note that this is a multi body model (left). In preparation for analysis, mid-surfaces have been placed in the middle of each spoke thickness and bodies defining spokes have been deleted (right).

Create a **Frequency** study and notice that the study folder contains two folders: **Solids** and **Shells**. Since surfaces do not contain information on thickness we must define this parameter. Select all surfaces in the *wheel* folder, right-click and select **Edit Definition** to open the **Shell definition** window. Use a **Thin** shell formulation and enter 2mm as the shell thickness – the thickness of the spokes (Figure 16-2).

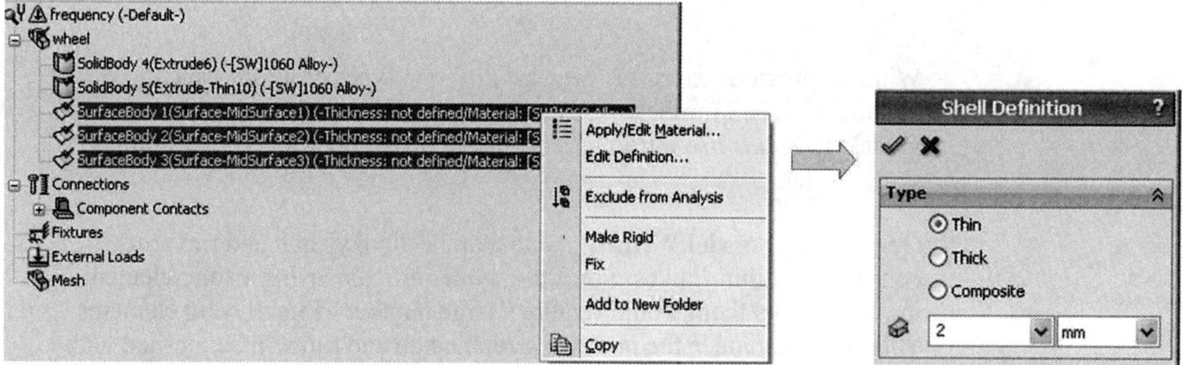

Figure 16-2: Defining shell thickness of spokes: 2 mm

A very important part of this exercise is definition of contact conditions. In a mixed mesh study, all global and component contact conditions are ignored and we must ensure connectivity between solid bodies to be meshed with solid elements and surface bodies to be meshed with shell elements by defining contact sets. Define two **Contact sets** as explained in Figure 16-3.

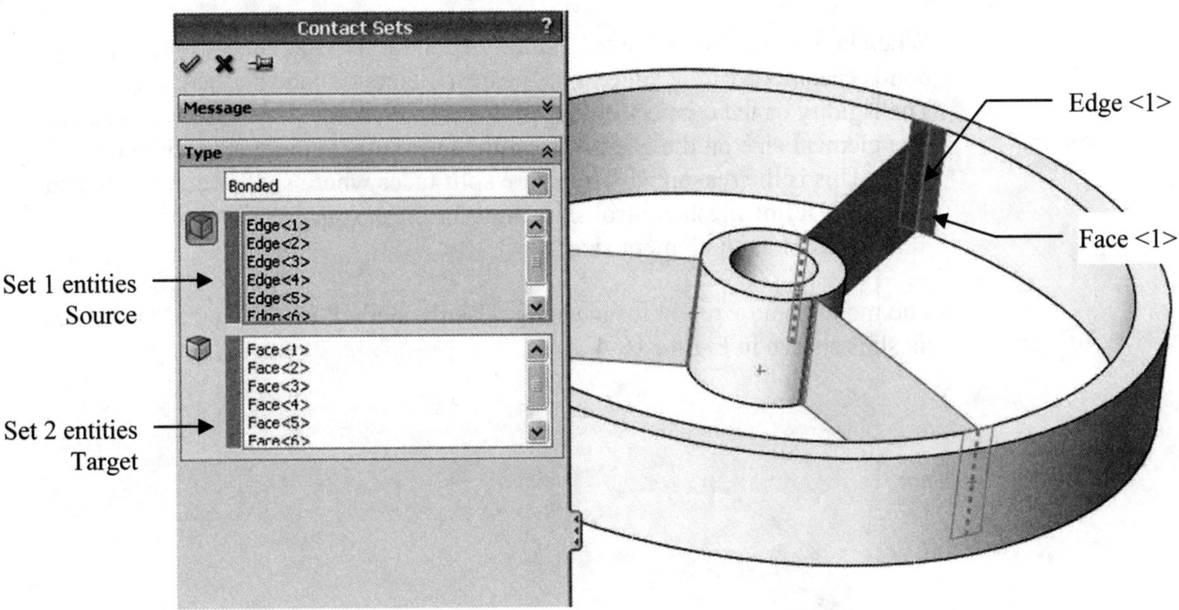

Figure 16-3: The Bonded contact condition is defined between the edge Edge<n> and the face Face<n> where n = 1,2,3,4,5,6

Contact sets enforce connectivity in six locations in total. In this case where shell elements will be connected to solid elements, the original angle between the shell or beam and the solid is maintained during deformation. By defining local contact conditions, we ensure connectivity of all components.

When bonding a shell edge to a solid or shell target face, the software rigidly bonds each node of the edge to the nearest element's face on the target. The rigidity of the connection depends on the element size near the interface. The element size on the target face should be equal to the thickness of the shell. This is the reason why there are split faces where spokes connect to rim and hub. Define mesh control size 2mm for these split faces and mesh the model with default element size.

The model is now ready for meshing. Use the default element size. The mixed mesh is shown in Figure 16-4.

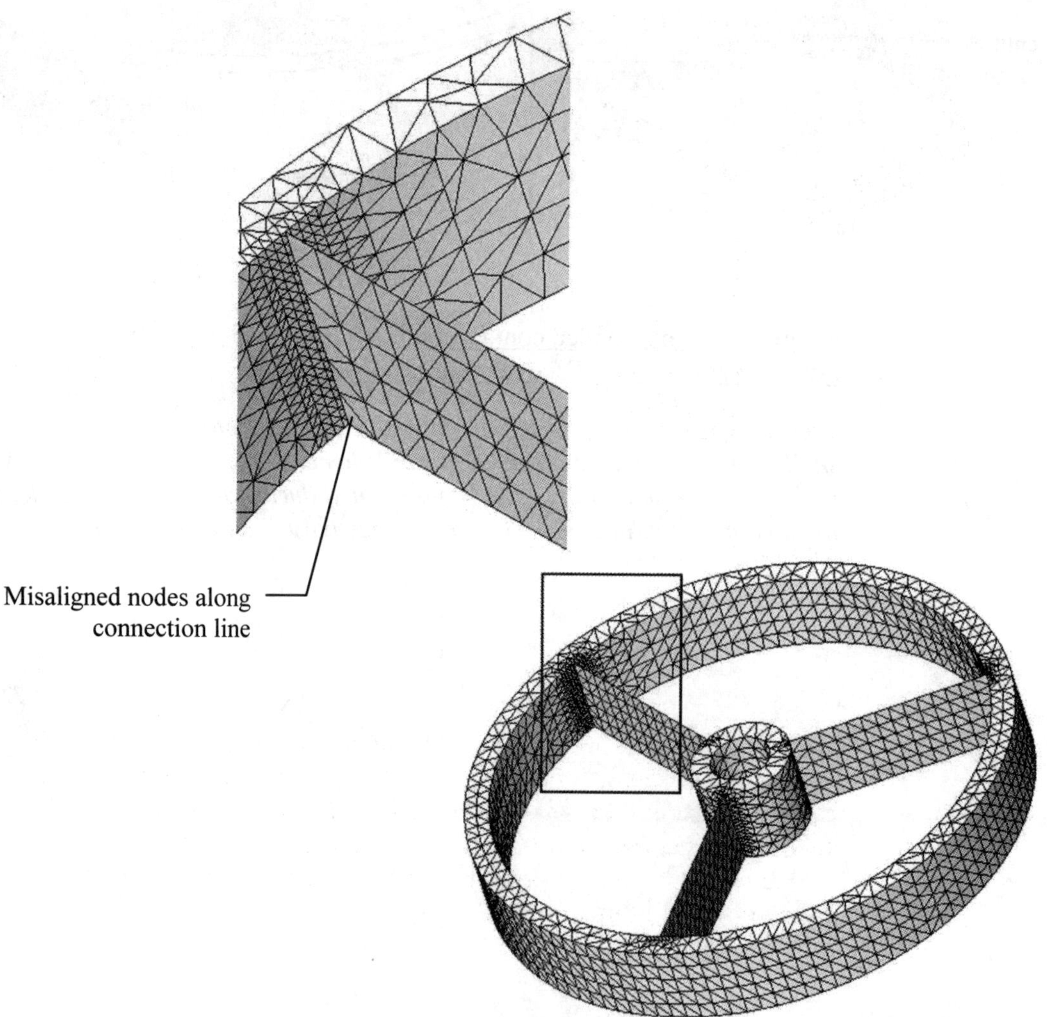

Figure 16-4: Mixed mesh: rim and hub are meshed with solid elements. Spokes are meshed with shell elements

Note that shell element mesh and solid element do not share nodes. The spokes would be disconnected from the rim if not for the contact set that enforces connection.

Before solving, apply a **Fixed** restraint to the hole in the hub.

The deformation pattern of the first two modes of vibration are shown in Figure 16-5.

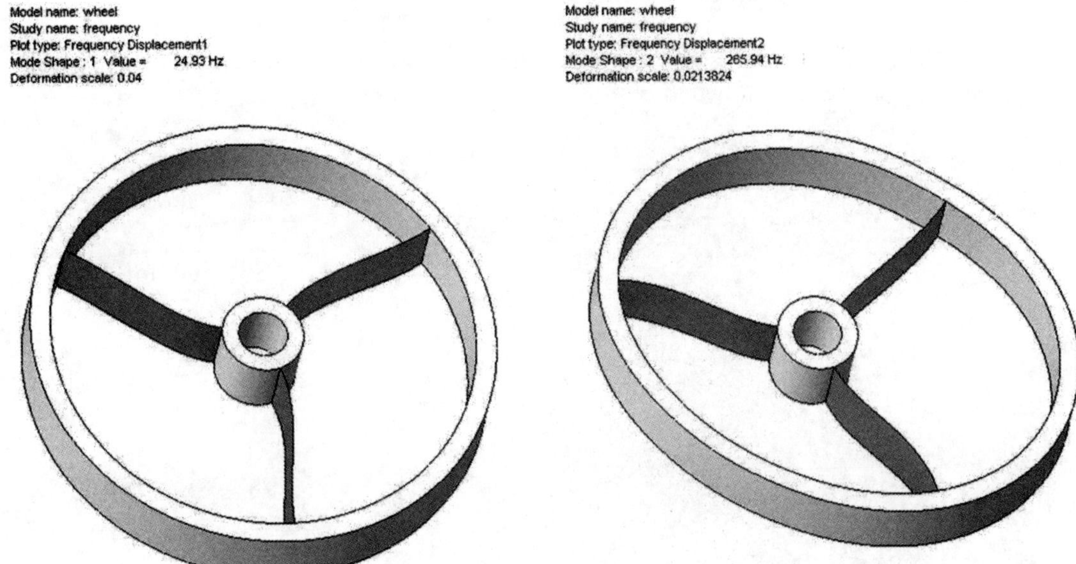

Figure 16-5: Deformation pattern corresponding to the first two modes of vibration

As you might have noticed, a model suitable for mixed meshing requires careful preparation of geometry in SolidWorks and definition of contact conditions in **Simulation**. But once the model is ready for analysis, it is easy to analyze the effect of different spoke thickness, no matter how thin. This would not require any geometry modification, only a change in **Shell Definition** and change in **Mesh Control** size.

Notes:

17: Analysis of a weldment using beam elements

Topics covered

- Different levels of idealization implemented in finite elements
- Preparation of SolidWorks model for analysis with beam elements
- Beam elements and truss elements
- Analysis of results using beam elements
- Limitations of analysis with beam elements

Project description

A Roll-Over Protective Structure (ROPS) is used to protect an operator of heavy equipment in case of roll-over. Open the ROPS model. It consists of eight hollow square tubes 3 x 3 x 0.25 (Figure 17-1). All tubes are created in SolidWorks as structural members.

We need to find the displacements and stresses of this structure under a load of 5000lb with all four legs restrained.

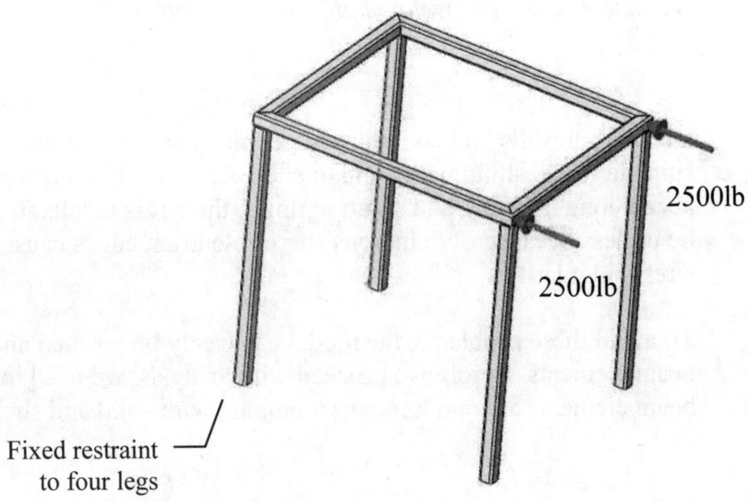

Figure 17-1: A ROPS cage is loaded in two corners with horizontal load 2500lb to each corner. All legs are restrained as shown.

The tube cross section and details of corner treatment and trims are shown in Figure 17-2.

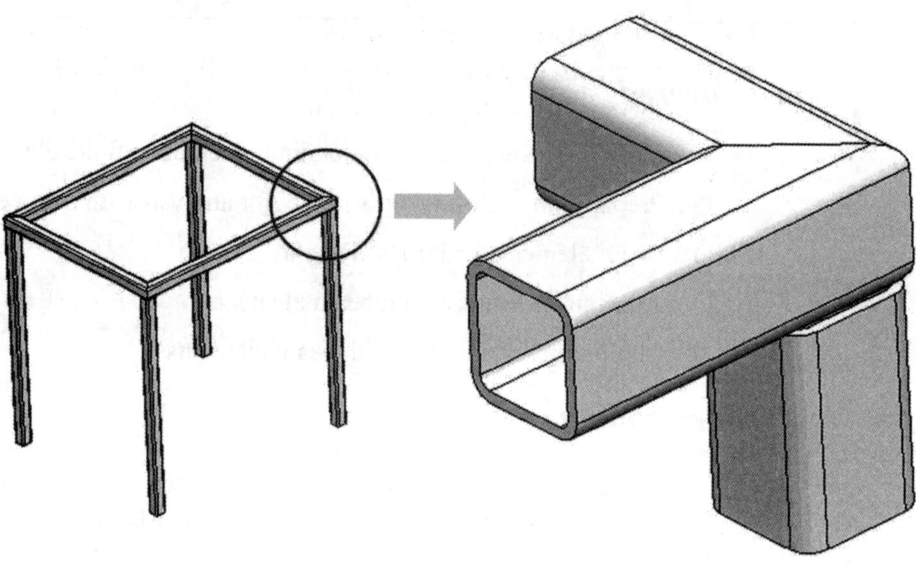

Figure 17-2: A detail of the corner; all tubes are 3″x3″x0.25″ with a 0.5″ radius

Corner treatments and trims are applied in the SolidWorks model using Weldment tools. The weld bead is not modeled.

Due to thin walls and complicated geometry in corners, this model is not suitable for meshing with solid or shell elements. Even if we were ready to accept long meshing and solution times, the stress results in the corners would be useless because of numerous sharp re-entrant edges causing numerous stress singularities.

To avoid these problems, the model can easily be meshed and analyzed with beam elements. Before we proceed with analysis, we need to explain what beam elements are and how they compare with solid and shell elements.

The differences between solid, shell and beam elements are summarized in the following table.

Element type	Idealizations made to geometry intended to be meshed with this element	Assumptions on stress distribution in the element
Solid	None; solid elements are created by meshing 3D solid geometry.	No assumptions on stress distribution need to be made
Shell	Shell elements are created by meshing a surface. Thickness is not present in the geometry and must be entered as a numerical value in the shell element definition.	Assumptions on stress distribution across thickness are made. In-plane stresses are assumed to be distributed linearly across the thickness. Transverse shear stresses are either assumed to have uniform distribution across element thickness (thin shell formulation), or to have parabolic distribution (thick shell formulation).
Beam	Curves are used to create beam elements. Curves represent beam geometry mathematically and do not physically model the cross section. In CAD terminology this is called wire frame geometry.	Assumptions about stress distribution must be made in two directions perpendicular to the curve. These assumptions are the same as in the beam theory: bending stresses are distributed linearly in both directions, and both axial and shear stresses are constant.

In summary, solid elements are a natural choice for meshing models with approximately the same size in all three dimensions, shells are the natural choice to mesh sheet metal models, and beams are the natural choice to mesh structural members.

Beam cross section geometry is only used to define beam element properties such as the area and second moments of inertia of the beam cross-section. It does not become part of the finite element model.

The information about beam cross sections is retrieved from the SolidWorks model which must be created as a Weldment. It is important to understand that solid geometry of a Weldment is not meshed when beam elements are used. What is meshed is the underlying wire frame geometry (Figure 17-3).

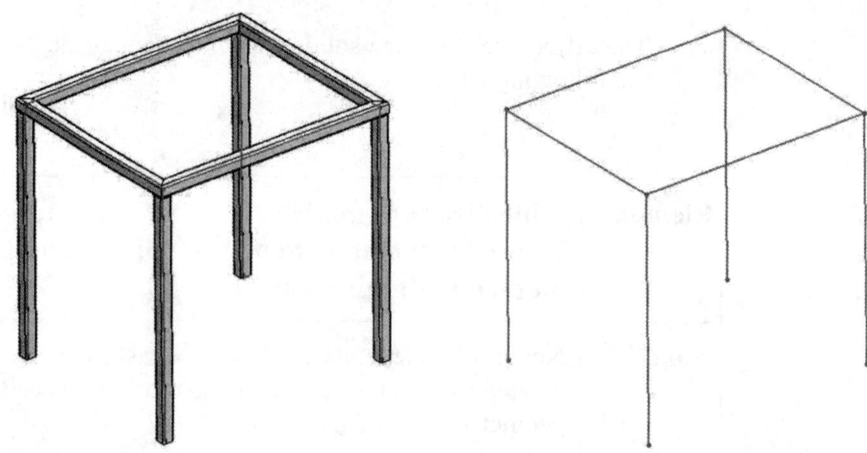

Figure 17-3: Solid model and the underlying wire frame geometry

Solid geometry is used only to define beam cross sections. Beam elements are created by meshing curves. You can think of beam elements as lines with assigned beam cross section properties. Currently, only straight lines can be meshed with beam elements.

Corner treatments and trims have no relevance in beam element models. Before creating study, change to configuration *02 no end treatment* where end treatment is suppressed (Figure 17-4).

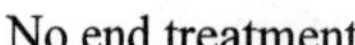

No end treatment

End treatment applied

Figure 17-4: Corner treatment and trims have no relevance in beam element models. Both geometries will produce the same finite element model when meshed with beam elements.

Procedure

Having examined the ROPS part, move to SolidWorks **Simulation** and create a **Static** study. Simulation recognizes the weldment geometry and anticipates that we intend to use beam elements. It creates a Solid Body for each structural member present in the geometry (Figure 17-5).

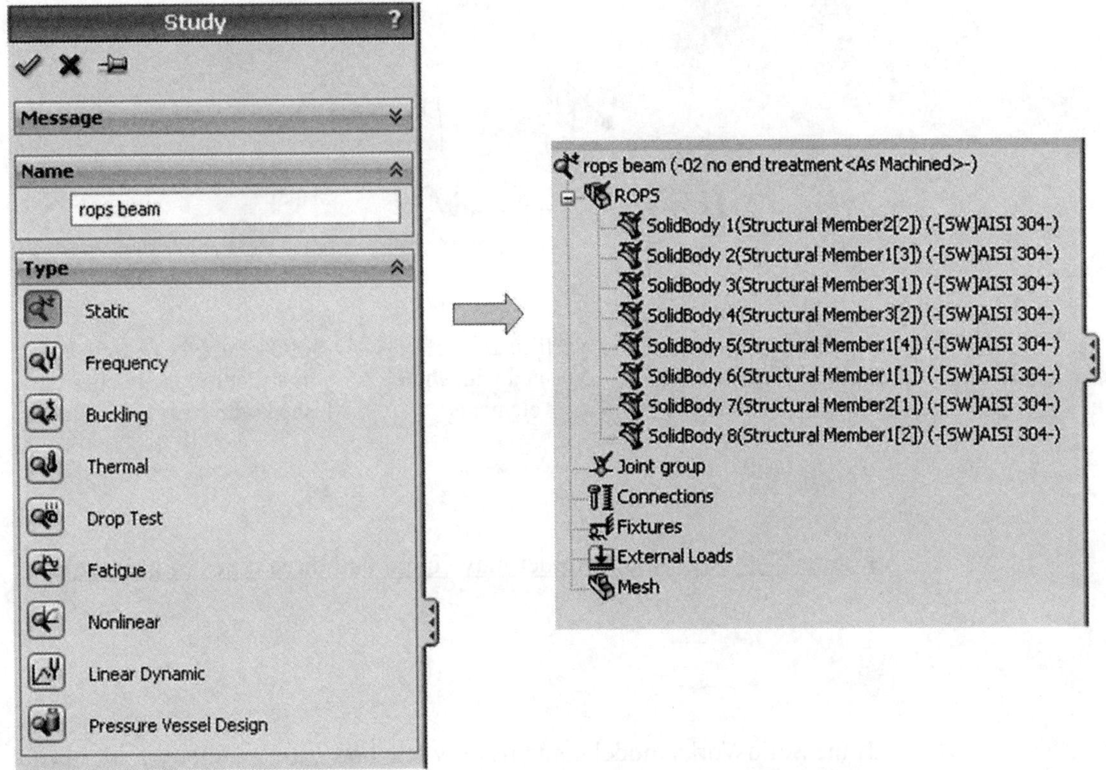

Figure 17-5: Study definition with beam elements

By default, the structural member is meshed with beam elements. You may change it by right-clicking and select Treat as Solid.

Material can be imported from the SolidWorks model or defined in SolidWorks Simulation individually to each or all beams. Here, material was imported from the SolidWorks model.

Recall Figure 4-2 which shows icons denoting geometry intended for Solid and Shell meshing. We may now append it by one more: Beam geometry (Figure 17-6).

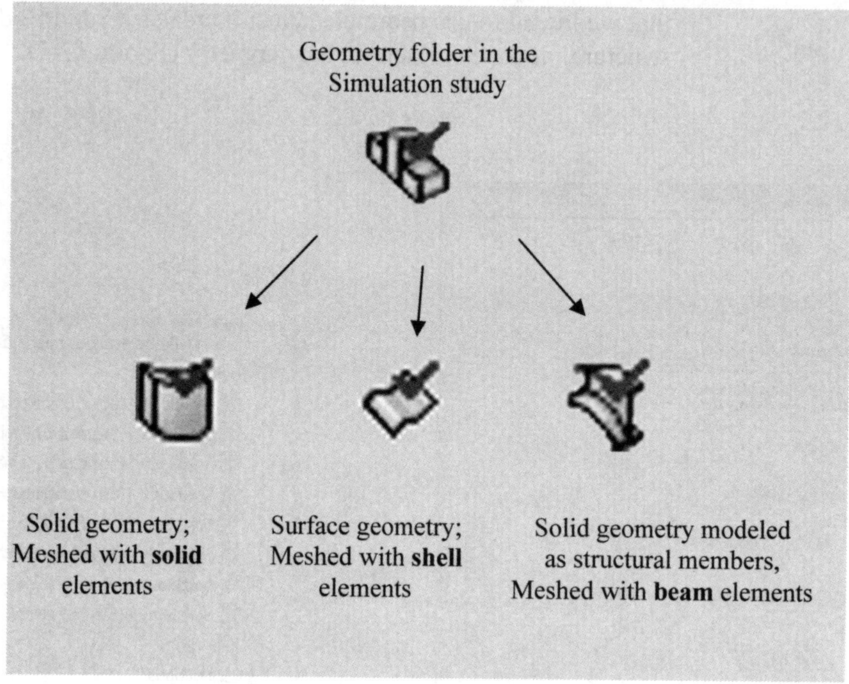

Figure 17-6: A geometry folder may contain all three types of geometries

If the SolidWorks model contains only one body, the geometry folder is not shown in the **Simulation** study. Otherwise, items in the geometry folder are marked by icons as shown in Figure 17-6. In many cases the automatic designation of geometry to one of three geometry types can be changed. **Beams** may be replaced by **Solids** and **Surfaces,** and sheet metal parts may be replaced by **Solids**. This is accomplished by right-clicking the geometry folder component and selecting the appropriate choice from the pop-up menu.

In this exercise we accept default assignment of all geometry to **Beam** elements. As Figure 17-5 indicates, the geometry folder holds eight bodies and they are all intended for meshing with beam elements.

The next step is the definition of connectivity between the soon to be created beams.

Right-click the *Joint Group* folder and select **Edit** from the pop-up menu to open the **Edit Joints** window which shows automatically created joints. If necessary, these automatically created joints may be edited in this window, Accept the default selection **All** beams and click **Calculate** to create joints automatically (Figure 17-7).

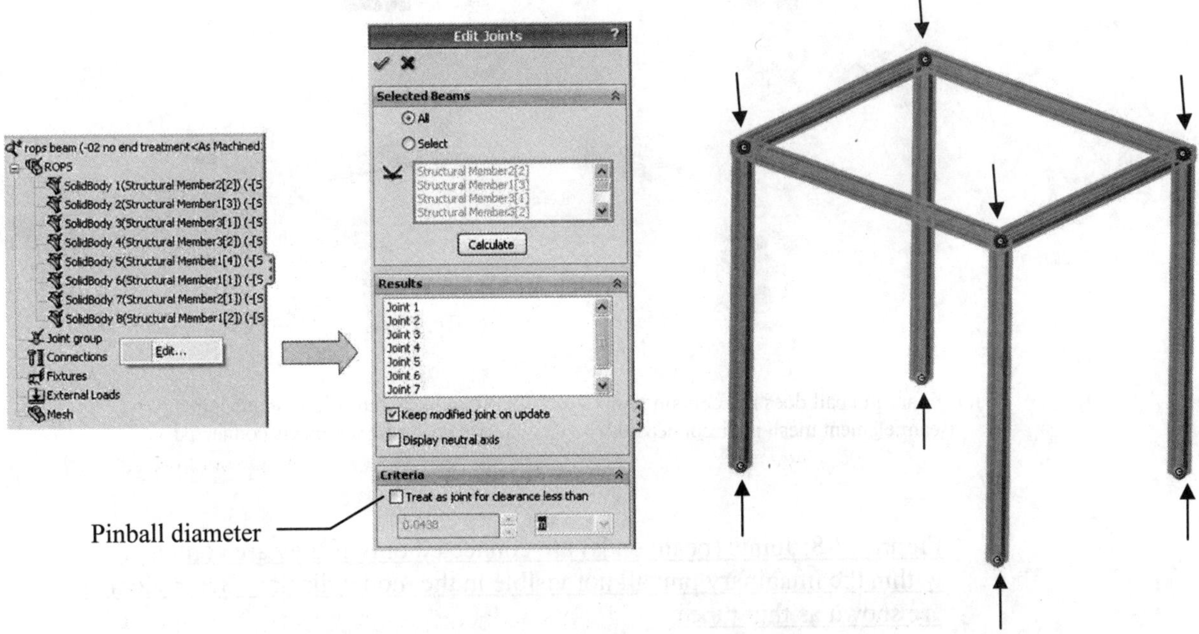

Figure 17-7: Joints are automatically created between. Arrows indicate joint positions.

No action is required in our case._Working with a simplified geometry facilitated automatic joint creation.

Joints (or beam ends) are connected to each other only if they are contained within the pinball diameter which can be changed in **Edit joints** window. It is recommended that beam ends intended to be connected are made coincident or very close. Non coincident beam ends can still be connected if they fall inside the pinball, but this may result in a "patch-up" beam element mesh (Figure 17-8).

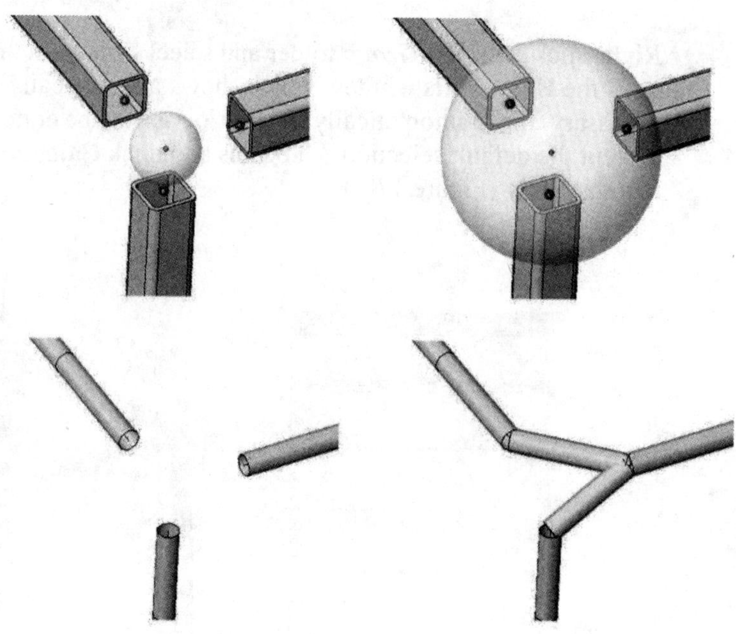

Imaginary pin ball does not contain joints.
Beam element mesh is disconnected

Imaginary pin ball contains joints.
Beam element mesh is connected

Figure 17-8: Joints (beam ends) are connected only if they are contained within the imaginary pinball not visible in the model display. Beam elements are shown as thin tubes

Beam elements are graphically depicted as round tubes, even though the beam elements are in fact just lines. The tube diameter is always the same, regardless of the actual cross-section size, shape and orientation.

Disjoined structural members can be connected if their ends fall within the volume of pinball (Figure 17-8 top right). However, the beam element mesh (bottom right) will then contain automatically created connecting elements. This may create unpredictable results.

Apply restraints to all four joints at the free ends (at the bottom) of the vertical members (Figure 17-9).

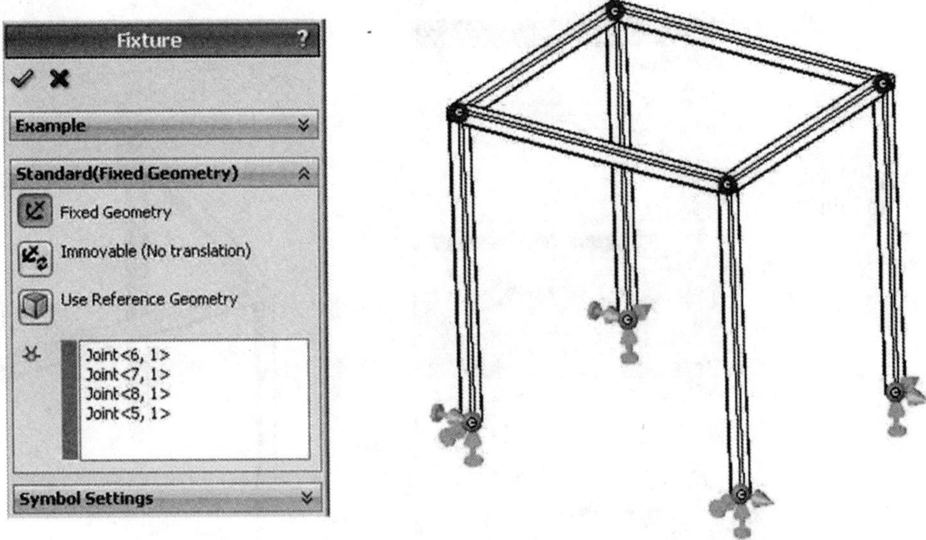

Figure 17-9: Fixed restraint applied to the free ends of vertical members

Note that beam elements have six degrees of freedom per node and, therefore, can distinguish between Fixed and Immovable restraint. Here, we need to apply a Fixed restraint.

Apply a 2500 lb load to two corners as shown in Figure 17-10.

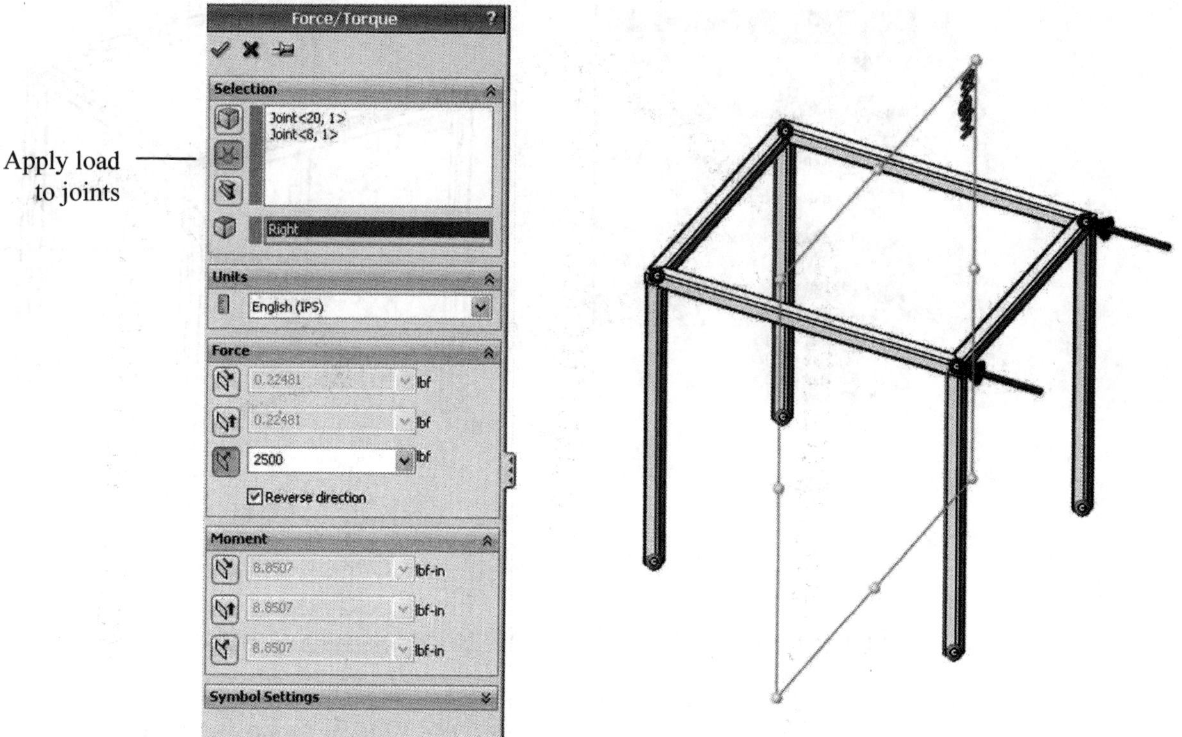

Figure 17-10: Force load applied to the corner joint

Note that beam elements have six degrees of freedom per node and therefore can be loaded with force as well as with moment load.

Now create the beam element mesh, noting that there are no user controlled mesh parameters. The beam element mesh is shown in Figure 17-11.

Figure 17-11: A beam element mesh is created from curves (here straight lines) used in the SolidWorks model to define Structural Members

A beam element is a line with cross-section properties taken from Structural Member cross section geometry. This is schematically illustrated in Figure 1-9.

Run the solution and create a displacement plot (Figure 17-12) as well as a stress plot (Figure 17-13). Note that while the undeformed model is shown as solid geometry, the displaced model is shown as "tubes".

Figure 17-12: Resultant displacement results of ROPS model

Figure 17-13: Stress plot of "Highest axial and bending" stresses showing the location of maximum stress.

The stress results 20800psi, compared with material yield strength of 30000psi indicates that structure is below yield.

Note that the "Highest axial and bending" stress is NOT von Mises stress. To understand what "worst case" stress is we need to review all stress results options available for beam elements.

The software provides the following options for viewing stresses (refer to Figure 17-14):

- Axial: Uniform axial stress = P/A
- Bending in local direction 1: Bending stresses due to moment M1 about axis 1.
- Bending in local direction 2: Bending stress due to moment M2 about axis 2
- Highest axial and bending
- Torsional
- Shear stress in DIR1
- Shear stress in DIR2

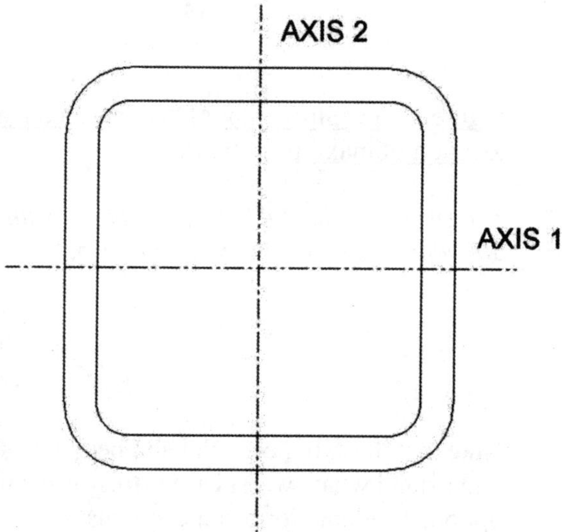

Figure 17-14: Positions of axis1 and axis2 for beam cross section used in this exercise

Axis1 and Axis2 cross the centroid of the cross section. The second moment of inertia of this cross section about each axis is the same due to the double symmetry of this cross section.

Highest axial and bending is calculated by combining axial stress and bending stresses due to moments M1 and M2. This is the default selection in the **Stress Plot** window.

Simulation offers ample ways of analyzing beam element results such as a beam diagram of bending moment, shown in Figure 17-15. Also, investigate listing **Beam Forces.**

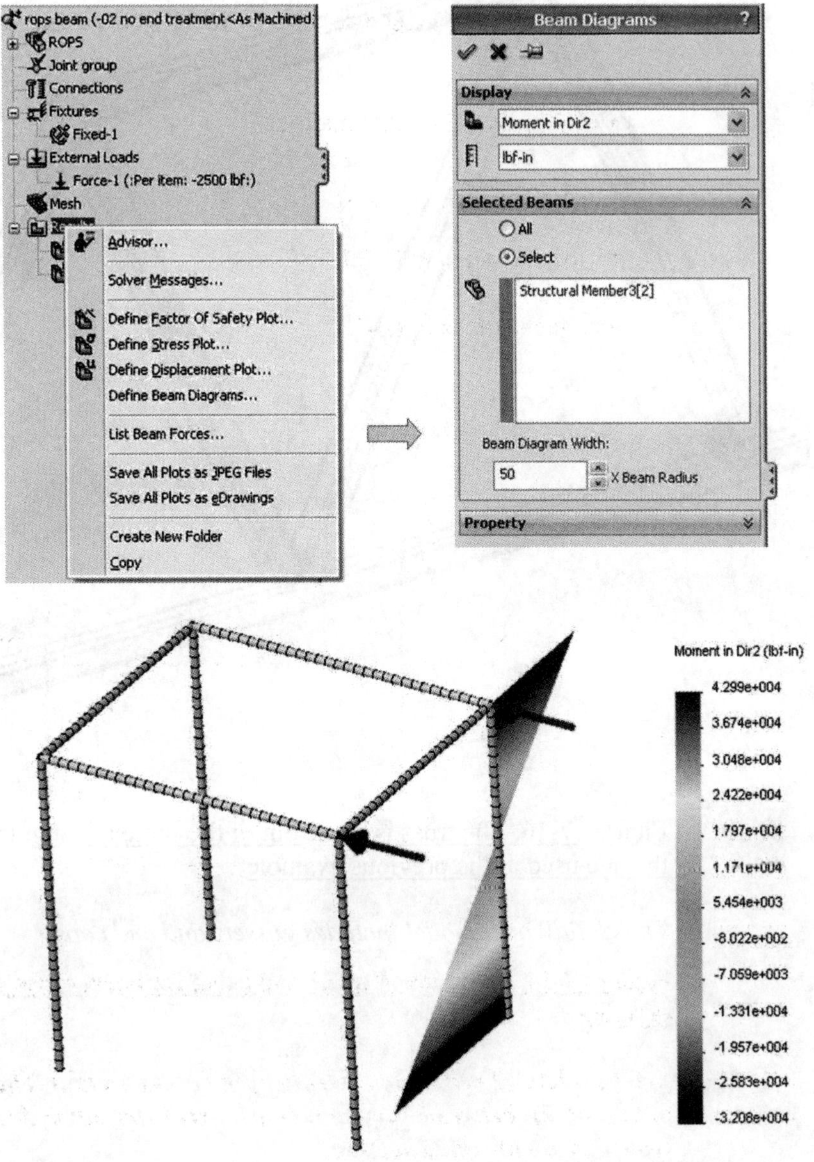

Figure 17-15: Bending Moments in direction 2 shown for one vertical beam

The Beam Diagrams window is called from the pop-up menu activated by right-clicking the Results folder.

For a better understanding of beam elements we will review another example shown in Figure 17-16. Open the part TRUSS.

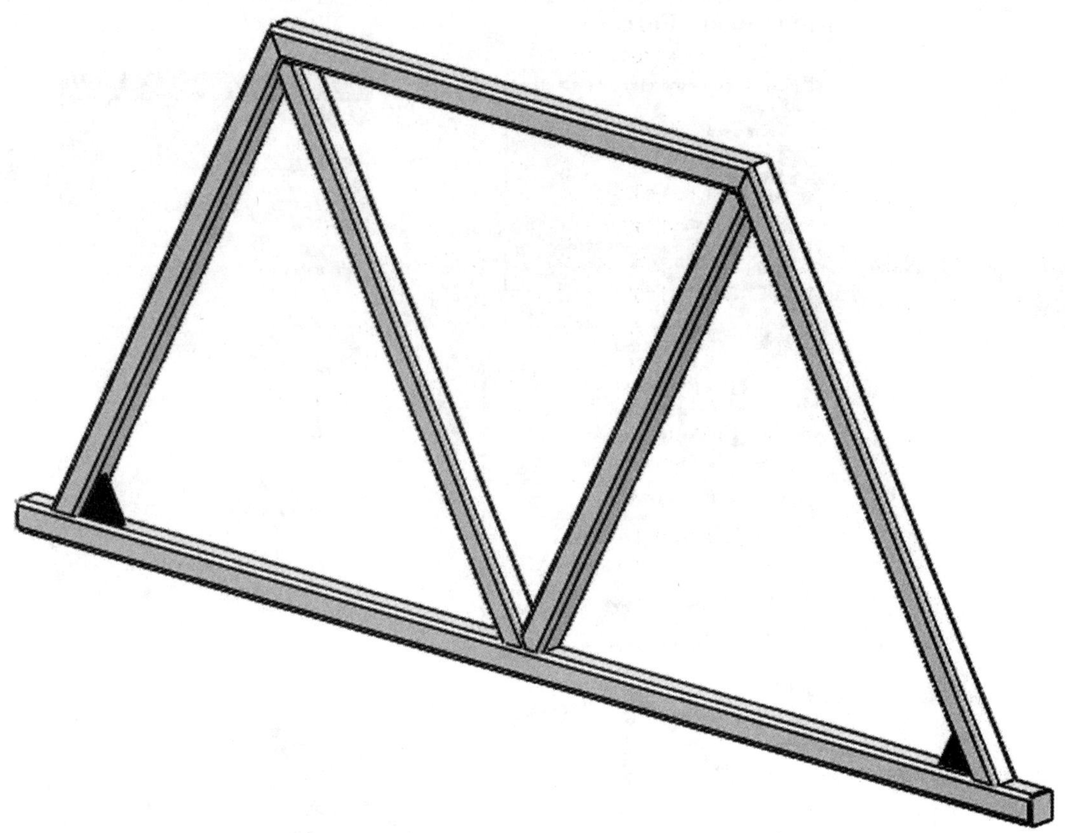

Figure 17-16: The truss is made out of the same rectangular hollow tube as the one used in the previous example

This SolidWorks model includes gussets and end caps.

Change the configuration of the SolidWorks to *03 no end treatment* to suppress gussets, end caps and end treatments. These details may interfere with the definition of joints in the beam mesh. Another way would be to remove them from analysis as shown in Figure 17-17.

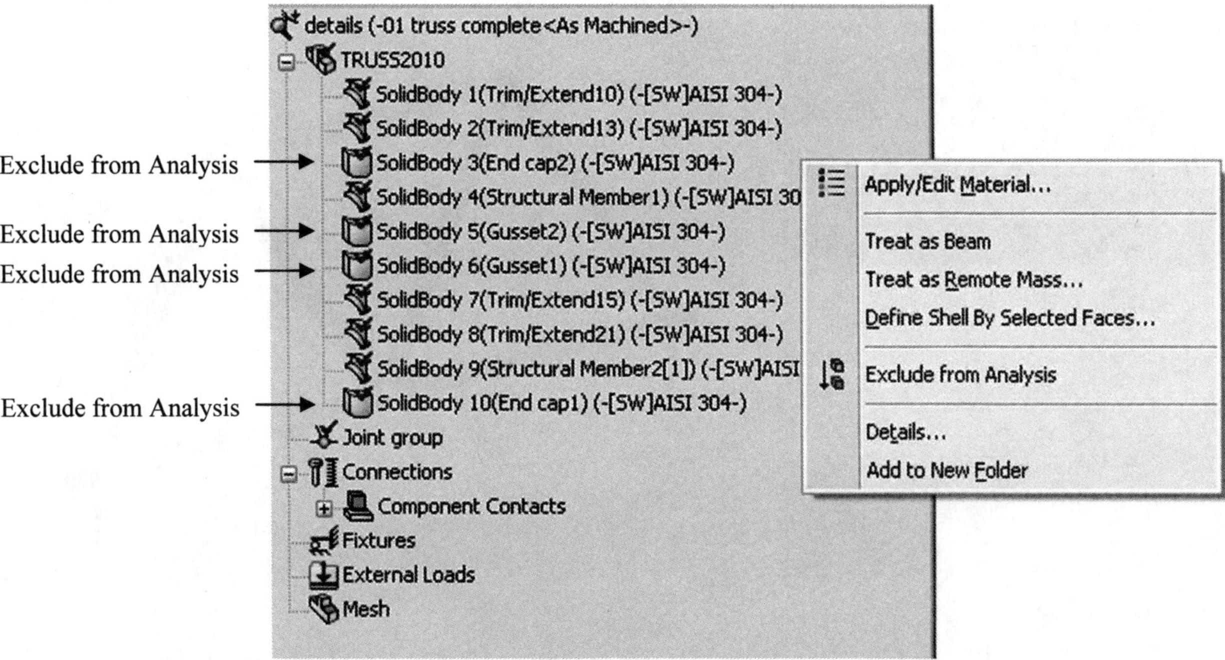

Figure 17-17: Details can be excluded from analysis by right-clicking the corresponding component in the geometry folder and selecting Exclude from Analysis

This is for information only. In this exercise we exclude details from the analysis by suppressing them in the SolidWorks Feature Manager.

Define a static study *weldment01.* Next, right-click the *Joint Group* folder and verify that seven joints have been correctly calculated (Figure 17-18).

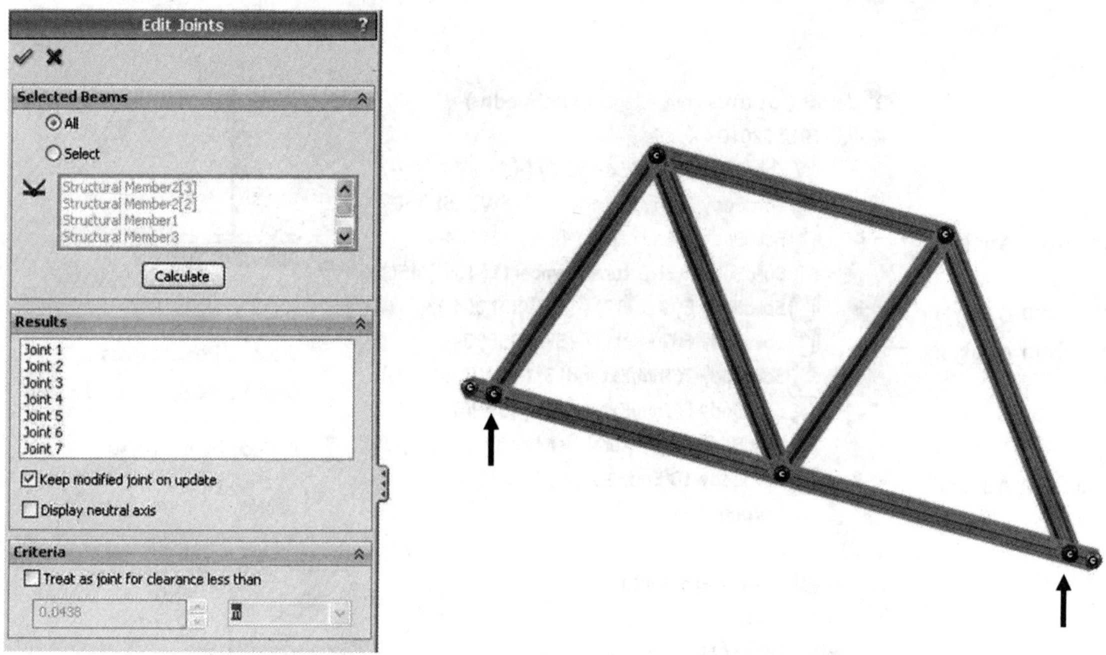

Figure 17-18: Seven joints (including two beam ends) were calculated

These joints have been calculated using configuration 03 no end treatment. Restraints (Figure 17-19) will be applied to the joints indicated by the arrows

Apply restraints and a load to the joints as shown in Figure 17-19.

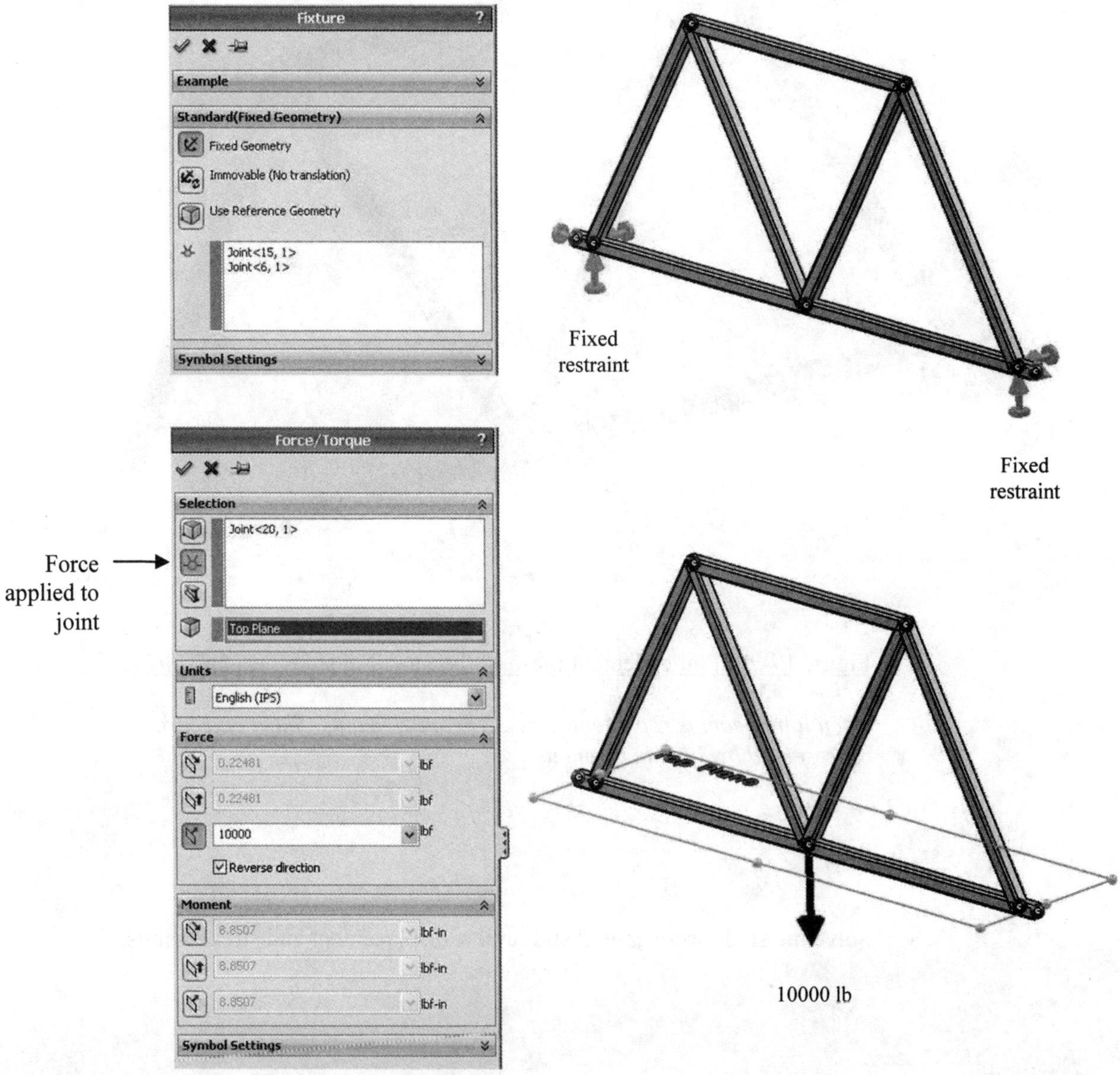

Fixture
Example
Standard(Fixed Geometry)
Fixed Geometry
Immovable (No translation)
Use Reference Geometry
Joint<15, 1>
Joint<6, 1>
Symbol Settings

Fixed restraint

Fixed restraint

Force applied to joint

Force/Torque
Selection
Joint<20, 1>
Top Plane
Units
English (IPS)
Force
0.22481 lbf
0.22481 lbf
10000 lbf
Reverse direction
Moment
8.8507 lbf-in
8.8507 lbf-in
8.8507 lbf-in
Symbol Settings

Top Plane

10000 lb

Figure 17-19: Restraints and loads applied to joints

Mesh the model to produce a mesh as shown in Figure 17-20.

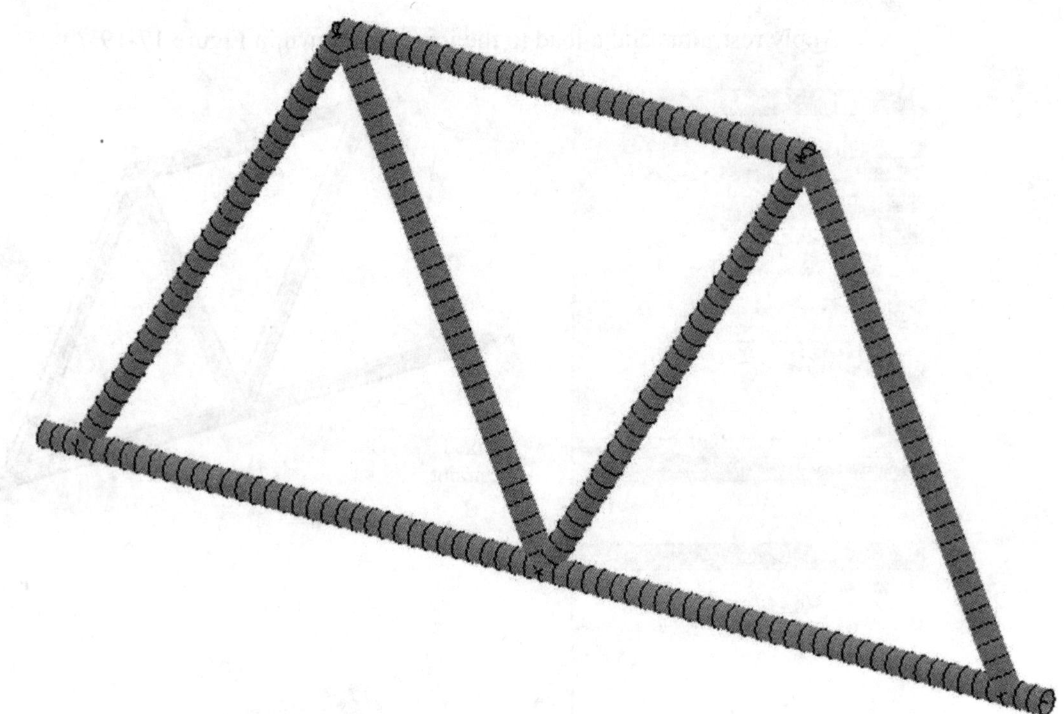

Figure 17-20: Finite element mesh of the model in study *weldment01*

Each long beam is represented by 32 beam elements. Short ends are represented by 3 beam elements.

Solve the study *weldment02* and review displacement and stress results.

Now copy study *weldment01* into study *weldment02*. In study *weldment02,* select all beams in the *truss* folder and right-click to open a pop-up menu. Select **Edit definition** to open the **Apply/Edit beam** window. Select **Truss** in the **Apply/Edit beam** window (Figure 17-21).

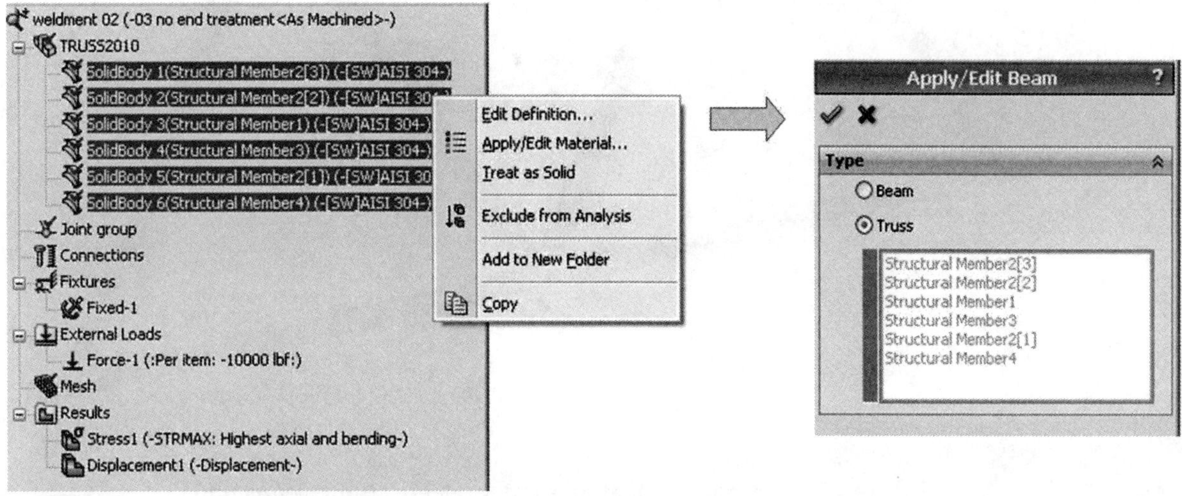

Figure 17-21: All beams are now defined as trusses

This can be done for all beams or individually for selected beams.

This redefines connectivity between beams from rigid to pin joints. While beams can be loaded with any combination of forces and moments, trusses can be only loaded with axial force. Trusses behave as a tension/compression springs and are meshed with only one element (Figure 17-22)

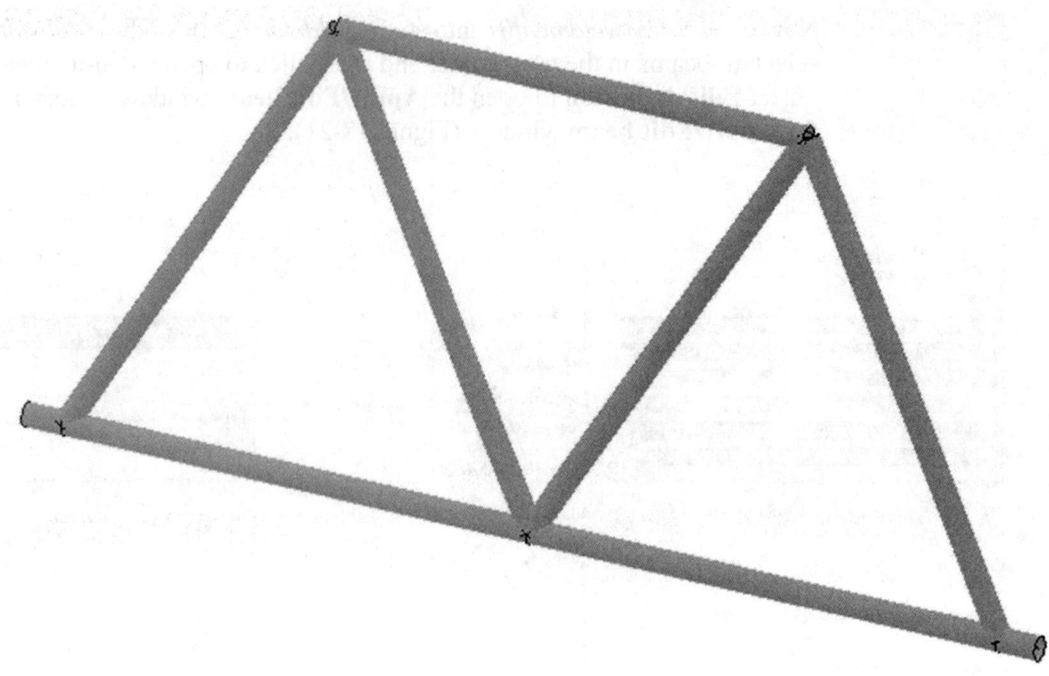

Figure 17-22: Finite element mesh of model in study *weldment03*

Each beam is represented by one truss element. There are nine elements in the model. They behave as if they were pin jointed and can be loaded only with axial load.

An attempt to run a solution of study *weldment03* displays an error message shown at the top of Figure 17-23.

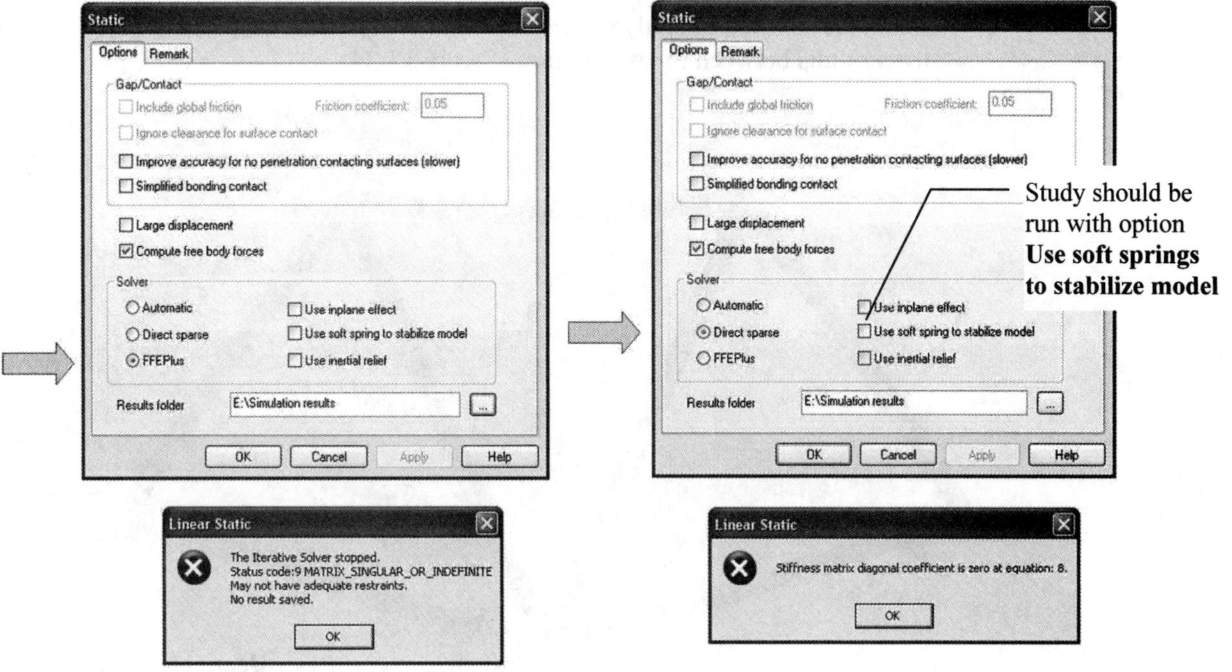

FFEPlus solver (iterative) | Direct Sparse solver

Figure 17-23: An attempt to run study *weldment02* brings up an error message which differs with the solver used but in either case is caused by Rigid Body Motions present in the model.

The study needs to be run with the option Use soft springs to stabilize model.

The supports are insufficient and allow rigid body motion of the model because truss elements have only three degrees of freedom and can not accept any restraints on rotations. Therefore, the entire model can spin about the line passing through the supports. The short ends can freely rotate about the joint where restraint is defined. To eliminate these rigid body motions we need to execute a solution with the **Use soft springs to stabilize model** option checked (Figure 17-23).

Obtain the solution of study *weldment02* and compare the displacement and stress results between the two studies (Figure 17-24).

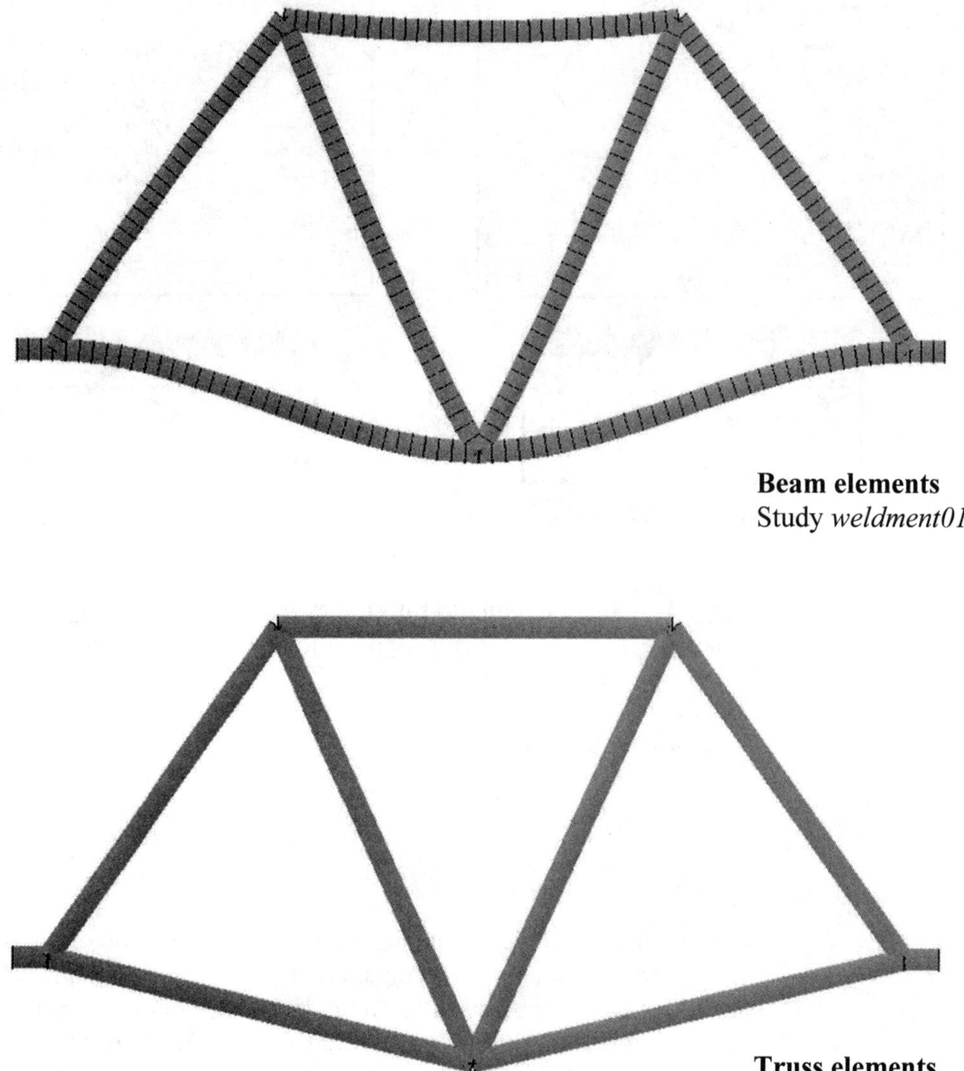

Figure 17-24: The deformation pattern of the model with beam elements (top) and truss elements (bottom)

Note that the short ends in models with truss elements do not experience displacements.

Bending of structural members observed in the beam element model proves that beam elements are rigidly connected to each other and transmit bending moments. Conversely, truss elements are connected by pin joints; they can not transmit bending. Deformation of truss elements can only take the form of stretching and compressing, therefore deformed truss elements remain straight.

Verify that the **Highest axial and bending stress** and **Axial** stress are the same for the truss element model. This is because axial stress is the only stress component present in the truss elements.

Notes:

18: Vibration Analysis - Modal Time History and Harmonic

Topics covered

- Modal Time History analysis (Time Response)
- Harmonic analysis (Frequency Response)
- Modal Superposition Method
- Damping

What is dynamic analysis?

In preparation for the dynamic analysis exercises, we need to clarify an important terminology issue. The term "Dynamic Analysis" applies to an analysis of both unrestrained and restrained bodies such as mechanisms and structures. "Dynamic Analysis" within the scope of FEA deals only with the vibration of deformable bodies about the position of equilibrium. A more appropriate term to use would be "Vibration Analysis" but the term "Dynamic Analysis" is well entrenched in the FEA literature. We will use the term understanding that Dynamic Analysis within FEA really means vibration analysis of structures.

All types of analyses that we have discussed so far have assumed that the load is not function of time. We will now lift this restriction to introduce two common types of dynamic analyses: **Modal Time History** and **Harmonic,** which are available in SolidWorks **Simulation** Advanced Professional. **Modal Time History** is also known as a Time Response analysis and **Harmonic** analysis as Frequency Response analysis or as Steady State Harmonic Response analysis. **Modal Time History** and **Harmonic analyses** both belong to the category of linear analyses.

Modal superposition method

The review of dynamic analyses needs to be preceded by a description of the modal superposition method on which both Time Response and Frequency Response analyses are most often based. The modal superposition method represents a dynamic response of a vibrating structure by using the superposition of responses that characterize single degree of freedom (1DOF) systems. The natural frequencies of these 1DOF systems correspond to the natural frequencies of the analyzed structure. The number of 1DOF contributing to a dynamic response is equal to the number of modes calculated by a pre-requisite modal (frequency) analysis. How many modes should then be calculated to represent dynamic responses using the modal superposition method? The first few modes are the most important, but the exact number of required modes is not known prior to analysis. One should use a convergence process to demonstrate that increasing the number of modes past a certain number no longer significantly affects results.

The modal superposition method is not always a prerequisite for dynamic analysis. Other methods, like the Direct Integration method, do not require modal analysis. SolidWorks **Simulation** uses the Direct Integration method in the **Drop test** study.

Modal Time History (Time Response) analysis

In a **Modal Time History** analysis, the applied load is an explicit function of time, mass and damping properties all of which are taken into consideration and the vibration equation appears in its full form:

$$[M]\ddot{d} + [C]\dot{d} + [K]d = F(t)$$

Where:

[M] known mass matrix

[C] known damping matrix

[K] known stiffness matrix

F(t) known vector of nodal loads, this vector is a function of time

d unknown vector of nodal displacements

Dynamic Time Response analysis requires the definition of a damping coefficient which is most often expressed as a percentage of critical damping. Readers are referred to (1) as listed in chapter 23 for selected numerical values of damping coefficients.

Dynamic time response analysis is used to model events of a short duration. A typical example would be an analysis of structure vibrations due to an impact load or acceleration applied to the base (called base excitation). Results of the Time Response analysis will capture both the response during the time when the load is applied, as well as the free vibration after the load has been removed.

Harmonic (Frequency Response) analysis

Harmonic analysis assumes that the load is a function of frequency rather than being directly dependent on time as is the case of a Time Response analysis.

$$[M]\ddot{d} + [C]\dot{d} + [K]d = F\sin(\omega t)$$

Frequency Response analysis models the structure's response to force excitation or base excitation (excitation applied to support) that is a sinusoidal function of time. It is assumed that the excitation frequency changes very slowly, hence the alternative name Steady State Harmonic Response is often used for this type of analysis. Frequency response analysis also uses the modal superposition method and requires that damping be defined, usually as a percentage of critical damping.

A typical application of frequency response analysis is a simulation of a shaker table, which we demonstrate later in this chapter.

Single Degree of Freedom Oscillator (1DOF)

To introduce **Modal Time History** and **Harmonic** analyses as implemented in SolidWorks **Simulation**, a very simple model is used to illustrate the physics of vibration. Open the assembly model 1DOF shown in Figure 18-1.

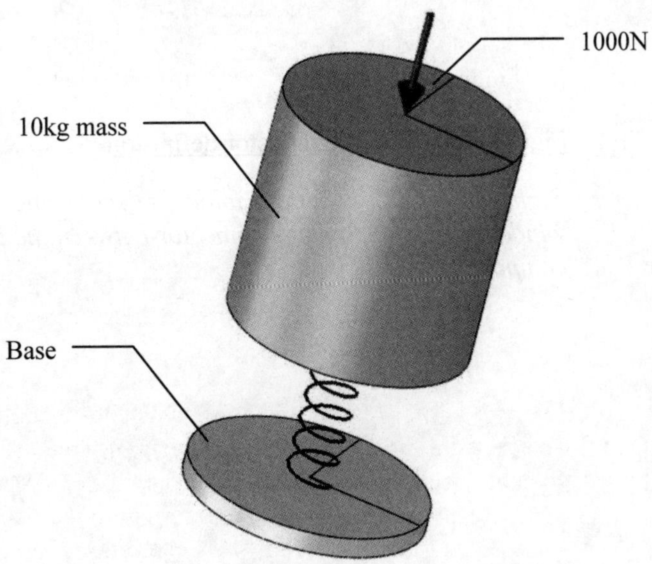

Figure 18-1: One degree of freedom oscillator

Verify that the mass of the cylinder is 10kg. Split lines form vertices which are used to attach the spring connector and to apply the excitation force.

To investigate the vibration of the 1DOF model, we start with a **Frequency** analysis. Create a **Frequency** study called *Modal*. In order to make the 1DOF model behave as a Single Degree of Freedom oscillator, apply a **Spring Connector** and **Restraint** as shown in Figure 18-2 and 18-3.

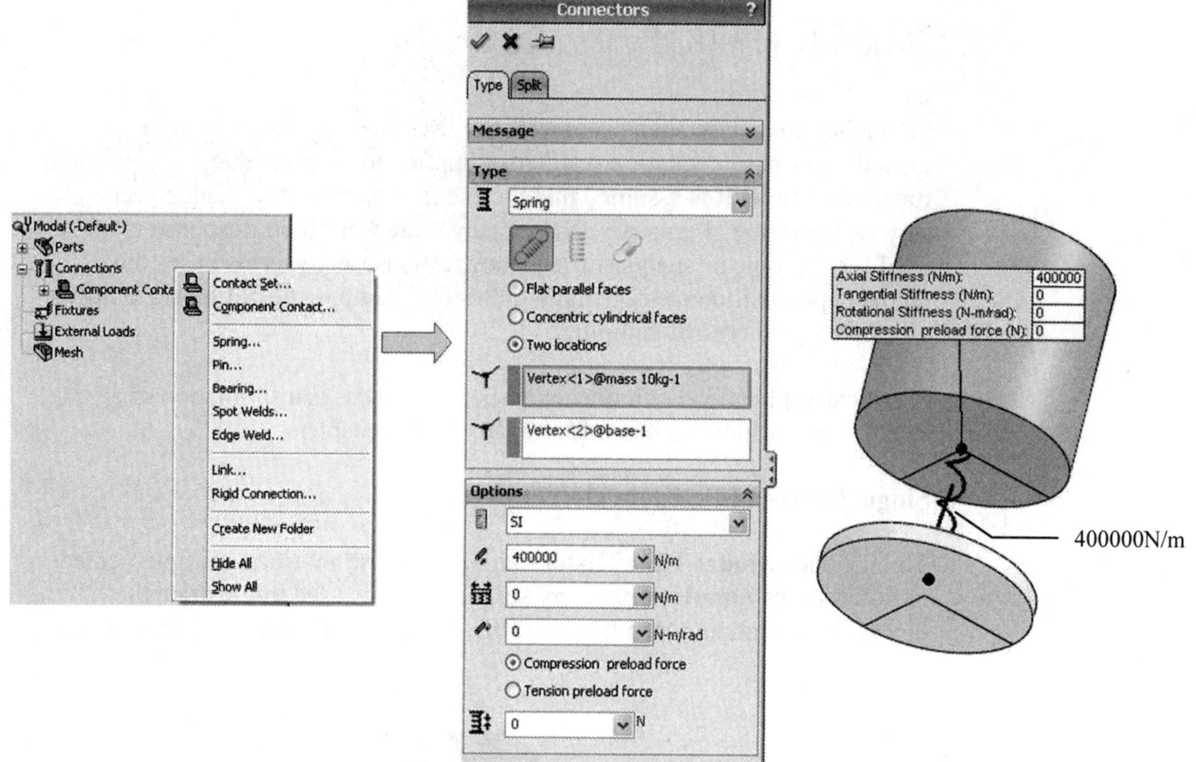

Figure 18-2: Spring connector definition

Right-click the Connections folder, select Spring to open the Connectors window. Define a Spring Connector between the center points of the two components.

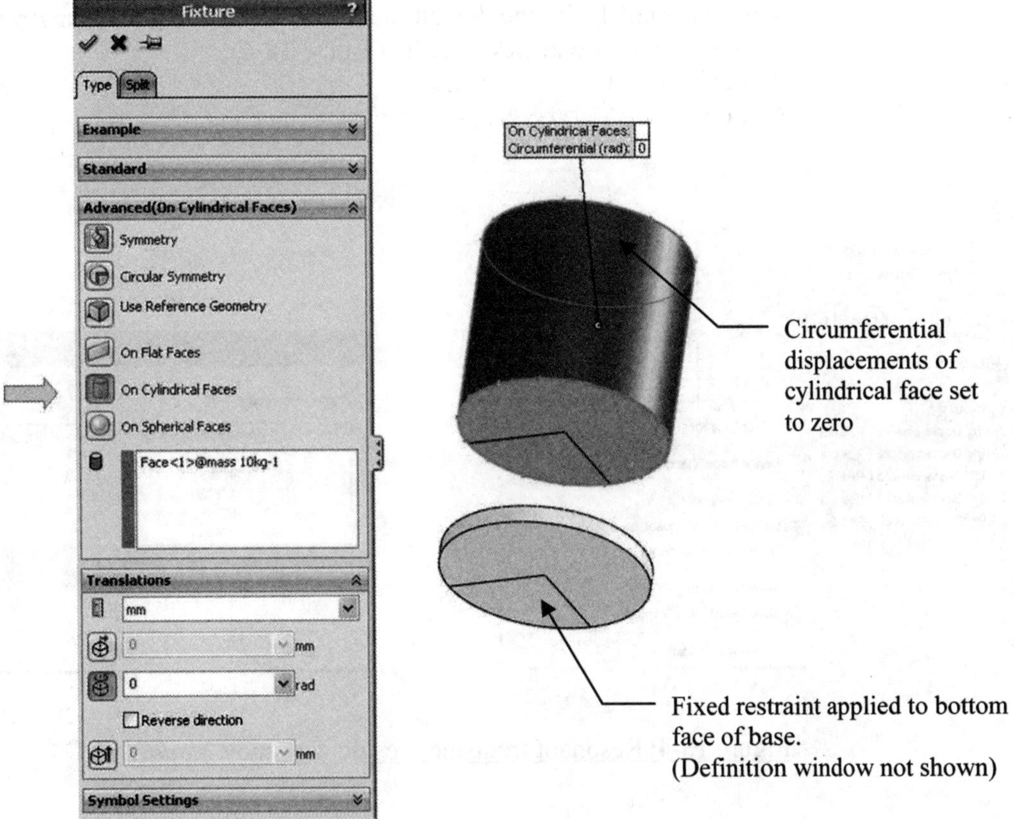

Figure 18-3: Restraints definition

Define restraints in the circumferential direction on the cylindrical face to prevent the mass from rotating. This way the 10kg mass can only move up and down.

Mesh the model with the default mesh size. Run *Modal* study and verify that the first natural frequency is 32Hz (Figure 18-4).

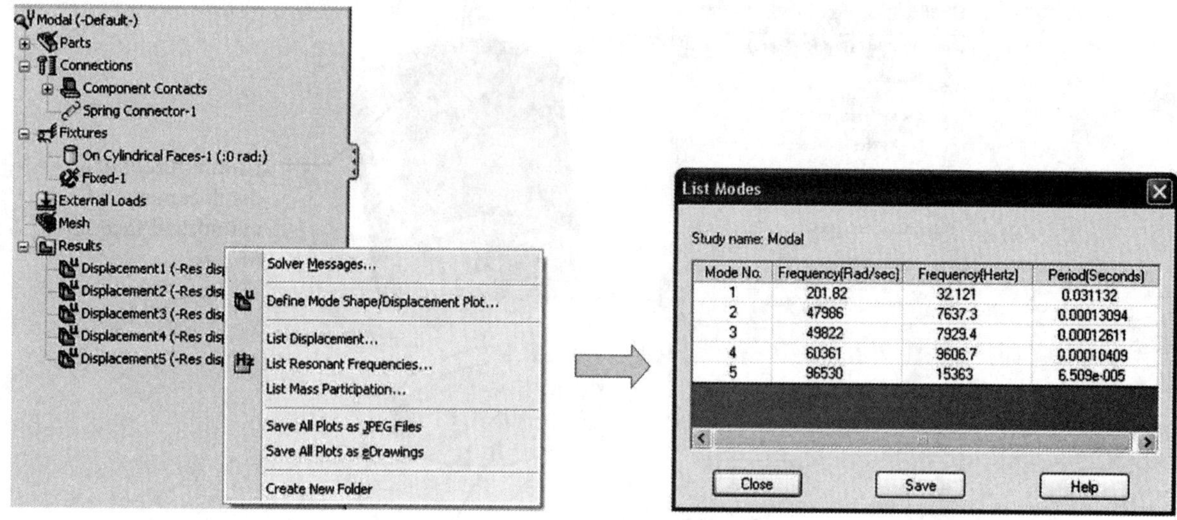

Figure 18-4: Resonant frequency results for study *Modal*

Recall from the theory of vibration that the natural frequency ω of a 1DOF is:

$$\omega = \sqrt{\frac{k}{m}} = \sqrt{\frac{400000}{10}} = 200 rad / s$$

To express the same in Hz:

$$f = \omega / 2\pi = 200 / 2\pi = 31.8 \text{ cycles/s}$$

SolidWorks **Simulation** results closely match analytical results. Note that the higher mode results shown in Figure 18-4 correspond to deformation of the cylinder, not the spring, and therefore are not related to 1DOF oscillations.

Now, create a **Modal Time History** study called *Time Response* as shown in Figure 18-5.

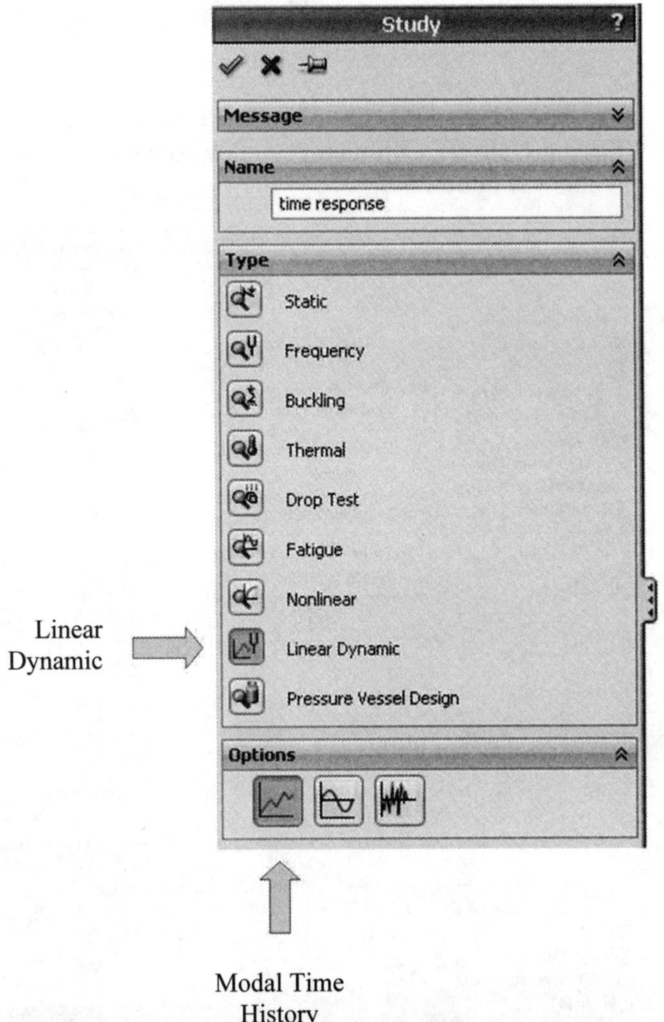

Figure 18-5 Defining a Modal Time History study

A Modal Time History study is created by selecting Linear Dynamic study with the Modal Time History option.

You can copy restraints from the modal study, but the **Spring Connector** must be defined in **Modal Time History** since its definition has an option to include damping. Damping can also be defined as modal damping which specifies damping as a fraction of critical damping. Oscillations no longer occur when the damping value is critical or above critical.

The critical damping for 1DOF is:

$$c_{cr} = 2\sqrt{km} = 4000\frac{Ns}{m}$$

To define damping as 5% of critical damping we can either enter 200 in the **Spring-Damper Connector** window, or as 0.05 in the **Global Damping** window (Figure 18-6).

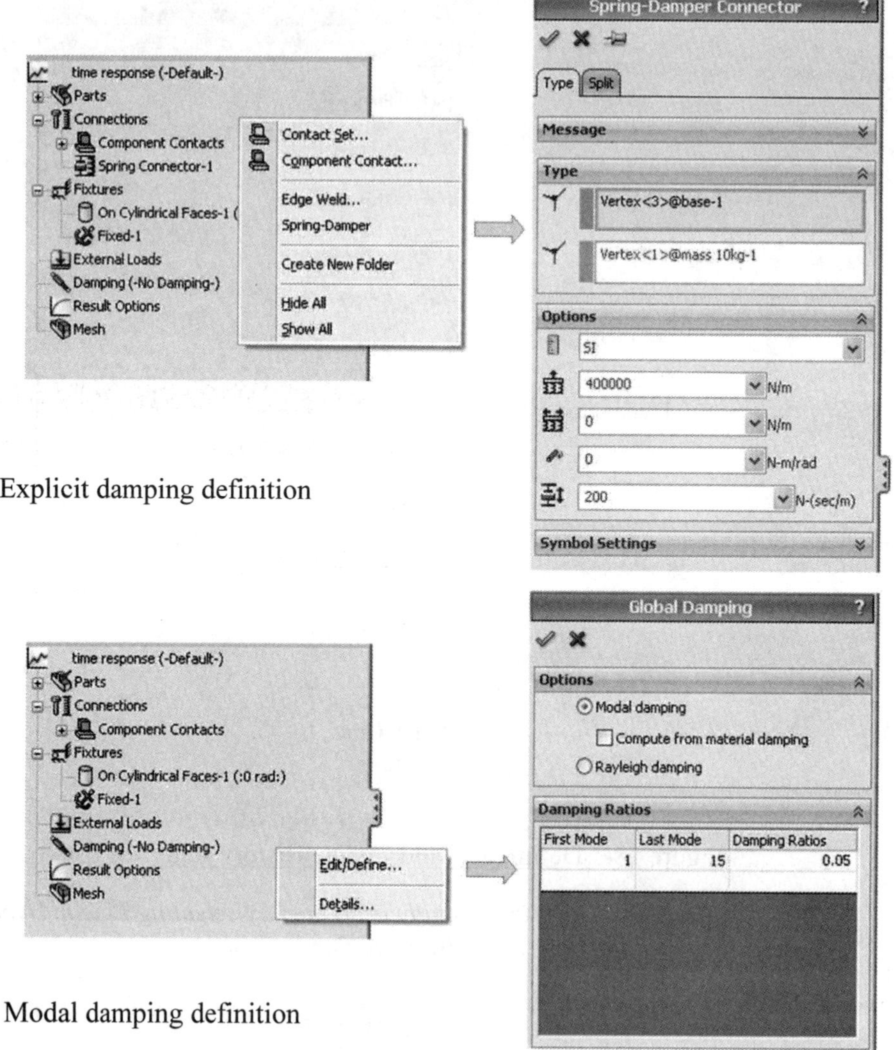

Figure 18-6: Damping can be defined explicitly (top) or as a fraction of critical damping (bottom). The entries in both windows define the same damping. In this example we use an explicit damping definition.

Modal damping makes it possible to define damping individually for each mode. Since we base analysis on one mode only, we define damping for this single mode.

Dynamic analysis requires a load defined as a function of time. To apply a 1000N force as shown in Figure 18-1 and define its time history, follow the steps explained in Figure 18-7.

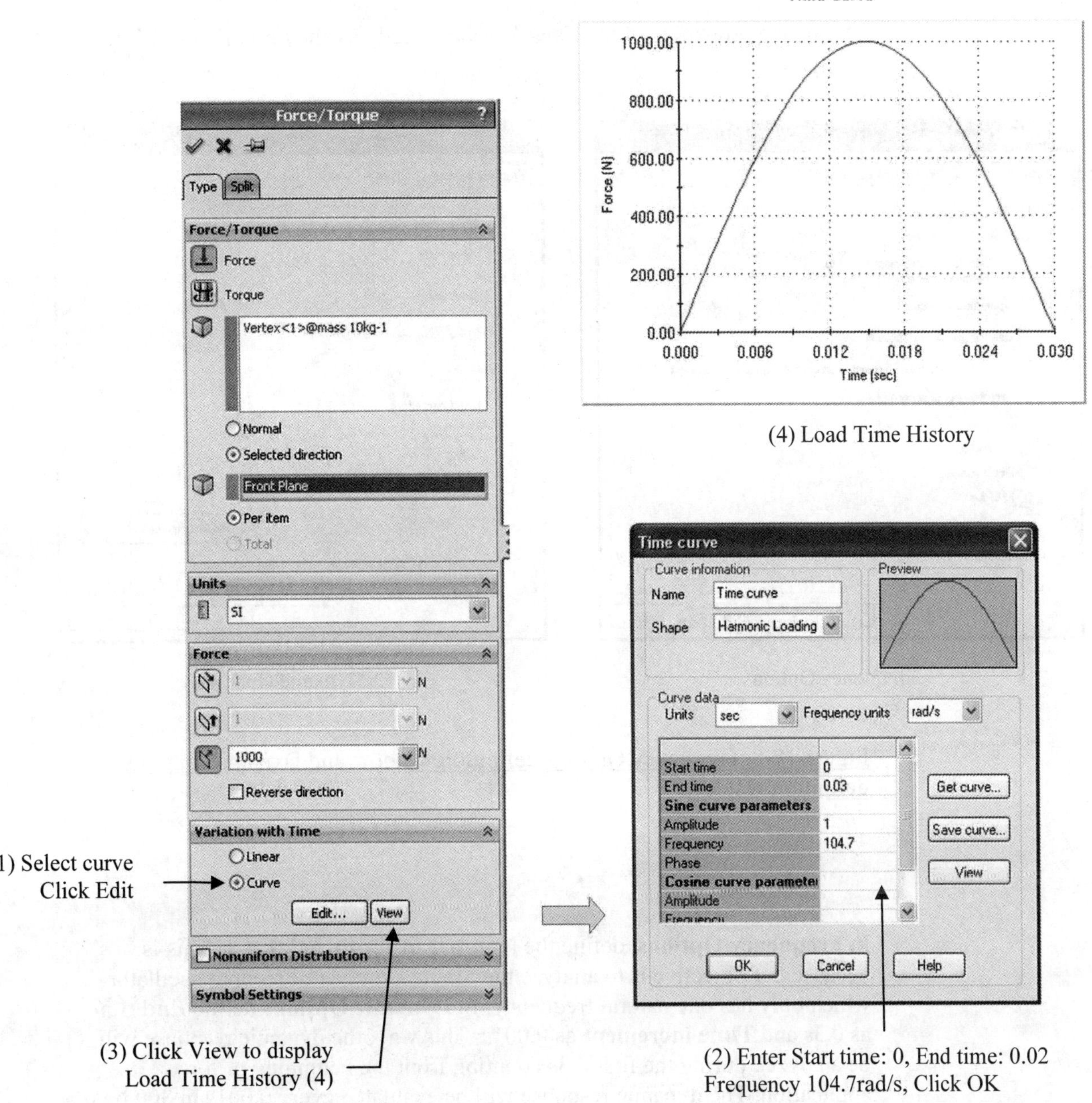

Figure 18-7: Defining load as a function of time. The force takes 0.015s to reach the maximum of 1000N, then another 0.015s to drop back to zero.

Select Variation with Time as Curve (1) and click Edit to open the Time curve definition window (2). Define the shape as harmonic loading and enter values as shown then click View (3 to examine the Load time history curve (4).

Note that neither the entry in the **Force** window nor the values defining the **Time curve** define the load time history on their own. The corresponding values are multiplied to calculate force magnitude as a function of time.

Define the properties of the *Time Response* study as shown in Figure 18-8.

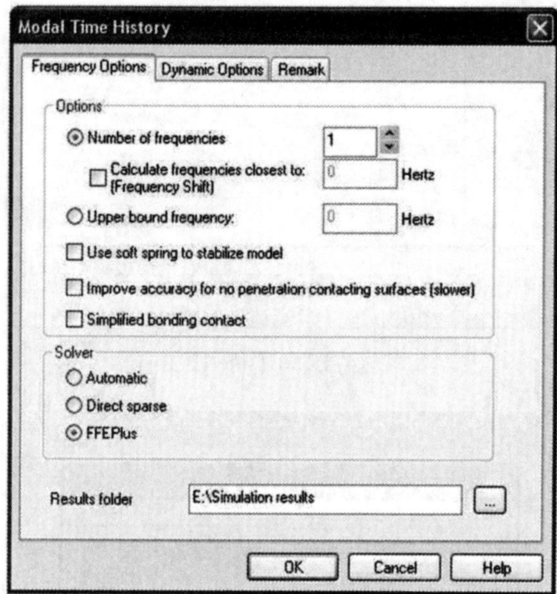

Frequency Options

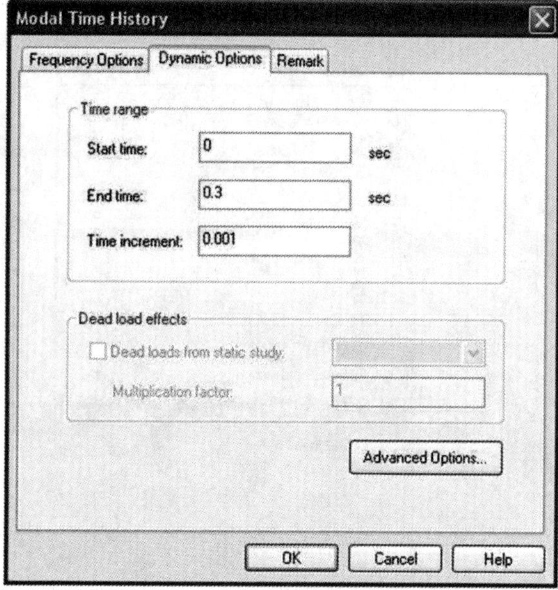

Dynamic Options

Figure 18-8: Frequency Options definition window and Dynamic Options definition window

In **Frequency Options**, define the **Number of frequencies** as 1. This is because our objective is to analyze the Single Degree of Freedom oscillator which only has one natural frequency. In **Dynamic Options** define **End time** as 0.3s and **Time increment** as 0.001s. This way, the dynamic response will be analyzed during the first 0.3s counting from the beginning of force application. The dynamic response will be evaluated every 0.001s in 300 time steps.

Note that the duration of the load is 0.03s (Figure 18-7), while the duration of analysis is 0.3s (Figure 18-8).

Define a **Sensor** as shown in Figure 18-9.

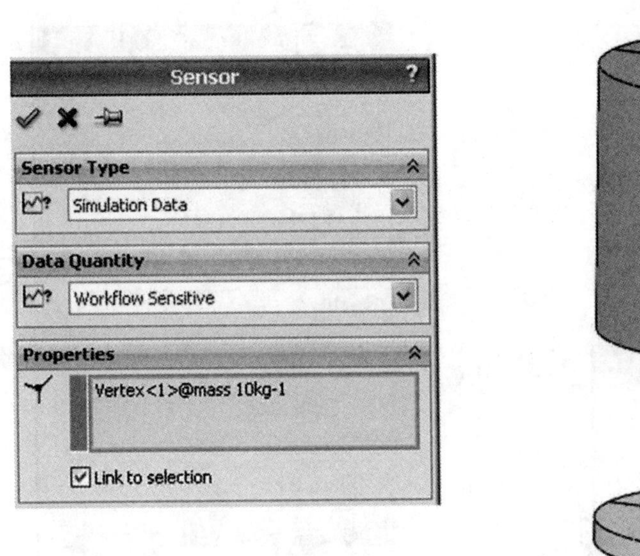

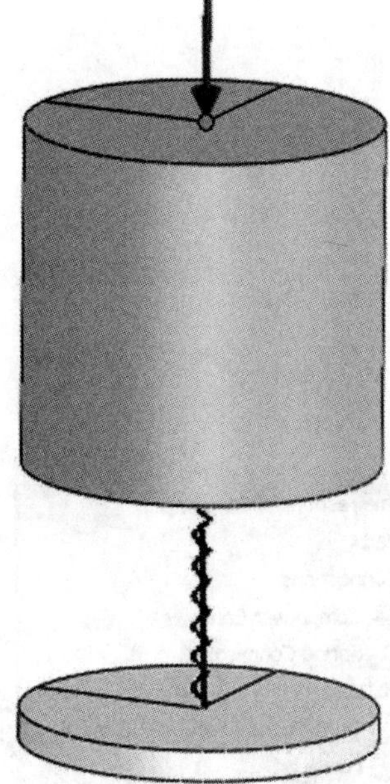

Figure 18-9: Sensor definition

Define a sensor in SolidWorks Feature Manager. Select the point where the load is applied.

Right-click the *Results Options* folder to define **Results Options,** as shown in Figure 18-10.

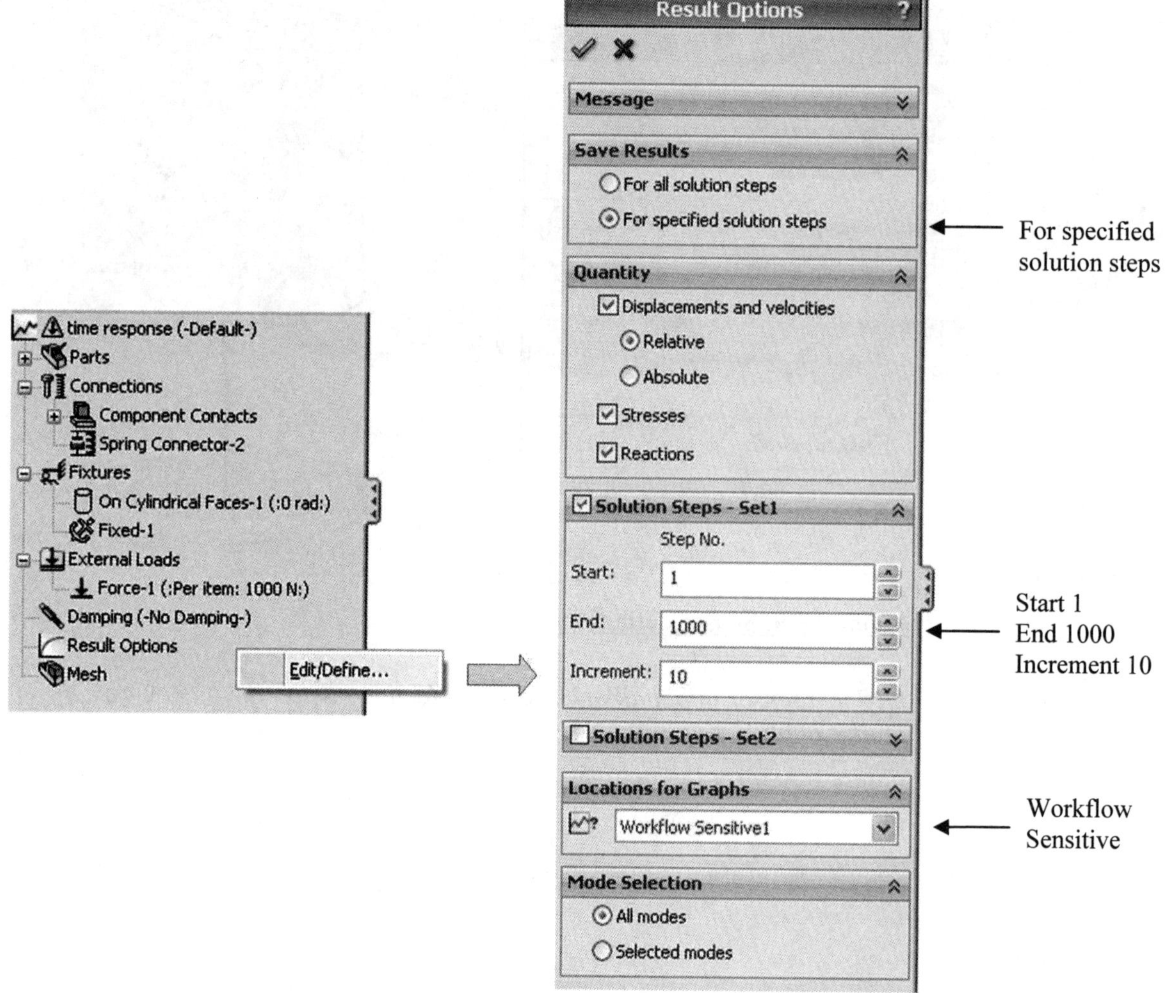

Figure 18-10 Results Options definition

Make the indicated selections in preparation for graphing results.

Mesh with a coarse mesh (element size 40mm) because accurate modeling of elastic properties of the cylinder and base is irrelevant in this exercise.

Run the *Time Response* study observing that each solution stage is completed in 300 steps as specified in study properties (Figure 18-8). Right-click the *Results* folder and follow the steps illustrated in Figure 18-11 to create a graph showing displacement in the sensor location as a function of time.

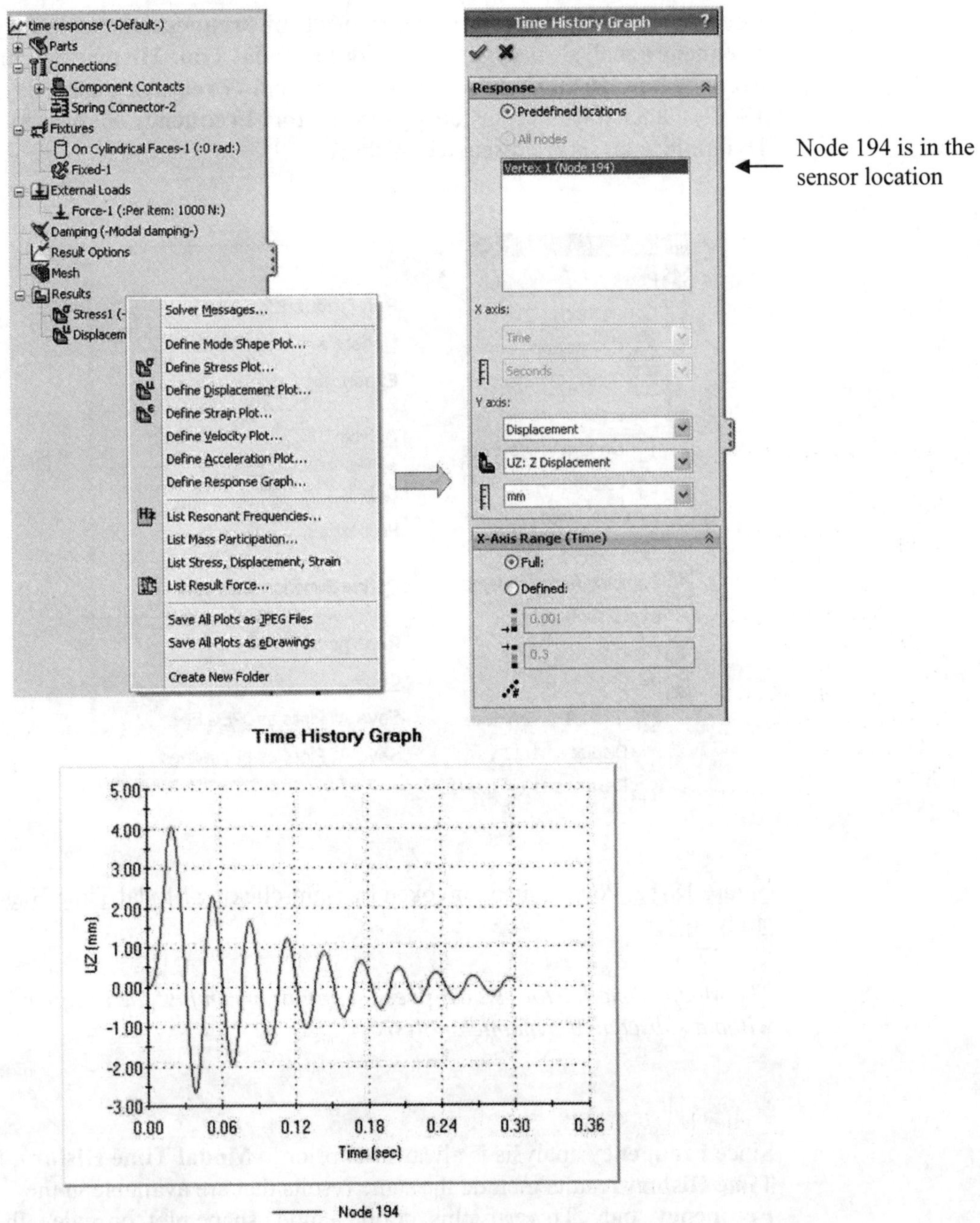

UZ displacement of node 194 as function of time

Figure 18-11: Displacement of cylinder (10kg mass) for the first 0.3s after load application

Note that after 0.03s, the load becomes zero and 1DOF performs free damped oscillations.

Since **Modal Time History** requires results of **Frequency** analysis, **Frequency** analysis is always run prior to **Modal Time History**. Within **Modal Time History** you may select to run only **Frequency** analysis (Figure 18-12). Other ways of transferring results from **Frequency** analysis to **Dynamic** analysis are discussed in chapter 19.

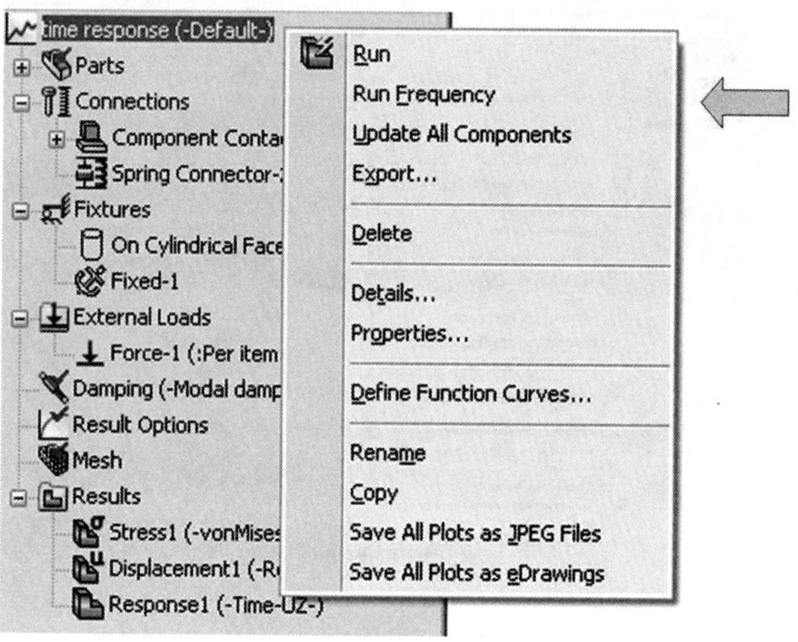

Figure 18-12: Pop-up menu invoked by right-clicking Modal Time History study folder

The Modal Time History study gives an option to run just the Frequency study without subsequent dynamic analysis.

Since **Frequency** analysis is always run prior to **Modal Time History**, **Modal Time History** results include the same results that are available in the **Frequency** study. To verify this, define a mode shape plot, or review the list of modal frequencies. Note that you will see only one frequency as specified in **Modal Time History** properties (Figure 18-8).

In continuation of the 1DOF analysis, create a **Harmonic** study called *frequency response 01* (Figure 18-13).

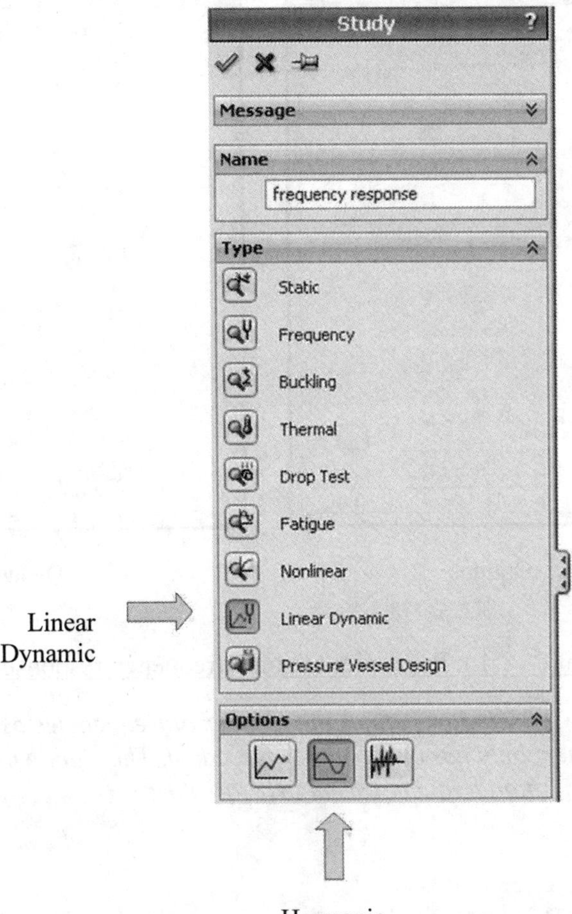

Figure 18-13: Defining a Harmonic study

A harmonic study is created by selecting a Linear Dynamic study with the Harmonic option.

We will investigate the dynamic response of 1DOF under an oscillating force with a 1000N magnitude, applied to the same point as in previous study. The frequency of oscillation will change from 0Hz to 100Hz. The excitation force is a function of frequency. We assume that force magnitude remains constant while the frequency of oscillations increases from 0Hz to 100Hz.

$$F = 1000\sin(2\pi ft)$$

$$0 \le f \le 100$$

Define *Frequency Response 01* study properties as shown in Figure 18-14.

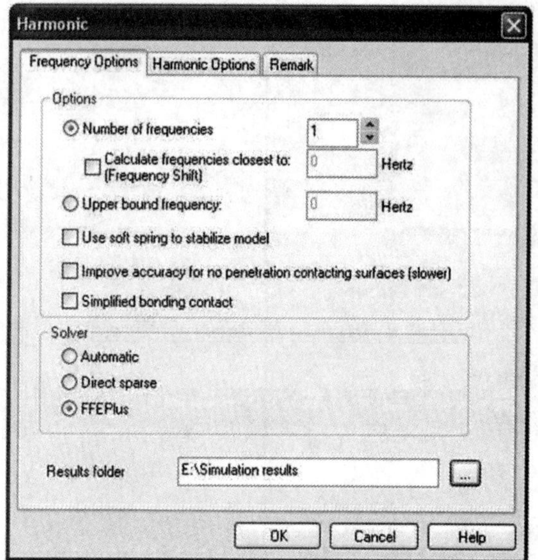

Frequency Options

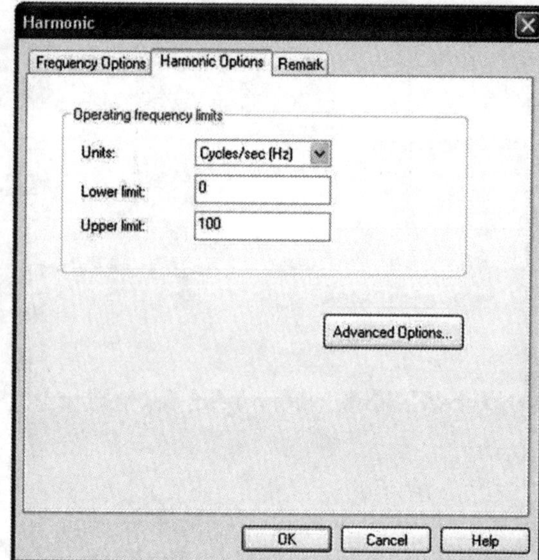

Dynamic Options

Figure 18-14: Properties of study frequency response 01

The left window defines the number of frequencies as 1 because the analyzed system only has one degree of freedom. The right window defines the range of oscillation frequency from 0Hz to 100Hz.

In a **Harmonic** analysis, the excitation load must be defined as a function of frequency.

Define identical restraints as in the study *Time Response*. To define the spring connector, damping and load, follow the steps explained in Figure 18-15.
In the **Harmonic** study, damping must be defined as **Global Damping**. Refer to Figure 18-15 and define it as 5% of critical damping.

Define default Results Options the same as in the previous *time response* study.

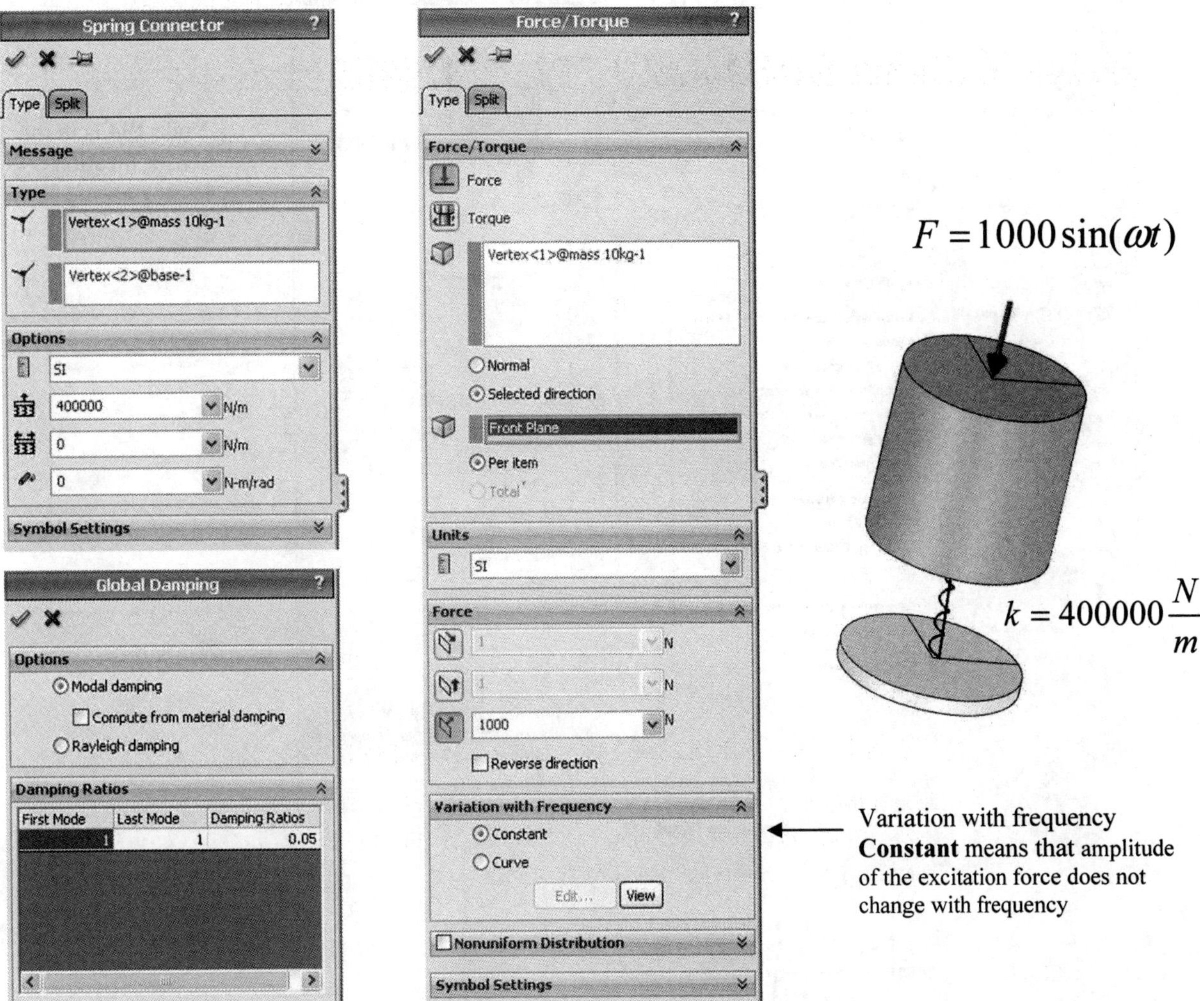

Figure 18-15: Definition of spring connector, global damping and load in study *frequency response 01*

Note that the Spring-Damper Connector in the Harmonic study does not include a definition of damping. Damping must be defined as global damping.

Define **Results Options** as explained in Figure 18-10. Run the study and define a **Response Graph** for the UZ displacement component following the steps in Figure 18-16.

The **Response Graph** shows the amplitude of vibration as a function of excitation frequency.

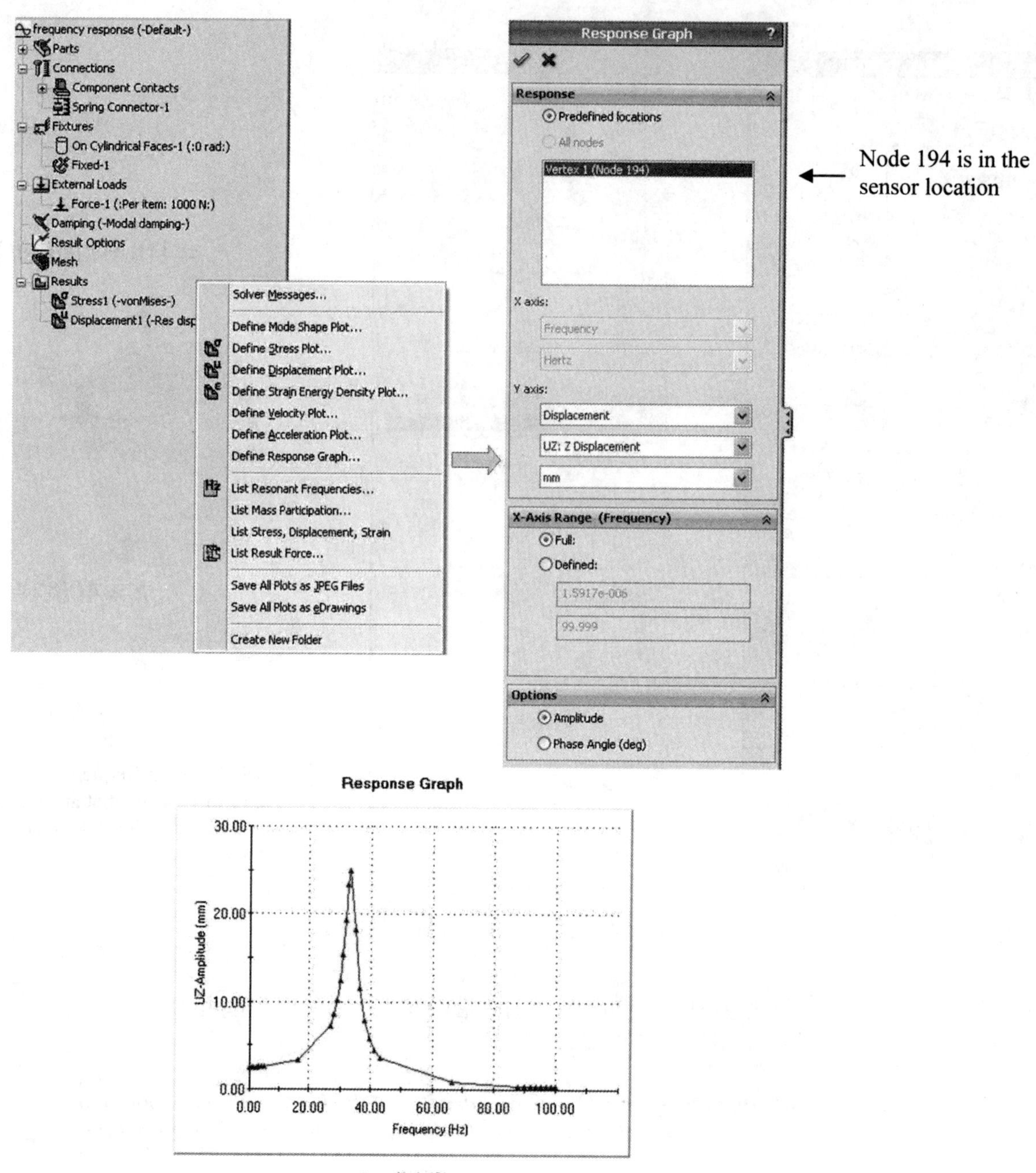

UZ displacement of node 194 as function of frequency

Figure 18-16: Definition of **Response Graph** showing the amplitude of vibration as a function of excitation frequency

Note that the amplitude at zero frequency is the static displacement of the spring under 1000N force. The maximum amplitude corresponds to the excitation frequency equal to the natural frequency of the 1DOF

The sharp peak in amplitude magnitude visible in Figure 18-16 is the 1DOF response under excitation frequency equal to the natural frequency of the 1DOF. This is called resonance. The amplitude of vibration in resonance is controlled only by damping. To demonstrate the relation between amplitude of vibration in resonance and damping, copy study *Frequency Response 01* into *Frequency Response 02* and increase **Global Damping** to 0.1. Define the same study properties. Run the solution and observe the much lower resonance amplitude. Repeat this exercise with **Global Damping** equal to 0.02. The graph in Figure 18-17 presents a summary of results for modal damping ζ = 0.02, 0.05, 0.10. The graph has been created in Excel using data exported from SolidWorks **Simulation** graphs.

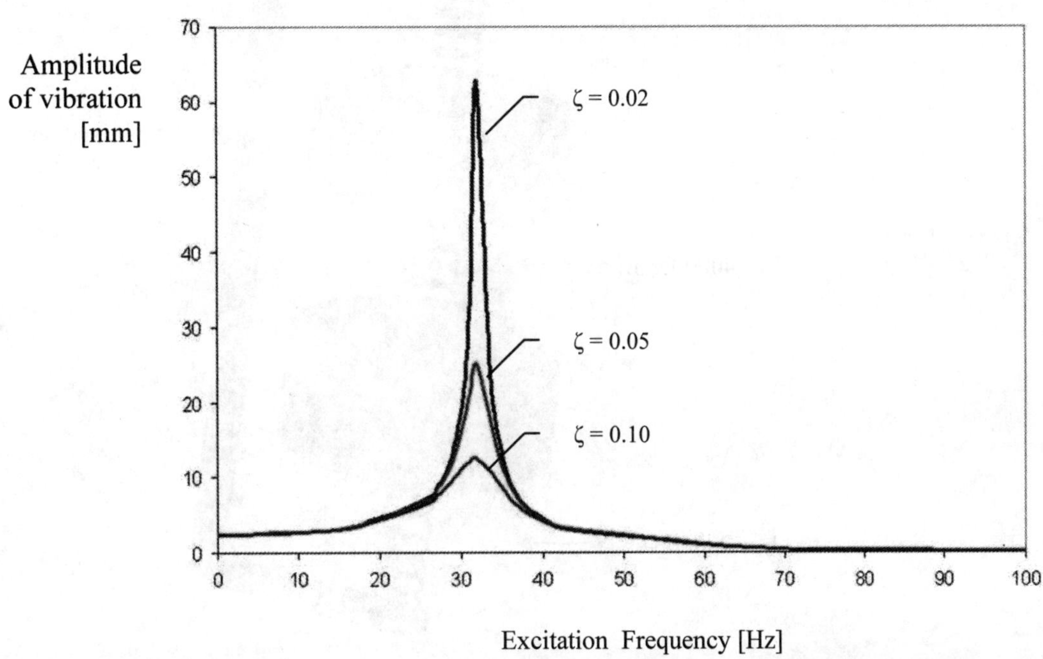

Figure 18-17: Amplitude of vibration as a function of the excitation frequency for different modal damping ratios

Note that damping strongly affects the amplitude for excitation frequencies close to the resonant frequency. It has no effect for excitation frequencies much lower or much higher than the resonant frequency.

Amplitude of vibration is measured from the neutral position, not between negative and positive peaks.

Now open the assembly model *2DOF* and create a **Frequency** study *2DOF frequency.* Verify that mass of cylinders is 99kg (top) and 149kg (bottom).

Define **Restraints** and **Spring Connectors** as shown in Figure 18-18. Run the **Frequency** study to verify that the system has two natural frequencies related to the deformation of the springs: 2.6Hz and 5.6Hz. These values may vary slightly depending on the solver used ((FFEPlus or Direct Sparse).

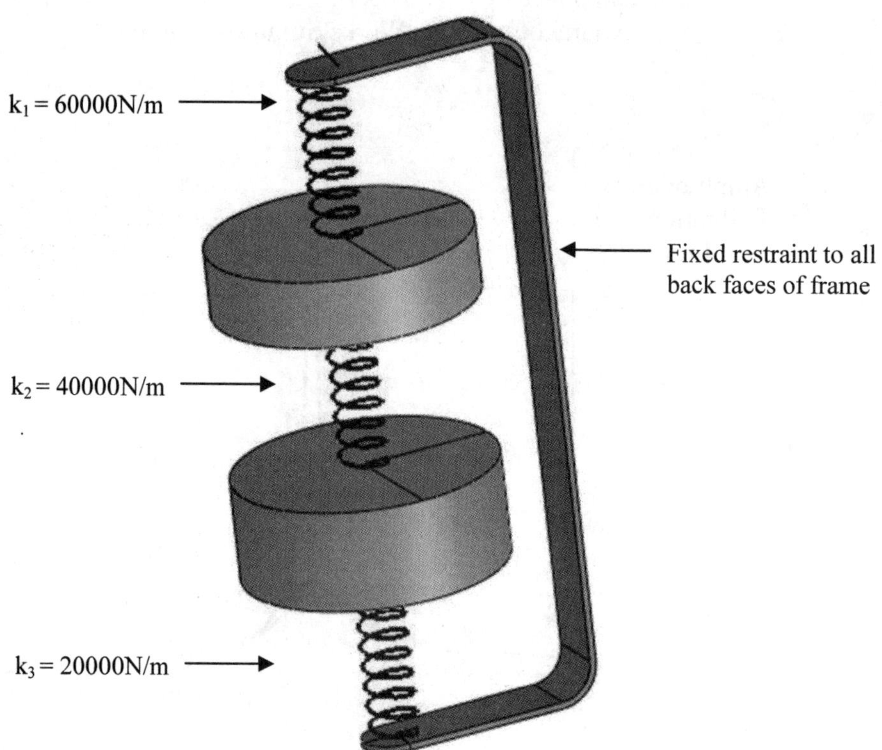

Figure 18-18: Restraints and Spring Connectors definition in 2DOF model

Restrain cylindrical faces of both masses the same way as in 1DOF example. Masses should only have the ability to move in the axial direction.

Restrain all back faces of the frame to make it practically rigid.

This example introduces a different way of loading the model called **Base Excitation**. The concept is presented in Figure 18-19.

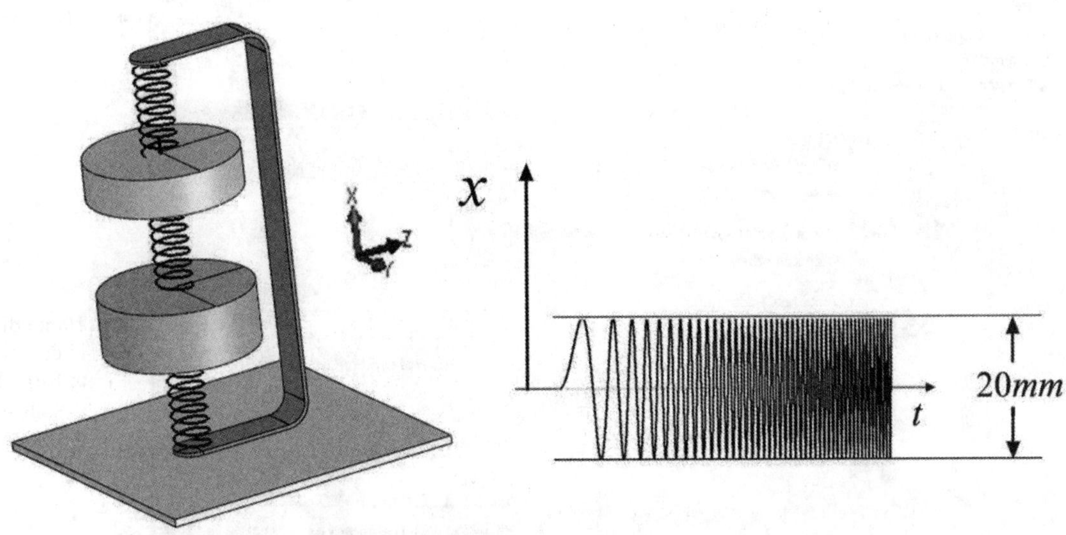

Figure 18-19: Concept of base excitation

The model sits on a shaker table which oscillates up and down with the amplitude of 10mm. The frequency of oscillation changes from 0Hz to 10Hz as defined in Figure 18-22.

Create a **Dynamic** study with the **Harmonic** option and call it *Shaker Table*. Copy restraints from the *2DOF frequency* study and define **Spring Connectors** the same way as in the *2DOF frequency* study.

To define base excitation, right-click the **Uniform Base Excitation** icon in the *Load/Restraint* folder. This opens the **Uniform Base Excitation** window. Define it as shown in Figure 18-20.

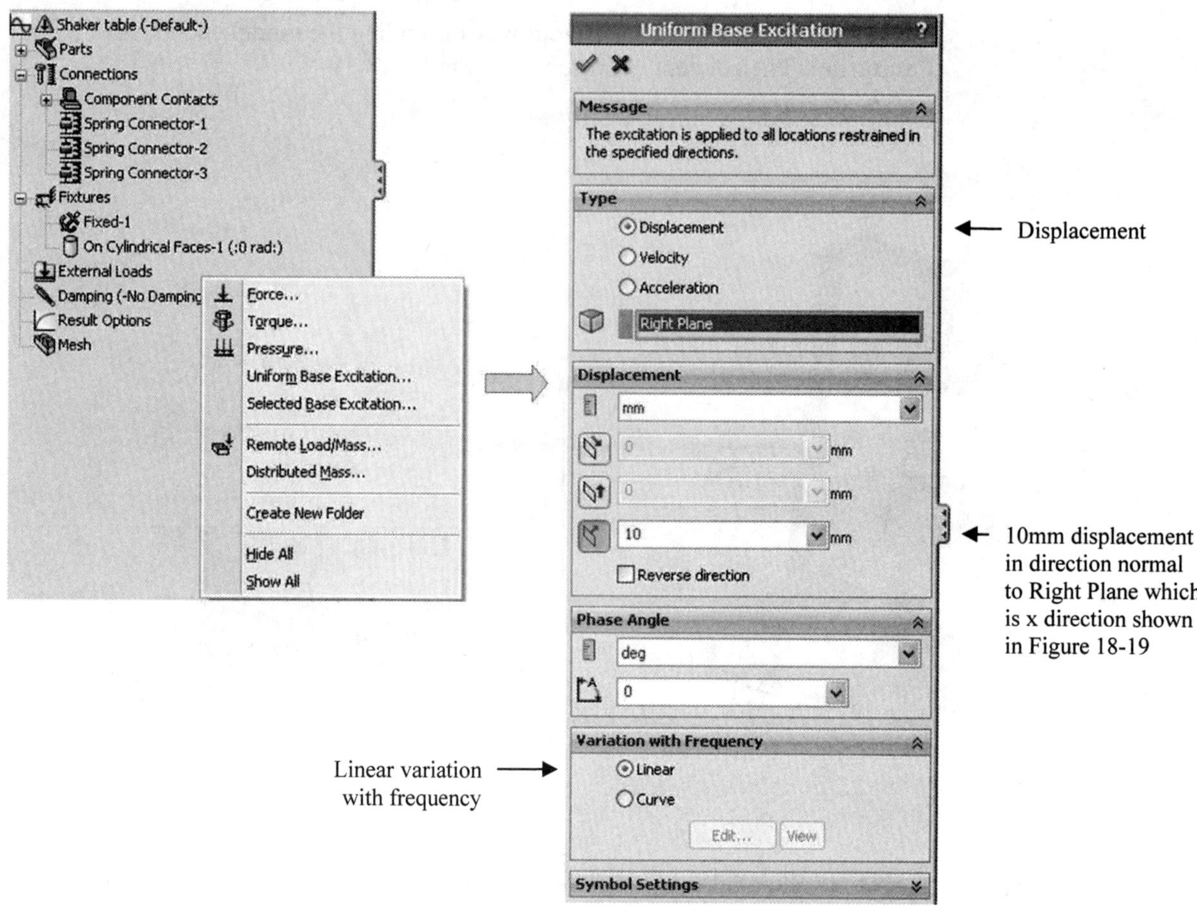

Figure 18-20: Defining base excitation in Uniform Base Excitation window

Base Excitation in the specified direction (here the direction of movement of masses) is applied to all restraints present in the model. Due to restraints on all outside faces, the frame moves "up and down" practically as a rigid body. Linear variation with frequency means the displacement does not change with frequency

Specify a modal damping of 0.05 (Figure 18-21).

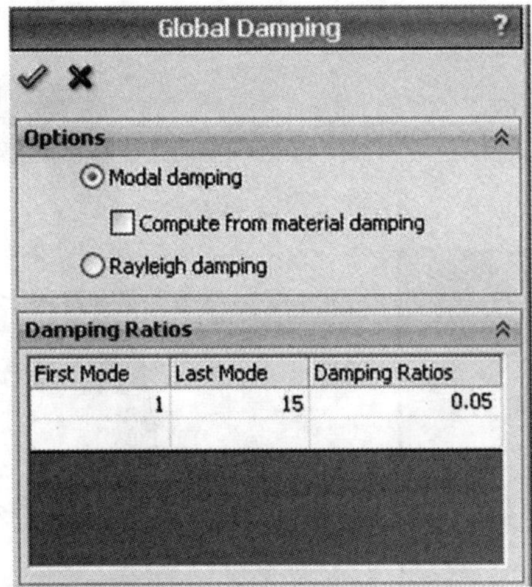

Figure 18-21: Definition of Modal Damping

A modal damping of 0.05 (5% of critical damping) defined for modes 1 and 2 considered in this analysis. Last mode 15 shown here has no relevance in this analysis which is based on two modes only.

Define study properties as shown in Figure 18-22.

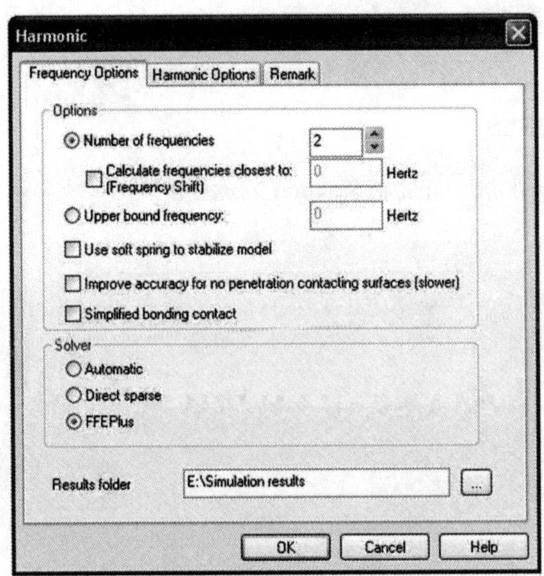

Frequency Options

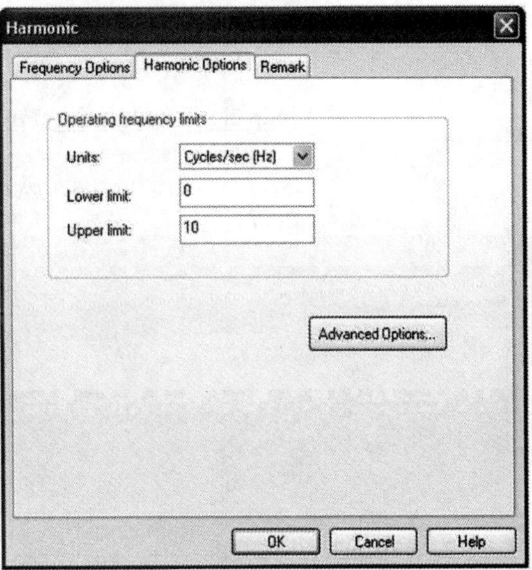

Dynamic Options

Figure 18-22: Properties of the frequency response study

Frequency Options tab (left) specifies that two frequencies will be included in the dynamic response. The Harmonic Options tab (right) specifies that excitation frequency will be changed from 0Hz to 10Hz.

Define Sensors at the two points to be included in detailed results as shown in Figure 18-23.

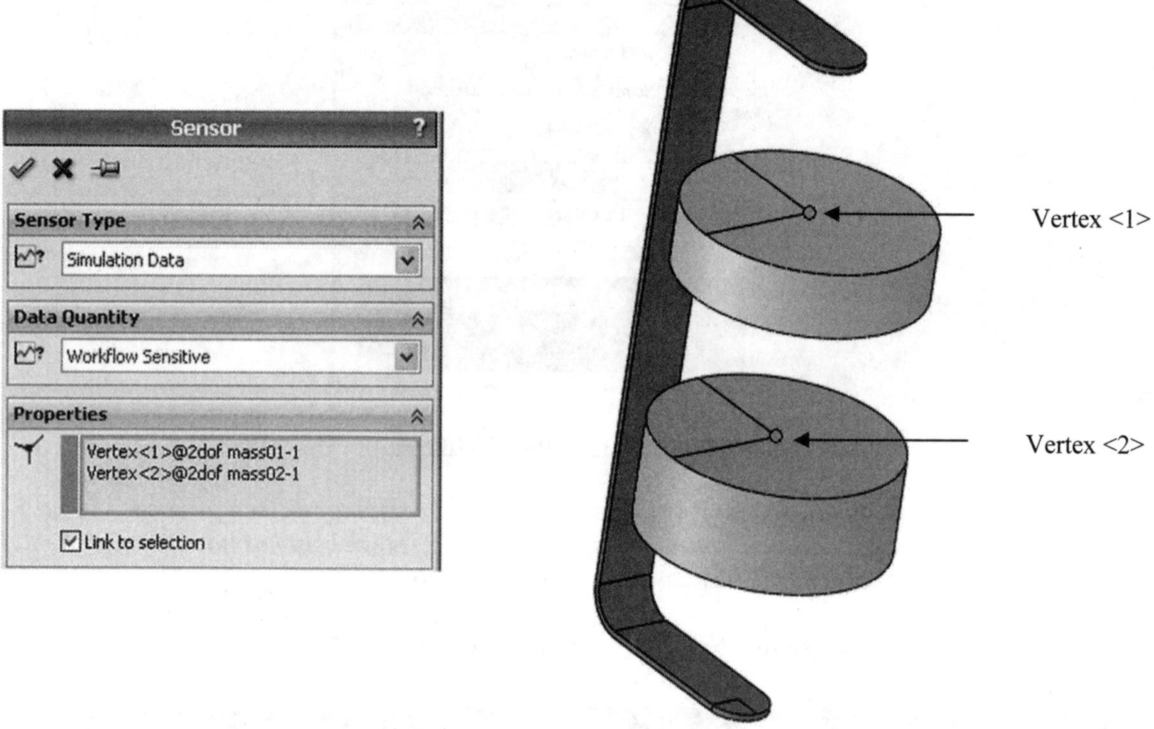

Figure 18-23: Definition of Sensors

Select vertices on the tops of each mass where Spring Connectors are attached.

Define **Results Options** as shown in Figure 18-24.

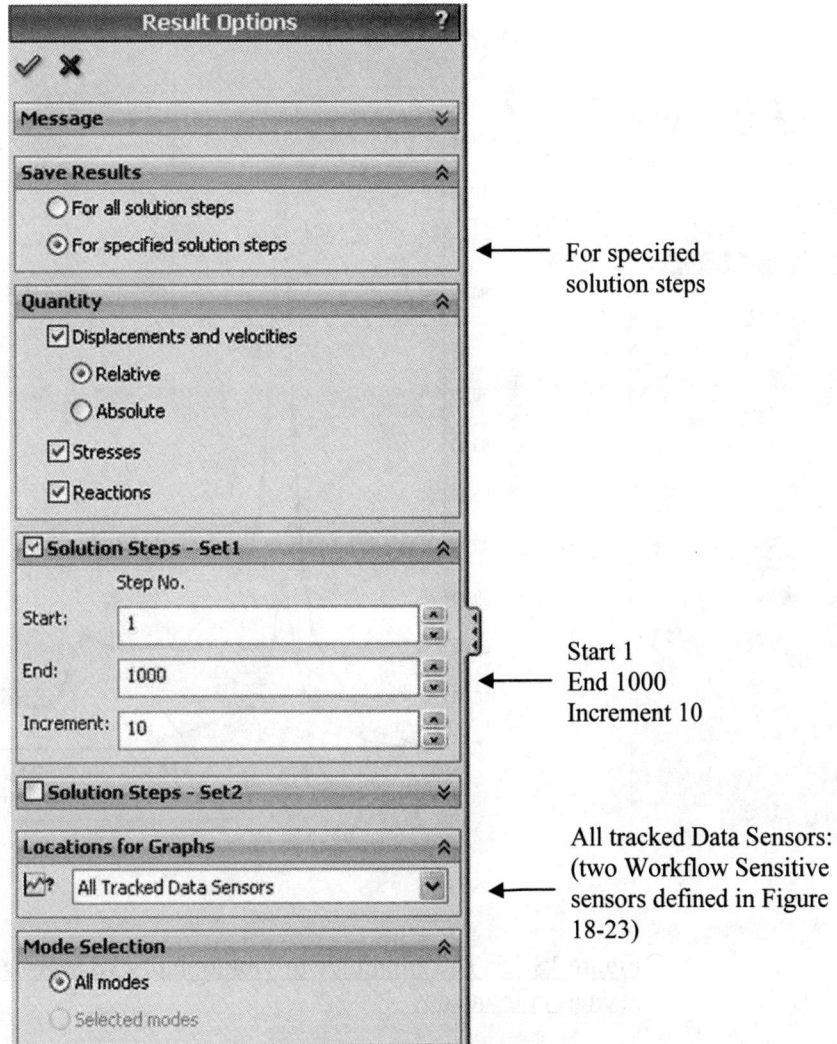

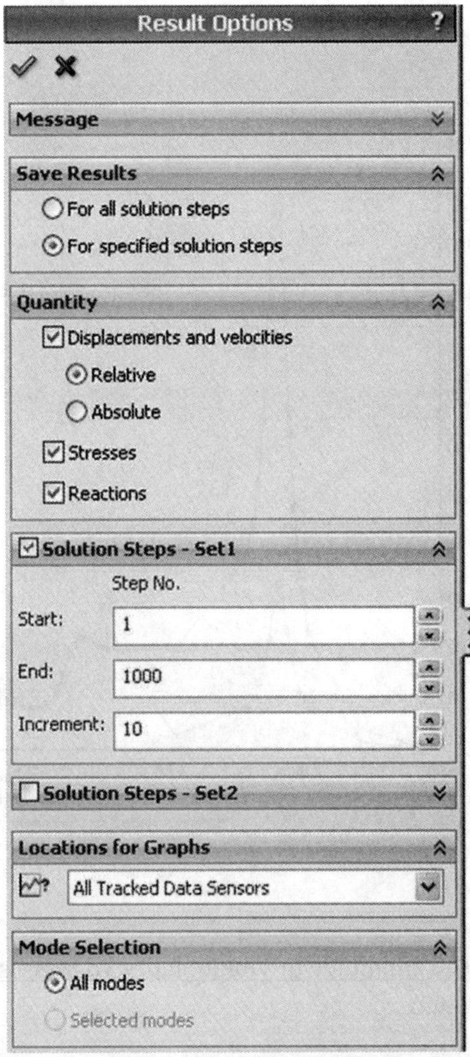

For specified solution steps

Start 1
End 1000
Increment 10

All tracked Data Sensors: (two Workflow Sensitive sensors defined in Figure 18-23)

Figure 18-24 Results Options definition

Make the indicated selections in preparation for graphing results.

Mesh model with a coarse mesh and run *Shaker table* study.

Create a response graph following steps shown in Figure 18-16, select both vertices and display the graph shown in Figure 18-25.

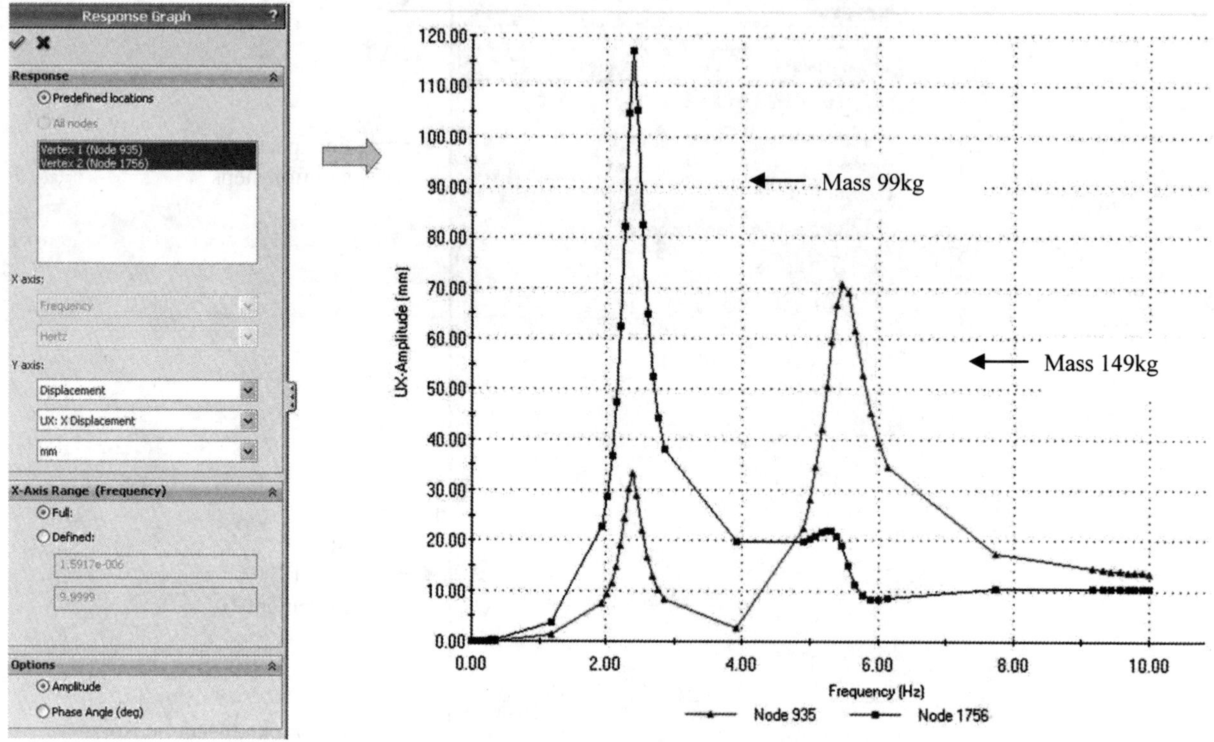

Figure 18-25: The amplitude of vibration of two masses as a function of excitation frequency

You can also create graphs individually for each mass.

The response graph in Figure 18-25 clearly shows that there are two peaks of amplitude response which correspond to the natural (resonant) frequencies of the model.

Repeat this exercise for different values of Modal Damping to study the effect of damping on the vibration amplitudes of the two masses.

19: Analysis of random vibration

Topics covered

- Random vibrations
- Power Spectral Density
- RMS results
- PSD results
- Modal excitation

Random vibration

Random vibrations are non-periodic. Knowing the history of random vibration, we can predict the probability of occurrence of acceleration, velocity and displacement magnitudes, but can not predict the precise magnitude at a specific time instant.

For most structural vibrations, the excitation such as force or base acceleration alternates about zero. Consequently, mean values characterizing the excitation as well as responses to that excitation such as displacement or stress are equal to zero. For this reason, results of random vibrations analysis are given in the form of Root Mean Square (RMS) values.

To explain the concept of RMS value, refer to the graph in Figure 19-1 which shows the acceleration time history (acceleration as a function of time) of random vibration expressed in gravitational acceleration [G]. As explained above, the acceleration time history has a zero mean value. However, if we multiply the function by itself, we obtain a function with a positive value. Its mean will no longer be zero and this squared function will be well suited to characterize the acceleration time history. This mean value of square acceleration time history is the mean square value and has units [G^2]. The square root of the mean value is the root-mean-square (RMS) acceleration and has units of [G]. The same applies to RMS displacement, velocity, stress etc.

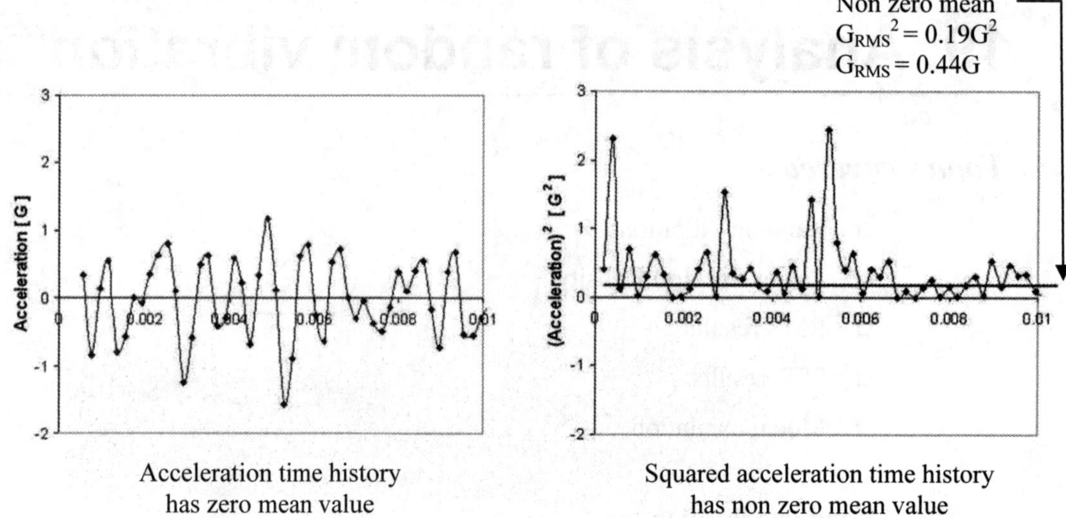

Figure 19-1: Squaring acceleration time history (left) function produces function with non zero mean (right)

Calculating the square root of mean square value gives $G_{RMS} = 0.44G$.

In random vibration, the magnitudes of acceleration, velocity, displacement etc. all follow a normal distribution. The RMS value corresponds to one standard deviation σ characterizing the normal distribution. To explain this, we refer again to Figure 19-1. The magnitude of acceleration, as characterized by the given acceleration time history, has 68% probability of remaining below 0.44G and above -0.44G. Consequently, it has a 32% probability of being less than -0.44G or more than 0.44G.

Random vibration is composed of a continuous spectrum of frequencies. The huge amount of time history data makes it impractical to run a dynamic time analysis (Figure 19-2).

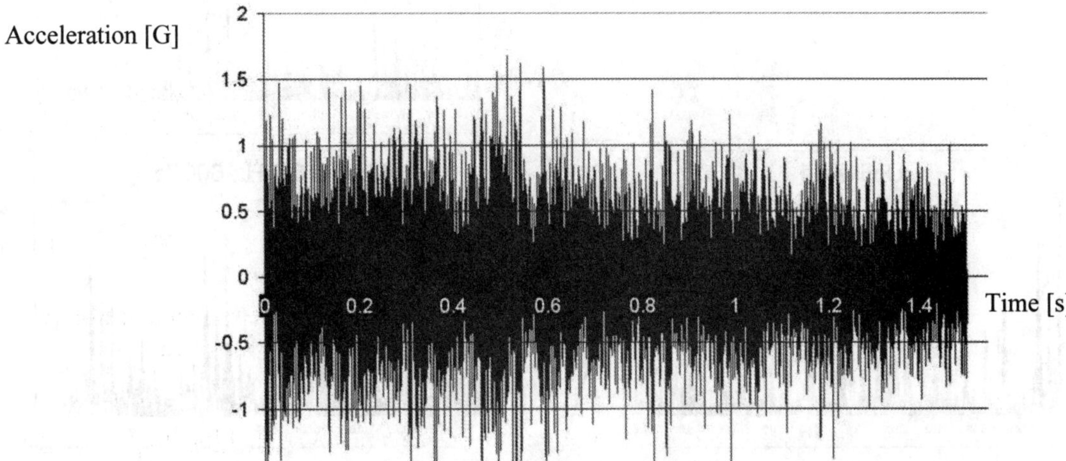

Figure 19-2: An example of acceleration time history data collected during 1.5s

Considering the sampling rate of 5000 samples per second, this time history curve contains 7500 data samples. The overall G_{RMS}^2 *is* $0.27G^2$*, the overall* G_{RMS} *is 0.52G.*

Acceleration Power Spectral Density

Let's assume that the acceleration time history in Figure 19-2 is a stationary random process where probability numbers characterizing this process do not change with time. In this case, acceleration time history can be used to calculate the Acceleration Power Spectral Density (PSD) curve (variation of any property with respect to frequency is called "spectrum").

The overall G_{RMS}^2 of random vibrations shown in Figure 19-2 is $0.27G^2$. However, random vibrations are composed of a large number of frequencies. Let's say we wish to investigate G_{RMS}^2 individually for a number of frequencies in the range from 0 to 2000Hz. Therefore, we divide the 0-2000Hz range into 20 sections, each 100Hz wide and calculate G_{RMS}^2 characterizing each section by filtering out all frequencies falling outside of the section (Figure 19-3).

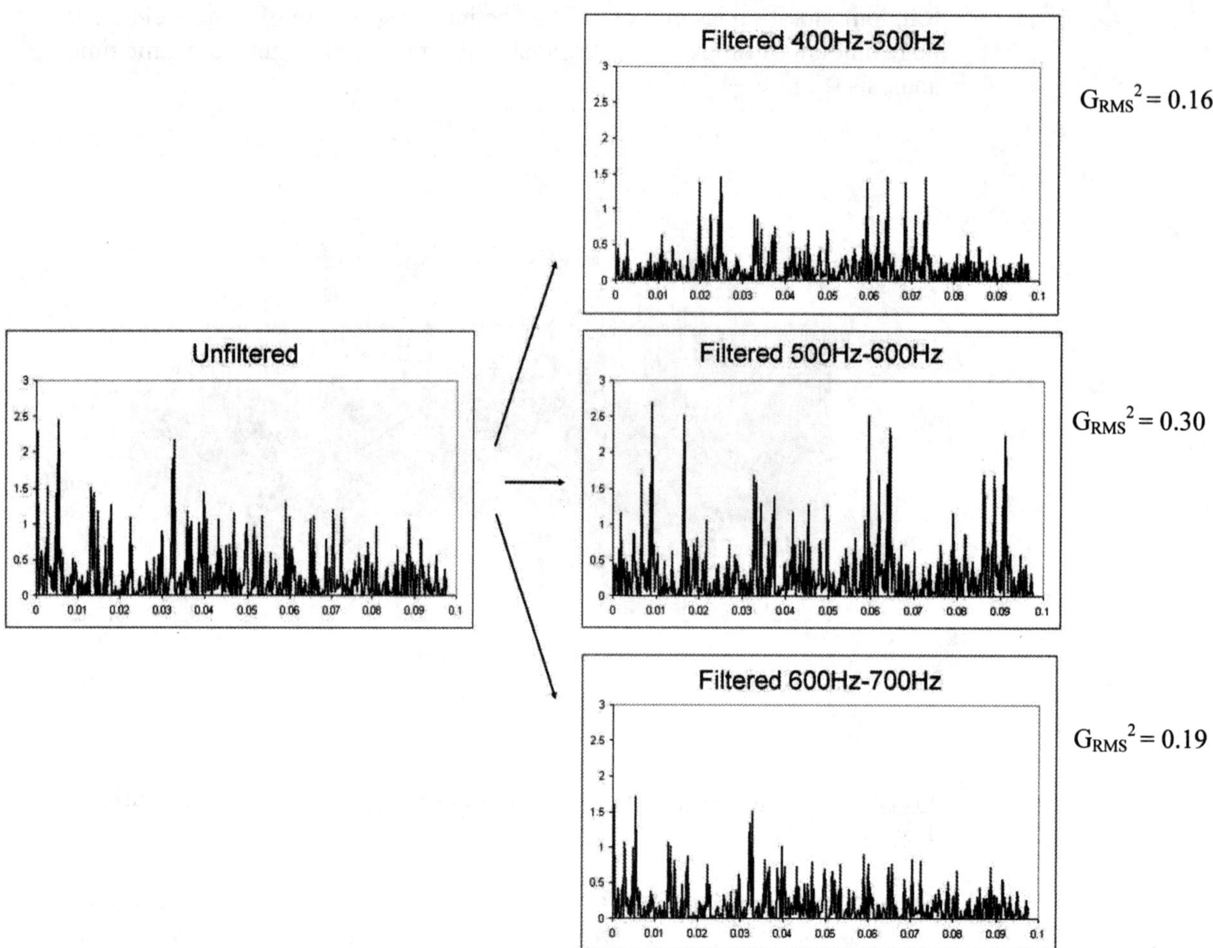

Figure 19-3: G_{RMS}^2 calculated individually for specified frequency ranges

The graph on the left shows squared acceleration time history from Figure 19-2. Only three frequency ranges (sections) are illustrated here for brevity (right).

Having found G_{RMS}^2 values obtained for each frequency range, we can now calculate individual "densities" of G_{RMS}^2 in each section by dividing G_{RMS}^2 in each section by the width of the section. Results obtained for all sections may be plotted as a function of the frequency in the center of each section. This function is the Acceleration Power Spectral Density (Figure 19-4).

BANDPAS FILTER	BAND CENTER	G_{RMS}^2	BANDWIDTH	ACCELERATION PSD
	Hz	$(m/s^2)^2$	Hz	G_{RMS}^2 / Hz
400Hz-500Hz	450	0.16	100	0.0016
500Hz-600Hz	550	0.30	100	0.003
600Hz-700Hz	650	0.19	100	0.0019

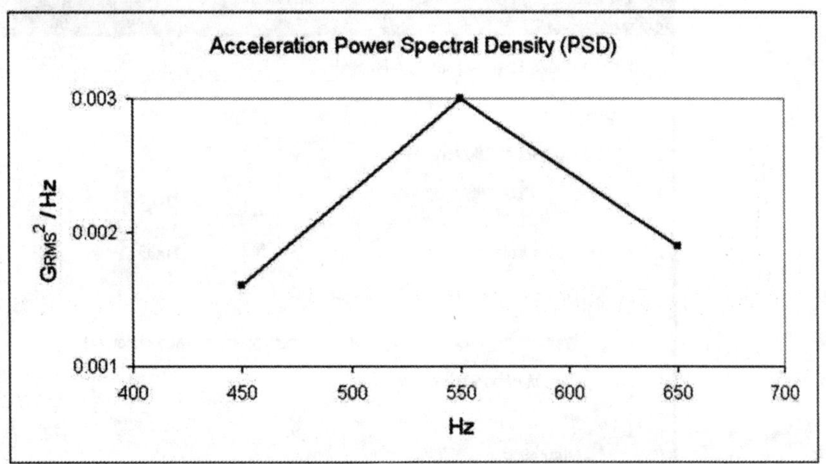

Figure 19-4: Constructing the Acceleration Power Spectral Density function (PSD)

Three points of the Acceleration PSD curve have been calculated by dividing G_{RMS}^2 *in each section (each frequency range) by the width of the section.*

The Acceleration Power Spectral Density (PSD) allows for compression of data and is commonly used to characterize a random process. In particular, mechanical vibrations are commonly described by the Acceleration Power Spectral Density, which is easily generated by testing equipment. Design requirements and test specifications of an apparatus subjected to random vibration are typically given in the form Acceleration PSD.

Analysis of random vibration of a hard drive head

With the short introduction on random vibration complete, we can now begin a random vibration analysis of a hard drive head. Open part HD HEAD and create a **Frequency** study with properties shown in Figure 19-5. Call the study Modal.

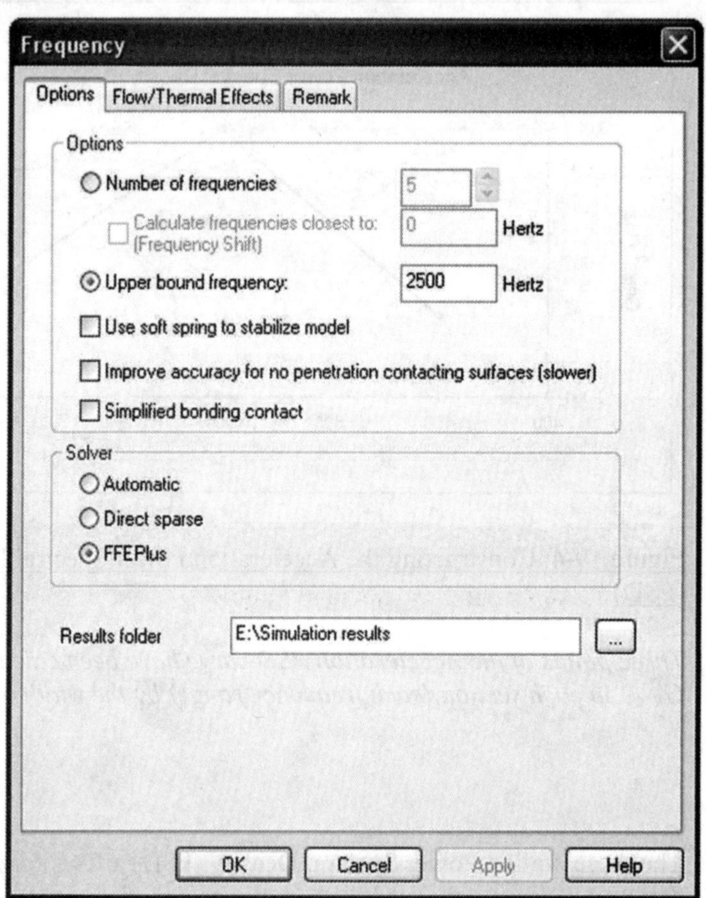

Figure 19-5: Properties of study *Modal*

All frequencies in the range of 0-2500Hz will be calculated.

Apply restraints as shown in Figure 19-6.

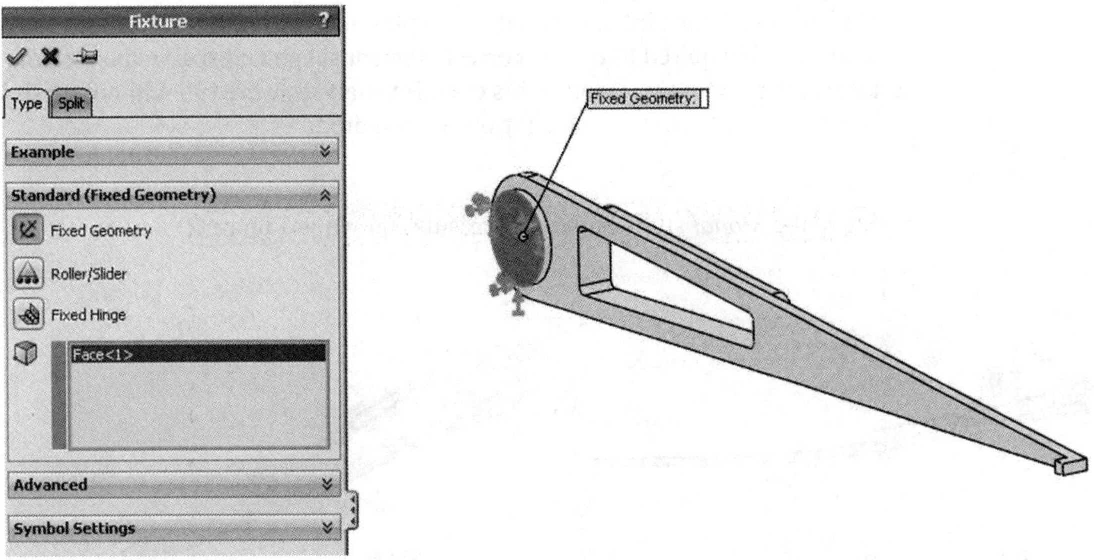

Figure 19-6: Restraints applied to a hard drive head model

Apply **Mesh Control** as shown in Figure 19-7 and mesh with default element size.

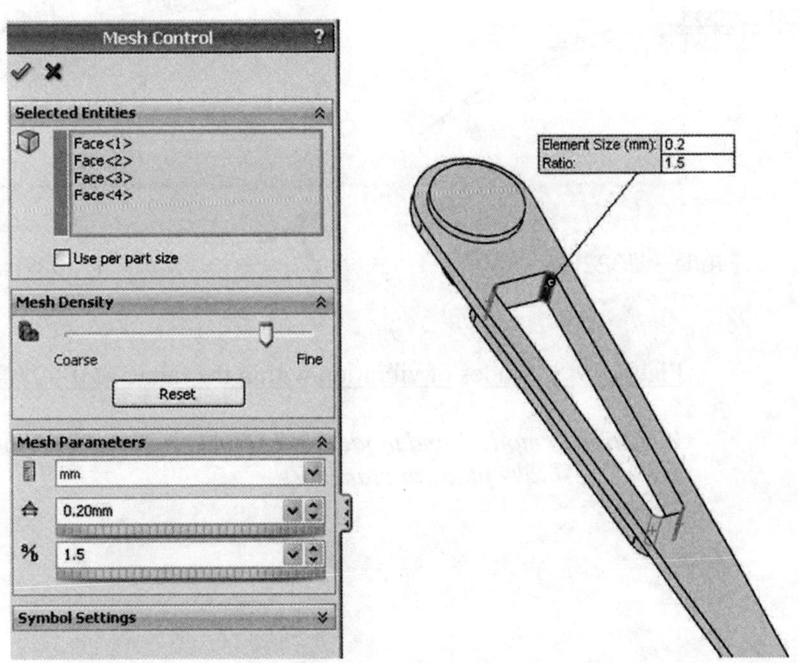

Figure 19-7: Mesh controls (0.2mm) applied to four fillets

If displacement results were our only objective, the default mesh would be acceptable for both Frequency Analysis and subsequent Random Analysis. However, since we intend to analyze displacements and stresses, mesh controls are required to ensure correct element shape and size in the area of stress concentrations. Prior to this exercise analyses were run without mesh controls to find where mesh controls are required.

Solve the *Modal* study and review results shown in Figure 19-8.

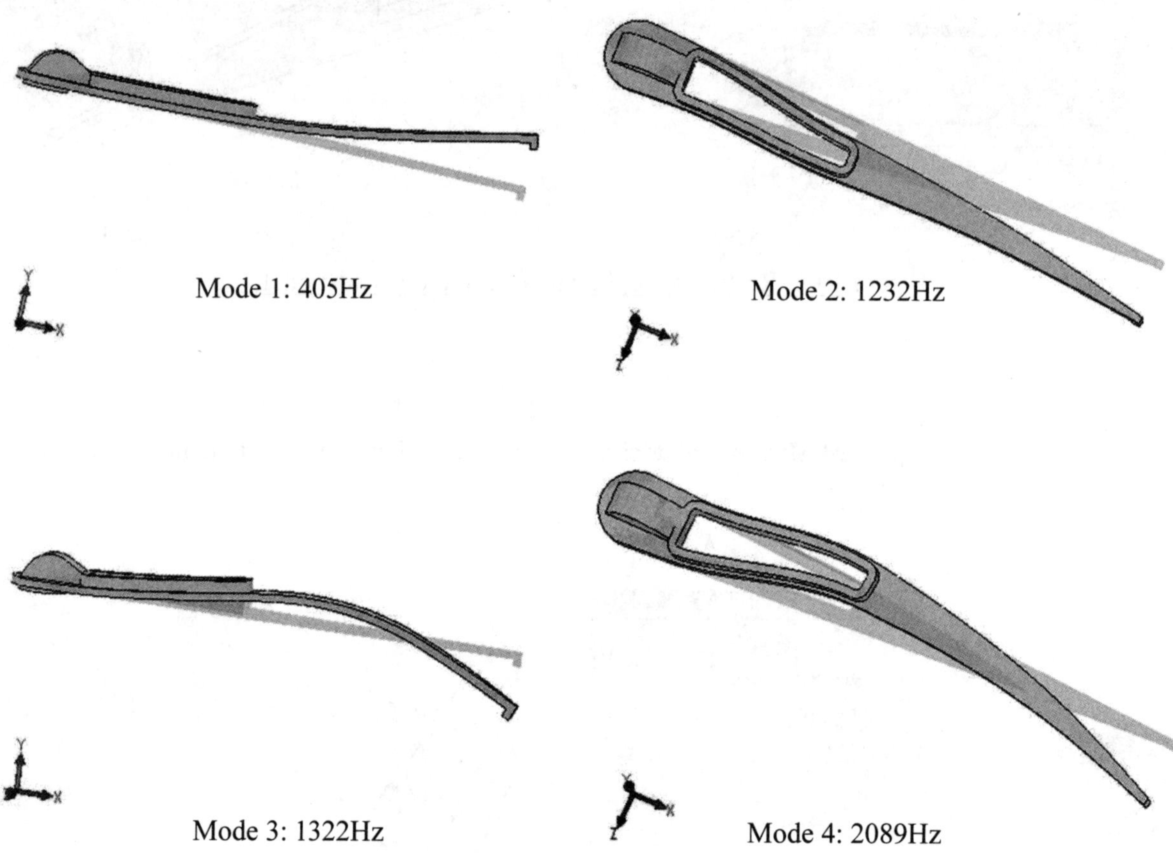

Figure 19-8: Modes of vibration within the range of 0 – 2500Hz

Vibration in mode 1 and mode 3 take place in plane XY, vibration in mode 2 and mode 4 take place in plane XZ.

Proceeding to the analysis of Random Vibration, we could create a new **Dynamic** study, independent from the just completed **Frequency** study, this time with the **Random** option selected. However, a **Frequency** analysis would then have to be repeated within a **Dynamic Random** study. To avoid this repetition, we can copy the results of the **Frequency** study into a **Dynamic Random** study as shown in Figure 19-9.

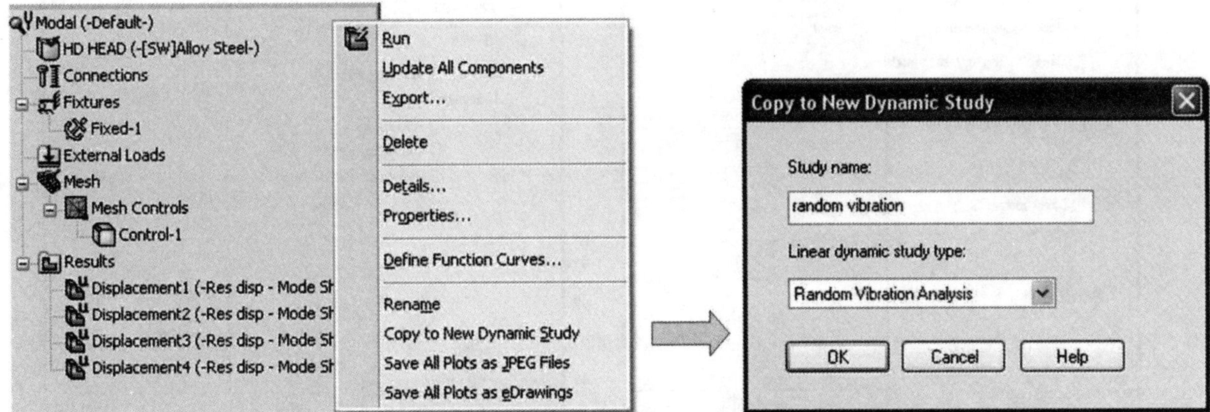

Figure 19-9: Results of Frequency study can be copied to a new Dynamic study

Right-click the Modal study folder and select Copy to New Dynamic Study. Select Random Vibration as the type of dynamic study. Name the study Random Vibration.

Copying the **Frequency** study into **Dynamic Random** study also copies mesh information and restraints.

The required properties of the **Random Vibration** study are shown in Figure 19-10.

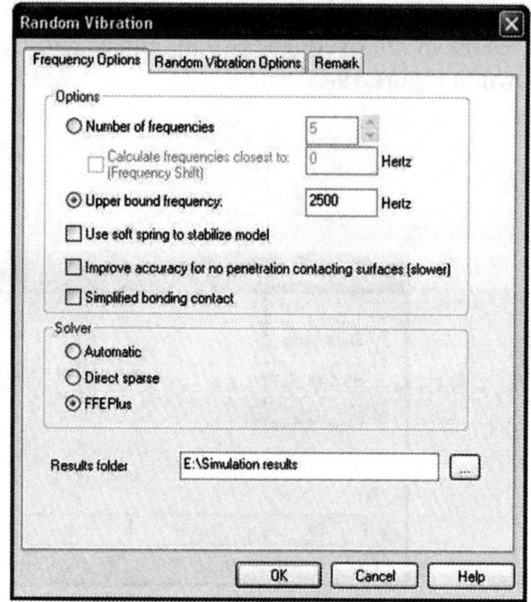

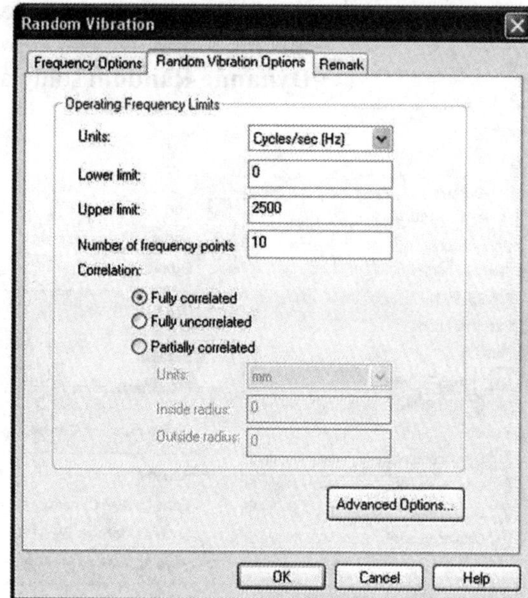

Frequency Options

Dynamic Options

Figure 19-10: Properties of the Random Vibration study

Frequency Options (left) come from the already run Frequency study. In the Random Vibration options, specify the Upper limit as 2500Hz to investigate responses to Random Vibration in the frequency range from 0 to 2500Hz.

Define Global Damping as shown in Figure 19-11.

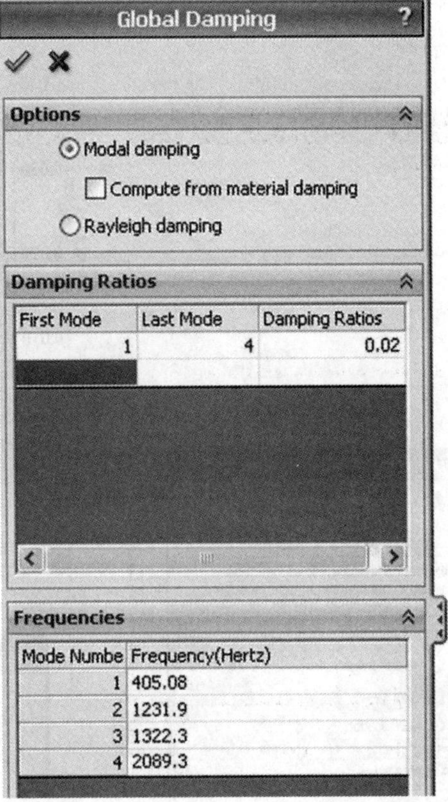

Figure 19-11: Global damping definition

Global damping is defined as 2% of critical damping. The number of modes (4) corresponds to the number of modes calculated in the preceding frequency analysis.

The load on the hard drive head comes from random excitation of the base in the global Y direction. Follow Figure 19-12 to define Acceleration PSD.

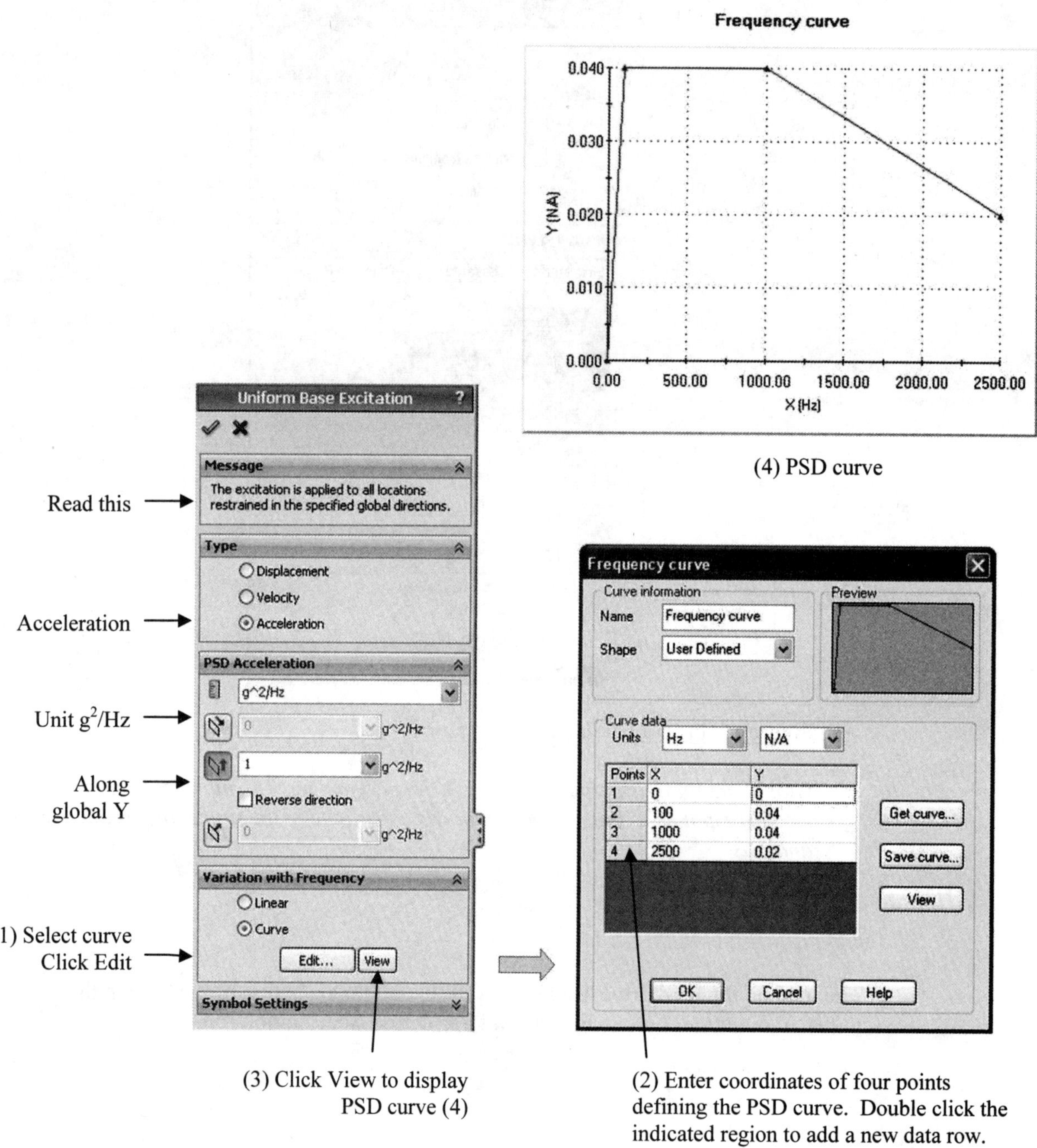

Figure 19-12: Uniform Base Excitation defined as Acceleration PSD in global Y direction acts on all restraints present in the model (here only one restraint is present)

Follow the above steps to create the PSD curve.

Define a **Sensor** as shown in Figure 19-13.

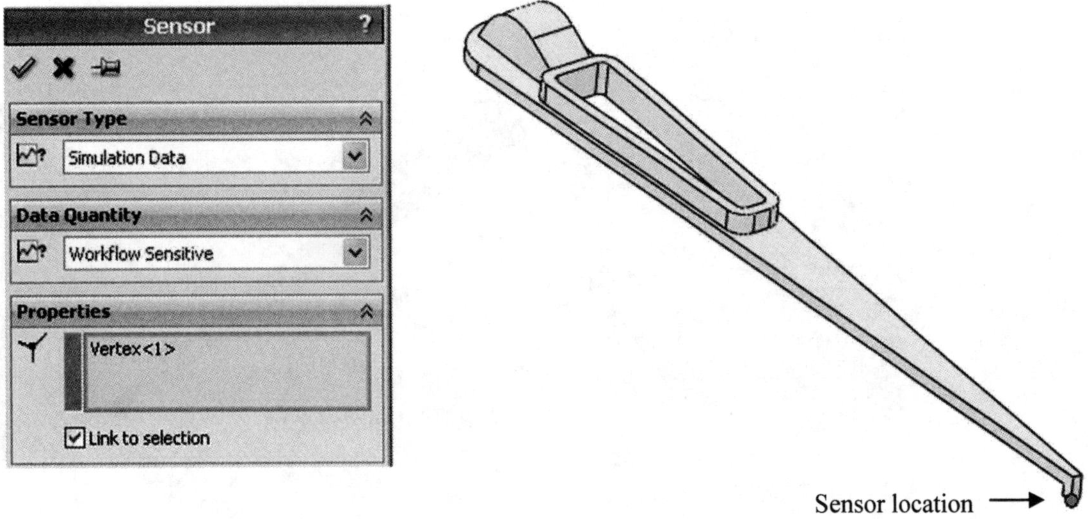

Figure 19-13: Sensor location

Select the vertex at the tip of the head.

Define **Result Options** as shown in Figure 19-10.

Obtain the solution and analyze RMS displacement results and PSD displacement results shown in Figure 19-14.

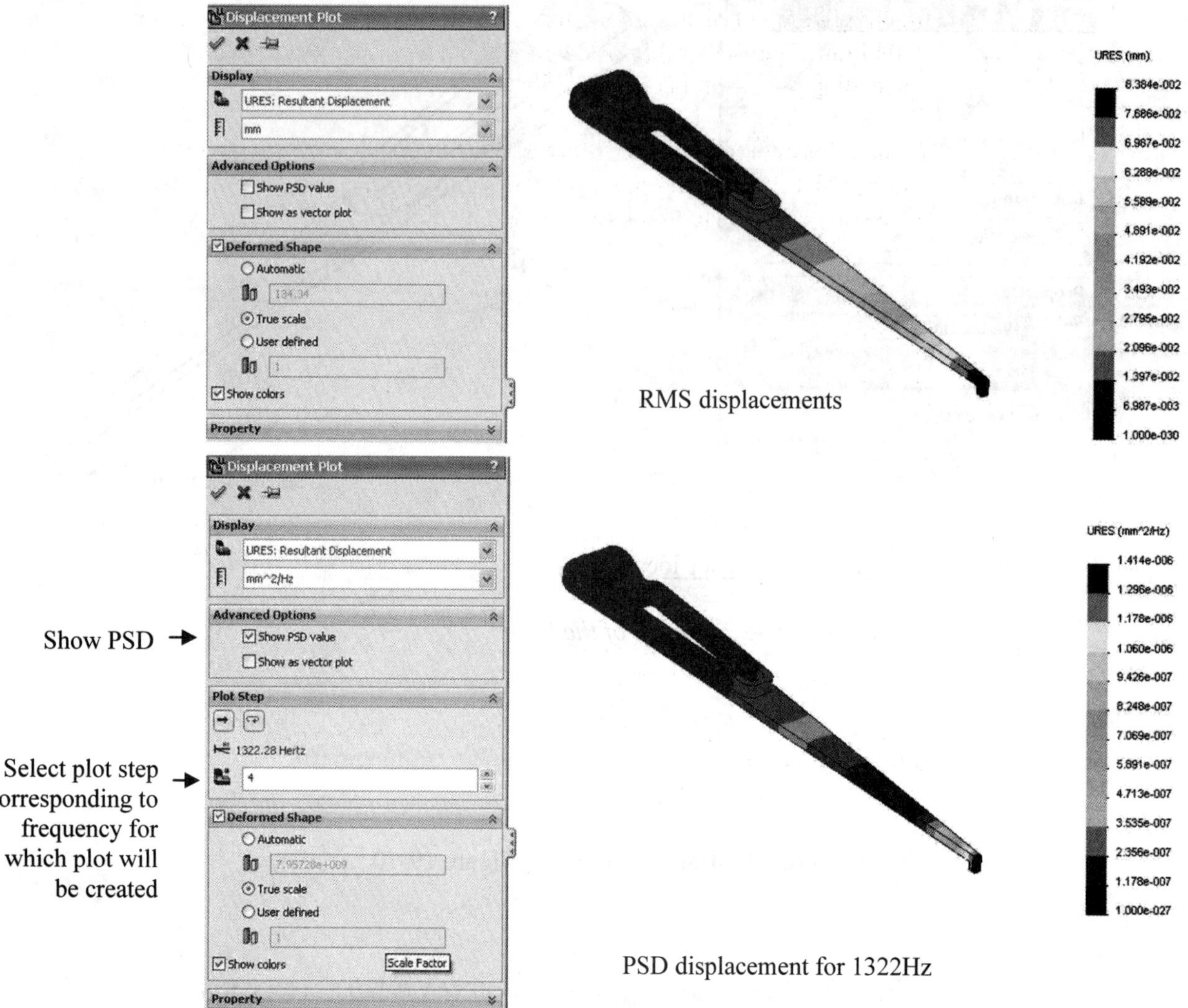

Figure 19-14: RMS displacement results (top) and PSD displacement results (bottom).

The maximum RMS displacement is 0.084mm.
PSD displacements are displayed in units of mm^2/Hz for the selected frequency.

It is important to understand the meaning of results in a Random Vibration analysis. The displacement results in Figure 19-14 top are the RMS displacements. The maximum RMS displacement is 0.084mm meaning that the magnitude of displacement has 68% probability of remaining under 0.084mm. The probability of the maximum displacement magnitude exceeding 0.084mm is of course 32%.

Remembering that the probability of a given displacement is defined by a normal distribution for which $\sigma = 0.084$mm, we can calculate the probability of displacement magnitude exceeding any defined value (Figure 19-15).

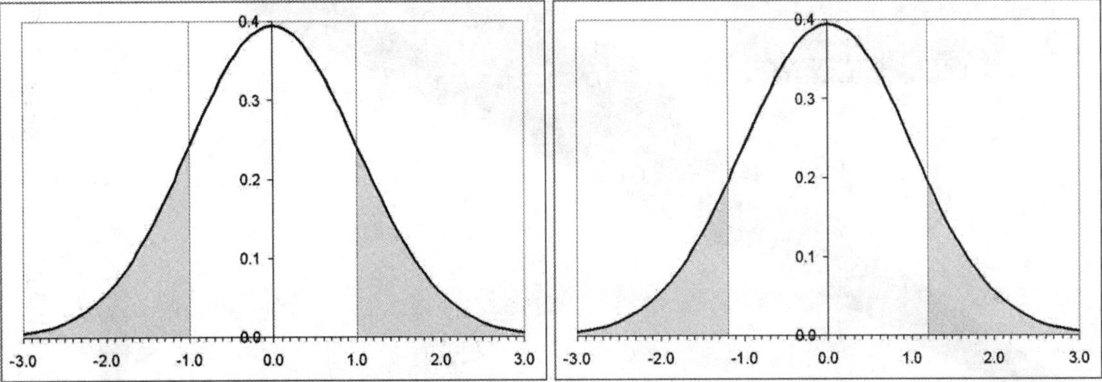

Figure 19-15: Total area under the normalized Gauss curve is 1. The probability of displacement magnitude exceeding $\pm\sigma$ (left) and $\pm 1.2\sigma$ (right) is equal to the shaded area.

The probability of displacement magnitude exceeding 1*RMS displacement (here 0.084mm) is given by the area outside $\pm$ 1σ which is 32% (left). Probability of displacement magnitude exceeding 1.2*RMS displacement (0.10mm) is given by the area outside $\pm$ 1.2σ which is 23% (right).

The same applies to all results of Random Vibration analysis. The RMS P1 stress result is shown in Figure 19-16.

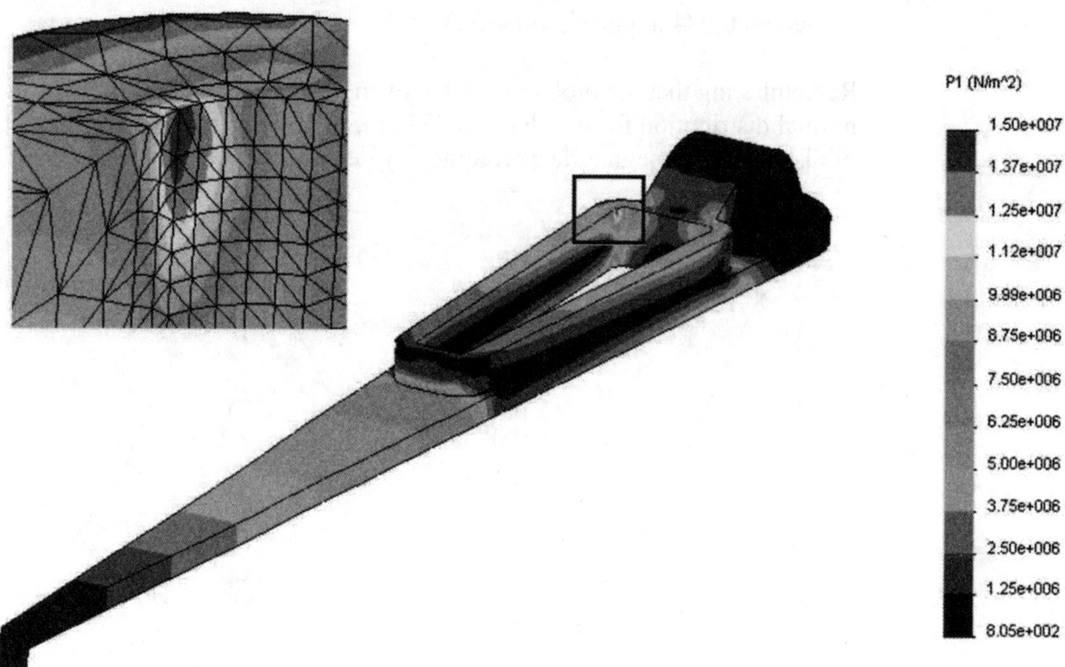

Figure 19-16: RMS P1 stress results.

The maximum P1 stress has a 68% probability of remaining below 15MPa.

Refer to Figure 19-16 and compare the size of elements to the size of stress concentration. Even with mesh controls applied, the mesh is at best marginal to model stress concentration. Repeat the analysis with a more aggressive mesh control.

The results of the Dynamic Random analysis presented as RMS values provide one result for the entire frequency range of excitation. All results (displacement, stresses etc.) can also be presented as PSD values (Figure 19-14 bottom), which are different for each excitation frequency. Examine the PSD options of displacements and stress result plots and notice that displacement results are given in mm^2/Hz, and stress results are given in MPa^2/Hz. These units are a consequence of the base excitation being defined as acceleration squared per frequency range, in our case $G_{RMS}{}^2$/Hz.

The most informative way to review PSD results is to graph them over the frequency range. Create a graph showing PSD displacement in the selected location shown in Figure 19-13. Define a Y Displacement **Response Graph** as shown in Figure 19-17.

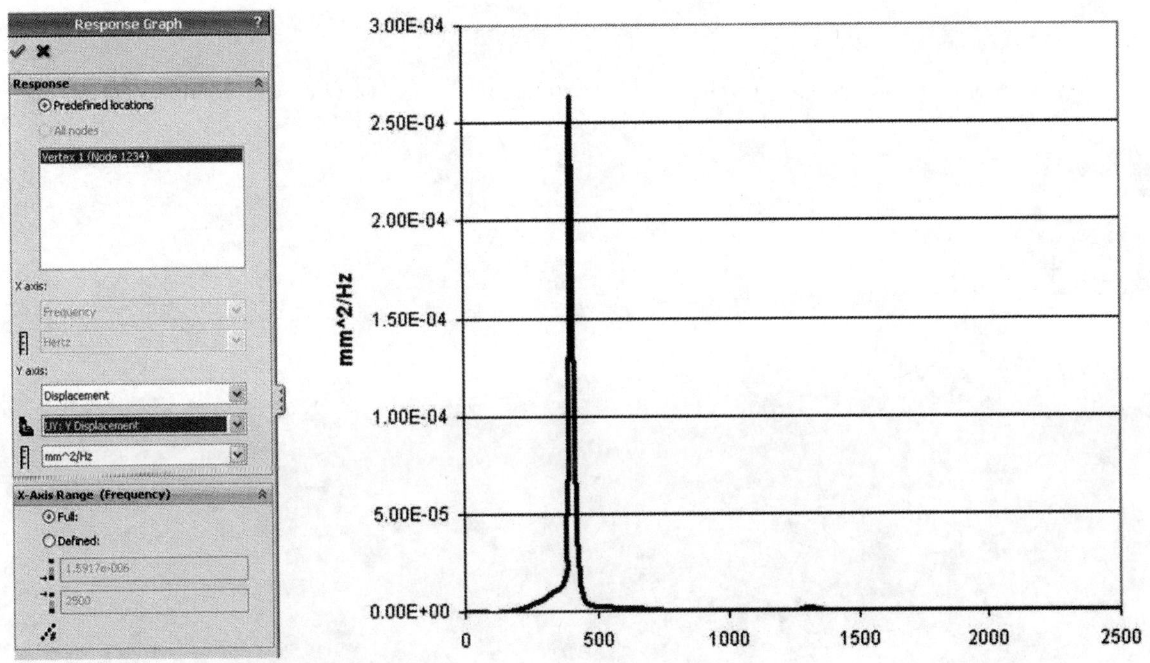

Figure 19-17: PSD displacement as function of excitation frequency

Mode 1 and mode 3 (barely visible) are excited. Verify that the area under the curve equals the RMS^2 displacement of the tip where the sensor has been defined.

Upon examination of the graph in Figure 19-17, we find that the applied base acceleration excites mode 1 and mode 3 because these modes occur in the XY plane. Mode 2 and mode 4 occur in plane XZ which is orthogonal to the direction of base acceleration and are therefore not excited.

Repeat this exercise with base excitation where direction is not orthogonal to any global direction to see that all four modes will be excited.

20: Miscellaneous topics

Topics covered

- Mesh quality
- Solvers and solvers options
- Displaying mesh in result plots
- Automatic reports
- E drawings
- Non uniform loads
- Bearing load
- Frequency analysis with pre-stress
- Shrink fit analysis
- Pin connector
- Bolt connector
- Remote Load/Mass
- Weld connector

The analysis capabilities of SolidWorks **Simulation** go beyond those we have discussed so far. In this chapter we review a variety of topics that have not been addressed in previous exercises. All models discussed in this chapter come complete with defined studies.

Mesh quality

The ideal shape of a tetrahedral element is a regular tetrahedron. The aspect ratio of a regular tetrahedron is assumed top be 1. Analogously, an equilateral triangle is the ideal shape for a shell element. During meshing, elements are mapped onto model geometry. This distorts the element shape. The aspect ratio becomes higher when the element departs further from its original shape (Figure 20-1). An aspect ratio that is too high causes element degeneration, which negatively affects the quality of results.

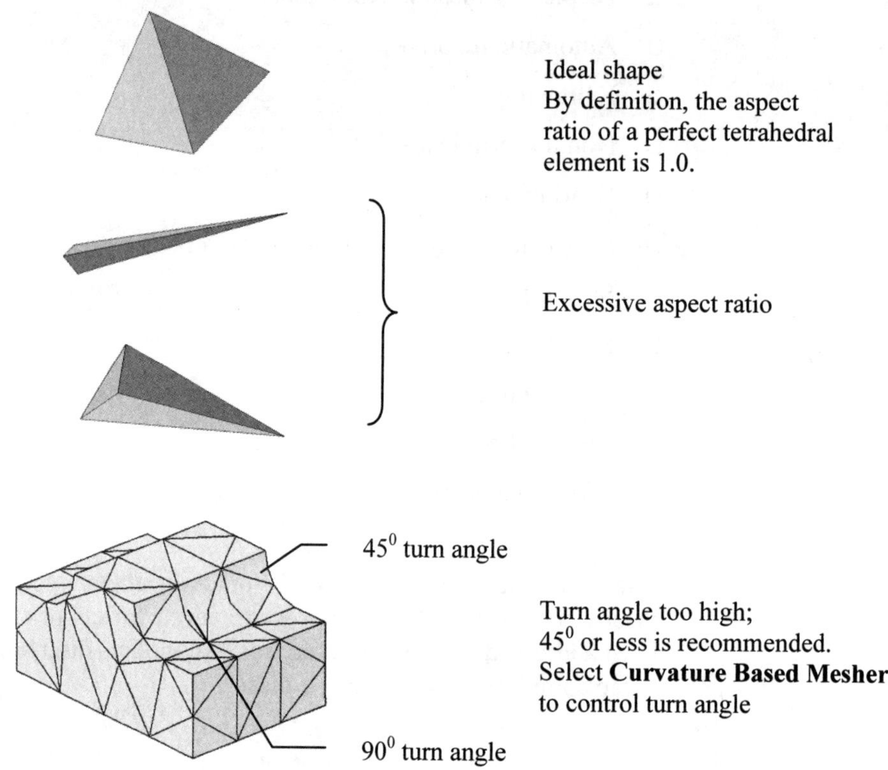
Ideal shape
By definition, the aspect ratio of a perfect tetrahedral element is 1.0.
Excessive aspect ratio
45^0 turn angle
Turn angle too high;
45^0 or less is recommended.
Select **Curvature Based Mesher** to control turn angle
90^0 turn angle

Figure 20-1: Tetrahedral element shapes: ideal and after mapping

A tetrahedral element with an ideal shape (top) has an aspect ration of 1. "Spiky" and "flat" elements shown in this illustration (middle) have excessively high aspect ratios. "Concave" elements (bottom) have excessive turn angles.

The aspect ratio of a perfect tetrahedral element is used as the basis for calculating the aspect ratios of other elements. While the mesher tries to create elements with aspect ratios close to 1, the nature of geometry sometimes makes it impossible to avoid high aspect ratios (Figure 20-2).

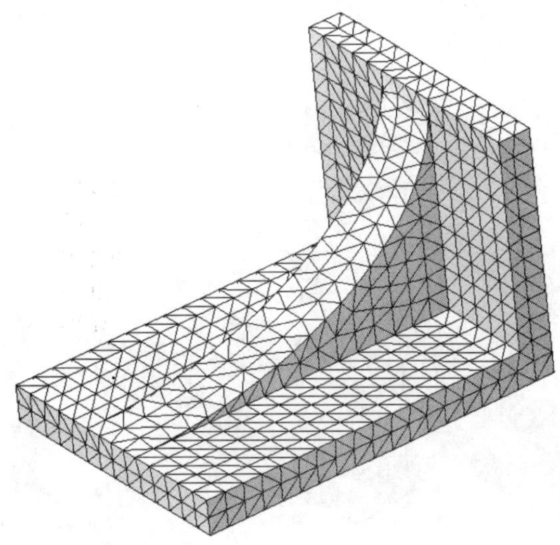

Figure 20-2: Mesh of an elliptical fillet

Meshing an elliptical fillet creates highly distorted elements near the tangent edges.

A failure diagnostic can be used to spot problem areas if meshing fails. To run a failure diagnostic, right-click the **Mesh** icon. This opens the associated pop-up window from which **Failure Diagnostic …** is selectable.

In the same menu you can **Create Mesh plot** showing the mesh itself or mesh quality measures such as **Aspect Ratio** and **Jacobian** explained in the table below and shown in Figure 20-3.

Aspect ratio	The aspect ratio of an element is defined as the ratio between an element's longest edge and the shortest height normalized with respect to a perfect tetrahedral. The aspect ratio check assumes straight edges connecting the four corner nodes. It can not differentiate between first order elements (straight edges) and second order elements which may have curved edges.
Jacobian	The Jacobian ratio is a measure of the quality of second order elements. Jacobian ratio of element, with all mid-side nodes located exactly at the middle of the straight edges, is 1.0. The Jacobian ratio increases as the curvatures of the edges increase. The Jacobian ratio at a point inside the element provides a measure of the degree of distortion of the element at that location. The software calculates the Jacobian ratio at the selected number of points for each element. The Jacobian of an extremely distorted element becomes negative. An element with a negative Jacobian causes the analysis program to stop.

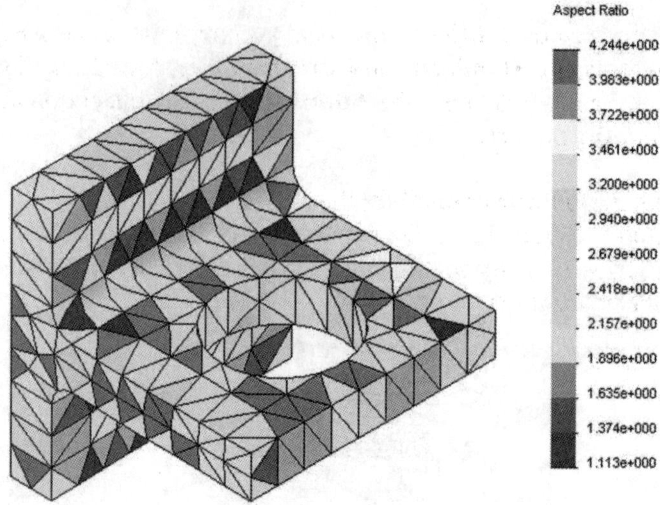

Plot of aspect ratio

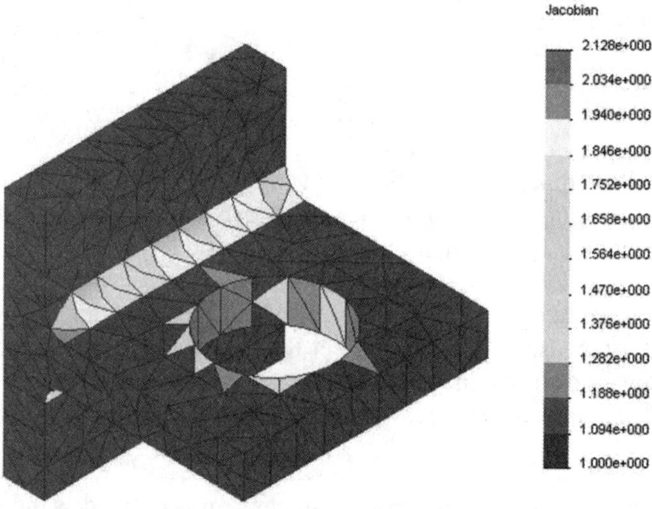

Plot of Jacobian ratio

Figure 20-3: Aspect ratio plot and Jacobian ratio plot

For clarity of illustrations a coarse mesh is used for these plots.

Meshing difficult geometries may sometimes result in degenerated elements without any warning. If mesh degeneration is only local, then we can simply not look at results (especially the stress results) produced by those degenerated elements. If degeneration affects large portions of the mesh, then even global results cannot be trusted.

We have studied different methods to control the mesh size such as **Mesh Controls** and **Standard** and **Curvature Based** meshers. Another way to control a mesh is to use the **Automatic Transition** option available in the **Standard** mesher.

With **Automatic transition**, the mesher applies mesh controls to small features (Figure 20-4). Do not use **Automatic transition** when meshing large models with many small features and details to avoid generating a very large number of elements

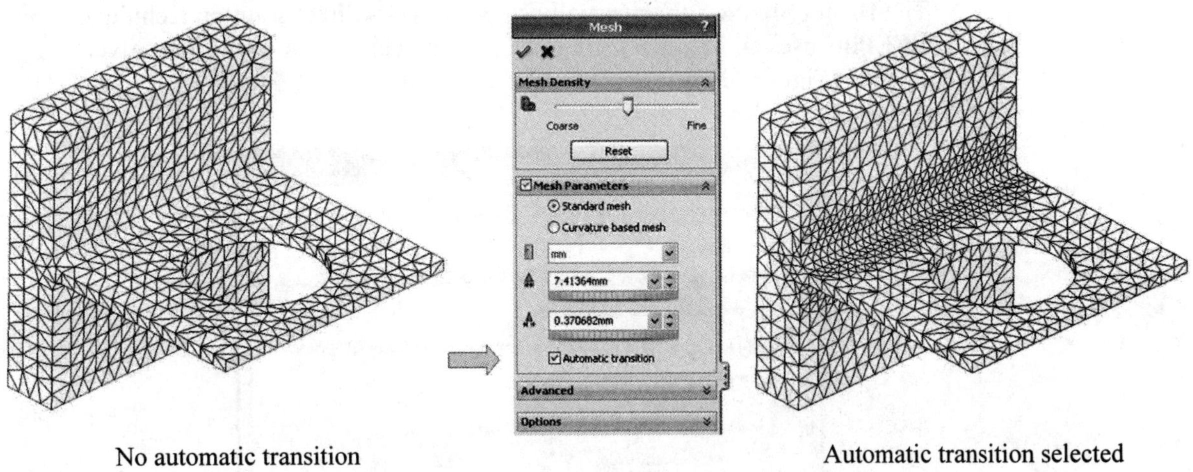

Figure 20-4: Mesh without Automatic Transition option (left) and mesh with Automatic Transition option (right)

Automatic transition has a similar effect to applying mesh control to the fillets.

Solvers and solvers options

In finite element analysis, a problem is represented by a large set of algebraic equations that must be solved simultaneously. There are two classes of solution methods: direct and iterative.

Direct methods solve equations using exact numerical techniques, while iterative methods solve equations using approximate techniques. With the iterative method, a solution is approximated iteratively and the associated errors are evaluated. The iterations continue until the errors become acceptable.

The **Direct Sparse** solver (usually slower) uses a direct solution technique, **FFEPlus** uses an iterative technique. A study can be run with three solver options (Figure 20-5).

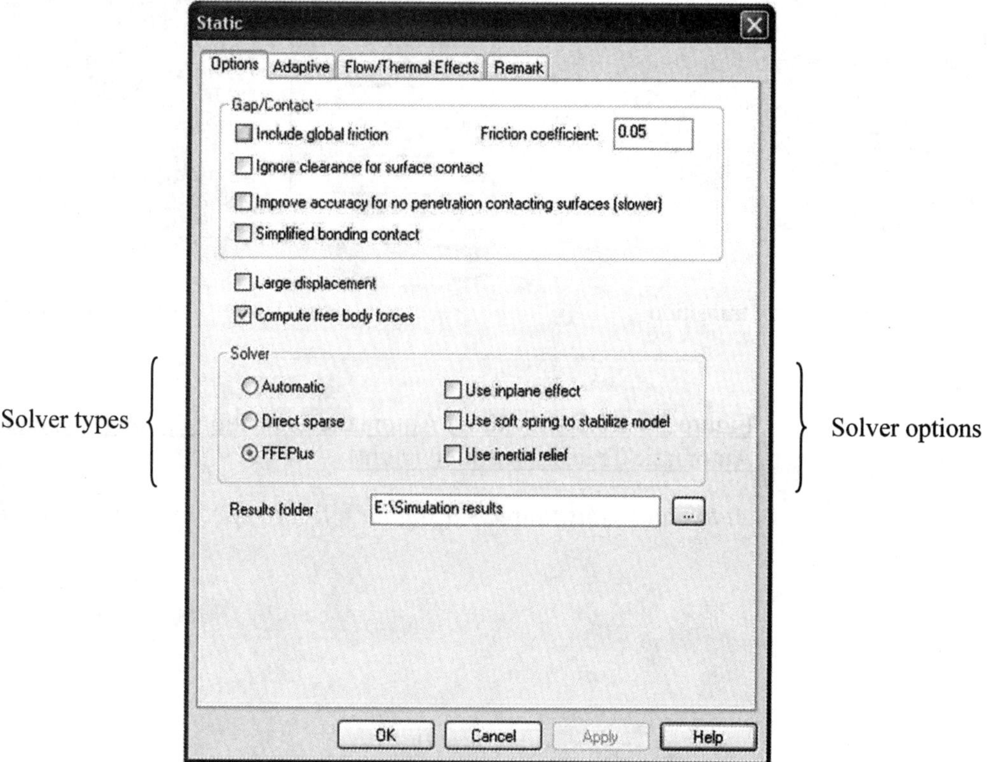

Figure 20-5: Different Solvers and Solver options are available in SolidWorks Simulation

Both **Direct sparse** and **FFEPlus** solvers give comparable results if the required options are supported. It is generally recommended to use the **Automatic** option to select the solver automatically based on user specified solver options.

If a solver requires more memory than available, then disk space is used to store and retrieve temporary data. When this situation occurs, a message is displayed which states that the solution is going out of core and the solution progress slows down very significantly. Three solver options are available:

Option	Purpose
Use in plane effect	In a static analysis, use this option to account for changes in structural stiffness due to the effect of stress stiffening (when stresses are predominantly tensile) or stress softening (when stresses are predominantly compressive).
Use soft springs to stabilize the model	Use this option primarily to locate problems with restraints that result in rigid body motion. If the solver runs without this option selected and reports that the model is insufficiently constrained (an error message appears), the problem can be re-run with this option selected (checked). Insufficient restraints can then be detected by animating the displacement results. An alternative to using this option is to run a frequency analysis, identify the modes with zero frequency (these correspond to rigid body modes), and animate them to determine in which direction the model is insufficiently constrained.
Inertial relief	Use this option if a model is loaded with a balanced load, but no restraints. Due to numerical inaccuracies, the balanced load will report a non-zero resultant. This option can then be used to restore model equilibrium. This option is most often used to balance a model with loads imported from Motion Simulation.

Several options are available when solving contact problems: **Include global friction**, **Ignore clearance for surface contact** and **Friction coefficient**. These options are defined in the study properties, as shown in the table below.

The five options are described below:

Option	Purpose
Include global friction	If selected (checked), friction between contacted surfaces is considered.
Ignore clearance for surface contact	Use this option to ignore the initial clearance that may exist between surfaces in contact. The contacting surfaces start interacting immediately without first canceling out the gap.
Improve accuracy for no penetration contacting surfaces	This method produces continuous and more accurate stresses in regions with definitions of no penetration contact. The method is used when defining contact between faces to faces and faces to edges.
Large displacement	See chapter 15.
Compute free body forces	Enables probing of forces and moments transmitted by nodes.

Displaying mesh in result plots

The default brightness of **Ambient** light, defined in SolidWorks Manager in the **Lighting** folder, is usually too dark to display the mesh, especially a high-density mesh. A clear display of mesh (Figure 20-6) requires increasing the brightness of ambient light.

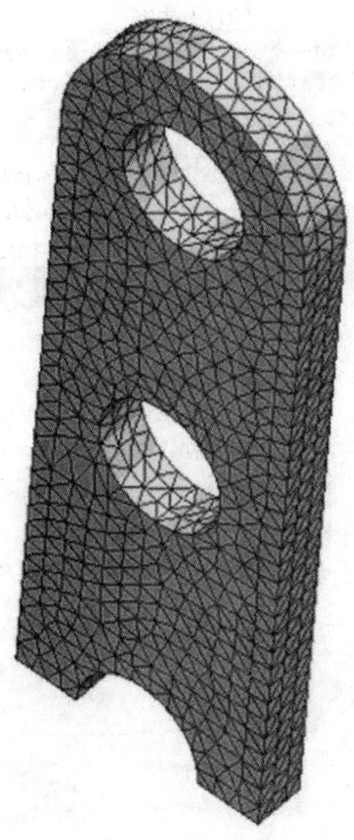

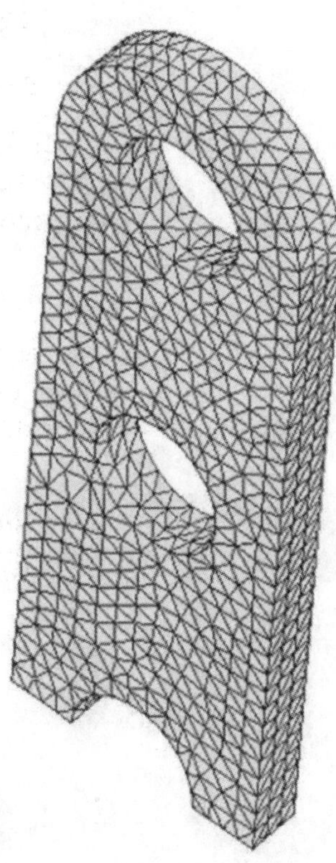

Figure 20-6: Mesh display in default ambient light (left) and adjusted ambient light (right)

A finite element mesh is displayed with ambient light brightness suitable for a CAD model (left), and with the brightness adjusted for the displaying the mesh (right).

Automatic reports

SolidWorks **Simulation** provides automated report creation. After a solution finishes, select **Report** from the **Simulation** Command Manager to define the report format and the items it will contain. The report is created in a few steps and contains all plots from the result folders (Figure 20-7).

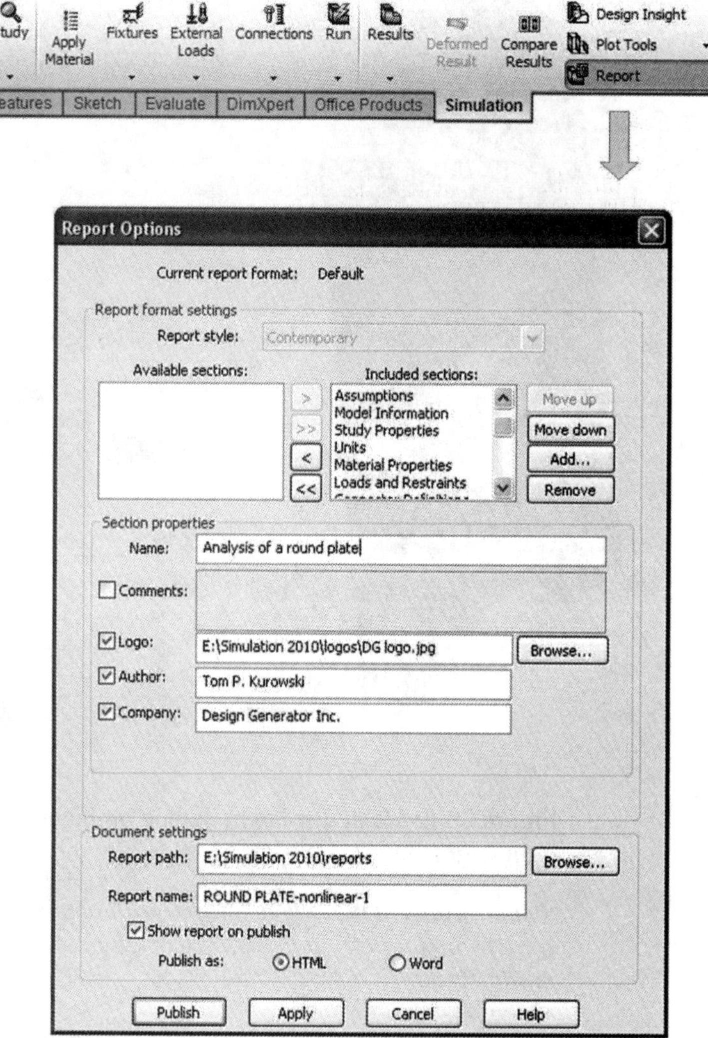

Figure 20-7: The Report Options window is activated by right-clicking the *Report* folder

A Report folder may contain several reports. A report can be created only after an analysis has been completed.

E drawings

Each result plot can be saved in various graphic formats, as well as in the SolidWorks eDrawing format. The eDrawing format offers a very convenient 3D way of communicating FEA results to people who do not have SolidWorks **Simulation** (Figure 20-8).

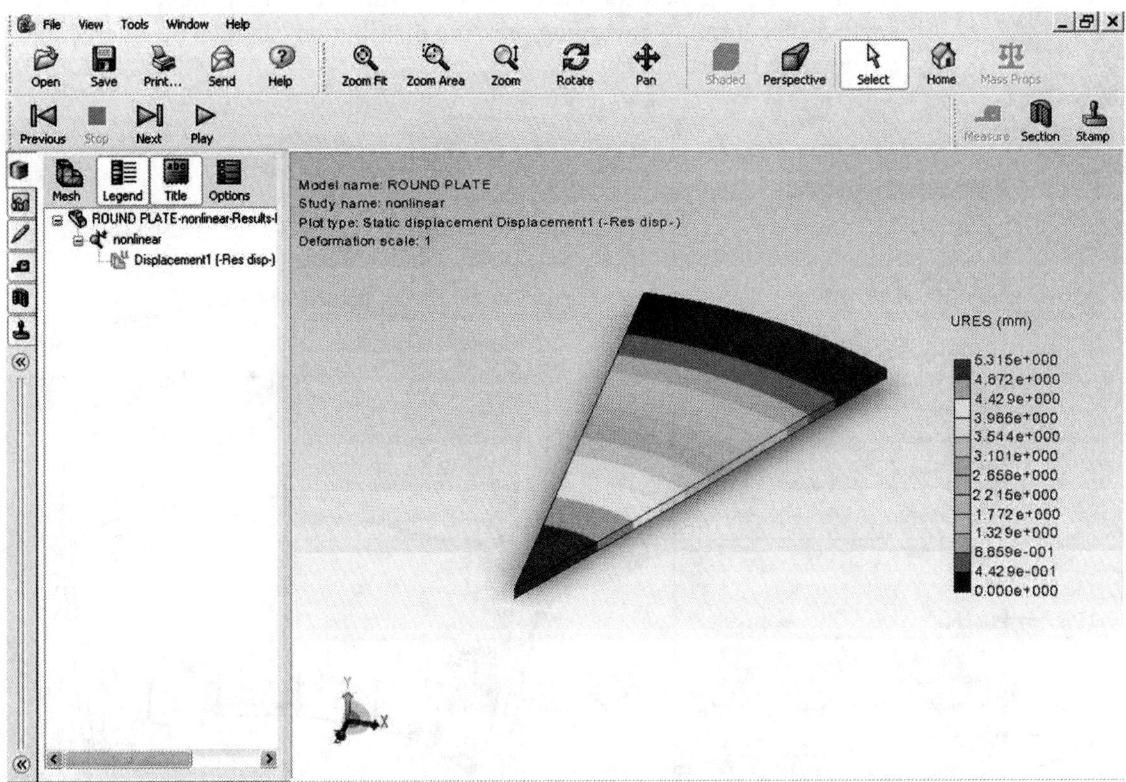

<u>Figure 20-8: Simulation results saved in eDrawing format can be viewed in 3D</u>

Review options offered by eDrawing results viewer.

Non-uniform loads

We will illustrate the use of non-uniformly distributed loads with an example of hydrostatic pressure acting on the walls of a 1.95m deep tank, presented in the SolidWorks part file called NON UNIFORM LOAD. Note that this model uses meters for the unit of length. The pressure magnitude expressed in [N/m^2] follows the equation p = 10000*x,* with *x* being the distance from the top of tank (where the coordinate system *cs1* is located). The pressure definition requires selecting the coordinate system and the face where pressure is to be applied. The formula governing pressure distribution can then be entered in, as shown in Figure 20-9.

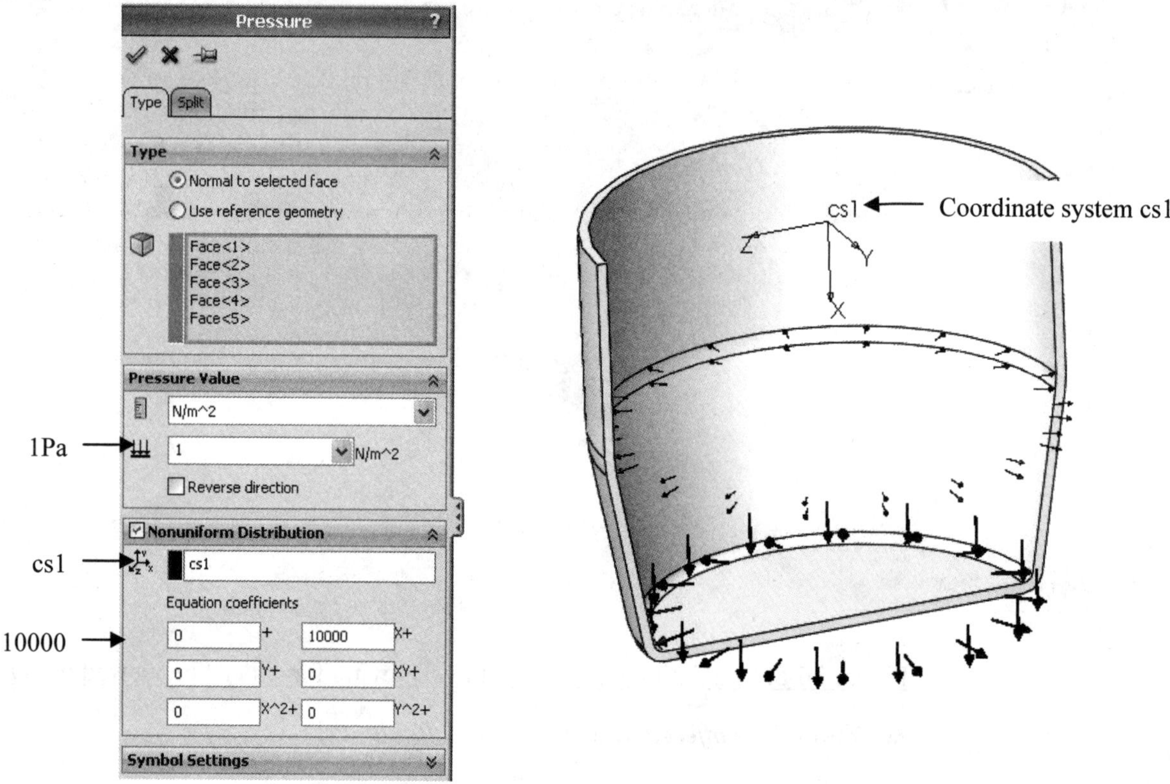

Figure 20-9: A water tank loaded with hydrostatic pressure requires linearly distributed pressure

This illustration uses a section view. Note that the vector lengths correspond to pressure magnitudes that vary with x coordinates of the cs1 coordinate system. This model uses meters as units of length, and Pascals as units of pressure.

You may want to complete this exercise by applying a **Fixed** restraint to the bottom of the tank and material of your choice. Note that the tank geometry makes it suitable for meshing with shell elements.

Frequency analysis with pre-stress

A frequency analysis of rotating machinery most often must account for stress stiffening. Stress stiffening is the increase in structural stiffness due to tensile loads. We will illustrate this concept with the example of a helicopter blade. Open part ROTOR which comes with assigned material properties and two defined SolidWorks **Simulation** studies: *no preload* and *preload.*

A load definition is not required in a **Frequency** analysis. However if loads are defined, their effect will be considered. Direct sparse is the only solver that accounts for the effect of loads in a **Frequency** analysis.

A centrifugal load is defined as shown in Figure 20-10. An axis or a cylindrical face is required as a reference to define a centrifugal load. Review the restraint, which is the same in both studies. Since ROTOR has three identical blades, switch to the *02 section* configuration, which will work with geometry containing only one blade. Restraints may be represented as **Fixed Geometry** restraints applied to faces created by the cut and to the section of central hole.

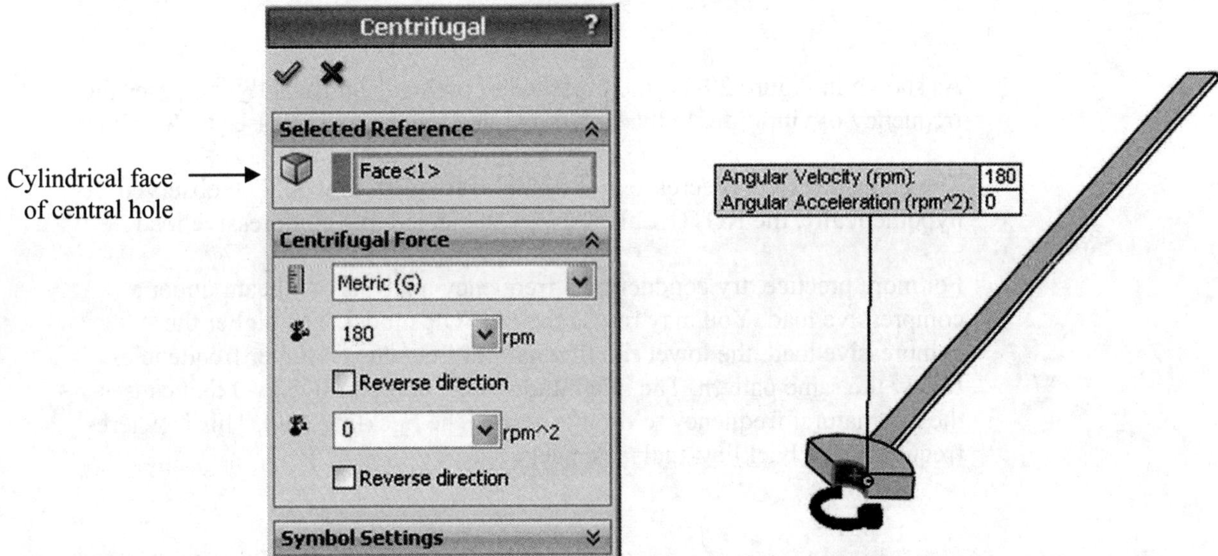

Figure 20-10: **Centrifugal** load window with centrifugal force defined

A centrifugal load resulting from an angular velocity of 180 rpm is applied to the model, simulating the effect of rotation about the axis of the cylindrical face. Angular acceleration can also be defined.

Solve both studies and compare frequency results (Figure 20-11) without and with the pre-stress effect caused by centrifugal force.

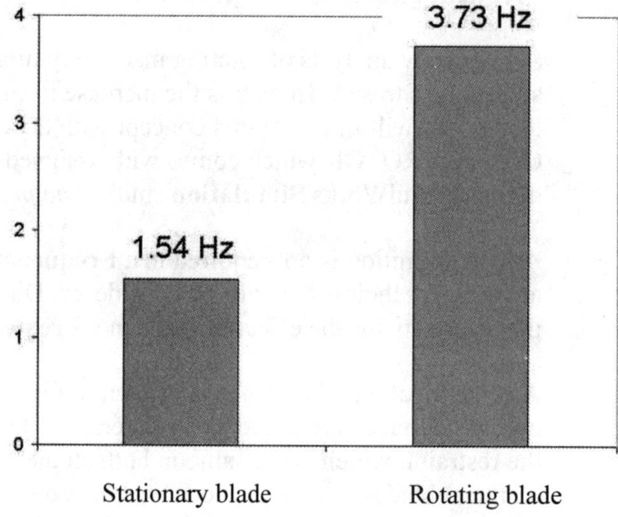

Figure 20-11: Frequency of the first mode of vibration without and with the effect of centrifugal load

As shown in Figure 20-11, the presence of preload significantly increases the frequency of vibration. In the first mode, the frequency increases by 2.4 times.

The opposite effect (decrease in the natural frequency) would be observed if, hypothetically, the ROTOR blades were subjected to a compressive load.

For more practice, try conducting a frequency analysis of a beam under a compressive load. You may re-use the ROTOR model. The higher the compressive load, the lower the first natural frequency. Higher frequencies follow the same pattern. The magnitude of the compressive load that causes the first natural frequency to drop to zero is the buckling load. This is where frequency and buckling analyses meet!

Shrink fit analysis

Shrink fit is another type of **Contact/Gaps** condition. We use it here to analyze stresses developed as a result of an interference (press fit) between two assembly components. Open the SolidWorks assembly SHRINK FIT. The definition of the shrink fit condition is shown in Figure 20-12. Review this model for definitions of restraints, supports and contact conditions.

Note that the contact condition does not include friction, therefore the inside cylindrical face of the pressed-in component has been restrained in circumferential and axial directions to prevent rigid body motions.

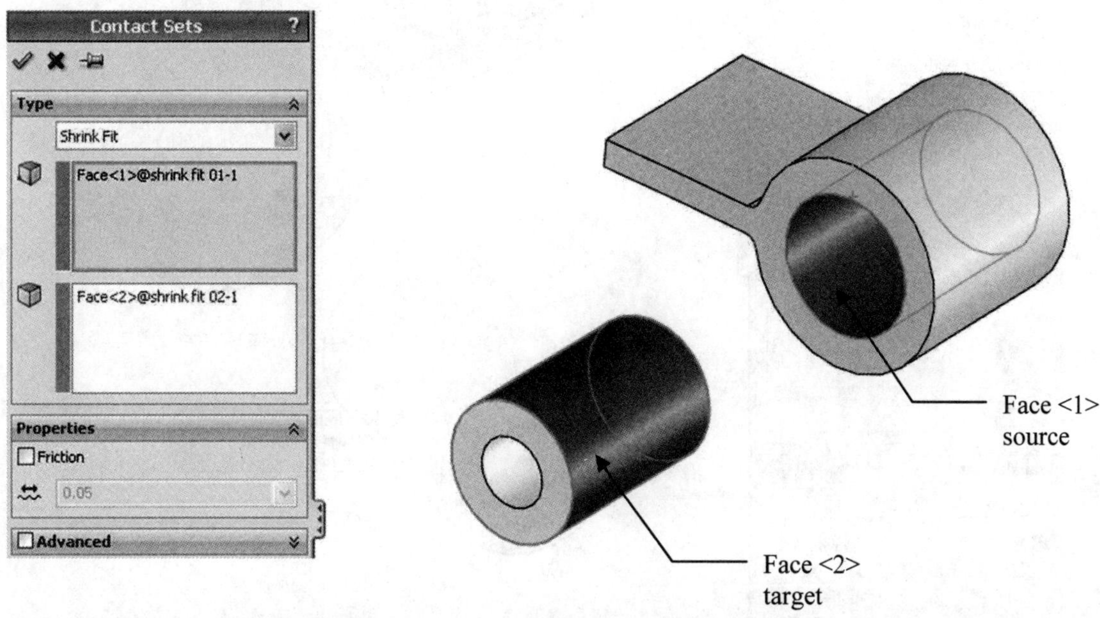

Figure 20-12: Cylindrical face <2> has a larger diameter than cylindrical face <1>. Solving the model with Shrink Fit contact condition eliminates this interference.

Exploded view should be used to select the interfering faces.

Apply a restraint to the "tail" of the housing and restraints to the hole of the shaft as shown in Figure 20-13. This is necessary to eliminate rigid body motions of the shaft.

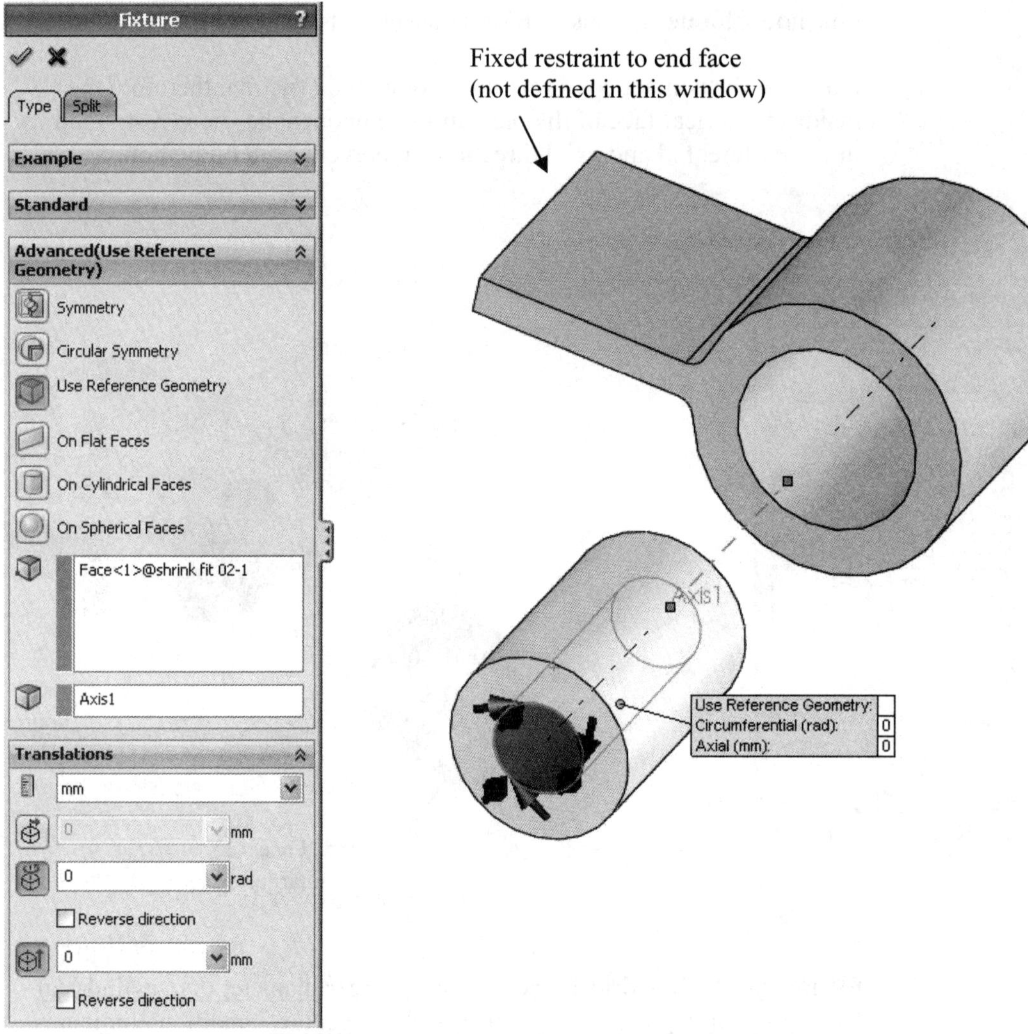

Figure 20-13: Restraints applied to the hole are required to eliminate rigid body motions

Restraints are applied in circumferential and axial directions. The radial direction is free so it does not prevent the hole from shrinking.

The same restraint could have been applied using an On Cylindrical Faces restraint.

Mesh the model with a default element size and obtain the solution. Display the SX stress plot using axis as reference geometry to convert it into radial stress (Figure 20-14). When stresses SX, SY, SZ are plotted using an axis as a reference, as in Figure 20-14, SX becomes radial stress, SY becomes circumferential stress and SZ becomes axial stress. The symbol in the lower right corner indicates that results are presented in a local cylindrical coordinate system.

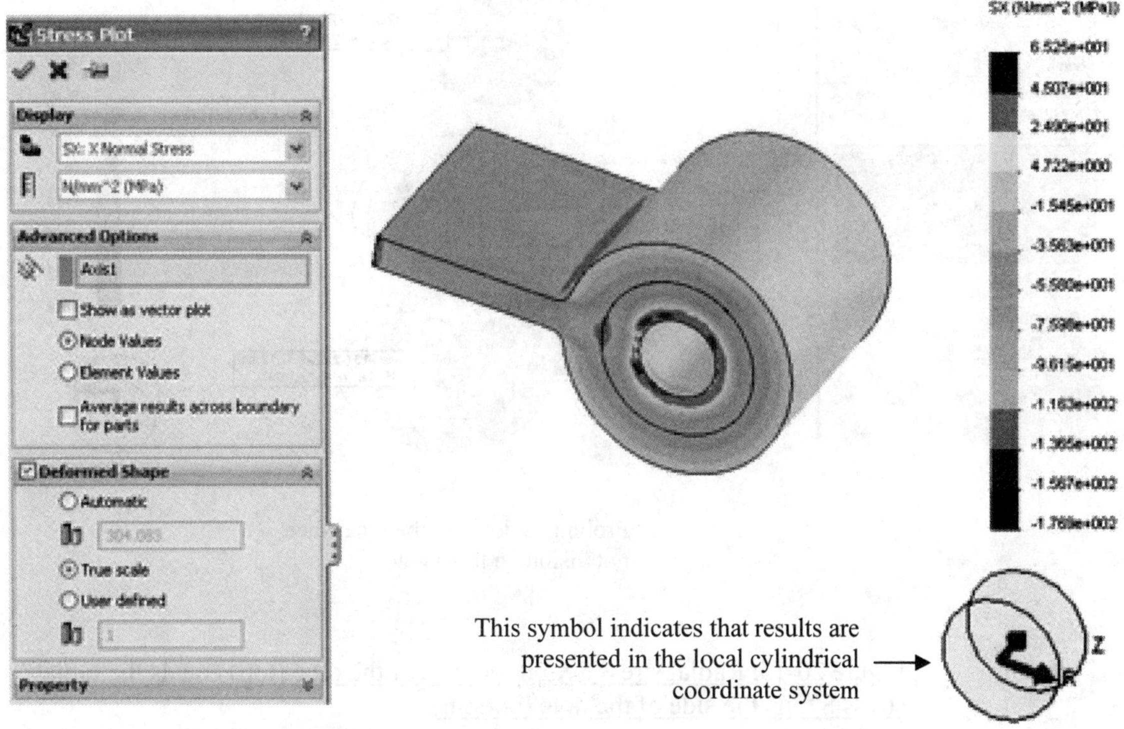

Figure 20-14: Radial stresses SX developed due to shrink fit

Note that on contacting faces, the absolute magnitude of contact stress equals the absolute magnitude of SX stress.

Review the options in the **Stress Plot** window in Figure 20-14 and try using the vector display option to visualize the radial direction of stress SX. This option does not work properly in some service pack of Simulaiton2010 where stress vectors are incorrectly aligned with the global coordinate system rather than with the cylindrical coordinate system. For this reason use a less informative fringe plot in Figures 20-14 and 20-15.

Explode the view and probe the radial stresses on both contacting faces approximately in the same location (Figure 20-15).

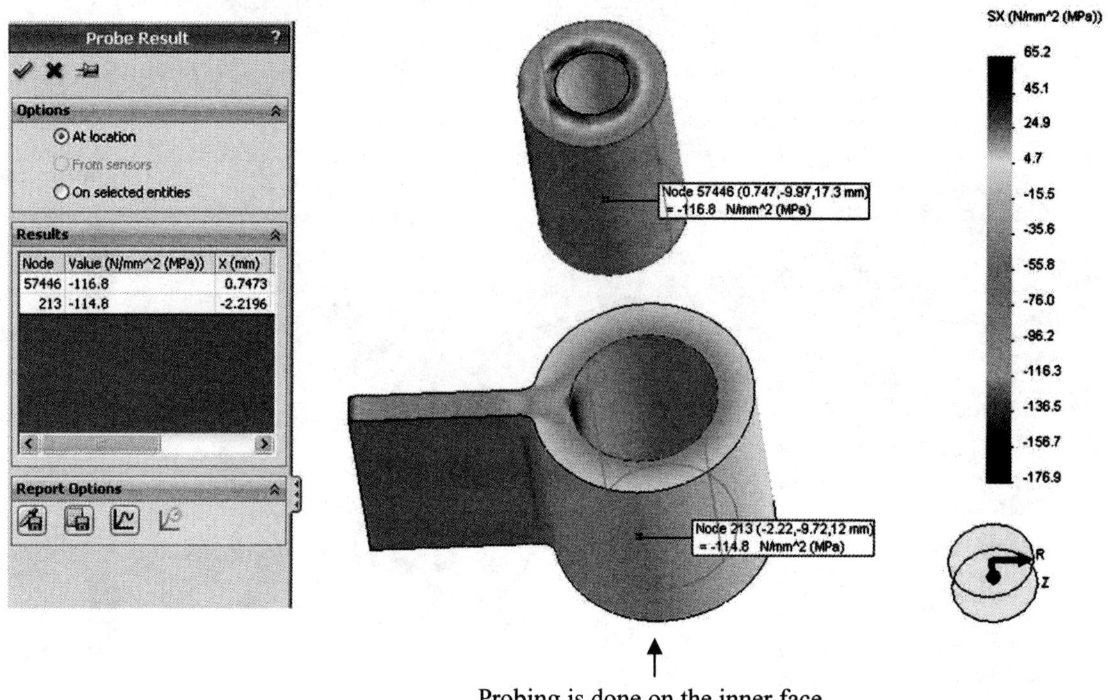

Probing is done on the inner face, not visible in this view

<u>Figure 20-15: Radial stress SX on the face of the tube (top) equals the radial stress SX on the side of the hole (bottom)</u>

Radial stresses correspond to contact pressure which is the same on both contacting faces due to the equilibrium conditions.

Connectors

A connector defines how an entity (vertex, edge, face) is connected to another entity or to the ground. Using connectors simplifies modeling because, in many cases, you can simulate the desired behavior without having to create the detailed geometry or define contact conditions.

SolidWorks **Simulation** offers several types of connectors such as: **Spring**, **Pin**, **Bolt**, **Bearing**, **Spot Welds**, **Edge Welds**, **Link** and **Rigid Connection**. Selected connectors are briefly introduced in this chapter. For more information refer to SolidWorks **Simulation** help which offers extensive explanations backed by examples. To learn about **Simulation** functionality (including connectors) you may also use **Advisor** which is located in the SolidWorks task pane.

A connector definition is called by right-clicking the *Connectors* folder and selecting the desired connector type (Figure 20-16).

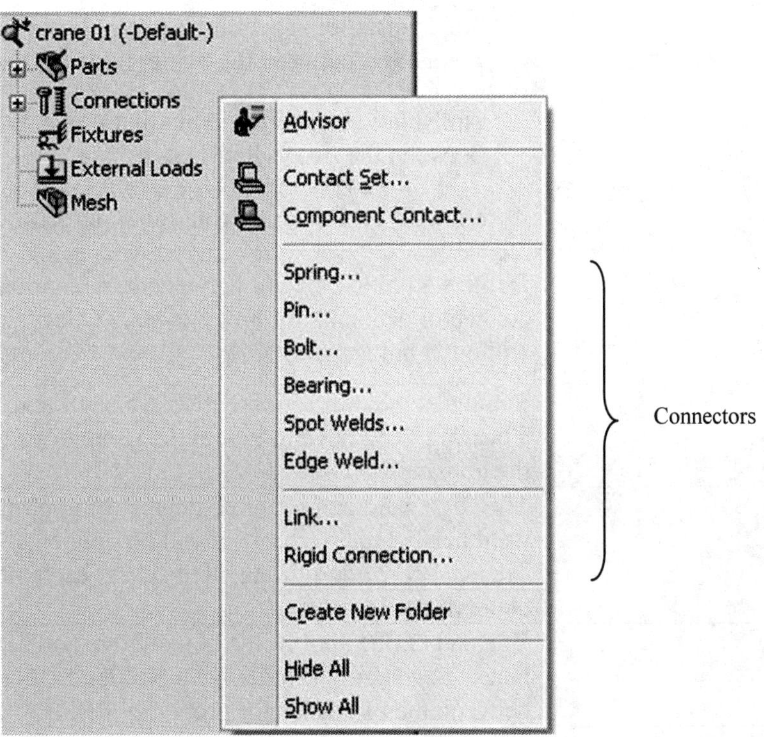

Figure 20-16: Connectors are called from the same pop-up menu as contact conditions

Connectors available in SolidWorks **Simulation** 2010 are summarized in the table below.

TYPE OF CONNECTOR	FUNCTION
Spring	Connects a face of a component to a face of another component by defining total stiffness or stiffness per area. Both normal and shear stiffness can be specified. The two faces must be planar and parallel to each other. Springs are introduced in the common area of the projection of one of the faces onto the other. You can specify a compressive or tensile preload for the spring connector.
Pin	A pin connects cylindrical faces of two components. Two options are available: No Translation: specifies a pin that prevents relative axial translation between the two cylindrical faces. No Rotation: specifies a pin that prevents relative rotation between the two cylindrical faces. Additionally, axial and/or rotational pin stiffness can be defined.
Bolt	Defines a bolt connector between two components. The bolt connector accounts for bolt pre-load. Configurations with and without a nut are available.
Bearing	Simulates the interaction between a shaft and a housing through a bearing. You have to model the geometries for the shaft and the housing.
Edge weld	The edge weld connector estimates the appropriate size of a weld needed to attach two metal components. The program calculates the appropriate weld size at each mesh node location along the weld seam.
Spot weld	You can define spot welds to weld two solid faces or two shell faces. You should also define a No Penetration contact condition between the two faces for proper modeling.
Link	The Link connector ties any two locations in the model by a rigid bar that is hinged at both ends. The distance between the two locations remains unchanged during deformation. The link connector is available for static, buckling, and frequency studies.
Rigid Connection	Defines a rigid link between the selected faces. Faces connected by a rigid link do not translate or rotate in relation to each other.

We will review the use of **Rigid Connection** and **Pin** using a model in the assembly CRANE. This model comes with a defined **Rigid Connection** and three **Pin** connectors.

The **Rigid** connector is shown in Figure 20-17.

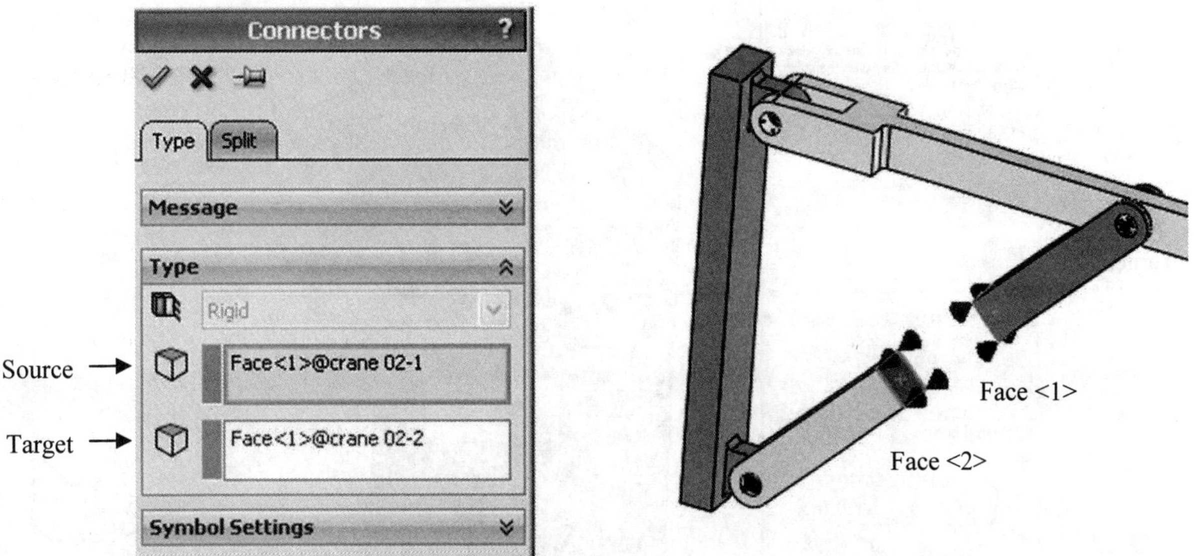

Figure 20-17: Rigid connector rigidly connects two faces

The selection of the face as a source and as a target is arbitrary.

One of the **Pin** connectors is shown in Figure 20-18.

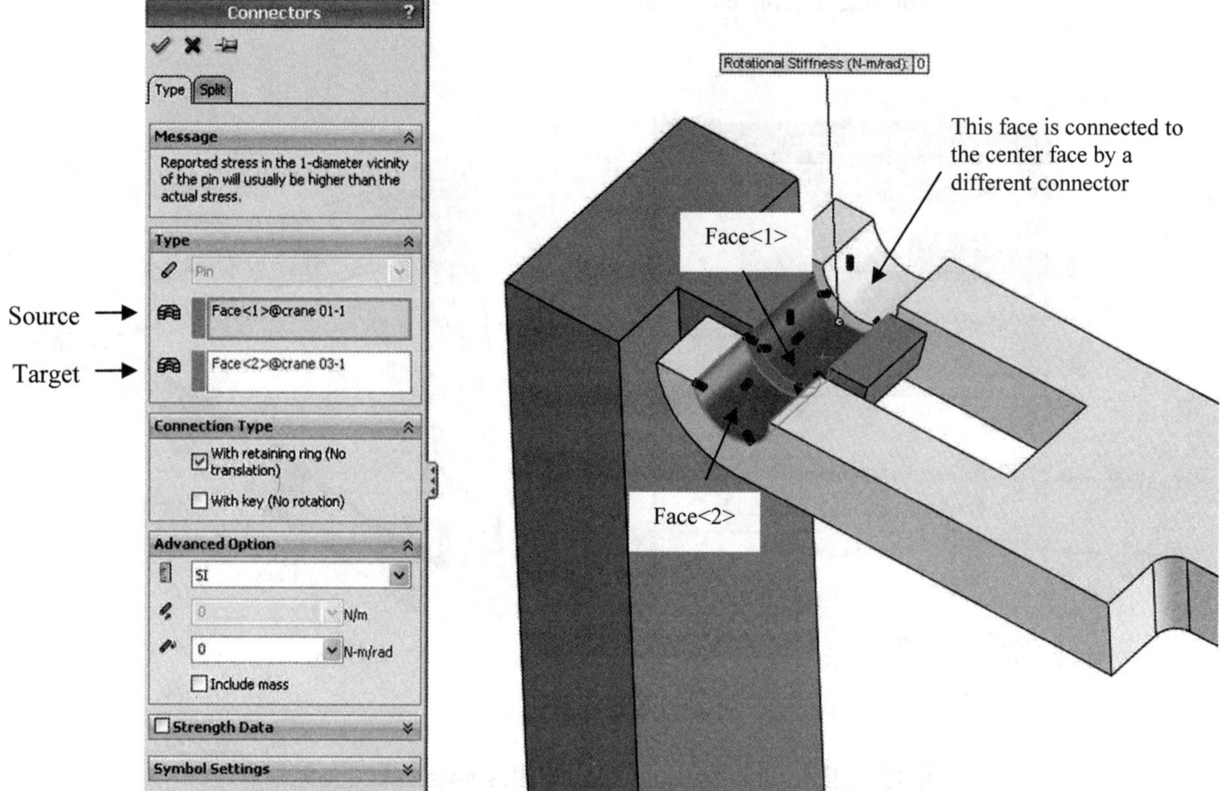

Figure 20-18: The Pin connector connects faces of two components

In this model, each location requires two Connectors. Only one connector is shown in this illustration.

Cross section view is used to show the connected faces.

Note that the torsional stiffness of the **Pin** connector shown in Figure 20-18 is specified as 0 (this is the default value). This means that **Pin** connectors allow for rotation between the two components. All degrees of freedom on the selected faces are coupled (must be the same) except for circumferential translations, which are disjoined.

Practice using **Pin** connectors using the assembly STAND. Our objective is to find the first mode of vibration of the assembly. This model has little relevance to real life devices but offers a good opportunity to practice **Pin** connectors.

Note that no **Global Contact** conditions exist in the study *Modal.* In the absence of **Global Contact** conditions all touching faces are treated as free, they are not bonded and penetration is allowed. Consequently, the four links are not bonded to the top and the bottom plate. They are connected to them by **Pin** Connectors

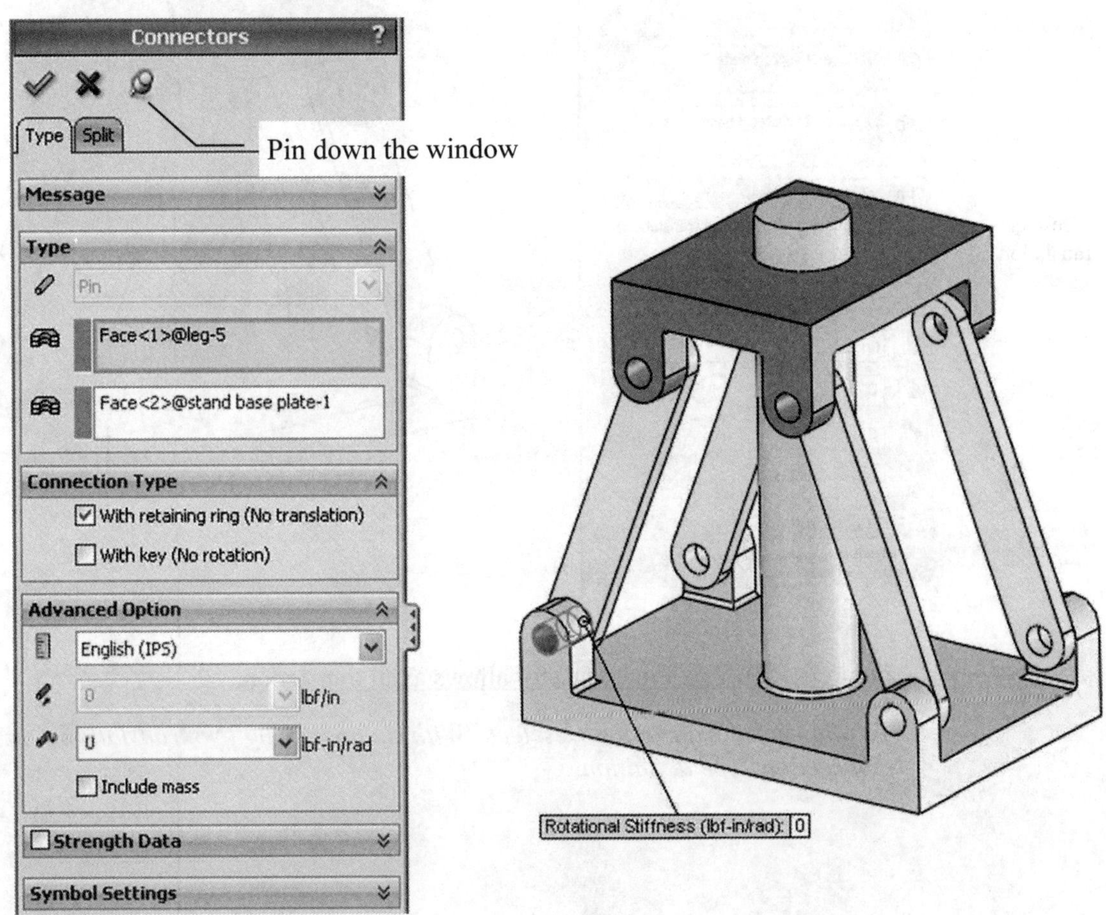

Figure 20-19: Definition of on of eight Pin connectors connecting legs with the top and bottom plate.

You may pin down the Connectors window to create a number of pins in one step. All connectors will then be placed is a separate folder. Note that "pin" as in "Pin down the window" has nothing to do with "pin" as in Pin connector.

The vertical shaft is connected by a **Pin** connector to the top plate. The important difference between this **Pin** connector and the previously discussed **Pin** connectors is explained in Figure 20-20.

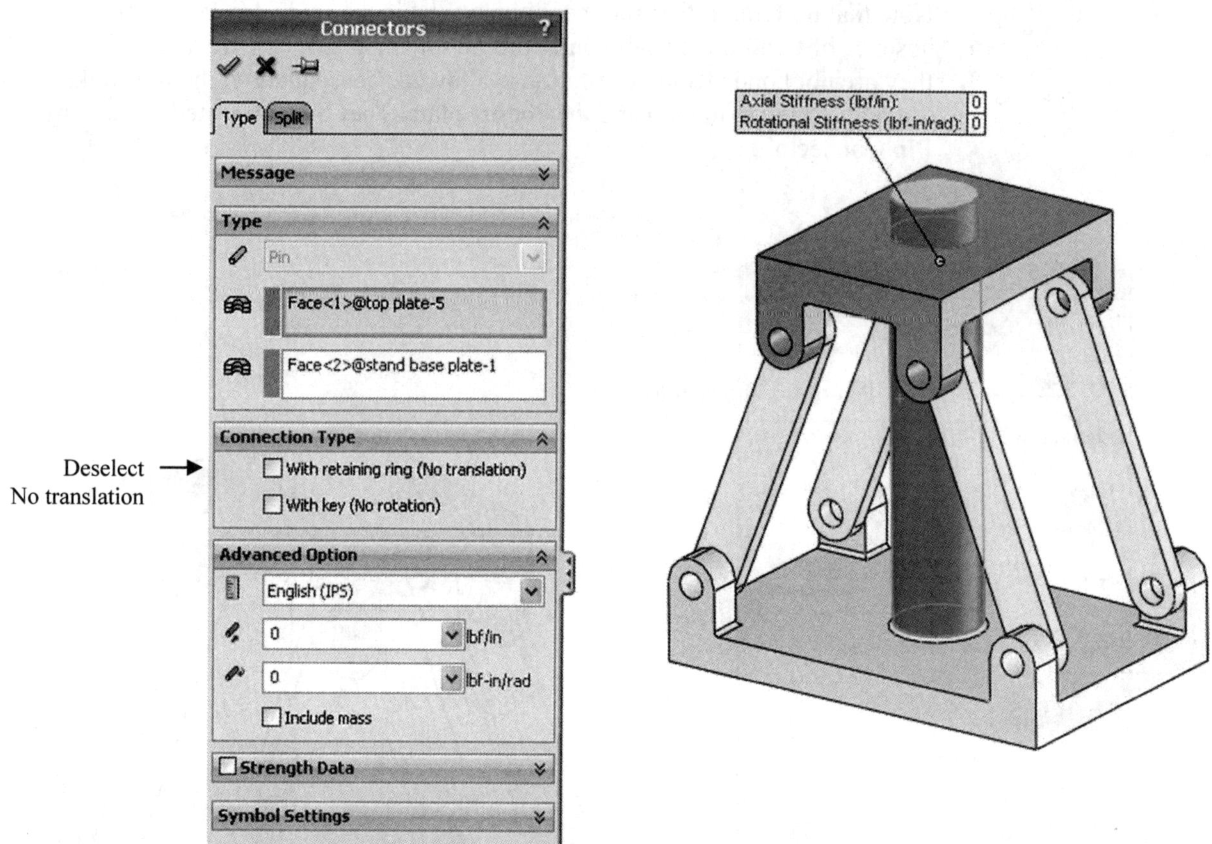

Figure 20-20: This Pin connector allows axial translation.

To allow axial translation, deselect "With retaining ring (No translation)" in Connection Type definition.

Review restraints of the model (bottom of the BASE PLATE is rigidly restrained) and run Modal analysis. The first mode of vibration is shown in Figure 20-21.

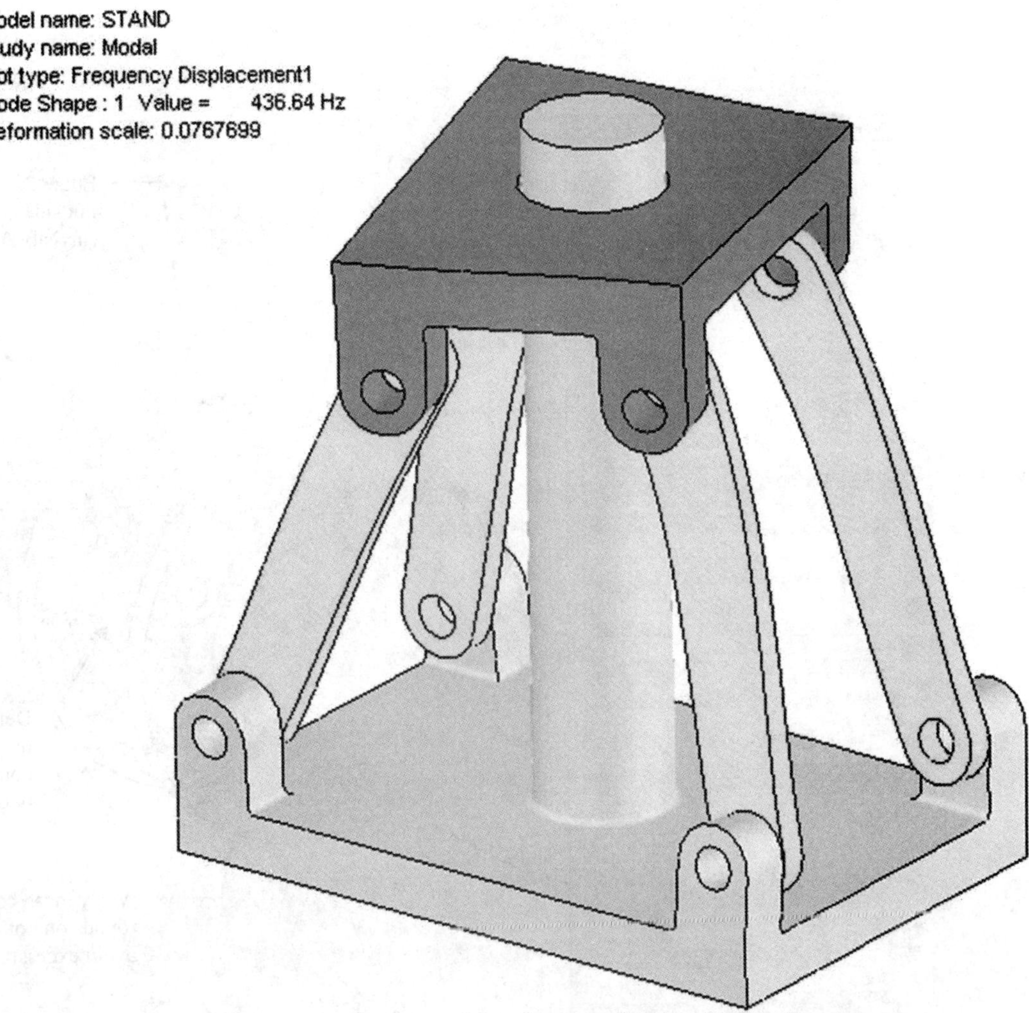

Figure 20-21: The first mode of vibration of STAND.

Note that this is an anti-symmetric, torsional mode.

To review the **Bolt** connector and a load type called **Remote Load**, open the assembly FLANGE, in the *01 long* configuration. The model comes with six bolt connectors already defined. Right-click one of the **Bolt Connector** icons and select **Edit Definition** to open the **Connectors** windows (Figure 20-22).

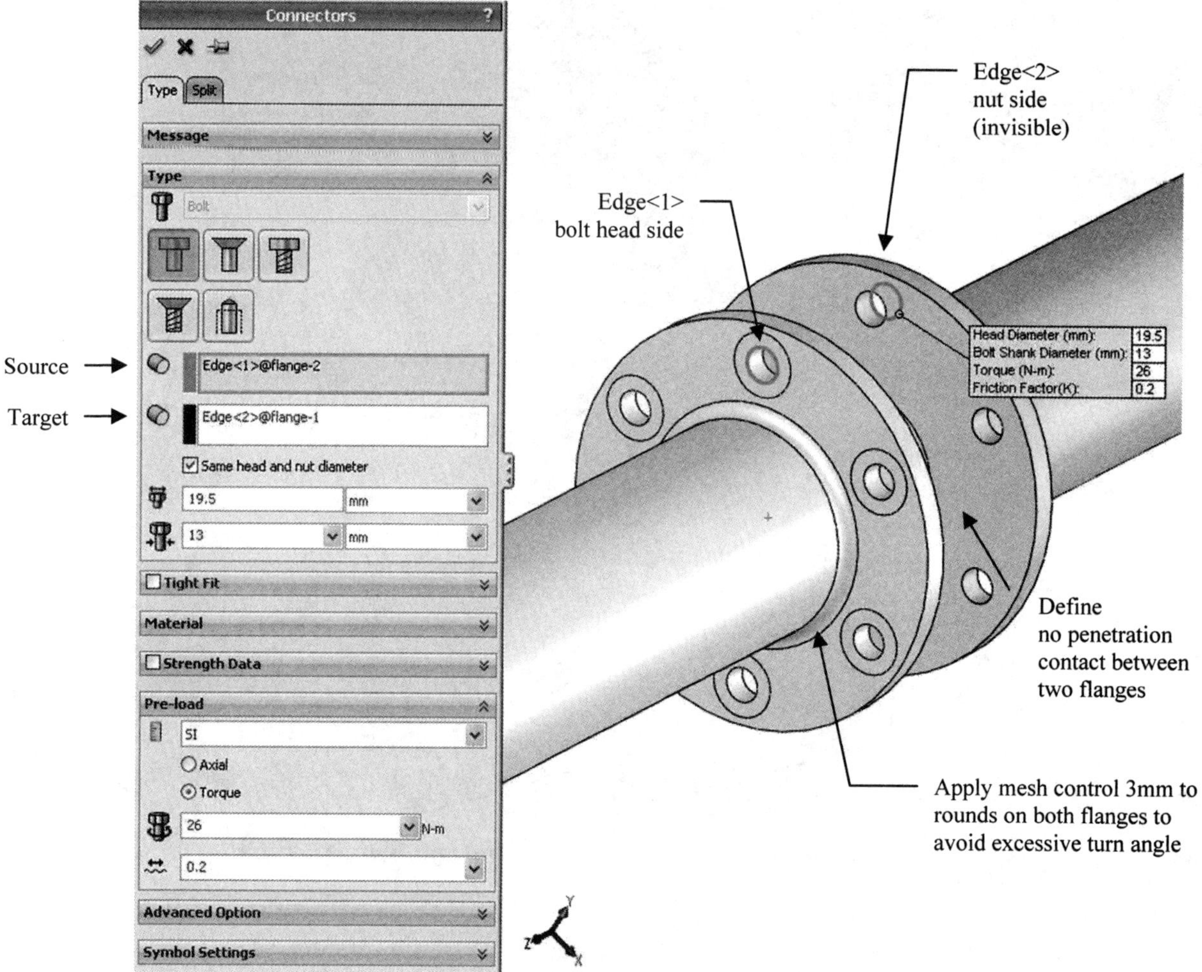

Figure 20-22: One of six bolt connectors in the FLANGE assembly model. Contact condition (no penetration) must be defined between touching faces of two flanges. Tight fit must be defined to transmit the shear force in the absence of friction between flanges.

The pre-load definition indicates that each bolt is loaded with 26Nm of torque, the coefficient of friction is 0.2.

Defining the **Bolt Connector** offers several options. In this example, we model the bolt with a nut. The bolt is made out of Alloy Steel, has a loose fit, and a diameter of 13mm. Automatically calculated diameters of the bolt head and nut are accepted. The bolt is preloaded with a torque 26Nm.

Review loads and restraints summarized in Figure 20-23.

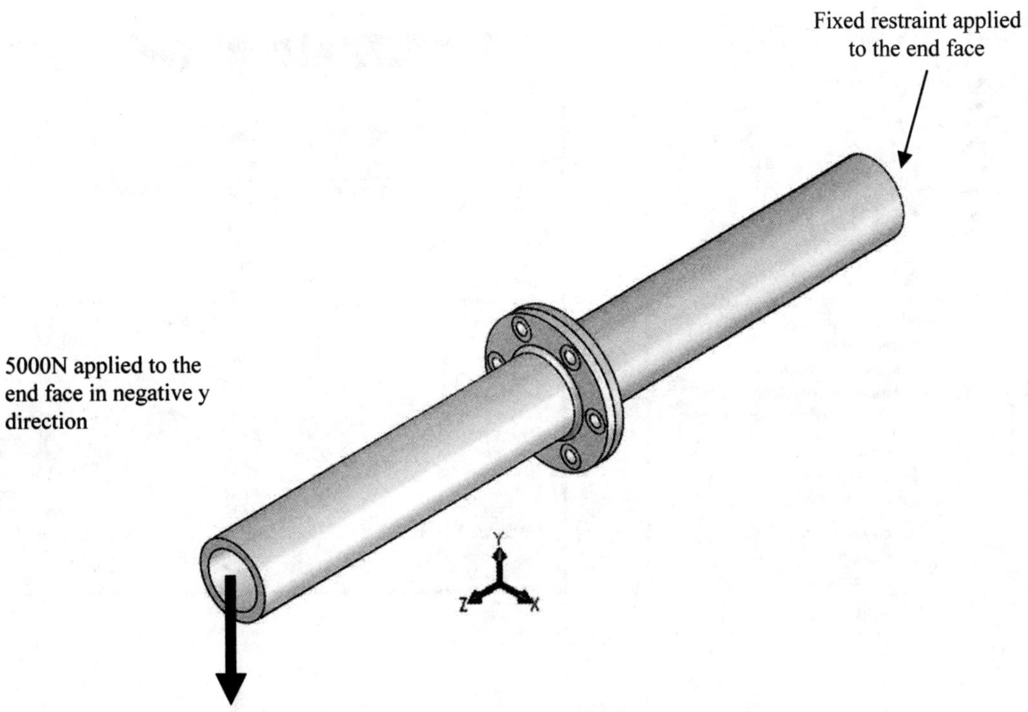

Figure 20-23: Load and restraint applied to FLANGE model.

Apply mesh controls 3mm to rounds as shown in Figure 20-21 and mesh the model with default mesh size, be prepared for a long solution. Upon solution, review bolt forces which are available by right-clicking on the *Results* folder and selecting **List Pin/Bolt/Bearing Force**. (Figure 20-24).

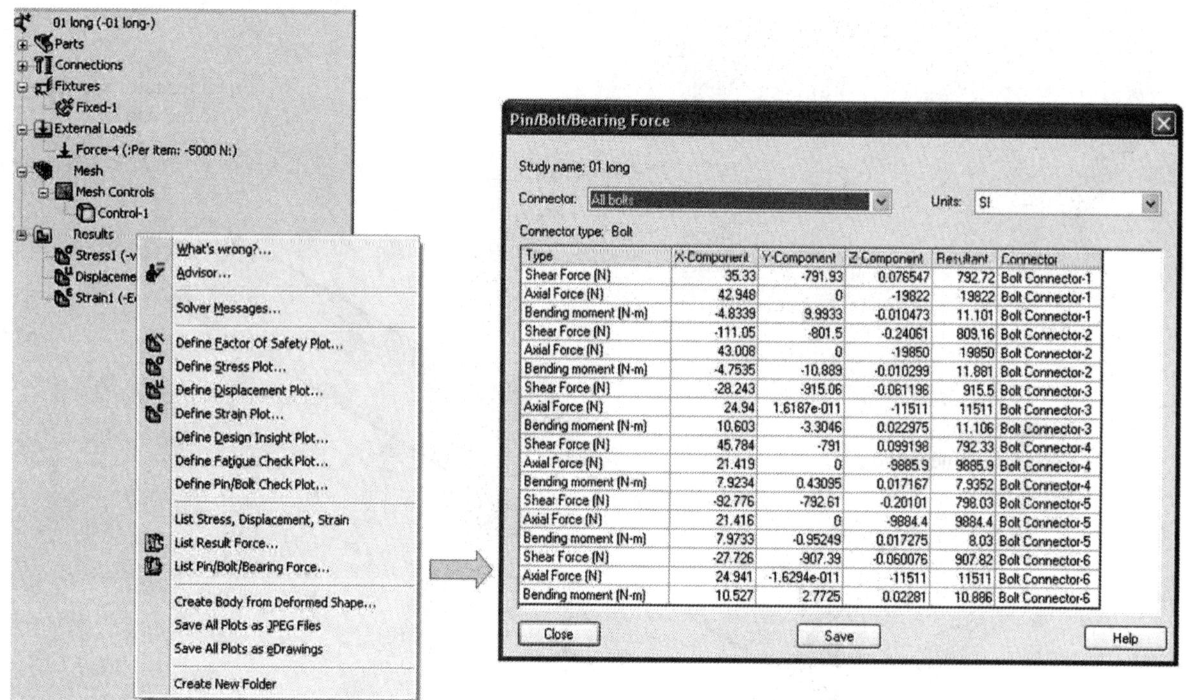

Type	X-Component	Y-Component	Z-Component	Resultant	Connector
Shear Force (N)	35.33	-791.93	0.076547	792.72	Bolt Connector-1
Axial Force (N)	42.948	0	-19822	19822	Bolt Connector-1
Bending moment (N-m)	-4.8339	9.9933	-0.010473	11.101	Bolt Connector-1
Shear Force (N)	-111.05	-801.5	-0.24061	809.16	Bolt Connector-2
Axial Force (N)	43.008	0	-19850	19850	Bolt Connector-2
Bending moment (N-m)	-4.7535	-10.889	-0.010299	11.881	Bolt Connector-2
Shear Force (N)	-28.243	-915.06	-0.061196	915.5	Bolt Connector-3
Axial Force (N)	24.94	1.6187e-011	-11511	11511	Bolt Connector-3
Bending moment (N-m)	10.603	-3.3046	0.022975	11.106	Bolt Connector-3
Shear Force (N)	45.784	-791	0.099198	792.33	Bolt Connector-4
Axial Force (N)	21.419	0	-9885.9	9885.9	Bolt Connector-4
Bending moment (N-m)	7.9234	0.43095	0.017167	7.9352	Bolt Connector-4
Shear Force (N)	-92.776	-792.61	-0.20101	798.03	Bolt Connector-5
Axial Force (N)	21.416	0	-9884.4	9884.4	Bolt Connector-5
Bending moment (N-m)	7.9733	-0.95249	0.017275	8.03	Bolt Connector-5
Shear Force (N)	-27.726	-907.39	-0.060076	907.82	Bolt Connector-6
Axial Force (N)	24.941	-1.6294e-011	-11511	11511	Bolt Connector-6
Bending moment (N-m)	10.527	2.7725	0.02281	10.886	Bolt Connector-6

Figure 20-24: Pop-up menu activated by right-clicking the Results folder (left) and Pin/Bolt/Bearing Force window.

Also investigate other results options in this menu.

Note that when you have a pin defined by two separate pin connectors then the sum of the two pins forces equal the forces on the overall pin

Review von Mises stress results to notice that mesh in the area of stress concentration is, at best, marginal (Figure 20-25).

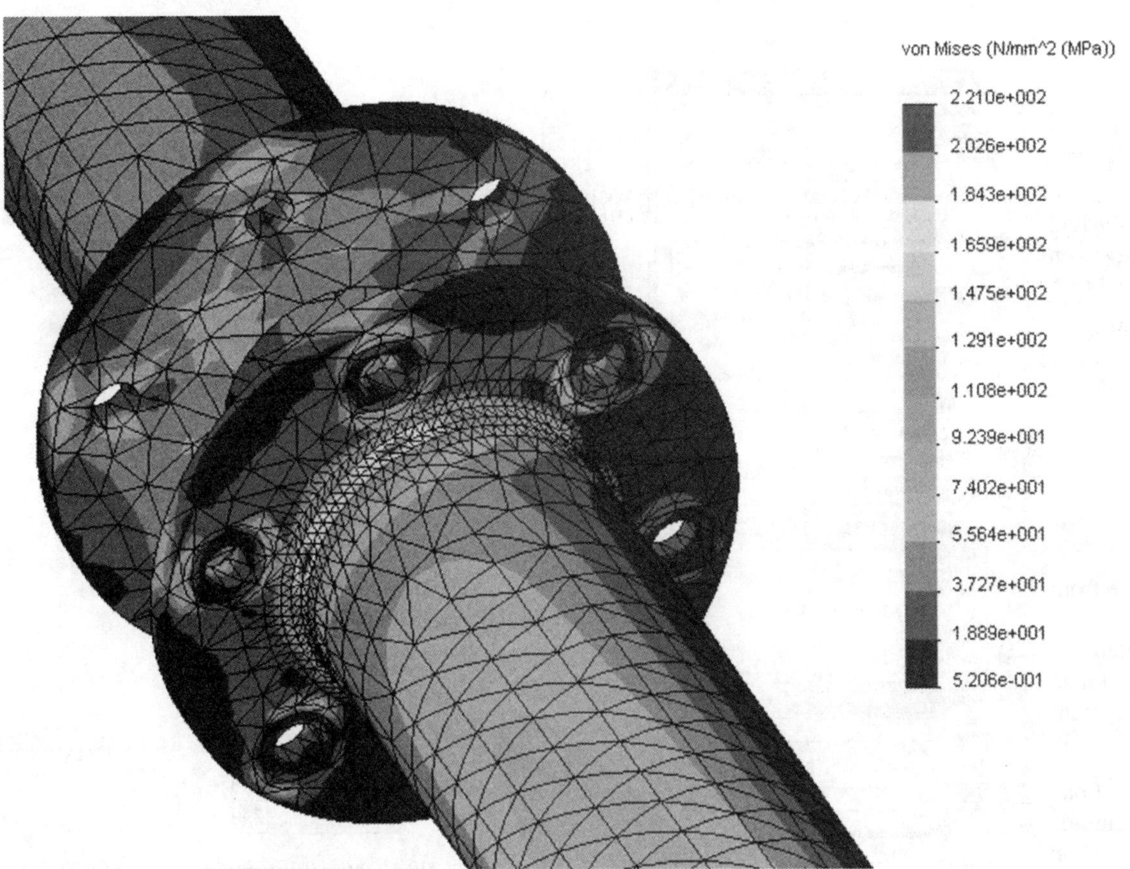

Figure 20-25: Review of stress concentrations indicate that the mesh should have been refined

Stress concentrations that are attracted to nodes and are smaller than the element size indicates the need for mesh refinement.

Considering that the mesh needs to be refined while the solution time should be kept short, we will reduce the model size using the **Remote Load** technique. Change to configuration *02 short* and create a new study. Copy all **Bolt Connectors** from the previous study.

Right click the *External loads* folder and select **Remote Load/Mass** from the pop-up menu to open the **Remote Load/Mass** window, make entries as shown in Figure 20-26.

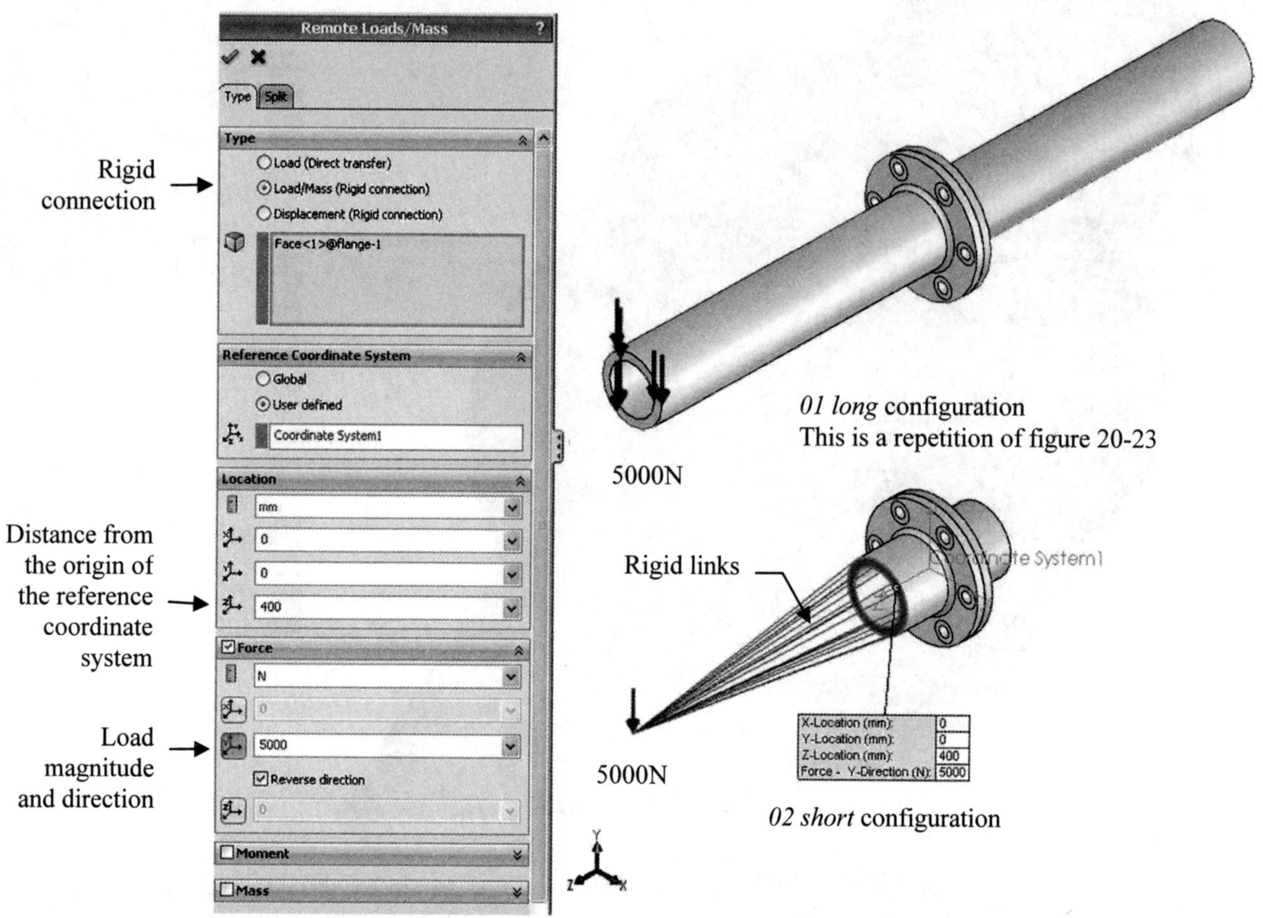

Figure 20-26: Load applied to the end face in configuration *01 long* (top) and Remote load applied to end face in configuration *02 short (bottom)*.

The Remote Loads/Mass window applies to configuration 02 short. Point of load application is connected to the end face by means of rigid links.

The use of **Remote load** allows us to reduce the model size by cutting the pipes short and applying a load as if these eliminated portions of the model were still there.

There are two types of Remote Load: **Direct Transfer** and **Rigid Connection**. The choice between these two types depends on the stiffness of the suppressed/eliminated component as compared to the rest of the model. For example a thin-walled tube would just transfer the load to the face of the link and therefore the **Direct transfer** would have to be specified. A thick wall pipe, as in our case, stiffens the end face of the short flange where it is attached, so we specify **Rigid connection**.

Load/Mass (Rigid connection) can also be used to define a remote mass. The **Displacement (Rigid connection)** option is used when displacement boundary conditions are specified.

No penetration contact between flanges; apply a fixed restraint to the opposite end of the model in configuration *02 short*. Note that this is analogous to applying load through rigid links and stiffens up the model as compared to the model in configuration *01 short*. Apply a mesh control of 2mm to both rounds and mesh the model with the default mesh size.

Von Mises stress results are shown in Figure 20-26. Even with a more aggressive mesh bias, the mesh is still at best, marginal. Repeat this exercise with several more mesh refinements until stress concentrations are modeled by 3 - 4 elements.

Von Mises stress results are shown in Figure 20-27.

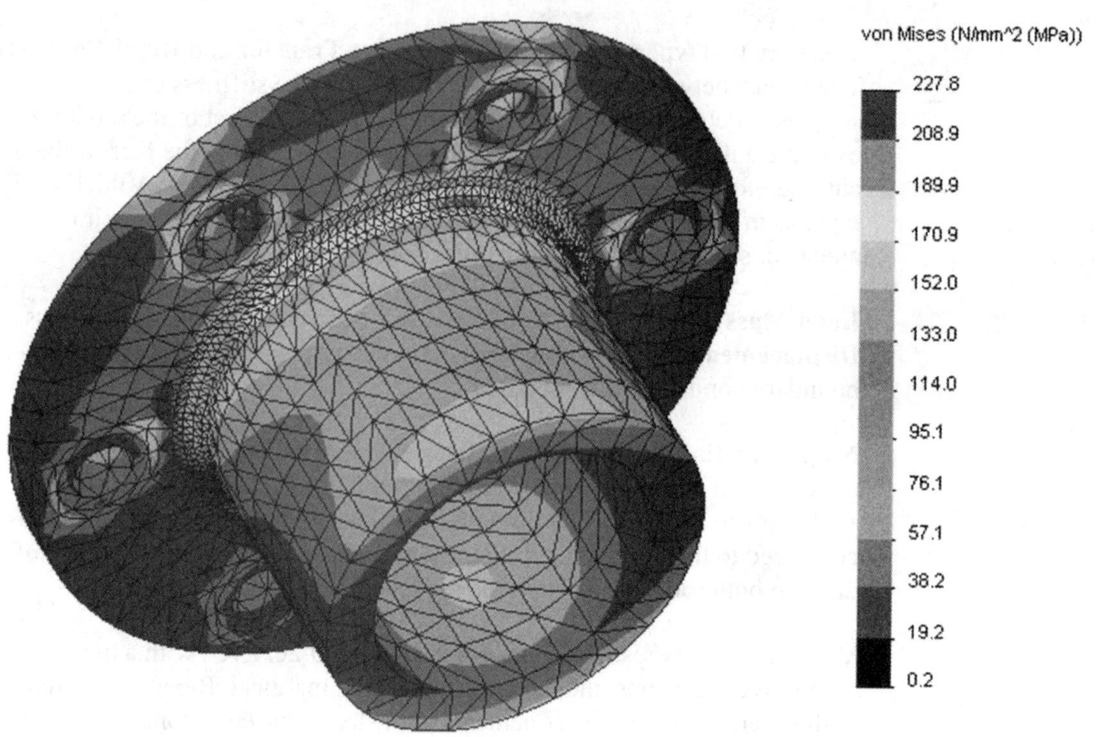

Figure 20-27: Von Mises stress results in the *02 short* configuration.

Note that the other assembly component is hidden.

To visualize the effect of clamping the two flanges with bolts repeat the analysis of model in the *02 short* configuration without any external load. The only loads are bolt clamping forces. Deformation results in a greatly exaggerated scale are shown in Figure 20-28.

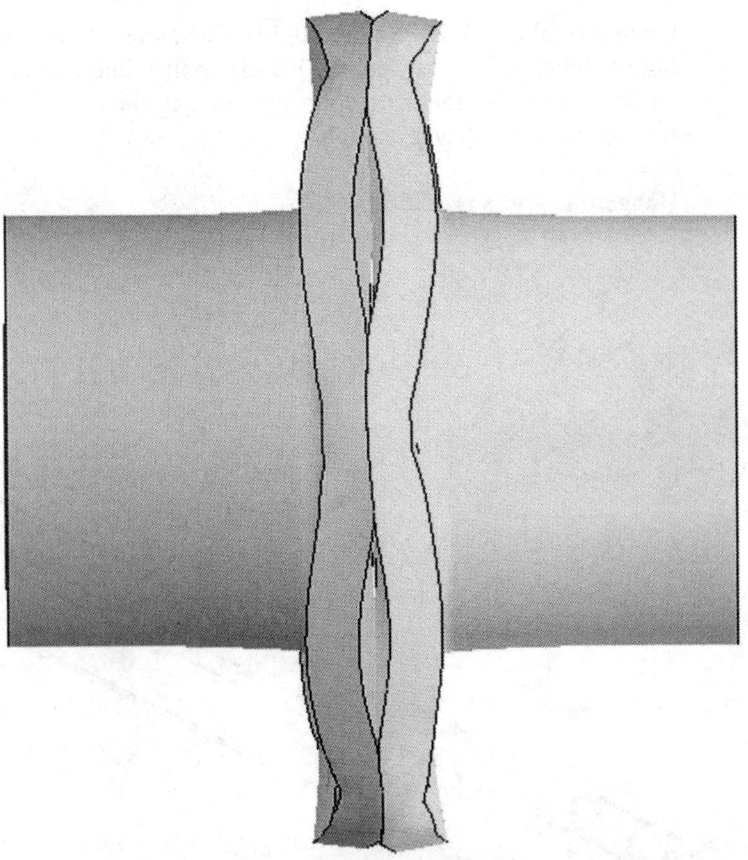

Figure 20-28: Deformation of model in the 02 short configuration.

Deformation scale is 8000:1.

Edge Weld connector

An **Edge Weld** connector is used to connect components of a welded assembly and calculate weld loads. Note that the actual weld is NOT modeled. **Edge Welds** model connections along a line where the weld would be located. Next, loads transmitted by those lines are calculated. These loads are then used to assess if the specified weld is adequate.

Open assembly TUBE (Figure 20-29). The assembly consists of a square hollow tube, endplate where the load is applied and two hangers modeled as surfaces. These hangers are connected to the tube by welds, we need to check if the welds are "strong enough".

Hanger thickness is 0.25″

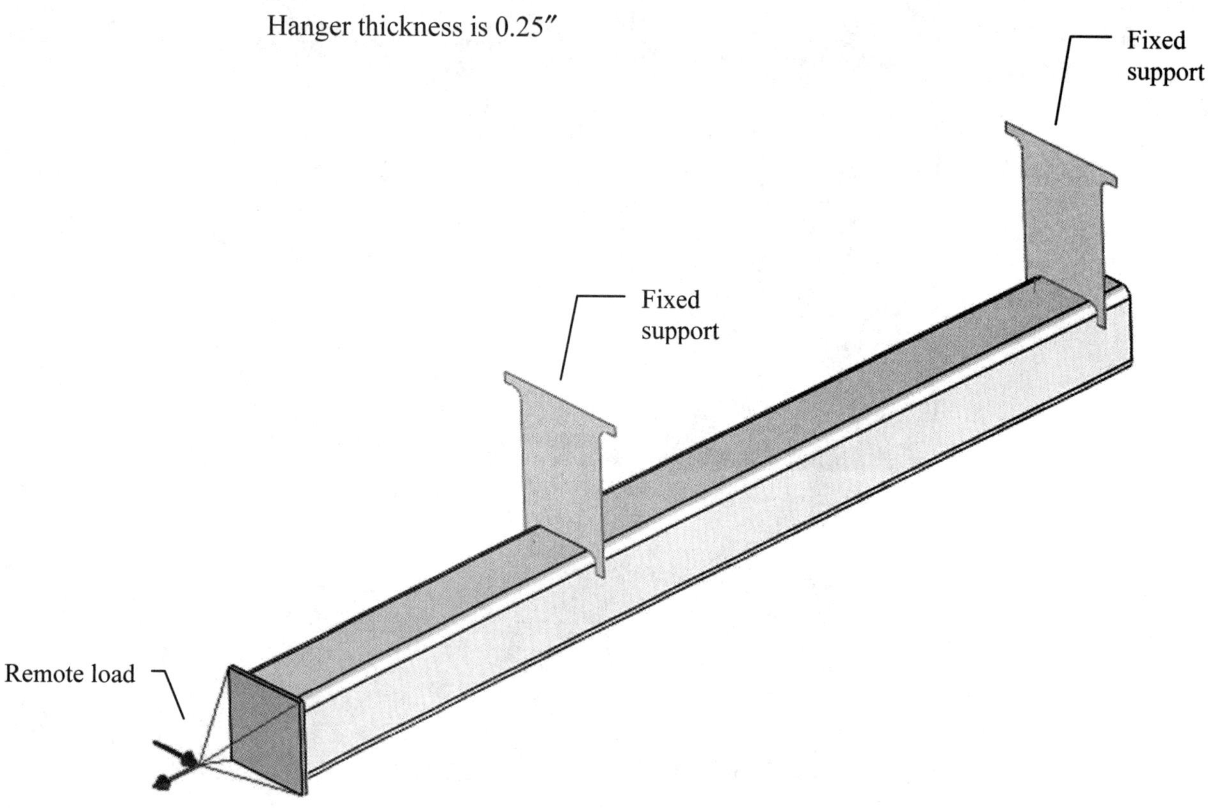

Figure 20-29: TUBE model intended for weld strength analysis.

The remote load applied to the model is explained in Figure 20-30.

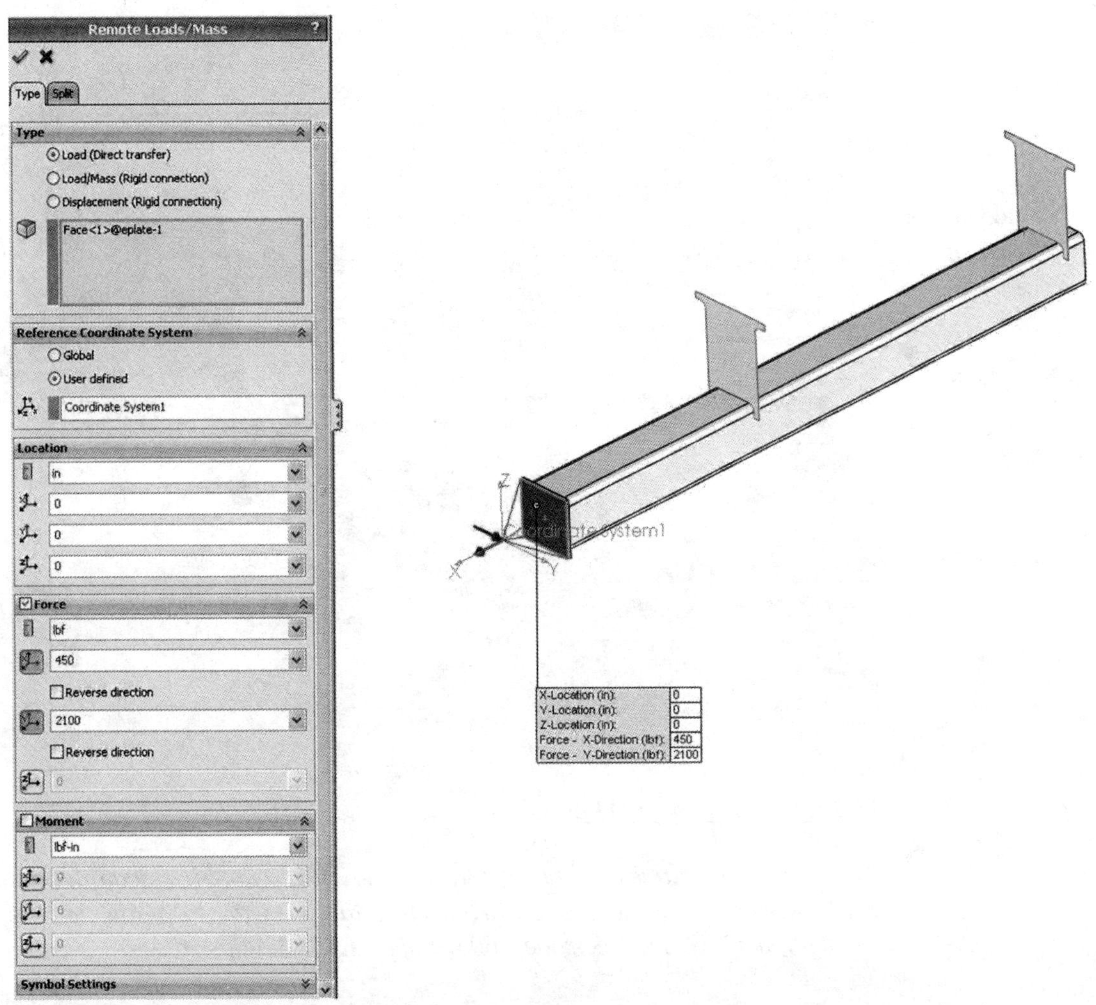

Figure 20-30: Remote load applied to the endplate.

Load is applied at the origin of the local coordinate system

Ten **Edge Weld** connectors have to be defined in the model. Figure 20-31 shows definition of one of them.

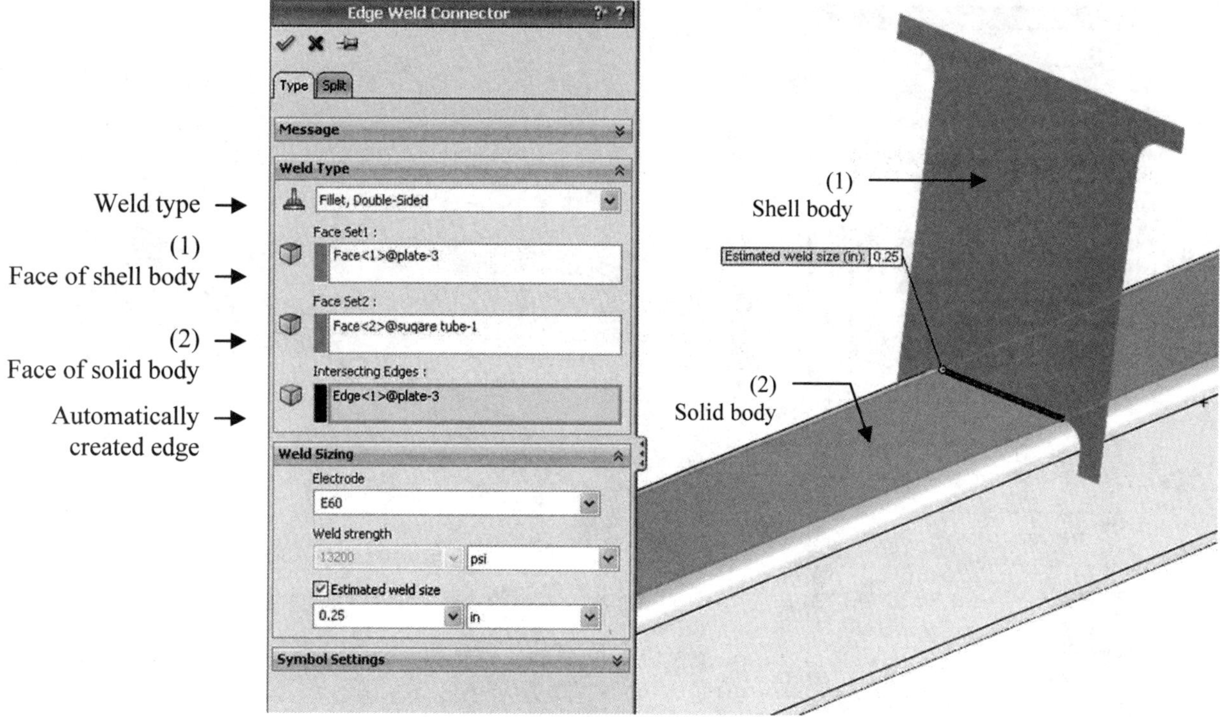

Figure 20-31: Edge weld definition

The definition includes weld type and size, here it is a double sided fillet weld 0.25″in size. It also includes electrode material type with the associated Weld strength, here we use electrode E60 with strength 13200psi.

Repeat the **Edge Weld** definition nine more times to define all weld connectors and apply restraints as shown in Figure 20-29. Run the analysis and display the **Weld Check** plot as shown in Figure 20-32.

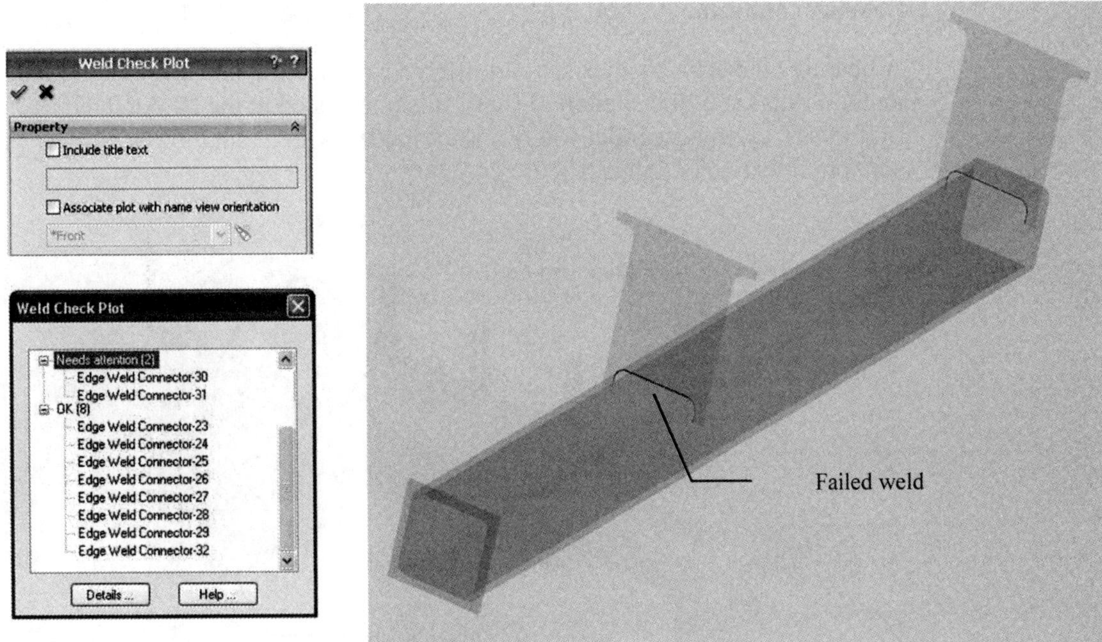

Figure 20-32: Weld Check plot

Welds that have passed the check are displayed in green, welds that failed are displayed in red. This is difficult to show in this B&W illustration. The plot is accompanied by a small window listing passed and failed plot.

Complete the analysis of TUBE by reviewing von Mises stress results and comparing them to the yield strength of assembly components.

Bearing connector

A bearing connector models support offered by a bearing and allows for some angular rotation of the supported shaft. It is introduced in the BEARING SUPPORT assembly model where a shaft loaded with a radial force is supported by two bearings (Figure 20-33).

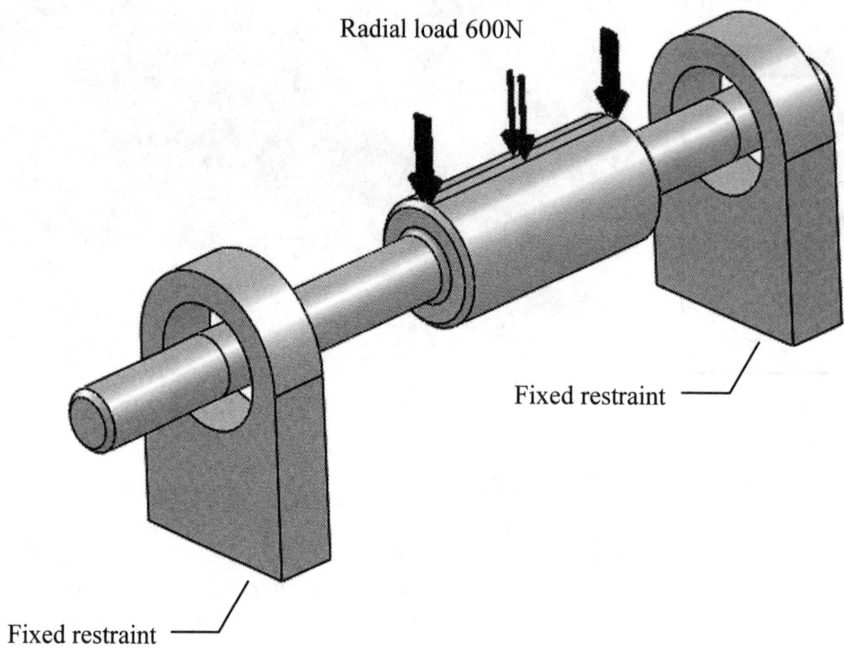

Figure 20-33: Shaft supported by two bearings

Each bearing support is modeled by a Bearing connector. Note that bearings are not modeled explicitly. The bearing connector connects the shaft to the bearing housings. Load is applied to the split face, restraints are applied to bottom faces of the bearing housings.

Definition of **Bearing connectors** is shown in Figure 20-34.

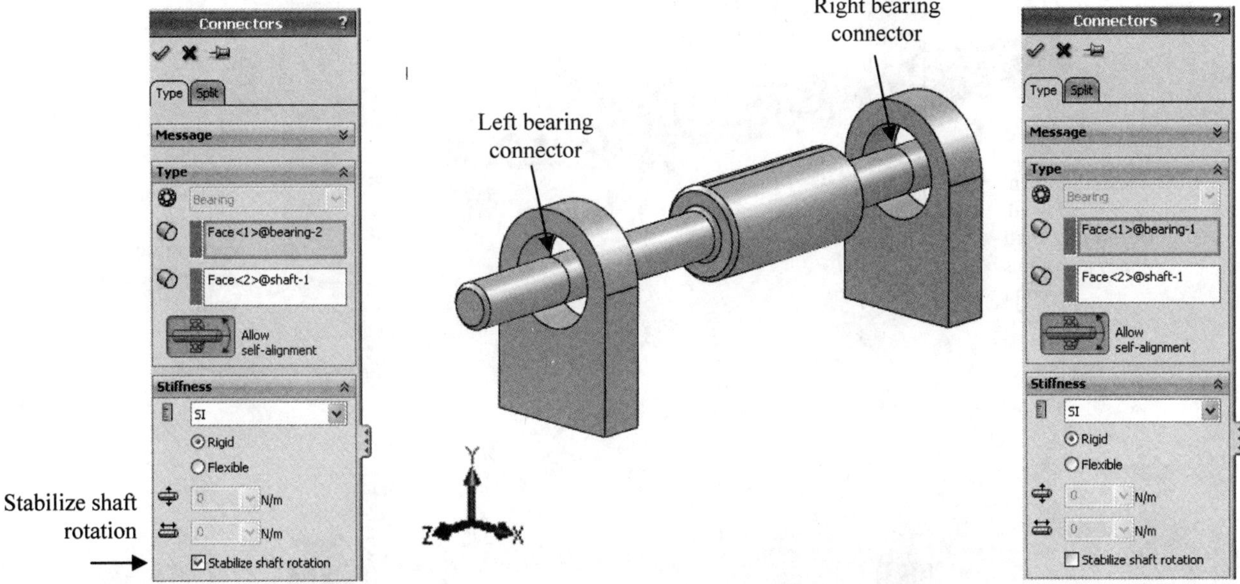

Figure 20-34: Definition of Bearing connectors

The stabilize shaft rotation option is selected in the left bearing connector. Bearing connector symbols are not shown.

The definition of the connectors on the left and the right sides differs because we need to eliminate the rotation of the shaft about the z axis because this would result in a rigid body motion. This can be done on one side only.

Both bearings are modeled as rigid. Self alignment is allowed meaning that the deflecting shaft can rotate about the centre of the imaginary bearing.

Mesh the model using mesh bias to ensure correct element shape and size in the regions of stress concentrations.

Complete the analysis of the BEARING SUPPORT assembly by repeating the analysis with one **Bearing Connector** without self-alignment.

Deformed shapes of the shafts are shown in Figure 2-35.

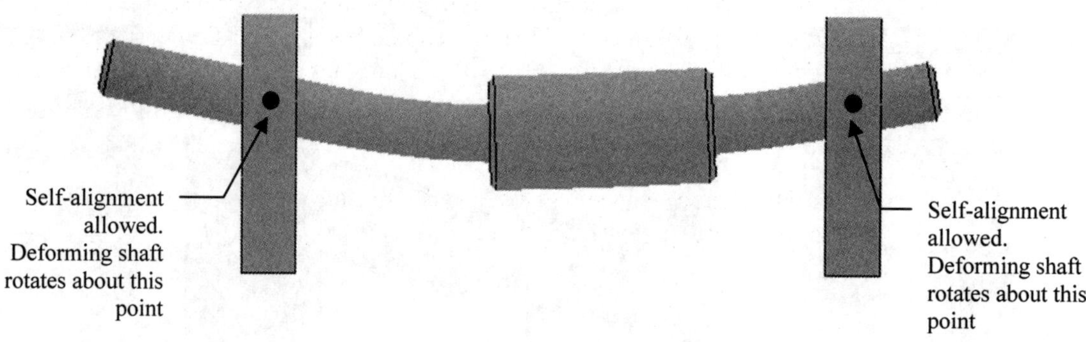
Self-alignment allowed. Deforming shaft rotates about this point
Self-alignment allowed. Deforming shaft rotates about this point

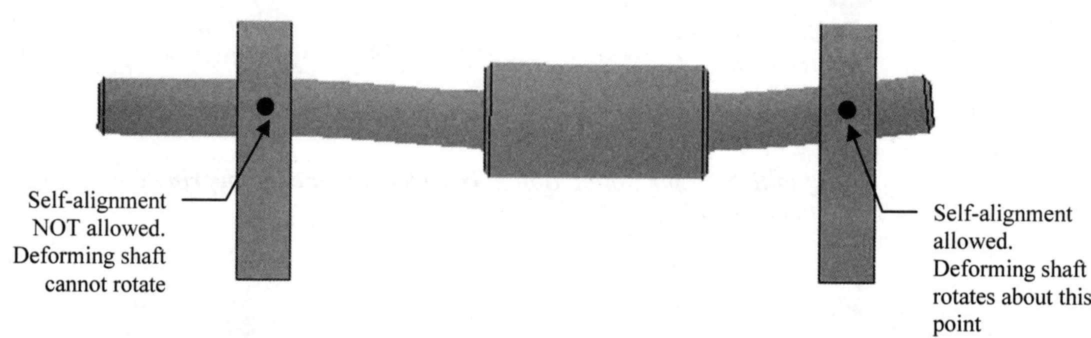
Self-alignment NOT allowed. Deforming shaft cannot rotate
Self-alignment allowed. Deforming shaft rotates about this point

Figure 20-35: Deformed shapes of the SHAFT with supports defined as Bearing connectors

Top: self alignment is allowed on both sides

Bottom: self alignment is allowed on the right side only.

Circular symmetry

The use of **Circular symmetry** simplifies the analysis of a model with circular patterns around an axis by modeling only one representative segment. The geometry, restraints, and loading conditions must be similar for all other segments making up the model. Typical examples of machine components suitable for analysis with circular symmetry include turbines, fans, flywheels, and motor rotors.

Note that geometry as well as loads and restraints must be characterized by the same circular pattern.

Open the part CIRCULAR and switch to the *02 section* configuration. Note that this is a 1/7th section of the complete geometry (Figure 20-36).

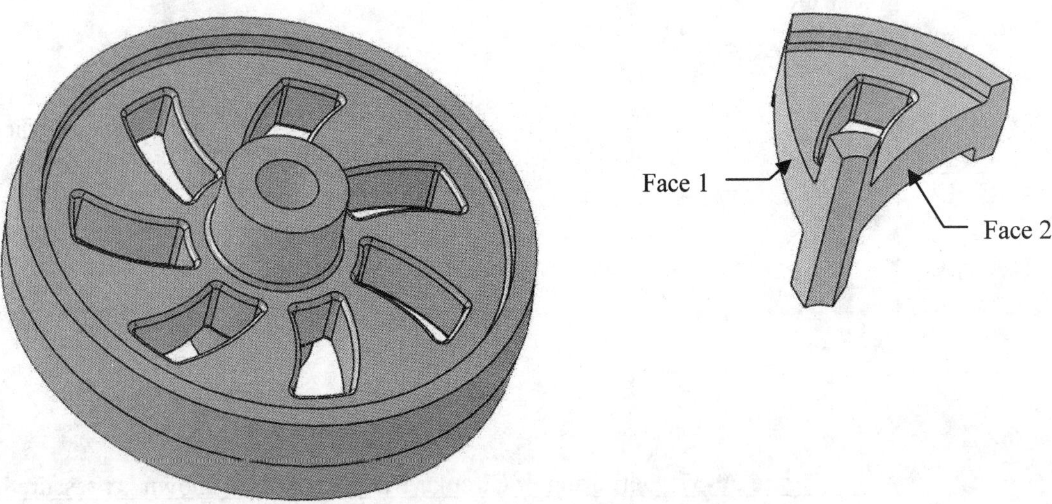

Figure 20-36: Complete model (left) and 1/7 section suitable for analysis with Circular symmetry

The program enforces equal displacements at each corresponding location on both faces. The faces where circular symmetry is enforced do not have to be of any particular shape. The only requirement is the segment is a part of a repetitive geometry.

Definition of circular symmetry is explained in Figure 20-37.

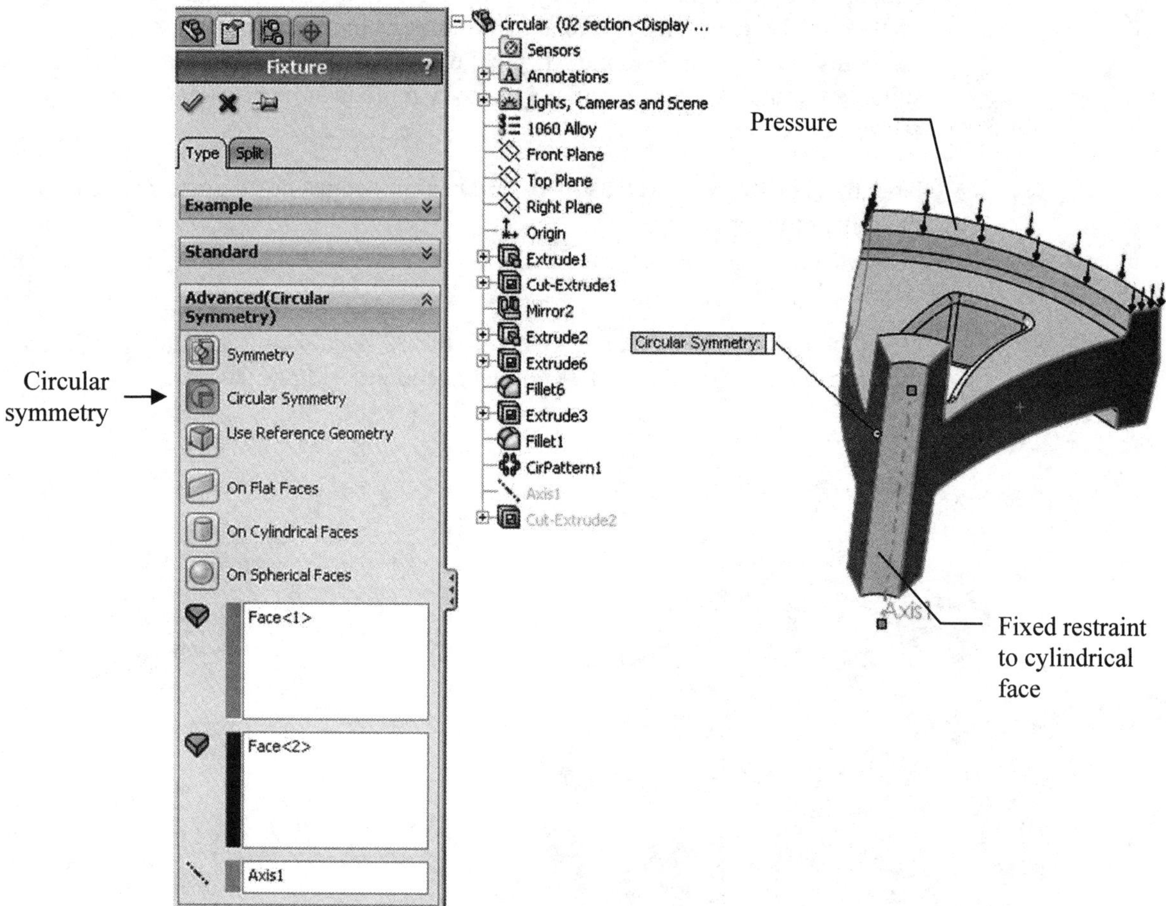

Figure 20-37: Definition of Circular Symmetry. Also shown is pressure load and fixed restraint to be applied to the central hole.

The definition requires a reference axis which is aligned with the central hole.

Apply a **Fixed** restraint to the central hole. Apply 10MPa **Pressure** to the rim and run the model. Analyze the stress results and decide if the mesh needs refinement. Compare results with those obtained using the model in configuration *01 full*.

21: Implementation of FEA into the design process

Topics covered

- Verification and Validation of FEA results
- FEA driven design process
- FEA project management
- FEA project checkpoints
- FEA report

VERIFICATION AND VALIDATION OF FEA RESULTS

Tools of Computer Aided Engineering (CAE) are now widely used to make design decisions. The reliance on CAE tools such as Finite Element Analysis (FEA) to make design decisions brings about the issue of how relevant results from FEA models are to real life design problems. To make sure that correct decisions are made, FEA results must be verified and validated.
The terms "verification" and "validation" are often used interchangeably in casual conversations.

In FEA, verification and validation pertain to different steps if the FEA modeling process. We will define and differentiate these terms while describing FEA modeling steps. We will repeat and expand the discussion found in chapter 1.

Step 1 Creation of a mathematical model

Every FEA project starts with the creation of a mathematical model. The mathematical model needs information on the geometry of a part or assembly that we analyze, material properties assigned to that geometry, loads and restraints. Definition of the type of analysis along with its simplifying assumptions (for example nonlinear static analysis, linear buckling analysis or transient thermal analysis) completes the creation of the mathematical model (Figure 21-1).

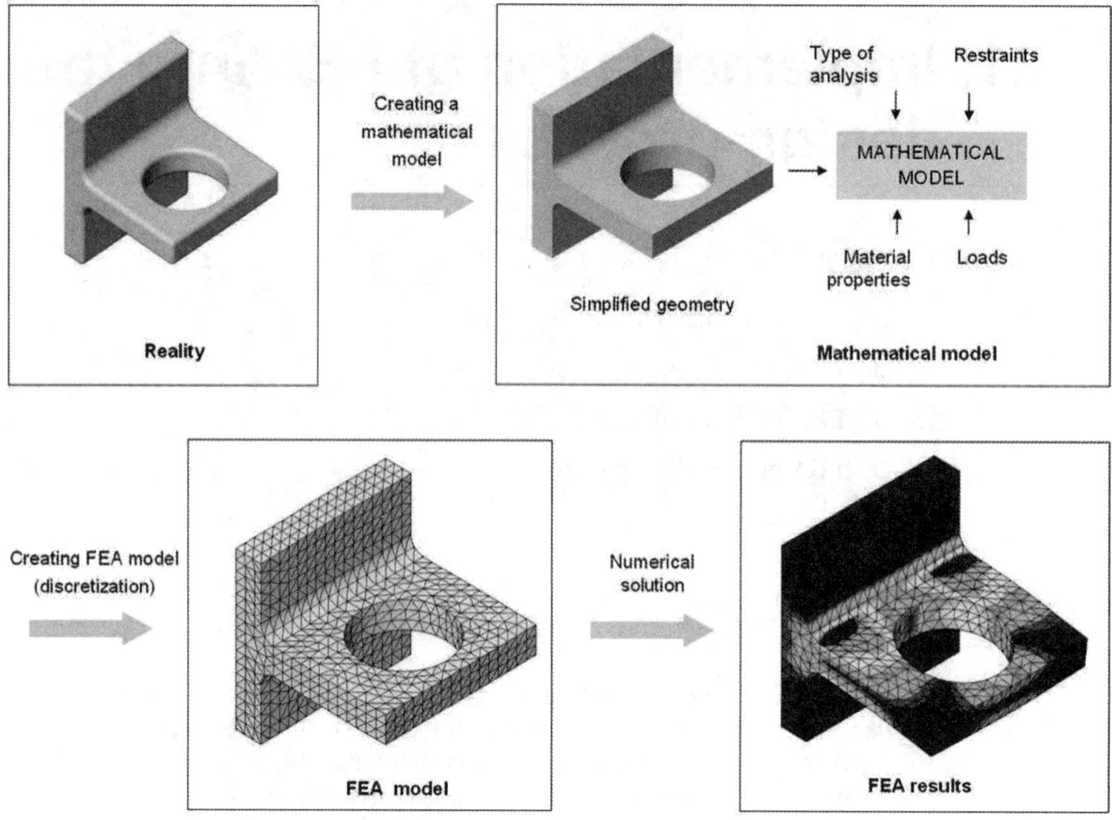

Figure 21-1: Steps in FEA project

All components of a mathematical model definition bring with them inherent simplifying assumptions which affect the results. A correctly formulated mathematical model captures the most important aspects of the real object. For example, analysis of a compliant link under a static load requires nonlinear formulation due to expected large displacements. Analysis of a cooling process requires transient thermal analysis and a drop test calls for nonlinear dynamic analysis.

Very serious errors result if the mathematical model does not capture the physics of the analyzed phenomenon. For example, if we neglect the large displacements and use a linear rather than nonlinear analysis to calculate beam displacement, we produce nonsensical results as shown in Figure 21-2.

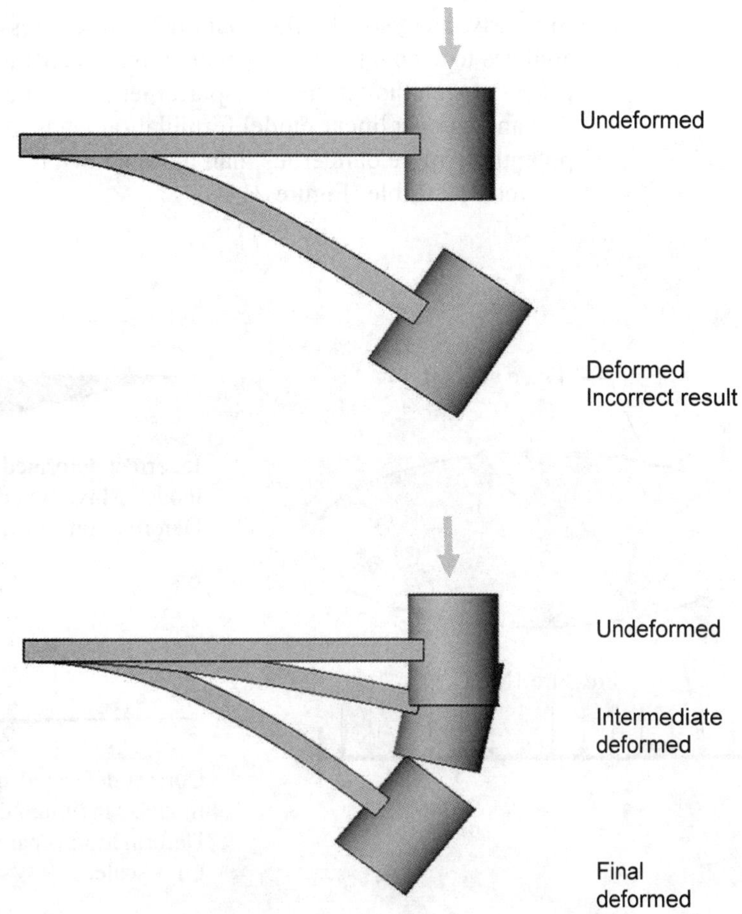

Figure 21-2: Cantilever beam in bending. Incorrect results are produced by a linear analysis (top). Correct results are produced by a nonlinear, large displacement analysis (bottom).

Similarly, analysis of a flat membrane under pressure requires nonlinear analysis to account for the change in model stiffness during the deformation process (even though these displacements may be very small). Neglecting this fact and using a linear model formulation leads to a very serious error and is potentially more dangerous than those shown in Figure 21-2 because results can look plausible (Figure 21-3).

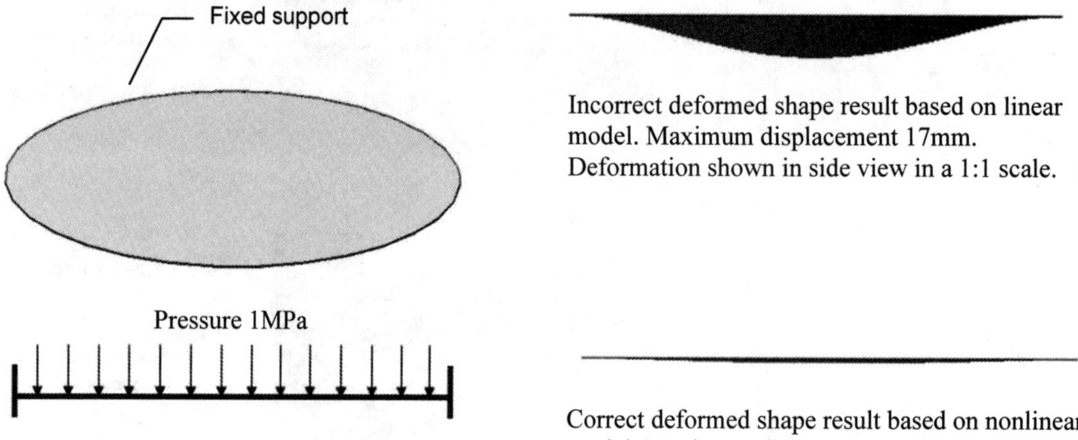

Fixed support
Pressure 1MPa
Incorrect deformed shape result based on linear model. Maximum displacement 17mm. Deformation shown in side view in a 1:1 scale.
Correct deformed shape result based on nonlinear model. Maximum displacement 1.8mm. Deformation is barely visible in the side view in a 1:1 scale.

Figure 21-3: Thin plate subjected to pressure load must be treated as nonlinear large displacement problem

Nylon membrane: diameter 200mm, thickness 0.5mm. Fixed support on circumference, pressure load 1MPa.

A very serious yet common modeling error is using a model with stress singularities to provide stress results in those singular locations (Figure 21-4).

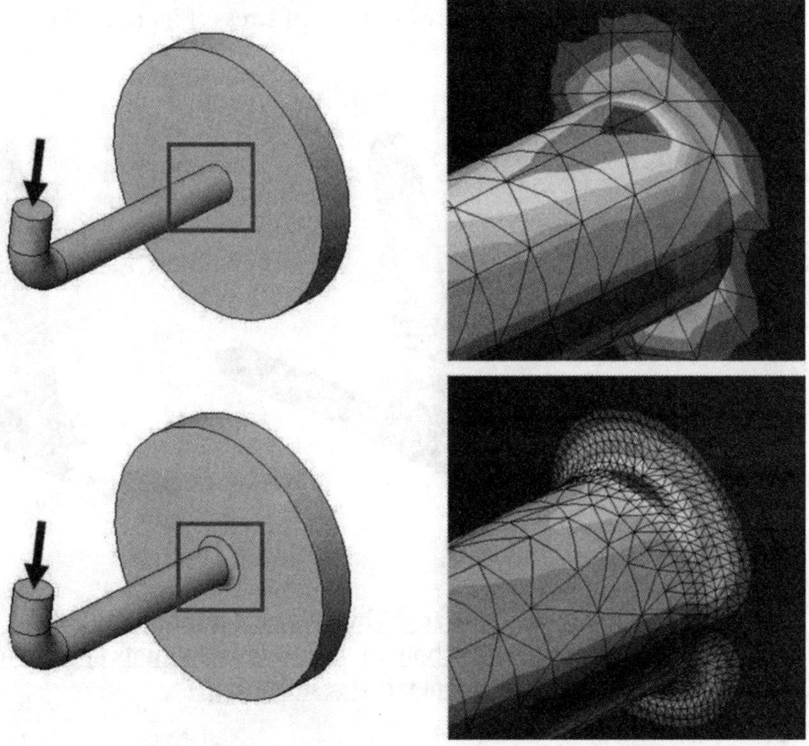

Figure 21-4: Stress singularities caused by sharp re-entrant edge (top). If stresses at the base of the cantilever are of interest, a fillet must be present in the analyzed geometry (bottom)

A mathematical model may also have more "trivial" errors such as incorrect loading or incorrect material properties. In the author's experience, errors are commonly found in the restraints definitions. For example, applying a rigid support to the entire back face of a support plate rather than to the bolt holes leads to severe underestimation of stress (Figure 21-5).

Figure 21-5 Errors caused by incorrect restraint definition. Restraints are applied to the entire bottom face (left). Restraints applied to only the holes produce very different stress results (right)

Even the definition of very simple mathematical models contains many assumptions and simplifications. For example to calculate the elongation, ΔL, of a rod under a tensile load, we use the equation $\Delta L = \dfrac{FL}{EA}$ where F is the tensile force, L is the length of the rod, A is the rod cross sectional area, and E is the modulus of elasticity of the rod material. By accepting this equation as a valid mathematical model to describe beam elongation, we assume that E is constant and does not change with strain, thus accepting a linear material model. We also assume that A is constant so we ignore the effect of Poisson's ratio, that tensile force does not change during the deformation process, and that the loading process is quasi static.

A mathematical model is never free of all errors. These unavoidable errors are known as the less intimidating term - simplifying assumptions. Every definition in making a mathematical model has some degree of simplifying assumptions which must be justified and are critical to the success of an analysis. It is our responsibility to assure that simplifying assumptions are not made "subconsciously" and that they do not prevent the model from providing trustworthy results.

Mathematical models are seldom simple enough to solve by hand and so we must use numerical approximations techniques to solve them. FEA is one of these numerical techniques which due to versatility and the ease of use, has dominated the commercial market of engineering analysis software.

Creation of an FEA model

As any other numerical technique, FEA works with a discretized model. Therefore, in preparation for a solution with FEA, the mathematical model must be discretized. In discretization, a continuous mathematical model is split into finite elements in the process commonly known as meshing. While a meshed model is easy to depict graphically, this graphical representation may be confusing because it implies that a mesh is imposed on model geometry. In fact there is nothing continuous left in the FEA model. Continuous geometry is replaced by discrete nodes and interaction between nodes is defined by elements connecting these nodes. Finite elements define relations between nodes. It is conceptually important to remember that loads and restraints are also discretized. Discrete loads and discrete restraints are applied to nodes. The model mass is no longer distributed continuously but rather, it is distributed among nodes. Unfortunately, FEA programs do not have graphical capabilities to show discretization of anything but geometry.

The process of discretization which converts the mathematical model into an FEA model has it own problems that add to errors in the mathematical model. Every discretization brings with it discretization errors which may be analyzed (and controlled) in the convergence process where we analyze the effect of element size on results. There are many "shades" of a convergence process. Most often a mesh is refined and the results are examined in terms of their sensitivity to the refinement. Many modern FEA programs have capabilities to perform convergence processes automatically.

Discretization of an FEA model leads to discretization of results. The result's nature depends on the type of elements used. The ability (or the lack) of elements to model the real displacement and stress distribution very strongly impact the results. A common error is to use too large elements which are unable to capture local stress concentrations (Figure 21-6).

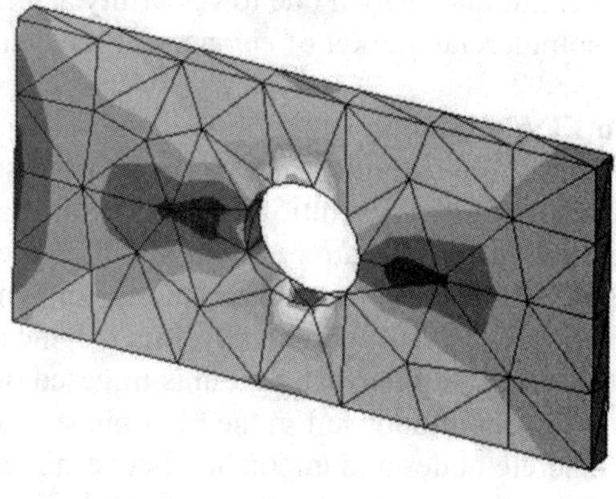

Too large elements
Maximum von Mises stress
304MPa

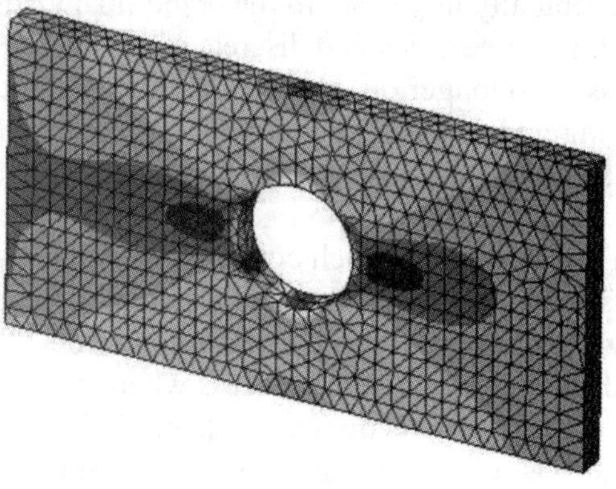

Correctly sized elements
Maximum von Mises stress
378MPa

Figure 21-6 Errors caused by incorrect meshing

Problems depicted in Figure 21-6 are easy to catch by a trained eye and can all be rectified by mesh refinement. In fact, understanding the discrete nature of results will prevent the use of inadequate meshes. Even though discretization errors are easily preventable, experience indicates that they still plague analysis reports.

Solution

Once an FEA model has been created, its solution is just a matter of solving a large number of linear algebraic equations. This can be done by a variety of solvers. The solution introduces numerical errors which are usually very low.

Interpretation of results

Finally, results must be analyzed and a design decision made. Incorrect interpretation of results is a topic for a separate article. Here we just mention a few common errors. Indiscriminate use of von Mises stress as a safety criterion is, in the author's opinion, on top of the list. Von Mises stress is a valid safety measure for materials showing distinct plasticity on a stress-strain curve. For example, using it to analyze results of a ceramic part makes no sense. Another mistake is the incorrect use of element versus nodal stress results, which results form the lack of understanding the difference between these two.

Each of the above steps takes us further away from the reality we are modeling. Errors can be made at each step, some of them are unavoidable errors inherent to the method, others may be grave errors of FEA "malpractice".

We are now in the position to define the terms verification and validation.

Verification is the process of determining that an FEA model correctly represents the modeler's conceptual description of the model and the solution of the model. In other words verification checks if the mathematical model, as submitted to be solved with FEA, has been correctly discretized and solved.

Validation is the process of determining if an FEA model correctly represents the reality from the perspective of the intended use of the model. It checks if results correctly describe the real life behavior of the analyzed object.

The difference between verification and validation is pictured in Figure 21-7.

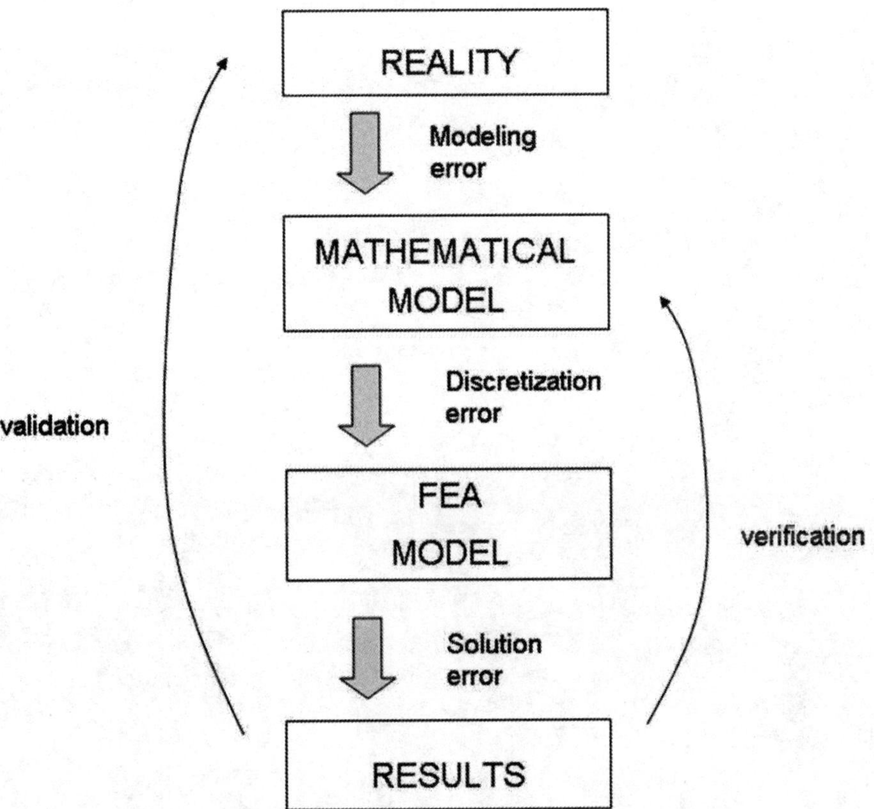

Figure 21-7 Verification and validation of FEA results

A model with meshing errors would not pass the verification test. For example, having been discretized into too large elements, the mathematical model would be solved incorrectly.

A model with incorrect load definitions would pass the verification test because verification only concerns itself with correctness of solution of the mathematical model, not if that model itself is correct. Verification fails if discretization and/or solution errors invalidate results. Convergence analysis will usually reveal problems causing verification test failure and those problems can be treated by mesh refinement or by using higher order elements.

Establishing the correctness of a mathematical model along with the correctness of its solution is the process of validation which should follow verification. Validation will fail because of conceptual errors in the definition of the mathematical model. These conceptual errors are much more dangerous than the errors of discretization. They may escape the modeler's attention, especially since there is no well defined structured process to reveal conceptual errors. Our only protection is the true understanding of the analyzed problem.

FEA DRIVEN DESIGN PROCESS

We have already stated that FEA should be implemented early in the design process and be executed concurrently with design activities in order to help make more efficient design decisions. This concurrent CAD-FEA process is illustrated in Figure 21-8.

Notice that the design begins in CAD geometry and FEA begins in FEA-specific geometry. Every time FEA is used, the interface line is crossed twice: the first time when modifying CAD geometry to make it suitable for analysis with FEA, and the second time when implementing results.

This significant interfacing effort can be avoided if the new design is started and iterated in FEA-specific geometry. Only after performing a sufficient number of iterations we switch to CAD geometry by adding all manufacturing specific features. This way, the interfacing effort is reduced to just one switch from FEA to CAD geometry as illustrated in Figure 21-8.

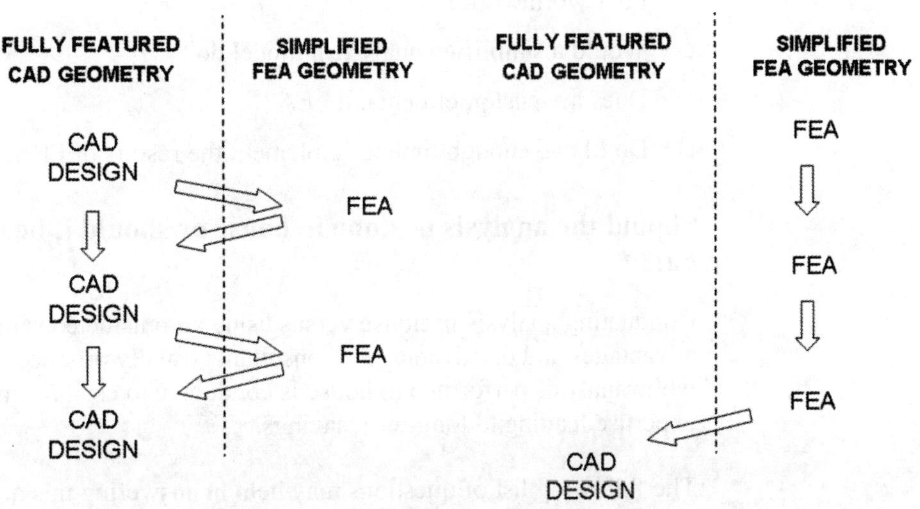

Figure 21-8: Concurrent CAD-FEA product development processes (left) and FEA driven product development process (right)

The CAD-FEA design process is developed in CAD-specific geometry, while FEA analysis is conducted in FEA-specific geometry. Interfacing between the two geometries requires substantial effort and is prone to error.

CAD-FEA interfacing efforts can be significantly reduced if the differences between CAD geometry and FEA geometry are recognized and the design process starts with FEA-specific geometry.

FEA PROJECT MANAGEMENT

Now let's discuss the steps in an FEA project from a managerial point of view. The steps in an FEA project that require the involvement of management are marked with an asterisk (*).

Do I really need FEA? *

This is the most fundamental question to address before any analysis starts. FEA is expensive to conduct and consumes significant company resources to produce results. Therefore, a decision to use FEA should be well justified.

Providing answers to the following questions may help to decide if FEA is worthwhile:

- Can I use previous test results or previous FEA results?
- Is this a standard design, in which case no analysis is necessary?
- Are loads, supports, and material properties known well enough to make FEA worthwhile?
- Would a simplified analytical model do?
- Does my customer demand FEA?
- Do I have enough time to implement the results of FEA?

Should the analysis be done in house or should it be contracted out? *

Conducting analysis in-house versus using an outside consultant has advantages and disadvantages. Consultants usually produce results faster while analysis performed in house is conducive to establishing company expertise leading to long-term savings.

The following list of questions may help in answering this question:

- How fast do I need to produce results?
- Do I have enough time and resources in-house to complete FEA before design decisions must be made?
- Is in-house expertise available?
- Do I have software that my customer wants me to use?

Establish the scope of the analysis*

Having decided on the need to conduct FEA, we need to decide what type of analysis is required. The following is a list of questions that may help in defining the scope of analysis.

Is this project:

- A standard analysis of a new product from an established product line?
- The last check of a production-ready new design before final testing?
- A quick check of design in-progress to assist the designer?
- An aid to an R&D project (particular detail of a design, gauge, fixture etc.)?
- A conceptual analysis to support a design at an early stage of development (e.g., R&D project)?
- A simplified analysis (e.g., only a part of the structure) to help make a design decision?

Other questions to consider are:

- Is it possible to perform comparative analyses?
- What is the estimated number of model iterations, load cases, etc.?
- What are applicable criteria to evaluate results?
- How will I know whether the results can be trusted?

Establish a cost-effective modeling approach and define the mathematical model accordingly

Having established the scope of analysis, the FEA model must now be prepared. The best model is of course the simplest one that provides the required results with acceptable accuracy. Therefore, the modeling approach should minimize project cost and duration, but should account for the essential characteristics of the analyzed object.

We need to decide on acceptable idealizations of geometry. This decision may involve simplification of CAD geometry by defeaturing, or idealization by using surface or wire frame representations. The goal is to produce a meshable geometry properly representing the analyzed problem.

Create a Finite Element model and solve it

The Finite Element model is created by discretization, or meshing, of a mathematical model. Although meshing implies that only geometry is discretized, discretization also affects loads and supports. Meshing and solving are both a largely automated step, but still require input, which depending on the software used, may include:

- Element type(s) to be used
- Default element size and size tolerance
- Definition of mesh controls (if any)

- Mesher type to be used
- Solver type and options to be used

Review results

FEA results must be critically reviewed prior to using them for making design decisions. This critical review includes:

- Verification of assumptions and assessment of results (an iterative step that may require several analysis loops to debug the model and to establish confidence in the results)
- Studying the overall mode of deformations and animating displacements to ensure that loads and restraints have been defined properly
- Checking for Rigid Body Motions
- Checking for overall stress levels (at least the order of magnitude) using analytical methods in order to verify the applied loads
- Checking for reaction forces and comparing them with free body diagrams
- A review of discretization errors (e.g. by comparing nodal and element stresses)
- Analysis of stress concentrations and the ability of the mesh to model them properly
- A review of results in difficult-to-model locations, such as thin walls, high stress gradients, etc.
- An investigation of the impact of element distortions on the data of interest

Analyze results*

The exact execution of this step depends, of course, on the objective of the analysis.

- Present displacement results
- Present modal frequencies and associated modes of vibration (if applicable)
- Present stress results and corresponding factors of safety
- Consider modifications to the analyzed structure to eliminate excessive stresses and to improve material utilization and manufacturability
- Discuss results, and repeat iterations until an acceptable solution is found

Produce report*

- Produce a report summarizing the activities performed, including assumptions and conclusions
- Append the completed report with a backup of relevant electronic data

FEA project management requires the involvement of the manager during project execution. The correctness of FEA results cannot be established by only reviewing the analysis of the results. A list of progress checkpoints may help a manager stay in the loop and improve communication with the person performing the analysis. Several checkpoints are suggested in Figure 21-9.

FEA PROJECT CHECKPOINTS

The following check points are especially recommended when junior engineers perform FEA (Figure 21-9).

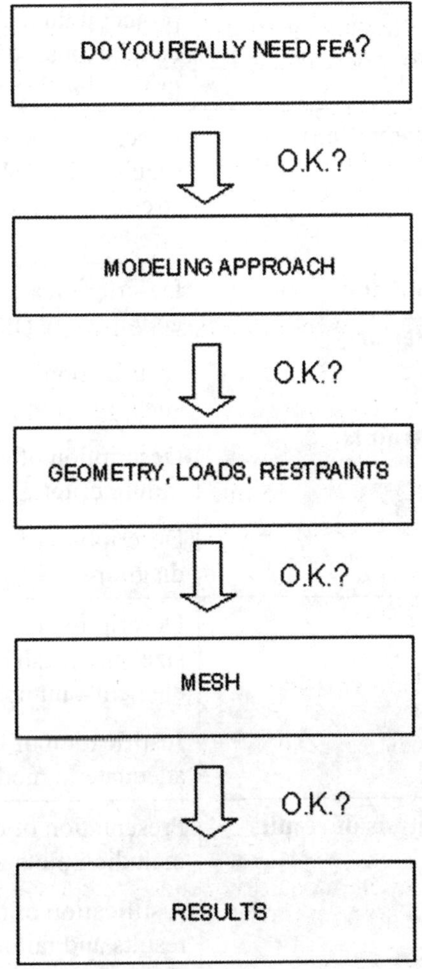

Figure 21-9: Checkpoints in an FEA project

Using the proposed checkpoints, the project is allowed to proceed only after the manager/supervisor has approved each step.

FEA REPORT

Even though each FEA project is unique, the structure of an FEA report follows similar patterns. The following are the major sections of a typical FEA report and their contents.

Section	Content
Executive Summary	Objective of the project, part/assembly number, project number, essential assumptions, results and conclusions, software used, information on where project backup is stored, etc.
Introduction	Description of the problem: Why did the project require FEA? What kind of FEA? (static, contact stress, frequency, etc.) What were the data of interest?
Geometry **Material** **Loads** **Restraints**	Description and justification of any simplification and/or idealization of geometry Justification of the modeling approach (e.g. solids, shells) Description of material properties and applicable failure criteria Description of loads and restraints, including load diagrams
Mesh	Description of the type of elements, global element size, any mesh control applied, number of elements, number of DOF, type of mesher used Justification of why this particular mesh is adequate to model the data of interest
Analysis of results	Presentation of displacement and stress results, including plots and animations Justification of the type of stress used to present results and failure criteria Discussion of errors in the results

Conclusions	Recommendations regarding structural integrity, necessary modifications, further studies needed Recommendations for follow-up testing procedure (e.g., strain-gauge test, fatigue life test) Recommendations on future similar analyses
Project documentation	Full documentation of design, design drawings, FEA model explanations, and computer back-ups Note that building in-house expertise requires very good documentation of the project besides the project report itself. Significant time should be allowed to prepare project documentation.
Follow-up	After completion of tests, append the report with test results Discussion of correlation between analysis results and test results Discussion of corrective action taken in case correlation is unsatisfactory (may involve revised model and/or tests)

Notes:

22: Glossary of terms

The following glossary provides definitions of terms used in this book.

Term	Definition
Beam element	A beam element is intended for meshing wire frame geometry. Nodes of beam elements have 6 degrees of freedom.
Boundary Element Method	An alternative to the FEA method of solving field problems, where only the boundary of the solution domain needs to be discretized. Very efficient for analyzing compact 3D shapes, but difficult to use on more "spread out" shapes.
CAD	Computer Aided Design
Clean-up	Removing and/or repairing geometric features that would prevent the mesher from creating a mesh or would result in an incorrect mesh.
Convergence criterion	Convergence criterion is a condition that must be satisfied in order for the convergence process to stop. In SolidWorks **Simulation** this applies to studies where an h-adaptive or a p-adaptive solution has been selected.

Term	Definition
Convergence process	This is a process of systematic changes in the mesh in order to see how the data of interest changes with the choice of the mesh and (hopefully) proves that the data is not significantly dependent on the choice of discretization. A convergence process can be preformed as h-convergence or p-convergence. An h-convergence process is done by refining the mesh, i.e., by reducing the element size in the mesh and comparing the results before and after mesh refinement. Reduction of element size can be done globally, by refining the mesh everywhere in the model, or locally, by using mesh controls. An h-convergence analysis takes its name from the element characteristic dimension h, which changes from one iteration to the next. A p-convergence analysis does not affect element size. Elements stay the same throughout the entire convergence analysis process. Instead, element order is upgraded from one iteration to the next. A p-convergence analysis is done automatically in an iterative solution until the user-specified convergence criterion is satisfied. Sometimes, the desired accuracy cannot be achieved even with the highest available p-element order. In this case, the user has to refine the p-element mesh manually in a fashion similar to traditional h-convergence, and then re-run the iterative p-convergence solution. This is called a p-h convergence analysis.
Defeaturing	Defeaturing is the process of removing (or suppressing) geometric features in CAD geometry in order to simplify the finite element mesh or make meshing possible.
Discretization	This defines the process of splitting up a continuous mathematical model into discrete "pieces" called elements. A visible effect of discretization is the finite element mesh. However, model mass, loads and restraints are also discretized.

Discretization error	This type of error affects FEA results because FEA works on an assembly of discrete elements (mesh) rather than on a continuous structure. The finer the finite element mesh, the lower the discretization error, but the solution takes more time.
Element stress	This refers to stresses at Gauss points of a given element. Stresses at different Gauss points are averaged amongst themselves (but not with stresses reported by other elements) and one value is assigned to the entire element. Element stresses produce a discontinuous stress distribution in the model.
Finite Difference Method	This is an alternative to the FEA method of solving a field problem, where the solution domain is discretized into a grid. The Finite Difference Method is generally less efficient for solving structural and thermal problems, but is often used in fluid dynamics problems.
Finite Element	Finite elements are the building blocks of a mesh, defined by the position of their nodes and by functions approximating distribution of sought after quantities, such as displacements or temperatures.
Finite Volumes Method	This is an alternative to the FEA method of solving a field problem, similar to the Finite Difference Method.
Frequency analysis	Also called modal analysis, a frequency analysis calculates the natural frequencies of a structure as the associated modes (shapes) of vibration. Modal analysis does not calculate displacements or stresses.
Gaussian points	These points are locations in the element where stresses are first calculated. Later, these stress results can be extrapolated to nodes.
h-adaptive solution	An iterative solution which involves mesh refinement. Iterations continue until convergence requirements are satisfied or the maximum number of iterations is reached.

h-element	An h-element is a finite element for which the order does not change during solution. Convergence analysis of the model using h-elements is done by refining the mesh and comparing results (like deflection, stress, etc.) before and after refinement. The name, *h-element*, comes from the element characteristic dimension *h*, which is reduced in consecutive mesh refinements.
Harmonic analysis	Dynamic analysis where excitation is a function of frequency.
Idealization	This refers to making simplifying assumptions in the process of creating a mathematical model of an analyzed structure. Idealization may involve geometry, material properties, loads and restraints.
Idealization error	This type of error results from the fact that analysis is conducted on an idealized model and not on a real-life object. Geometry, material properties, loads, and restraints are all idealized in models submitted to FEA.
Linear material	This is a type of material where stress is a linear function of strain.
Mesh diagnostic	This is a feature of SolidWorks **Simulation** that determines which geometric entities prevented meshing when meshing fails.
Meshing	This refers to the process of discretizing the model geometry. As a result of meshing, the originally continuous geometry is represented by an assembly of finite elements.
Modal analysis	See Frequency analysis.
Modal Time History analysis	Dynamic analysis where excitation is an explicit function of time.
Modeling error	See Idealization error.
Nodal stresses	These stresses are calculated at nodes by extrapolating stress from Gauss points and then averaging stresses (coming from different elements) at nodes. Nodal stresses are "smoothed out" and, by virtue of averaging, produce continuous stress distributions in the model.
Numerical error	This is round-off error accumulated by the solver.

p-element	P-elements are elements that do not have pre-defined order. Solution of a p-element model requires several iterations while element order is upgraded until the difference in user-specified measures (e.g., total strain energy, RMS stress) becomes less than the requested accuracy. The name *p-element*, comes from the *p-order* of polynomial functions which defines the displacement field in the element. This order is upgraded during the iterative solution.
p-adaptive solution	This refers to an option available for static analysis with solid elements only. If the p-Adaptive solution is selected (in the properties window of a static study), SolidWorks **Simulation** uses p-elements for an iterative solution. A p-adaptive solution provides results with narrowly specified accuracy.
Pre-load	A pre-load is a load that modifies the stiffness of a structure. A pre-load may be important in a static or frequency analysis if it significantly changes structure stiffness.
Power Spectral Density	A function describing random excitation as a function of frequency.
Principal stress	Principal stress is the stress component that acts on the side of an imaginary stress cube in the absence of shear stresses. A general 3D state of stress can be represented either by six stress components (normal stresses and shear stresses) expressed in an arbitrary coordinate system or by three principal stresses and three angles defining the cube orientation in relation to that coordinate system.
Random analysis	Dynamic analysis of system response to a random signal.
Rigid body mode or **Rigid body motion**	This refers to a mode of vibration with zero frequency found in structures that are not fully restrained or not restrained at all. A structure with no supports has six rigid body modes. A rigid body mode is the ability to move without elastic deformation. In the case of a fully supported structure, the only way it can move under load is by deforming its shape. If a structure is not fully supported, it can move as a rigid body without any deformation. Rigid body motions are only allowed in Frequency analyses.

RMS stress	Root Mean Square stress. RMS stress may be used as a convergence criterion if the p-adaptive solution method is used.
Shell element	Shell elements are intended for meshing surfaces. The shell element that is used in SolidWorks **Simulation** is a triangular shell element. Triangular shell elements have three corner nodes. If this is a second order triangular element, it also has mid-side nodes, making the total number of nodes equal to six. Each node of a shell element has 6 degrees of freedom.
Small Displacement assumption	Analysis based on small displacements assumes that displacements caused by loads are small enough to not significantly change structure stiffness. Analysis based on this assumption of small deformations is also called linear geometry analysis or small displacement analysis. However, the magnitude of displacements itself is not the deciding factor in determining whether or not those deformations are indeed small. What matters, is whether or not those displacements significantly change the stiffness of the analyzed structure.
Steady state thermal analysis	Steady state thermal analysis assumes that heat flow has stabilized and no longer changes with time.
Structural stiffness	Structural stiffness is a function of shape, material properties, and restraints. Stiffness characterizes structural response to an applied load.
Symmetry boundary conditions	These refer to displacement conditions defined on a flat model boundary allowing only for in-plane displacement and restricting any out-of-plane displacement components. Symmetry boundary conditions are very useful for reducing model size if model geometry, load, and supports are all symmetric.

Tetrahedral solid element	This is a type of element used for meshing solid models. A tetrahedral element has four triangular faces and four corner nodes. If used as a second order element ("high quality" in SolidWorks **Simulation** terminology) it also has mid-side nodes, making the total number of nodes equal to 10. Each node of a tetrahedral element has 3 degrees of freedom.
Thermal analysis	Thermal analysis finds temperature distribution, temperature gradient and heat flux in a structure.
Transient thermal analysis	Transient thermal analysis is an option in a thermal analysis. It calculates temperature, temperature gradient and heat flow changes over time as a result of time dependent thermal loads and thermal boundary conditions.
Ultimate strength	The maximum stress that may occur in a structure. If the ultimate strength is exceeded, failure will take place (the part will break). Ultimate strength is usually much higher than yield strength.
Von Mises stress	This is a stress measure that takes into consideration all six stress-components of a 3D state of stress. Von Mises stress, also called Huber stress, is a very convenient and popular way of presenting FEA results because it is a scalar, non-negative value and because the magnitude of von Mises stress can be used to determine safety factors for materials exhibiting elasto-plastic properties, such as most types of steel.
Yield strength	The maximum stress that can be allowed in a model before plastic deformation takes place.

Notes:

23: Resources available to FEA users

Many sources of FEA expertise are available to users. Sources include, but are not limited to:

- Engineering textbooks
- Software manuals
- Engineering journals
- Professional development courses
- FEA users' groups
- Government organizations

Readers of this book may wish to review the book "Finite Element Analysis for Design Engineers" which expands on many topics discussed in this book (Figure 23-1).

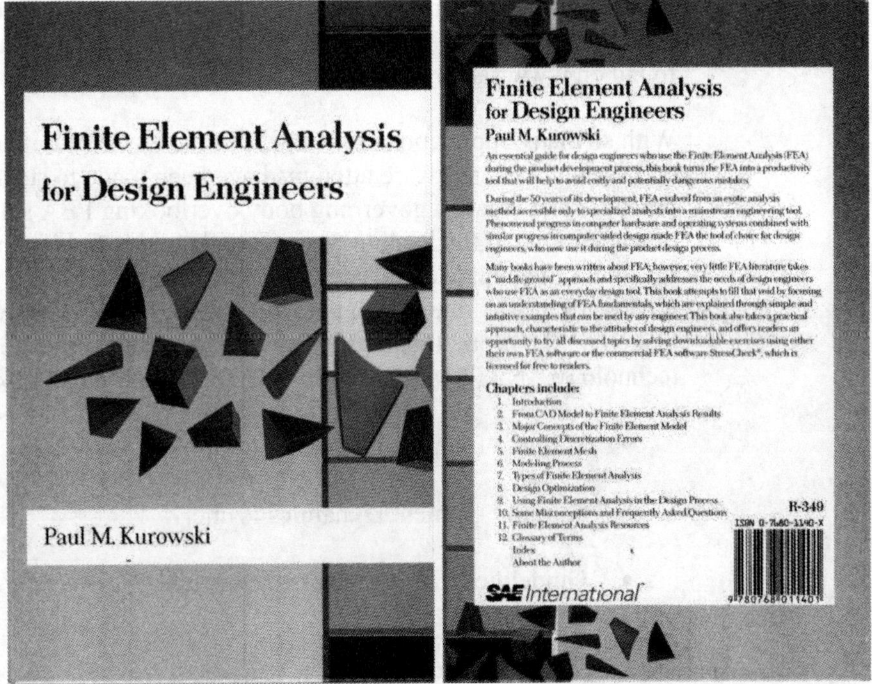

Figure 23-1 "Finite Element Analysis for Design Engineers" book

"Finite Element Analysis for Design Engineers" is available through the Society of Automotive Engineers website (www.sae.org).

Engineering literature offers a large selection of FEA-related books, a few of which are listed here.

1. Adams V., Askenazi A. "Building Better Products with Finite Element Analysis", OnWord Press, 1998.

2. Logan D. "A First Course in the Finite Element Method", Brooks/Cole 2002

3. Macneal R. "Finite Elements: Their Design and Performance", Marcel Dekker, Inc., 1994.

4. Spyrakos C. "Finite Element Modeling in Engineering Practice", West Virginia University Printing Services, 1994.

5. Szabo B., Babuska I. "Finite Element Analysis", John Wiley & Sons, Inc., 1991.

6. Zienkiewicz O., Taylor R. "The Finite Element Method", McGraw-Hill Book Company, 1989.

Several professional organizations like the Society of Automotive Engineers (SAE) and the American Society of Mechanical Engineers (ASME) offer professional development courses in the field of the Finite Element Analysis. More information on FEA related courses offered by SAE and ASME can be found on www.sae.org and www.asme.org.

With so many applications for FEA, various levels of importance of analysis, and various FEA software attempts have been made to standardize FEA practices and create a governing body overlooking FEA standards and practices. One of the leading organizations in this field is the National Agency for Finite Element Methods and Standards, better know by its acronym NAFEMS. It was founded in the United Kingdom in 1983 with a specific objective "To promote the safe and reliable use of finite element and related technology." NAFEMS has published many FEA handbooks such as:

- A Finite Element Primer
- A Finite Element Dynamics Primer
- Guidelines to Finite Element Practice
- Background to Benchmarks

The full list of these excellent publications can be found on www.nafems.org.

Another internet site with a number of FEA related publications is presented by Design Generator Inc. Publications related to FEA fundamentals, training and implementation can be found at:

http://www.designgenerator.com/publications.htm

Notes:

Notes:

Notes:

Notes:

Notes:

Notes:

Notes: